Lecture Notes in Computer Science 10581

Commenced Publication in 1973
Founding and Former Series Editors:
Gerhard Goos, Juris Hartmanis, and Jan van Leeuwen

Editorial Board

More information about this series at http://www.springer.com/series/7410

Editors
Sheng Wen
Deakin University
Geelong
China

Aniello Castiglione
University of Salerno
Fisciano
Italy

Wei Wu
Fujian Normal University
Fuzhou Shi
China

ISSN 0302-9743   ISSN 1611-3349 (electronic)
Lecture Notes in Computer Science
ISBN 978-3-319-69470-2   ISBN 978-3-319-69471-9 (eBook)
https://doi.org/10.1007/978-3-319-69471-9

Library of Congress Control Number: 2017957553

LNCS Sublibrary: SL4 – Security and Cryptology

Printed on acid-free paper

This Springer imprint is published by Springer Nature
The registered company is Springer International Publishing AG
The registered company address is: Gewerbestrasse 11, 6330 Cham, Switzerland

Sheng Wen · Wei Wu
Aniello Castiglione (Eds.)

Cyberspace Safety and Security

9th International Symposium, CSS 2017
Xi'an, China, October 23–25, 2017
Proceedings

 Springer

Preface

This volume contains the papers presented at CSS 2017: The 9th International Symposium on Cyberspace Safety and Security held during October 23–25, 2017, in Xi'an, China.

Security and safety are two aspects of security research that strongly interact and complement each other; one focuses more on cyberspace techniques, and the other focuses more on the impacts of security research on communities. The series of International Symposiums on Security and Safety (CSS) is a forum for presentation of theoretical and applied research papers, case studies, implementation experiences, as well as work-in-progress results in these two disciplines. Since its inception nine years ago, the CSS symposium has attracted national and international researchers, engineers, practitioners, and learners from industry, government, and academia.

The 2017 conference brought together approximately 100 attendees from diverse locations across the US East and West Coast and Europe among others. Hence, the opportunities created by this symposium to bring world-class knowledge to the ongoing efforts in cybersecurity research are significant. The conference especially invites young researchers and PhD students, who have an opportunity to share their results with colleagues, invited keynote lectures, and the Program Committee (PC) members actively participating in conference sessions.

The 2017 conference comprised 31 regular papers selected from 120 submissions. Each regular paper concerns an area in security and safety, and addresses a critical problem in a related topic. There were another 10 short papers, which dealt with recent problems in cybersecurity. All the accepted papers were examined by at least three reviewers (prestigious PC members). Decisions about final paper acceptance were reviewed and approved by the Organizing Committee.

We hereby thank the invited speakers for enriching the program with their presentations. We thank Prof. Yang Xiang, Chair of the CSS Steering Committee, for his advice throughout the conference preparation process. We also thank Prof. Yu Yong for the contributions to the local arrangements, which helped make this conference happen in Xi'an. Last but not least, we thank EasyChair for making the entire process of the conference convenient.

We hope you find these proceedings educational and enjoyable!

September 2017

Sheng Wen
Wei Wu
Aniello Castiglione

Organization

Honorary Chairs

Bo Yang   Shaanxi Normal University, China
Kui Ren   State University of New York at Buffalo, USA
Shangping Wang   Xi'an University of Technology, China

General Chairs

Wanlei Zhou   Deakin University, Australia
Hui Li   Xidian University, China
Xiujuan Lei   Shaanxi Normal University, China

Program Chairs

Sheng Wen   Deakin University, Australia
Wei Wu   Fujian Normal University, China
Aniello Castiglione   University of Salerno, Italy

Organizing Chairs

Yong Yu   Shaanxi Normal University, China
Jianfeng Wang   Xidian University, China

Publication Chairs

Yu Wang   Deakin University, Australia
Shigang Liu   Deakin University, Australia

Publicity Chair

Jun Zhang   Deakin University, Australia

Steering Committee

Yang Xiang   Deakin University, Australia

Track Chairs

First Track (Privacy Preserving)

Tianqing Zhu	Deakin University, Australia
Rongxing Lu	University of New Brunswick, Canada
Zhe Liu	University of Luxembourg, Luxembourg

Second Track (Intrusion Detection and Forensics)

Shuyuan Jin	Sun Yat-sen University, China
Tian Wang	Xiamen Huaqiao University, China
Xuyun Zhang	The University of Auckland, New Zealand

Third Track (Cyber Physical System Security)

James Xi Zheng	Deakin University, Australia
Mohammod Sayad Haghighi	University of Tehran, Iran

Fourth Track (Big Data Security)

Kaitai Liang	Manchester Metropolitan University, UK
Jianzhong Qi	The University of Melbourne, Australia
Hongzhi Yin	The University of Queensland, Australia

Fifth Track (Mobile Security)

Zhen Ling	Southeast University, China
Lucas Hui	The University of Hong Kong, SAR China
Md Zakirul Alam Bhuiyan	Fordham University, USA

Program Committee

Raffaele Pizzolante	University of Salerno, Italy
Catuogno Luigi	University of Salerno, Italy
Arcangelo Castiglione	University of Salerno, Italy
Zhen Peng	College of William and Mary, USA
Yongxuan Lai	Xiamen University, China
Zhitao Guan	North China Electric Power University, China
Changli Zhou	Huaqiao University, China
Yiqiao Cai	Huaqiao University, China
Weiqing Wang	The University of Queensland, Australia
Xingzhong Du	The University of Queensland, Australia
Saeid Hosseini	Singapore University of Technology and Design, Singapore
Lei Zhu	The University of Queensland, Australia
Wei Zhang	East China Normal University, China
Clemente Galdi	University of Naples, Italy

Francesco Moscato	Second University of Naples, Italy
Francesco Colace	University of Salerno, Italy
Vincenzo Moscato	University of Naples, Italy
Christian Esposito	University of Salerno, Italy
Massimo Ficco	Second University of Naples, Italy
Xiapu Luo	Hong Kong Polytechnic University, SAR China
Xiaobo Ma	Xi'an Jiaotong University, China
Xuejun Li	Anhui University, China
Huiting Liu	Anhui University, China
Chao Zhang	Anhui University, China
Flora Amato	University of Naples, Italy
Fei Chen	Shenzhen University, China
Jinguang Han	Nanjing University of Finance and Economics, China
Yuan Zhang	Nanjing University, China
Jianfeng Lu	Zhejiang University, China
Ruan Na	Shanghai Jiaotong University, China
Tao Xiang	Chongqing University, China
Yuexin Zhang	Deakin University, Australia
Ding Wang	Peking University, China
Shaojun Yang	Fujian Normal University, China
Rongmao Chen	National University of Defense Technology, China
Xiaoyang Liu	Columbia University, USA
Ping Xiong	Zhongnan University of Economics and Law, China
Cao Yuan	Wuhan Polytechnic University, China
Jiageng Chen	Central China Normal University, China
Abdorasoul Ghasemi	K. N. Toosi University of Technology, Iran
Carsten Rudolf	Monash University, Australia
Xiaoliang Fan	Lanzhou University, China
Masud Moshtaghi	University of Melbourne, Australia
Chuanwen Li	Northeastern University, China
Zeyi Wen	National University of Singapore, Singapore
Liangfu Lv	Tianjin University, China
Zhiyuan Tan	Edinburgh Napier University, UK
Deepak Puthal	University of Technology Sydney, Australia
Lianyong Qi	Qufu Normal University, China
Chi Yang	Unitec, New Zealand
Gaofeng Zhang	Hefei University of Technology, China
Zoe Lin Jiang	Harbin Institute of Technology, China
An Wang	Beijing Institute of Technology, China
Richard Overill	King's College London, UK
Lin Li	Beijing Jiaotong University, China
Junbin Fang	Jinan University, China
Donghai Tian	Beijing Institute of Technology, China
Zhe Yang	Northwestern Polytechnical University, China
Xiaolong Xu	Nanjing University, China
Chen Jing	Wuhan University, China

Contents

Detection of Lurkers in Online Social Networks

Flora Amato[1], Aniello Castiglione[1,3], Vincenzo Moscato[1,2],
Antonio Picariello[1,2], and Giancarlo Sperlì[1(✉)]

[1] Dipartimento di Ingegneria Elettrica e Tecnologie dell'Informazione,
University of Naples "Federico II", Via Claudio 21, 80125 Naples, Italy
{flora.amato,vmoscato,picus,giancarlo.sperli}@unina.it,
castiglione@ieee.org
[2] CINI - ITEM National Lab, Complesso Universitario Monte Santangelo,
80125 Naples, Italy
[3] University of Salerno, Via Giovanni Paolo II, 132, 84084 Fisciano, SA, Italy

Abstract. In this work, we propose a novel data model that integrates
and combines information on users belonging to one or more heterogeneous Online Social Networks (OSNs), together with the content that
is generated, shared and used within the related environments, using
an hypergraph-based approach. Then, we discuss how the most diffused
centrality measures – that have been defined over the introduced model
– can be efficiently applied for a number of data privacy issues, such
as lurkers detection, especially in "interest-based" social networks. Some
preliminary experiments using the Yelp dataset are finally presented.

1 Introduction

Social networks have been studied fairly extensively over two decades within
the general context of analyzing interactions among people: the final goal is to
derive "useful" knowledge from network data that can effectively support a large
variety of applications.

Generally, social networks can be seen as particular structures whose nodes
represent people or other entities embedded in a social context, and whose
edges represent interactions, collaboration, or influence between entities. Natural examples of social networks include the set of all scientists in a particular
discipline, with edges joining pairs who have coauthored articles; the set of all
employees in a large company, with edges joining pairs working on a common
project; or a collection of business leaders, with edges joining pairs who have
served together on a corporate board of directors.

In the last years, the research trend has focused on *Online Social Networks*
(OSNs), in which the social network is enabled as an Internet application. In fact,
the use of OSNs is rapidly growing allowing people, living in different places, to
make friends and to share, comment and observe different types of content. OSNs
have thus produced a tremendous amount of data showing *Big Data* features,
mainly due to their high change rate, their large volume, and the intrinsic heterogeneity, especially if we try to combine information coming from different
OSNs [19].

© Springer International Publishing AG 2017
S. Wen et al. (Eds.): CSS 2017, LNCS 10581, pp. 1–15, 2017.
https://doi.org/10.1007/978-3-319-69471-9_1

Actually, modern OSNs can be defined either in the context of systems such as Facebook and Twitter which have been explicitly designed for social interactions, or in terms of other applications such as Flickr, Instagram, YouTube and Last.fm which have been born for different aims such as multimedia content sharing, but which also embed an extensive level of social interaction (not "directed", but obtained by means of the shared multimedia content). Eventually, other kinds of social networks have as main purpose to share comment and opinions on specific topics (e.g., Yelp, IMDB, etc.), to suggest objects or places of interest (e.g., TripAdvisor, Foursquare, etc.) or to provide social environments able to facilitate particular tasks (e.g., the search of a job as in LinkedIn, the answer to research questions as in ResearchGate, etc.), just to cite the most diffused and known social networks. *Social Network Analysis* (SNA) methodologies [31] have been recently introduced to study the properties of social networks with the aim of supporting a wide range of applications: information retrieval, influence analysis, recommendation, viral marketing, event recognition, expert finding, community detection, user profiling, security and social data privacy and so on [8,9]. The majority of SNA techniques mainly exploit "user to user" interactions, leveraging the graph theory as powerful tool to support the different kinds of analytics. More recently, according to a *data-centric* view of OSN, also "user to content" relationships have been considered together with content features to provide more advanced forms of analysis. In particular, the SNA techniques can be inspired by two different approaches [1]: (i) *Linkage-based and Structural Analysis*, in which we construct an analysis of the linkage behavior of the network in order to determine important nodes, communities, links, and evolving regions of the network and *Content-based Analysis*, in which the tremendous amount of content (multimedia and tags) contained in OSNs can be leveraged in order to improve the quality of the analysis. In the security related applications, SNA – especially *link prediction* methodologies – can be used to identify hidden groups of terrorists and criminals in social networks. Moreover, other kinds of analytics can be profitably exploited to guarantee data privacy [3,10,11] in correspondence of unauthorized intrusion or to detect *lurkers* and *fake* accounts.

In this paper we describe a novel data model based on hypergraph for *Heterogeneous Social Networks*. Exploiting the feature of the proposed data model, we develop an algorithm for lurker detection based on the "Follow the Leader strategy" [30]. The paper is organized as in the following. Section 2 presents the related work about the proposed techniques to identify lurkers in an Online Social Network. Section 3 describes in details our model with its properties and foundations; moreover we analyze the most diffused centrality measures on the proposed model and introduce a new centrality measures based on the concept of "neighborhood". In the Sect. 4 we introduce a simple heuristics to cope the problem of lurkers' detections. Section 5 shows the obtained experimental results using Yelp data, while Sect. 6 reports conclusions and the future work.

2   Related Works

In Online Social Networks silent and passive members, corresponding to large amount of users called "lurkers", have attracted the interest of different researchers; in fact, in the study [7] the authors recognize that the 90% of the actions in OSNs corresponds to the simple browsing. Lurkers differ significantly from posters, especially in their willingness to give information and exchange social support [29]. A first definition of lurkers is given by Nonnecker et al. [28], that define them as non public participants in Online social communities. In the literature, they are also defined as users that do not contribute to produce knowledge but only to reshare it [27]. Moreover, Kollock and Smith [25] indicate that lurkers might have a negative influence on an Online community because many people regard them as free raiders. Another definition is provided in [17,26], where the concept of a lurker is related to a sort of peripheral participation. In particular, in the second paper the authors show both qualitatively and quantitatively how peripheral contributors add value to an open community. In addition, an interesting definition has been given under individual information strategy of microlearning [6]. In turn, within P2P sharing systems [13], a lurker user corresponds to a leeching that wastes valuable bandwidth by downloading much more than what s/he uploads.

Many works have been then proposed with the goal of analyzing the lurkers' behavior in social networks. The authors in [28] provide a demographic analysis of lurking in email based list. In this analysis they note that lurkers have an sporadic participation. In [14], the authors provide a different view of lurker problem that is useful to understand the reason that led them to avoid to actively contribute to the communities. Moreover, Amichai-Hamburger et al. [5] make a review to better understand why the majority of participants in an Online social communities remain silent, identifying different factors such as need for gratification, personality dispositions, time available and self-efficacy, social-group processes (such as socialization, type of community, tendency toward social loafing, responses to delurking and the quality of responses), technological setting factors (technical design flaws, privacy and safety of the online group and so on). Faazen et al. [16] classify OSN users into the following four classes: *leaders*, *lurkers*, who are generally inactive, but occasionally follow some tweets, *spammers* and *close associate*. In [23], the evolutionary game theory is used for proposing a Lurker game, in which active users are regarded as cooperators and lurkers as defectors to analyze the transitions from a lurking to a non-lurking (i.e., active) user role, and vice-versa. Cooperators contribute to the system by adding information in the shape of virtual coins, while defectors do not contribute. The total amount of virtual coins in the common pool increases according to two key aspects: (i) the collective effort of cooperators and (ii) the different impact that information naturally has on each agent, depending on her/his preferences. Due to lurkers acquire knowledge form a social context, delurking strategies assume growing importance. In [21], Interdonato et al. develop a delurking-oriented targeted influence maximization problem under the linear threshold (LT) model, defining an objective function based on lurking scores associated with the nodes in the final active set. A greedy algorithm called DEvOTION is developed to compute a k-node set that maximizes the value of the delurking-capital-based objective function for a given minimum lurking score threshold. In a successive work [20], the authors try to improve the task of delurking in social networks exploiting the boundary spanning theory. Firstly, they analyze how the lurkers are related to users that take the role of bridges between different communities, unveiling insights into the bridging nature of lurkers and their tendency to acquire information from outside their own community. Successively, they also analyze how the learning of users that can best engage lurkers is related to the community structure. In particular they found that the best users to engage lurkers belong to the adjacent communities. Eventually, Interdonato et al. [22] try to understand and quantify the relationships that involve lurkers for protecting the active users from untrustworthy or undesired interactions and encouraging lurkers to more actively participate in the community life through the guidance of active users.

3   Data Model

To properly manage the large amount of heterogeneous data generated by Online Social Networks, we use a *Heterogeneous Social Network* (HSN) model, that allows to integrate in a unified model the interactions among users and among the generated content and users [4]. In particular, the vertices set is composed by the following types of entities:

- **Users** - i.e., the set of persons and organizations constituting one or more social communities. Several information concerning their profile, interests, preferences, etc. can be opportunely taken into account.
- **Objects** - the set of user-generated items that are of interest within a given social community. In the most diffused online large-scale social networks, as Twitter, Google$^+$ and Facebook, objects are represented by different types of heterogeneous content such as tweets, posts, but also videos, photos and so on. In other kinds of social networks (e.g., Instagram, Flickr, Youtube, Last.fm, etc.) objects are essentially multimedia data (i.e., images, video and audio contents). Finally, in some interest-based social networks (e.g., Yelp, Imdb, etc.) or location-based social networks (e.g., TripAdvisor, Foursquare) objects correspond to specific items that are usually rated for recommendation purposes (e.g. restaurants in TripAdvisor, movies in Imdb, business objects in Yelp, places of interest in Foursquare, etc.). Objects can be obviously described using *metadata* and different annotation schemata. In addition, in our model also multimedia data low-level *features* can be properly used.
- **Topics** - i.e., the most significant terms or named entities - whose definition can be retrieved from dictionaries, ontologies and so on - of one or more domains, exploited by users to describe objects and eventually derived from the analysis of textual annotations, mainly tags but also keywords, comments,

reviews etc. Clearly, such kind of information cannot be always correctly and automatically inferred: thus, such information could be not available for all kinds of applications.

3.1 Basic Definitions

We leverage the *hypergraph* formalism to model HSN due to the heterogeneity and complexity of relationships that can be established among the described vertices; for instances, a user publishes a photo tagging his friends, a user listen a song, a user write a review for a given restaurant and so on. Thus, in our vision a HSN is a weighted and undirected hypergraph, defined as in the following.

Definition 1 (HSN). *An* Heterogeneous Social Network *HSN is a triple $(HV; HE = \{he_i : i \in I\}; \omega)$, HV being a finite set of* vertices, *HE a set of* hyperedges *with a finite set of indexes I and $\omega : HE \rightarrow [0,1]$ a weight function. The set of vertices is defined as $HV = U \cup O \cup T$, U being the set of OSN users, O the set of objects and T the set of topics. Each hyperedge $he_i \in HE$ is in turn defined by a ordered pair $he_i = (he_i^+ = (HV_{he_i}^+, i); he_i^- = (i, HV_{he_i}^-))$. The element he_i^+ is called the* tail *of the hyperarc he_i whereas he_i^- is its* head, *$HV_{he_i}^+ \subseteq HV$ being the set of vertices of he_i^+, $HV_{he_i}^- \subseteq HV$ the set of vertices of he_i^- and $HV_{he_i} = HV_{he_i}^+ \cup HV_{he_i}^-$ the subset of vertices constituting the whole hyperedge.*

In our model, vertices and hyperedges are considered as *abstract data types* to model the entities involved in several social networks and the related relationships by a set of properties (attributes and methods); in particular, we use the "dot notation" to manage the attributes of a given vertex or hyperedge, for instances we can represent the id, name, timestamp, type of OSN and type of relationships by e_i.id, e_i.name, e_i.time, e_i.source and e_i.type. Moreover, it is possible to associate the weight function the "confidence" of a given relationship in terms of probability.

We can also define the *incidence matrix I* of an HSN in the following way:

$$i(v, he_i) = \begin{cases} 1, & \text{if } v \in HV_{e_i} \\ 0, & \text{otherwise} \end{cases} \tag{1}$$

The social paths, composed by sequences of hyperedges, represent a means to connect the entities of our model.

Definition 2 (Social Path). *A social path between two vertices v_{s_1} and v_{s_k} of an OSN is a sequence of distinct vertices and hyperedges $sp(v_{s_1}, v_{s_k}) = v_{s_1}, he_{s_1}, v_{s_2}, ..., he_{s_{k-1}}, v_{s_k}$ such that $\{v_{s_i}, v_{s_{i+1}}\} \subseteq HV_{he_{s_i}}$ for $1 \leq i \leq k - 1$. The length γ of the hyperpath is $\alpha \cdot \sum_{i=1}^{k-1} \frac{1}{\omega(he_{s_i})}$, α being a normalizing factor. We say that a social path contains a vertex v_h if $\exists he_{s_i} : v_h \in he_{s_i}$.*

Thus, the different types of relationships, described in Sect. 3.2, allow to define several social paths between two nodes: two users can be "directly" connected by a given path respectively because they are members of same groups or are friends, or "indirectly" if they have shared the same image or commented the same video.

Other useful definitions in our model are those related to concepts of *distance* between two nodes and *nearest neighbors* of a node.

Definition 3 (Distances). *We define* minimum distance $(d_{min}(v_k, v_j))$, maximum distance $(d_{max}(v_k, v_j))$ *and* average distance $(d_{avg}(v_k, v_j))$ *between two vertices of an HSN the length of the shortest hyperpath, the length of the longest hyperpath and the average length of the hyperpaths between v_k and v_j, respectively. In a similar manner, we define the* minimum distance $(d_{min}(v_k, v_j | v_z))$, maximum distance $(d_{max}(v_k, v_j | v_z))$ *and* average distance $(d_{avg}(v_k, v_j | v_z))$ *between two vertices v_k and v_j, for which there exists a hyperpath containing v_z.*

Definition 4 (λ-Nearest Neighbors Set). *Given a vertex $v_k \in V$ of an HSN, we define the λ-Nearest Neighbors Set of v_k the subset of vertices NN_k^λ such that $\forall v_j \in NN_k^\lambda$ we have $d_{min}(v_k, v_j) \leq \lambda$ with $v_j \in U$. Considering only the constrained hyperpaths containing a vertex v_z, we denote with NN_{iz}^λ the set of nearest neighbors of v_k such that $\forall v_j \in NN_{iz}^\lambda$ we have $\tilde{d}_{min}(v_k, v_j | v_z) \leq \lambda$.*

Using the above definition, we can define λ-*Nearest Users Set* and λ-*Nearest Objects Set*, denoted as NNU^λ and NNO^λ, considering as neighbors only vertices that belong to respectively users and objects type.

3.2   Relationships

We classify the relationships that can be established in the well-known Online Social Networks in the following three categories: (i) **User to User** relationships, describing user actions towards other users; (ii) **Similarity** relationships, describing a relatedness between two objects, users or topics and (iii) **User to Object** relationships, representing the action made by users on objects, that can be involved some topics or other users. In the following, we provide the definition for each type of relationships with some examples.

Definition 5 (User to User relationship). *Let $\hat{U} \subseteq U$ a subset of users in an OSN, we define* user to user relationship *each hyperedge he_i with the following properties: (1) $HV_{he_i}^+ = u_k$ such that $u_k \in \hat{U}$, (2) $HV_{he_i}^- \subseteq \hat{U} - u_k$.*

Examples of "user to user" relationships are properly represented by *friendship*, *following* or *membership* of some online social networks (see Fig. 1). For this kind of relationships, we can set $\omega(he_i)$ to a value in [0,1] that is function of the specific relationship and depends on the particular supported application. In the opposite, a general strategy can assign the value 1 to each user to user relationship.

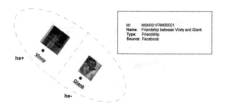

Fig. 1. Friendship relationship.

Definition 6 (Similarity relationship). *Let $v_k, v_j \in V$ $(k \neq j)$ two vertices of the same type of an OSN, we define* similarity relationship *each hyperedge he_i with $HV^+_{he_i} = v_k$ and $HV^-_{he_i} = v_j$. The weight function for this relationship returns similarity value between the two vertices.*

It is possible to compute a similarity value: between two users (by considering different types of features (interests, profile information, preferences, etc.)); between two objects (using the well-known high and low level features and metrics proposed in the literature); between two topics (by the well-known metrics on vocabularies or ontologies). In our model, a similarity hyperedge is effectively generated if $\omega(he_i) \geq \eta$, η being a given threshold (see Fig. 2).

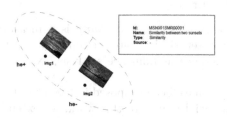

Fig. 2. Multimedia similarity relationship.

Definition 7 (User to Object relationship). *Let $\widehat{U} \subseteq U$ a set of users, $\widehat{T} \subseteq T$ a set of topics and $\widehat{O} \subseteq O$ a set of objects in a OSN, we define* user to object relationship *each hyperedge he_i with the following properties: (1) $HV^+_{he_i} = u_k$ such that $u_k \in \widehat{U}$, (2) $HV^-_{he_i} \subseteq \widehat{O} \cup \widehat{T} \cup \widehat{U}$.*

Examples of "user to object" relationships (see Fig. 3) are represented, *publishing, reaction, annotation, review, comment* (in the last three cases the set $HV^-_{e_i}$ can also contains one or more topics) or *user tagging* (involving also one ore more users) activities. For this kind of relationships, we set $\omega(he_i)$ to a value in $[0,1]$ that is function of the specific relationship and depends on the particular supported application. In the opposite, a general strategy can assign the value 1 to each user to object relationship.

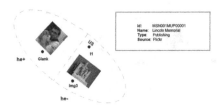

Fig. 3. Multimedia tagging relationship.

3.3 Hypergraph Building

The proposed hypergraph building process, in part inspired by the methodology proposed in [15], consist of three different stages. In the first step, called *hypergraph structure construction*, the crawled information about objects, users and their relationships is used to construct the hypergraph structures in terms of nodes and hyperedges. Successively, in the *topic learning* phase, we use the LDA approach, proposed in [12], to learn the most important topics and to infer relations between topics and textual annotations. In the last stage, called *similarity computation*, a similarity values between users, objects and topics are eventually determined using proper strategies.

3.4 Centrality Measures

In the Social Network Analysis, the *centrality* is a measure to represent the "importance" of a given user within related community that is possible to exploit for several applications, such as influence analysis, expert finding, community detection and so on.

Several measures [24] have been proposed in literature to determine the centrality of a node in a social graph. In this work, we extend the most diffused ones (in the case of undirected graphs) on the introduced hypergraph-based HSN model and define a new centrality measure based on the concept of "neighborhood" among users.

Definition 8 (Degree Centrality). *Let $v_k \in V$ a vertex of an HSN and I the related incidence matrix, we define the* degree centrality *of v_k as:*

$$dc(v_k) = \sum_{he_i \in HE} i(v_k, he_i) \tag{2}$$

In other terms, the degree centrality of a given node corresponds to the number of social relationships in which the node is involved.

Definition 9 (Closeness Centrality). *Let $v_k \in HV$ a vertex of an HSN, we define the* closeness centrality *of v_k as:*

$$cc(v_k) = \frac{1}{\sum_{v_j \in V} d_{min}(v_k, v_j)} \tag{3}$$

In this case, the closeness centrality of a node depends on the sum of distances respect to all the other nodes. The nodes from which is more simple to reach the other ones are those more important.

Definition 10 (Betweenness Centrality). *Let* $v_k \in HV$ *a vertex of an HSN, we define the* betweenness centrality *of* v_k *as:*

$$bc(v_k) = \frac{\sum_{v_j \neq v_z \in V} \sigma_{v_j v_z}(v_k)}{\sigma_{v_j v_z}} \tag{4}$$

$\sigma_{v_j v_z}(v_k)$ *being the number of shortest hyperpaths connecting* v_j, v_z *and passing through* v_k, *while* $\sigma_{v_j v_z}$ *is the total number of shortest hyperpaths between* v_j, v_z,

In other terms, the betweenness centrality measures the number of times that a node is present in the shortest hyperpaths between each pair of distinct vertices of a hypergraph.

In addition to the discussed measures, we have introduced a novel centrality measure that exploits the concept of λ-Nearest Neighbors Set.

Definition 11 (Neighborhood Centrality). *Let* $v_k \in HV$ *a vertex of an HSN and* λ *a given threshold, we define the* neighborhood centrality *of* v_k *as:*

$$nc(v_k) = \frac{\left| NN_{v_k}^{\lambda} \cap HV \right|}{|HV| - 1} \tag{5}$$

NN_k^{λ} *being the* λ-Nearest Users Set *of* v_k.

The neighborhood centrality of a given node can be measured by the number of nodes that are "reachable" within a certain number of steps using the available social paths among the different social entities.

Except for the degree centrality, the other introduced measures can be computed locally with respect to a community of users $(\widehat{U} \subseteq U \subseteq HV)$ and considering only vertices of user type for the end-to-end nodes of hyperpaths. In this manner, centrality is refereed to user importance within the related community. We define *user centrality* such kind of measure. In addition, in order to give more importance to user-to-content relationships during the computation of distances for the user neighborhood centrality, we can apply a *penalty* if the considered hyperpaths contain some users; in this way, all the distances can be computed as $\tilde{d}(v_k, v_j) = d(v_k, v_j) + \beta \cdot N$, N being the number of user vertices in the hyperpath between v_i and v_j and β a scaling factor[1]. Eventually, we can obtain a *topic-sensitive centrality* for the closeness, betweenness and neighborhood measures considering in the distances' computation only hyperpaths that contain a given topic node. Just as an example, the *topic-sensitive user neighborhood centrality* for a given user community is:

$$nc(u_k | \widehat{U}, t_z) = \frac{\left| NNU_{u_k t_z}^{\lambda} \cap \widehat{U} \right|}{\left| \widehat{U} \right| - 1} \tag{6}$$

---

[1] Such strategy is necessary to penalize *lurkers*, i.e., users of an HN that do not directly interact with content but through user to user relationships.

$\widehat{U}$ being a user community, u_k a single user and t_z a given topic.

3.5 HSN Computation

Generally, hypergraphs are very complex data structures to manage, and for computational reasons, different approaches have been introduced to deal with their intrinsic complexity [18], especially for large graphs. In this work, we have chosen to adopt the methodology that transforms the MSN hypergraph into a *bi-partite* graph. In particular, each hyperedge is mapped into a subgraph with the following characteristics (see Fig. 4): (i) each hypergraph vertex corresponds to a subgraph vertex; (ii) the hyperedge generates a new vertex: each vertex in $V_{e_i}^+$ and $V_{e_i}^-$ is separately connected to the new vertex by a directed edge; (iii) the hyperedge weight is uniformly distributed over each path connecting the vertex in $V_{e_i}^+$ to the vertices in $V_{e_i}^-$.

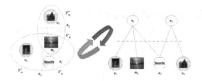

Fig. 4. HSN mapping on bi-partite graph.

4 Lurker Detection Algorithm

In this section we describe our approach based on HSN model to address the lurker problem. We propose a two steps algorithm based on the "Follow the Leader strategy" [30], an intuitive sequential prediction strategy; firstly, it detects the most influential people in a network and successively identify the lurker as the user that is attached to the central node only for receiving information, without producing any further knowledge. To better explain our idea, we consider the subnet described in the Hypergraph representation showed in Fig. 5[2]. It's easily noted in Fig. 5 that the *Mr x* user is a lurker; in fact he is able to reach all users in HSN through *Giank* node. Table 1 reports the user centrality measures' values related to the HSN representation. We can note as the introduced centrality measure can be effectively detect possible lurkers.

Considering the proposed neighborhood measure, it is possible to note that the node *Mister X* is a *candidate* lurker: in fact, it has a minimal neighborhood centrality linked to a node having maximal neighborhood centrality. In the following, we report the proposed algorithm that describes the previous intuitions.

---

[2] We have also considered the most important topics within the reviews.

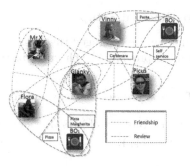

Fig. 5. Example of HSN.

Table 1. Example of user centrality measures

	Degree	Closeness	Betweenness	Neighborhood ($\lambda = 2$, $\beta = 1.5$)
Vinny	2.00	0.14	0.0	0.25
Picus	2.00	0.14	0.0	0.25
Giank	5.00	0.25	0.6	0.75
MisterX	2.00	0.16	0.0	0.0
Flora	3.00	0.16	0.0	0.25

Algorithm 1. Identify lurker candidate set L

Require: HSN
Ensure: $L = \{s_1, s_2, \ldots, s_k\}$
$NC \leftarrow ComputeCentrality$
$P_h = \max \{NC\}$
$P_l = \min \{NC\}$
for $p_l \in P_l$ **do**
   for $p_h \in P_h$ **do**
      if $\exists he : i(p_l, he) = 1 \wedge i(p_h, he) = 1$ **then**
         Add p_l to L
      end if
   end for
end for
return L

---

5 Evaluation

In this section we present the experimental evaluation aiming at evaluating efficiency and effectiveness of our approach for lurkers detection. First, we analyzed efficiency for the proposed HSN data model, showing both the elapsed times to build a bipartite graph implementation of an HSN hypergraph and computation times for the discussed user centrality measures, varying the dimension of the graph. In the second phase, we evaluated the recall and precision in the lurkers detection task with respect to a given ground truth.

5.1   Dataset and Experimental Setup

For our experimental campaign, we leveraged the *Yelp Challenge Dataset*[3], provided by Yelp in 2014. Table 2 provides the characterization of our dataset.

Table 2. Dataset characterization

Dataset	Users	Business objects	Reviews	Tips
Yelp	1 M	144 K	4.1 M	947 K

In particular, we exploited the following information to build of our HSN: (i) users' friendships: they have been used to instantiate user-to-user relationships; (ii) users' reviews: they have been used to instantiate user-to-content relationships (topics were extracted form the textual information attached to the different reviews using the LDA-based approach [12]); (iii) business objects' geographical coordinates: they have been used to instantiate objects' similarity relationships based on a "closeness distance"; (iv) for each user the number of reviews, compliments and friends and the number of votes assigned to her/his reviews: such data have been used to obtain a Yelp users' ranking, adopted as ground-truth for our experiments. All the experiments were performed using the *Databricks* platform[4], a cloud-based [2] big data processing environment based on Spark. We exploited 5 computing nodes each one composed by 8 cores and 15 GB RAM. All the algorithms have been implemented in Apache Spark using Scala 2.11.

5.2   Efficiency

Figure 6(a) shows loading times for the HSN bipartite graph varying its size (total number of edges and nodes); in turn, Fig. 6(b) reports elapsed times for computing the different centrality measures on the bipartite data structure.

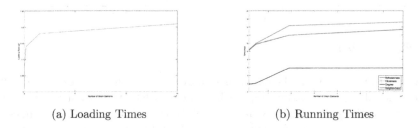

(a) Loading Times   (b) Running Times

Fig. 6. Efficiency for the bipartite graph.

---
[3] https://www.yelp.com/dataset_challenge.
[4] https://databricks.com/.

5.3 Effectiveness

Due to the lacks of ground-truth for lurker detection we adopted an approach based on data-driven methodology as suggested in [32] and used it to assess the proposed and competing methods. We first generated a ground-truth using different information contained in the Yelp dataset. In particular, the ground truth represents a sort of ranking for Yelp users, where the rank or popularity of each user has been computed as a linear and weighted combination of the following four parameters: (i) the number of reviews, (ii) the number of compliments, (iii) the number of friends and (iv) the number of votes assigned by other users to her/his reviews.

Successively, we used Algorithm 1 on the generated ground truth to identify the set of possible lurkers (that correspond to the most inactive users). Then, we evaluated how each user centrality measure allows to detect lurkers with respect to the ground-truth above defined by leveraging the following measures of *Recall* and *Precision*:

$$R = \frac{|\hat{U} \cap \tilde{U}|}{|\hat{U}|} \qquad P = \frac{|\hat{U} \cap \tilde{U}|}{|\tilde{U}|}$$

where $\hat{U}$ corresponds to the set of lurkers in the ground-truth and $\tilde{U}$ is the set of lurkers computed by a specific centrality measure.

In the Table 3 we show the values of recall and precision for each kind of user centrality considering the whole Yelp dataset. The results were obtained as average values varying the cardinality of the set of lurkers from 50 to 200[5].

Table 3. Recall and precision measures

	Recall	Precision
Degree	0.13	0.25
Closeness	0.24	0.29
Betweenness	0.33	0.30
Neighborhood	0.48	0.55

6 Conclusion

In this paper we described a data model for *Heterogeneous Social Networks*, combining information on users together with the generated content. Inspired by hypergraph based approaches, our model provides a solution for representing HSNs sufficiently general with respect to: (i) a particular social information network, (ii) the different kinds of entities, (iii) the different types of relationships, (iv) the different applications. Moreover, we implemented an algorithm for lurker detection based on concept of neighborhood among users exploiting the features of this model.

---

[5] For the Neighborhood centrality, we set $\lambda = 6$ and $\alpha = 1.5$.

As future work, we are planning to: (i) compare our approach with others proposed in literature; (ii) develop more sophisticated algorithms for lurkers detections; (iii) design and develop more algorithms for other data privacy and security problems on the top of the implemented system.

References

1. Aggarwal, C.C.: An introduction to social network data analytics. In: Aggarwal, C. (ed.) Social Network Data Analytics, pp. 1–15. Springer, Boston (2011). doi:10.1007/978-1-4419-8462-3_1
2. Amato, F., Mazzeo, A., Moscato, V., Picariello, A.: A framework for semantic interoperability over the cloud, pp. 1259–1264 (2013)
3. Amato, F., Castiglione, A., De Santo, A., Moscato, V., Picariello, A., Persia, F., Sperlí, G.: Recognizing human behaviours in online social networks. Comput. Secur. (2017)
4. Amato, F., Moscato, V., Picariello, A., Sperlì, G.: Multimedia social network modeling: a proposal. In: 2016 IEEE Tenth International Conference on Semantic Computing (ICSC), pp. 448–453 (2016)
5. Amichai-Hamburger, Y., Gazit, T., Bar-Ilan, J., Perez, O., Aharony, N., Bronstein, J., Dyne, T.S.: Psychological factors behind the lack of participation in online discussions. Comput. Hum. Behav. **55**, 268–277 (2016)
6. Ardichvili, A.: Learning and knowledge sharing in virtual communities of practice: motivators, barriers, and enablers. Adv. Develop. Hum. Resour. **10**(4), 541–554 (2008). doi:10.1177/1523422308319536
7. Benevenuto, F., Rodrigues, T., Cha, M., Almeida, V.: Characterizing user navigation and interactions in online social networks. Inf. Sci. **195**, 1–24 (2012)
8. Carullo, G., Castiglione, A., De Santis, A.: Friendship recommendations in online social networks. In: 2014 International Conference on Intelligent Networking and Collaborative Systems, pp. 42–48, September 2014
9. Carullo, G., Castiglione, A., De Santis, A., Palmieri, F.: A triadic closure and homophily-based recommendation system for online social networks. World Wide Web **18**(6), 1579–1601 (2015). doi:10.1007/s11280-015-0333-5
10. Castiglione, A., Cattaneo, G., De Santis, A.: A forensic analysis of images on online social networks. In: 2011 Third International Conference on Intelligent Networking and Collaborative Systems, pp. 679–684, November 2011
11. Castiglione, A., D'Alessio, B., De Santis, A.: Steganography and secure communication on online social networks and online photo sharing. In: 2011 International Conference on Broadband and Wireless Computing, Communication and Applications, pp. 363–368, October 2011
12. Colace, F., De Santo, M., Greco, L., Amato, F., Moscato, V., Picariello, A.: Terminological ontology learning and population using latent dirichlet allocation. J. Vis. Lang. Comput. **25**(6), 818–826 (2014)
13. Dhungel, P., Wu, D., Schonhorst, B., Ross, K.W.: A measurement study of attacks on bittorrent leechers. IPTPS **8**, 7 (2008)
14. Edelmann, N.: Reviewing the definitions of "lurkers" and some implications for online research. Cyberpsychology Behav. Soc. Netw. **16**(9), 645–649 (2013)
15. Fang, Q., Sang, J., Xu, C., Rui, Y.: Topic-sensitive influencer mining in interest-based social media networks via hypergraph learning. IEEE Trans. Multimedia **16**(3), 796–812 (2014)

16. Fazeen, M., Dantu, R., Guturu, P.: Identification of leaders, lurkers, associates and spammers in a social network: context-dependent and context-independent approaches. Soc. Netw. Anal. Min. **1**(3), 241–254 (2011)

17. Halfaker, A., Keyes, O., Taraborelli, D.: Making peripheral participation legitimate: reader engagement experiments in Wikipedia. In: Proceedings of the 2013 Conference on Computer Supported Cooperative Work, CSCW 2013, NY, USA, pp. 849–860 (2013). doi:10.1145/2441776.2441872

18. Heintz, B., Chandra, A.: Beyond graphs: toward scalable hypergraph analysis systems. ACM SIGMETRICS Perform. Eval. Rev. **41**(4), 94–97 (2014)

19. Hoang Long, N., Jung, J.J.: Privacy-aware framework for matching online social identities in multiple social networking services. Cybern. Syst. **46**(1–2), 69–83 (2015)

20. Interdonato, R., Pulice, C., Tagarelli, A.: Community-based Delurking in social networks. In: 2016 IEEE/ACM International Conference on Advances in Social Networks Analysis and Mining (ASONAM), pp. 263–270. IEEE (2016)

21. Interdonato, R., Pulice, C., Tagarelli, A.: Got to have faith!: the devotion algorithm for Delurking in social networks. In: Proceedings of the 2015 IEEE/ACM International Conference on Advances in Social Networks Analysis and Mining 2015, pp. 314–319. ACM (2015)

22. Interdonato, R., Tagarelli, A.: To trust or not to trust lurkers?: evaluation of lurking and trustworthiness in ranking problems. In: Wierzbicki, A., Brandes, U., Schweitzer, F., Pedreschi, D. (eds.) NetSci-X 2016. LNCS, vol. 9564, pp. 43–56. Springer, Cham (2016). doi:10.1007/978-3-319-28361-6_4

23. Javarone, M.A., Interdonato, R., Tagarelli, A.: Modeling evolutionary dynamics of lurking in social networks. In: Cherifi, H., Gonçalves, B., Menezes, R., Sinatra, R. (eds.) Complex Networks VII. SCI, vol. 644, pp. 227–239. Springer, Cham (2016). doi:10.1007/978-3-319-30569-1_17

24. Kang, C., Molinaro, C., Kraus, S., Shavitt, Y., Subrahmanian, V.: Diffusion centrality in social networks. In: Proceedings of the 2012 International Conference on Advances in Social Networks Analysis and Mining (ASONAM 2012), pp. 558–564. IEEE Computer Society (2012)

25. Kollock, P., Smith, M.: Managing the virtual commons. Comput.-Mediated Commun. Linguist. Soc. Cross-Cult. Perspect. 109–128 (1996)

26. Lave, J., Wenger, E.: Situated Learning: Legitimate Peripheral Participation. Cambridge University Press, Cambridge (1991)

27. Muller, M., Shami, N.S., Millen, D.R., Feinberg, J.: We are all lurkers: consuming behaviors among authors and readers in an enterprise file-sharing service. In: Proceedings of the 16th ACM International Conference on Supporting Group Work, pp. 201–210. ACM (2010)

28. Nonnecke, B., Preece, J.: Lurker demographics: counting the silent. In: Proceedings of the SIGCHI Conference on Human Factors in Computing Systems, pp. 73–80. ACM (2000)

29. Ridings, C., Gefen, D., Arinze, B.: Psychological barriers: lurker and poster motivation and behavior in online communities. Commun. Assoc. Inf. Syst. **18**(1), 16 (2006)

30. de Rooij, S., van Erven, T., Grunwald, P.D., Koolen, W.M.: Follow the leader if you can, hedge if you must. J. Mach. Learn. Res. **15**, 1281–1316 (2014)

31. Scott, J.: Social Network Analysis. Sage, London (2012)

32. Tagarelli, A., Interdonato, R.: Lurking in social networks: topology-based analysis and ranking methods. Soc. Netw. Anal. Min. **4**(1), 1–27 (2014)

Static Taint Analysis Method for Intent Injection Vulnerability in Android Applications

Bin Xiong[1], Guangli Xiang[1]([✉]), Tianyu Du[2], Jing (Selena) He[3], and Shouling Ji[2]

[1] College of Computer Science and Technology,
Wuhan University of Technology, Wuhan, China
`13072799038@163.com, glxiang@whut.edu.cn`
[2] College of Computer Science and Technology,
Zhejiang University, Hangzhou, China
`tydusky@gmail.com, sji@zju.edu.cn`
[3] Department of Computer Science, Kennesaw State University,
Marietta, GA 30060, USA
`jhe4@kennesaw.edu`

Abstract. In the component communication of Android application, the risk that Intent can be constructed by attackers may result in malicious component injection. To solve this problem, we develop IntentSoot, a prototype for detecting Intent injection vulnerability in both public components and private components for Android applications based on static taint analysis. It first builds call graph and control flow graph of Android application, and then tracks the taint propagation within a component, between components and during the reflection call to detect the potential Intent injection vulnerability. Experimental results validate the effectiveness of IntentSoot in various kinds of applications.

Keywords: Static taint analysis · Call graph · Control flow graph · Intent injection vulnerability

1 Introduction

With the growing momentum of the Android operating system, thousands of applications (also called apps) emerge every day on the official Android market (Google Play) and other alternative markets. In the second quarter of 2016, Android devices occupied 86.2% of total sales on mobile operating system, and 2600 thousand apps have been installed from Google Play store in December 2016. Due to the fact that many application developers have poor security awareness and application markets do not take comprehensive security testing measures, there are various security vulnerabilities in a large number of applications, which brings security risks to users.

In order to enhance application security, each application is assigned a user ID (UID) and runs in an isolated virtual machine. However, applications need to share data with others in a collaborative environment, so Android provides a

© Springer International Publishing AG 2017
S. Wen et al. (Eds.): CSS 2017, LNCS 10581, pp. 16–31, 2017.
https://doi.org/10.1007/978-3-319-69471-9_2

flexible communication mechanism named Inter-Process Communication (IPC), which takes place in Binder or Intent [11]. Among them, Intent can transfer messages between the same or different application components as a message container (including action, data, type, extras and other properties), which achieves Inter Component Communication (ICC). A large number of studies have shown that the introduction of ICC mechanism will expose applications to a variety of external stressful conditions, and therefore applications is likely to receive a large number of untrusted data, which causes security vulnerabilities. Intent injection is an ICC application vulnerability. Generally, the application with an intent injection contains a public component. The application can receive a malicious intent message. Intent injection vulnerability is a relatively common ICC vulnerability. Applications with this type of vulnerability typically contain a public component. After the application receives a maliciously constructed Intent message, it does not perform valid security authentication and directly parses out the parameters for some security-sensitive operations, resulting in malicious behaviors such as privilege elevation, information leakage, and even remote code execution.

Related Work. Methods for detecting Intent injection vulnerability can be roughly divided into two kinds, including dynamic analysis and static analysis [14]. Dynamic analysis sends random input to the target application to identify potential vulnerabilities by monitoring software anomalies. JarJarBink modified the ICC parameters according to a custom variation strategy and sent them to the target application component to evaluate the ICC [7]. Intent Fuzzer used a new method combined with static analysis and test case generation [10]. For all the public components of the application, the data structure of Intent is obtained by static analysis, and then the corresponding fields are randomly changed. Compared with JarJarBinks, Intent Fuzzer can detect exceptions from deeper logic of code segments. However, it is difficult for the Fuzzing method to find available vulnerabilities along with a lot of empty pointer exceptions. Without running the practical application, static analysis directly analyzes Dalvik bytecode of the application and extracts potential malicious behaviors. ComDroid [1] used static analysis to detect ICC problems, but they believed that as long as the component is exposed and there is no privilege protection, there are Intent injection attacks. This coarse-grained analysis method will lead to a quantity of false positives. CHEX found data flow between application components by connecting all the code segments from the entry point to detect component hijacking vulnerabilities [6]. However, due to the absence of data flow analysis between components, they cannot detect the injection of private components, leading to false negatives. Epicc [8] transformed the ICC issue to an IDE problem [9], but there are still a lot of false positives. At the Blackhat conference in 2014, Daniele proposed a static detection approach for Intent message vulnerabilities in Android applications [7], but it only detects vulnerabilities in a single Activity component, which exists false negatives. Recently, IccTA proposed a static detection method for ICC problems [4,5], which can be modified to directly connect components but cannot detect the vulnerability during reflection calls. Since component exposure does not imply the presence of Intent injection and Intent injection exists not only in public components, the above-mentioned studies is common in false positives or false negatives and cannot effectively analyze the dynamic loading as well as reflection mechanism in Android.

Our Contribution. In this paper, we present IntentSoot, a prototype to effectively detect the Intent injection vulnerability in Android applications based on static taint analysis. By defining the Intent message as a taint source and tracking the propagation of taint data within a component, IntentSoot can effectively reduce the number of false positives and false negatives between components and during reflection calls.

Roadmap. The rest of this paper is organized as follows. Section 2 introduces the communication process security analysis in Android applications. Section 3 presents the overall structure of IntentSoot. Section 4 details the principles of IntentSoot. Section 5 shows the datasets and experimental results. Section 6 concludes the paper.

2   Communication Process Security Analysis in Android Application

2.1   Component Communication Mechanism

Android applications have four types of components, including Activity, Service, BroadcastReceiver and ContentProvider. Except ContentProvider, the communication between the other three components requires an Intent message. Intent is a media for ICC process to convey messages. Intent contains both the explicit and the implicit, among which explicit Intent specifies the receiving component by name, so the Intent is sent to a particular application component. However, implicit Intent's receiver can be all components that meet the conditions, and the Android system determines which application can receive the Intent. Intent-filter tag can be added to a component in AndroidManifest file, thus receiving different Intent by defining action, category and data. In addition, all components that have the intent-filter tag and do not have the attribute "exported" valued false are public by default, and other applications can send Intent messages to public components.

2.2   Intent Injection Vulnerability in Application Communication Process

The Intent injection vulnerability was proposed in literature [2] at the first time, and an application with such vulnerability typically has a public component that can receive external Intent messages. The logic of internal processing in application directly uses the parameter information parsed from the Intent message for some security-sensitive operations without validation. If the Intent message is carefully constructed by the attacker, it will cause Intent injection. The threat model of Intent injection contains two roles, including attackers and victims, as shown in Fig. 1.

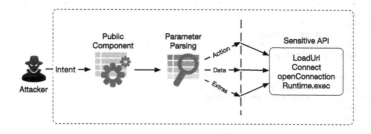

Fig. 1. Threat model for Intent injection attack

2.3   Intent Injection Example

Intent injection vulnerability means that, the taint data may not only flow within a component and between components in the process of taint data propagation, but also flow during the refection calls, as shown in Listing 1.1. Assuming that doSomethingBad1 and doSomethingBad2 are two security-sensitive API functions, then there are two Intent injection vulnerabilities in this example. The first vulnerability exists in the public component Activity01, where the parameter s1 is passed directly to the method doSomethingBad1 without any security check. The second vulnerability exists in the private component Activity02, where the parameter s4 is passed to the method sendMSG in the class SendMessage, and then passed to the method doSomethingBad2 without any security check. The Next-Intent attack described in [13] utilized the Dropbox application's private components. The presence of the Intent injection vulnerability in the VideoPlayerActivity caused the leak of token information of a large quantity of Drophox accounts. However, previous studies [1,3,6,8] were unable to detect Intent injection vulnerabilities in private components. Therefore, the purpose of this paper is to develop a static analysis tool which can detect Intent injection vulnerability in both public components and private components for Android applications through the static taint analysis method.

3   Overall Design for IntentSoot

This section systematically introduces our tool named IntentSoot, whose overall structure and flow chart is shown in Fig. 2. We make some definitions first to facilitate further description.

- **Source method:** The method where the caller is located, is represented by Sm. As shown in Listing 1.1, the onCreate method in Activity02 is a source method.
- **Source class:** The class where the source function is located, is represented by Sc.
- **Target method:** The called method, is represented by Tm. As shown in Listing 1.1, the sendMSG method in SendMessage is a target method.

```
1  //Activity01
2  onCreate(Bunlde ...){...
3    Intent i1 = this.getIntent();
4    String s1 = i1.getData().getQueryParameter("key1"); //source
5    String s2 = i1.getStringExtra("key2"); //source
6    ...
7    doSomethingWith(s1);
8    Intent i2 = new Intent();
9    i2.setClass(..., BroadcastReceiver01.class);
10   i2.putExtra("key2", s2);
11   sendBroadcast(i2);
12 }
13 Public void doSomethingWith(String value){
14   doSomethingBad1(value);//sink
15 }
16 //BroadcastReceiver01
17 OnReceive(Context c, Intent i3){...
18   Intent i4 = new Intent(c, Activity02.class);
19   String s3 = i3.getStringExtra("key2");
20   I4.putExtra("key3",s3);
21   C.startActivity(i4);
22 }
23 //Activity02
24 onCreate(Bunlde){...
25   Intent i5 = getIntent();
26   String s4 = i5.getStringExtra("key3");
27   File file = new File("/adcard/DynamicLoadClient.apk");
28   if (file.exist()){
29     DexClassLoader cl = new DexClassLoader(file.toString(), ...);
30     try{
31        Class<?> myClass = cl.loadClass("com.dynamicloadclient.SendMessage");
32        Constructor<?> constructor = myClass.getConstructor(new Class[]{String.class});
33        Object object = constructor.newInstance(new Object[]{"MessageMark"});
34        Method action = myClass.getMethod("SendMSG", new Class[]{String.class});
35        action.invoke(object, s4);
36     } catch (Exception e) {
37        e.printStackTrace();
38     }
39   }
40 }
41 //SendMessage
42 public void sendMSG(String content){
43   doSomethingBad2(content);//sink
44 }
```

Listing 1.1. The Intent injection example for apps without reflection

- **Target class:** The class where the called function is located, is represented by Tc. As shown in Listing 1.1, the SendMessage class is a target class.
- **Reflection method:** The method used by the caller to implement the reflection mechanism, including the newInstance and invoke methods, is represented by Rm. As shown in Listing 1.1, the newInstance method in line 33 and the invoke method in line 35 are reflection methods.

IntentSoot mainly consists of two parts: dynamic execution module (IntentSoot-D) and static analysis module(IntentSoot-S).

IntenSoot first runs IntentSoot-D, installing the app into the Android device. After installing the app, IntentSoot runs the app file and cyclically reads the system's log output to get information about the dynamic loading and reflection calls. When capturing the dynamic loading behaviors, IntentSoot sends an adb downloading command to the Android device, and then downloads the loaded

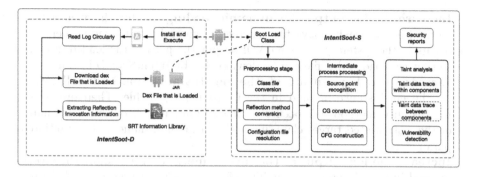

Fig. 2. Overall structure and flow chart of IntentSoot

dex file to the local computer. When capturing the reflection call behaviors, IntentSoot extracts the information such as Sm, Rm and Tm corresponding to the reflection call from the log, and stores the information in the form of a triple group of <Sm, Rm, Tm> in the local computer's file called SRT library. The downloaded dex file and SRT library will be used for subsequent static taint analysis.

When the dynamic execution module is finished, IntentSoot runs IntentSoot-S. IntentSoot-S is actually an improvement version of Soot [12]. It makes up Soot's defects by adding the dynamic execution module outputs, namely dex file and the SRT library, to static taint analysis. Meanwhile, the mapping table between ICC method and lifecycle method of target component is supplied to make up the defect that Soot cannot handle component communication. IntentSoot-S consists of three stages, including preprocessing stage, intermediate processing stage and taint analysis stage.

4 Principle Introduction for IntentSoot

4.1 Principle Introduction for IntentSoot-D

IntentSoot-D includes running the app, downloading the dex file to the local computer and collecting a triple group <Sm, Rm, Tm> of reflection call information into the SRT library. The downloaded dex files and the SRT library will be used for subsequent static taint analysis.

4.1.1 The Modifications for Android Source Code

We modify the Android source code according to the literature [15], and the modified Android version is 4.4. The main modifications include:

– **The modification of elements stored in the method call stack.** The method call stack in the source code only stores the class name and method name. In order to get complete information, we modified it to store parameters and return values of the method.

- **Increase the log output for dynamic loading.** Modify the openDexFile method in the DexFile.java file. Therefore, when dynamic loading behavior occurs in the system, the system will output the path of the loaded dex file, so that the loaded dex file can be downloaded by IntentSoot-D in time.
- **Increase the log output of the newInstance method call.** Modify the newInstance method in the Constructor.java file. Therefore, when newInstance method call occurs in the system, it will output class name of the instantiated target class, instantiated method name and instantiated parameters.
- **Increase the log output of the invoke method call.** Modify the invoke method in the Method.java file. Therefore, when invoke method call occurs in the system, it will output class name of the target class, method name and parameters of the target method.

The items 2-4 above corresponds to the log output, which includes not only the descripted log output but also the additional output, including log ID, uid number, operation number and call stack information, etc. The log ID is used to identify which log information need to be parsed by IntentSoot-D. Through the uid number, IntentSoot-D can identify which log output is generated by the application. The operation number is used to identify the type of monitored program behavior. According to the difference of called method, we set the newInstance, invoke, openDexFile method corresponding to the number 1, 2, 3. In addition, the Android system outputs not only the log information of the three items above but also the information of the Android method call stack in the current thread, which will assist the IntentSoot-D to get the information of source method and reflection method. The details will be described in Sect. 4.2.

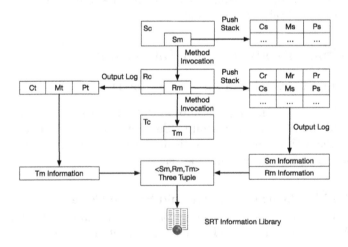

Fig. 3. Schematic diagram of log analysis

4.1.2 Log Analysis

After installing and running the application, IntentSoot can get the app's uid number. The app's running requires actual use, as well as triggering dynamic loading and reflection call as much as possible. IntentSoot-D will cyclically read the phone's log information, extracting the log informations of the app according to the uid. When reading a record of dynamically loading dex files, IntentSoot-D downloads the dex file to the specified folder in the local computer. When capturing the output information of the newInstance method or the invoke method, the IntentSoot extracts the information of the corresponding source method Sm, the reflection method Rm and the target method Tm, which will be stored in <Sm, Rm, Tm>.

The extraction principle of the information is described in Fig. 3. We use Cx, Mx, and Px to represent class name, method name and method parameter name, respectively. X can be a value of s, r or t, representing the source, the reflection and the target. For example, Cs represents the class name of the source class. According to the modification in Sect. 4.1.1, we can get the information of Tm directly from log when newInstance or invoke method is called. Similarly, we can get the information about Sm and Rm through the Android method call stack in current thread. The Android method call stack stores the method call sequence from the current method call in chronological order. The method information currently being called is stored on the top of the stack, and the last method call from the current method call is stored on the second unit. Thus, when a reflection method call occurs, the method at the top of the stack is usually the information of the reflection method Rm, and the second unit in the stack is the information of the source method Sm. According to the modification of the elements stored in the method call stack of Android system in Sect. 4.1.1, we can obtain the information of Sm, including Cs, Ms, Ps and the information of Rm, including Cr, Mr, Pr through the output stack information when the reflection method call occurs. Finally, IntentSoot-D will store Sm, Rm and Tm to the SRT library in the form of a triple group.

4.2 Principle Introduction for IntentSoot-S

When the dynamic execution module is finished, IntentSoot runs IntentSoot-S. First, the necessary Java class files in the apk file and in the dex file are loaded into memory and converted into Soot's internal representation–Jimple. Then the reflection method is converted according to SRT library while the source point is identified. Finally, IntentSoot builds correct CG and CFG and starts static taint analysis.

4.2.1 Class Loading

Soot's static analysis method is based on Soot's Jimple language. Soot loads all the classes contained in the apk file into memory, then builds the main method and constructs the function call graph and the control flow graph. In order to reduce the burden of memory, by using on-demand loading way, IntentSoot-S

```
1  $r14 = new array(java.lang.Object)[1]
2  $r14[0] = "MessageMark";
3  $r15 = virtualinvoke $r13.<java.lang.reflect.Constructor:java.lang.Object newInstance(
       java.lang.Object[])>($r14);
4  ...
5  $r14 = new array(java.lang.Object)[1];
6  $r14[0] = $r7
7  $r5 = virtualinvoke $r15.<java.lang.reflect.Method:java.lang.Object invoke(java.lang.
       Object, java.lang.Object)>($r5, $r14);
```

Listing 1.2. The Jimple code before the transformation of newInstance and invoke

loads the corresponding class in the loaded dex file. In other words, IntentSoot-S only loads the source classes and the target classes in the SRT library. When constructing the function call graph, Soot automatically loads the extra necessary classes according to the extension of the function call graph. The target method may exist either in the loaded dex file or in the class of the app or in the Android system library named android.jar, and these possible files will serve as the base class for Soot.

4.2.2 Modification Algorithm for Source Method

We first give the following definitions to facilitate the description of our algorithm.

- **Target reflection object.** The object of instantiating the target class through reflection mechanism, is represented by Fo, such as the "object" object that is shown in the 33rd line of Listing 1.1.
- **Target object.** The object of directly instantiating target class, is represented by To.
- **Target reflection parameter.** The parameter that is passed to the target method through the reflection mechanism, is represented by Fp, such as the $r14 array shown in the third line and seventh line of Listing 1.2.
- **Reflection object.** The object of instantiating reflection class, is represented by Ro, such as the "constructor" object in 32nd line and the "action" object in the 34th line of Listing 1.1.

An algorithm flow chart for specific source method modification is shown in Fig. 4. For SRT mapping, IntentSoot-S first judges whether the reflection method is newInstance or invoke method. For the invoke method, IntentSoot-S first transforms the target reflection parameter Fp into the target parameter Tp, then determines whether the target reflection object is empty. If it is empty, IntentSoot constructs a static target method call. If it is not empty, IntentSoot-S defines the object To of the target class type, and casts the target reflection object Fo to To, finally executes a non-static method call. The newInstance method contains two types of parameters and no parameters. For the newInstance method with parameters, IntentSoot-S first defines and creates a target object To, then casts the target reflection parameter Fp to the target parameter Tp, invokes the target method Tm (init ()) and instantiates it, finally reassigns the To object to the original target reflection object Fo to ensure that Fo is

```
 1 $r14 = new array(java.lang.Object)[1]
 2 $r14[0] = "MessageMark";
 3 $i1 = 0;
 4 if $i1==0 goto label08;
 5 $r18 = new com.dynamicloadclient.SendMessage;
 6 special invoke $r18.<com.dynamicloadclient.SendMessage:void<init>(java.lang.String)>("
       SendMessage");
 7 $r5 = $r18;
 8 goto label09;
 9 label08:
10 $r5 = virtualinvoke $r13.<java.lang.reflect.Constructor:java.lang.Object newInstance(
       java.lang.Object[])>($r14);
11 label09:
12 ...
13 $r14 = new array(java.lang.Object)[1];
14 $r14[0] = $r7
15 $i0 = 0;
16 if $i0==0 goto label14;
17 $r17 = (com.dynamicloadclient.SendMessage)$r5;
18 $r5 = virtualinvoke $r17.<java.lang.reflect.Method:java.lang.Object invoke(java.lang.
       Object, java.lang.Object)>($r5, $r14);
19 goto label15;
20 label14:
21 $r5 = virualinvoke $r15.<java.lang.reflect. Method:java.lang.Object invoke(java.lang.
       Object, java.lang.Object)>($r5, $r14);
22 label15:
```

Listing 1.3. The Jimple code after the transformation of newInstance and invoke

passed normally in the program. The source code of the 33rd and 35th line in Listing 1.1 corresponds to the Jimple code in Listing 1.2. Listing 1.3 shows the result of the modified source method in Listing 1.2.

4.2.3   Source and Sink Definitions

IntentSoot uses the static taint analysis method to detect the sensitive operation (Sink) by marking the untrusted input data (Source) and statically tracking the propagation path of the taint data. The Source and Sink are defined as follows.

- **Source method:** the GET method of the Intent object that is used to extract information about the Data and Extras fields, such as getStringExtra(), get-Data() and so on.
- **Sink method:** some security-sensitive operations that are related to the API, such as the page loading-loadUrl(), the command execution-Runtime.exec(), the database query-query() and so on.

4.2.4   Build CG and CFG

CG is a directed graph, of which the nodes represent the functions and the edges represent call points. In order to build a function call graph, IntentSoot needs to determine the entry function of the program first. However, in the lifecycle management of the components in Android, one of the lifecycle methods (e.g., onCreate) is likely to be the entry function of the program.

Since Intent injection vulnerability detection focuses primarily on the delivery of external Intent messages, when a public component receives an Intent message, the extraction of Intent object fields information is usually done in a

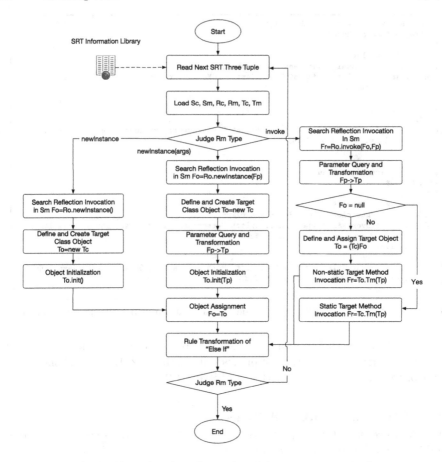

Fig. 4. Algorithm flow chart of modifying source method

specific lifecycle method. According to this feature, we defined the correspondence between different component types and the component entry methods, as listed in Table 1. IntentSoot selects the corresponding component entry method as the entry point of the CG and then analyzes all the function call statements from the CG entry.

CFG is also a directed graph. The nodes in CFG are basic blocks, and the edges in the graph represent the conditional information from one basic block to another basic block. IntentSoot traverses all nodes through Depth-first search algorithm and then generates a CFG for each function in CG.

4.3 Static Taint Analysis

Static taint analysis is based on the constructed CG and CFG, including the taint data trace within a component and between the components.

Table 1. Component entry method

Component type	Component entry method
Activity	void OnCreate(BundlesavedInstanceState);
Service	void OnBind(); void OnStartCommand();
BroadcastReceiver	void OnReceive();

4.3.1   The Taint Data Trace Within a Component

When the taint data within a component is tracked, IntentSoot identifies the relevant fields information of the Intent object as the taint source, then performs the taint data trace in program analysis to detect whether the taint data flows into Sink method. The taint analysis are analyzed from the entry point of the CG, traversing the CFG of each function. When the method call is encountered, IntentSoot analyzes the taint data propagation in the method call through the binding relationship between formal parameters and actual parameters.

4.3.2   The Taint Data Trace Between the Components

If the method call is an ICC method and its parameter Intent is taint data, it is necessary to track the propagation of the taint information between the components. As shown in the example application of Listing 1.1, when the program is analyzed into the sendBroadcast method in component Activity01, it is necessary to track the propagation of the taint data between components and then continue the taint analysis within the BroadcastReceiver01 component since parameter i2 is the taint data. It is also necessary to track the propagation of taint information between the BroadcastReceiver01 component and the Activity02 component. However, the fact that communication between components is performed by the operating system results in discontinuities of control flow graph between components, as shown in Fig. 5. There are no explicit call process between the sendBroadcast method of the Activity01 component and the onReceive method of the BroadcastReceiver01 component, so static analysis cannot track the data flow information between components.

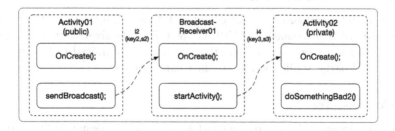

Fig. 5. ICC control flow for example application

To achieve the taint data trace between the components, IntentSoot should first determine the target components. When analyzing the ICC method, we can parse the Intent or the AndroidManifest.xml file to determine the target component. When the target component is determined, IntentSoot achieves the continuity of control flow and data flow between components by constructing a mapping table between the ICC methods and the lifecycle methods, as listed in Table 2. When an ICC method is invoked, it is automatically replaced with the corresponding lifecycle method, and the Intent is passed to the corresponding method for taint data trace.

Table 2. Mapping table between ICC methods and lifecycle methods of target component

Target component type	ICC method	Lifecycle method	Intent information pass
Activity	startActivity(Intent i) startActivityForResult(Intent i,···)	OnCreate(Bundle ···)	i→getIntent()
Service	startService(Intent i) bindService(Intent i,···)	OnStartCommand(Intent intent,···) OnBind(Intent intent)	i→Intent i→Intent
Broadcast receiver	sendBroadcast(Intent i) sendBroadcast(Intent i,···) sendOrderedBroadcast(Intent i, ···) sendOrderedBroadcast(Intent i,···) sendStickyBroadcast(Intent i) sendStickyOrderedBroadcast(Intent i,···)	OnReceive(···, Intent intent)	i→Intent

4.3.3   Vulnerability Detection

Intent injection vulnerability detection occurs in the process of tracking taint. When IntentSoot analyzes the internal Jimple statement, if the current statement contains a function call, IntentSoot will first determine whether the method is in the defined list of the Sink methods. If so, it further determines whether the relevant parameters are taint data. If so, it means there is a potential Intent injection vulnerability. Then data dependence graph of the parameters is generated, according to which the path of taint trace from the Source to the Sink is recorded.

5   Experimental Results

5.1   Experimental Environment

The experimental platform is 64-bit Ubuntu 14.04 operating system. The number of processor is 6. The frequency of CPU is 2.50 GHZ. The size of physical memory is 6 GB. We selects two sample sets that include the standard test application and the third party application to conduct experiments.

5.2   Contrast Test

In order to evaluate the performance of IntentSoot, we designed five types of standard test applications that contain public component C1, private component C2 and reflection calls, as listed in Table 3.

Table 3. Five types of standard test applications

Application type	Public component C1	Private component C2	Reflection call	Whether exists Intent vulnerability	Intent Soot	Epicc	Average analysis time
A	exist source and sink	-	-	yes	✓	✓	51/65
B	exist source	sink	-	yes	✓	missed positives	52/56
C	exist source	-	sink	yes	✓	missed positives	54/61
D	no source	-	-	no	✓	false positives	12/45
E	exist source, no sink	-	-	no	✓	false positives	46/51

In this experiment, IntentSoot and Epicc were used to analyze the five types of standard applications. Experimental results are shown in Table 3. We can find that Epicc can only detect C-type applications, while IntentSoot can correctly detect all five kinds of applications in terms of detection capability. Since Epicc supposed that there are Intent injection vulnerabilities in all public components, it didn't perform fine-grained analysis for applications. In addition, the average analysis time of IntentSoot is significantly less than Epicc, because IntentSoot analyzes only the public components in the application and the private components on demand, not handling the code of event response function in the process of handling a single component. However, Epicc needs to analyze all the components and all the code within a single component, causing large performance overhead.

5.3   Function Test

We not only analyzed the standard test applications but also collected 60 applications of 10M from third party application market (HiMarket) as test samples, including security management applications, social applications and mobile shopping applications. We found that seven test samples have the path from the Source to Sink. We manually created an exploit trigger to prove that there are indeed Intent injection vulnerabilities, and the test results are listed in Table 4. From the table, we can find that there are a large number of public components in each application. Furthermore, there are Intent injection vulnerabilities in a public component of sample1. The public component can load any page, and the WebView implements the *addJavaScriptInterface* interface, therefore it can embed the JavaScript code to execute remote command. Sink points in Sample3 occur in private components, so IntentSoot requires taint data trace between components. In addition, the number of public components in Sample6 is 11, and the analysis time of Sample6 is significantly more than any other applications, mainly because the code of each public component in Sample6 is much more complex than any other applications, and there may be codes such as reflection calls.

Table 4. Detection results for third party application vulnerability

Sample	Public component numbers/Total component numbers	Sink type	Within components/Between components	Analysis time (s)
Sample1	7/43	Open the web page (Can execute remote commands)	Within components	93
Sample2	8/63	Execute remote commands	Within components	111
Sample3	13/51	Open the web page	Between components	187
Sample4	8/52	Write the specified file	Within components	109
Sample5	8/49	Modify the database	Within components	55
Sample6	11/63	Send a text message to the specified number	Within components	257
Sample7	13/72	Modify the database	Within components	172

6   Conclusion

We proposed IntentSoot, a prototype for detecting Intent injection vulnerability of Android application based on static taint analysis, which considers the taint data trace within a component, between the components and during reflection calls. Compared with previous detection methods, experimental results shows that IntentSoot can effectively reduce false positives and false negatives while reducing performance overhead through only focusing on code snippets from the outside application's Intent message processing. However, IntentSoot does not consider taint propagations of JNI call in the program code, which we will study in the future.

Acknowledgments. This work was partly supported by NSFC under No. 61772466, the Provincial Key Research and Development Program of Zhejiang, China under No. 2017C01055, the Fundamental Research Funds for the Central Universities, the Alibaba-Zhejiang University Joint Research Institute for Frontier Technologies (A.Z.F.T.) under Program No. XT622017000118, and the CCF-Tencent Open Research Fund under No. AGR20160109.

References

1. Chin, E., Felt, A.P., Greenwood, K., Wagner, D.: Analyzing inter-application communication in android. In: International Conference on Mobile Systems, pp. 239–252. ACM (2011)
2. Enck, W., Octeau, D., McDaniel, P., Chaudhuri, S.: A study of android application security. In: USENIX Security, vol. 2, p. 21 (2011)
3. Gallingani, D.: Static detection and automatic exploitation of intent message vulnerabilities in android applications (2014)
4. Li, L., Bartel, A., Bissyandé, T.F., Klein, J., Le Traon, Y., Arzt, S., Rasthofer, S., Bodden, E., Octeau, D., McDaniel, P.: IccTA: detecting inter-component privacy leaks in android apps. In: International Conference on Software Engineering, vol. 1, pp. 280–291. IEEE (2015)
5. Li, L., Bartel, A., Klein, J., Traon, Y.L., Arzt, S., Rasthofer, S., Bodden, E., Octeau, D., Mcdaniel, P.: I know what leaked in your pocket: uncovering privacy leaks on android apps with static taint analysis. Computer Science (2014)

6. Lu, L., Li, Z., Wu, Z., Lee, W., Jiang, G.: Chex: statically vetting android apps for component hijacking vulnerabilities. In: ACM Conference on Computer and Communications Security, pp. 229–240. ACM (2012)
7. Maji, A.K., Arshad, F.A., Bagchi, S., Rellermeyer, J.S.: An empirical study of the robustness of inter-component communication in android. In: The 42nd Annual IEEE/IFIP International Conference on Dependable Systems and Networks (DSN), pp. 1–12. IEEE (2012)
8. Octeau, D., McDaniel, P., Jha, S., Bartel, A., Bodden, E., Klein, J., Le Traon, Y.: Effective inter-component communication mapping in android with epicc: an essential step towards holistic security analysis. In: USENIX Security, pp. 543–558 (2013)
9. Sagiv, M., Reps, T., Horwitz, S.: Precise interprocedural dataflow analysis with applications to constant propagation. Theor. Comput. Sci. **167**(1), 131–170 (1996)
10. Sasnauskas, R., Regehr, J.: Intent fuzzer: crafting intents of death. In: Joint International Workshop on Dynamic Analysis, pp. 1–5. ACM (2014)
11. Singapati, S.: Inter process communication in android (2012). https://dspace.cc.tut.fi/dpub/bitstream/handle/123456789/21105/singapati.pdf
12. Soot[eb/ol], G.: https://sable.github.io/soot/
13. Wang, R., Xing, L., Wang, X., Chen, S.: Unauthorized origin crossing on mobile platforms: threats and mitigation. In: ACM SIGSAC Conference on Computer & Communications Security, pp. 635–646. ACM (2013)
14. Yuqing, Z., Zhejun, F., Kai, W., Zhiqiang, W., Hongzhou, Y., Qixu, L.: Survey of android vulnerability detection. Comput. Res. Dev. **52**, 2167–2177 (2015)
15. Zhauniarovich, Y., Ahmad, M., Gadyatskaya, O., Crispo, B., Massacci, F.: Stadyna: addressing the problem of dynamic code updates in the security analysis of android applications. In: ACM Conference on Data and Application Security and Privacy, pp. 37–48. ACM (2015)

Achieving Differential Privacy of Data Disclosure from Non-intrusive Load Monitoring in Smart Grid

Hui Cao[1,3($\boxtimes$)], Shubo Liu[1], Zhitao Guan[2], Longfei Wu[4], and Tian Wang[5]

[1] School of Computer, Wuhan University, Wuhan 430072, China
2013102110071@whu.edu.cn
[2] School of Control and Computer Engineering,
North China Electric Power University, Beijing 102206, China
[3] North China Branch of State Grid Corporation of China, Beijing 10053, China
[4] Department of Mathematics and Computer Science,
Fayetteville State University, Fayetteville, NC 28301, USA
[5] College of Computer Science and Technology, Huaqiao University,
Xiamen 361021, China

Abstract. In smart grid, large quantities of smart meters are installed in customers' homes to collect electricity usage data, which can then be used to draw the load curve versus time of a day, and develop a plan or model for power generation. However, such data can also reveal customer's daily activities. In addition, a non-intrusive load monitoring (NILM) device can monitor an electrical circuit that contains a number of appliances which switch on and off independently. If an adversary analyzes the meter readings together with the data measured by NILM device, the customer's privacy will be disclosed. In this paper, we propose an effective privacy-preserving scheme for electric load monitoring, which can guarantee differential privacy of data disclosure in smart grid. In the proposed scheme, an energy consumption behavior model based on Factorial Hidden Markov Model (FHMM) is established. In addition, Laplace noise is added to the behavior parameter, which is different from the traditional methods that usually add noise to the energy consumption data. The analysis shows that the proposed scheme can get a better trade-off between utility and privacy compared with other popular methods.

Keywords: Differential privacy · Non-intrusive load monitoring · Factorial Hidden Markov Model · Kullback–Leibler divergence · Smart grid

1 Introduction

As a new generation of power grid, smart grid integrated with advanced information and communication technology is regarded as an efficient and robust grid. To optimize the energy utilization, lots of smart meters installed at users' households are connected to the communication network [1], and send their power consumption to the control center of smart grid at a fine granularity.

© Springer International Publishing AG 2017
S. Wen et al. (Eds.): CSS 2017, LNCS 10581, pp. 32–42, 2017.
https://doi.org/10.1007/978-3-319-69471-9_3

However, the fine-grained energy consumption data collected by smart meter may disclose the detailed information regarding the power consumption patterns of the household appliances, which raises serious concerns about the user's privacy [2]. Non-intrusive appliance load monitoring (NILM) is an advanced power signature analysis tool, which is often used to break down the aggregate energy consumption data into individual appliances [3]. Given a user's load profile, an adversary can track the states (ON or OFF) of all appliances with NILM. Based on the extracted device-level energy consumption data, the adversary can further infer lots of privacy-sensitive information about the user's habits and behaviors.

In fact, there is a significant body of work analyzing the users' privacy-preservation [4]. The major privacy-preserving solutions can be classified into homomorphic encryption [5–8], flattening energy signatures by battery-based load hiding (BLH) [9–12] and noise addition [13–15]. However, schemes based on homomorphic encryption need to spend huge computational cost and always need a third party for key distribution and management [15]. In addition, the credibility of the third party is difficult to guarantee. The privacy-preserving schemes based on rechargeable battery are limited to the battery capacity and may conflict with the user's economic interest [17]. Zhao [13] adopts the BLH method to preserve user's privacy-sensitive information and uses differential privacy to measure the privacy-preserving performance. Noise addition is a common solution to provide differential privacy which is a novel standard whose outcome is not significantly affected by the removal or addition of single participants.

However, most schemes based on differential privacy are mainly used to protect individual information for a statistical dataset, and current schemes applying differential privacy mainly focus on the privacy-preservation of smarting data during the data aggregation among multiple consumers. There is less work contributing on preserving device-level data against NILM [12]. Therefore, designing a reasonable data obfuscation algorithm which can apply the differential privacy to preserve the device-level data against NILM is the focus of our paper. We summarize our contributions as follows:

(1) Differing from traditional differential privacy schemes, we add noise into the switch states of each appliance to provide differential privacy.
(2) We use the basic properties of differential privacy to prove the effectiveness of our scheme in privacy-preservation.
(3) Motivated by the lower bound on utility which is called discriminant proposed by Kifer [18], we define a measurement to prove the better performance of our scheme in data-utility.
(4) We adopt the information theory of differential privacy proposed by Cuff [19] to measure the trade-off between utility and privacy in our scheme.

The rest of this paper is organized as follows. Section 2 introduces the background and related work. In Sect. 3, our scheme is stated. In Sect. 4, security analysis is given. In Sect. 5, the performance of our scheme is evaluated. In Sect. 6, the paper is concluded.

2   Background and Related Work

2.1   Notations

Table 1. Notations in our scheme

Acronym	Descriptions
ε	Privacy budget
$<D, D'>$	Adjacent datasets
π_i	Initial probability of appliance i
A_i	Transition probability of appliance i
B_i	Emission probability of appliance i
N	The number of appliances
X_i	Hidden states sequence of appliance i
Y_i	Observed states sequence of appliance i
Y_{sum}	Aggregate observed state sequence
Y_{train}	Training energy consumption data
$x_t^{(i)}$	Hidden state of appliance i at time t
$x_t^{(i)'}$	Obfuscated hidden state of appliance i at time t
$y_t^{(i)}$	Observed state of appliance i at time t
$y_t^{(i)'}$	Obfuscated observed state of appliance i at time t
$\hat{y}_t'$	Aggregate obfuscated observed state at time t
λ	The set of parameters A, B, π
LS_f	Local sensitivity

2.2   Differential Privacy

Dwork [20] has proposed the notion of differential privacy for general datasets and shows how to realize differential privacy by adding noise [21]. The property of differential privacy and application in smart grid are discussed in [22–27] (Table 1).

Definition of differential privacy

M is a randomized algorithm. For any datasets D_i and D' differing from at most one element, and all subsets of possible answers $S \subseteq Range(M)$, M satisfies ε-differential privacy if both of the datasets satisfy the following condition:

$$P_r\{M(D) \in S\} \leq e^{\varepsilon} \times P_r\{M(D') \in S\} \tag{1}$$

Property1: Parallel Composition [22]

$M_1, M_2 \ldots M_n$ are different randomized algorithms with the privacy budgeting parameters $\varepsilon_1, \varepsilon_2 \ldots \varepsilon_n$. Then, the combined algorithm $M(M_1(D_1), M_2(D_2) \ldots M_n(D_n))$.provides $(\max \varepsilon_i)$.-differential privacy for the disjoint datasets $D_1, D_2 \ldots ._n$.

Property2: Stable Transformation [22]

For any two databases E and F, we say T provides c-stable if it meets the following condition.

$$|T(E) \oplus T(F)| \leq c \times |E \oplus F| \tag{2}$$

Here, $\oplus$ represents the XOR operation. If the privacy preserving mechanism M provides ε-differential privacy and T is a c-stable transformation, the combination $M \circ T$ provides $(\varepsilon \times c)$-differential privacy.

2.3 Factorial Hidden Markov Model

As an extension of HMMs, FHMM [28] is used to model multiple independent hidden state sequences in different times. X_i represents independent hidden states sequence. Y_i represents corresponding observed states sequence. Y_{sum} represents the aggregated observed states sequence.

3 Our Scheme

3.1 Design Goal

The design goals of the proposed scheme are given as follows.

Besides inherited from Barbosa's [15] three design goals, our schemes also focus on the following aspects:

(1) The entropy of the final obfuscated data should not be far from the original data.
(2) There is no outlier in the final obfuscated load profile.

3.2 System Model

We show the system model of our scheme in Fig. 3. The load signature is extracted from the power consumption data. Then, each appliance's switch state related with consumer's behavior is estimated based on the FHMM. Differing from the traditional schemes which add noise into active power data, we add noise into the consumer's behaviors (switch states) to realize the differential privacy (Fig. 1).

3.3 Appliance Modeling

As we analyzed before, the energy consumption behavior can be modeled by the FHMM, in which the aggregated active power sequence of the entire appliances is regarded as the observed state and the switch state sequence of each appliance is regarded as the hidden state. To estimate the hidden state, we need to estimate the related parameters in FHMM firstly.

The related parameters of appliance i in FHMM contain the initial probabilities $\pi_i = P(x_1^{(i)})$, the conditional probabilities $A_i = P(x_t^{(i)}|x_{t-1}^{(i)})$, emission probabilities $B_i = P(y_t^{(i)}|x_t^{(i)})$. To simplify the analysis, we use λ_i to denote the set of parameters.

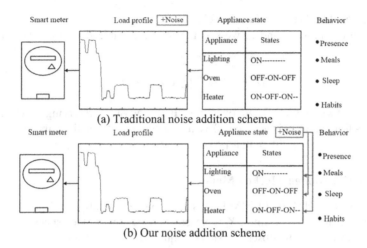

Fig. 1. The architecture of our scheme

Based on the related parameters, we can calculate the initial probability $\pi = \prod_{i=1}^{N} \pi_i = \prod_{i=1}^{N} P(x_1^{(i)})$, transition probability $A = \prod_{i=1}^{N} A_i = \prod_{i=1}^{N} P(x_t^{(i)}|x_{t-1}^{(i)})$, emission probability $A = \prod_{i=1}^{N} A_i = \prod_{i=1}^{N} P(x_t^{(i)}|x_{t-1}^{(i)})$ and the conditional probability of switch state $P(Y, X|\lambda_i, 1 \le i \le N)$ as follows:

$$P(Y, X|\lambda_i, 1 \le i \le N) = \pi AB \tag{3}$$

N denotes the number of appliances. Expectation Maximization algorithm (EM) is a common solution to estimate these parameters by using an auxiliary function until the convergence to a local maximum occurs. In our paper, we don't adopt EM. Instead, we take partial energy consumption data from all kinds of appliances as the training data Y_{train} and estimate the parameters by Maximum Likelihood Estimation.

Given a series of energy consumption data Y_{sum} from a smart meter, we can estimate all the appliances' switch state sequences based on our FHMM model. With the Maximum Likelihood Estimation, we can estimate all the appliances' switch state sequences as follows:

$$X_1 X_2 ... X_N = \arg \max P(Y_{sum}, X|\lambda) \tag{4}$$

3.4   Noise Addition

Definition 1. Adjacent datasets. Instantiated by the notion of differential privacy proposed by Dwork [20], we propose the notion of differential privacy for datasets of the behavior signatures. We call switch D and D' differing in at most one element adjacent datasets, if the differential element is an additional behavior signature.

Definition 2. Local sensitivity. For a mapping $f : D \rightarrow R^k$, in which R^k denotes a k-dimensional vector and D' is an arbitrary adjacent dataset of D, the local sensitivity of f is

$$LS_f = \max_{D} \|f(D) - f(D')\|_1 \tag{5}$$

For all the D and D' differing in one appliance's switch state.

Theorem 1. For $f : D \rightarrow R^k$, the mechanism that adds noise with distribution $Lap(LS_f/\varepsilon)$ provides ε-differential privacy.

After getting the switch state sequences of appliance i in time t, we add Laplace into the switch states of each appliance to generate the obfuscated switch state $x_t^{(i)'}$. The detailed process can be expressed as follows:

$$x_t^{(i)'} = x_t^{(i)} + lap\left(LS_f/\varepsilon\right) \tag{6}$$

3.5   Data Re-aggregation

After we get the obfuscated switch state sequence, we can generate the obfuscated active power sequence based on the FHMM. While, considering the data-utility, we adjust the obfuscated active power as follows:

$$y_t^{(i)'} = \begin{cases} y_t^{(i)} & x_t^{(i)'} = x_t^{(i)'} \cap x_t^{(i)'} \neq 0 \\ 0 & x_t^{(i)'} = 0 \\ CP & x_t^{(i)'} \neq x_t^{(i)'} \cap x_t^{(i)'} \neq 0 \end{cases} \tag{7}$$

When $x_t^{(i)'} = x_t^{(i)}$ and $x_t^{(i)'} \neq 0$, the obfuscated active power based on FHMM is similar to the average value of the energy consumption data in a time slot. To reflect the real energy consumption, we take the original energy consumption data as the obfuscated active power in this time slot.

When $x_t^{(i)'} = 0$, theoretically, the obfuscated active power should be zero. However, as the relationship between the switch states and observed states is estimated by FHMM and may be nonzero value when $x_t^{(i)'} = 0$. Therefore, we set $y_t^{(i)'} = 0$ in this situation.

In fact, the active power of an appliance is a little different even in the same switch state. When $x_t^{(i)'} \neq x_t^{(i)}$ and $x_t^{(i)'} \neq 0$, to reflect the real energy consumption, we take the value from the energy Consumption Profile (CP) whose switch state is equal to $x_t^{(i)'}$ as our obfuscated active power. The final aggregated active power in time t can be calculated as follows:

$$\hat{y}_t' = \sum_{i=1}^{N} y_t^{(i)'} \tag{8}$$

4 Security Analysis

4.1 Privacy Analysis

Theorem 2: Our scheme provides ε-differential privacy.

Proof: The process of our scheme T_{sum} can be expressed as follows:

$$T : Y \xrightarrow{FHMM} x^{(i)}$$

(1) As the mapping T_b representing the FHMM can be regarded as a linier mapping approximately and $|E \oplus F|$ represent the number of different elements between E and F. Therefore,

$$|T(E) \oplus T(F)| \leq |E \oplus F|$$

Thus, the map T is c-stable and the value of c is one.

According to the property of differential privacy, transformation T provides ε-differential privacy.

4.2 Utility Analysis

Theorem 3: our scheme satisfies $(k\theta, 0)$ -utility.

Proof: In this paper, D can be regarded as the real switch states of an appliance in different time slots. D' can be regarded as the noisy switch states. Q represents the FHMM algorithm.

k and b are linear parameters

$$||Q(D') - Q(D)||_1 = k||\Delta D||_1 = k \sum_{i}^{n} \Delta d_i$$

As each noise $\Delta d_i \sim laplace(0, \frac{LS_f}{\varepsilon})$, the value of $\sum_{i}^{n} \Delta d_i$ will converge to zero when the value of n is large enough. Therefore, we have

$$||Q(D') - Q(D)||_1 \leq k\theta$$

Therefore, our scheme is proved to satisfy $(k\theta, 0)$-utility.

5   Performance Evaluation

In this section, we use F1-score [29] to measure the performance of our scheme in terms of the level of privacy-preservation and adopt Kullback–Leibler divergence [30] to measure the level of data-utility based on the REDD data set [31] with the tool NILMTK [32]. As shown in Fig. 2, we compare our scheme with Barbosa's scheme and Sankar's scheme as follows.

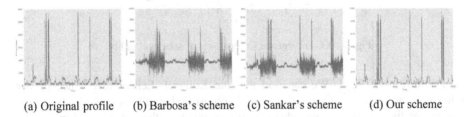

  (a) Original profile   (b) Barbosa's scheme   (c) Sankar's scheme   (d) Our scheme

Fig. 2. Energy consumption profiles processed by different schemes (multiple appliances) $\varepsilon = 10$

5.1   Privacy-Preserving Level of Our Scheme

We adopt FHMM to estimate the switch states from the active power data obfuscated by Barbosa's scheme, Sankar's scheme and our scheme. As shown in Fig. 3, the F1-score [29] of our scheme is less than the other schemes, which means that our scheme has a higher level of privacy preservation.

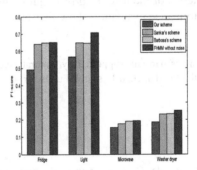

Fig. 3. F1-score Comparison of schemes' preservation.

5.2   Data-Utility of Our Scheme

Kullback–Leibler divergence is a measure of how one probability distribution diverges from another expected probability distribution.

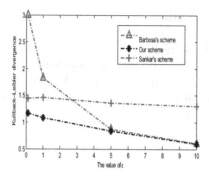

Fig. 4. KL-Divergence Comparison of schemes' utility

As shown in Fig. 4, We can find that the Kullback–Leibler divergence of our scheme is the lowest one and our scheme's obfuscated profile is very similar to the original profile. Therefore, our scheme outperformes the others in data-utility.

6 Conclusion

In this paper, we propose a privacy-preserving scheme based on the obfuscated switch states to realize the differential privacy in smart grid. We adopt the Factorial Hidden Markov Model to estimate the switch states of each appliance. Then, noise is added into the switch state to achieve the differential privacy. Based on the obfuscated switch states, we generate the obfuscated observed states and adjust them to guarantee the data-utility. At last, we analyze the performance of our scheme, and compare it with other similar schemes in terms of the level of privacy-preserving and data-utility. The security analysis and performance evaluation show that our scheme provides a better utility-privacy tradeoff.

Acknowledgment. This work is partially supported by Natural Science Foundation of China under grant 61402171, and the Fundamental Research Funds for the Central Universities under grant 2016MS29.

References

1. Savi, M., Rottondi, C., Verticale, G.: Evaluation of the precision-privacy tradeoff of data perturbation for smart metering. IEEE Trans. Smart Grid **6**(5), 2409–2416 (2015)
2. Grid, N.S.: Guidelines for Smart Grid Cyber Security, vol. 2, Privacy and the Smart Grid (2010)
3. Hart, G.W.: Nonintrusive appliance load monitoring. Proc. IEEE **80**(12), 1870–1891 (1992)
4. Wang, T., Cai, Y., Jia, W., et al.: Maximizing real-time streaming services based on a multi-servers networking framework. Comput. Netw. **93**, 199–212 (2015)
5. Du, X., Xiao, Y., Guizani, M., et al.: An effective key management scheme for heterogeneous sensor networks. Ad Hoc Netw. **5**(1), 24–34 (2007)

6. Du, X., Guizani, M., Xiao, Y., et al.: A routing-driven elliptic curve cryptography based key management scheme for heterogeneous sensor networks. IEEE Trans. Wireless Commun. **8**(3), 1223–1229 (2009)

7. Chu, C.K., Liu, J.K., Wong, J.W., et al.: Privacy-preserving smart metering with regional statistics and personal enquiry services. In: ACM SIGSAC Symposium on Information, Computer and Communications Security, pp. 369–380 (2013)

8. Lu, R., Liang, X., Li, X., et al.: EPPA: an efficient and privacy-preserving aggregation scheme for secure smart grid communications. IEEE Trans. Parallel Distrib. Syst. **23**(9), 1621–1631 (2012)

9. Kalogridis, G., Efthymiou, C., Denic, S.Z., et al.: Privacy for smart meters: towards undetectable appliance load signatures. In: IEEE International Conference on Smart Grid Communications, pp. 232–237 (2010)

10. Du, X., Lin, F.: Maintaining differentiated coverage in heterogeneous sensor networks. Wireless Commun. Networking **5**(4), 565–572 (2005)

11. Zhao, J., Jung, T., Wang, Y., et al.: Achieving differential privacy of data disclosure in the smart grid. In: IEEE International Conference on Computer Communications, pp. 504–512 (2014)

12. Zhang, Z., Qin, Z., Zhu, L., et al.: Toward practical differential privacy in smart grid with capacity-limited rechargeable batteries. Mathematics (2015)

13. Rastogi, V., Nath, S.: Differentially private aggregation of distributed time-series with transformation and encryption. In: International Conference on Management of Data, pp. 735–746 (2010)

14. Sankar, L., Rajagopalan, S.R., Mohajer, S., et al.: Smart meter privacy: a theoretical framework. IEEE Trans. Smart Grid **4**(2), 837–846 (2013)

15. Barbosa, P., Brito, A., Almeida, H.: A Technique to provide differential privacy for appliance usage in smart metering. Inform. Sci. **370–371**, 355–367 (2016)

16. Du, X., Rozenblit, M., Shayman, M.: Implementation and performance analysis of SNMP on a TLS/TCP base. In: IFIP/IEEE International Symposium on Integrated Network Management, pp. 453–466 (2001)

17. Mclaughlin, S., Mcdaniel, P., Aiello, W.: Protecting consumer privacy from electric load monitoring. In: ACM Conference on Computer and Communications Security, pp. 87–98. ACM (2011)

18. Kifer, D., Machanavajjhala, A.: No free lunch in data privacy. In: ACM SIGMOD International Conference on Management of Data, Special Interest Group on Management of Data, pp. 193–204 (2011)

19. Cuff, P., Yu, L.: Differential privacy as a mutual information constraint. In: ACM SIGSAC Conference on Computer and Communications Security, pp. 43–54 (2016)

20. Dwork, C.: Differential privacy. In: Bugliesi, M., Preneel, B., Sassone, V., Wegener, I. (eds.) ICALP 2006. LNCS, vol. 4052, pp. 1–12. Springer, Heidelberg (2006). doi:10.1007/11787006_1

21. Dwork, C., Mcsherry, F., Nissim, K.: Calibrating noise to sensitivity in private data analysis. In: Theory of Cryptography Conference, pp. 265–284 (2006)

22. Eibl G, Engel D. Differential privacy for real smart metering data. Comput. Sci. Res. Dev., 1–10 (2016)

23. Xiao, Y., Chen, H.H., Du, X., et al.: Stream-based cipher feedback mode in wireless error channel. IEEE Trans. Wireless Commun. **8**(2), 662–666 (2009)

24. Ács, G., Castelluccia, C.: I Have a DREAM! (DiffeRentially privatE smArt Metering). In: Filler, T., Pevný, T., Craver, S., Ker, A. (eds.) IH 2011. LNCS, vol. 6958, pp. 118–132. Springer, Heidelberg (2011). doi:10.1007/978-3-642-24178-9_9

25. McSherry, F.D.: Privacy integrated queries: an extensible platform for privacy-preserving data analysis. In: International Conference on Management of Data, pp. 19–30. ACM (2009)
26. Won, J., Ma, C.Y.T., Yau, D.K.Y., et al.: Privacy-assured aggregation protocol for smart metering: a proactive fault-tolerant approach. In: IEEE Conference on Computer Communications, pp. 2804–2812 (2014)
27. Shi, Z., Sun, R., Lu, R., et al.: Diverse grouping-based aggregation protocol with error detection for smart grid communications. IEEE Trans. Smart Grid 6(6), 2856–2868 (2015)
28. Ghahramani, Z., Jordan, M.I.: Factorial hidden markov models. Mach. Learn. 29(2), 245–273 (1997)
29. Kim, H.S.: Unsupervised disaggregation of low frequency power measurements. In: SIAM International Conference on Data Mining, pp. 28–30 (2011)
30. Anderson, K.D., Berges, M.E., Ocneanu, A., et al.: Event detection for Non Intrusive load monitoring. In: IEEE Industrial Electronics Society, pp. 3312–3317 (2012)
31. Kolter, J.Z., Johnson, M.J.: REDD: a public data set for energy disaggregation research. In: KDD Workshop on Data Mining Applications in Sustainability, vol. 25, pp. 59–62 (2011)
32. Batra, N., Kelly, J., Parson, O., et al.: NILMTK: an open source toolkit for non-intrusive load monitoring. In: International Conference on Future Energy Systems, pp. 265–276 (2014)

Protecting In-memory Data Cache with Secure Enclaves in Untrusted Cloud

Yuxia Cheng[1]([✉]), Qing Wu[1], Bei Wang[2], and Wenzhi Chen[2]

[1] School of Computer Science and Technology, Hangzhou Dianzi University,
Hangzhou, China
`yuxia_cheng@163.com`
[2] College of Computer Science and Technology, Zhejiang University,
Hangzhou, China

Abstract. Protecting data security and privacy is one of the top concerns in the public cloud. As the cloud infrastructure is complex, and it is difficult for cloud users to gain trust. Particularly, how to guarantee the confidentiality and integrity of in-memory user private data in untrusted cloud faces big challenges. The in-memory data is typically used for online processing that requires high performance and plaintext access in CPU, therefore simple data encryption is infeasible for in-memory data security protection. In this paper, we propose a secure in-memory data cache scheme based on the memcached key-value store system and leverage the new trusted Intel SGX processors to protect sensitive operations. Firstly, we build a secure enclave and design a trusted channel protocol using remote attestation mechanism. Secondly, we propose a cache server partitioning method that decouples the sensitive key-value operations with enclave protection. Thirdly, we implement a secure client library to maintain the original cache semantics for application compatibility. The experimental result showed that the proposed solutions achieves comparable performance with the traditional key-value store systems, while improves the level of data security in untrusted cloud.

Keywords: Data security · Cloud computing · In-memory caching · Trusted computing

1 Introduction

Cloud computing are prevalent nowadays. There is a great amount of private data existing in the public cloud. Data security is one of the top concerns when we use the cloud services. Cloud users have to rely on both the providers and their globally distributed cloud infrastructures (including software and hardware platform) to not expose their privacy.

However, the traditional public cloud architecture is based on a hierarchical multi-layer security model. In this hierarchical model, the security mechanisms mainly target at protecting the more privileged codes (of cloud providers) from untrusted application codes (of cloud users), and seldom aim at protecting user

© Springer International Publishing AG 2017
S. Wen et al. (Eds.): CSS 2017, LNCS 10581, pp. 43–56, 2017.
https://doi.org/10.1007/978-3-319-69471-9_4

data from being accessed by the privileged codes [1]. Therefore, the users must trust: (i) the provider's hardware used to run their applications; (ii) the cloud provider's software, including privileged system software (host OS, hypervisor, firmware) and the full stack of cloud management software; (iii) the system administrators and other staffs that have entitlements to access cloud facilities. From this point of view, the trusted computing base (TCB) to the cloud user is very large and uncertain. And there were many data leakage incidents [2,3] happened due to software and administrative vulnerabilities.

With the increasing security concerns in the cloud industry, new hardware technologies for trusted computing have evolved rapidly. Trusted execution environments (TEEs) can provide applications with a secure execution context. Even if the rest of software (hypervisor, OS, etc.) are compromised, the application inside TEE can still remain trusted. The recent Intel Software Guard Extensions (SGX) [4] and the ARM TrustZone [5] are among the promising techniques that protect user's security code and data against malicious software that attempts to compromise its integrity and confidentiality.

Our objective is to provide cloud users a trusted self-controlled manner to protect their sensitive in-memory data in the public cloud. In this paper, we aim to protect in-memory key-value caching data based on the new trusted mode of hardware processors. Cloud users need only trust the hardware and their own applications, thus reducing TCB to the minimum. By design and implementation of secure key-value in-memory caching system, we focus on achieving the following goals: (i) Users' code and data are guaranteed to reside in the memory of the cloud provider's trusted physical machine. (ii) Confidentiality and integrity of user's private data are protected even if the cloud provider's software stack is compromised and controlled by adversaries. (iii) The performance gap between the secure in-memory caching system and the original system without the security enhancements should be kept small.

Reaching the above three goals faces some challenges. First of all, establishing trust between the cloud servers and the user clients involves intricate attestation mechanisms. And partitioning the key-value caching system into trusted and untrusted parts to minimize TCB is non-trivial. Secondly, the interaction between trusted parts and the rest of the system should be carefully examined to prevent potential attacks, such as the Iago attacks [6]. Finally, context switches into in the trusted mode of hardware processor incur high performance overhead.

In this paper, we propose a secure in-memory data cache scheme that uses the new Intel SGX processors to protect user private data in the public cloud. The main contributions of this paper is described as follows:

(1) To establish trust between the cloud servers and the user clients, we build a secure enclave and design a trusted channel protocol using the Intel SGX CPU extensions and remote attestation mechanism. The user's confidential code and data are stored in the enclave, and other malicious software cannot access the enclave protected by the trusted hardware.

(2) To reduce the trusted computing base (TCB) and maintain high performance, we propose a cache server partitioning mechanism that decouples the

sensitive key-value operations into the enclave region and the non-sensitive operations outside the enclave. The sensitive operations that involve modifying data content of key-value pairs are executed in the secure enclave region, while the rest of operations are executed in the normal application space.

(3) We provide a secure client library to maintain the original caching semantics for application compatibility. The key-value pairs are encrypted using hardware accelerated crypto instructions. We use the AES-GCM [7] encryption scheme to guarantee the confidentiality, integrity, and authenticity of the encrypted key-value pairs that stored in the remote server's memory.

The experimental result showed that the proposed solutions achieves comparable performance with the traditional key-value store systems, while improves the level of data security in untrusted cloud.

The rest of this paper is organised as follows. Section 2 provides background of Intel SGX. Section 3 describes secure key-value store system design and implementation. Section 4 presents performance evaluation. Section 5 describes the related work. And finally, Sect. 6 concludes our work.

2   Background

2.1   SGX Overview

Enclave Protection. The confidentiality and integrity of enclave's code and data are protected by the processor. The SGX processor is responsible for the linear to physical address mappings of each enclave. An enclave is created by invoking an ECREATE instruction that sets up a control structure (named as SECS, SGX Enclave Control Structure) in the protected memory region. After the creation of an enclave, the pre-allocated memory pages are added into the enclave by using the EADD instructions. The pages added into the enclave region are named as EPC (Enclave Page Cache) pages. The EPC pages must be mapped to a real physical memory region. For each EPC page, the processor maintains contents in the EPCM (Enclave Page Cache Mapping) structure, which tracks the EPC page's status of validity and accessibility, its enclave ID, page type (regular, SECS, etc.), the linear addresses of the enclave that are allowed to access the page, and permissions (read/write/execute). EPC page contents are encrypted and integrity protected when reside in memory after they leave out of the processor cache. The contents reside in the processor caches are protected by CPU access controls.

Attestation. SGX provides CPU-based attestation and sealing mechanisms [8]. The remote attestation in SGX enables a remote user to validate that the user's designated code and data have been actually loaded into an SGX enclave. Through establishing shared secrets between enclave and the remote user, the user can gain confidence of having an end-to-end trusted communication channel with the enclave. In the process of the enclave construction, SGX computes a secure hash digest of the enclave's initial state. The sealing mechanism [8] enables each enclave to get unique keys that are derived from the processor hardware and the enclave's digest, and retrieve a report signed by the processor to prove its identity to another local enclave (named local attestation). To support remote attestation, a special quoting enclave (QE) is provisioned in each SGX-enabled processor. Only the QE can access a unique asymmetric private key that is manufactured within the processor. The QE can sign a hash digest of a local enclave together with the digest of enclave contents to create a quote. Using the trusted QE, a remote user can obtain the quote that proves the report is sent from the specific SGX-enabled enclave. Like the TPM, the hardware manufacture is the root of trust for attestation.

2.2   Key-Value Store System

The in-memory key-value store systems are widely used in the cloud. To speed up the process of data retrieving, most frequently accessed data is cached in memory in the form of $\langle key, value \rangle$ pairs. As shown in Fig. 1, the key-value store systems (using memcached [9] as an example) typically have both server side and client side. In the server side, $\langle key, value \rangle$ pairs are efficiently structured in linked list. Hash functions are deployed to accelerate the process of searching keys, and cache replacement algorithms are used to evict less frequently accessed data when memory capacity is limited. Commonly, there are multiple distributed cache servers to form an aggregated pool of memory caching resources. In the client side, using the predefined protocols, clients can issue commands via network (TCP/UDP), such as set/get/add/replace/append, to operate on the data stored in remote cache servers.

However, this kind of key-value store systems have multiple security vulnerabilities. First, most $\langle key, value \rangle$ pairs are plaintexts reside in memory, which can easily cause information leakage to adversaries. Second, $\langle key, value \rangle$ pairs are sent through networks, which may occur man-in-the-middle attacks.

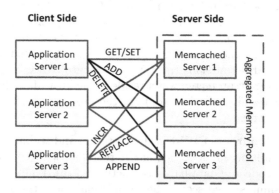

Fig. 1. The key-value in-memory store system. The data caching servers are distributed in the cloud data center, which forms an aggregated memory resource pool. The clients issue commands to store/retrieve key-value pairs.

Finally, even if the $\langle key, value \rangle$ pairs are encrypted, processing them online still need to be decrypted, and how to protect the private key in the public cloud faces a big challenge. Therefore, designing a secure and high performance key-value store systems to guarantee the confidentiality and integrity of the data is an urgent request in the public cloud.

2.3 Threat Model

We assume that the key-value caching system is deployed in an untrusted public cloud environment, in which the attacker may compromise the whole software stack of the cloud platform. The compromised software includes hypervisors, host/guest OSes, and other resource management and administration software. This assumption can be found in the cloud when an attacker exploited vulnerabilities in the hypervisor or OS kernel and gained the privilege of accessing the user-level data resides in memory, in storage devices, or in the network. In the hardware level, the attacker may take control of physical machines and may read/write data after it leaves the processor by using hardware means, such as probing, DMA, or inject arbitrary network packages. We assume that the attacker could not physically explore and compromise the SGX-enabled processors as long as the processor packages are manufactured without security defects. However, in this paper, we do not guarantee the availability of the key-value store system, which is another hot research topic. The Denial-of-Service (DoS) attack and side-channel attacks are also beyond the scope of this paper.

3   Secure In-memory Data Cache

3.1   Overview

Our goal is to design a secure in-memory data cache system in the untrusted cloud. To guarantee the confidentiality and integrity of key-value pairs stored in remote cloud servers, the proposed system has two major parts: secure cache servers and secure clients. Based on SGX-enabled processors, we propose the attestation and key exchange protocol to build an end-to-end trusted channel between servers and clients. In the secure cache servers, we partition the key-value store system into trusted enclave region and non-enclave region. The confidential operations related to updating key-value pairs are executed in the enclave region, while other operations are executed in the non-enclave region. We store key-value pairs encrypted and authenticated in the non-enclave memory region. In this design, cache servers can maintain most of the caching operations in native speed while guarantee data confidentiality and integrity. In the client side, a secure client library is implemented that other applications can use it to access the remote cache servers with APIs as defined in general key-value store protocols. The following sections will describe the trusted channel protocol, the cache server partitions mechanism, and the secure client library design respectively.

3.2   Trusted Channel Protocol

To establish an end-to-end trusted communication channel between servers and clients, we present the trusted channel protocol in Fig. 2. The protocol consists of four major phases, we show the detailed descriptions as follows:

Phase (1): At the beginning, the client prepares the code of cache server which consists of trusted code in the enclave region (denoted as C_{ecl}) and the rest of code in the non-enclave region (C_{ecl-}). As the Eq. (1) shows, the first message sent from the client to the server (denoted as CS_1) includes C_{ecl}, C_{ecl-}, as well as the client's public key (denoted as pk_u). We use '|' to denote the concatenation of two messages.

$$CS_1 = C_{ecl}|C_{ecl-}|pk_u \tag{1}$$

Phase (2): The server receives the CS_1 message, then extracts C_{ecl}, C_{ecl-}, and pk_u. After obtaining the C_{ecl} code, the server checks integrity of the code and initialises an enclave with C_{ecl}. Once the enclave is successfully initialised, the server enters into the enclave. In the enclave mode, C_{ecl} generates a symmetric key k_s and encrypts it using pk_u as Eq. (2) shows. The symmetric key k_s is used for secure communication between the enclave and the client after the remote attestation process succeeds.

$$m_s = \mathbf{Enc}_{pk_u}\{k_s\} \tag{2}$$

To certify the integrity of CS_1 to the client, C_{ecl} uses HMAC (keyed-hash message authentication code) [cite] to generate an authenticated digest of CS_1 using k_s as shown in Eq. (3).

In the remote attestation process, C_{ecl} uses the SGX QE to generate a `quote` which certifies that the message is sent from a genuine SGX enclave (as described in Sect. 2.1). However, the quote from QE only proves that the code is running on the SGX-enabled server, but lacks the evidence that the server is located in the authentic cloud provider's data center rather than in other places controlled by the adversary. Therefore, we propose to create an additional cloud quoting enclave (CQE) (similar in [10]) in each server to sign the report that the message is sent from the cloud provider's SGX server.

$$SC_2 = m_s|\mathbf{H}_{MAC}\{k_s, CS_1\}|\mathbf{QE}_{ecl}\{m_s\}|\mathbf{CQE}_{ecl}\{m_s\} \tag{3}$$

Overall, the second message sent from the server to the client is shown in Eq. (3), which includes the encrypted symmetric key m_s, the HMAC of CS_1, the quote from SGX QE, and the quote from Cloud QE.

Phase (3): The client receives the CS_2 message, then extracts m_s, $\mathbf{H}_{MAC}\{k_s, CS_1\}$, $\mathbf{QE}_{ecl}\{m_s\}$, and $\mathbf{CQE}_{ecl}\{m_s\}$. The client uses its private key ps_u to decrypt m_s and obtains the symmetric key k_s. Then, the client can verify the integrity of CS_1 using $\mathbf{H}_{MAC}\{k_s, CS_1\}$. After the code integrity check succeeds, the client uses the public keys of both QE and CQE to verify that the message m_s is sent from the enclave which resides in the SGX-enabled provider's physical server.

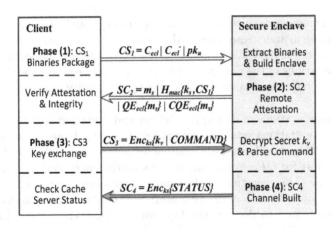

Fig. 2. A brief overview of the trusted channel protocol. The grey arrows represent encrypted communications.

Once all verifications succeed, the third message is sent from the client to the server as shown in Eq. (4). CS_3 includes a symmetric key k_v generated for crypto-operations of key-value pairs and the COMMAND used to launch the rest part of the code resides in cache server. The message is encrypted using the symmetric key k_s.

$$CS_3 = \mathbf{Enc}_{k_s}\{k_v|COMMAND\} \tag{4}$$

Phase (4): The server receives the CS_3 message, then decrypts and extracts k_v and COMMAND in the enclave using k_s. The symmetric key k_v is protected within the enclave and never leaves out of the enclave. The enclave checks the integrity of C_{ecl-}, parses the COMMAND, and launches the rest part of the key-value cache system. The enclave collects the STATUS of the system and sends a message SC_4 back to the client. This message is also encrypted using the symmetric key k_s.

$$SC_4 = \mathbf{Enc}_{k_s}\{STATUS\} \tag{5}$$

After completing the above four major steps, the trusted channel is established between the server and the client. And the enclave created in the server acts as a trusted control knob associated with the remote cloud users for the key-value store operations. All encryptions in the protocol uses the AES-GCM [7] scheme to provide confidentiality, integrity, and authenticity assurances on the data.

3.3 Cache Server Partitions

The key-value store system in the cache server is partitioned into enclave region and non-enclave region. The enclave region involves processing confidential data, while the non-enclave region is responsible for the data-oblivious maintenance work. In the cache server, the major functions of key-value store system includes:

(1) allocating memory resources; (2) storing/retrieving/updating key-value pairs; and (3) recycling memory resources used to store key-value pairs. Considering the large overhead of memory allocation/deallocation in enclave mode, we choose to put these operations in the non-enclave region. The cache server should response to the client's request in time to meet the QoS (Quality of Service) of cloud applications.

As for the operations of storing/retrieving and updating key-value pairs, we classify these operations into two categories: the type I operations (short for OP_I) that involve modifying data content of key-value pairs and the type II operations (short for OP_{II}) that only process on the encrypted data as a whole. Specifically, the OP_I operations include append/prepend, increase/decrease, and the OP_{II} operations include set, add, get, replace, delete, touch. The OP_I operations need to decrypt the key-value pairs, update the data, and re-encrypt the data. Therefore, the OP_I operations have to be executed inside the enclave. While the OP_{II} operations do not involve decrypting the key-value pairs in the server side, these operations can be executed in the non-enclave region.

The communications between enclave region and non-enclave region may bring new attack surfaces. To minimize the attack surfaces, we depend on the in-enclave library. However, some functions may rely on the potentially malicious OS system calls, which may return a forged input to the enclave (usually known as Iago attacks [6]). To prevent such attacks, we uses the secure enclave-host communication protocol [11]. The protocol defines a narrow interface to the enclave and is driven by the trusted enclave in a strict communication manner.

3.4   Secure Client Library

In the traditional key-value store system, the clients communicate with the cache servers through TCP connections. The cache servers listen on some configurable ports; the cache clients connect to these ports, send operation commands to the servers, read the responses from servers, and finally close the connections. To ease deployment, we introduce a secure client library that supports secure communication with the cache servers. The main functions of the secure client library include: (i) secure encryption and decryption of key-value pairs; (ii) support of the client and server communication protocol.

For example, the client decides to send a $\langle key, value \rangle$ pair to store in the cache server. The client first calls the library function of the SET command. Inside the SET command function, the key and the $\langle key, value \rangle$ pair are encrypted respectively using the established symmetric key k_v (described in Sect. 3.2). The encrypted key is used for indexing and hashing operations in the cache server, and the encrypted $\langle key, value \rangle$ pair as a whole is stored as the new value. Once the encryption is done, the SET command function sends the command and the encrypted $\langle key, value \rangle$ pair to the server. The server parses the command and stores the data in memory. When the client decides to retrieve the previously stored $\langle key, value \rangle$ pair in the server, it calls the library function of the GET command. The GET command function sends the command to the server and parses the received responses. Then, the library function uses the AES-GCM scheme to decrypt the received $\langle key, value \rangle$ pair and also check the integrity and authenticity of the data. Once the decrypted $\langle key, value \rangle$ pair passes the check, the library function returns it to the client application.

4 Performance Evaluation

4.1 Experiment Platform

In this section, we evaluate the proposed secure key-value store system (short for SeKV) using the Intel SGX processor and real-life memcached benchmarks. Firstly, we describe the experimental platform. The physical server is configured with a 2.70 GHz Intel Core i5-6400 processor (code name Skylake), 32 GB of RAM, and a 1 TB disk storage. The ethernet controller is the Intel Corporation Ethernet Connection (2) I219-V (rev 31). The client machine is configured with a 2.6 GHz Intel Core i5-4570 processor, 8 GB of RAM, and 256 GB SSD storage. Both machines are installed with the Ubuntu 14.04.5 64-bit OS, the Linux kernel version is 4.7.0.

To evaluate the performance of the SeKV system, we use the following two configurations of key-value cache systems for comparison.

(1) **BaseKV** runs the default memcached [9] server daemon and the client sends plaintext key-value pairs to the server. The BaseKV system has no performance penalties of enclave overhead, crypto operations overhead and secure communication overhead.

(2) **EncKV** runs the default memcached server daemon and the client sends encrypted key-value pairs to the server. In the server side, there is no enclave module to guarantee that the crypto operations are executed in a trusted environment. In the client side, the key-value pairs are encrypted/decrypted the same as the SeKV system. But there is no secure communication channel between the client and the enclave.

We use the synthetic and real-life benchmarks to test the performance of key-value cache systems. The synthetic key-value requests are generated using the twemperf tool. And we use the Cloud Suite data caching benchmark as the real-life applications for the key-value systems.

4.2 Overall Performance Comparison

To compare the overall performance of key-value systems, we use the data caching benchmark in the CloudSuite [12]. The data caching benchmark deploys the memcached key-value systems for caching the real-life applications of the Twitter dataset. The original dataset consumes 300 MB of server memory, and we scaled the dataset up to 10 GB of main memory using the loader tool in the benchmark.

Figure 3 shows the overall performance of three key-value systems: (a) the BaseKV; (b) the EncKV; (c) the SeKV. To deploy the proposed SeKV system in the data caching benchmark, we replace the default memcached server with the

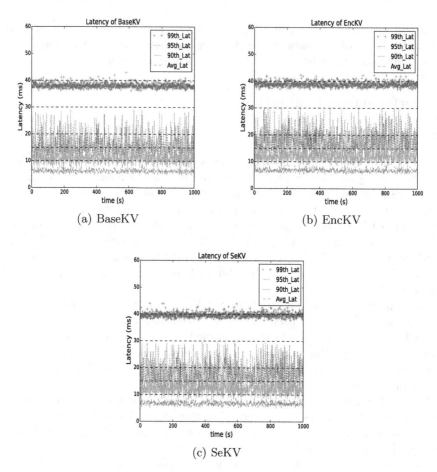

Fig. 3. The performance comparison of three key-value systems: (a) the BaseKV; (b) the EncKV; and (c) the SeKV. The performance metrics include: the average latency (*Avg_Lat*) of key-value operations, the 90-percentile (*90th_Lat*), the 95-percentile (*95th_Lat*), and the 99-percentile (*99th_Lat*) latencies.

SeKV server and modify the client code to integrate secure client library. The performance metrics include: the average latency (*Avg_Lat*) of key-value operations in a period of time (1s in the experiment setting), the 90-percentile latency (*90th_Lat*) of key-value operations (which means the latency of 90% operations are lower than the value of *90th_Lat* during a period of time), and similarly the 95-percentile latency (*95th_Lat*) and the 99-percentile latency (*99th_Lat*). In the experiment, we adopt the default GET/SET ratio of 4:1 and set 4 client worker threads with 40 TCP connections. The client threads issue 16000 requests per second to the cache server.

From the experimental result, we can observe that the performance difference among the BaseKV, the EncKV and the SeKV is modest. The *Avg_Lat* of all

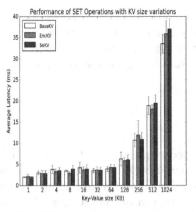
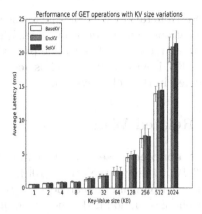

(a) The SET operations latency distribution

(b) The GET operations latency distribution

Fig. 4. The Key-Value operation performance comparisons between BaseKV, EncKV and SeKV. Figure (a) represents the SET operations average latency due to the key-value size variations; and Figure (b) represents the GET operations average latency due to the key-value size variations.

three systems are kept below 10 ms, which is acceptable in the typical key-value caching system deployment. As Fig. 3 shows, the *90th_Lat* of the BaseKV is slightly lower than the EncKV and the SeKV, which is due to the encryption overhead in the EncKV and SeKV systems. The *95th_Lat* and *99th_Lat* in the three systems are increased up to 40 ms. This is because some large size of key-value pairs in the dataset are transmitted between the client and the server. The network communication latencies dominate in the operations of the large size key-value pairs. Therefore, 1% to 5% of the key-value operations have relatively high latencies as shown in the figure.

4.3 Key-Value Size Variation Impact

The size of key-value pair varies depending on the caching dataset. To study the performance impact of the key-value size variation on the SeKV system, we set the experiment to manually increase the size of key-value pairs and record their average latencies. We vary the key-value size from 1 KB to 1024 KB to show the different performance impact.

Figure 4(a) shows the performance of the SET operations with different key-value sizes under the three systems. From the experimental result, we can observe that the average latencies of the SET operations in all the three systems increase as the sizes of key-value pairs increase. The reason is that the network transmission time increases due to the data size increases. However, the latency gap between the BaseKV and the SeKV also increases as the crypto operations on larger dataset cost more CPU time. As Fig. 4(b) shows, the trend is similar in the GET operations. The average latency of the GET operation is smaller than the SET operation, which is due to the GET operations need fewer network communications and the decryption time is also shorter than the encryption time. For the largest size of key-value pair, the latency gap between the BaseKV and the SeKV is within 10%, which is acceptable considering the security guarantees provided in the SeKV system.

5   Related Work

SGX enabled research. The Intel SGX technique was first introduced in [8,13,14]. A few of projects [1,10] have conducted SGX-related research in the cloud environment. Researchers in [1] proposed the architecture named Haven that enables unmodified windows applications to run on the SGX mode in an untrusted cloud. Haven loads both a trusted application and a trusted library OS into an enclave. Haven achieves application security with good compatibility, but its TCB is still relatively large for common cloud users. F. Schuster etc. [10] suggested using SGX for trustworthy data analytics in the cloud. They proposed VC3 that only protects user's MapReduce code and data in SGX enclaves, but keeps the Hadoop software, OS, and hypervisor out of the TCB. They further proposed methods [15] of observing and preventing leakage in MapReduce using VC3. R. Sinha et al. [16] proposed a approach of verifying confidentiality of enclave programs. Prerit Jain et al. [11] established an open source project OpenSGX that emulates Intel SGX hardware components at the instruction level with the QEMU emulator. It also provides OS components and toolchains for SGX research and development. [17,18] were the preliminary studies on the OpenSGX platform that leverages SGX to develop trusted network applications.

Hardware based solutions. Besides the recently introduced Intel SGX, existing hardware technologies for trusted computing, known as trusted execution environments (TEEs), include TPM [19], Intel TXT [20], and ARM TrustZone [5], etc. Researchers used these TEEs in many different scenarios [21–24]. For example, J. M. McCune etc. [25] proposed Flicker that time-mutiplexes the whole system between trusted Flicker sessions and untrusted host OS using TPMs. TrInc [21] provides trustworthy computation by using TPM for distributed systems. The performance overhead in TPM based implementations are very high, thus preventing the TPM adoption in most performance sensitive applications. Recently, V. Costan et al. [26] presented a detailed analysis of SGX design and then proposed a new hardware extensions [27] that achieve stronger security isolation and have good performance.

6   Conclusion

In this paper, we proposed the secure in-memory data cache scheme based on the Intel SGX processor. We proposed a trusted channel protocol to establish trust between the cache server deployed in the public cloud and the cloud user client. Then, we proposed a cache server partitioning mechanism to decouple the secret operations into the enclave region and the non-secret operations outside the enclave. In this manner, the cache server not only provides the guarantees of data confidentiality and integrity, but also keeps the performance close to the traditional key-value store systems. We also provided a secure client library to maintain the original cache semantics so that users can easily deploy the secure system using the same library APIs as in the traditional key-value systems. The experimental results showed that the proposed solution achieves near native performance compared with the default and the encrypted versions of key-value caching systems. In the future, we plan to design more advanced security features for key-value store systems, such as the high availability with multi-cloud support.

References

1. Baumann, A., Peinado, M., Hunt, G.: Shielding applications from an untrusted cloud with Haven. ACM Trans. Comput. Syst. **33**(3), 1–26 (2015)
2. Fernandes, D.A.B., Soares, L.F.B., Gomes, J.V., Freire, M.M., Inácio, P.R.M.: Security issues in cloud environments: a survey. Int. J. Inf. Secur. **13**(2), 113–170 (2013)
3. Ardagna, C.A., Asal, R., Damiani, E., Vu, Q.H.: From security to assurance in the cloud. ACM Comput. Surv. **48**(1), 1–50 (2015)
4. Intel corporation: Intel® Software Guard Extensions Programming Reference, pp. 1–186, October 2014
5. ARM Ltd.: ARM Security Technology: Building a Secure System using TrustZone Technology. White paper (2009)
6. Checkoway, S., Shacham, H.: Iago attacks: why the system call API is a bad untrusted RPC interface. In: Proceedings of the Eighteenth International Conference on Architectural Support for Programming Languages and Operating Systems (ASPLOS), pp. 253–264 (2013)
7. McGrew, D., Viega, J.: The Galois/counter mode of operation (GCM). Submission to NIST Modes of Operation Process (2004)
8. Hoekstra, M., Lal, R., Pappachan, P., Phegade, V.: Innovative technology for CPU based attestation and sealing. In: Proceedings of the 2nd International Workshop on Hardware and Architectural Support for Security and Privacy (HASP), pp. 1–11 (2013)
9. Memcached Opensource Project. https://memcached.org/
10. Schuster, F., Costa, M., Fournet, C., Gkantsidis, C., Peinado, M., Mainar-Ruiz, G., Russinovich, M.: VC3: Trustworthy data analytics in the cloud using SGX. In: IEEE Symposium on Security and Privacy (S&P), pp. 38–54 (2015)
11. Prerit, J., Soham, D., Seongmin, K., et al.: OpenSGX: an open platform for SGX research. In: Proceedings of the Network and Distributed System Security Symposium (NDSS), pp. 1–16, December 2016
12. Ferdman, M., et al.: Clearing the clouds: a study of emerging scale-out workloads on modern hardware. In: Proceedings of the Seventeenth International Conference on Architectural Support for Programming Languages and Operating Systems (ASPLOS), pp. 37–48 (2012)

13. Hoekstra, M., Lal, R., Pappachan, P., Phegade, V., del Cuvillo, J.: Using innovative instructions to create trustworthy software solutions. In: Proceedings of the 2nd International Workshop on Hardware and Architectural Support for Security and Privacy (HASP), pp. 1–11 (2013)
14. McKeen, F., Alexandrovich, I., Berenzon, A., Rozas, C.V., Shafi, H., Shanbhogue, V., Savagaonkar, U.R.: Innovative instructions and software model for isolated execution. In: Proceedings of the 2nd International Workshop on Hardware and Architectural Support for Security and Privacy (HASP), pp. 1–10 (2013)
15. Olga, O., Manuel, C., Cédric, F., Christos, G., Markulf, K., Divya, S.: Observing and preventing leakage in mapreduce. In: The ACM Conference on Computer and Communications Security (CCS) (2015)
16. Rohit, S., Sriram, R., Sanjit A., S., Kapil, V.: Moat: verifying confidentiality of enclave programs. In: The ACM Conference on Computer and Communications Security (CCS) (2015)
17. Shih, M.W., Kumar, M., Kim, T., Gavrilovska, A.: S-NFV: securing NFV states by using SGX. In: Proceedings of the 2016 ACM International Workshop on Security in Software Defined Networks & Network Function Virtualization, pp. 45–48 (2016)
18. Kim, S., Shin, Y., Ha, J., Kim, T., Han, D.: A first step towards leveraging commodity trusted execution environments for network applications. In: Proceedings of the 14th ACM Workshop on Hot Topics in Networks, pp. 1–7 (2015)
19. Trusted Computing Group: Trusted Platform Module (TPM) Specifications. Technical report (2011)
20. Greene, J.: Intel corporation: Intel® Trusted Execution Technology. White paper (2012)
21. Levin, D., Douceur, J.R., Lorch, J.R., Moscibroda, T.: TrInc: small trusted hardware for large distributed systems. In: Proceedings of the 6th USENIX Symposium on Networked Systems Design and Implementation (NSDI), pp. 1–14 (2009)
22. Azab, A.M., Ning, P., Zhang, X.: SICE: a hardware-level strongly isolated computing environment for x86 multi-core platforms. In: Proceedings of the ACM SIGSAC Conference on Computer and Communications Security (CCS), pp. 375–388 (2011)
23. Owusu, E., Guajardo, J., McCune, J.M., Newsome, J., Perrig, A., Vasudevan, A.: OASIS: on achieving a sanctuary for integrity and secrecy on untrusted platforms. In: Proceedings of the ACM SIGSAC Conference on Computer & Communications Security (CCS), pp. 13–24 (2013)
24. Sun, K., Wang, J., Zhang, F., Stavrou, A.: SecureSwitch: BIOS-assisted isolation and switch between trusted and untrusted commodity OSes. In: Proceedings of the Network and Distributed System Security Symposium (NDSS) (2012)
25. McCune, J.M., Parno, B., Perrig, A., Reiter, M.K., Isozaki, H.: Flicker: an execution infrastructure for TCB minimization. In: Proceedings of the 3rd European Conference on Computer Systems (EuroSys), pp. 315–328 (2008)
26. Costan, V., Devadas, S.: Intel SGX Explained. Technical report, February 2016
27. Costan, V., Lebedev, I., Devadas, S.: Sanctum: minimal hardware extensions for strong software isolation. In: Proceedings of USENIX Security Symposium (2016)

An Anonymization Method to Improve Data Utility for Classification

Jianmin Han[1(⊠)], Juan Yu[2], Jianfeng Lu[1], Hao Peng[1], and Jiandang Wu[1]

[1] Department of Computer Science and Technology, Zhejiang Normal University, Jinhua 321004, China
{hanjm,lujianfeng}@zjnu.cn, hpeng@zjnu.edu.cn,
295692223@qq.com
[2] Smart City Research Center, Hangzhou Dianzi University,
Hangzhou 310018, China
yujuan@hdu.edu.cn

Abstract. k-anonymity is a popular method to preserve privacy in microdata, which sacrifices data utility for preserving individuals' privacy. Therefore, how to preserve privacy with high data utility has been becoming a hot topic in k-anonymity area. Existing anonymization methods seldomly consider the data utility for specific data mining. To address the problem, we define a novel attribute weight measurement for determining the generalization order, and further propose a new anonymization algorithm based on the weight measurement using global generalization, called Weighted Full-Domain Anonymization (WFDA) Algorithm. The main idea of the algorithm is to generalize attributes with large weights to lower levels, and attributes with small weights to high levels. The proposed algorithm can reserve data utility for classification to a large extent. Experiments show that anonymous data resulted from the proposed method retains higher utility, i.e., has better classification accuracy, than that generated by other anonymization methods.

Keywords: Privacy preservation · k-anonymity · Classification · Generalization

1 Introduction

Microdata play an increasingly important role in data mining. Many organizations are collecting and publishing microdata. However, as publishing microdata may threaten individuals' privacy, privacy preservation has become a hot topic recently. Simply removing the attributes that identify individuals cannot effectively protect their privacy, because adversaries could make use of the released public data to re-identify individuals. Sweeney [1] pointed out that there were about 87% of Americans can be uniquely identified through the combination of their gender, birthday and postcode.

To address the problem, Samarati and Sweeney [2] proposed the k-anonymity model. It requires that each record is indistinguishable from at least $k-1$ other records with respect to quasi-identifier (QID) attributes in an anonymized table. The k-

© Springer International Publishing AG 2017
S. Wen et al. (Eds.): CSS 2017, LNCS 10581, pp. 57–71, 2017.
https://doi.org/10.1007/978-3-319-69471-9_5

anonymity can protect individuals' identities from being re-identified with larger than $1/k$ probability. But it can not resist homogeneity and background knowledge attacks, and therefore many other enhanced privacy preservation models have been proposed, such as l-diversity [3], t-closeness [4], $k^{\tau,\varepsilon}$-anonymity [5], P-sensitive k-anonymity [6].

Generalization [2] is a typical technique to achieve anonymity models. The idea of generalization is to replace original values of quasi-identifier attributes with less specific but semantically consistent values. As generalization distorts the original microdata, it deteriorates the utility of the data. Thus, how to reserve the data utility of anonymous data has become a hot topic in privacy preservation area [7]. So far, various generalization methods have been proposed, but only a few of them are focus on specific data mining tasks, such as Yin et al. [8], Tsai et al. [9]. Iyengar [10] proposed an optimization approach to minimize class impurity in data generalization. However, the method is impractical for large sized datasets. Wang et al. [11] proposed a bottom-up anonymization method for classification, but it can only handle categorical values. TDS [12] (top-down specialization method) is an improved version of the bottom-up method in [11], which is efficient and keeps high classification accuracy. TDR [13] (Top-Down Refinement) is a further improvement on the TDS. It can not only handle categorical attributes with taxonomy, categorical attributes without taxonomy, and continuous attributes, but also handle data with multiple quasi-identifiers. Kisilevich et al. [14] proposed a multi-dimensional suppression approach for classification-aware anonymization, called KACTUS. The method makes use of a decision tree, i.e. C4.5, as a base for deciding multi-dimensional regions to be suppressed. And Lefevre et al. [15] proposed the notion of multidimensional k-anonymity, called Mondrian. Mondrian has then been extended to InfoGain Mondrian [16] for a specific task such as classification. InfoGain Mondrian has been shown to achieve better classification accuracy than the TDS [12]. Li et al. [17] proposed an IACK (Information based Anonymization for Classification given k) algorithm. The method first determines the generalization level of each attribute according to its distribution. However, they did not consider the fact that different attributes have different impact on building classifiers.

Motivated by the fact that the attribute generalization level should be determined by the classification capability instead of the privacy requirement, we propose a new anonymization method for classification, which is able to ensure that the attribute generalization level be more appropriate for classification and to avoid over-generalizing attributes that are important for classification. Major contributions of the paper are as follows.

(1) We develop an attribute weight measurement based on the information gain ratio of the attribute, and use it as the criteria to determine the order of generalization on QI attributes.
(2) We introduce the attribute level weight and firstly use it as the metric to determine the best generalization level during the generalization process.
(3) We propose a Weighted Full-Domain Anonymization (WFDA) Algorithm incorporating global generalization and data suppression to achieve anonymization.

2 Preliminaries

Definition 1 (Quasi-identifier). A quasi-identifier (QID) is a set of publicly-accessible attributes that each individual attribute cannot uniquely identify a person, but the combination of these attributes can yield unique identification. For example, in the data set in Table 1, {Gender, Age, Pcode} compose a quasi-identifier.

Table 1. Global recording example

(a) A raw table				(b) 2-anonymous view by global recoding.			
Gender	Age	Pcode	Class	Gender	Age	Pcode	Problem
female	35	4661	stress	*	[20,39]	466*	stress
male	36	4663	obesity	*	[20,39]	466*	obesity
female	37	4663	obesity	*	[20,39]	466*	obesity
female	21	4354	stress	*	[20,39]	435*	stress
female	25	4354	obesity	*	[20,39]	435*	obesity
female	55	4331	stress	*	[40,59]	433*	stress
female	57	4331	obesity	*	[40,59]	433*	obesity
female	67	4652	stress	*	[60,79]	465*	stress
female	69	4653	obesity	*	[60,79]	465*	obesity
male	68	4653	stress	*	[60,79]	465*	stress
male	48	4354	obesity	*	[40,59]	435*	obesity
male	54	4354	stress	*	[40,59]	435*	stress

Definition 2 (Anonymous Equivalent Class). An anonymous equivalent class of a table with respect to a set of attributes is a set of tuples with the same attribute values.

For example, tuples 1, 2, 3 in Table 1(b) form an equivalent class with respect to the attribute set {Gender, Age, Pcode}, whose corresponding values are identical.

Definition 3 (k-anonymity). If each record in a table has at least $k - 1$ other records with the same QID values, the table satisfies k-anonymity, and the table is called a k-anonymized table.

According to the definitions, k-anonymity requires that the size of each equivalent class with respect to quasi-identifier is at least k. For example, Table 1(b) is a 2-anonymized table of Table 1(a), where the quasi-identifier is {Gender, Age, Pcode}.

Definition 4 (Generalization). Generalization is one of the most popular approaches for k-anonymizing microdata. The main idea of generalization is to replace the original values of Quasi-identifier with less specific values which are semantically consistent with the original values.

Generalization can be divided two categories: global recoding and local recoding. For global recording, once an attribute value is generalized, each occurrence of the value should be replaced by the new generalized value. Figure 1 shows the generalization hierarchy of the attribute Pcode. Incognito [2] is a typical global-recoding algorithm. Table 1(b) is a global recoding version of the original table (a). It is easy to see that global recoding may over-generalization microdata.

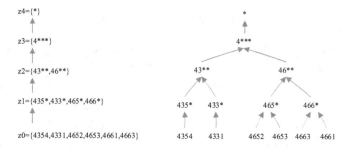

Fig. 1. The procedure of generalization

Definition 5. Entropy [18] is used to measure the uncertainty of events. Let D be a training set. Suppose the label attribute has m distinct values which partition D into m classes, i.e. $C_1, C_2, \ldots, C_m$. Let $|C_{i,D}|$ and $|D|$ denote the number of tuples in C_i and D respectively. The entropy of D can be defined as Eq. (1).

$$Info(D) = \sum_{i=1}^{m} (p_i \log(1/p_i)) \tag{1}$$

where p_i is the probability that a tuple belongs to C_i, which can be calculated as $|C_{i,D}|/|D|$. The base of the log function is 2, because the information is encoded in bits.

Suppose that an attribute A of a table D has v distinct discrete values, $\{a_1, a_2, \ldots a_v\}$. The table can be partitioned into v subsets, i.e. $(D_1, D_2, \ldots D_v)$, where D_i contains those tuples whose values of attribute A is a_i. If attribute A is used as the test attribute, the new expected information required to classify a tuple based on attribute A can be measured by Eq. (2).

$$Info_A(D) = \sum_{i=1}^{v} \frac{|D_i|}{|D|} \times Info(D_i) \tag{2}$$

where $\frac{|D_i|}{|D|}$ is the weight of the i-th partition, $Info_A(D)$ denotes the expected information.

Definition 6. Information gain [18] is defined as the difference between the original expected information (i.e., based on just the proportion of classes) and the new expected information (i.e., obtained after partitioning on A), which can be calculated by Eq. (3).

$$Gain\,(A) = Info\,(D) - Info_A(D) \tag{3}$$

The greater the information gain of an attribute is, the greater the uncertainty information it contains. As data classification is favorable of the uncertainty information of attributes, the ID3 classification algorithm can use information gain as the attribute selection metric.

3 The WFDA Algorithm for Classification

Generalization can be divided into two categories, namely global recoding and local recoding. Local recoding can preserve more information than global recoding. But value consistency is very important for classification. For example, local recoding may generalize values of the Age attribute into 23, 10–15, 18, 20–30, 40–60, and the generalized values are not suitable for most classification tools as overlapping intervals brings challenges to classification tasks. That is to say, attribute values are preferred to be within the same domain for most classification tasks. Therefore, global recoding is preferred to achieve k-anonymity for classification applications, for the reason that it can generalize attribute values into the domain with non-overlapping values, such as 10–20, 20–30, 30–40 and so on.

To preserve the quality of anonymized data for classification, we propose a new method to anonymize datasets based on global recording, called Weighted Full-Domain Algorithm (WFDA). The goal of the proposed algorithm is to generalize attributes with large weights to lower levels, and attributes with small weights to high levels. To achieve this goal, two problems should be considered: (1) how to determine the order of attributes to be generalized; and (2) how to select the best generalization levels for each attribute. For the first problem, we propose attribute weight measurements based on information gain and generalize attributes according to their weights. For the second one, we introduce a method to adaptively determine the best generalization level for each attribute.

3.1 Determination of Attribute Weight

Generally, the attribute with the highest information gain is chosen as a splitting attribute preferentially. The higher the information gain an attribute has, the more important it is for classification analysis. So we propose an attribute weight measurement based on information gain of the attribute, which is defined as an exponential function of its information gain, seeing Eq. (4),

$$w_A = e^{Gain(A)} \tag{4}$$

where A is an attribute, Gain(A) is the information gain of A, e is the mathematical constant (the base of the natural logarithm).

For example, a data table includes four attributes A, B, C, D, suppose Gain(A) is 0.8, Gain(B) is 1.2, Gain(C) is 0.3, and Gain(D) is 0.5. Then the corresponding attribute weights are shown in Table 2.

Table 2. The attribute weights of different attributes

/	A	B	C	D
Information gain	0.8	1.2	0.3	0.5
Weight (w_A)	2.226	3.320	1.349	1.649

The information gain measurement prefers to select the attribute with a large value domain. However, this attribute might be useless for classification. Thus, information gain ratio [18] is proposed for selecting classification attributes. Information gain ratio is defined as follows.

$$GainRatio(A) = Gain(A)/SplitI(A) \tag{5}$$

where $SplitI(A) = \sum_{i=1}^{v} (p_i \log(1/p_i))$.

Information gain works fine for most cases, unless there are a few attributes with a large number of values (or has a large value domain). Information gain is biased towards choosing attributes with large value domains as root nodes. Information gain ratio is a modification of information gain. It overcomes the shortage of information gain by taking into account the number of branches that would result before making the split. That is to say that the bias of information gain could be avoided by taking the intrinsic information of a split into account.

Accordingly, we propose an attribute weight measurement based on the information gain ratio, and define it as Eq. (6).

$$w_A = e^{GainRatio(A)} \tag{6}$$

where A is an attribute, GainRatio(A) is the information gain ratio of A, e is the mathematical constant (the base of the natural logarithm). The higher the information gain ratio of an attribute is, the more important the attribute is for classification.

3.2 Selection of Attribute Generalization Levels

Information gain or information gain ration can be used as the metric to select generalization levels of attributes. For an attribute, different generalization levels results in different information gains or information gain rations. Let denote the attribute levels weight on attribute A at the generalization level i, which can be calculated using Eq. (6).

For instance, Fig. 2 shows the generalization taxonomy of a given attribute A, there are 8 values at level 1, 4 values at level 2, and 2 values at level 3. Table 3 lists of the attribute A at different generalization levels, which are calculated according to the Eq. (6). During generalization, we can select the best generalization level as the one with the largest weight.

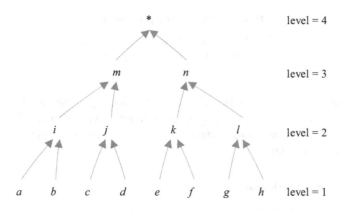

Fig. 2. The generalization taxonomy of attribute A

Table 3. w_A^i of the attributes at different generalization level

Level	InfoGainRatio	w_A^i
1	0.55	1.733
2	1.22	3.386
3	1.05	2.857

3.3 Suppression Ratio

In practical, the generalization cannot often make all tuples satisfy anonymous constraints, and those tuples not satisfying anonymous constraints are often suppressed to satisfy the predefined anonymous constrains. Whereas simply suppress tuples could result in high information loss. To make information loss as less as possible, we proposed a suppression policy. Let n' denote the number of tuples which do not satisfy anonymous constraints, n be the tuples number of the whole dataset, then the suppression ratio r can be calculated as

$$r = n'/n. \tag{7}$$

The suppression policy is that if the suppression ratio r is smaller than a given threshold r_0, we suppress these tuples which do not satisfy anonymous constraints; otherwise, we generalize these tuple to the highest level. Generally, our goal is to generalize attributes with large weights to lower levels, and attributes with small weights to high levels. Thus, we choose the attribute with the smallest w_A^i first to be generalized in the anonymization algorithm. In this paper we set $r_0 = 0.08$.

For example, for Table 1(a), attributes {*age, race, education, worktime*} are generalized to levels {2, 1, 2, 2} respectively, and their corresponding weights are listed in Table 4.

Table 4. The w_A^i after generalization

/	Age	Race	Education	Worktime
w_A^i	2.224	1.561	1.602	1.751

If the suppression ratio r is larger than the threshold r_0, attributes should be generalized in ascending order according to their weights. For example, for the given attributes {*age, race, education, worktime*}, the order we choose to generalize is *race, education, worktime, age*.

3.4   Algorithm Description

The proposed WFDA algorithm first generalizes the original data into the favor levels for classification, and then suppresses tuples not satisfying anonymous constraints according to the suppression policy. The detailed description of the algorithm is described in Algorithm 1.

Algorithm 1 Weighted Full-Domain algorithm(WFDA)

Input: A original dataset T, a suppression threshold r_0.

Output: an anonymized dataset T'

Steps:

for $i = 1$ to m do //m is attributes number of quasi-identifier
    compute information gain ratio and w_A^i for each hierarchical level of A_i;

    find l_i' that maximizes the w_A^i ;

    generalize attribute A_i to the level l_i';

end for

    $r=n/n_0$;

    // n_0 is the tuple number of D, n is the number of tuple which do not satisfy the k anonymity constraints

while ($r > r_0$) **do**

  generalize the attribute A' that the attribute levels weight is minimum to the next levels

end while

    return anonymous table T'

---

4   Experiments

We use the Adult dataset from UCI Machine Learning Repository [19] as the testing dataset. Adult dataset is US census data and has been a benchmark dataset for comparing anonymity algorithm. We treat the 6 attributes described in Table 5 as quasi-identifiers and the salary attribute as the sensitive information. We discretize salary as 50K and >50K. The Adult dataset includes 30801 records. We use JAVA to implement the algorithm. All experiments were conducted on an Intel Core(TM)Duo 2.00 GHz PC with 4-Gbyte RAM. For classification analysis, we use C4.5 Classifier,

Table 5. Attribute description of adult

Num	Attribute	Attribute type	Numerical range	Levels
1	Age	Numeric	74	5
2	Work class	Categorical	8	3
3	Gender	Categorical	2	2
4	Race	Categorical	5	3
5	Education	Categorical	16	4
6	Work time	Numeric	80	5

NaiveBayes Classifier, logistic classifier and AD tree classifier in weka (Waikato Environment for Knowledge Analysis) [20].

4.1 Selection of the Generalization Level

For an attribute A, the generalization level is determined by its level weights calculated according to the Eq. (6). We assume that the larger the weight w_A^i is, the more favorable for the classification algorithms are. Thus, we select the level with the maximal wight w_A^i as its generalization level. Figure 3 shows the weights of different levels of attributes in the Adult dataset. From the figure we can see that, the weight variable of attribute age reaches the peak at level 2, the weight variable of attribute workclass is peaked at level 1, the weight variable of attribute race is peaked at level 2, gender peaks at 1, education peaks at 2, and worktime peaks at 2.

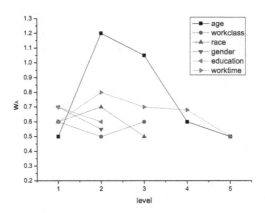

Fig. 3. The values of w_A^i at different levels

4.2 Data Quality

In this experiment, our goal is to show that the proposed method can generate high quality anonymous datasets while anonymizing the dataset satisfying a broad range of anonymity requirements. Specifically, we compare the accuracies of classification on the original dataset, on anonymous datasets resulting from Incognito Full-Domain algorithm, and on anonymous dataset generated by the Weighted Full-Domain Algorithm (WFDA) using the C4.5 classifier, Naive Bayesian classifier, respectively. Comparison results are shown in Figs. 4, 5, 6 and 7. Classification accuracy of anonymous dataset generated by the WFDA is very close to that of the original data, and is higher than that of anonymous dataset generated by Incognito on C4.5 classifier, Naive Bayesian classifier, logistic classifier and AD tree classifier.

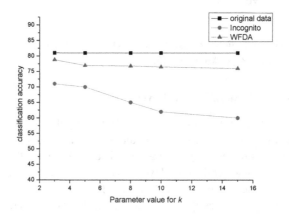

Fig. 4. The classification accuracy in the C4.5 classifier

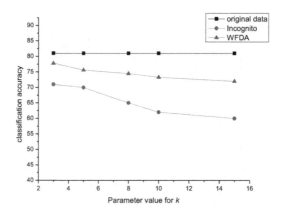

Fig. 5. The classification accuracy in the Naive Bayesian classifier

Figures 8 and 9 show the classification accuracy of C4.5 classifier and Naive Bayesian classifier on k anonymized dataset resulted from WDFA and IACk [17] in comparison against the accuracy on the original dataset. The classification accuracy on the anonymous dataset generated by WFDA is slightly higher than the accuracy on the dataset resulted from the IACk.

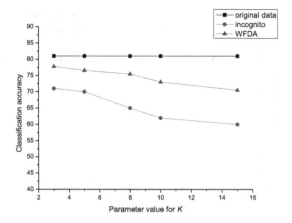

Fig. 6. The classification accuracy in the logistic classifier

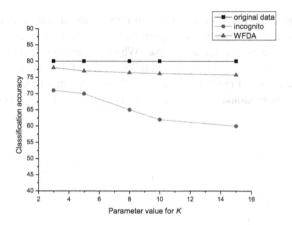

Fig. 7. The classification accuracy in the ADtree classifier

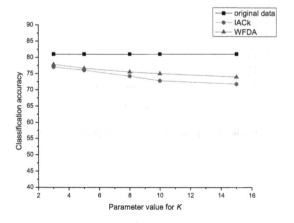

Fig. 8. The classification accuracy in the C4.5 classifier

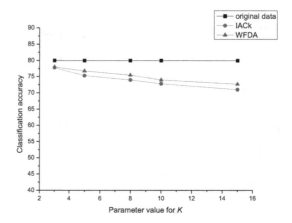

Fig. 9. The classification accuracy in the Naive Bayesian classifier

To implement k-anonymity, the IACk algorithm might directly suppress equivalent class with tuples not satisfying the anonymity constraints. when k growing larger, the IACk algorithm cause more information loss. Whereas, the WFDA algorithm continues to generalize attributes with small weights until $r < r_0$, and then inconsistent values are subsequently suppressed. Figure 10 shows that the percentage of the suppressed tuples by WFDA which is obviously lower than the percentage of the suppressed tuples by IACk.

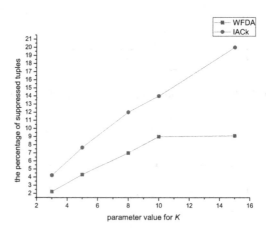

Fig. 10. The percentage of the suppressed tuples

4.3 Efficiency

Figure 11 shows the running time of the WFDA and IACk algorithms with various k. From the figure we can observe that the running time of WFDA is slightly higher than that of the IACk algorithm, as the attribute generalization level control is added in the WFDA. We consider that the increment of computational cost is acceptable.

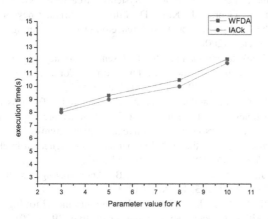

Fig. 11. Running time

5 Conclusion

The problem of anonymizing microdata for classification is considered in the paper, and a new anonymization algorithm, which takes the importance of attributes on classification into account, is proposed. Experiments show that the proposed method can generate anonymous dataset with better classification results than existing k-anonymization methods.

This paper focuses on designing methods to preserve the data utility of anonymous datasets for classification. In the future, we plan to find effective methods to anonymize datasets for other data mining tasks, such as association rules, clustering etc.

Acknowledgment. We thank anonymous reviewers for constructive comments, which lead to a substantial improvement of this paper. This work is supported by National Natural Science Foundation of China (Grant No. 61402418, 61503342, 61672468, 61602418), the Young Scientists Fund of the National Natural Science Foundation of China (Grant No. 61702148), MOE (Ministry of Education in China) Project of Humanity and Social Science (Grant No. 12YJCZH142, 15YJCZH125), Social development project of Zhejiang provincial public technology research (Grant No. 2016C33168), Zhejiang Provincial Natural Science Foundation of China (Grant No. LY15F020013, LQ13F020007, LY16F030002, LQ16F020002), Key Lab of Information Network Security, Ministry of Public Security (Grant No. C15610), and Opening Fund of Shanghai Information Security Key Laboratory of Integrated Management of Technology (Grant No. AGK2013003).

References

1. Sweeney, L.: k-anonymity: a model for protecting privacy. Int. J. Uncertainty Fuzziness Knowl. Based Syst. **10**(5), 557–570 (2002)
2. Samarati, P., Sweeney, L.: Generalizing data to provide anonymity when disclosing information (abstract). In: Proceedings of the 17th ACM-SIGMOD-SIGACT-SIGART Symposium on the Principles of Database Systems, Piscataway, NJ, p. 188. IEEE (1998)
3. Machanavajjhala, A., Gehrke, J., Kifer, D.: l-diversity: privacy beyond k-anonymity. In: Proceedings of the 22nd International Conference on Data Engineering, Atlanta, pp. 24–35. IEEE Computer Society (2006)
4. Li, N., Li, T., Venkatasubramanian, S.: t-Closeness: privacy beyond k-anonymity and l-diversity. In: Proceedings of the 23rd International Conference on Data Engineering (ICDE), Istanbul, Turkey, pp. 106–115. IEEE Press (2007)
5. Gramaglia, M., Fiore, M., Tarable, A., et al.: $k^{\tau,\varepsilon}$-anonymity: Towards Privacy-Preserving Publishing of Spatiotemporal Trajectory Data (2017). arXiv preprint: arXiv:1701.02243
6. Jia, J., Yan, G., Xing, L.: Personalized sensitive attribute anonymity based on P - sensitive K anonymity. In: Proceedings of the 2016 International Conference on Intelligent Information Processing, New York, NY, USA, pp. 54:1–54:7 (2016)
7. Gong, Q., Luo, J., Yang, M., Ni, W., Li, X.-B.: Anonymizing 1:M microdata with high utility. Knowl. Based Syst. **115**, 15–26 (2017)
8. Yin, C., Zhang, S., Xi, J., et al.: An improved anonymity model for big data security based on clustering algorithm. Concurrency Comput. Pract. Exp. **29**(7) (2017)
9. Tsai, Y.-C., Wang, S.-L., Song, C.-Y., Ting, I.-H.: Privacy and utility effects of k-anonymity on association rule hiding. In: Proceedings of the 3rd Multidisciplinary International Social Networks Conference on Social Informatics 2016, Data Science 2016, New York, NY, USA, pp. 42:1–42:6 (2016)
10. Iyengar, V.S.: Transforming data to satisfy privacy constraints. In: Proceedings of the 8th ACM SIGKDD International Conference on Knowledge Discovery and Data Mining, Edmonton, AB, Canada, pp. 279–288, July 2002
11. Wang, K., Yu, P.S., Chakraborty, S.: Bottom-up generalization: a data mining solution to privacy protection. In: Proceedings of the Fourth IEEE International Conference on Data Mining, pp. 205–216 (2004)
12. Fung, B.C.M., Wang, K., Yu, P.S.: Top-down specialization for information and privacy preservation. In: Proceedings of the 21st International Conference on Data Engineering (ICDE 2005), pp. 205–216, April 2005
13. Fung, B.C.M., Wang, K., Yu, P.S.: Anonymizing classification data for privacy preservation. IEEE Trans. Knowl. Data Eng. **19**(5), 711–725 (2007)
14. Kisilevich, S., Rokach, L., Elovici, Y., Shapira, B.: Efficient multidimensional suppression for k-anonymity. IEEE Trans. Knowl. Data Eng. **22**(3), 334–347 (2010)
15. LeFevre, K., DeWitt, D.J., Ramakrishnan, R.: Mondrian multidimensional k-anonymity. In: International Conference on Data Engineering (ICDE 2006), p. 25. IEEE Computer Society (2006)
16. LeFevre, K., DeWitt, D.J., Ramakrishnan, R.: Workload-aware anonymization techniques for large-scale datasets. ACM Trans. Database Syst. **33**(3), 1–47 (2008)
17. Li, J., Liu, J., Baig, M.: Information based data anonymization for classification utility. Elsevier, 18 July 2011

18. Han, J., Kamber, M.: Data Mining Concepts and Techniques. Morgan Kaufmann Publishers Inc. (2005)
19. Blake, E.K.C., Merz, C.J.: UCI repository of machine learning databases (1998). http://www.ics.uci.edu/mlearn/MLRepository.html
20. Witten, I.H., Frank, E., Hall, M.A.: Data Mining Practical Machine Learning Tools and Techniques. China Machine Press, Beijing (2012)

A Fair Three-Party Contract Singing Protocol Based on Blockchain

Hui Huang[1], Kuan-Ching Li[2], and Xiaofeng Chen[1(✉)]

[1] State Key Laboratory of Integrated Service Networks (ISN),
Xidian University, Xi'an, People's Republic of China
hhui323@163.com, xfchen@xidian.edu.cn
[2] Department of Computer Science and Information Engineering,
Providence University, Taichung, Taiwan
kuancli@gm.pu.edu.tw

Abstract. Contract signing allows two or more mutual distrust entities to sign a predefined digital contract in a fair and effective way. It is a significant cryptographic service in commercial environment, where the crucial property for contract signing protocols is fairness. The existing solutions involved a trusted third party (TTP) to solve the problem of fairness. However, the existence of TTP become a bottleneck, since it can be a single point of failure or suffer from external or internal attack. In this paper, we propose a fair three-party contract singing protocol based on the primitive of blockchain, which provides a novel solution to design a fair protocol without a TTP. Our proposed construction makes use of the verifiable encrypted signature and the blockchain to accomplish the fair exchange. As result, a dishonest party will be monetarily penalized as it aborts after receiving the current output. Moreover, the privacy of the contract content can be preserved on the public chain.

Keywords: Contract signing · Blockchain · Verifiable encrypted signature · Penalty

1   Introduction

A contract signing protocol is a communication protocol which allows two or more participants to sign a digital contract. An important property of contract signing protocol is fairness, permitting the participants to exchange signed contract in an all-or-nothing way. Namely, the involved participants either obtain a valid contract or nothing useful at the end of the protocol. It means that dishonest participants can not get more advantage than honest ones. The fairness is very easy to achieve in face-to-face contract signing. However, due to lack of trust in computer network, there are many security threats that can not be ignored [12,13,23]. Therefore, signing contract electronically in a fair way has become a challenging problem.

A number of electronic contract signing schemes have been proposed in the literature [5,10,11,14,16–18], and there are two major solutions to solve the

ⓒ Springer International Publishing AG 2017
S. Wen et al. (Eds.): CSS 2017, LNCS 10581, pp. 72–85, 2017.
https://doi.org/10.1007/978-3-319-69471-9_6

problem of fairness in existing protocols. The first one is TTP-free protocol [15], that is, the participants exchange their signatures on a contract by means of "bit by bit". In this scenario, parties in the protocol release their secrets gradually in multiple rounds. If any of the parties fails to complete the exchange, they can still complete by searching the remaining bits of signatures. It had the advantage of removing the TTP, though it was not suitable for real world application due to its high communication cost. Another solution is to introduce a trusted third party (TTP), who is online or offline to mediate the exchange of signature. In contract-signing protocols, a TTP can make the execution of the signing process simpler and efficient. In the online-TTP setting [6], the main problem is that the TTP becomes a bottleneck of the system when there are multiple participants in the system. Contract signing protocols with an offline TTP [2,3,5,10,14,16,17] are more practical, in which TTP is only involved in the case of dispute, called optimistic contract signing.

It seems that existing solutions have disadvantages. Among these protocols, some require participants to run an extra protocol to guarantee the fairness, which could be much more expensive (especially in the communication cost) than a standard protocol; some need an external party who must be trusted, e.g. in the optimistic protocol, the party needs to contact with a trusted third party each time a dispute occurs. In summary, all these protocols exist the weakness that the honest party has to make extra effort to prevent adversary from cheating. Blockchain provides a solution to solving the trust problem, which was proposed as the underlying technology of Bitcoin [19]. Bitcoin is a peer-to-peer decentralized digital currency system and uses the cryptography tools to build a currency system without a trusted third party. Its novel and open design has attracted more and more attention. Due to the advantage of Bitcoin system, it is applicable to design fair protocol. Recently, Andrychowicz [1] showed how the advantages of Bitcoin can be used in designing fair multiparty computations. To the best of our knowledge, it seems that there is no similar investigation on fair contract signing protocol based on Bitcoin blockchain.

1.1 Our Contributions

In this paper, we propose a fair three-party contract singing protocol based on blockchain. Different from previous works, the proposed protocol does not need a third party to guarantee the fairness. The contributions of this paper are as follows:

– We construct a fair three-party contract signing protocol with penalties. The proposed protocol combines threshold public key encryption with verifiable encryption to protect the privacy of contract content. Also, it uses the blockchain to finish the fair exchange. The proposed protocol enables a dishonest party to be monetarily penalized when he aborts after receiving the current output. Different from previous works, there is not a bank or a trusted third party to guarantee the fairness. The setting of proposed structure is more practical than existing ones.

– The privacy of the contract against the blockchain can be preserved in our proposed protocol. The parties only publish the decryption shares to the blockchain. As a result, the nodes on the public chain only learn some decryption shares. Since the nodes never get the encrypted items, they can not decrypt the encryption of signed contract. At last, the contract signing protocol required only constant number of communication rounds. The setting of the proposed structure is more efficient than previous ones.

1.2 Organization

The rest of paper is organized as follows. Some preliminaries are given in Sect. 2, and the proposed fair three-party contract singing protocol is given in Sect. 3. The security analysis and performance analysis is given in Sect. 4, and finally, conclusion remarks in Sect. 5.

2 Preliminaries

In this section, we first give an overview of threshold ElGamal encryption and verifiable encryption signature. Then, we introduce some notion of blockchain.

2.1 Threshold ElGamal Encryption

As [16], a threshold encryption scheme consists of four probabilistic polynomial time algorithms: *Key Generation, Verification, Decryption* and *Encryption*. In this paper, we will adopt the *ElGamal* threshold encryption (i.e., $k = n$) scheme to build our protocol. Assume there are n participants in the scheme. They have previously agreed on the primes p and q, where $q \mid p - 1$. Let g be a generator of $\mathbb{Z}_q^*$, $\mathbb{Z}_p$ is a group with the large prime order p.

– *Key Generation:* Each party randomly chooses $x_i \in \mathbb{Z}_p$ and the set of private keys are $SK = \{x_1, x_2, \cdots x_n\}$. Computes $h_i = g^{x_i}$. As [16,20] done, each party commits to h_i and broadcasts to all participants. Denote these public verification key as $PVK = \{h_1, \cdots, h_n\}$. The public key $PK = (g, h)$, where $h = \prod_{i=1}^{n} = g^{\sum x_i}$.
– *Encryption:* Given a message m, the party randomly chooses $r \in \mathbb{Z}_q$ and computes $a = g^r, b = mh^r$. The ciphertext is $E = (a, b)$.
– *Verification:* The verification algorithm is run by given the verification key PVK, the ciphertext E and the decryption share $d_i = g^{rx_i}$ belonging to party i. If $log_g h_i = log_g d_i$, it outputs *valid*. Otherwise, it outputs *invalid*.
– *Decryption:* The decryption algorithm takes input the n decryption $d_i, i \in \{1, \cdots n\}$. Then, it computes $d = \prod d_i$ and decrypts the ciphertext as:

$$m = \frac{b}{d} = \frac{mh^r}{g^{r \sum x_i}} = \frac{mh^r}{h^r}$$

2.2 Verifiable Encrypted Signature

The verifiable encrypted signature allows a party to encrypt his message signature and the recipient can verify the signature without performing any decryption. Asokan et al. [4] formally introduced the notion of verifiable encrypted signature. Boneh et al. [8] presented the first non-interactive verifiable encrypted signature scheme by verifiably encrypting the BLS signature [9]. Recently, Shao et al. [21] proposed the first verifiably encrypted discrete-log signature scheme. In this section, we will combine Shao's verifiable encrypted signature with the threshold encryption to describe the scheme.

As described in Sect. 2.1, considering a k out of n threshold encryption scheme, a single public key is used to perform the encryption on a message, though the corresponding secret key is shared among a set of n decrypter. Only k of them work together, they can decrypt a message. Assume every party has obtained the public key h and the corresponding secret key has been distributed between them. Here, we consider $k = n$. The party P_1 wants to run a verifiable encrypted signature scheme to send his encrypted signature to P_2. P_2 can use the public key h and the public key of P_1 to verify the signature without performing decryption. A verifiably encrypted signature scheme consists of four probabilistic polynomial time algorithms: *Setup, KeyGen, VEsign, VEVerify, Decryption* [8,21].

- *Setup:* On input the secure parameters, generates public hash functions and the system parameters.
- *KeyGen:* Given the system parameters, the participants generates key pair (x'_i, y_i), which is used for signing the contract. Then, they work together to generate the public key of threshold encryption h.
- *VEsign:* For a message $M \in \{0,1\}^*$, the signer P_i computes a signature (M, σ) with his private key x'_i, then generates a VES_i with the public key of threshold encryption h.
- *VEVerify:* After receiving the verifiable encrypted signature of the message M, the verifier checks the verification equations for the VES_i with the respect to the public key y_i and h.
- *Decryption:* The decryption algorithm takes input the n decryption shares of all participants. Then, each participant extracts the signature with the decryption shares.

2.3 Blockchain

A blockchain is essentially a distributed database on the peer-to-peer network. It maintains continuously growing blocks which record the data and can prevent these data from tampering and revision. The blockchain was firstly used in Bitcoin, which was conceptualised by Satoshi Nakamoto in 2008 [19]. It was a core component of the Bitcoin system. The invention of the blockchain enabled Bitcoin to become the first electronic currency without the use of a trusted authority [22].

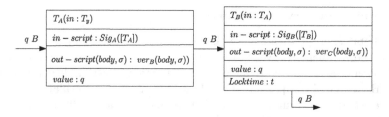

Fig. 1. The graph gives the relationship of two transaction. Assume T_A and T_B are two related transactions produced by two users. A and B are two public key. T_y is a previous transaction can be redeemed by A. $[T_A]$ denotes messages contained the input script of T and all content of T_A except the output script. This example describes that T_A can be redeemed by the public key B in time t.

Addresses and transactions are two components of Bitcoin system. Every user in the system has a key pair. A bitcoin address is the hash of the user's public key. The private key is used for signing the transactions, and the public key is used for verifying the signatures. A transaction has some input and output. The input script of the transactions is a signature, and the output script is a verification algorithm, which controls the conditions weather the coins can be redeemed or not. In a real system, users can define the condition flexibly. In the standard transaction, input-script is just a signature with the sender's secret key, and out-script implements a signature verification with the recipient's public key. If the time t is 0, it means the transaction is locked and final. As an example, Fig. 1 gives the relationship of two transaction.

3   The Proposed Fair Contract Signing Protocol

In this section, we introduce a concrete construction of three-parties contract signing protocol. The three participants are denoted by P_A, P_B, P_C. We assume all participants can be either honest or malicious. We define that the party P_A obtains a valid contract only if P_A has received the other two parties' signature on the contract. If P_A only received one party's signature, say P_B, then the contract is invalid. Our proposed fair contract signing protocol should satisfy the security of *completeness, fairness, timeliness, non-repudiation,* and *confidentiality* [3].

We assume all messages between the participants are reliably transferred. Our protocol does not need the messages to be transferred in sequence. We also assume the communication channel between the participants is resilient. The property of resilient refers to asynchronous communication model without global clocks, in which the messages can be delayed arbitrarily but will reach eventually in finite time. In order to avoid disputes, the deadline time in our protocol should include the time to be delayed in the communication channel.

3.1 Our Protocol

In this section, we present a fair three-parties contract signing protocol with penalties. Before describing our protocol in detail, we introduce some notations first. There are three parties involved in our protocol, denote by $P_i, i \in \{A, B, C\}$. They have agreed on a contract M in advance. Denote by σ_i the signature on contract M with the secret key of the party $P_i, i \in \{A, B, C\}$. VES_i is a verifiable encrypted signature of P_i's signed contract under the public key h. In our protocol, we use blockchain network to guarantee the fairness. In the following, we use T_i to denote a bitcoin transaction. $P_i \xrightarrow[q,t]{S} P_j$ denote a deposit transaction produced by P_i with q coins and it can be calimed by P_j only if it provides S_j. After the time t, P_i can get back the deposit.

Note that we do not describe the agreement on the contract and the amount of the coins in detail. It may require a number of rounds of communication between the involved parties through a security channel. All parties should agree on the deadline for each phase in the protocol. Our protocol has four phases. The details are as below.

- **Key Generation.** In this phase, all parties join together to generate a public key for the verifiable encrypted signature algorithm. They firstly agree on a prime p−order subgroup $\mathbb{Z}_p \subset \mathbb{Z}_q^*$, q is a large prime. Assume g is a generator of $\mathbb{Z}_p$. Then each $P_i, i \in \{A, B, C\}$ does:
  - Firstly, Party P_A randomly chooses $x_1 \in \mathbb{Z}_p$ as his secret key. He computes $h_1 = g^{x_1}$. Then he randomly selects a string r_1 and makes commitment $C_1 = C(h_1, r_1)$ to h_1 as [16,20] done. Sends C_1 to party P_B and P_C.
  - When all the two parties have received the commitment, P_A opens the commitment C_1. P_B and P_C obtain P_A's h_1.
  - P_B and P_C repeat the same process as P_A does. At the end, all the parties have the public key set $\{h_1, h_2, h_3\}$. The threshold encryption's public key h is computed as:
  $$h = \prod_1^3 h_i = \prod_1^3 g^{x_i} = g^{\sum_i x_i} = g^x.$$
  Here, we let $x = \sum_i x_i$.
  Note that all parties know the public key, but they cannot find the secret key $x = \sum_i x_i$ unless they all work together.
- **Signature Exchange.** In this phase, each $P_i, i \in \{A, B, C\}$ computes a signature σ_i on the contract M. And then, it runs the verifiable encrypted signature scheme described in Sect. 2.2 to encrypt σ_i. At last, P_i sends the encrypted signature VES_i to other parties. Assume the system has produced two public hash functions: $H : \{0,1\}^* \to \mathbb{Z}_q^*$, $H_1 : \mathbb{Z}_P \to \mathbb{Z}_p^*$. P_i generates the verifiable encrypted signature as follows.
  - Firstly, the party P_A randomly chooses $x_1' \in \mathbb{Z}_q^*$ as his private key and computes $y_1 = g^{x_1'}$. h is the public key which has been generated in phase 1.

- For a contract $M \in \{0,1\}^*$, the party P_A randomly chooses three integers $r_1, t_{11}, t_{12} \in Z_q^*$. Computes the signature $\sigma_1 = H(M)^{x_1'}$, $a_1 = y_1^{r_1}$, $b_1 = h^{r_1}$, $c_1 = \sigma_1 b_1^{x_1'}$, $r_{11} = g^{t_{11}}$, $r_{12} = (H(M)b)^{t_{11}}$, $r_{13} = y_1^{t_{12}}$, $r_{14} = h^{t_{12}}$, $h_{11} = H_1(H(M), g, y_1, h, r_{11}, r_{12}, r_{13}, r_{14})$, $s_{11} = t_{11} - h_{11}x_1'$, $s_{12} = t_{12} - h_{11}r_1$, The verifiable encrypted signature of the contract M is $VES_1 = (a_1, b_1, c_1, h_{11}, s_{11}, s_{12})$.
- After receiving the contract M's verifiable encrypted signature $VES_1 = (a_1, b_1, c_1, h_{11}, s_{11}, s_{12})$, the recipient $P_j, j \in \{B, C\}$ computes $r_{11}' = y_1^{h_{11}} g^{s_{11}}$, $r_{12}' = c_1^{h_{11}} (H(M)b_1)^{s_{11}}$, $r_{13}' = a_1^{h_{11}} y_1^{s_{12}}$, $r_{14}' = b_1^{h_{11}} h^{s_{12}}$, $h_{11}' = H_1(H(M), g, y_1, h, r_{11}', r_{12}', r_{13}', r_{14}')$. If $h_{11} = h_{11}'$, P_j accepts the encrypted signature. Otherwise, he aborts the protocol.
- $P_j, j \in \{B, C\}$ repeat the same process as P_A does. At the end, each $P_i, i \in \{A, B, C\}$ receives the verifiable encryption signature sets $VES_i, i \in \{1, 2, 3\}$.

If anything goes wrong up to the time t_1, that is, other participant does not receive the verifiable encryption VES_i, he can abort the protocol.

- **Shares Exchange.** In this phase, each party will send the decryption shares to other parties to decrypt each VES_i. Here, we will use the special nature of bitcoin to guarantee the fairness of the exchange. If a dishonest party aborts after receiving all shares, he will be monetarily penalized. First, each P_i should make a deposit transaction via Bitcoin system to commit that he will reveal the share $S_i = (a_1^{x_i}, a_2^{x_i}, a_3^{x_i})$. If he does not reveal the secret share S_i by deadline, he will be punished and the other parties will be compensated. After all parties make the deposit, they reveal their secret share S_i via a claim transaction step by step. The process of deposit and claim is shown in Fig. 3, as well the detailed descriptions.
  - **Deposit.** This process begins when each party receives all verifiable encryptions signatures VES_i from the other one. If anything goes wrong or the protocol exchange has been aborted, it cannot be run. The process of deposit protocol can be described as [7]:

$$P_A \xrightarrow[q, \tau_3]{S_1 \wedge S_2 \wedge S_3} P_C \tag{1}$$

$$P_B \xrightarrow[q, \tau_3]{S_1 \wedge S_2 \wedge S_3} P_C \tag{2}$$

$$P_C \xrightarrow[2q, \tau_2]{S_1 \wedge S_2} P_B \tag{3}$$

$$P_B \xrightarrow[q, \tau_1]{S_1} P_A \tag{4}$$

It can be divided in two steps. Formulas (1) and (2) are the first step. That is, parties P_A, P_B make a deposit of q coins to recipient P_C at the same time. This deposit transaction can be claimed by P_C only if he can produce the secret value S_1, S_2, S_3 in round τ_3. As second step, party P_C

makes a deposit of $2q$ coins to recipient P_B, which can be claimed by P_B when he produces S_1, S_2 in round τ_2. Party P_B makes a deposit of q coins to recipient P_A, which can be claimed by P_A when he produces S_1 in round τ_1. Here, $\tau_3 < \tau_2 < \tau_1$. The details are described in the following.
* For $i \in \{A, B\}$, P_i does the following.
   1. P_A prepares an unredeemed transaction T^1 that can be redeemed with a key known only to P_A. Then P_A builds a new transaction T^1_{dep} with q coins according to some condition described in Fig. 2. And he keeps it private and create another transaction T^1_{ref} which has a locked time τ_3.
   2. P_A sends the body $[T^1_{ref}]$ to P_C and asks P_C to sign. P_C signs $[T^1_{ref}]$ and sends back the signed transaction to P_A. If the signed $[T^1_{ref}]$ does not reach P_A by deadline, P_A aborts. After receiving the signed $[T^1_{ref}]$, P_A posts the transaction T^1_{dep} to the Ledger. This show that P_A can get his deposit back when P_C is dishonest.
   3. P_B makes the deposit transaction T^2_{dep} at the same time. The process is the same as the above step. In order to get a better understanding of this step, Fig. 2 shows the details of this step in bitcoin syntax.
* This is the second step. This step begins after the transactions $\{T^i_{dep}, i \in \{1, 2\}\}$ appear on the ledger. For $k = C$ to B, P_k does the following:
   1. The party P_C prepares an unredeemed transaction T^3 that can be redeemed with a key known only to P_C. Then P_C builds a new transaction T^3_{dep} with $2q$ coins according to some condition which are different from Step 1. P_C creates another transaction T^3_{ref} which has a locked time τ_2. P_C sends the body $[T^3_{ref}]$ to P_B and asks P_B to sign. P_B signs $[T^3_{ref}]$ and sends back the signed transaction to P_C. If the signed $[T^3_{ref}]$ does not reach P_C by deadline, then P_C aborts. After receiving the signed $[T^3_{ref}]$, P_C posts the transaction T^3_{dep} to the Ledger. Figure 3 shows the details of this step.

   2. The party P_B also prepares another unredeemed transaction $T^{2'}$ and builds a new transaction $T^{2'}_{dep}$ with q coins. Then he repeats the same process as P_C does. P_B posts the transaction $T^{2'}_{dep}$ to the Ledger. This step is illustrated in Fig. 4.

If anything goes wrong up to the time t_2, that is, other participant does not make deposit, the protocol can be aborted.
• **Claim.** Wait until all parties have made deposit, all parties begin to make claim transaction in the reverse direction.
   * The party P_A firstly makes claim transaction as described next. He prepares a transaction $T^{2'}_{cla}$ and posts it to the ledge. When the transaction appears on the ledger, P_B, P_C collect S_1. If the transaction $T^{2'}_{cla}$ does not appear on the ledger, P_B gets his deposit back wait by round $\tau_1 + 1$.

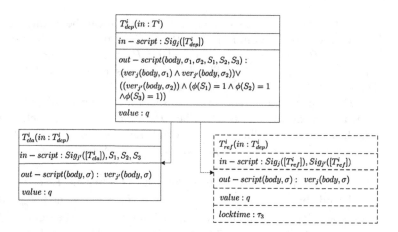

Fig. 2. Description of Formula (1) and (2) in bitcoin syntax. Here, $i = 1, 2$ and $j' = C$. When $i = 1$, $j = A$. When $i = 1$, $j = B$.

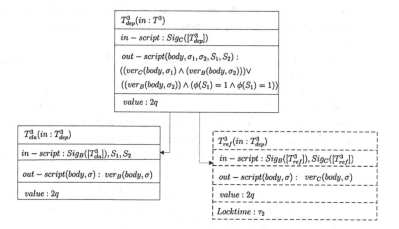

Fig. 3. Description of Formula (3) in bitcoin syntax.

* Then, the party P_B uses S_1 and S_2 to create the transaction T^3_{cla} to claim his deposit. When the transaction appears on the ledger, P_A, P_C collect S_2. If the transaction T^3_{cla} does not appear on the ledger, P_B gets his deposit back wait by round $\tau_2 + 1$.

* At last, the party P_C uses S_1, S_2 to create the transaction T^1_{cla} and T^2_{cla} to claim his deposit. When the transaction appears on the ledger, P_A, P_B collect S_3. If the transaction T^1_{cla} and T^2_{cla} does not appear on the ledger, P_A and P_B get their deposit back wait by round $\tau_3 + 1$. P_A posts the transaction T^1_{ref} and gets his deposit back wait by round $\tau_3 + 1$.

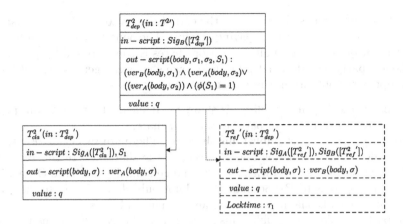

Fig. 4. Description of Formula (4) in bitcoin syntax.

If anything goes wrong up to the time t_3, that is, if any participants does not make claim transaction, it means that the decryption share of someone has not revealed, then the protocol can be aborted.

- **Decryption.** In this phase, P_i can decrypt each VES_i after receiving all the necessary values. He can get the other parties signature on the contract M. The decryption for σ_i is as follows:

$$\sigma_i = c_i / \prod_1^3 a_i^{x_k} = \sigma_i b_i^{x_i'} / a_i^{\sum_1^3 x_k} = \sigma_i b_i^{x_i'} / a_i^x = \sigma_i a_i^x / a_i^x$$

4 Analysis of Our Proposed Scheme

4.1 Security Analysis

Theorem 1. *The proposed three-parties contract signing protocol satisfies the property of fairness.*

Proof. In our protocol, the property of fairness is guaranteed by: (1) All participant obtain valid signed contract or they only obtained the others verifiable signature on the contract. (2) If a dishonest party does not abide by the protocol, then the honest party is compensated and the dishonest one has to pay a fine.

We prove the first one. Assuming that threshold encryption scheme and the verifiable signature scheme are all secure. We assume the party P_i is dishonest. He refused to send his VES_i to other two parties after receiving the other's in the phase of signature exchange. In this case, the other two parties wait until the deadline time and then they can abort the protocol. According to the protocol, the following phase can not be run. Despite P_i has obtained other parties' VES_j, but he did not have the shared key for the ciphertext. Therefore, if the phase 3 does not run, they only obtain others verifiable signature on the contract.

Next, we prove the second one. At the end of the protocol, all honest parties will receive all shares S_i without paying any fine. The honest party who publishes his share but does no obtain all decryption shares is compensated by q coins. If each honest party who does not publish his own shares can get his deposit back, no corrupt party obtains all shares. There are three cases:

- The party P_A does not publish his share S_1. It means that the Claim phase has not been executed. No party obtains all share.
- The party P_B does not publish his share S_2. There are two cases. First, P_A has made claim transaction and P_B receives the shares S_1. In this case, P_B only needs to publish his own shares S_2 and gets his deposit back. Otherwise, he will pay q coins to P_A. Second, P_A did not publish his shares. In this case, P_B does not make claim transaction and no party obtains S_2.
- The party P_C does not publish his share S_3. In this case, it means that P_C is the first party who obtains all shares. If P_C is dishonest and it aborts the protocol, then P_A and P_B do not obtain P_C's shares. But both of them get the deposit after time τ_3. This is due to, as when P_A published S_1, it gets q coins from P_B. While P_B gets $2q$ coins from P_C when he publishes S_2. At this point, both of them has been compensated.

4.2   Performance Analysis

In the following, we present the performance analysis of our proposed protocol. In our protocol, each party P_i sends one verifiable encryption to the other two parties. In the end, he broadcasts the transactions containing the decryption shares to the blockchain. The number of messages which every party P_i sends is $O(n)$, where n is the numbers of parties. If there are n parties, the total message complexity is $O(n^2)$. Besides, our protocol only needs a constant number of rounds. Table 1 presents the comparison between our protocol and the previous works.

Table 1. Comparison with the previous scheme.

Scheme	Communication complexity	Message complexity	TTP
Scheme [5]	$O(n^3)$	$O(n^2)$	Yes
Scheme [14]	$O(n^3)$	$O(n)$	Yes
Scheme [17]	$O(n^3)$	$O(n)$	Yes
Scheme [18]	$O(n^2)$	$O(n)$	Yes
Our scheme	$O(n^2)$	$O(1)$	No

Firstly, our proposed protocol is based on blockchain without a TTP, unique model compared to all others that need a TTP to resolve the dispute. The existence of TTP become a bottleneck, since it can be a single point of failure or suffer from external or internal attacks. Second, [14] is the first solution for fair optimistic multi-party contract signing protocol. In this protocol, the total number of messages needed is $O(n^3)$ and the communication complexity is $O(n^2)$ rounds, where n is the number of the participants. Though, Garay's [14] solution was very inefficiency. Another scheme proposed in [5], which efficiency depends on the number of dishonest parties. We consider the worst case that the number of dishonest parties is $n-1$, it needs $(n+1)n(n+1)$ $(O(n^3))$ messages and $n+1$ rounds. The round complexity was decreased by [18] to $O(n^3)$, but also need $O(n^3)$ messages. It is introduced in [17] a linear fair multi-party contract signing protocol based on the optimistic model with a lower bound on the message complexity of $O(n^2)$, as well the round complexity was not constant. In summary, the proposed protocol is more efficient than existing ones.

Table 2. Comparison among schemes.

Properties	Scheme				
	Scheme [5]	Scheme [14]	Scheme [17]	Scheme [18]	Our scheme
Fairness	Weak	X	√	√	√
Timeliness	√	√	√	√	√
Non-repudiation	X	√	√	√	√
Confidentiality	X	√	X	√	√

As seen in Table 2, scheme [14] was introduced by Chadha et al. [10] that did not satisfy the fairness property when $n > 4$. Scheme [5] assumed that TTP should know the number of the dishonest parties and all honest parties could not abort the protocol. In case that, if some honest parties want to abort, fairness could not be guaranteed for other honest ones, and therefore, scheme [5] was weak in fairness. In summary, our proposed scheme can satisfy all of the security properties.

5   Conclusions

Multi-party contract signing is a practical applications of electronic data interchange. A crucial property for a contract signing protocol is fairness. The existing solutions to solve the problem of fairness need a trusted third party (TTP) to involve in the dispute. Blockchain, as the underlying technology of bitcoin, provides a solution to solve the trust problem of the third party. In this paper, we propose a fair three-party contract singing protocol based on blockchain. The proposed construction allows the participants to sign a contract in a fair way without needing a arbitrator. Meanwhile it can protect the privacy of the contract content.

Acknowledgments. This work is supported by the National Natural Science Foundation of China (No. 61572382), China 111 Project (No. B16037), and the Natural Science Basic Research Plan in Shaanxi Province of China (No. 2016JZ021).

References

1. Andrychowicz, M., Dziembowski, S., Malinowski, D., Mazurek, L.: Secure multi-party computations on bitcoin. In: Proceedings of 2014 Symposium on Security and Privacy, SP 2014, pp. 443–458, Berkeley, CA, USA. IEEE (2014)
2. Asokan, N., Schunter, M., Waidner, M.: Optimistic protocols for fair exchange. In: Proceedings of the 4th ACM Conference on Computer and Communications Security, pp. 7–17. ACM (1997)
3. Asokan, N., Shoup, V., Waidner, M.: Optimistic fair exchange of digital signatures. In: Nyberg, K. (ed.) EUROCRYPT 1998. LNCS, vol. 1403, pp. 591–606. Springer, Heidelberg (1998). doi:10.1007/BFb0054156
4. Asokan, N., Shoup, V., Waidner, M.: Optimistic fair exchange of digital signatures. IEEE J. Sel. Areas Commun. 18(4), 593–610 (2000)
5. Baum-Waidner, B., Waidner, M.: Round-optimal and abuse-free optimistic multi-party contract signing. In: Montanari, U., Rolim, J.D.P., Welzl, E. (eds.) ICALP 2000. LNCS, vol. 1853, pp. 524–535. Springer, Heidelberg (2000). doi:10.1007/3-540-45022-X_44
6. Ben-Or, M., Goldreich, O., Micali, S., Rivest, R.L.: A fair protocol for signing contracts. IEEE Trans. Inf. Theory 36(1), 40–46 (1990)
7. Bentov, I., Kumaresan, R.: How to use bitcoin to design fair protocols. In: Garay, J.A., Gennaro, R. (eds.) CRYPTO 2014. LNCS, vol. 8617, pp. 421–439. Springer, Heidelberg (2014). doi:10.1007/978-3-662-44381-1_24
8. Boneh, D., Gentry, C., Lynn, B., Shacham, H.: Aggregate and verifiably encrypted signatures from bilinear maps. In: Biham, E. (ed.) EUROCRYPT 2003. LNCS, vol. 2656, pp. 416–432. Springer, Heidelberg (2003). doi:10.1007/3-540-39200-9_26
9. Boneh, D., Lynn, B., Shacham, H.: Short signatures from the weil pairing. J. Cryptology 17(4), 297–319 (2004)
10. Chadha, R., Kremer, S., Scedrov, A.: Formal analysis of multiparty contract signing. J. Autom. Reasoning 36(1–2), 39–83 (2006)
11. Chen, X., Zhang, F., Tian, H., Wu, Q., Mu, Y., Kim, J., Kim, K.: Three-round abuse-free optimistic contract signing with everlasting secrecy. In: Sion, R. (ed.) FC 2010. LNCS, vol. 6052, pp. 304–311. Springer, Heidelberg (2010). doi:10.1007/978-3-642-14577-3_23
12. Du, X., Lin, F.: Maintaining differentiated coverage in heterogeneous sensor networks. EURASIP J. Wireless Commun. Networking 2005(4), 565–572 (2005)
13. Du, X., Xiao, Y., Guizani, M., Chen, H.-H.: An effective key management scheme for heterogeneous sensor networks. Ad Hoc Netw. 5(1), 24–34 (2007)
14. Garay, J.A., MacKenzie, P.: Abuse-free multi-party contract signing. In: Jayanti, P. (ed.) DISC 1999. LNCS, vol. 1693, pp. 151–166. Springer, Heidelberg (1999). doi:10.1007/3-540-48169-9_11
15. Goldreich, O.: A simple protocol for signing contracts. In: Chaum, D. (ed.) Advances in Cryptology, pp. 133–136. Springer, Boston (1984). doi:10.1007/978-1-4684-4730-9_11
16. Kılınç, H., Küpçü, A.: Optimally efficient multi-party fair exchange and fair secure multi-party computation. In: Nyberg, K. (ed.) CT-RSA 2015. LNCS, vol. 9048, pp. 330–349. Springer, Cham (2015). doi:10.1007/978-3-319-16715-2_18
17. Mauw, S., Radomirovic, S., Dashti, M.T.: Minimal message complexity of asynchronous multi-party contract signing. In: 22nd IEEE Computer Security Foundations Symposium, CSF 2009, pp. 13–25. IEEE (2009)

18. Mukhamedov, A., Ryan, M.D.: Fair multi-party contract signing using private contract signatures. Inf. Comput. **206**(2–4), 272–290 (2008)
19. Nakamoto, S.: Bitcoin: A peer-to-peer electronic cash system (2008)
20. Pedersen, T.P.: A threshold cryptosystem without a trusted party. In: Davies, D.W. (ed.) EUROCRYPT 1991. LNCS, vol. 547, pp. 522–526. Springer, Heidelberg (1991). doi:10.1007/3-540-46416-6_47
21. Shao, Z., Gao, Y.: Practical verifiably encrypted signatures based on discrete logarithms. Secur. Commun. Netw. (2017)
22. Economist Staff: Blockchains: The great chain of being sure about things. The Economist. Retrieved 18 2016
23. Yao, X., Han, X., Du, X., Zhou, X.: A lightweight multicast authentication mechanism for small scale iot applications. IEEE Sens. J. **13**(10), 3693–3701 (2013)

Securely Outsourcing Decentralized Multi-authority Attribute Based Signature

Jiameng Sun[1], Jing Qin[1,2(✉)], and Jixin Ma[3]

[1] School of Mathematics, Shandong University, Jinan, China
`sunjiameng1991@163.com,qinjing@sdu.edu.cn`
[2] State Key Laboratory of Information Security,
Institute of Information Engineering, Chinese Academy of Sciences,
Beijing 100093, China
[3] School of Computing and Mathematical Sciences,
Centre for Computer and Computational Science,
University of Greenwich, London, UK
`j.ma@greenwich.ac.uk`

Abstract. Attribute based signature (ABS) is a novel primitive of digital signature that allows the signer to endorse a piece of message with a set of certain attributes in order to preserve the privacy of the signer's identity. There are multiple authorities that issue different secret keys for signer's various attributes. And a central authority is usually established to manage all these attribute authorities. This brings a huge workload to compute a signature and also a threat to security and privacy if the central authority is compromised. In this paper, we present an outsourced decentralized multi-authority attribute based signature (ODMA-ABS) scheme. Compared with existing multi-authority attribute based signature schemes, the ODMA-ABS scheme achieves a stronger notion of attribute privacy and authority collusion resistance. And the workload to compute a signature is further reduced by utilizing the outsourcing technique, which makes our scheme more practical in reality.

Keywords: Attribute based signature · Outsourcing computation · Decentralization · Distributed computation

1 Introduction

Attribute based signature (ABS) is a primitive that derives from identity based signature [1]. It enables a signer to endorse a message on behalf of a set of attributes rather than his (her) unique identity, which brings development to the harmony between message endorsement and identity privacy-preserving. This is of great significance since privacy has now become an important-but-fragile part for individuals, especially in this Big Data Age. As an example to show the application of ABS, consider an e-voting scenario, the voter has to be someone whose identity satisfies certain requirements. Then he (she) is able to generate a signature of the candidate he (she) would like to elect as the ballot. However

© Springer International Publishing AG 2017
S. Wen et al. (Eds.): CSS 2017, LNCS 10581, pp. 86–102, 2017.
https://doi.org/10.1007/978-3-319-69471-9_7

using his (her) identity as the signing private key will simultaneous reveal his (her) vote. Under such circumstance, an ABS protocol is competent for both requirements of candidate election and voter privacy. Other applications of ABS lie in different aspects like fulfilling security requirement in attribute based messaging system [2], providing access control in anonymous authentication system [3], etc.

In an ABS, the user takes his attribute set to query the attribute authority for secret keys corresponding to certain attributes. Since an individual may have various kinds of attributes, e.g. gender, profession, address, etc., there are usually multiple attribute authorities that handle different kinds of attribute key requests. These different authorities may not communicate with or trust each other, even may not be aware of each other. This multi-authority setting greatly relieves the computational workload of single authority, and more importantly, enhances the security since one or some of the authorities' compromission or corruption may not affect the others.

However, multi-authority setting brings a difficulty on how to generate a common secret now that authorities may not trust or communicate with each other. A feasible way is to build a central authority to manage each authority and allocate different part of a shared secret to them. But this brings us back to the drawback of single authority scenario because once the central authority is compromised, the whole system will be no longer secure. So a crucial point in attribute based signature is decentralization.

Efficiency is another crucial point for the practice of ABS. Actually, the multi-authority setting does not reduce workload the signer has to do, or even increase it in some ways because now the signer has to interact with multiple authorities to obtain the secret keys associated to his whole attributes. This situation may become even worse when the signer would like to perform the message endorsing action on some portable device, like the mobile phone. Fortunately, with the development of cloud computing, the signer can choose to outsource the heavy computational workload in the singing phase to the cloud to enjoy the unlimited computational resource of the cloud in a pay-per-use manner. This motivates us to construct an efficient, secure and attribute-private ABS scheme.

1.1 Related Works

Attribute Based Signature. ABS was first defined and constructed in 2008 by Maji et al. [2], where they present a scheme supporting predicate described by monotone span program. Later, a (n, n)-threshold predicate construction was proposed by Li and Kim [4], after which Shahandashti and Safavi-Naini [5] improved the predicate to (k, n)-threshold. In 2010, Li et al. [6] proposed another construction that achieves better efficiency than that in [4,5]. What is more, they also proposed a construction for multi-authority (MA) scenario. There are other works that focus on MA-ABS [7–9]. In 2013, Okamoto and Takashima [10] proposed the first decentralized multi-authority attribute-based signature (DMA-ABS) scheme in the random oracle model, which removes the trusted central authority of the MA-ABS scheme. Though their scheme was as efficient as former MA-ABS, the size of the private keys or signature is still very large.

Outsourcing Computation. Outsourcing computation (OC) was first proposed by Hohenberger and Lysyanskaya [11] and formally defined by Gennaro et al. [12]. Gennaro et al. presented a way to use Gentry's [13] fully homomorphic encryption (FHE) together with Yao's [14] 2-party computation to securely outsource any circuit evaluation. Since operating FHE costs too much, the scheme is not very practical. Later other works [15–17] were proposed to improve the performance of using FHE, yet the cost still can not be very ideal.

To avoid using FHE, some works have been done to seek secure ways to outsource specific kind of computation. As for attribute based cryptography, Green et al. [18] proposed a scheme to outsource the decryption phase of attribute based encryption (ABE) scheme, and [19] proposed a scheme to outsource the encryption and decryption of ABE. In 2014, Li et al. [20] proposed an outsourced attribute based signature (OABS) scheme. They use the blinding technique to make attribute private piecewise and thus will not reveal attribute privacy in the outsourcing paradigm. However their construction is in single attribute model. Recently, Ren et al. [21] proposed another OABS scheme that achieves correctness verification of the outsourced singing operation, yet still a single authority proposal.

1.2 Our Contribution

In this paper, we propose a new model called outsourced decentralized multi-authority attribute based signature (ABS). It captures both the security requirements of an ABS protocol and the efficiency requirement of an OC protocol. We present the specific construction of an ODMA-ABS scheme and give the corresponding analysis of each property, like correctness, unforgeability, attribute privacy, efficiency, etc. We also provide a comparison among some existing MA-ABS schemes and ours.

1.3 Paper Organization

The remaining parts of the paper are organized as follows. Some necessary preliminaries are provided for the proposed schemes in Sect. 2. The model of decentralized multi-authority attribute based signature (DMA-ABS) scheme is defined in Sect. 3. The proposed outsourced decentralized multi-authority attribute based signature is presented and analyzed in Sect. 4. Section 5 concludes the paper and shows future work.

2 Preliminaries

In this section, we provide the definitions of pseudorandom function (PRF) and Bilinear Map. We also provide the computational assumption that is used for the construction of our scheme, the co-CDH assumption and XDH assumption.

2.1 Pseudorandom Function

Our construction takes use of the pseudorandom function (PRF), which was first introduced by Goldreich et al. [22]. Informally speaking, a PRF takes as input a random value in the domain and outputs a value that is computational indistinguishable from a truly random value in the range. We give the specific definition of the pseudorandom function family below.

Definition 1 (Pseudorandom function family). *Let* $\mathcal{F} = \{f_s | s \in \{0,1\}^\lambda\}_{\lambda \in \mathbb{N}}$. *Then* $\mathcal{F}$ *is called a family of* $(X(\lambda), Y(\lambda))$ *pseudorandom function if the following holds,*

- $\forall \lambda \in \mathbb{N}, \forall s \in \{0,1\}^\lambda, f_s : \{0,1\}^{X(\lambda)} \to \{0,1\}^{Y(\lambda)};$
- $\forall \lambda \in \mathbb{N}, \forall s \in \{0,1\}^\lambda, f_s$ *can be computed in polynomial time;*
- *Pseudorandomness: for any probabilistic polynomial time algorithm* $\mathcal{A}$, *there holds*

$$|Pr[\mathcal{A}^{f_s}(1^\lambda) = 1 | s \xleftarrow{U} \{0,1\}^\lambda] - Pr[\mathcal{A}^g(1^\lambda) = 1 | g \xleftarrow{U} \mathcal{R}(X(\lambda), Y(\lambda))]| \le negl(\lambda),$$

where $\mathcal{R}(X(\lambda), Y(\lambda))$ *is the set of all possible functions* $g : \{0,1\}^{X(\lambda)} \to \{0,1\}^{Y(\lambda)}$.

2.2 Bilinear Map

Our constructions also utilize the bilinear map. The bilinear map is a powerful tool in non-interactive authentication and has been widely applied in both signature and outsourcing computation schemes [23,24].

Definition 2 (Bilinear Map). *Let* $\mathbb{G}_1, \mathbb{G}_2$ *and* $\mathbb{G}_T$ *be finite cyclic multiplicative groups of prime order* p, *and* g_1, g_2 *be generators of* $\mathbb{G}_1$ *and* $\mathbb{G}_2$ *respectively. A map* $\hat{e} : \mathbb{G}_1 \times \mathbb{G}_2 \to \mathbb{G}_T$ *is called a bilinear map if it satisfies the following properties:*

- *Bilinearity: it holds that*

$$\hat{e}(g_1^a, g_2^b) = \hat{e}(g_1, g_2)^{ab} \tag{1}$$

for all $a, b \in \mathbb{Z}_p$.
- *Non-degeneracy: There exist* $G_1 \in \mathbb{G}_1, G_2 \in \mathbb{G}_2$ *such that* $\hat{e}(G_1, G_2) \ne 1$.
- *Computability: There exists an efficient algorithm to compute* $\hat{e}(G_1, G_2)$ *for any* $G_1 \in \mathbb{G}_1, G_2 \in \mathbb{G}_2$.

We say that the bilinear group is symmetric if there exists an efficiently computable isomorphism ϕ from $\mathbb{G}_1$ to $\mathbb{G}_2$ and an efficiently computable isomorphism ϕ' from $\mathbb{G}_2$ to $\mathbb{G}_1$. Similarly, we say that the bilinear group is asymmetric if such ϕ' does not exist. (ϕ from $\mathbb{G}_1$ to $\mathbb{G}_2$ may or may not exists.) Our construction is based on asymmetric group where such ϕ exists.

2.3   Threshold Predicate

Our construction applies to threshold predicate. We present the specific definition.

Definition 3 (Threshold Predicate). *Let U^* be an attribute set of size d, and k be an integer in $[1, d]$, a threshold predicate is a monotone boolean function that is defined as follows.*

$$\Upsilon_{k,U^*}(U) = \begin{cases} 1, & |U \cap U^*| \geq k \\ 0, & otherwise \end{cases}$$

We say that an attribute set U satisfies a predicate Υ if $\Upsilon(U) = 1$.

2.4   Lagrange Coefficient

Our construction also utilize the Lagrange interpolation.

Definition 4 (Lagrange coefficient). *Let $p(\cdot)$ be a $d - 1$ degree polynomial, and $p(1), \cdots, p(d)$ be the corresponding values in d points. Write $S = \{1, \cdots, d\}$. We define the Lagrange coefficient in the computation $p(x)$ as*

$$\Delta_{i,S}(x) = \prod_{j \in S, j \neq i} \frac{x - j}{i - j}$$

Then the polynomial $p(x)$ can be represented as

$$p(x) = \sum_{i=1}^{d} p(i)\Delta_{i,S}(x) \tag{2}$$

2.5   Computational Assumption

Our construction of the scheme is based on the standard assumption, the co-CDH assumption and the XDH assumption.

Definition 5 (co-CDH Assumption). *Let $\mathcal{G}_B$ be a bilinear group generator that takes as input a parameter λ and outputs a description of a bilinear group $(p, g_1, g_2, \mathbb{G}_1, \mathbb{G}_2, \mathbb{G}_T, \hat{e})$, where p is the order, g_1, g_2 the generators of $\mathbb{G}_1, \mathbb{G}_2$ respectively, and $\hat{e}$ the bilinear map from $\mathbb{G}_1 \times \mathbb{G}_2$ to $\mathbb{G}_T$. We say that the co-CDH assumption (t, ϵ) holds if for any probabilistic polynomial t-time algorithm $\mathcal{A}$ there holds*

$$|Pr[\mathcal{A}(p, g_1, g_2, g_1^a, g_2^b) = g_2^{ab}]| \leq \epsilon,$$

where $a, b \in_R \mathbb{Z}_p$.

Definition 6 (XDH Assumption). *Let* $(p, g_1, g_2, \mathbb{G}_1, \mathbb{G}_2, \mathbb{G}_T,$
$\hat{e}, \phi)$ *be an asymmetric bilinear tuple where* ϕ *is a one way map from* $\mathbb{G}_1$ *to*
$\mathbb{G}_2$. *We say that the XDH assumption* (t, ϵ) *holds in* $\mathbb{G}_2$ *if for any probabilistic*
polynomial t-time algorithm $\mathcal{A}$ *there holds*

$$|Pr[\mathcal{A}(p, \hat{e}, \phi, g_1, g_2, g_2^a, g_2^b, g_2^{ab}) = 1] - Pr[\mathcal{A}(p, \hat{e}, \phi, g_1, g_2, g_2^a, g_2^b, g_2^c) = 1| \le \epsilon,$$

where $a, b, c \in_R \mathbb{Z}_p$.

Notice that the XDH assumption does not hold in symmetric bilinear groups. This is obvious since that one can map g_2^a into $\mathbb{G}_1$ and use bilinear map $\hat{e}$ to distinguish the XDH tuple. The same thing also holds for group $\mathbb{G}_1$ in asymmetric setting since ϕ exists.

3 Modeling ODMA-ABS

In this section, we present some relative notitions of the ODMA-ABS. Generally speaking, an ODMA-ABS enjoys the property of trusted authority free while maintaining the unforgeability and attributes privacy of an ABS protocol, and the computational efficiency and security of an outsourcing computation protocol.

3.1 Definitions

Definition 7 (Outsourced Decentralized Multi-authority Attribute Based Signature). *An Outsourced decentralized multi-authority attribute based signature scheme* π *is defined via the following five algorithms.*

- $(PP, MSK) \leftarrow$ **Setup**(λ, N): *The randomized system setup algorithm takes as input a secure parameter* λ, *the number of attribute authorities* N, *and outputs the public parameter* PP *and the master secret key* MSK *for each attribute authority. This is done by the multiple authorities.*
- $(OK_k, SK_k) \leftarrow$ **AKeyGen**$(PP, MSK, A_{k,u})$: *The randomized key generation algorithm takes as input the public parameter* PP, *the master secret key* MSK, *the attribute set* $A_{k,u}$ *of user* u *and outputs the outsourcing key* OK_k *and the private key* SK_k. *This is done individually by each attribute authority.*
- $\sigma_{part} \leftarrow$ **Sign**$_{out}(OK, A_u, \Upsilon_{n_k, C_k^*})$: *The randomized outsourced signing algorithm takes as input the outsourcing key* OK *of all attribute authorities, the user's attribute set* A_u, *a set of predicate* Υ_{n_k, C_k^*} *and outputs the partial signature* σ_{part}. *This is done by the signing cloud server (SCS).*
- $\sigma \leftarrow$ **Sign**$(SK, m, \sigma_{part}, \Upsilon_{n_k, C_k^*})$: *The randomized signing algorithm takes as input the private key* SK, *the message to-be-signed* m, *the partial signature* σ_{part}, *the set of predicate* Υ_{n_k, C_k^*} *and outputs the formal signature* σ. *This is done by the user.*
- $b \leftarrow$ **Verify**$(PP, \sigma, m, \Upsilon_{n_k, C_k^*})$: *The deterministic verification algorithm takes as input the public parameter* PP, *the signature* σ *with signed message* m *and predicate* Υ_{n_k, C_k^*} *and outputs 1 if it the signature is valid and 0 otherwise. This is done by the verifier.*

Definition 8 (Correctness). *An ODMA-ABS scheme is correct if for all* $(PP,$ $MSK) \xleftarrow{R} \textbf{Setup}(\lambda, N)$, *all attribute sets* $\{A_k\}$, *all* $(OK_k, SK_k) \xleftarrow{R} \textbf{AKeyGen}$ $(PP, MSK, A_{k,u})$, *all predicate* Υ_{n_k, C_k^*}, *all* $\sigma_{part} \xleftarrow{R} \textbf{Sign}_{out}(OK, A_u, \Upsilon_{n_k, C_k^*})$, *all messages* m, *and all* $\sigma \xleftarrow{R} \textbf{Sign}(SK, m, \sigma_{part}, \Upsilon_{n_k, C_k^*})$, *the verification algorithm outputs 1 with probability* $1 - \epsilon$ *where* ϵ *is negligible.*

An ODMA-ABS protocol is supposed to satisfy the unforgeability property. Consider the unforgeablity experiment between a challenger $\mathcal{C}$ and an adversary $\mathcal{F}$ in a selective predicate model.

- **Initial.** $\mathcal{C}$ receives a corrupted authorities set $\mathbb{K}_c \subseteq \{1, \cdots, N\}$ and challenge predicate Υ_{n_k, C_k^*}, where $k \notin \mathbb{K}_c$.
- **Setup.** $\mathcal{C}$ runs the **Setup**(λ, N) algorithm. It sends PP to $\mathcal{F}$ and keeps MSK.
- **Query.** $\mathcal{F}$ is allowed to perform a series of the following queries to the oracle.
  - *Private key query:* $\mathcal{F}$ can query $\mathcal{C}$ for SK with an identity u.
  - *Outsourcing key query:* $\mathcal{F}$ can query $\mathcal{C}$ for SK with attribute set $\{A_k\}_{k \notin \mathbb{K}_c}$.
  - *Signing query:* $\mathcal{F}$ can query $\mathcal{C}$ for signature with message m and predicate Υ.
- **Forgery.** $\mathcal{F}$ outputs a tuple $(m^*, \sigma^*, \Upsilon_{n_k, C_k^*})$.

We say that $\mathcal{F}$ wins if (i) $(m^*, \sigma^*, \Upsilon_{n_k, C_k^*})$ passes the verification algorithm; (ii) $\Upsilon_{n_k, C_k^*}(A_k) = 1$ for any A_k that has been submitted to the *Outsourcing key query* oracle; (iii) $(m^*, \Upsilon_{n_k, C_k^*})$ has not been submitted to the *Signing query* oracle. Define the probability of $\mathcal{F}$ in winning the experiment as $Exp_{\mathcal{F}}^{\text{ODMA-ABS}}$.

Definition 9 (Unforgeability). *An ODMA-ABS scheme is* $(t, \epsilon, n, q_P, q_O,$ $q_S)$-*unforgeable if no probabilistic polynomial* t *time adversary* $\mathcal{F}$ *can win the unforgeability experiment over* ϵ *when at most* n *attribute authorities are corrupted, with at most* q_p, q_O, *and* q_S *times of private key query, outsourcing key query and signing query respectively.*

An ODMA-ABS protocol is supposed to realize attribute privacy for the signer. Informally, attribute privacy requires that the signature reveals nothing about user's identity or attribute set except for what is revealed explicitly.

Definition 10 (Attribute privacy). *An ODMA-ABS scheme is attribute private if for all* $(PP, MSK) \xleftarrow{R} \textbf{Setup}(\lambda, N)$, *any* A_{u1} *and* A_{u2} *that satisfy* $\Upsilon(A_{ui}) = 1$ *and any* $\sigma_{part,i} \leftarrow \textbf{Sign}_{out}(OK_i, A_{ui}, \Upsilon)$ *for* $(i = 1, 2)$, *the distribution of* $\sigma_1 \leftarrow \textbf{Sign}(SK_1, m, \sigma_{part,1}, \Upsilon)$ *and* $\sigma_2 \leftarrow \textbf{Sign}(SK_2, m, \sigma_{part,2}, \Upsilon)$ *are equal.*

As an outsourcing scheme, the ODMA-ABS is also supposed to satisfy the efficiency property.

Definition 11 (Efficiency). *An ODMA-ABS scheme is efficient if the total computation cost on the signer side is less than the cost to generate the signature all by the user.*

4 The Proposed ODMA-ABS Scheme

4.1 Anonymous Key Issue Protocol

Our construction takes use of an anonymous key issue (AKI) protocol proposed in [25]. We would like to give a brief introduction first.

The AKI is an interactive protocol executed between user side and attribute authority side. In the AKI, the user U and attribute authority A have access to some common known values, while keeping some secret values as well, and they jointly compute a value via the following steps.

- **Step 1:** Set up the public parameters including a group $\mathbb{G}$ of order p and two group elements $g, h \in \mathbb{G}$.
- **Step 2:** A general 2-party computation protocol is executed on input (u, a_1) from u and β from A, where u is the hash value of the user's identity GID, and $(a_1, \beta) \in_R \mathbb{G}$. Such 2-party computation can be realized via the proposal in [26]. As a result, A obtains $x := (\beta + u)a_1 \mod p$.
- **Step 3:** A computes $X_1 := g^{\tau/x} \ X_2 := h^{\alpha\tau}$ and sends X_1, X_2 to U, where $\alpha, \tau \in_R \mathbb{Z}_p$.
- **Step 4:** On receiving X_1, X_2, U picks $a_2 \in_R \mathbb{Z}_p$ and computes $Y := (X_1^{a_1} X_2)^{a_2}$. Then send Y to A.
- **Step 5:** On receiving Y, A picks a $\gamma \in_R \mathbb{Z}_p$ and computes $Z := Y^{\gamma/\tau}$. Then send Z to U.
- **Step 6:** Finally, on receiving Z, U computes $Z^{1/a_2} = (h^\alpha g^{1/(\beta+u)})^\gamma$.

The correctness of the above protocol is easy to verified by the following equation.

$$Z^{1/a_2} = Y^{\gamma/(\tau/a_2)} = (X_1^{a_1\gamma/\tau} X_2^{\gamma/\tau}) = (g^{a_1\gamma/x} h^{\alpha\gamma}) = (h^\alpha g^{1/(\beta+u)})^\gamma \quad (3)$$

The above protocol is secure under DDH assumption assuming that the underlying 2-party computation is secure. The proof can be found in [25].

Now we are about to utilize the AKI protocol to construct the signature scheme.

4.2 ODMA-ABS Construction

The construction is based on the signature scheme of Li et al.'s [6]. We will present the specific steps of our scheme. Let the Lagrange coefficients be as that in Definition 4. Then the proposed ODMA-ABS scheme is shown as follows.

- **Setup**(λ, N): On input the security parameter λ, and a common reference string (CRS), the N attribute authorities generate an admissible asymmetric bilinear group denoted by $e = (p, g_1, g_2, \mathbb{G}_1, \mathbb{G}_2, \mathbb{G}_T, \hat{e}(\cdot, \cdot), \phi(\cdot))$ and two collision resistant Hash functions (CRHF) $H : \{0, 1\}^* \to \mathbb{Z}_p$, $H' : \{0, 1\}^* \to \mathbb{G}_2$.

The former maps user's global identity to an element in $\mathbb{Z}_p$ (denoted by u) and the latter maps the message to be signed to an element in $\mathbb{G}_2$. Select an admissible $G_2 \in_R \mathbb{G}_2$ among the authorities.

Then, for each attribute authority $k \in \{1, \cdots, N\}$, redefine the attributes in universe $\{\mathcal{U}_k\}_{k \in \{1, \cdots, N\}}$ as elements in $\mathbb{Z}_p$, and define a d_k-element default attribute set C_k. Choose a CRHF $H_k : \{0,1\}^* \rightarrow \mathbb{G}_2$, which maps each attribute i to the element in $\mathbb{G}_2$. Select $x_k, v_k \in_R \mathbb{Z}_p$ and compute $y_k = G_2^{x_k}, Y_k = g_1^{v_k}, Z_k = \hat{e}(Y_k, G_2)$.

Next the authorities pairwise engage a two party key exchange protocol such that authority k and j share a unique seed $s_{kj} \in \mathbb{Z}_p$, which is only known to them two but not to any other authority $i \notin \{k, j\}$. Specially, define $s_{kj} = s_{jk}$. Then the pseudorandom function between authority k and j for user u is defined as

$$\mathrm{PRF}_{kj}(u) = G_2^{x_k x_j / (s_{kj} + u)}, u \in \mathbb{Z}_p \tag{4}$$

Finally, the public parameter

$$PP = (\{y_k, Y_k, Z_k, H_k, d_k\}_{k \in \{1, \cdots, N\}}, H, H', e, G_2),$$

and the master secret key

$$MSK = (\{x_k, v_k, \{s_{kj}\}_{j \in \{1, \cdots, N\} \setminus \{k\}}\}_{k \in \{1, \cdots, N\}}).$$

– **AKeyGen**$(PP, MSK, A_{k,u})$: To generate the key on attribute set $A_{k,u}$, user u executes independently $N - 1$ anonymous key issuing protocol with authority k that works as follows.

1. For $j \in \{1, \cdots, N\} \setminus \{k\}$, let

$$g = y_j^{x_k}, h = G_2, a = \delta_{kj} R_{kj}, b = s_{kj}, c = \delta_{kj},$$

where R_{kj} is selected randomly from $\mathbb{Z}_p$ by k, $\delta_{kj} = 1$ if $k > j$ and $\delta_{kj} = -1$ otherwise. As a consequence, u gets

$$D_{kj} = G_2^{R_{kj}} \mathrm{PRF}_{kj}(u), k > j$$
$$D_{kj} = G_2^{R_{kj}} / \mathrm{PRF}_{kj}(u), k < j$$

2. k randomly selects a $d_k - 1$ degree polynomial $p_k(\cdot)$ such that

$$p_k(\cdot) = v_k - \sum_{j \in \{1, \cdots, N\} \setminus \{k\}} R_{kj} \tag{5}$$

and for each $i \in A_{k,u} \cup C_k$ and each $r_{k,i}$ randomly selected from $\mathbb{Z}_p$, computes

$$d_{k,i0} = G_2^{p_k(\cdot)} H_k(i)^{r_{k,i}}, d_{k,i1} = g_1^{r_{k,i}}.$$

Finally, k outputs the outsourcing key

$$OK_k = (\{d_{k,i0}, d_{k,i1}\}_{i \in A_{k,u} \cup C_k}),$$

and the user's private key

$$SK_k = (\{D_{kj}\}_{j \in \{1, \cdots, N\} \setminus \{k\}}).$$

- **Sign$_{\text{out}}$**$(OK, A_u, \Upsilon_{n_k, C_k^*})$: For the outsouced signing query from user u, with $OK_k = (\{d_{k,i0}, d_{k,i1}\}_{i \in A_{k,u} \cup C_k})$, $A_u = \{A_{k,u}\}_{k \in \{1, \cdots, N\}}$ and predicate $\Upsilon_{n_k, C_k^*}(\cdot)$, where $|C_k^*| = m_k$ and n_k could be 0, the SCS works as follows.
  1. For each $k \in \{1, \cdots, N\}$, select a random n_k-element attribute subset $A_k' \subseteq A_{k,u} \cap C_k^*$, and a $(d_k - n_k)$-element default attribute subset $C_k' \subseteq C_k$. Define $S_k = A_k' \cup c_k'$, $|S_k| = d$.
  2. Select $m_k + d - n_k$ random values $s_{k,1}, \cdots, s_{k,m_k+d-n_k}$ from $\mathbb{Z}_p$, and compute the following items

$$\sigma_0' = \prod_{1 \le k \le N} (\prod_{i \in S_k} d_{k,i0}^{\Delta_{i,S_k}(0)} \prod_{i \in C_k^* \cup C_k'} H_k(i)^{s_{k,i}})$$

$$\sigma_{k,i}' = \begin{cases} d_{k,i1}^{\Delta_{i,S_k}(0)} g_1^{s_{k,i}}, & i \in S_k \\ g_1^{s_{k,i}}, & i \in C_k^* \setminus A_k' \end{cases}$$

  3. Output the partial signature

$$\sigma_{\text{part}} = (\sigma_0', \{\{\sigma_{k,i}'\}_{i \in C_k^* \cup C_k'}\}_{k \in \{1, \cdots, N\}})$$

- **Sign**$(SK, m, \sigma_{\text{part}}, \Upsilon_{n_k, C_k^*})$: To generate the formal signature after receiving σ_{part} from SCS, u works as follows.
  1. Compute

$$D_u = \prod_{(k,j) \in \{1, \cdots, N\} \times \{1, \cdots, N\} \setminus \{k\}} D_{k,j}$$

  2. Select a random value s from $\mathbb{Z}_p$ and compute

$$\sigma_0 = D_u \cdot \sigma_0' \cdot H'(m \| \Upsilon_{n_k, C_k^*})^s$$
$$\sigma_s = g_1^s, \qquad \sigma_{k,i} = \sigma_{k,i}'$$

  3. Output the final signature as

$$\sigma = (\sigma_0, \sigma_s, \{\{\sigma_{k,i}\}_{i \in C_k^* \cup C_k'}\}_{k \in \{1, \cdots, N\}})$$

- **Verify**$(PP, \sigma, m, \Upsilon_{n_k, C_k^*})$: On input the signature σ, the message m with predicate Υ and let $v = H'(m \| \Upsilon_{n_k, C_k^*})$, the verification is processed by checking the following equation

$$\hat{e}(g_1, \sigma_0) \stackrel{?}{=} \prod_{1 \le k \le N} [\prod_{i \in C_k^* \cup C_k'} Z_k \hat{e}(\sigma_{k,i}, H_k(i))] \cdot \hat{e}(\sigma_s, v) \qquad (6)$$

Output 1 and accept the signature if the above equation holds; otherwise 0 and reject the signature.

4.3 Security Analysis

We now give a specific analysis of correctness, unlinkability, unforgeability and attribute privacy.

Correctness. Correctness is shown in the following theorem.

Theorem 1. *The proposed ODMA-ABS scheme is correct.*

Proof. Let $D_u = \prod_{(k,j)\in\{1,\cdots,N\}\times\{1,\cdots,N\}\setminus\{k\}} D_{k,j}$, $S_k = A'_k \cup c'_k$ and $v = H'(m\|\Upsilon_{n_k,C^*_k})$. The correctness of our proposed scheme derives from the following equation.

$$
\begin{aligned}
\hat{e}(g_1,\sigma_0) &= \hat{e}(g_1, D_u \cdot \prod_k (\prod_{i\in S_k} d_{k,i0}^{\Delta_{i,S_k}(0)} \prod_{i\in C^*_k \cup C'_k} H_k(i)^{s_{k,i}}) \cdot v^s) \\
&= \hat{e}(g_1, g_2^{\sum_k v_k} \prod_k (\prod_{i\in S_k} H_k(i)^{r_{k,i}\Delta_{i,S_k}(0)} \prod_{i\in C^*_k \cup C'_k} H_k(i)^{s_{k,i}}) \cdot v^s) \\
&= \hat{e}(g_1, g_2^{\sum_k v_k} \prod_k (\prod_{i\in C^*_k \cup C'_k} \hat{e}(\sigma_{k,i}, H_k(i))) \cdot v^s) \\
&= \prod_{k\leq N} [\prod_{i\in C^*_k \cup C'_k} \hat{e}(\sigma_{k,i}, H_k(i))] \cdot \hat{e}(\sigma_s, v)
\end{aligned}
\tag{7}
$$

Unlinkablity. Our construction achieves authority unlinkability.

Theorem 2. *The proposed ODMA-ABS scheme is an authority unlinkable ABS when at most $N-2$ attribute authorities are corrupted, under the XDH assumption.*

Informally speaking, the property of unlinkability requires that the corrupted authorities cannot collude with each other to reconstruct the user's private key by pooling their secrets together when at least some authorities are honest. And it is obvious to see that based on the discrete logarithm assumption, the corrupted authorities can only see the published value $G_2^{x_j}$ of the honest authority j, but have no idea of the secret value x_j. What is more, the underlying AKI protocol in Sect. 4. A is secure under the DDH assumption [25]. Thus the unlinkability holds for our ODMA-ABS scheme.

Unforgeability. Our scheme achieves unforgeability. We have the following theorem.

Theorem 3. *The proposed ODMA-ABS scheme is unforgeable under co-CDH assumption.*

Proof. Let $\mathcal{F}$ be an adversary that has a non-negligible advantage ϵ in breaking the unforgeability of the proposed ODMA-ABS scheme. And suppose that $\mathcal{F}$ makes at most $q_{H_k}, q_{H'}, q_P, q_O$ and q_S times of queries to the hash functions H_k (of authority k), H', the private key generation oracle, the outsourcing key generation oracle and the signing oracle respectively. Given a co-CDH tuple (g_1^a, g_2^b, e) and to compute $g_2^a b$, the challenger $\mathcal{C}$ sets $A = g_1^a, B = g_2^b$. Then execute the simulation as follows.

Initial. $\mathcal{C}$ receives a corrupted authorities set $1, \cdots, N \backslash \{k\}$ and a challenge predicate Υ_{n_k, C_k^*}. Here the predicate is restricted for only authority k since other authorities are corrupted and can generate the corresponding signature for any predicate.

Setup. Let the default attribute set denoted by C_k for authority k. $\mathcal{C}$ selects a $d_k - n_k$ subset $C_k' \subseteq C_k$ and publishes $G_1 = g_1^a, G_2 = g_2^b$ to $\mathcal{F}$. k picks $x_k \in_R \mathbb{Z}_p$ and interacts with other $k-1$ authorities and shares the secret seeds s_{kj}. Publish $y_k = G_2^{x_k}$ to $\mathcal{F}$.

Query. $\mathcal{C}$ initializes an integer $j = 0$, an empty table L and an empty set U, $\mathcal{F}$ is allowed to issue queries as follows.

- H_k-*query.* $\mathcal{C}$ maintains a list $\mathcal{L}_1$ to store the answers to the hash oracle H_k. On receiving a query i, $\mathcal{C}$ first checks the list $\mathcal{L}_1$ and returns the corresponding answer if the same value has been queried. Otherwise, $\mathcal{C}$ simulates as follows.
  1. If $i \in C_k^* \cup C_k'$, it chooses a $\beta_{k,i} \in \mathbb{Z}_p$ and answers $H_k(i) = g_2^{\beta_{k,i}}$.
  2. If $i \notin C_k^* \cup C_k'$, it chooses $\alpha_{k,i}, \beta_{k,i} \in \mathbb{Z}_p$ and answers $H_k(i) = G_2^{\alpha_{k,i}} g_2^{\beta_{k,i}}$
  After returning $H_k(i)$, $\mathcal{C}$ adds the tuple $(i, H_k(i))$ onto the list $\mathcal{L}_1$.
- H'-*query.* $\mathcal{C}$ picks a value $\delta \in_R \{1, \cdots, q_{H'}\}$ and maintains a list $\mathcal{L}_2$ to store the answers to the hash oracle H'. On receiving the l-th query $m_l \parallel \Upsilon_{n_{k,l}, C_{k,l}^*}$ for $1 \le l \le q_2$ and $1 \le n_{k,l} \le d_k$, $\mathcal{C}$ first checks the list $\mathcal{L}_2$ and returns the corresponding answer if the same value has been queried. Otherwise, $\mathcal{C}$ simulates as follows.
  1. If $l = \delta$, it chooses a $\beta_{k,\delta}' \in \mathbb{Z}_p$ and answers $H'(m_l \parallel \Upsilon_{n_{k,l}, C_{k,l}^*}) = g_2^{\beta_{k,\delta}'}$.
  2. If $l \ne \delta$, it chooses $\alpha_{k,l}, \beta_{k,'l} \in \mathbb{Z}_p$ and answers $H'(m_l \parallel \Upsilon_{n_{k,l}, C_{k,l}^*}) = G_2^{\alpha_{k,l}'} g_2^{\beta_{k,l}'}$
  After returning $H'(m_l \parallel \Upsilon_{n_{k,l}, C_{k,l}^*})$, $\mathcal{C}$ adds the tuple $(m_l \parallel \Upsilon_{n_{k,l}, C_{k,l}^*}, H'(m_l \parallel \Upsilon_{n_{k,l}, C_{k,l}^*}))$ onto the list $\mathcal{L}_2$.
- *Private key query.* On receiving a private key query of identity u, $\mathcal{C}$ first sets $U = U \cup \{u\}$ and maintains a list $\mathcal{L}_3$. Then it checks if (u, SK_k) exists in L. If so, return SK_k. Otherwise, $\mathcal{C}$ performs the same operation as that in the scheme. This is because the secret key x_k is not invalid. As a consequence, $\mathcal{F}$ receives $D_{kj} = G_2^{R_{kj}} \mathrm{PRF}_{kj}(u)$ for $k > j$ and $D_{kj} = G_2^{R_{kj}} / \mathrm{PRF}_{kj}(u)$ for $k < j$, where R_{kj} is randomly selected from $\mathbb{Z}_p$ by $\mathcal{C}$. Finally, after returning SK_k, $\mathcal{C}$ adds the tuple (u, SK_k) onto the list $\mathcal{L}_3$.
- *Outsourcing key query.* On receiving an outsourcing key request on attribute set A_k, $\mathcal{C}$ sets $j = j + 1$ and maintains a list $\mathcal{L}_4$. Then it simulates as follows.

1. If $|A_k \cap C_k^*| < n_k$, it chooses three sets Γ, Γ', S such that $\Gamma = (A_k \cap C_k^*) \cup C_k'$, $|\Gamma'| = d_k - 1$ and $\Gamma \subseteq \Gamma' \subseteq A_k \cup C_k'$, $S = \Gamma' \cup \{0\}$. Here we assume $|A_k| > n_k$. Then for $i \in \Gamma'$, it chooses $\tau_{k,i}, r_{k,i} \in_R \mathbb{Z}_p$ and simulates

$$\begin{cases} d_{k,i0} = \phi(G_1)^{\tau_{k,i}} H_k(i)^{r_{k,i}} \\ d_{k,i1} = g_1^{\tau_{k,i}} \end{cases}$$

For $i \in (A_k \cup C_k) \backslash \Gamma'$, let $R_k = \sum_{j \in \{1,\cdots,N\} \backslash \{N\}} R_{kj}$, $r_{k,i} = r'_{k,i} - \frac{a \Delta_{i,S}(0)}{\alpha_{k,i}}$ where $r'_k, i \in_R \mathbb{Z}_p$ and simulate

$$\begin{cases} d_{k,i0} = \phi(G_1)^{\sum_{j \in \Gamma'} \tau_{k,j} \Delta_{j,S}(i) - (R_k + \frac{\beta_{k,i}}{\alpha_{k,i}}) \Delta_{0,S}(i)}. \\ \qquad G_2^{\alpha_{k,i} r'_{k,i}} g_2^{\beta_{k,i} r'_{k,i}} \\ d_{k,i1} = G_1^{-\frac{\Delta_{0,S}(i)}{\alpha_{k,i}}} g_2^{r'_{k,i}} \end{cases}$$

2. If $|A_k \cap C_k^*| \geq n_k$, it chooses a_1 and a random polynomial $p_k(\cdot)$ with $p_k(0) = a_1$ and simulates OK_k for $i \in A_k \cup C_k$ as

$$(d_{k,i0}, d_{k,i1}) = (\phi(G_1)^{p_k(\cdot)} H_k(i)^{r_{k,i}}, g_1^{r_{k,i}})$$

where $r_{k,i} \in_R \mathbb{Z}_p$.

– *Signing Query.* On receiving a signing request on $(m, \Upsilon_{n'_k, C_k^*})$, $\mathcal{C}$ first simulates the outsourced signing phase for corrupted authorities $j \in \{1, \cdots, N\} \backslash \{k\}$. Since all keys corresponding to corrupted authorities are well prepared, the simulation of $\sigma_{j,0}$ and $\sigma_{j,i}$ executes just the same as that in the outsourced signing phase of the proposed scheme, where $\sigma_{j,0}$ represents the factors to construct σ'_0 except the part generated from authority k's OK. To simulate the part of k's with request $(m, \Upsilon_{n'_k, C_k^*})$, $\mathcal{C}$ checks whether $|A_k \cap C_k^*| < n_k$. If so, it executes the above private key query and outsourcing key query once again and generate a signature with other $k - 1$ part normally as that in the proposed scheme. Otherwise, i.e. $|A_k \cap C_k^*| \geq n_k$, if $H'(m \| \Upsilon_{n_k, C_k^*}) = g_2^{\beta'_{k,\delta}}$, the query is aborted. Otherwise, assume that $H'(m \| \Upsilon_{n_k, C_k^*}) = G_2^{\alpha'_{k,l}} g_2^{\beta'_{k,l}}$ and $\mathcal{C}$ selects a n'_k-element subset $\hat{C}^* \subseteq C_k^*$ and a $(d_k - n'_k)$-element subset $C_k'' \subseteq C_k$. Let $s_{k,i} = s'_{k,i} - \frac{a}{\alpha'_{k,l}}$, $S_k = \hat{C}^* \cup C_k''$ and simulate the signature as follows:

$$\sigma_0 = \prod_{j \in \{1,\cdots,N\} \backslash \{k\}} \sigma_{j,0} \prod_{i \in S_k} [H_k(i)^{r_{k,i} \Delta_{i,S}(0)}]$$

$$\prod_{j \in C_k^* \cup C_k''} [H_k(i)^{s_{k,i}}] G_2^{\alpha'_{k,l} s'_{k,l}} \phi(G_1)^{-\frac{\beta'_{k,l}}{\alpha'_{k,l}}} g_2^{\beta'_{k,l} s'_{k,l}},$$

$$\sigma'_{k,i} = \begin{cases} g_1^{r_{k,i} \Delta_{i,S_k}(0) + s_{k,i}}, & i \in S_k \\ g_1^{s_{k,i}}, & i \in C_k^* \backslash \hat{C}^* \end{cases}$$

$$\sigma_s = G_1^{-\frac{1}{\alpha'_{k,l}}} g_1^{s'}$$

where $s', r_{k,i}, s_{k,j} \in_R \mathbb{Z}_p$ for $i \in \hat{C}^* \cup C_k''$ and $j \in C^* \cup C_k''$. For part of the signature the corrupted Finally, $\mathcal{C}$ returns simulated signature $(\sigma_0, \sigma_s, \{\{\sigma_{k,i}\}_{i \in C_k^* \cup C_k''}\}_{k \in \{1, \cdots, N\}})$ to $\mathcal{F}$.

Forgery. After performing the query phase, $\mathcal{F}$ outputs a forged signature σ^* on message m^* with predicate Υ_{n_k, C_k^*}. If the associated default attribute set is not C_k' or $H'(m, \Upsilon_{n_k', C_k^*}) \neq g_2^{\beta_{k,\delta}'}$, $\mathcal{C}$ will abort. Otherwise the forged signature passes the verification algorithm which means,

$$
\begin{aligned}
\hat{e}(g_1, \sigma_0^*) &= \prod_{1 \leq k \leq N} [\prod_{i \in C_k^* \cup C_k'} Y_k \hat{e}(\sigma_{k,i}^*, H_k(i))] \\
&\quad \hat{e}(\sigma_s^*, H'(m^*, \Upsilon_{n_k', C_k^*})) \\
&= \prod_{1 \leq k \leq N} [\prod_{i \in C_k^* \cup C_k'} \hat{e}(\sigma_{k,i}^*, H_k(i))] \\
&\quad \prod_{1 \leq k \leq N} Z_k \hat{e}(\sigma_s, H'(m^*, \Upsilon_{n_k', C_k^*})) \quad (8) \\
&= \prod_{1 \leq k \leq N} [\prod_{i \in C_k^* \cup C_k'} \hat{e}(\sigma_{k,i}^*, g_2^{\beta_{k,i}})] \\
&\quad \hat{e}(G_1, G_2) \prod_{j \in \{1, \cdots, N\} \setminus \{k\}} Z_j \hat{e}(\sigma_s^*, g_2^{\beta_{k,\delta}'}))
\end{aligned}
$$

Then $\mathcal{C}$ can compute g_2^{ab} as,

$$
g_2^{ab} = \frac{\sigma_0^*}{\prod_{j \in \{1, \cdots, N\} \setminus \{k\}} G_2^{v_j} \prod_{i \in C_k^* \cup C_k'} (\phi(\sigma_{k,i}^*)^{\beta_{k,i}}) \phi(\sigma_s^*)^{\beta_{k,\delta}'}} \quad (9)
$$

Assume that $\mathcal{F}$ breaks the unforgeability of the proposed ODMA-ABS scheme in t time with probability ϵ. Then we can build an algorithm to solve the co-CDH problem in t' time with probability ϵ', where $t' \approx (\sum_k q_{H_k} + q_{H'} + N(N-1)q_P + 2|\overline{A_O}|q_O + \frac{3}{2} \sum_k (|\overline{C_k^*}| + d_k - \overline{n_k})q_S)t_e$ and $\epsilon' = \frac{\epsilon}{q_{H'}\binom{d_k - n_k}{d_k - 1}}$. Here $\overline{A_O}$ represents the average number of attributes in queried set in *outsourcing key query*, $\overline{C_k^*}$ and $\overline{n_k}$ represent the average parameter of the predicate in *signing query*, $\frac{1}{q_{h'}}$ and $\frac{1}{\binom{d_k - n_k}{d_k - 1}}$ represent the probability of which the cases 'the associated default attribute set is C_k' and $H'(m, \Upsilon_{n_k', C_k^*}) = g_2^{\beta_{k,\delta}'}$' happen respectively. What is more, t_e represents the time to perform a single-based exponentiation operation in $\mathbb{G}_1$ or $\mathbb{G}_2$, and we assume without loss of reasonability that one multi-based exponentiation which multiples up to 2 single-based exponentiation takes roughly the same as a single-based exponentiation [20].

Attribute Privacy. Our construction also achieves attribute privacy.

Theorem 4. *The proposed ODMA-ABS scheme is attribute private.*

Proof. The proof of the theorem is simple. In fact, the core of our construction is that any of the values of d attribute points can reconstruct the polynomial

Table 1. Comparison of the three ABS schemes

	DMA-ABS [10]	OABS [17]	ODMA-ABS
Authority involved	Multiple	Single	Multiple
Decentralization	$\times$	$\perp$	$\checkmark$
Corrupted authorities tolerance	Weak	No	Strong $(N-1)$
Key size	$15i\|G\|$	$SK : 2\|G\|$ $OK : 2(d+i-1)$	$SK : \|G\|$ $OK : 2(i+N\|\overline{d_k}\|)\|G\|$
Signature size	$13i\|G\|$	$(3+m+d-n)\|G\|$	$(2+(\overline{m_k}+\overline{d_k}-\overline{n_k})N)\|G\|$
Computation cost of the signer	$(14i+ri^2)M$	$4(M+E)$	$2E+(N^2-N+2)M$

by Lagrange interpolation. And we simply take k from the user's attribute set (also belong to the predicate attribute set) and $d-k$ from the default attribute set. Thus, it is obvious that for attribute sets A_{u1} and A_{u2} that both satisfy the predicate, they both catch such k elements that together with some $d-k$ elements from the default attribute set can retrieve the value of the polynomial at point 0 and furthermore generate a valid signature. This indicates that the attribute privacy holds. Here we omit the formal proof since it is similar with that in [20].

Efficiency. Now we analyze the efficiency of the scheme. In fact, the efficiency is obvious since that if no SCS exists, the signer will operate the same procedure as the $\mathbf{Sign_{out}}$ algorithm but in an outsourcing paradigm this part of computation is delegated to the SCS without producing extra computation. Here we need to assume the SCS to be semi-honest, which honestly perform the computation it is advertised but try to discover as much information as what it is not supposed to know. When it comes to the case that the SCS is malicious, the verification procedure need to be added to check whether the SCS has honestly performed the computation. We will discuss this in the extended version of this paper.

4.4   Performance

Now we compare our scheme to Li et al.'s [17] OABS and Okamato and Takashima's [10] DMA-ABS in Table 1, where $i = |A_u|$, d, n, m represent the corresponding d_k, n_k, m_k in our multi-authority setting, $\overline{d_k}, \overline{n_k}, \overline{m_k}$ represent the average of d_k, n_k, m_k in our scheme, $|G|$ represents the length of a group element, r represents the parameter usually smaller than i. M and E represents multiplication and exponentiation operation in the group. From the table we can see that our scheme enjoys a better security properties, and if we assume that N is small, which is reasonable in some scenario, like e-voting, our scheme also achieves a better efficiency.

5   Conclusion

In this paper, we have presented an outsourced decentralized multi-authority attribute based signature scheme. The ODMA-ABS achieves a strong notion of singer's privacy and can tolerant the collusion of at most $N - 1$ authorities. Furthermore, by outsourcing heavy computation workload to a singing cloud server, the scheme also achieves good performance in efficiency. We have proved the security properties and made a comparison to some existing schemes to show the efficiency.

Acknowledgment. This work is supported by the National Nature Science Foundation of China under Grant No.: 61272091, 61772311.

References

1. Shamir, A.: Identity-based cryptosystems and signature schemes. In: Blakley, G.R., Chaum, D. (eds.) CRYPTO 1984. LNCS, vol. 196, pp. 47–53. Springer, Heidelberg (1985). doi:10.1007/3-540-39568-7_5
2. Maji, H., Prabhakaran, M., Rosulek, M.: Attribute based signatures: achieving attribute privacy and collusion-resistance (2008). http://eprint.iacr.org/2008/328
3. Belenkiy, M., Chase, M., Kohlweiss, M., Lysyanskaya, A.: P-signatures and noninteractive anonymous credentials. In: Canetti, R. (ed.) TCC 2008. LNCS, vol. 4948, pp. 356–374. Springer, Heidelberg (2008). doi:10.1007/978-3-540-78524-8_20
4. Li, J., Kim, K.: Attribute-based ring signatures (2008). http://eprint.iacr.org/2008/394
5. Shahandashti, S.F., Safavi-Naini, R.: Threshold attribute-based signatures and their application to anonymous credential systems. In: Preneel, B. (ed.) AFRICACRYPT 2009. LNCS, vol. 5580, pp. 198–216. Springer, Heidelberg (2009). doi:10.1007/978-3-642-02384-2_13
6. Li, J., Au, M.H., Susilo, W., Xie, D., Ren, K.: Attribute-based signature and its applications. In: ACM Symposium on Information, Computer and Communications Security. ACM, pp. 60–69 (2010)
7. Maji, H.K., Prabhakaran, M., Rosulek, M.: Attribute-based signatures. In: Kiayias, A. (ed.) CT-RSA 2011. LNCS, vol. 6558, pp. 376–392. Springer, Heidelberg (2011). doi:10.1007/978-3-642-19074-2_24
8. Cao, D., Zhao, B., Wang, X., Su, J., Ji, G.: Multi-authority attribute-based signature. In: Third International Conference on Intelligent Networking and Collaborative Systems. IEEE Computer Society, pp. 668–672 (2011)
9. Chen, Y., Chen, J., Yang, G.: Provable secure multi-authority attribute based signatures. J. Converg. Inf. Technol. **8**(2), 545–553 (2013)
10. Okamoto, T., Takashima, K.: Decentralized attribute-based signatures. In: Kurosawa, K., Hanaoka, G. (eds.) PKC 2013. LNCS, vol. 7778, pp. 125–142. Springer, Heidelberg (2013). doi:10.1007/978-3-642-36362-7_9
11. Hohenberger, S., Lysyanskaya, A.: How to securely outsource cryptographic computations. In: Kilian, J. (ed.) TCC 2005. LNCS, vol. 3378, pp. 264–282. Springer, Heidelberg (2005). doi:10.1007/978-3-540-30576-7_15
12. Gennaro, R., Gentry, C., Parno, B.: Non-interactive verifiable computing: outsourcing computation to untrusted workers. In: Rabin, T. (ed.) CRYPTO 2010. LNCS, vol. 6223, pp. 465–482. Springer, Heidelberg (2010). doi:10.1007/978-3-642-14623-7_25
13. Gentry, C.: Fully homomorphic encryption using ideal lattices. In: STOC 2009, pp. 169–178 (2009)
14. Yao, A.C.: Protocols for secure computations. FOCS **82**, 160–164 (1982)

15. Gentry, C.: Computing arbitrary functions of encrypted data. Commun. ACM **53**(3), 97–105 (2010)
16. Fiore, D., Gennaro, R., Pastro, V.: Efficiently verifiable computation on encrypted data. In: ACM SIGSAC Conference on Computer and Communications Security, pp. 844–855. ACM (2014)
17. Lai, J., Deng, R.H., Pang, H., Weng, J.: Verifiable computation on outsourced encrypted data. In: Kutyłowski, M., Vaidya, J. (eds.) ESORICS 2014. LNCS, vol. 8712, pp. 273–291. Springer, Cham (2014). doi:10.1007/978-3-319-11203-9_16
18. Green, M., Hohenberger, S., Waters, B.: Outsourcing the decryption of ABE ciphertexts. In: USENIX Conference on Security, p. 34. USENIX Association (2011)
19. Zhou, Z., Huang, D.: Efficient and secure data storage operations for mobile cloud computing. Cryptology ePrint Archive, Report 2011/185 (2011)
20. Chen, X., Li, J., Huang, X., Li, J., Xiang, Y., Wong, D.S.: Secure outsourced attribute-based signatures. IEEE Trans. Parallel Distrib. Syst. **25**(12), 3285–3294 (2014)
21. Ren, Y., Jiang, T.: Verifiable outsourced attribute-based signature scheme. Multimedia Tools Appl. 1–11 (2017). doi:10.1007/s11042-017-4539-7
22. Goldreich, O., Goldwasser, S., Micali, S.: How to construct Randolli functions. In: 25th Annual Symposium on Foundations of Computer Science, pp. 464–479. IEEE (1984)
23. Boneh, D., Mironov, I., Shoup, V.: A secure signature scheme from bilinear maps. In: Joye, M. (ed.) CT-RSA 2003. LNCS, vol. 2612, pp. 98–110. Springer, Heidelberg (2003). doi:10.1007/3-540-36563-X_7
24. Benabbas, S., Gennaro, R., Vahlis, Y.: Verifiable delegation of computation over large datasets. In: Rogaway, P. (ed.) CRYPTO 2011. LNCS, vol. 6841, pp. 111–131. Springer, Heidelberg (2011). doi:10.1007/978-3-642-22792-9_7
25. Chow, S.M.: New privacy-preserving architectures for identity-/attribute-based encryption. Doctoral dissertation, Courant Institute of Mathematical Sciences New York (2010)
26. Belenkiy, M., Camenisch, J., Chase, M., Kohlweiss, M., Lysyanskaya, A., Shacham, H.: Randomizable proofs and delegatable anonymous credentials. In: Halevi, S. (ed.) CRYPTO 2009. LNCS, vol. 5677, pp. 108–125. Springer, Heidelberg (2009). doi:10.1007/978-3-642-03356-8_7

Efficient CCA2 Secure Revocable Multi-authority Large-Universe Attribute-Based Encryption

Dawei Li, Jie Chen, Jianwei Liu$^{(\boxtimes)}$, Qianhong Wu$^{(\boxtimes)}$, and Weiran Liu

School of Electronic and Information Engineering, Beihang University, Beijing 100191, China
{lidawei,jonathon_cj,liujianwei,qianhong.wu}@buaa.edu.cn,
liuweiran900217@gmail.com

Abstract. We propose an efficient revocable multi-authority large-universe attribute-based encryption system deployed to cloud storage service, which supports multiple authorities issuing secret keys for users with attributes from different domains in considering of privacy preserving and efficiency. In addition, it supports large-universe attributes allowing attributes denoted as any string in a large universe. Furthermore, it realizes an efficient revocation of attributes with less computation of key updating and data re-encryption. For this system, we define the security notion named indistinguishability against selective authority and access policy and statically chosen ciphertext attacks (IND-sAA-sCCA2), which can meet the majority of current security needs. Finally, a concrete scheme supporting ciphertext verifiability is constructed on prime-order groups to improve computing efficiency. We prove that the scheme satisfies IND-sAA-sCCA2 security with the help of a Chameleon hash function.

1 Introduction

Cloud storage provides a convenient way for data owners to store huge amount of data and share files with others. With the development of cloud storage, preserving data security is an important factor to concern. Traditional public key cryptosystems can realize encryption of shared files to ensure security while only the one with corresponding secret key has the ability to decrypt it, which is not flexible enough for one-to-many data sharing [1]. Thus attribute-based encryption (ABE) [2] was proposed to achieve fine-grained access control, with which the data owners can encrypt files according to the attributes of the target recipients without knowing their exact identities.

In an ABE system, the authority generates secret keys for users corresponding to their attributes. However, different kinds of attributes might be authorized by different departments, and these departments might not want to share authentication information to a unified third-party authority [3]. For example, Alice shares a file with the access policy ("Google Employees" and "Facebook

S. Wen et al. (Eds.): CSS 2017, LNCS 10581, pp. 103–118, 2017.
https://doi.org/10.1007/978-3-319-69471-9_8

Employees"), where the attributes should be authorized by Google and Facebook, but they cannot share out all of their employees' information to preserve privacy. To solve this obstacle, multi-authority ABE (MA-ABE) [4] was proposed to allow users get secret keys from multiple authorities associating with their varies attributes. Besides, to enable any meaningful string to act as an attribute and to expand the attribute universe, large-universe multi-authority ABE was then proposed to further improve the function of ABE. Most of the large-universe MA-ABE schemes were constructed on composite-order groups, seriously affecting the operational efficiency [5]. Then Rouselakis and Waters [6] proposed the efficient version based on prime-order groups with statical security.

However, once some data visitors are deprived of their certain attributes or have leaked their secret keys occasionally, the associating authority has to generate secret keys to all users under it and require the data owners to re-encrypt and re-upload the shared files whose access policy is associated with such attributes [7]. In this case, the computation load is linearly related to the users' number and it brings a heavy burden to all users. To make things worse, a large number of users share their files through the mobile intelligent devices with limited computing power, which has a high demand for computational efficiency. What's more, a practical revocable large-universe MA-ABE with higher security, like CCA2, is urgently needed to ensure the cloud storage operators provide more secure services.

1.1   Our Contributions

We define a new efficient revocable multi-authority large-universe attribute-based encryption system on prime-order groups with IND-sAA-sCCA2 security. Our main contributions are summarized as follows.

We formalized the security notion, indistinguishability against selective authority and access policy and statically chosen ciphertext attacks (IND-sAA-sCCA2) for revocable multi-authority large-universe ABE. In this security notion, an adversary should declare an access policy that it will attack as well as a set of corrupted authorities. Then the adversary can play a statical CCA2 security game with the challenger, but it cannot guess out which is the encrypted message with a more than negligible probability. We use Chameleon hash function to prevent the challenge ciphertext tampered and we treat the hashed value as an on-the-fly dummy attribute to finish the simulation of the CCA2 game.

We construct a concrete revocable multi-authority large-universe CP-ABE scheme on prime-order groups, which has an efficient performance in encryption and supports ciphertext verifiability by cloud server [8]. The subset-cover revocation framework is used in this scheme to achieve efficient and flexible revocation of users and reduce the computation cost in updating keys from linearly to logarithmically correlated with the number of users. Besides, only one part of the shared files need to be re-encrypted by the cloud server to prevent the revoked users from decrypting them.

Above all, the proposed revocable multi-authority large-universe CP-ABE system can meet almost all of the current function, efficiency and security needs for cloud storage service, and thus it is suitable for real deployment in cloud storage.

1.2 Related Work

ABE was first proposed by Sahai and Waters [2], and Goyal et al. introduced and distinguished ABE (KP-ABE) and ciphertext-policy ABE (CP-ABE). In KP-ABE, secret keys are associated with access policies and ciphertexts are associated with attributes, while in CP-ABE the ciphertexts are associated with access policies and secret keys are associated with attributes. Then KP-ABE was proposed by Goyal et al. [9] and CP-ABE was proposed by Bethencourt et al. [10]. And many ABE scheme was proposed to enhance the security [11–14]. Okamoto et al. [15] and Lewko et al. [16] proposed fully secure constructions in the standard model. Multi-authority ABE was proposed by Chase [4] which allows multiple attribute authorities. Since then, many multi-authority ABE [17–20] have been proposed with improvement in efficiency or security. Lewko et al. [21] proposed a new multi-authority CP-ABE with adaptive security, and Liu et al. [22] proposed a fully secure version without random oracles.

The first large-universe ABE was proposed in [23] on composite order groups and the first large universe KP-ABE on prime order groups was then proposed in [24] by Lewko. And Rouselakis et al. [25] proposed large-universe CP-ABE and KP-ABE with selective security in standard model. Rouselakis and Waters then proposed an efficient large universe multi-authority attribute-based encryption scheme with statical security. Revocation of ABE can be realized with two methods: direct and indirect revocation [26]. [27] proposed the revocable KP-ABE with indirect method by updating keys. And Sahai et al. proposed the revocable ABE by updating keys and updating ciphertext [28]. And Tsuchida et al. [29] constructed the revocable multi-authority ABE with CPA security.

To enhance security of ABE, several approaches have been proposed to realize CCA2 security [30]. Caneti-Halevi-Katz [31] approach was proposed which can convert the KP-ABE in [9] with CPA security to CCA2 security. Yamada et al. [32] came up with a generic construction to transform CPA-secure ABE to CCA2-secure ABE if the ABE satisfies delegatability or verifiability. Chen et al. [33] and Ge et al. [34] constructed ABE schemes without one-time signature, which is used in above approaches, with limitation that it only supports threshold access policies. And recently, Liu et al. [35] proposed CCA2-secure KP-ABE with the help of a Chameleon hash function.

2 Preliminaries

2.1 Computational Assumption

To prove security of the scheme, we use the assumption on prime order bilinear groups in [6] which is a modified version of the q-Decisional Parallel Bilinear Diffie-Hellman Exponent (q-DPBDHE) Assumption [14] and named q-DPBDHE2. The assumption is defined as follows.

q-DPBDHE2 Problem. Let $\mathbb{G}$ and $\mathbb{G}_T$ be the bilinear groups of order p, $e :$ $\mathbb{G} \times \mathbb{G} \rightarrow \mathbb{G}_T$, and g be a generator of $\mathbb{G}$. Pick $s, a, b_1, b_2, \ldots, b_q \xleftarrow{R} \mathbb{Z}_p$ and $R \xleftarrow{R} \mathbb{G}_T$ and a tuple

$$D = (\mathbb{G}, p, e, g, g^s, \{g^{a^i}\}_{\substack{i \in [2q], \\ i \neq q+1}}, \{g^{b_j a^i}\}_{\substack{(i,j) \in [2q,q], \\ i \neq q+1}}, \{g^{s/b_i}\}_{i \in [q]}, \{g^{s a^i b_j / b_{j'}}\}_{\substack{(i,j,j') \in [q+1,q,q] \\ j \neq j'}})$$

Given the tuple $(D, e(g,g)^{s a^{q+1}})$ or (D, R), an algorithm $\mathcal{B}$ outputs a bit $b \in \{0, 1\}$. We define that $\mathcal{B}$ has advantage ϵ in solving q-DPBDHE2 problem if

$$|\Pr[\mathcal{B}(D, e(g,g)^{s a^{q+1}}) = 0] - \Pr[\mathcal{B}(D, R) = 0]| \geq \epsilon$$

where the probability is over the random choice of $g \in \mathbb{G}, R \in \mathbb{G}_T, s, a, b_1, b_2, \ldots,$ $b_q \in \mathbb{Z}_p$ and random bits used in $\mathcal{B}$.

q-DPBDHE2 Assumption. The q-DPBDHE2 assumption holds in $\mathbb{G}$ if there is no algorithm that has advantage at least ϵ in solving the (t, ϵ, q)-DPBDHE2 problem in polynomial time t.

2.2 Linear Secret Sharing Schemes

Definition 1 (*Linear Secret Sharing Schemes (LSSS)* [25,27]). *Let $\mathcal{U}$ be the attribute universe. A secret sharing scheme Π with domain of secrets $\mathbb{Z}_p$ for realizing access structure on $\mathcal{U}$ is linear if:*

1. *The shares of a secret z for each attribute form a vector over $\mathbb{Z}_p$*
2. *There exists a matrix $A \in \mathbb{Z}_p^{\ell \times n}$ for each access structure $\mathbb{A}$. For all $i \in [\ell]$, we define the function $\delta(i)$ that labels the i-th row of A with attributes from $\mathcal{U}$. When we consider the column vector $\overrightarrow{v} = (z, r_2, r_3, \ldots, r_n)^\top$, where $r_2, r_3, \ldots, r_n \xleftarrow{R} \mathbb{Z}_p$, the vector of ℓ shares of the secret z according to Pi is equal to $\lambda = A \bullet \overrightarrow{v} \in \mathbb{Z}_p^{\ell \times 1}$. And the share λ_i belongs to the attribute $\delta(i)$ for $i \in [\ell]$.*

We refer to the tuple (A, δ) as the access structure $\mathbb{A}$ encoded by the LSSS-policy. All secret sharing schemes should satisfy the requirements [27] including reconstruction requirement that the secret can be reconstructed efficiently for authorized sets and security requirement that it's hard to reveal any partial information about the secret for any unauthorized sets. These requirements are used in out setting. Let S denote an authorized set of attributes and let I be the set of rows whose labels are in S. The reconstruction requirement states that there exists constants $\{\omega_i \in \mathbb{Z}_p\}_{i \in I}$ such that for any valid shares $\{\lambda_i = (A\overrightarrow{v})_i\}_{i \in I}$ of a secret z according to Π, we have that $\sum_{i \in I} \omega_i \lambda_i = z$. Additionally, the constants $\{\omega_i\}_{i \in I}$ can be calculated in time polynomial in the size of the matrix A. For unauthorized sets S', no such constants $\{\omega_i\}_{i \in I}$ exist, but there exists a vector $\overrightarrow{d} \in \mathbb{Z}_p^{1 \times n}$ such that its first component $d_1 = 1$ and $\overrightarrow{A_i} \bullet \overrightarrow{d} = 0$ for all $i \in I'$.

2.3 Chameleon Hash

The Chameleon hash is used in our scheme to prove the security. A Chameleon hash function consists of three algorithms, and only some one knowing the secret key can find collisions for its inputs.

- $KeyGen_{ch}(1^\lambda) \to (SK_{ch}, PK_{ch})$: It takes in the security parameter $\lambda \in \mathbb{N}$ then outputs the secret key and the public key.
- $H_{ch}(PK_{ch}, M, r_{ch}) \to V$: It takes in the public key PK_{ch}, the message M and an auxiliary parameter r_{ch}, then outputs the hashed value V.
- $UForge_{ch}(SK_{ch}, M, r_{ch}, M') \to r'_{ch}$: It takes in the secret key SK_{ch}, a message M with its auxiliary parameter r_{ch} and a new message M', then outputs a new auxiliary parameter r'_{ch} such that the hashed value of M with r_{ch} is equal to the hashed value of M' with r'_{ch}, i.e., $H_{ch}(PK_{ch}, M, r_{ch}) = H_{ch}(PK_{ch}, M', r'_{ch})$.

2.4 Subset-Cover Revocation Framework

Let v denote a non-leaf node, and let v_L (v_R) denote the left (right) child of v. In the binary tree BT, each user is assigned to a leaf node, and if it is revoked on time T_i, it will be added into the revocation list RL. For a current time T, the KUNode(BT, RL) function is defined as follows:

$$
\begin{aligned}
&\text{KUNode}(BT, RL) \\
&\quad X, Y \leftarrow \emptyset \\
&\quad \forall (v_i, T_i) \in RL \\
&\qquad \text{if } T_i \leq T \text{ then add Path}(v_i) \text{ to } X \\
&\quad \forall x \in X \\
&\qquad \text{if } x_L \notin X, \text{ then add } x_L \text{ to } Y \\
&\qquad \text{if } x_R \notin X, \text{ then add } x_R \text{ to } Y \\
&\quad \text{if } Y = \emptyset, \text{ then add root to } Y \\
&\quad \text{Return } Y
\end{aligned}
$$

3 Revocable Multi-authority CP-ABE

3.1 System Model

There are four roles in this system, named cloud server, authorities, data owners and data visitors, as described in Fig. 1. And this system consists of nine polynomial time algorithms defined as follows.

- $GSetup(1^\lambda) \to Param$: The cloud server runs this algorithm to set up this system. It takes in the security parameter and outputs the system parameters.
- $ASetup(\theta) \to (PK_\theta, SK_\theta)$: The authority θ runs this algorithm to set up the authority's public key and private key.
- $KeyGen(\text{ID}, \theta, att, SK_\theta) \to SK_{\text{ID},att}$: The authority runs this algorithm to generate private key to the data visitor ID with attribute att.

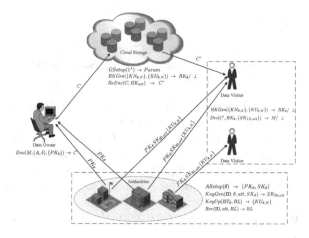

Fig. 1. System model

- $KeyUp(BT_\theta, RL) \rightarrow \{KU_{\theta,N}\}$: The authority runs this algorithm to update keys to unrevoked data visitors. It takes in the revocation list and a binary tree, and outputs the updated re-encryption part of private keys, which is then sent to the unrevoked data visitors and the cloud server.
- $RKGen(\{KN_{\theta,N}\}, \{KU_{\theta,N}\}) \rightarrow RK_\theta / \perp$: The cloud server and unrevoked data visitors run this algorithm to get the updated re-encryption keys. It takes in $\{KU_{\theta,N}\}$, and $\{KN_{\theta,N}\}$ that is a part of $SK_{\text{ID},att}$, and outputs the resulting re-encryption keys.
- $Enc(M, (A, \delta), \{PK_\theta\}) \rightarrow C$: The data owner runs this algorithm to encrypt message with corresponding access policy.
- $ReEnc(C, RK_{att}) \rightarrow C'$: The cloud server runs this algorithm to re-encrypt ciphertext to prevent revoked users from decrypting it.
- $Dec(C', RK_\theta, \{SK_{ID,att}\}) \rightarrow M / \perp$: The data visitor runs this algorithm to decrypt the ciphertext and if the data visitor does not satisfy the access policy or some of its corresponding attributes have been revoked, it cannot decrypt the ciphertext correctly.
- $Rev(\text{ID}, att, RL) \rightarrow RL$: The authority runs this algorithm to add the revoked users ID with attribute att into the revocation list.

3.2   Security Model

We define the indistinguishability against selective authority and access policy and statically chosen ciphertext attacks (IND-sAA-sCCA2) for this revocable multi-authority large-universe CP-ABE. In this security model, the adversary can query for secret keys associated with any access policy and query for decryption of any ciphertext, except that it cannot query for decryption of the challenge ciphertext and if it queries for secret keys associated with its selected access policy, it can only do this at phase 1 and it has to revoke one of the selected attributes immediately. Formally, the IND-sAA-sCCA2 security model is defined through the following game played between an adversary $\mathcal{A}$ and a challenger $\mathcal{B}$.

Init. $\mathcal{A}$ selects a challenge access policy (A^*, δ^*) and selects a set of corrupt authorities $\mathcal{C}_\theta$, then sends them to challenger $\mathcal{B}$.

Setup. $\mathcal{B}$ sends to $\mathcal{A}$ the public parameter $Param$.

Phase 1. $\mathcal{A}$ statically issues queries including $AuthoritySetupQueries$, $SecretKeyQueries$, $RevocationQueries$, $Re-EncryptionQueries$, $DecryptionQueries$. If the queried attributes set satisfies the selected access policy, $\mathcal{A}$ has to revoke one of the attributes from all users.

Challenge. $\mathcal{A}$ submits two messages M_0, M_1 with equal length to $\mathcal{B}$. Then $\mathcal{B}$ flips a random coin $b \in \{0, 1\}$ and encrypts M_b with the selected access policy. After being re-encrypted by the latest re-encryption keys, the re-encrypted ciphertext is returned to $\mathcal{A}$.

Phase 2. $\mathcal{A}$ and $\mathcal{B}$ processes the same as in **Phase 1** except that $\mathcal{A}$ cannot make secret key query for the selected access policy or decryption query for the challenge ciphertext.

Guess. Finally, $\mathcal{A}$ outputs a guess $b' \in \{0, 1\}$, and wins in the game if $b' = b$.

4   Concrete Scheme

The proposed scheme is as follows.

- $GSetup(1^\lambda) \rightarrow Param$: The cloud server runs this algorithm and takes as input the system security parameter 1^λ. It picks a prime order bilinear group generator $\mathcal{G}$, and runs $(\mathbb{G}, p, g) \xleftarrow{R} \mathcal{G}(1^\lambda)$. It randomly picks exponents $\alpha_0, \beta_0 \xleftarrow{R} \mathbb{Z}_p$ as the master key, and computes $PK_0 = (e(g, g)^{\alpha_0}, g^{\beta_0})$ as the public key. For identity and attribute are usually in the form of strings, it chooses a function H mapping identity ID to elements of $\mathbb{G}$, and another function F mapping attributes to elements of $\mathbb{G}$. Then it defines the attribute universe $\mathcal{U}$ and the authority universe $\mathcal{U}_\theta$, and $T :$ $\mathcal{U} \rightarrow \mathcal{U}_\theta$ is a publicly computable function mapping each attribute to a unique authority, which means that, for example, T maps the attribute "$att_i@\theta_i$" to its authority "θ_i". It initializes a revocation list $RL = \emptyset$. Finally, it picks a Chameleon hash function $H_{ch} : \{0, 1\}^* \rightarrow \mathcal{U}$ and runs the $KeyGen_{ch}(1^\lambda) \rightarrow (SK_{ch}, PK_{ch})$. Thus the global parameters are $Param = (p, \mathbb{G}, g, H, F, T, H_{ch}, \mathcal{U}, \mathcal{U}_\theta, PK_0, PK_{ch}, RL)$, which is the input for all of the following algorithms but we omit for simplicity.
- $ASetup(\theta) \rightarrow (PK_\theta, SK_\theta)$: The authority runs this algorithm and takes as input the global parameters $Param$ and the index of the authority $\theta \in \mathcal{U}_\theta \setminus \{0\}$. It randomly picks two exponents $\alpha_\theta, \beta_\theta \xleftarrow{R} \mathbb{Z}_p$, then publishes the public key $PK_\theta = (e(g, g)^{\alpha_\theta}, g^{\beta_\theta})$, and keeps the private key $SK_\theta = (\alpha_\theta, \beta_\theta)$.

- $KeyGen(\text{ID}, \theta, att, SK_\theta) \rightarrow SK_{\text{ID},att}$: To generate private keys for the user ID with attribute $att \in \mathcal{U}$, the authority runs this algorithm as follows. Firstly, it sets up a binary tree BT_θ if BT_θ has not yet existed, where each user with attribute $T(att) = \theta$ is assigned as a leaf node and it increases the height as the number of users increases. For each node N in binary tree BT_θ, it randomly picks $\{KN_{\theta,N}\} \xleftarrow{R} \mathbb{Z}_p$. Then the authority θ randomly picks $r \xleftarrow{R} \mathbb{Z}_p$ and computes $K_{\text{ID},att} = g^{\alpha_\theta} H(\text{ID})^{\beta_\theta} F(att)^r$, $K'_{\text{ID},att} = g^r$. Finally, it outputs $SK_{\text{ID},att} = (K_{\text{ID},att}, K'_{\text{ID},att}, \{KN_{\theta,N}\}_{N \in Path(\text{ID})})$, gives $SK_{\text{ID},att}$ to the user ID, and gives $(BT_\theta, \{KN_{\theta,N}\}_{N \in Path(\text{ID})})$ to the cloud server.
- $KeyUp(BT_\theta, RL) \rightarrow \{KU_{\theta,N}\}$: This algorithm is run by the authority θ. It takes as input the revocation list RL and the binary tree BT_θ kept by θ, and randomly picks $RK_\theta \xleftarrow{R} \mathbb{Z}_p$ for BT_θ, and publishes $\{KU_{\theta,N}\} = \{RK_\theta \times KN_{\theta,N}\}_{N \in KUNode(BT_\theta, RL)}$.
- $RKGen(\{KN_{\theta,N}\}, \{KU_{\theta,N}\}) \rightarrow RK_\theta / \perp$: This algorithm is run by the user ID and cloud server to generate the re-encryption key RK_θ for all unrevoked user with attribute $T(att) = \theta$. If $Path(\text{ID}) \cap KUNode(BT_\theta, RL) = \emptyset$, it returns $\perp$, otherwise, calculates the node $N \in Path(\text{ID}) \cap KUNode(BT_\theta, RL)$ and computes the re-encryption key $RK_\theta = \frac{KU_{\theta,N}}{KN_{\theta,N}}$.
- $Enc(M, (A, \delta), \{PK_\theta\}) \rightarrow C$: This algorithm is run by the message sender. It takes as input a message M, an access policy (A, δ) with $A \in \mathbb{Z}_p^{\ell \times n}$, and the public keys $\{PK_\theta\}$ of the relevant authorities, where $\theta = T(att)$. We defines a function $\rho : [\ell] \rightarrow \mathcal{U}_\theta$ as $\rho(\cdot) = T(\delta(\cdot))$ to map rows to authorities. Then it randomly picks $z, v_2, \ldots, v_n, \omega_2, \ldots, \omega_n \xleftarrow{R} \mathbb{Z}_p$ and creates vectors $\overrightarrow{v} = (z, v_2, \ldots, v_n)^\top$ and $\overrightarrow{\omega} = (0, \omega_2, \ldots, \omega_n)^\top$. We let $\lambda_x = \overrightarrow{A_x} \bullet \overrightarrow{v}$ denote the share of z corresponding to row x, and $\omega_x = \overrightarrow{A_x} \bullet \overrightarrow{\omega}$ denote the share of 0, where $\overrightarrow{A_x}$ is the x-th row of matrix A. Let $\omega_0 = \sum_{x \in \ell} \omega_x$. For each row x of A, it randomly picks exponent $t_x \xleftarrow{R} \mathbb{Z}_p$ and $t_0 \xleftarrow{R} \mathbb{Z}_p$, and computes the ciphertext $C = (C_0, \{C_{1,x}, C_{2,x}, C_{3,x}, C_{4,x}\}_{x \in [0,\ell]}, r_{ch})$ as follows:

$$C_0 = M \cdot e(g,g)^z, C_{1,0} = e(g,g)^z e(g,g)^{\alpha_0 t_0}, C_{2,0} = g^{-t_0}, C_{3,0} = g^{\beta_0 t_0} g^{\omega_0},$$

$$V = H_{ch}(PK_{ch}, PK_{ch} \parallel C \setminus C_{4,0}, r_{ch}), C_{4,0} = F(V)^{t_0},$$

$$\{C_{1,x} = e(g,g)^{\lambda_x} e(g,g)^{\alpha_{\rho(x)} t_x}, C_{2,x} = g^{-t_x}, C_{3,x} = g^{\beta_{\rho(x)} t_x} g^{\omega_x}, C_{4,x} = F(\delta(x))^{t_x}\}_{x \in [\ell]}$$

- $ReEnc(C, RK_{att}) \rightarrow C'$: This algorithm is run by the cloud server. It firstly computes $V' = H_{ch}(PK_{ch}, PK_{ch} \parallel C \setminus C_{4,0}, r_{ch})$ and verifies the validity of the ciphertext by computing:

$$e(C_{4,x}, g) \cdot e(C_{2,x}, F(att)) \overset{?}{=} 1 \tag{1}$$

$$e(C_{4,0}, g) \cdot e(C_{2,0}, F(V')) \overset{?}{=} 1 \tag{2}$$

$$\frac{\prod_{x \in [\ell]} (e(C_{2,x}, g^{\beta_{\rho(x)}}) \cdot e(C_{3,x}, g))}{e(C_{2,0}, g^{\beta_0}) \cdot e(C_{3,0}, g)} \overset{?}{=} 1 \tag{3}$$

If the equation holds, it means that the ciphertext is encrypted exactly by the attribute att, and it has not been tampered maliciously. The cloud server

re-encrypts the ciphertext by computing $C' = (C_0, C_{1,0}, C_{2,0}, C_{3,0}, C_{4,0},$
$\{C_{1,x}, C_{2,x}, C_{3,x}, C_{4,x}^{RK_{T(\delta(x))}}\}_{x\in[\ell]}, r_{ch})$. Then the re-encrypted ciphertext C'
would be stored securely on the cloud server.

- $Dec(C', RK_\theta, \{SK_{ID,att}\}) \to M/ \perp$: This algorithm is run by the decryptor ID with attributes att. It firstly computes the original ciphertext $C = C'$ except that $\{C_{4,x}\}_{x\in[\ell]} = \{C'^{RK_{T(\delta(x))}^{-1}}_{4,x}\}_{x\in[\ell]}$. Then it verifies the validity of the ciphertext with the Eqs. (1), (2) and (3) in the algorithm $ReEnc$. If the equation holds, it means that the ciphertext is encrypted exactly by the attribute att, and it has not been tampered maliciously or the attributes att have not been revoked for this decryptor ID. Let (A, δ) be the access policy of the ciphertext. It computes:

$$C_{1,x} \cdot e(K_{ID,\delta(x)}, C_{2,x}) \cdot e(H(ID), C_{3,x}) \cdot e(K'_{ID,\delta(x)}, C_{4,x}) = e(g,g)^{\lambda_x} \cdot e(H(ID), g)^{\omega_x}$$

Then it calculates a constants $c_x \in \mathbb{Z}_p$ such that $\sum_x c_x \overrightarrow{A_x} = (1, 0, \cdots, 0)$. For $\lambda_x = \overrightarrow{A_x} \bullet \overrightarrow{v}$ and $\omega_x = \overrightarrow{A_x} \bullet \overrightarrow{w}$, $(1, 0, \cdots, 0) \bullet \overrightarrow{v} = z$ and $(1, 0, \cdots, 0) \bullet \overrightarrow{w} = 0$. Finally, the decryptor computes:

$$M = \frac{C_0}{\prod_x (e(g,g)^{\lambda_x} e(H(ID), g)^{\omega_x})^{c_x}} = \frac{M \cdot e(g,g)^z}{e(g,g)^z}$$

- $Rev(ID, att, RL) \to RL$: This algorithm is run by each authority to revoke a certain attribute att from a user ID. It just add this user's identity and revoked attribute into the revocation list RL.

5 Security Analysis

In this section, we prove that the proposed scheme is IND-sAA-sCCA2 secure. At the Init phase, the adversary first selects a target access policy (A^*, δ^*) and a set of corrupted authorities $\mathcal{C}_\theta$ that it will attack, with limitation that $\rho[\ell] \nsubseteq \mathcal{C}_\theta$. At the setup phase, the simulator randomly picks a message M^* and an auxiliary parameter r^* to compute the ciphertext C^* ahead of time, where the Chameleon hash function V^* in $C^*_{4,0}$ acts as the challenge on-the-fly dummy attribute. At the challenge phase, the simulator ignores the contribution of the rows belonging to the corrupted authorities based on "zero-out" lemma. Given the challenge message M_0 and M_1, the simulator replaces M^* with M_b in C^*, while the V^* remains unchanged because of Chameleon hash function. At phase 1 and phase 2, the adversary should statically output all queries (ID_i, S_i) about a single ID_i at once, where $S_i = \{att_1, \ldots, att_{|S_i|}\}$ is a set of all attributes that ID has. Then the simulator splits the unknown parameters into two parts to continue the simulation process. Besides, the adversary can make $KeyGen$ queries for (ID_i^*, S_i^*) whose attributes S_i^* satisfies (A^*, δ^*) only at phase 1, but it has to revoke at least one attribute $att^* \in S_i \setminus \{T(att) \in \mathcal{C}_\theta\}$ for all user who has attribute att^* to prevent them from being colluded by the adversary before the challenge phase. If the attacker attempts to modify the challenge ciphertext to query for decryption, the simulator will verify the consistency of the ciphertext and then detect this malicious tamper. We review the "zero-out" lemma whose proof can be found in [6].

Lemma 1. *Let* $(A^* \in \mathbb{Z}_p^{\ell \times n}, \delta^*)$ *be the selected challenge access policy, and* $\mathcal{C}_\theta$ *be a set of corrupted authorities, where* $\mathcal{C} \subseteq [\ell]$ *denotes the set of rows corresponding to the attributes in* $\mathcal{C}_\theta$, *and* c *denotes the dimension of the subspace spanned by the rows of* $\mathcal{C}$. *Then the distribution of the shares* $\{\lambda_x\}_{x \in [\ell]}$ *sharing the secret* $z \in \mathbb{Z}_p$ *generated by* A^* *is the same as the distribution of the shares* $\{\lambda'_x\}_{x \in [\ell]}$ *sharing the secret* z *generated by* A', *where* $A'_{x,j} = 0$ *for all* $(x, j) \in \mathcal{C} \times [n' = n - c]$. *And for each row* $A'_{x \in \mathcal{C}}$, *there is only one "1" in one of the last* c *positions, and "0" in others.*

Theorem 1. *Let* $\mathcal{G}$ *be a prime-order bilinear group generator and* $\Pi = \{GSetup, ASetup, KeyGen, KeyUp, RKGen, Enc, ReEnc, Dec\}$ *be a concrete scheme. The proposed concrete scheme* Π *is IND-sAA-sCCA2 secure if the* $(q+1)$-*DPBDHE2 assumption holds on* $\mathcal{G}$, *the employed Chameleon hash function is secure, and the size of selected matrix is at most* $q \times q$.

Proof. Suppose that there is a probabilistic polynomial time adversary $\mathcal{A}$ who has advantage ϵ to break our concrete scheme in the security game. We construct a simulator $\mathcal{B}$ that can solve the $(q+1)$-DPBDHE2 problem on $\mathcal{G}$ with the tuple (D, T) as input and interact with $\mathcal{A}$ as follows.

Init. Algorithm $\mathcal{A}$ selects a challenge access policy (A^*, δ^*) which means an attribute set $S^* = \{att_1, \ldots, att_{|S^*|}\}$, and selects a set of corrupt authorities $\mathcal{C}_\theta$, then sends them to $\mathcal{B}$. We have that A^* is a matrix whose size $\ell \times n$ is at most $q \times q$ and $\delta^* : [\ell] \to \mathbb{Z}_p$.

Setup. Algorithm $\mathcal{B}$ gets the tuple (D, T) from $(q+1)$-DPBDHE2 challenger and substitutes A^* with the matrix A' according to "zero-out" lamma. It randomly picks a challenge message $M^* \xleftarrow{R} \mathbb{G}_T$ and sets $C_0^* = M^* \cdot T$. It calls a secure Chameleon hash function $H_{ch} : \{0,1\}^* \to \mathcal{U}$ and runs the $KeyGen_{ch}(1^\lambda) \to (SK_{ch}, PK_{ch})$. It randomly picks an auxiliary parameter $r^* \xleftarrow{R} \mathbb{Z}_p$ and computes $V^* = H_{ch}(PK_{ch}, C_0^*, r_{ch}^*)$. Then V^* is regarded as a challenge on-the-fly dummy attribute authorized by θ_0 controlled by $\mathcal{B}$, and $\mathcal{B}$ calculates a matrix $A_{\ell+1} \in \mathbb{Z}_p^{1 \times n}$ representing the access policy of V^*. $\mathcal{B}$ randomly picks $\alpha_0', \beta_0' \xleftarrow{R} \mathbb{Z}_p$ and sets $\alpha_0 = \alpha_0' + \sum_{x \in X \cup \{\ell+1\}} b_x a^{q+2}$, $\beta_0 = \beta_0' + \sum_{x \in X \cup \{\ell+1\}} \sum_{j=2}^{n'} b_x a^{q+3-j} A_{\ell+1,j}$. Thus it calculates $PK_0 = (e(g,g)^{\alpha_0}, g^{\beta_0}) = (e(g,g)^{\alpha_0'} e(g^{b_{\ell+1}a}, g^{a^{q+1}})^{A_{\ell+1,1}}, g^{\beta_0'} \prod_{j=2}^{n'} (g^{b_{\ell+1}a^{q+3-j}})^{A_{\ell+1,j}})$. $\mathcal{B}$ sends to $\mathcal{A}$ the public parameter $Param = (p, \mathbb{G}, g, , T, H_{ch}, \mathcal{U}, \mathcal{U}_\theta, PK_0, PK_{ch}, RL)$, where the random oracles H and F are programmed by the simulator and $RL = \emptyset$.

Phase 1. Algorithm $\mathcal{A}$ statically issues following queries.

Authority Setup Queries: $\mathcal{A}$ outputs a set of non-corrupted authorities $\mathcal{N}_\theta \in \mathcal{U}_\theta$, and $\mathcal{N}_\theta \cap \mathcal{C}_\theta = \emptyset$. For each $\theta \in \mathcal{N}_\theta$, there are two cases:

- If $\theta \notin \rho[\ell]$, $\mathcal{B}$ randomly picks $\alpha_\theta, \beta_\theta \overset{R}{\leftarrow} \mathbb{Z}_p$ and outputs the public key $(e(g,g)^{\alpha_\theta}, g^{\beta_\theta})$.
- If $\theta \in \rho[\ell] \backslash \mathcal{C}_\theta$, let $X = \{x | \rho(x) = \theta\}$, which means the $x-th$ row of A is corresponding to θ. $\mathcal{B}$ randomly picks $\alpha'_\theta, \beta'_\theta \overset{R}{\leftarrow} \mathbb{Z}_p$, and computes $(e(g,g)^{\alpha_\theta}, g^{\beta_\theta})$

$$= (e(g,g)^{\alpha'_\theta} \prod_{x \in X \cup \{\ell+1\}} e(g^{b_x a}, g^{a^{q+1}})^{A'_{x,1}}, g^{\beta'_\theta} \prod_{x \in X \cup \{\ell+1\}} \prod_{j=2}^{n'} (g^{b_x a^{q+3-j}})^{A'_{x,j}})$$

where the secret key is $(\alpha_\theta, \beta_\theta)$ for $\alpha_\theta = \alpha'_\theta + \sum_{x \in X \cup \{\ell+1\}} b_x a^{q+2} A'_{x,1}$ and $\beta_\theta = \beta'_\theta + \sum_{x \in X \cup \{\ell+1\}} \sum_{j=2}^{n'} b_x a^{q+3-j} A'_{x,j}$.

H-Oracle Queries: $\mathcal{A}$ queries to oracle H for identity ID_i with attribute set S_i. If there is no row x such that $\delta(x) \in S_i$, $\mathcal{B}$ randomly picks $h'_i \overset{R}{\leftarrow} \mathbb{Z}_p$ and computes $H(\mathrm{ID}_i) = g^{h'_i} \cdot g^a \dots g^{a^{n'-1}} = g^{h'_i} \cdot \prod_{k=2}^{n'} g^{a^{k-1}}$. Otherwise, for some rows $X' = \{x | \delta(x) \in S_i \cap [\ell]\}$ and $X_C = \{x | T(\delta(x)) \in \mathcal{C}_\theta \cap [\ell]\}$, $\mathcal{B}$ can find a vector $\overrightarrow{d_i} \in \mathbb{Z}_p^{n \times 1}$ with $d_{i,1} = 1$ such that $\overrightarrow{A_x^*} \bullet \overrightarrow{d_i} = 0$ and $\overrightarrow{A_x'} \bullet \overrightarrow{d_i} = 0$ for all $x \in X' \cup X_C$ and then $\mathcal{B}$ computes $H(\mathrm{ID}_i) = g^{h'_i} \cdot (g^a)^{d_{i,2}} \dots (g^{a^{n'-1}})^{d_{i,n'}} = g^{h'_i} \cdot \prod_{k=2}^{n'} (g^{a^{k-1}})^{d_{i,k}}$.

F-Oracle Queries: $\mathcal{A}$ queries to oracle F for attribute att whose authority is $\theta = Tatt$. If $\theta \notin \rho[\ell]$ or $\theta \in \mathcal{C}_\theta$, $\mathcal{B}$ randomly picks $F(att) \overset{R}{\leftarrow} \mathbb{Z}_p$. If $\theta \in \rho[\ell]$, let $X'' = \{x | \rho[x] = \theta\} \backslash \{x | \delta(x) = att\}$. Then $\mathcal{B}$ randomly picks $u_{att} \overset{R}{\leftarrow} \mathbb{Z}_p$ and outputs $F(att) = g^{u_{att}} g^{\sum_{x \in X'' \cup \{\ell+1\}} \sum_{j \in [n']} b_x a^{q+2-j} A'_{x,j}} = g^{u_{att}} \prod_{x \in X'' \cup \{\ell+1\}} \prod_{j \in [n']} (g^{b_x a^{q+2-j}})^{A'_{x,j}}$.

Secret Key Queries: $\mathcal{A}$ makes secret key queries for (ID_i, S_i), and $\mathcal{B}$ computes secret key $(K_{\mathrm{ID}_i, att}, K'_{\mathrm{ID}_i, att}, \{KN_{\theta, N}\}_{N \in Path(\mathrm{ID}_i)})$ for every $att \in S_i$. There are three cases:

- $T(att) = \theta \notin \rho[\ell]$: $\mathcal{B}$ randomly picks $r, \alpha_\theta, \beta_\theta \overset{R}{\leftarrow} \mathbb{Z}_p$ and $\{KN_{\theta, N}\}_{N \in Path(\mathrm{ID}_i)} \overset{R}{\leftarrow} \mathbb{Z}_p$ if it has not been stored. Then it outputs $K_{\mathrm{ID}_i, att} = g^{\alpha_\theta} H(\mathrm{ID}_i)^{\beta_\theta} F(att)^r$, $K'_{\mathrm{ID}_i, att} = g^r, \{KN_{\theta, N}\}_{N \in Path(\mathrm{ID}_i)}$.
- $T(att) = \theta \in \rho[\ell]$ and $S_i \cap \delta[\ell] = \emptyset$: If the attribute att belongs to the authority θ who has other attributes in the challenge policy, but none of this users' attributes is in the challenge policy, for $H(\mathrm{ID}_i) = g^{h'_i} \cdot \prod_{k=2}^{n'} g^{a^{k-1}}$ and $F(att) = g^{u_{att}} \prod_{x \in X \cup \{\ell+1\}} \prod_{j \in [n']} (g^{b_x a^{q+2-j}})^{A'_{x,j}}$, $\mathcal{B}$ randomly picks $t \overset{R}{\leftarrow} \mathbb{Z}_p$, sets $r = t - \sum_{k \in [n']} a^k$ and computes

$$K_{\mathrm{ID}_i,att} = g^{\alpha_\theta} H(\mathrm{ID}_i)^{\beta_\theta} F(att)^r = g^{\alpha'_\theta} \prod_{x \in X \cup \{\ell+1\}} \prod_{j=2}^{n'} (g^{b_x a^{q+3-j}})^{-A'_{x,j}} H(\mathrm{ID}_i)^{\beta'_\theta}$$

$$\cdot (g^{\beta_\theta})^{h'_i} \prod_{x \in X \cup \{\ell+1\}} \prod_{k=2}^{n'} (g^{b_x a^{q+1+k}})^{-A'_{x,1}} \cdot (g^r)^{u_{att}} \prod_{x \in X \cup \{\ell+1\}} \prod_{k \in [n']} (g^{b_x a^{q+2-k}})^{tA'_{x,k}}$$

$$K'_{\mathrm{ID}_i,att} = g^r = g^t \prod_{k \in [n']} (g^{a^k})^{-1}$$

and randomly picks $\{KN_{\theta,N}\}_{N \in Path(\mathrm{ID}_i)} \xleftarrow{R} \mathbb{Z}_p$ if it has not been stored.

- $T(att) = \theta \in \rho[\ell]$ and $S_i \cap \delta[\ell] \neq \emptyset$: If the attribute att belongs to the authority θ who has other attributes in the challenge policy, and some of this users' attributes are in the challenge policy, for $H(\mathrm{ID}_i) = g^{h'_i} \cdot \prod_{k=2}^{n'} g^{a^{k-1}d_{i,k}}$ and $F(att) = g^{u_{att}} \prod_{x \in X'' \cup \{\ell+1\}} \prod_{j \in [n']} (g^{b_x a^{q+2-j}})^{A'_{x,j}}$, $\mathcal{B}$ randomly picks $t \xleftarrow{R} \mathbb{Z}_p$, sets $r = t - \sum_{k \in [n']} a^k d_{i,k}$ and computes $K_{\mathrm{ID}_i,att}$ and $K'_{\mathrm{ID}_i,att}$ as follows, where $X \setminus X'' = \{x | \delta(x) = att\}$ means the rows that map to att, and if $att \notin \delta[\ell]$, the related multiplication factor part is equal to 1. Then it randomly picks $\{KN_{\theta,N}\}_{N \in Path(\mathrm{ID}_i)} \xleftarrow{R} \mathbb{Z}_p$ if has not been stored.

$$K_{\mathrm{ID}_i,att} = g^{\alpha_\theta} H(\mathrm{ID}_i)^{\beta_\theta} F(att)^r = H(\mathrm{ID}_i)^{\beta'_\theta} \prod_{x \in X \setminus X''} \prod_{j,k=2,j \neq k}^{n',n'} (g^{b_x a^{q+2+k-j}})^{-A_{x,1}d_{i,k}}$$

$$\cdot g^{\alpha'_\theta} \prod_{x \in X \cup \{\ell+1\}} \prod_{j=2}^{n'} (g^{b_x a^{q+3-j}})^{-A'_{x,j}} \cdot (g^{\beta_\theta})^{h'_i} \prod_{x \in X \cup \{\ell+1\}} \prod_{k=2}^{n'} (g^{b_x a^{q+1+k}})^{-A'_{x,1}d_{i,k}}$$

$$\cdot (g^r)^{u_{att}} \prod_{x \in X'' \cup \{\ell+1\}} \prod_{j \in [n']} (g^{b_x a^{q+2-j}})^{tA'_{x,j}}$$

$$K'_{\mathrm{ID}_i,att} = g^r = g^t \prod_{k \in [n']} (g^{a^k})^{-1}$$

Revocation Queries: $\mathcal{A}$ makes revocation queries for (ID_i, att), and $\mathcal{B}$ adds (ID_i, att) to RL. Then $\mathcal{B}$ runs the $KeyUp$ algorithm to update keys for unrevoked users and runs the $ReEnc$ algorithm to get the latest ciphertext C'.

Re-Encryption Queries: $\mathcal{A}$ makes re-encryption queries for ciphertext C to get the resulting re-encrypted ciphertext C'. $\mathcal{B}$ runs the $RKGen$ algorithm and takes it as input to run the $ReEnc$ algorithm to get C'.

Decryption Queries: $\mathcal{A}$ makes decryption queries for C' with (A, δ). $\mathcal{B}$ first restores C' to the original ciphertext C with the latest RK_θ. Then $\mathcal{B}$ computes $V = H_{ch}(PK_{ch}, PK_{ch} \parallel C \setminus C_{4.0}, r_{ch})$ and determines whether the ciphertext is valid by checking Eqs. (1), (2) and (3). If either of the equalities does not hold, the ciphertext is invalid and $\mathcal{B}$ outputs $\perp$. Otherwise, it decrypts the ciphertext with the corresponding secret keys to get M.

Challenge. $\mathcal{A}$ submits two messages $M_0, M_1 \in \mathbb{G}_T$ with equal length to $\mathcal{B}$. $\mathcal{B}$ flips a random coin $b \in \{0,1\}$ and calculates $C'^*_0 = M_b \cdot T$, where T the challenge term might be $e(g,g)^z = e(g,g)^{sa^{q+2}}$ or a random element $R \xleftarrow{R} \mathbb{G}_T$. $\mathcal{B}$ sets $\overrightarrow{v} = (sa^{q+2}, 0, \ldots, 0)^\top \in \mathbb{Z}_p^n$ and $\overrightarrow{w} = (0, sa^{q+1}, \ldots, sa^{q-n'+3}, 0, \ldots, 0)^\top \in \mathbb{Z}_p^n$.

- For a row $x^* \in [\ell]$ that $T(\delta(x^*)) \in \mathcal{C}_\theta$, we have that $\lambda_{x^*} = 0, \omega_{x^*} = 0$ because $A'_{x^*,i} = 0$ for $i \in [n']$. $\mathcal{B}$ randomly picks $t_{x^*} \xleftarrow{R} \mathbb{Z}_p$ and computes

$$C_{1,x^*} = e(g,g)^{\lambda_{x^*}} e(g,g)^{\alpha_{\rho(x^*)} t_{x^*}} = (e(g,g)^{\alpha_{\rho(x^*)}})^{t_{x^*}},$$

$$C_{2,x^*} = g^{-t_{x^*}}, C_{3,x^*} = g^{\beta_{\rho(x^*)} t_{x^*}} g^{\omega_{x^*}} = (g^{\beta_{\rho(x^*)}})^{t_{x^*}}, C_{4,x^*} = F(\delta(x^*))^{t_{x^*}}$$

- For a row $x^* \in [\ell]$ that $T(\delta(x^*)) \notin \mathcal{C}_\theta$, we have that $\lambda_{x^*} = sa^{q+2} \cdot A'_{x^*,1}, \omega_{x^*} = \sum_{j=2}^{n'} sa^{q+3-j} \cdot A'_{x^*,j}$. $\mathcal{B}$ sets $t_{x^*} = -s/b_{x^*}, t_0 = -s/b_{\ell+1}$ and computes

$$C_{1,x^*} = e(g,g)^{\lambda_{x^*}} e(g,g)^{\alpha_{\rho(x^*)} t_{x^*}} = e(g,g)^{sa^{q+2} A'_{x^*,1} - \sum_{x \in X \cup \{\ell+1\}} sb_x a^{q+2} A'_{x^*,1}/b_{x^*}}$$

$$= \prod_{x \in X \cup \{\ell+1\} \setminus \{x^*\}} e(g, g^{sb_x a^{q+2}/b_{x^*}})^{-A'_{x^*,1}}$$

$$C_{2,x^*} = g^{-t_{x^*}} = g^{s/b_{x^*}}$$

$$C_{3,x^*} = g^{\beta_{\rho(x^*)} t_{x^*}} g^{\omega_{x^*}} = \prod_{x \in X \cup \{\ell+1\} \setminus \{x^*\}} \prod_{j=2}^{n'} (g^{sb_x a^{q+3-j}/b_{x^*}})^{-A'_{x^*,j}}$$

$$C_{4,x^*} = F(\delta(x^*))^{t_{x^*}} = \prod_{x \in X'' \cup \{\ell+1\}} \prod_{j \in [n']} (g^{sb_x a^{q+2-j}/b_{x^*}})^{-A'_{x^*,j}}$$

$$C_{1,0^*} = Te(g,g)^{\alpha_0 t_0}, C_{2,0^*} = g^{-t_0}, C_{3,0^*} = g^{\beta_0 t_0 + \sum_{x^* \in [\ell]} \omega_{x^*}}, C_{4,0^*} = F(V^*)^{t_0}$$

To re-randomize the ciphertext due to the distribution of t_{x^*}, $\mathcal{B}$ randomly picks $z', t'_{x^*}, t'_0 \xleftarrow{R} \mathbb{Z}_p$ and random vectors $\overrightarrow{v'}, \overrightarrow{w'}$ with the first elements z' and 0. Then it computes the re-randomized ciphertext C^*

$$(C'^*_0, \{C^*_{1,x^*}, C^*_{2,x^*}, C^*_{3,x^*}, C^*_{4,x^*}\}_{x^* \in [0,\ell]}) = (C'^*_0 e(g,g)^{z'}, C_{1,0^*} e(g,g)^{z' + \alpha_0 t'_0},$$

$$C_{2,0^*} g^{-t'_0}, C_{3,0^*} g^{\beta_0 t'_0} g^{\sum_{x^* \in [\ell]} \overrightarrow{A}_{x^*} \bullet \overrightarrow{w'}}, C_{4,0^*} F(V^*)^{t'_0}, \{C_{1,x^*} e(g,g)^{\overrightarrow{A}_{x^*} \bullet \overrightarrow{v'} + \alpha_{\rho(x^*)} t'_{x^*}},$$

$$C_{2,x^*} g^{-t'_{x^*}}, C_{3,x^*} g^{\beta_{\rho(x^*)} t'_{x^*}} g^{\overrightarrow{A}_{x^*} \bullet \overrightarrow{w'}}, C_{4,x^*} F(\delta(x^*))^{t'_{x^*}}\}_{x^* \in [\ell]})$$

In order to keep V^* unchanged, $\mathcal{B}$ runs $r_b^* \leftarrow UForge_{ch}(SK_{ch}, C_0^*, r_{ch}^*, PK_{ch} \| C^* \setminus C^*_{4,0^*})$ such that $V^* = H_{ch}(PK_{ch}, PK_{ch} \| C^* \setminus C^*_{4,0^*}, r_b^*)$. Then $\mathcal{B}$ re-encrypts $(C^*, r_b^*, (A^*, \delta^*))$ with the latest re-encryption keys and returns the re-encrypted ciphertext to $\mathcal{A}$.

Phase 2. Algorithm $\mathcal{B}$ processes the same as in **Phase 1**.

Guess. Finally, $\mathcal{A}$ outputs a guess $b' \in \{0,1\}$. If $T = e(g,g)^z = e(g,g)^{sa^{q+2}}$, the ciphertext is well encrypted such that $\mathcal{B}$ plays the proper security game with $\mathcal{A}$, and the advantage $\mathcal{A}$ wins in this game is ϵ. Otherwise, if $T \xleftarrow{R} \mathbb{G}_T$, the ciphertext is a random element in $\mathbb{G}_T$, and the advantage that $\mathcal{A}$ wins in this game is 0. Therefore, if $\mathcal{A}$ has advantage $Adv_{\mathcal{A}}(\lambda) \geq \epsilon$ in breaking this concrete scheme, $\mathcal{B}$ would break the (q+1)-DPBDHE2 problem on $\mathcal{G}$ with advantage $Adv_{\mathcal{B}}(\lambda) \geq \epsilon$. This completes the proof.   □

6   Conclusion

We formalized a revocable multi-authority large-universe CP-ABE system to meet the function requirement and a security notion IND-sAA-sCCA2 to meet the security requirement of cloud storage service. Then we constructed a concrete scheme shown to be IND-sAA-sCCA2 secure under (q+1)-DPBDHE2 assumption. For this scheme constructed on prime-order groups, it has remarkable efficiency improvement compared with others on composite-order groups, and it can be applied in practical cloud storage system to provide efficient, flexible and fine-grained access control for file sharing.

Acknowledgment. This paper is supported by the Natural Science Foundation of China through projects 61672083, 61370190, 61772538, 61532021, 61472429, 61402029, and 61702028, by the National Cryptography Development Fund through project MMJJ20170106, by the planning fund project of ministry of education through project 12YJAZH136 and by the Beijing Natural Science Foundation through project 4132056.

References

1. Huang, X., Liu, J.K., Tang, S., Xiang, Y., Liang, K., Xu, L., Zhou, J.: Cost-effective authentic and anonymous data sharing with forward security. IEEE Trans. Comput. **64**(4), 971–983 (2015)
2. Sahai, A., Waters, B.: Fuzzy identity-based encryption. In: Cramer, R. (ed.) EURO-CRYPT 2005. LNCS, vol. 3494, pp. 457–473. Springer, Heidelberg (2005). doi:10.1007/11426639_27
3. Yao, X., Han, X., Du, X., Zhou, X.: A lightweight multicast authentication mechanism for small scale iot applications. IEEE Sens. J. **13**(10), 3693–3701 (2013)
4. Chase, M.: Multi-authority attribute based encryption. In: Vadhan, S.P. (ed.) TCC 2007. LNCS, vol. 4392, pp. 515–534. Springer, Heidelberg (2007). doi:10.1007/978-3-540-70936-7_28
5. Xiao, Y., Chen, H., Du, X., Guizani, M.: Stream-based cipher feedback mode in wireless error channel. IEEE Trans. Wirel. Commun. **8**(2), 622–626 (2009)
6. Rouselakis, Y., Waters, B.: Efficient statically-secure large-universe multi-authority attribute-based encryption. In: Böhme, R., Okamoto, T. (eds.) FC 2015. LNCS, vol. 8975, pp. 315–332. Springer, Heidelberg (2015). doi:10.1007/978-3-662-47854-7_19
7. Du, X., Xiao, Y., Guizani, M., Chen, H.: An effective key management scheme for heterogeneous sensor networks. Ad Hoc Netw. **5**(1), 24–34 (2007)
8. Chen, X., Li, J., Huang, X., Ma, J., Lou, W.: New publicly verifiable databases with efficient updates. IEEE Trans. Dependable Sec. Comput. **12**(5), 546–556 (2015)
9. Goyal, V., Pandey, O., Sahai, A., Waters, B.: Attribute-based encryption for fine-grained access control of encrypted data. In: CCS 2006, Alexandria, VA, USA, October 30–November 3, pp. 89–98 (2006)

10. Bethencourt, J., Sahai, A., Waters, B.: Ciphertext-policy attribute-based encryption. In: S&P 2007, Oakland, California, USA, 20–23 May 2007, pp. 321–334 (2007)
11. Cheung, L., Newport, C.C.: Provably secure ciphertext policy ABE. In: CCS 2007, Alexandria, Virginia, USA, 28–31 October 2007, pp. 456–465 (2007)
12. Ostrovsky, R., Sahai, A., Waters, B.: Attribute-based encryption with non-monotonic access structures. In: CCS 2007, Alexandria, Virginia, USA, 28–31 October 2007, pp. 195–203 (2007)
13. Liang, X., Cao, Z., Lin, H., Xing, D.: Provably secure and efficient bounded ciphertext policy attribute based encryption. In: ASIACCS 2009, Sydney, Australia, 10–12 March 2009, pp. 343–352 (2009)
14. Waters, B.: Ciphertext-policy attribute-based encryption: an expressive, efficient, and provably secure realization. In: Proceedings of PKC 2011, Taormina, Italy, 6–9 March 2011, pp. 53–70 (2011)
15. Okamoto, T., Takashima, K.: Fully secure functional encryption with general relations from the decisional linear assumption. In: Rabin, T. (ed.) CRYPTO 2010. LNCS, vol. 6223, pp. 191–208. Springer, Heidelberg (2010). doi:10.1007/978-3-642-14623-7_11
16. Lewko, A., Okamoto, T., Sahai, A., Takashima, K., Waters, B.: Fully secure functional encryption: attribute-based encryption and (hierarchical) inner product encryption. In: Gilbert, H. (ed.) EUROCRYPT 2010. LNCS, vol. 6110, pp. 62–91. Springer, Heidelberg (2010). doi:10.1007/978-3-642-13190-5_4
17. Chase, M., Chow, S.S.M.: Improving privacy and security in multi-authority attribute-based encryption. In: CCS 2009, Chicago, Illinois, USA, 9–13 November 2009, pp. 121–130 (2009)
18. Lin, H., Cao, Z., Liang, X., Shao, J.: Secure threshold multi authority attribute based encryption without a central authority. In: Chowdhury, D.R., Rijmen, V., Das, A. (eds.) INDOCRYPT 2008. LNCS, vol. 5365, pp. 426–436. Springer, Heidelberg (2008). doi:10.1007/978-3-540-89754-5_33
19. Müller, S., Katzenbeisser, S., Eckert, C.: Distributed attribute-based encryption. In: Lee, P.J., Cheon, J.H. (eds.) ICISC 2008. LNCS, vol. 5461, pp. 20–36. Springer, Heidelberg (2009). doi:10.1007/978-3-642-00730-9_2
20. Li, D., Liu, J., Liu, W.: Secure and anonymous data transmission system for cluster organised space information network. In: SmartCloud 2016, New York, NY, USA, 18–20 November 2016, pp. 228–233 (2016)
21. Lewko, A., Waters, B.: Decentralizing attribute-based encryption. In: Paterson, K.G. (ed.) EUROCRYPT 2011. LNCS, vol. 6632, pp. 568–588. Springer, Heidelberg (2011). doi:10.1007/978-3-642-20465-4_31
22. Liu, Z., Cao, Z., Huang, Q., Wong, D.S., Yuen, T.H.: Fully secure multi-authority ciphertext-policy attribute-based encryption without random oracles. In: Atluri, V., Diaz, C. (eds.) ESORICS 2011. LNCS, vol. 6879, pp. 278–297. Springer, Heidelberg (2011). doi:10.1007/978-3-642-23822-2_16
23. Lewko, A., Waters, B.: Unbounded HIBE and attribute-based encryption. In: Paterson, K.G. (ed.) EUROCRYPT 2011. LNCS, vol. 6632, pp. 547–567. Springer, Heidelberg (2011). doi:10.1007/978-3-642-20465-4_30
24. Lewko, A.: Tools for simulating features of composite order bilinear groups in the prime order setting. In: Pointcheval, D., Johansson, T. (eds.) EUROCRYPT 2012. LNCS, vol. 7237, pp. 318–335. Springer, Heidelberg (2012). doi:10.1007/978-3-642-29011-4_20
25. Rouselakis, Y., Waters, B.: Practical constructions and new proof methods for large universe attribute-based encryption. In: CCS 2013, Berlin, Germany, 4–8 November 2013, pp. 463–474 (2013)

26. Attrapadung, N., Imai, H.: Attribute-based encryption supporting direct/indirect revocation modes. In: Proceedings of IMA 2009, Cirencester, UK, 15–17 December 2009, pp. 278–300 (2009)

27. Beimel, A.: Secure schemes for secret sharing and key distribution. Ph.D. thesis, Department of Computer Science, Technion (1996)

28. Sahai, A., Seyalioglu, H., Waters, B.: Dynamic credentials and ciphertext delegation for attribute-based encryption. In: Safavi-Naini, R., Canetti, R. (eds.) CRYPTO 2012. LNCS, vol. 7417, pp. 199–217. Springer, Heidelberg (2012). doi:10.1007/978-3-642-32009-5_13

29. Tsuchida, H., Nishide, T., Okamoto, E., Kim, K.: Revocable decentralized multi-authority functional encryption. In: Dunkelman, O., Sanadhya, S.K. (eds.) INDOCRYPT 2016. LNCS, vol. 10095, pp. 248–265. Springer, Cham (2016). doi:10.1007/978-3-319-49890-4_14

30. Wu, Q., Qin, B., Zhang, L., Domingo-Ferrer, J., Farràs, O., Manjón, J.A.: Contributory broadcast encryption with efficient encryption and short ciphertexts. IEEE Trans. Comput. **65**(2), 466–479 (2016)

31. Canetti, R., Halevi, S., Katz, J.: Chosen-ciphertext security from identity-based encryption. In: Cachin, C., Camenisch, J.L. (eds.) EUROCRYPT 2004. LNCS, vol. 3027, pp. 207–222. Springer, Heidelberg (2004). doi:10.1007/978-3-540-24676-3_13

32. Yamada, S., Attrapadung, N., Hanaoka, G., Kunihiro, N.: Generic constructions for chosen-ciphertext secure attribute based encryption. In: Catalano, D., Fazio, N., Gennaro, R., Nicolosi, A. (eds.) PKC 2011. LNCS, vol. 6571, pp. 71–89. Springer, Heidelberg (2011). doi:10.1007/978-3-642-19379-8_5

33. Chen, C., Zhang, Z., Feng, D.: Efficient ciphertext policy attribute-based encryption with constant-size ciphertext and constant computation-cost. In: Boyen, X., Chen, X. (eds.) ProvSec 2011. LNCS, vol. 6980, pp. 84–101. Springer, Heidelberg (2011). doi:10.1007/978-3-642-24316-5_8

34. Ge, A., Zhang, R., Chen, C., Ma, C., Zhang, Z.: Threshold ciphertext policy attribute-based encryption with constant size ciphertexts. In: Susilo, W., Mu, Y., Seberry, J. (eds.) ACISP 2012. LNCS, vol. 7372, pp. 336–349. Springer, Heidelberg (2012). doi:10.1007/978-3-642-31448-3_25

35. Liu, W., Liu, J., Wu, Q., Qin, B., Zhou, Y.: Practical direct chosen ciphertext secure key-policy attribute-based encryption with public ciphertext test. In: Kutyłowski, M., Vaidya, J. (eds.) ESORICS 2014. LNCS, vol. 8713, pp. 91–108. Springer, Cham (2014). doi:10.1007/978-3-319-11212-1_6

CloudDPI: Cloud-Based Privacy-Preserving Deep Packet Inspection via Reversible Sketch

Jie Li[1], Jinshu Su[1,2(✉)], Xiaofeng Wang[1], Hao Sun[1], and Shuhui Chen[1]

[1] School of Computer, National University of Defense Technology,
Changsha, Hunan 410073, China
{lijie13d,sjs,xf_wang,haosun4257,shchen}@nudt.edu.cn
[2] National Key Laboratory for Parallel and Distributed Processing,
National University of Defense Technology, Changsha, Hunan 410073, China

Abstract. Hardware-based middleboxes are ubiquitous in computer networks, which usually incur high deployment and management expenses. A recently arsing trend aims to address those problems by outsourcing the functions of traditional hardware-based middleboxes to high volume servers in a cloud. This technology is promising but still faces a few challenges. First, the widely adopted data encryption techniques contradict with payload inspection needs of some middleboxes such as DPI and IDS devices. Second, the inspection rules of middleboxes may be commercial properties, thus the middlebox providers want to keep their rules confidential under third-party cloud environments, and this creates hindrances for the cloud to perform outsourced middlebox functions. Third, performance of the outsourced middlebox is an inevitable issue that needs deliberate consideration. In this paper, we propose a cloud-based DPI middlebox implementation which performs payload inspection over encrypted traffic while preserving the privacy of both communication data and inspection rules. Our design employs a modified reversible sketch structure which is used for efficient error-free membership testing, and we utilize unkeyed one-way hash functions instead of complex cryptographic protocols to achieve the privacy preservation requirements. CloudDPI supports a wide range of real-world inspection rules, we conduct evaluations on ClamAV rule set and the experiment results demonstrate the effectiveness of our proposal.

Keywords: Network function virtualization · DPI outsourcing · Privacy preservation

1 Introduction

Network contains large numbers of various hardware appliances or middleboxes and it is increasingly difficult to design, integrate and operate the complex hardware-based appliances to launch a new network service [1]. Moreover, hardware-based middleboxes have short lifecycles, which requires the procure-design-integrate-deploy cycle to be repeated with little or no benefits [1]. In 2011,

ⓒ Springer International Publishing AG 2017
S. Wen et al. (Eds.): CSS 2017, LNCS 10581, pp. 119–134, 2017.
https://doi.org/10.1007/978-3-319-69471-9_9

Justine Sherry et al. [2] surveyed 57 network administrators regarding middleboxes and came to the conclusion that middlebox deployments are large and incur high capital expenses, complex management requirements, and they often lack scalability and fault-tolerance.

A recent trend of NFV aims to address the above mentioned problems by outsourcing the middlebox functions as virtualized services residing in a cloud, shifting the heavy middlebox management burdens from local network managers to the cloud service providers, which lowers the deployment and management expenses for enterprises and provides the middlebox as a more flexible and fault-tolerant service. However, there are still a few challenges which need profound solutions.

1. Various security oriented protocols such as HTTPS and SSL are adopted by network users to protect their data privacy, and these encryption techniques almost completely disable functions of middleboxes like DPI and IDS devices.
2. The inspection rules of the outsourced middlebox can be enterprise properties or they may infer sensitive commercial information. Consider an exfiltration detection system customized by an enterprise, the inspection rules may contain sensitive keywords such as product names. Thus, the enterprise wants to protect the rules from leakage if the cloud providing middlebox service is not fully trusted. However, intuitively the cloud will not be able to perform middlebox functions if the rules are hidden from it.
3. Last but not least, inspection accuracy, delay and throughput are important middlebox performance criterions, performance optimization of the outsourced middlebox will always be an important problem.

Consider the following usage scenario: a trusted user Alice unfortunately became a victim of the notorious extortion virus WannaCry [3], after the tragedy she realized the importance of her computer's security and she wants all traffic that flows into her computer be checked first, but meanwhile she does not want to risk the confidentiality of her private emails or instant messages, so she would adopt SSL protocol when communicating with other hosts. Probably being an unprofessional, Alice does not want to deploy her own DPI device and bother herself with the complex configuration details. Also taking flexibility, cost efficiency, fault tolerance and scalability into account, buying DPI as a virtualized service provided by a cloud like Amazon may be her optimal choice. The inspection rules generator or middlebox provider in our usage scenario could be some professional vendors like Kaspersky Lab or McAfee, which is different from the general purposed cloud computation service provider like Amazon, the inspection rules are commercial properties so the middlebox provider wants to protect them from the semi-trusted cloud.

BlindBox [4] is the first outsourced middlebox which enables inspection over encrypted traffic. But it does not consider the privacy of the inspection rules, and it involves sophisticated cryptographic techniques including garbled circuit [5,6] and oblivious transfer [7,8], thus BlindBox incurs heavy computational burdens and is not feasible for practical use. Yuan et al. [9] address the problems with BlindBox and build an outsourced middlebox which performs inspection on encrypted data and provides protection on both packet payloads and inspection rules. However, their work focuses more on *token matching* instead of *rule matching*, if all the tokens of a packet are checked without a match, the packet is considered legitimate and allowed through, on the other hand, if a token is matched, the corresponding action is taken. In practice, however, there is a big gap between token matching and rule matching, an inspection rule usually contains multiple signature fragments of different lengths, it is infeasible for the communication parties to generate tokens of different sizes, otherwise it will incur too much computation and network overhead. Besides, the Cuckoo hash table adopted in [9] has a major drawback: insertion failures might occur after certain number of insert operations, and this will definitely affect the inspection accuracy of the outsourced middlebox. Moreover, [9] still utilizes some complex cryptographic mechanisms including broadcast encryption [10] and secret sharing [11], and as a result, the performance of the outsourced middlebox will suffer.

Our work basically shares the same goal with [9], that is to build an outsourced DPI middlebox which performs inspection over encrypted traffic while preserving the privacy of both packet payloads and the inspection rules. But our work differs from [9] in the following ways:

- We come up with a complete solution including the customized reversible sketch [12,13] data structure and a suit of algorithms on rule matching instead of single token matching.
- The reversible sketch in our system is efficient and does not have Cuckoo hash table's insertion failure problem, together with the first factor, this makes our system more accurate on packet inspection.
- Our system only utilizes a set of hash functions and does not involve any heavy-computational cryptographic techniques, deliberately designed, we make our system more efficient and still satisfy the privacy preservation requirements.
- We provide more elegant, unified and simplified ways to support rules with multiple conditions, rules with content position modifiers and field attributes, and cross-connection inspection.

2   Related Work

Shi et al. [14] present privacy-preserving outsourcing firewalls in SDN environment. They exploit CLT multilinear maps to build their system, which has security flaws [15], and what is more, they assume the cloud provider for the enterprise is its ISP, and does not consider protecting the packet payloads from the cloud. Melis et al. [16] propose two constructions on generic network functions outsourcing, the middleboxes considered in their paper include firewalls, load balancers, IDS and NAT. Their constructions are based on partial homomorphic encryption [16] and public-key encryption with keyword search [17], and it takes 250 ms and 1208 ms respectively to process 10 rules, which indicates that their system is not suitable for practical deployment.

APLOMB [2] is based on a survey of 57 enterprise networks, from the survey results the authors draw the conclusion that outsourcing middleboxes to a cloud can bring benefits including cost reduction, easy management, elasticity and fault-tolerance. APLOMB also introduces 3 approaches for traffic redirection, that is, bounce redirection, IP redirection and DNS redirection [2], these techniques can be directly adopted by us and serve as a complement to our work. However, APLOMB has to decrypt the encrypted traffic first before further processing, which is vulnerable for man-in-the-middle attacks [18].

As mentioned before, BlindBox [4] is the first work makes deep packet inspection over encrypted traffic possible. It contains three protocols of different complexity and functionality, the simplest protocol I supports single signature keyword matching and can be used in data exfiltration detection and parental filtering applications. Protocol II is based on protocol I, it supports rules which contain multiple keywords and offset information within the packet. Protocol III enables full IDS functionality, it supports rules with complex regular expressions by allowing the outsourced middlebox to decrypt the encrypted traffic if a suspicious keyword is found. While effective, this approach also sacrifices the confidentiality of packet payloads.

Embark [19] allows enterprises to outsource middleboxes to the cloud while keeping their network traffic confidential. For packet payload inspection, Embark directly adopts the schemes in BlindBox. For inspection on packet header fields such as IP addresses, Embark introduces a novel encryption scheme Prefix-Match [19], which enables the outsourced middlebox to tell if an encrypted IP address lies in an encrypted range, and at the same time, the outsourced middlebox can not learn the exact values of the IP address and the range. Our work differs from Embark in the user scenario setting and focuses only on the packet payload inspection part, while Embark provides a wider functionality, it also has the flaws of BlindBox on packet payload inspection.

3   System Architecture

Figure 1 depicts our system architecture. The system contains four entities: a trusted user (Alice) who wishes to adopt the outsourced DPI service; an untrusted user which is communicating with the trusted user; a trusted inspection rules generator who outsources DPI middlebox and a semi-trusted cloud which actually performs functions of the outsourced middlebox. During connection setup, both the trusted and untrusted users run the standard SSL protocol to establish an encrypted communication channel. Meanwhile, both of them communicate with the trusted rule generator, the latter builds up a reversible sketch for this connection, it transforms its secret inspection rules into hashed tokens by an unkeyed cryptographic one-way hash function and feeds the hashed tokens into the reversible sketch. After that, the rule generator outsources the DPI middlebox to the cloud by transmitting the reversible sketch just built, and it sends both the trusted and untrusted users the one-way hash function it used during tokenizing the inspection rules.

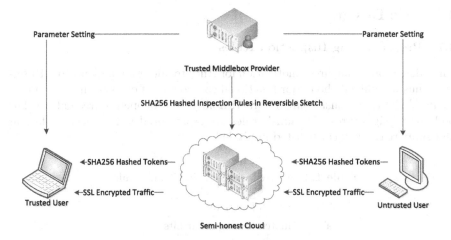

Fig. 1. System architecture

In our work, we properly modify reversible sketch into an efficient error-free data structure for membership testing of a given set, and use it for packet payload inspection instead of change detection. The reversible sketch used in our work contains H hash tables of size M, and each hash table has K randomly chosen 2-universal hash functions. The reversible sketch is stored as a 2-dimensional matrix of size $H \times M$, and each cell is associated with a sentinel bit and a list of buckets to store the hashed tokens of the inspection rules. Our modified reversible sketch can be regarded as a combination form of Bloom Filters and traditional hash tables, when testing membership of a certain message, H Bloom Filters are first consulted, then one of the bucket lists is traversed to confirm the message's existence if necessary. Our modified reversible sketch is fast, and brings no false positives or false negatives.

During communication, the trusted and untrusted users will communicate normally as SSL protocol specified with three alterations. Fist, the untrusted user is required to process his packet payloads into fixed-length tokens and hash them using the one-way hash function received from the rules generator during connection setup. Second, the untrusted user sends both SSL encrypted packets and the hashed tokens to the outsourced middlebox instead of directly to the trusted user. The outsourced middlebox performs inspection on the hashed tokens and relays the traffic if none of the rules is matched. Third, when received SSL encrypted traffic and the hashed tokens, the trusted user can verify the integrity of the untrusted user by regenerating the hashed tokens and comparing them with the ones it received, regeneration of the hashed tokens can be easily done since the trusted user is able to decrypt SSL encrypted packets and he also owns the one-way hash function provided by the rules generator. Note that we still assume the cloud to be semi-trusted, verification of the outsourced middlebox service will be covered in our near future work.

4   Basic Design

4.1   Preprocessing Inspection Rules

Virus detection is the direct motivation for Alice to adopt an outsourced DPI service, thus we make it the major functional component of our system. We employ ClamAV [20] rules considering its practicability and its open source nature. The body-based signatures of ClamAV rules are represented in hexadecimal format and support the wildcards listed in Table 1.

Table 1. Supported wildcards in ClamAV rules

??	match any byte
a?	match the high four bits
?a	match the low four bits
*	match any number of bytes
{n}	match n bytes
{-n}	match n or less bytes
{n-}	match n or more bytes
{m-n}	match between m and n bytes

Take the rule "Win.Worm.Mimail-8" in Fig. 2 for example, this rule is matched if byte sequence "9090909089c890909090f7f7909090" is found first, then after arbitrary length of content byte sequence "9090" is matched, and after another two bytes "90" is found, etc.

Win.Worm.Mimail-8:9090909089c890909090f7f7909090*9090????
90??9090*909190909090905890*9031309090909001f890909090e2
??90909090*67e9ed60ffff

Fig. 2. Rule Win.Worm.Mimail-8

ClamAV's body-based rule set contains approximately 100K rules, but they are not directly usable to our system due to the complex syntax. We make the rules compatible to CloudDPI by taking a few transformations. Again take the previous mentioned rule for example, this rule can be partitioned into eight *signature fragments* by the wildcards *, ? and {}, and we define *distance relationship* between two adjacent signature fragments according to the grammar of ClamAV rules. The five types of distance relationships we defined are listed in Table 2.

Partition of a rule and distance relationship assignment of the signature fragments should be straightforward. The first signature fragment is always assigned

Table 2. Distance relationship between signature fragments

arbitrary	any number of bytes apart
exact(n)	exactly n bytes apart
min(n)	at least n bytes apart
max(n)	at most n bytes apart
range(m, n)	between m and n bytes apart

arbitrary. For the rest, we assign distance relationship according to the wildcard between the current signature fragment and its previous one. Suppose the number of occurrences of "??" is n, we set the distance relationship to *exact(n)*. We set distance relationship to *min(n)* for {n-}, set *max(n)* for {-n} and set *range(m, n)* for {m-n} respectively. We ignore wildcards "a?" and "?a" since their occurrences are not encountered during system implementation. The result of partition and distance relationship assignment of rule "Win.Worm.Mimail-8" is shown in Table 3.

Table 3. Rule "Win.Worm.Mimail-8" after partition

Signature fragment	Distance relationship
9090909089c890909090f7f790909090	*arbitrary*
9090	*arbitrary*
90	*exact(2)*
9090	*exact(1)*
909190909090905890	*arbitrary*
9031309090909001f890909090e2	*arbitrary*
90909090	*exact(1)*
67e9ed60ffff	*arbitrary*

During connection set up, the signature fragments are again segmented into fixed-length tokens, and the tokens are hashed and fed into the reversible sketch. If the length of a signature fragment is less than that of a token, we need to delete this signature fragment from the rule and recalculate distance relationship between its predecessor and successor. We denote the length of a signature fragment sf by $len(sf)$, the distance relationship between two signature fragments sf_1 and sf_2 by $DR(sf_1, sf_2)$, and the signature fragment deleted by $deleted\_sf$, the signature fragment before it by $prev\_sf$, and the signature fragment after it by $next\_sf$. The new distance relationship between the deleted signature's previous and next signature fragments $DR(prev\_sf, next\_sf)$ is determined by three factors, namely $len(deleted\_sf)$, $DR(prev\_sf, deleted\_sf)$ and $DR(deleted\_sf, next\_sf)$. Deletion of short signature fragments and recalculation of distance relationships are performed in a linear fashion: we scan the inspection rule from the first signature fragment to the last one, if a signature fragment is too short, it is deleted and distance relationship between its previous and next signature fragments is recalculated.

4.2   Building Reversible Sketch

Now we are ready to build the reversible sketch for the outsourced middlebox. For each rule r in the rule set S, we use a sliding window of size w to segment each signature fragment sf of r into a set of tokens with length w bytes, namely, $sf \rightarrow \{t_1, t_2, ...t_{l-w+1}\}$, where l is the length of sf. Then for each generated token t, we hash it and store the hashed token ht in one of the $H \times K$ cells of the reversible sketch, the hashed token is associated with the signature fragment sf it belongs to. Since different signature fragments may generate same tokens, a certain hashed token ht may belong to multiple signature fragments, thus we associate each hashed token bucket with a list sf_ptr_list of pointers which point to the corresponding signature fragments. To maintain the correlation between signature fragments and rules, we store in each signature fragment a pointer $rule\_ptr$ pointing to the related rule, a pointer $prev\_sf$ pointing to the previous signature fragment and another pointer $next\_sf$ pointing to the next signature fragment, in each rule we store a pointer $first\_sf$ which points to its first signature fragment. To summarize, the structure of our reversible sketch is shown in Fig. 3.

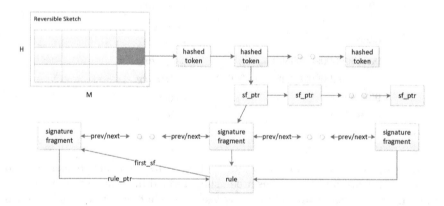

Fig. 3. Reversible sketch

We denote the one-way hash function used to hash the generated tokens as h, the $H \times K$ hash functions of reversible sketch as h_{ij}, where $i \in [H]$ and $j \in [K]$, and the two hash functions which determine the position of the cell storing a hashed token as h_{row} and h_{column}. The algorithm for inserting a signature fragment into the reversible sketch is represented in Algorithm 1. We associate with each signature fragment a list ht_ptr_list of pointers which point to the generated hashed tokens from it. The algorithm begins by segmenting the signature fragment into a set of tokens, and initializing ht_ptr_list to be empty. When inserting each hashed token of a signature fragment, we first check if the hashed token is already in the reversible sketch. If so, we again check if the signature fragment is already in the hashed token's sf_ptr_list because a token may appear multiple times in a signature fragment, if the signature fragment is not found, a new sf_ptr pointing to it is generated and added to the sf_ptr_list. If the hashed token is not found in the reversible sketch, we first set the sentinel bits using the $H \times K$ hash functions, then the hashed token is inserted into the cell chosen by the two hash functions h_{row} and h_{column}, we associate a sf_ptr_list to the hashed token and add a new sf_ptr pointing to the signature fragment to the list. For every generated hashed token, we add a ht_ptr node which points to the hashed token in the corresponding signature fragment's ht_ptr_list.

Algorithm 1. Signature Fragment Insertion

Input: signature fragment to be inserted

  generate tokens set S_t for sf

  initialize ht_ptr_list of sf to be empty

  for each token $t \in S_t$ **do**

    $ht = h(t)$

    lookup ht in reversible sketch

    if found ht **then**

      lookup sf in the sf_ptr_list

      if not found sf **then**

        add a sf_ptr which points to sf in sf_ptr_list

      end if

    else

      for each $i \in [H]$ **do**

        for each $j \in [K]$ **do**

          $RS[i][h_{ij}(ht)].sentinel = 1$

        end for

      end for

      insert ht into cell $RS[h_{row}(ht)][h_{column}(ht)]$

      associate an empty sf_ptr_list to ht

      add a sf_ptr which points to sf in sf_ptr_list

    end if

    add a ht_ptr which points to ht in ht_ptr_list of sf

  end for

Lookup for a hashed token in the reversible sketch is done by first checking the $H \times K$ sentinel bits, if one of the sentinel bits is not set, we know that the hashed token is not in the reversible sketch. Only if all the sentinel bits are set, we traverse the list of buckets of cell $RS[h_{row}(ht)][h_{column}(ht)]$ to confirm the hashed token's existence, this additional check eliminates the false positives brought by Bloom Filter and makes the lookup algorithm fast and accurate.

4.3 Inspection on Hashed Tokens

Taking both inspection delay and throughput into consideration, we developed batch inspection algorithm on the untrusted user's hashed tokens. The function is called when every *batch_size* tokens are received, as shown in Algorithm 2. The algorithm can be divided into three phases. The first phase begins by initializing an empty set S_{sf} of signature fragments and an empty set S_r of rules. Then we lookup each received hashed token *uht* in the reversible sketch to see if it is suspicious, we associate with each signature fragment a list *uht_list* of matched hashed tokens, and *uht* is added to this list of every signature fragment found in *sf_ptr_list* if *uht* is in the reversible sketch, and the corresponding signature fragments are added to set S_{sf} for further checking. The second phase checks every signature fragment *sf* in S_{sf} to see if it is matched, and the corresponding rule of a matched signature fragment is added to set S_r for further processing. The last phase checks every rule in set S_r and the corresponding actions of the matched rules are taken.

Algorithm 2. Batch Inspection

Input: a set S_{uht} of received hashed tokens from untrusted user
    initialize an empty set S_{sf} of signature fragments
    initialize an empty set S_r of matched rules
    for each *uht* $\in S_{uht}$ **do**
      lookup *uht* in reversible sketch
      if found *uht* **then**
        for each signature fragment *sf* in *sf_ptr_list* **do**
          add *uht* to *uht_list* of *sf*
          add *sf* to S_{sf}
        end for
      end if
    end for
    for each *sf* $\in S_{sf}$ **do**
      check if *sf* is matched
      if *sf* is matched **then**
        add the corresponding rule *r* to S_r
      end if
    end for
    for each *r* $\in S_r$ **do**
      check if *r* is matched
      if *r* is matched **then**
        take the corresponding actions of *r*
      end if
    end for

In our system, the untrusted user actually sends tuples of form $(offset, ht)$ to the cloud for inspection, $offset$ is the offset of the corresponding token in the payload data. Adding this field enables the cloud to accurately check if a signature fragment is matched and perform inspection on rules with content position modifiers (Sect. 5). To check if a signature fragment is matched, we first check if the $offset$ values of the received tokens in uht_list are consecutive, then we compare the received tokens with the tokens generated from inspection rules in ht_ptr_list.

Verifying if a rule is matched is done by first checking if all its signature fragments are matched, then if the distance relationship between every two adjacent signature fragments are satisfied.

5   Optimizations

5.1   Handling Rules with Position and Field Modifiers

In Snort rules, the 'content' keyword specifies a specific content pattern to search in the packet payload. More complex and accurate rules can be generated by attaching position modifiers to the content patterns. To support rules with position modifiers, we make the untrusted user send offset of the corresponding data segment together with the hashed token to the cloud. For modifiers $depth$ and $offset$, we modify the distance relationship of the first signature fragment in CloudDPI compatible rules from $arbitrary$ to $range(offset, depth - len(sf))$, and check if the first hashed token's offset falls into this range. Modifier $distance$ is directly transformed into distance relationship $exact(distance)$ for a signature fragment, and modifier $within$ is transformed to $range(0, within)$. The 'content' keyword in Snort rules can also be modified by packet field modifiers such as 'http_client_body' and 'http_header', for these kind of rules, we transform them into rules with $depth$ and $offset$ modifiers since these fields of a packet are usually in a relatively fixed position. And we note that rules with multiple conditions are naturally supported by CloudDPI.

5.2   Hiding Equality of Hashed Tokens

In our current design, the same hashed tokens will be generated for multiple appearances of the same data segment because the one-way hash function is deterministic. To avoid this problem, we took a similar course as [9] by trading space for efficiency. But we note that in [9] their Cuckoo hash table will grow much larger and two new problems will be caused. First, more insertion failures will happen as more tokens are inserted into the Cuckoo hash table. And second, it will take more time to lookup a token in the hash table because of its growth. Suppose the upper bound for the number of appearances of a certain data segment is C, in our approach the middlebox provider will build C reversible sketches instead of a single very large one during connection setup. For each token t generated by the sliding window, we associate it with a counter ctr to count the number of its appearances, and insert $h(t||ctr)$ into the ctr^{th} reversible sketch. During communication, we make the untrusted user send tuples of form $(offset, ctr, h(t||ctr))$ to the cloud for inspection, then cloud will lookup the ctr^{th} reversible sketch for this received hashed token and the time complexity will remain unchanged. Our approach naturally avoids the first problem caused by [9] since our reversible sketch structure does not introduce insertion failures.

5.3   Handling Cross-Connection Inspection

As stated in [9], cross-connection inspection is useful in detecting attacks such as brute-force logins. We also take the rule in Fig. 4 as an example:

> Snort rule #1633: alert tcp $EXTERNEL NET$ any → $HOME NET$
> 110 (flow: to server, established; content:"USER"; count 30, seconds 30;)

Fig. 4. Snort rule #1633

The rule triggers an alert when the keyword "USER" appears 30 times in 30 seconds across different established TCP connections. In [9], cross-connection is supported by introducing a universal message authentication code for all connections, which contradicts to the principle of hiding equality of tokens. The problem is solved in a much simpler and more elegant way by CloudDPI, we attach an additional pointer to the above rule in each connection's reversible sketch, these pointers point to a global structure which contains a counter counting the number of occurrences of keyword "USER" in different connections, and a down counting timer started at the first occurrence of the keyword. Whenever keyword "USER" appears in a connection, the counter in the global structure is increased, and if the counter reaches 30 before the timer timeouts, an alert is triggered. Our approach needs little modification to the existing design, it supports cross-connection inspection effectively and still hides equality of the hashed tokens.

6   Security Discussions

A hash function is usually used to transform a message M of message space $[2^m]$ into another element e of message space $[2^n]$ where $m > n$, and collisions will happen if enough number of messages are hashed. In CloudDPI, we use the one-way hash function *reversely*: the tokens of a signature fragment are hashed into a larger message space, namely, $m < n$. We get two benefits from this design, first, suppose the hash function maps each token to space $[2^n]$ with an equal possibility, and the number of tokens generated from the rule set is N, then the possibility of no collisions after hashing of N tokens will be $\prod_{i=1}^{N-1}(1 - i/2^n)$. If the hash space is large enough and the hash function we adopted is good enough, no collision is possible.

And second, our simple design utilizes the preimage resistance property of the unkeyed cryptographic one-way hash function to achieve the privacy preservation requirements of CloudDPI. When the rules of the middlebox provider and the data of the untrusted user are transformed into hashed tokens, it is computationally infeasible for the cloud to recover the inspection rules or communication data from the hashed tokens even the cloud has knowledge about the one-way hash function. Our exquisite design eliminates need of complex cryptographic mechanisms, which makes CloudDPI more computationally efficient and easier for system implementation.

7   Experimental Evaluation

Experiment setup: We implemented a prototype of CloudDPI with 3K lines of C code. For evaluation, we adopted ClamAV's signature based rule set, which contains approximately 100K rules for malware detection. We captured traffic from our campus network and size of our data set is about 2.3 GB. We deploy the outsourced middlebox on a server with Intel Xeon CPU(8 cores, 2.53 GHz), 32 GB memory and CentOS 5.6 installed. The client is deployed on a desktop PC with Core i3 CPU(3.4 GHz), 4 GB memory and Ubuntu 15.10 operating system.

Supported rules: ClamAV's signature based rules support specification for external detection engines, and these rules are not supported by CloudDPI for now. As shown in Table 4, there are totally 100541 rules in our adopted rule set, 276 of them specify external detection engines and are not supported by CloudDPI. When building the outsourced middlebox, 3635 rules are eliminated because their lengths are less than that of a token. Finally, 96630 rules are left and inserted into the reversible sketch. The percentage of supported ClamAV rules by CloudDPI is 96.11%, which indicates that our system is quite practical.

Table 4. Supported ClamAV rules

Total	Unsupported	Deleted	Left
100541	276	3635	96630

Middlebox build time: As show in Fig. 5, the time consumption of building the outsourced middlebox grows linearly with the number of inspection rules used, which illustrates the scalability of our proposal. When building middlebox with the whole rule set, it takes about 4 min, this is unsatisfying and we plan to optimize in the future. But we also note that the problem can be solved by pre-building a pool of middleboxes for unestablished connections and cache them in the cloud, and when a connection is setting up, the middlebox provider simply needs to assign a pre-built middlebox for this connection and notify the cloud of that information.

Middlebox transmission: In this subsection we evaluate the network consumption of transmitting the built middlebox. As show in Fig. 6, the size (also the network transmission consumption) of the built middlebox also grows linearly with the number of rules used, which again demonstrates CloudDPI's scalability.

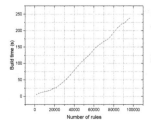 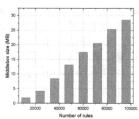 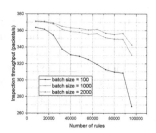

Fig. 5. Middlebox build time

Fig. 6. Middlebox transmission consumption

Fig. 7. Inspection throughput (Color figure online)

When all the inspection rules are used, the size increases to 28.5 MB, which is not an issue for most computer networks.

Inspection throughput: Now we evaluate the inspection throughput of Cloud-DPI by changing the number of rules used and taking different values of $batch\_size$. As show in Fig. 7, when $batch\_size$ is fixed, throughput drops as the number of rules increases, this is expected since more rules are needed to be checked. But we note that the performance degradation is acceptable: take the blue line with $batch\_size$ set to 2000 for example, inspection throughput is 371 packets per second when processing 8000 rules, and it drops to 342 packets per second when processing 96000 rules, the number of rules is increased by 11 times while inspection throughput only declines by 8.08%.

When the number of rules is fixed, CloudDPI's inspection throughput increases as $batch\_size$ increases, this illustrates the effectiveness of Algorithm 2, which decreases the overhead of processing individual packets by handling them as a batch. Also note that inspection throughput increases dramatically when $batch\_size$ changed from 100 to 1000, and increases only a little when $batch\_size$ changes from 1000 to 2000. This is because in our data set, the average size of captured packets is approximately 800 bytes, thus 100 tokens are too few for malware detection in a packet, while 1000 tokens are quite enough.

8   Conclusion

In this paper we propose a complete solution on outsourcing a DPI middlebox which performs inspection over encrypted traffic while protecting the privacy of both payload data and inspection rules. We modify reversible sketch into an efficient error-free data structure for membership testing instead of change detection, and design a corresponding suit of algorithms for packet inspection. During connection setup, the middlebox provider utilizes an unkeyed cryptographic one-way hash function to hash its private rules into tokens and build the reversible sketch. During communication, the untrusted user is required to process his traffic into hashed tokens by the one-way hash function and the outsourced middlebox performs detection on the hashed tokens.

References

1. Network functions virtualization, an introduction, benefits, enablers, challenges and call for action. N Operators - SDN and OpenFlow SDN and OpenFlow World Congress (2012)
2. Sherry, J., Hasan, S., Scott, C., Krishnamurthy, A., Ratnasamy, S., Sekar, V.: Making middleboxes someone else's problem: network processing as a cloud service. ACM SIGCOMM Comput. Commun. Rev. **42**(4), 13–24 (2012)
3. Wikipedia: Wannacry ransomware attack — wikipedia, the free encyclopedia (2017). [Online; Accessed 19 June 2017]
4. Sherry, J., Lan, C., Popa, R.A., Ratnasamy, S.: Blindbox: deep packet inspection over encrypted traffic. ACM SIGCOMM Comput. Commun. Rev. **45**, 213–226 (2015). ACM
5. Yao, A.C.C.: How to generate and exchange secrets. In: 27th Annual Symposium on Foundations of Computer Science, pp. 162–167. IEEE (1986)
6. Lindell, Y., Pinkas, B.: A proof of security of yaos protocol for two-party computation. J. Cryptology **22**(2), 161–188 (2009)
7. Naor, M., Pinkas, B.: Oblivious transfer with adaptive queries. In: Wiener, M. (ed.) CRYPTO 1999. LNCS, vol. 1666, pp. 573–590. Springer, Heidelberg (1999). doi:10.1007/3-540-48405-1_36
8. Asharov, G., Lindell, Y., Schneider, T., Zohner, M.: More efficient oblivious transfer and extensions for faster secure computation. In: Proceedings of the 2013 ACM SIGSAC Conference on Computer & Communications Security, pp. 535–548. ACM (2013)
9. Yuan, X., Wang, X., Lin, J., Wang, C.: Privacy-preserving deep packet inspection in outsourced middleboxes. In: IEEE INFOCOM 2016-The 35th Annual IEEE International Conference on Computer Communications, pp. 1–9. IEEE (2016)
10. Fiat, A., Naor, M.: Broadcast encryption. In: Stinson, D.R. (ed.) CRYPTO 1993. LNCS, vol. 773, pp. 480–491. Springer, Heidelberg (1994). doi:10.1007/3-540-48329-2_40
11. Bruce, S.: Applied Cryptography: Protocols, Algorithms, and Source Code in C. John Wiley & Sons, Inc., New York (1996)
12. Schweller, R., Li, Z., Chen, Y., Gao, Y., Gupta, A., Zhang, Y., Dinda, P.A., Kao, M.Y., Memik, G.: Reversible sketches: enabling monitoring and analysis over high-speed data streams. IEEE/ACM Trans. Networking (ToN) **15**(5), 1059–1072 (2007)
13. Sun, H., Wang, X., Buyya, R., Su, J.: Cloudeyes: Cloud-based malware detection with reversible sketch for resource-constrained internet of things (IoT) devices. Softw. Pract. Exp. **47**, 421–441 (2016)
14. Shi, J., Zhang, Y., Zhong, S.: Privacy-preserving network functionality outsourcing (2015). arXiv preprint: arXiv:1502.00389
15. Cheon, J.H., Han, K., Lee, C., Ryu, H., Stehlé, D.: Cryptanalysis of the multilinear map over the integers. In: Oswald, E., Fischlin, M. (eds.) EUROCRYPT 2015. LNCS, vol. 9056, pp. 3–12. Springer, Heidelberg (2015). doi:10.1007/978-3-662-46800-5_1
16. Melis, L., Asghar, H.J., De Cristofaro, E., Kaafar, M.A.: Private processing of outsourced network functions: feasibility and constructions. In: Proceedings of the 2016 ACM International Workshop on Security in Software Defined Networks & Network Function Virtualization, pp. 39–44. ACM (2016)

17. Boneh, D., Di Crescenzo, G., Ostrovsky, R., Persiano, G.: Public key encryption with keyword search. In: Cachin, C., Camenisch, J.L. (eds.) EUROCRYPT 2004. LNCS, vol. 3027, pp. 506–522. Springer, Heidelberg (2004). doi:10.1007/978-3-540-24676-3_30

18. Huang, L.S., Rice, A., Ellingsen, E., Jackson, C.: Analyzing forged SSL certificates in the wild. In: 2014 IEEE symposium on Security and Privacy (SP), pp. 83–97. IEEE (2014)

19. Lan, C., Sherry, J., Popa, R.A., Ratnasamy, S., Liu, Z.: Embark: securely outsourcing middleboxes to the cloud. In: 13th USENIX Symposium on Networked Systems Design and Implementation (NSDI 2016), pp. 255–273. USENIX Association (2016)

20. Wikipedia: Clam antivirus — wikipedia, the free encyclopedia (2017). [Online; Accessed 20 June 2017]

Noisy Smoothing Image Source Identification

Yuying Liu[1], Yonggang Huang[1(✉)], Jun Zhang[2], Xu Liu[1], and Hualei Shen[3]

[1] School of Computer Science and Technology, Beijing Engineering Research Center of High Volume Language Information Processing and Cloud Computing Applications, Beijing Institute of Technology, Beijing 100081, China
liuyuying0205@163.com, yonggang.h@gmail.com, liouliooo@163.com
[2] School of Information Technology, Deakin University, Melbourne, VIC 3125, Australia
jun.zhang@deakin.edu.au
[3] College of Computer and Information Engineering, Henan Normal University, Xinxiang 453007, China
shenhualei@henannu.edu.cn

Abstract. Feature based image source identification plays an important role in the toolbox for forensics investigations on images. Conventional feature based identification schemes suffer from the problem of noise, that is, the training dataset contains noisy samples. To address this problem, we propose a new Noisy Smoothing Image Source Identification (NS-ISI) method. NS-ISI address the noise problem in two steps. In step 1, we employ a classifier ensemble approach for noise level evaluation for each training sample. The noise level indicates the probability of being noisy. In step 2, a noise sensitive sampling method is employed to sample training samples from original training set according to the noise level, producing a new training dataset. The experiments carried out on the Dresden image collection confirms the effectiveness of the proposed NS-ISI. When the noisy samples present, the identification accuracy of NS-ISI is significantly better than traditional methods.

1 Introduction

With the popularity of digital cameras and development of digital technologies, massive images are producing in everydays' life. Digital images are now being used as evidence to make decisions by many governmental, legal, scientific, and news media organizations [1]. Identifying the source camera of an image would be a fundamental requirement in those scenarios.

There are three categories of image source identification approaches: image header based, watermark based and feature based. The image header based approach relies on investigating the image source related information embedded in the image header [2], such as camera brand, model, date, and time. However, the image header is very easy to be manipulated in practice. The watermark based approach [3,4] aims to embed into the image a watermark, which carries the source related information. The feature based approach firstly extracts features on intrinsic hardware artifacts or software-related fingerprints left during the

S. Wen et al. (Eds.): CSS 2017, LNCS 10581, pp. 135–147, 2017.
https://doi.org/10.1007/978-3-319-69471-9_10

image acquisition process, and casts the identification as a classification problem [2,5–8]. Then, the statistical learning tools, such as support vector machine (SVM) [9,10], are used as classifiers for the identification task. In this paper, we focus on the feature based approach.

In the field of feature based camera model identification, researchers have been devoted to develop sophisticate features [7,11,12], or applied state-of-art statistical learning tools for the identification task [13,14]. Those studies always assumes that the training datasets are well-labelled. That is, all the samples in the training dataset are associated with the right labels of their capture devices. However, in the real world, this assumption may be not the truth, and some noisy samples may exist in the training datasets. The reason for noisy samples is as follows. It is time-consuming and expensive to collect enough training samples via taking pictures for a large number of models. Meanwhile, massive images are published on on-line sites with device information, such as Facebook[1] and Instagram[2]. Those online sites can be served as important source for collecting the training samples. While most training samples collected from on-line sites are labelled correctly, some noisy images with wrong labels present. The noisy images are introduced because of intentionally or mistakenly manipulation. Those noisy samples can severely cause negative influence on the identification performance.

In this paper, we focus on the problem of noisy samples, and a Noisy Smoothing Image Source Identification (NS-ISI) method is proposed. NS-ISI deals with noisy samples within two steps. In step 1, a classifier ensemble approach is developed for noise level evaluation. The noise level is assigned according to the number of classifiers that predict the sample as negative. In step 2, a noise sensitive sampling method is employed to sample training samples from original training set. The samples with less noise levels have more probabilities to be chosen as training samples.

The remainder of the paper is structured as follows. Some related work is briefly reviewed in Sect. 2. Section 3 presents the new noise smoothing camera model identification method. Section 4 reports the experiments and results. Finally, the paper is concluded in Sect. 5.

2   Related Work

2.1   Features for Image Source Identification

There are two main features related to camera model identification, features on hardware-related and features on software-related fingerprints. These hardware-related are mainly included pattern noise [15–21], lens radial distortion [22–24], chromatic aberration [25], and sensor dust [26,27]. The software-related fingerprints include image-related features [7], and characters of color filter array [6].

Kharrazi *et al.* [7] proposed a total of 34 features to capture the differences in the underlying color characteristics for different cameras. Lyu *et al.* [11] adopted

---

[1] http://www.facebook.com/.
[2] http://instagram.com/.

two sets of features. The first feature set includes variance, skewness and kurtosis of the subband coefficients. And the second set is based on the coefficient error. Choi *et al.* [22] observed that most digital cameras are equipped with lenses owing spherical surfaces. Therefore, they use lens radial distortion for camera identification. Van *et al.* [25] noticed the presence of chromatic aberration in the image. They treated the parameters that affect chromatic aberration as the features for camera model identification. Li *et al.* [28] proposed a new way of extracting Photo Response Non-Uniformity (PRNU), called Colour-Decoupled PRNU (CD-PRNU). The method extracts features by distinguishing the physical and artificial color components of the image. They use a color filter array to interpolat an artificial color components from a physical color ones.

2.2 Statistical Leaning Based Image Source Identification

After the feature extraction, the camera model identification is transformed into a multi-classification problem. Support Vector Machine is a commonly used tools, because of its empirical performance. Liu *et al.* [29] proposed a graph based approach for camera identification. In this work, the identification problem is transformed into the segmentation problem of graph. Li *et al.* [30] developed an unsupervised learning approach. In their approach, firstly, Sensor Pattern Noise (SPN) is extracted as fingerprints of the cameras. Secondly, unsupervised learning is performed on the small training set of randomly selected SPNs. Then, clustering are carried out on the randomly selected training set, and the centroids of the clusters are used as training data set for identification classifiers. Tuama *et al.* [31] proposed a method of camera model identification based on convolution neural network (CNN) [32]. They added a layer of preprocessing into the CNN model. The added layer consists of a high-pass filter applied to the input image. Before training, they checked the CNN model with residuals. Then the recognition scores of each camera model are outputed after convolution.

2.3 The Problem of Noise

Traditional classification task usually assumes that the data set is clean. However, in real-life world, the training dataset may contain noisy samples that seriously affect the performance of the classifier. Few works have contributed to the problem of noisy data. Wang *et al.* [33] argued noisy training sample may exist in the scenario of network traffic classification. They developed a robust classification approach to address this issue, namely, Unclean Traffic Classification (UTC), consisting of noise cancellation and suspected noise reweight. Pyun *et al.* [34] proposed an improved HMGMM program to solve the problem of noise. In order to alleviate the influence of noise, they adjusted the covariance matrix in the Gaussian mixed vector quantization codebooks to minimize the overall minimum recognition information distortion.

3 Noisy Smoothing Image Source Identification

In this section, we present the proposed new Noisy Smoothing Image Source Identification (NS-ISI) method in detail.

3.1 System Model

Since the noisy samples can severely decrease the identification performance, in this paper, we propose a new NS-ISI method to alleviate the influence of noisy samples. The system model of NS-ISI is shown in Fig. 1. As we can see, NS-ISI has three core components: noise level evaluation, noise sensitive sampling, and multi-class classification. Noise level evaluation aims to associate each sample with a noise level, which indicates the probability of being noisy. Noise sensitive sampling sample training dataset according to the noise level, producing a new cleaned training dataset. Finally, multi-class classification is performed with traditional statistical tools. In this paper, support vector machine is used.

The new developed two components of NS-ISI are depicted in detail in next two subsections.

3.2 Noise Level Evaluation

Noisy samples can cause negative influence on the identification accuracy. In this section, we employ a classifier ensemble approach to evaluate the noise level of each sample in the training data set. The underline idea is as follows. For each class of samples, treating the samples in the class i as positive samples, and other samples as negative samples, an ensemble of two-class classifiers is constructed. Then, the classifiers in the ensemble are used to classify the images in class i. The noise level is assigned based on the number of classifiers that predict the sample as negative.

Suppose the data set is $T = \{T_1, \ldots, T_k\}$, where T_i represent the sample set of class i, and k represents the class number. The training dataset can be reorganized as $TT = \{TT_1, \ldots, TT_k\}$, where TT_i represents a division of the training dataset. In division TT_i, the samples of class i is regarded as positive samples, and the rest in T is treated as negative samples. $EA = \{F_1, \ldots F_M\}$ is the set of classifier ensembles. After noise level evaluation, the dataset is represented as $TS = \{TS_1, \ldots, TS_{M/2}\}$, where TS_l represents the samples of noise level l.

The overall process of the classifier ensemble based noise level evaluation is presented in Algorithm 1. In this paper, Random Forest (RF) [35] and Ensemble Support Vector Machine [36] are used as ensemble classifier algorithm. Here, we introduce the algorithm using RF as example. Firstly, regarding TT_i as training dataset, we construct the ensemble classifier F_i using RF algorithm. Then, all the base classifiers in F_i are used to classify samples in T_i. Suppose there are M classifiers in F_i. For each sample in T_i, if it is classified as negative by more than M/2 classifiers, the data is directly identified as noise and discarded. Otherwise, the noise level is set as,

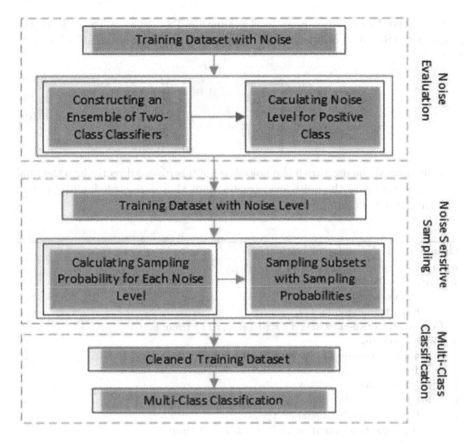

Fig. 1. System model

$$nl = \sum_{j=1}^{M} b_j^i \tag{1}$$

where nl represents the noise level, b_j^i is 1 for the negative output, 0 for the positive output. And the data is assigned to the set TS_{nl}. If the outputs of all base classifiers are positive, the noise level is 0 and the data is put directly to the final set T^*. T^* is a cleaned training data set for training classifiers.

3.3 Noise Sensitive Sampling

After noise level evaluation, each sample is associated with a noise level, which reflects the probability of being noisy. In this section, we develop a new novel noise sensitive sampling method to sample training samples from original training set.

Given the dataset after noise level evaluation $TS = \{TS_1,...,TS_{M/2}\}$, for the sample set TS_l with noise level l, the sampling portability is calculated as Formula (2).

$$P_{nl} = \begin{cases} 0, nl > \dfrac{M}{2} \\ (\dfrac{M-nl}{M})^{nl}, nl \leq \dfrac{M}{2} \\ 1, nl = 0 \end{cases} \tag{2}$$

In summary, the data with the noise level of 0 is placed directly into the final set T^*, the data with the noise level greater than M/2 is discarded, and the data from the set TS are sampled according to Algorithm 2.

Algorithm 1. Noise Level Evaluation

Input: Data set with noise $T=\{T_1,...,T_k\}$.
Output: Noise level nl,
　　　　　Data set with noise level TS,
　　　　　Final training data T^*.
1: Convert T to two-class sets $TT=\{TT_1...,TT_k\}$ from T.
2: **for** i=1 to k **do**
3:　　Train an ensemble of classifier F_i with TT_i.
4: **end for**
5: **for** i=1 to k **do**
6:　　**for** j=1 to length(T_i) **do**
7:　　　　Use F_i to predict instance $T_i^{(j)}$.
8:　　　　**if** all the base classifiers in F_i predict as 0 **then**
9:　　　　　　nl ← 0
10:　　　　　$T^* \leftarrow T^* \cup T_i^{(j)}$.
11:　　　　**else**
12:　　　　　**if** n base classifiers predict as 1 (n≤M/2) **then**
13:　　　　　　　Calculate noise level according to Formula (1).
14:　　　　　　$TS_n \leftarrow TS_n \cup T_i^{(j)}$
15:　　　　　**else**
16:　　　　　　**if** more than M/2 base classifiers predict 1 **then**
17:　　　　　　　　discard $T_i^{(j)}$.
18:　　　　　　**end if**
19:　　　　　**end if**
20:　　　　**end if**
21:　　**end for**
22: **end for**

Algorithm 2. Noise Sensitive Sampling

Input: Data set with noise level TS.
Output: Cleaned training data T*.
1: **for** i=1 to M/2 **do**
2:    Calculate probability for data set with noise level P_i according to Formula (2).
3:    Sampling data $TS_i^{(j)}$ from TS_i according to probability P_i.
4:    $T^* \leftarrow T^* \cup TS_i^{(j)}$.
5: **end for**

---

4   Experiments and Results

4.1   Dataset

In this paper, the Dresden image collection [37] is used for the empirical study. This open image collection was specifically built for the purpose of development and benchmarking of camera-based digital forensic techniques. We randomly divided the whole image collection into two subsets. 10,000 images are used as training data, and the remaining 6960 images are used as testing data. The noisy data are randomly introduced with the wrong label according to certain noisy data rate varying from 0.05 to 0.5.

$$noisy\ data\ rate = \frac{\#mislabelled\ training\ data}{\#training\ data} \tag{3}$$

4.2   Evaluation Metrics

In this paper, the accuracy is used to measure the performance of camera model identification. Accuracy is the number of all correctly classified images divided by the sum of all testing images. This metric is used to measure the accuracy of the classifier for the entire test data.

$$Accuracy = \frac{\#correctly\ classified\ images}{\#testing\ images} \tag{4}$$

4.3   Features

We extracted 34 features proposed by Kharrazi *et al.* [7] for the identification task. Those 34 features include:

1. Average Pixel Value. The measure is based on the assumption of the gray world. This assumption means that if the image has sufficient color change, the average of the RGB channels of the image should be gray. Therefore, the average of the three RGB channels are taken as features (3 features).
2. RGB Pair Correlation. Because the structure of the camera is different, the correlation between the different ribbons may change. There are three related pairs, RG, RB, GB (3 features).

3. Neighbor Distribution Center of Mass. The number of pixel neighborhoods for each pixel value is first calculated, where the pixel neighborhoods are defined as all pixels having a difference of 1 or −1 from the pixel value in question. Then the measure is calculated for each color band separately (3 features).
4. RGB Pairs Energy Ratio. This measure is required for white point correction, which is an integral part of the camera pipe. The calculation formulas of the 3 features are shown in Formula (5).

$$E_1 = \frac{|\,G\,|^2}{|\,B\,|^2}, E_2 = \frac{|\,G\,|^2}{|\,R\,|^2}, E_3 = \frac{|\,B\,|^2}{|\,R\,|^2} \tag{5}$$

5. Wavelet Domain Statistic. The color bands are decomposed by using separable quadratic mirror filters [11], each of which is broken down into three subbands. Then the average of each subband is calculated (9 features).
6. Image Quality Metrics (IQM). Different cameras produce varied image quality. The visual difference prompts people to use IQM as features to help identify the image source. IQM includes 13 features that can be divided into three categories. The first is based on the measurement of pixel difference, such as mean square error, mean absolute error, modified infinity norm. The second is based on the correlation of measurements, such as normalized cross correlation, Czekonowski correlation. The last is based on the measure of the spectral distance, such as spectral phase and magnitude errors.

4.4   The Effect of Noise Data

It can be seen from Fig. 2 that the presence of noise data has an adverse effect on the performance of the classifier. Baseline is the accuracy of the traditional camera model identification method. The traditional method does not denoise the data set. SVM is used in this experiment. And the more noise data exists, the worse the performance of the classifier is. When the noisy data rate is 0.1, the accuracy of the classifier is 0.86. But when the noisy data rate is 0.45, the accuracy of the classifier drops to 0.6.

4.5   Methods Comparison

In the experiment, two integrated algorithms are adopted, namely Random Forest (RF) and Ensemble SVM. As shown in Fig. 3, the performance of the classifier has been greatly improved after noise processing using RF and Ensemble SVM. Moreover, with the increase of noisy data rate, the increase in RF is increasing. When the noise ratio is 0.2, the accuracy is increased by 8%, but when the noise ratio increases to 0.45, the accuracy is increased by 15%.

4.6   The Effect of Parameter

Now let's take a look at the effect of the parameters on the experimental results. We use RF as an example to analyze. The main parameter affecting the RF

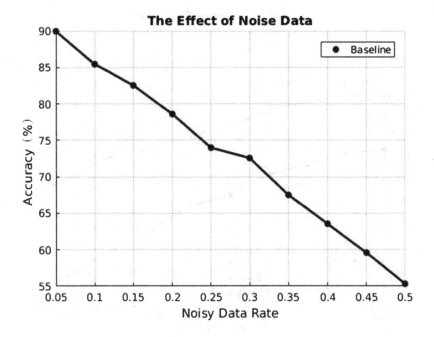

Fig. 2. The effect of noise.

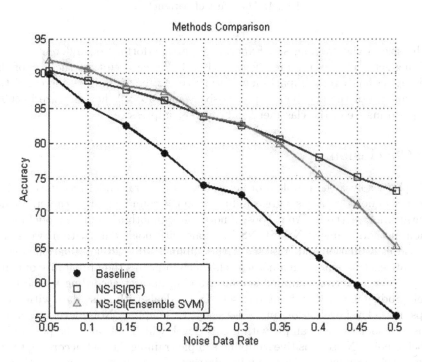

Fig. 3. Methods comparison.

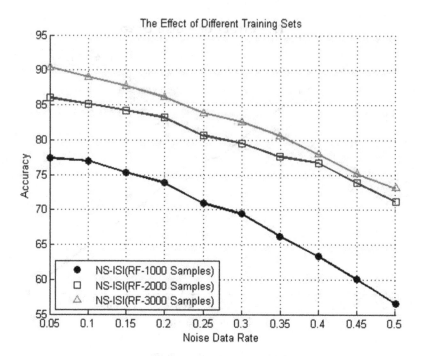

Fig. 4. The effect of parameter.

is the size of the training set. Experiments are performed on different sizes of training sets. The results are shown in Fig. 4. We can see that the size of the training set has a great impact on performance. As the training set increases, the performance of the classifier is progressively increased. When the size is 3000, the performance of the classifier has been very impressive.

5   Conclusion

This paper solves the problem of noise data in camera model recognition. The presence of noise data has a great influence on the commonly used camera model identification methods. We propose a new noise smoothing camera model recognition method, namely, NS-ISI. NS-ISI deals with noisy data within two steps, noise level evaluation and noise sensitive sampling. Noise level evaluation aims to associate each sample with a noise level, which indicates the probability of being noisy. Noise sensitive sampling sample training dataset according to the noise level, producing a new training dataset. NS-ISI deals with noisy data within two steps, noise level evaluation and noise sensitive sampling. Noise level evaluation aims to associate each sample with a noise level, which indicates the probability of being noisy. Noise sensitive sampling sample training dataset according to the noise level, producing a new training dataset. To evaluate the new method, a large number of experiments were carried out on a real-world image collection.

The results demonstrate that the proposed NS-ISI significantly outperforms traditional method when noisy data present.

Acknowledgment. This work was supported by the National Natural Science Foundation of China (No. 61300077 & No. 61502319).

References

1. Stamm, M.C., Liu, K.J.R.: Forensic detection of image manipulation using statistical intrinsic fingerprints. IEEE Trans. Inf. Forensics Secur. **5**(3), 492–506 (2010)
2. Celiktutan, O., Sankur, B., Avcibas, I.: Blind identification of source cell-phone model. IEEE Trans. Inf. Forensics Secur. **3**(3), 553–566 (2008)
3. Jain, L.C., Pan, J.S.: [1]. In: Cox, I.J., Miller, M.L., Bloom, J.A. (eds.) Digital Watermarking and Fundamentals. Morgan Kaufmann, San Francisco (2002)
4. Schyndel, R.G.V., Tirkel, A.Z., Osborne, C.F.: A digital watermark. In: Proceedings of IEEE International Conference on Image Processing, ICIP-94, vol. 2, pp. 86–90 (2002)
5. Committee, C.: Exchangeable image file format for digital still cameras: Exif version 2.3. (2010)
6. Bayram, S., Sencar, H., Memon, N., Avcibas, I.: Source camera identification based on CFA interpolation. In: IEEE International Conference on Image Processing, vol. 3, pp. 69–72 (2009)
7. Kharrazi, M., Sencar, H.T., Memon, N.: Blind source camera identification (2004)
8. Peng, F., Shi, J., Long, M.: Comparison and analysis of the performance of PRNU extraction methods in source camera identification. J. Comput. Inf. Syst. **9**(14), 5585–5592 (2013)
9. Castiglione, A., Cattaneo, G., Cembalo, M., Petrillo, U.F.: Experimentations with source camera identification and online social networks. J. Ambient Intell. Humanized Comput. **4**(2), 265–274 (2013)
10. Cortes, C., Vapnik, V.: Support-Vector Networks. Kluwer Academic Publishers, Boston (1995)
11. Lyu, S., Farid, H.: Detecting hidden messages using higher-order statistics and support vector machines. In: Revised Papers from the International Workshop on Information Hiding, pp. 340–354 (2002)
12. Wahid, A., Wahab, A., Ho, A.T.S., Li, S.: Inter-camera model image source identification with conditional probability features. In: Proceedings of IIEEJ Image Electronics & Visual Computing Workshop (2012)
13. Wang, B., Kong, X., You, X.: Source camera identification using support vector machines. In: Peterson, G., Shenoi, S. (eds.) DigitalForensics 2009. IAICT, vol. 306, pp. 107–118. Springer, Heidelberg (2009). doi:10.1007/978-3-642-04155-6_8
14. Roychowdhury, A., Lin, T.Y., Maji, S., Learnedmiller, E.: Face identification with bilinear CNNs, pp. 1–9 (2015)
15. Lukas, J., Fridrich, J., Goljan, M.: Digital camera identification from sensor pattern noise. IEEE Trans. Inf. Forensics Secur. **1**(2), 205–214 (2006)
16. Sutcu, Y., Bayram, S., Sencar, H.T., Memon, N.: Improvements on sensor noise based source camera identification. In: IEEE International Conference on Multimedia and Expo, pp. 24–27 (2007)
17. Li, C.T.: Source camera identification using enhanced sensor pattern noise. IEEE Trans. Inf. Forensics Secur. **5**(2), 280–287 (2010)

18. Li, C.T., Li, Y.: Color-decoupled photo response non-uniformity for digital image forensics. IEEE Trans. Circ. Syst. Video Technol. **22**(2), 260–271 (2012)
19. Kang, X., Li, Y., Qu, Z., Huang, J.: Enhancing source camera identification performance with a camera reference phase sensor pattern noise. IEEE Trans. Inf. Forensics Secur. **7**(2), 393–402 (2012)
20. Kang, X., Chen, J., Lin, K., Peng, A.: A context-adaptive spn predictor for trustworthy source camera identification. EURASIP J. Image Video Process. **2014**(1), 19 (2014)
21. Tsai, M.J., Wang, C.S., Liu, J., Yin, J.S.: Using decision fusion of feature selection in digital forensics for camera source model identification. Comput. Stand. Interfaces **34**(3), 292–304 (2012)
22. Choi, K.S., Lam, E.Y., Wong, K.K.: Automatic source camera identification using the intrinsic lens radial distortion. Opt. Express **14**(24), 11551–11565 (2006)
23. Kai, S.C., Lam, E.Y., Wong, K.K.Y.: Source camera identification using footprints from lens aberration. In: Proceedings of SPIE - The International Society for Optical Engineering, vol. 6069, pp. 60690J–60690J-8 (2006)
24. Min, G.H., Har, D.H., Park, H.J.: Source camera identification based on interpolation via lens distortion correction. Aust. J. Forensic Sci. **46**(1), 98–110 (2014)
25. Van, L.T., Emmanuel, S., Kankanhalli, M.S.: Identifying source cell phone using chromatic aberration. In: IEEE International Conference on Multimedia and Expo, pp. 883–886 (2007)
26. Dirik, A.E., Sencar, H.T., Memon, N.: Digital single lens reflex camera identification from traces of sensor dust. IEEE Trans. Inf. Forensics Secur. **3**(3), 539–552 (2008)
27. Dirik, A.E., Sencar, H.T., Memon, N.: Source camera identification based on sensor dust characteristics. In: IEEE Workshop on Signal Processing Applications for Public Security and Forensics, SAFE 2007, pp. 1–6 (2007)
28. Li, C.T., Li, Y.: Digital camera identification using colour-decoupled photo response non-uniformity noise pattern. In: IEEE International Symposium on Circuits and Systems, pp. 3052–3055 (2010)
29. Liu, B.B., Lee, H.K., Hu, Y., Choi, C.H.: On classification of source cameras: a graph based approach. In: IEEE International Workshop on Information Forensics and Security, pp. 1–5 (2010)
30. Li, C.T.: Unsupervised classification of digital images using enhanced sensor pattern noise. In: IEEE International Symposium on Circuits and Systems, pp. 3429–3432 (2010)
31. Tuama, A., Comby, F., Chaumont, M.: Camera model identification with the use of deep convolutional neural networks. In: IEEE International Workshop on Information Forensics and Security (2016)
32. Chen, Y.N., Han, C.C., Wang, C.T., Jeng, B.S., Fan, K.C.: The application of a convolution neural network on face and license plate detection. In: International Conference on Pattern Recognition, pp. 552–555 (2006)
33. Wang, B., Zhang, J., Zhang, Z., Luo, W., Xia, D.: Robust traffic classification with mislabelled training samples. In: IEEE International Conference on Parallel and Distributed Systems, pp. 328–335 (2015)
34. Pyun, K., Lim, J., Gray, R.M.: A robust hidden Markov Gauss mixture vector quantizer for a noisy source. IEEE Trans. Image Process. **18**(7), 1385–1394 (2009). IEEE Signal Processing Society
35. Breiman, L.: Random forest. Mach. Learn. **45**, 5–32 (2001)

36. Chatterjee, S., Dash, A., Bandopadhyay, S.: Ensemble support vector machine algorithm for reliability estimation of a mining machine. Qual. Reliab. Eng. Int. **31**(8), 1503–1516 (2016)
37. Gloe, T.: The 'Dresden image database' for benchmarking digital image forensics. In: ACM Symposium on Applied Computing, pp. 1584–1590 (2010)

Privacy-Preserving Comparable Encryption Scheme in Cloud Computing

Qian Meng[1], Jianfeng Ma[2(✉)], Kefei Chen[3], Yinbin Miao[2], and Tengfei Yang[2]

[1] School of Telecommunication Engineering, Xidian University, Xi'an 710071, China
mengqian@stu.xidian.edu.cn
[2] School of Cyber Engineering, Xidian University, Xi'an 710071, China
jfma@mail.xidian.edu.cn, ybmiao@xidian.edu.cn, yangtf@stu.xidian.edu.cn
[3] School of Science, Hangzhou Normal University, Hangzhou 310036, China
kfchen@hznu.edu.cn

Abstract. Data owners encrypt and outsource large size of data to cloud servers to reduce storage and management overhead. In traditional database, it is difficult for users to make comparable queries over ciphertexts. A **S**hort **C**omparable **E**ncryption (SCE) scheme has been emerged as a fundamental solution to enable data owners to conduct comparable queries over encrypted data. Unfortunately, it infers high computational and storage overhead as well as economic burden. In this paper, we first propose a basic **S**hort **C**omparable **E**ncryption scheme based on **S**liding **W**indow method, namely SCESW, which can relief computational and storage burden as well as enhance work efficiency by utilizing sliding window method. However, since the cloud server is always provided by semi-trusted third-party, auditing technology can be applied to protect data integrity. To this end, we improve SCESW scheme to present an enhanced auditing of SCESW scheme called PA-SCESW. Formal security analysis proves that PA-SCESW and SCESW schemes can guarantee data security, integrity as well as weak indistinguishability in standard model. Actual performance evaluation shows PA-SCESW scheme's feasibility and efficiency in practice applications, especially for users with constrained computing resources and capacities.

Keywords: Comparable encryption · Sliding window method · Integrity · Weak indistinguishability

1 Introduction

Cloud computing, envisioned as a novel computing paradigm [1], has been received increasing attention in many practical fields, such as e-Health [2], on-line shopping [3], image retrieval [4], etc. Considering its almost infinite storage and computation capabilities, the **D**ata **O**wner (DO) usually outsources amounts of data to the **C**loud **S**erver (CS) to relief local data storage and computational burden. As the CS is not completely credible, data usually encrypt before outsourcing to the CS to guarantee security. Nevertheless, the concerns on making

© Springer International Publishing AG 2017
S. Wen et al. (Eds.): CSS 2017, LNCS 10581, pp. 148–162, 2017.
https://doi.org/10.1007/978-3-319-69471-9_11

comparable operations over ciphertexts as well as data integrity protection in cloud computing remain rather challenging tasks, especially for users with constrained computing capabilities and resources, as illustrated in Fig. 1. To this end, studies on comparable encryption over ciphertexts and data integrity have been extensively explored by scholars and experts.

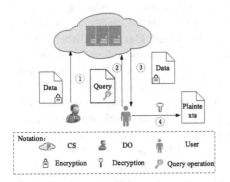

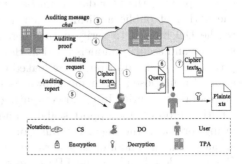

Fig. 1. An example of outsourcing data in cloud computing

Fig. 2. An example of outsourcing data in cloud computing

There exists some scenes like e-Health and stock exchange which need to compare numeric data over ciphertexts. For comparable query operations over ciphertexts, Agrawal et al. proposed an **O**rder **P**reserving **E**ncryption (OPE) scheme for digital query operations over ciphertexts [5]. Unfortunately, if all numbers are encrypted via an OPE, plaintexts can be easily derived from ciphertexts. Therefore, it is urgent to enhance its security. To address this problem, Furukawa introduced a request-based comparable encryption scheme by utilizing the idea of **P**refix **P**reserving **E**ncryption (PPE) [6]. Although the scheme surprisingly enhances the security of OPE scheme to a certain extent, it still produces significant computational and storage overhead. Aiming at reducing the amount of computation and storage costs, Chen Peng et al. discussed an efficient request-based comparable encryption scheme by utilizing sliding window method [7]. This scheme infers the idea of sliding window to allocate the binary form of the data, which fortunately reduces computational and storage overhead. To further reduce the ciphertext storage space, Furukawa presented SCE scheme by using PPE ideas [8]. A comparison between the request-based comparable scheme and the SCE scheme is made. Because of encrypting each bit into 3-ary, SCE scheme can significantly reduce the ciphertext storage space. As a consequence, SCE scheme can dramatically reduce the ciphertext length as well as enhance work efficiency. As the CS is not completely honest entity which may maliciously execute a fraction of operations and forge some ciphertexts, we should check the correctness of outsourced data in order to ensure data integrity.

How to efficiently verify the correctness of outsourced data without utilizing local copy of data files is becoming a big challenge for data security in cloud computing. For example, a remote integrity checking scheme which is based on modular-exponentiation cryptographic techniques was introduced by Deswarte et al. [9] Unfortunately, the new scheme has high computing complexity. To tackle this problem, Filho et al. [10] propose a scheme by utilizing an RSA-based secure hash function in order to achieve safe data transfer transaction through a trusted third party. However, this protocol is still vulnerable to the collusion attack in a P2P environment [10] as well as most of existing schemes cannot prevent the user data from being leaked to external auditors. Recently, the notion of public auditing, which allows the **T**hird **P**arty **A**uditor (TPA) or the DO himself to verify data integrity, has been proposed under different systems and security models [11–14]. However, most of existing schemes cannot prevent the user data from being leaked to external auditors. To this end, Wang et.al. [15] proposed a scheme known as privacy-preserving public auditing for data storage security in cloud computing, which is the first privacy-preserving auditing protocol to support scalable and auditing in the cloud computing. In Wang' protocol, the linear combination of sampled blocks in the CS's response is masked with randomness generated by a **P**seudo **R**andom **F**unction (PRF). Due to random blinding, the TPA cannot obtain all information by constructing an accurate group of linear equations, thereby preventing TPA from gaining the original data except for the linear equations [15]. As a result, this can achieve the privacy-preserving for data.

Aiming at the numeric data [16], we first propose an efficient short comparable encryption scheme based on the sliding window method, namely SCESW which can significantly reduce the high computational and storage overhead. Due to the fact that sometimes the CS is a semi-trusted entity which can obtain some sensitive information and then derive plaintexts, we further present an enhanced scheme named PA-SCESW to verify the stored data integrity. Table 1 shows comparison among various schemes. It is worth highlighting the following contributions made in this paper:

- Combining with sliding window method and SCE scheme, we first put forward the basic SCESW scheme, which can relief computational burden and storage overhead as well as enhance work efficiency.
- To further protect data integrity, we then introduce the enhanced PA-SCESW scheme, which allows the DO to check the correctness of stored cloud data.
- Experimental results demonstrate that PA-SCESW and SCESW schemes can guarantee data security, integrity as well as weak indistinguishability in standard model and our PA-SCESW scheme is feasible and efficient in practice applications.

2   Preliminaries

2.1   Sliding Window Method

Sliding window method is one of the extensively utilized methods for exponentiation proposed by Koc [17]. For example, if we want to compute x^e, e can be

Table 1. Comparisons among various schemes

	SCE scheme	SCESW scheme	PA-SCESW scheme
Storage overhead	Larger	Smaller	Smaller
Computational overhead	Larger	Smaller	Smaller
Efficiency	Lower	Higher	Higher
Sliding window method	No	Yes	Yes
Public auditing	No	No	Yes

represented by its binary code, such as $e = (b_{n-1}, \ldots, b_1, b_0), b_i \in \{0, 1\}, i = 0, 1, \ldots, n - 1$. According to the value of b_i, $(b_{n-1}, \ldots, b_1, b_0)$ is divided into a series of zero windows and nonzero windows. Utilizing sliding window method can bring the reduction in the amount of computation and management overhead. Details of sliding window method can refer to reference [7].

In our schemes, a digital number is considered as a sequence of its binary codes. However, not distinguishing zero windows or nonzero windows, we assume that all the windows have the fixed window size. The specific window size is decided by the users' security level requirements.

2.2 Notations

- $F-$ A sequence of m blocks $(f_0, f_1, \ldots, f_{m-1})$ of ciphertext file.
- $\Psi_{key}(\cdot)-$ Pseudorandom permutation (PRP) is defined as: $\{0, 1\}^{\log_2(n)} \times mkey \to \{0, 1\}^{\log_2(n)}$.
- $y_{key}(\cdot)-$ Pseudorandom function (PRF) is defined as: $\{0, 1\}^* \times mkey \to Z_p$.

3   Problem Statement

In this section, we mainly introduce system model and definitions of SCESW scheme.·

3.1   System Model

Figure 2 considers the main four entities involved in our PA-SCESW scheme, which are shown as follows:

1. DO: It has twofold responsibilities. Firstly, the DO encrypts large amounts of data files through SCESW scheme to be stored in the CS and shares the data with others, as shown in step ①. Secondly, the DO sends auditing request to the TPA in order to check the integrity of ciphertexts, as illustrated in Step ②.
2. CS: It can provide infinite storage and computation resources to the DO and the user. After executing auditing challenge, the CS sends auditing proof to the TPA, as shown in Step ④.

3. User: It has threefold responsibilities. Firstly, the user submits a query to compare the relationship of two ciphertexts $ciph$ and $ciph^*$, as shown in Step ⑥. Secondly, once doing Cmp operation, the CS returns the relationship of two numeric ciphertexts, as illustrated in Step ⑦. Last but not least, Step ⑧ is that the user can derive two numeric plaintexts relationship from two ciphertexts relationship.

4. TPA: It has twofold responsibilities. Firstly, the TPA submits auditing challenge to the CS, as shown in Step ③. Secondly, The TPA returns the results of the auditing report in Step ⑤. If the result of Step ⑤ is correctness, system continues the following steps. Otherwise, the scheme shows ciphertexts is not integrity and system stops to work.

As for the DO, the TPA and the user, these entities are considered to be fully trusted. Nevertheless, the CS is the semi-trusted entity which may execute a fraction of operations and forge some false ciphertexts.

3.2 Definitions of SCESW Scheme

The SCESW scheme consists of five algorithms involving (KeyGen,Par,Der,Enc and Cmp). KeyGen algorithm is run by the DO to initialize system. Par algorithm is utilized by the DO to generate the num num which adopts the sliding window method. Der algorithm is run by the DO to produce the token of the num num. Enc algorithm is used by the DO to generate ciphertexts of the num num. Cmp algorithm is employed by the user to compare the relationship of the number num and num^* from $ciph$ and $ciph^*$.

SCESW system definition can be defined as listed below.

- KeyGen: An algorithm that, given a security parameter $k \in N$ and the range parameter $n \in N$, outputs a parameter $param$ and a master key $mkey$.
- Par: An algorithm that, given a number num, outputs a number num' rewritten through its binary code by utilizing sliding window method.

$$num = (b_0, \ldots, b_{n-1}) = \sum_{0 \le i \le n-1} b_i 2^i; num' = (B_0, \ldots, B_{m-1}) = \sum_{0 \le i \le m-1} B_i (2^t)^i$$

where $num = num'$, t represents the window size, $m = n/t$ is the number of blocks.
- Der: An algorithm that, given a security parameter $k \in N$, the range parameter $n \in N$, a master key $mkey$ and a num $0 \le num \le 2^n$, outputs a token $token$.
- Enc: An algorithm that, given a security parameter $k \in N$, the range parameter $n \in N$, a master key $mkey$ and a num $0 \le num \le 2^n$, outputs a ciphertext $ciph$.
- Cmp: An algorithm that, given a parameter $param$, two ciphertexts $ciph$ and $ciph^*$, and a token $token$, outputs $-1, 0, 1$.

4   Proposed Basic and Enhanced Schemes

To facilitate understanding, we first introduce the basic SCESW scheme, followed by the enhanced PA-SCESW scheme. Before presenting concrete constructions of these schemes outlined above, we show some notations utilized in the whole paper, which is shown in Table 2.

Table 2. Notation descriptions in our schemes

Notations	Descriptions	Notations	Descriptions
$mkey$	Master key	Φ	Set of signature
$resp$	Challenge response	n	Length of number
$chal$	Challenge information	I	k bits random number
m	Number of window blocks	σ_i	Signature for each block f_i
H_i	$Hash_i, (i = 1, 2, 3, 4, 5)$ function	k_{prf}	Randomly chosen permutation key

4.1   The SCESW Scheme

We set the window size as a constant number to introduce the SCESW scheme, which is composed of five algorithms including (KeyGen,Par,Der,Enc and Cmp) algorithms. Specifically, we set the window size as t, which means each block has t bits. We assume n is a multiple of t and n can be an arbitrary number. If n is not a multiple of t, we make n be a multiple of t by adding zero in the end of the n's binary code. A detail description of SCESW scheme is given as follows.

- KeyGen$(k, n) \rightarrow (param, mkey)$: Suppose a security parameter $k \in N$ and the range parameter $n \in N$ are given. KeyGen randomly selects Hash functions defined as $H_1(.), H_2(.), H_3(.) : \{0,1\}^k \times \{0,1\}^* \rightarrow \{0,1\}^k$. Next, KeyGen outputs a master key $mkey \in \{0,1\}^k$ and $param = (n, H_1, H_2, H_3)$. KeyGen outputs a parameter $param = (n, H_1, H_2, H_3)$ and a master key $mkey$.

- Par$(num, t) \rightarrow (num')$: An original number num can be rewritten through its binary code by utilizing sliding window method. That is

$$num = (b_0, \ldots, b_{n-1}); num' = (B_0, \ldots, B_{m-1}) = \sum_{0 \leq i \leq m-1} B_i(2^t)^i \quad (1)$$

where $num = num'$, t represents the window size, $m = n/t$ is the number of blocks.

- Der$(param, mkey, num) \rightarrow (token)$: Suppose that $param = (n, H_1, H_2, H_3)$, a master key $mkey$ and a number $num = (B_0, \ldots, B_{m-1}) = \sum_{0 \leq i \leq m-1} B_i(2^t)^i$ are given. where

$$B_0 = (b_0, b_1, \ldots, b_{t-1}), \ldots, ; B_{m-1} = (b_{n-t}, b_{n-t+1}, \ldots, b_{n-1})$$

Der sets $B_m = 0$ and generates

$$d_i = H_1(mkey, B_m, \ldots, B_i), i = 1, 2, \ldots, m \tag{2}$$

Der outputs $token = (d_1, d_2, \ldots, d_m)$.

- Enc$(param, mkey, num) \to (ciph)$: Suppose that $param = (n, H_1, H_2, H_3)$, a master key $mkey$ and a number

$$num = (B_0, \ldots, B_{m-1}) = \sum_{0 \le i \le m-1} B_i (2^t)^i$$

are given. Enc randomly selects $token = (d_1, d_2, \ldots, d_m)$ and a random number $I \in \{0, 1\}^k$.

Next Enc generates

$$f_i = H_3(d_{i+1}, I) + H_2(mkey, d_{i+1}) + B_i mod(2^{(t+1)} - 1)(i = m-1, \ldots, 0) \tag{3}$$

Enc finally outputs ciphertexts $ciph = (I, (f_0, f_1, \ldots, f_{m-1}))$. The DO sends $ciph$ to the CS.

Here, $(f_0, f_1, \ldots, f_{m-1})$ can be encoded into an integer

$$F_t = \sum_{0 \le i \le m-1} f_i(2^{(t+1)} - 1))^i$$

to make ciphertexts short.

- Cmp$(ciph, ciph^*, token) \to (Cmp)$: Suppose that a pair of ciphertexts $ciph = (I, (f_0, f_1, \ldots, f_{m-1}))$, $ciph^* = (I', F^*) = (I', (f'_0, f'_1, \ldots, f'_{m-1}))$ and a token $token = (d_1, d_2, \ldots, d_m)$ are given.
  - Cmp sets $j = m - 1$ and keeps producing c_j by decreasing j by 1 at each step.

$$c_j = f_j - f'_j - H_3(d_{j+1}, I) + H_3(d_{j+1}, I')mod(2^{(t+1)} - 1) \tag{4}$$

This repetition stops when Cmp generates c_j such that $c_j \ne 0$ or when $c_j = 0$ for all $i = m-1, m-2, \ldots, 0$. If $1 \le c_j \le 2^t - 1$, then it means $num > num^*$. If $2^t \le c_j \le 2^{(t+1)} - 2$, then it means $num < num^*$. If $c_j \equiv 0$, then it means $num = num^*$. Then we have the following equations.

$$Cmp = \begin{cases} -1 & if & 1 \le c_j \le 2^t - 1 \\ 0 & if & c_j \equiv 0 \\ 1 & if & 2^t \le c_j \le 2^{(t+1)} - 2 \end{cases} \tag{5}$$

4.2   The PA-SCESW Scheme

In this section, we improve our basic SCESW scheme to efficiently support public auditing and the new scheme is called PA-SCESW. The PA-SCESW scheme is composed of four phases **(Setup, Enc, Audit and Cmp)**. The definition of PA-SCESW scheme is defined as follows:

1. Definition of PA-SCESW scheme

Setup phase

The DO chooses a random $x \leftarrow Z_p$, a random element $u \leftarrow G_1$, a security parameter $k \in N$ and the range parameter $n \in N$ to output a master key $mkey$ and a parameter $param$. The DO runs KeyGen to produce the secret parameter sk and the public parameter pk. This Setup phase contains KeyGen algorithm in SCESW scheme. Setup phase outputs the secret parameter sk, the public parameter pk, a parameter $param$ and a master key $mkey$.

Enc phase

- Par,Der: System models are similar to SCESW scheme, as shown in Fig. 2.
- Enc: A probabilistic algorithm that, given a security parameter $k \in N$, the range parameter $n \in N$, a master key $mkey$ and a num $0 \leq num \leq 2^n$, outputs a ciphertext $ciph$ and a ciphertext file F. Then the DO runs SignGen to compute signature σ_i for each block of F. Finally the DO sends $ciph, \{F, \Phi\}$ to the CS.

Audit phase

- GenProof: Upon receiving challenge $chal$, the CS runs GenProof to generate a response $resp$ proof of data storage correctness.
- VerifyProof: After receiving $resp = \{\mu, \sigma, R\}$, the TPA checks the verification equation for auditing ciphertexts integrity from the CS.

  If the verification is correctness, then system continues to complete the algorithm Cmp.

Cmp phase

- Cmp: System model is similar to SCESW scheme, as illustrated in Fig. 2.

2. Scheme Details

Let G_1, G_2 and G_T be multiplicative cyclic group of prime order p, $e : G_1 \times G_2 \rightarrow G_T$ be a bilinear map, g be a generator of G_2. Hash functions define $H_1(.), H_2(.), H_3(.) : \{0,1\}^k \times \{0,1\}^* \rightarrow \{0,1\}^k$. $H_4(.)$ is a secure map-to-point Hash function: $\{0,1\}^* \rightarrow G_1$, which maps strings randomly and uniformly to G_1. Another Hash function $H_5(.) : G_1 \rightarrow Z_p$, which maps strings uniformly to G_1 that maps group element of G_1 uniformly and randomly to Z_p. A number can be written $num = (b_0, b_1, \ldots, b_{n-1}) = \sum_{0 \leq i \leq n-1} b_i 2^i$. The process of generating $num^*, F^*, ciph^*$ is similar to the process of generating $num, F, ciph$.

Setup phase

Setup(1^λ) $\rightarrow$ ($pk, sk, param, mkey$): The DO selects a random $x \leftarrow Z_p$, a random element $u \leftarrow G_1$, a security parameter $k \in N$, the range parameter

$n \in N$ and H_1, H_2, H_3 to output a master key $mkey \in \{0,1\}^*$. Then he computes $v \leftarrow g^x$, $w \leftarrow u^x$. Besides, he defines $param = (n, H_1, H_2, H_3)$. The DO runs KeyGen to generate the system's public parameters $pk = (v, w, g, u)$, the system's secret parameters $sk = (x)$. This Setup phase contains KeyGen algorithm in SCESW scheme.

Setup phase outputs the secret parameter, the public parameter, a parameter $param$ and a master key $mkey$.

Enc phase

– Par$(num) \rightarrow (num')$, Der$(param, mkey, num) \rightarrow (token)$: Algorithms are similar to SCESW scheme.
– Enc$(param, mkey, num) \rightarrow (ciph)$: Suppose that $param = (n, H_1, H_2, H_3)$, a master key $mkey$ and a number

$$num = (B_0, \ldots, B_{m-1}) = \sum_{0 \leq i \leq m-1} B_i(2^t)^i$$

are given. Enc randomly selects $token = (d_1, d_2, \ldots, d_m)$ and a random number $I \in \{0,1\}^k$.
Next Enc generates

$$f_i = H_3(d_{i+1}, I) + H_2(mkey, d_{i+1}) + B_i mod(2^{(t+1)} - 1)(i = m - 1, \ldots, 0)$$

Enc finally outputs ciphertexts $ciph = (I, (f_0, f_1, \ldots, f_{m-1}))$. Here, $(f_0, f_1, \ldots, f_{m-1})$ can be encoded into an integer

$$F_t = \sum_{0 \leq i \leq m-1} f_i \cdot (2^{(t+1)} - 1))^i$$

to make ciphertexts short.
Then we get ciphertexts file $F = (f_0, f_1, \ldots, f_{m-1})$, the DO runs SignGen to compute signature σ_i for each block $f_i : \sigma_i = (H_4(i) \cdot u^{f_i})^x \in G_1, (i = 0, 1, \ldots, m - 1)$. Let us denote the set of signature by $\Phi = \{\sigma_i\}_{0 \leq i \leq m-1}$. The DO sends $ciph, \{F, \Phi\}$ to the CS.

Audit phase

– GenProof $(chal) \rightarrow (resp)$: In order to generate the audit message $chal$, the TPA randomly elaborates a m-element set $\Theta = \{s_1, s_2, \ldots, s_m\}$, where $s_q = \Psi_{k_{prp}}(q)$ for $1 \leq q \leq m$ and k_{prp} is a randomly chosen permutation key by the TPA for each auditing. Assume that $s_1 \leq \ldots \leq s_m$ is defined. For each element $i \in \Theta$, the TPA also selects a random value v_i (of a relative small bit length compared to $|p|$). And then he TPA sends the $chal = \{(i, v_i)\}_{i \in \Theta}$ to the CS.
Once receiving auditing challenge $chal = \{(i, v_i)\}_{i \in \Theta}$, the CS runs GenProof to generate a response $resp$ proof of data integrity. Specifically, the CS randomly chooses an element $r \leftarrow Z_p$ through $r = y_{k_{prf}}(chal)$, where k_{prf} is

the randomly selected PRF key by the CS for each auditing. Then the CS computes $R = (w)^r = (u^x)^r \in G_1$. Let $\mu' = \sum_{i \in \Theta} v_i \cdot m_i$ infer the linear combination of sampled blocks. For the purpose of masking μ' with r, the CS calculates $\mu = \mu' + rH_5(R) \in Z_p$ and also computes an aggregated signature $\prod_{i \in \Theta} \sigma_i^{v_i} \in G_1$. And then it sends $resp = \{\mu, \sigma, R\}$ to the TPA to prove of storage correctness.

- VerifyProof$(resp = \{\mu, \sigma, R\}) \rightarrow$ (correctness): After receiving $resp = \{\mu, \sigma, R\}$, the TPA checks whether the following verification equation holds.

$$e(\sigma \cdot (R^{H_5(R)}), g) \stackrel{?}{=} e(\prod_{i=s_1}^{i=s_m} H_4(i)^{v_i} \cdot u^\mu, v) \tag{6}$$

If the verification result is 0, the CS outputs $\perp$. This means the system stops and not continues the algorithm Cmp. Otherwise, the result is 1. Then the verifier believes that the integrity of all the blocks in shared data F is intact and system continues the algorithm Cmp.

Cmp phase

- Cmp$(ciph, ciph^*, token) \rightarrow (Cmp)$: Cmp algorithm is similar to SCESW scheme.

5   Security Analysis

In this section, we evaluate the security of the PA-SCESW scheme by analyzing the storage correctness, completeness and weak indistinguishability, shown in Theorems 1, 3 and 4. Then we will give properties of completeness and weak indistinguishability in PA-SCESW scheme by theoretical analysis with SCESW scheme similar to PA-SCESW scheme.

Theorem 1. Given shared data F and signatures, a verifier is able to correctly check the integrity of shared data F.

Proof. So as to prove the correctness of PA-SCESW scheme is equivalent to proving Eq. (6)'s correctness. According to the properties of bilinear maps, the correctness of Eq. (6) can be derived as follows.

$$e(\sigma \cdot (R^{H_5(R)}), g) = e(\prod_{i=s_1}^{i=s_m} \sigma_i^{v_i} (u^x)^{rH_5(R)}, g) = e(\prod_{i=s_1}^{i=s_m} (H_4(i)^{v_i} u^{f_i v_i} \cdot (u^{rH_5(R)}), g)^x$$

$$= e(\prod_{i=s_1}^{i=s_m} (H_4(i)^{v_i} \cdot (u^{\mu' + rH_5(R)}), g^x) = e(\prod_{i=s_1}^{i=s_m} H_4(i)^{v_i} \cdot u^\mu, v)$$

Theorem 2. From the cloud's response $\{\mu, \sigma, R\}$, no information of μ' will be leaked to the TPA [15].

Theorem 3. The PA-SCESW scheme is completeness as long as H_1, H_2 and H_3 are pseudorandom functions.

Proof. We consider *ciph* is generated from *num* and *ciph** generated from *num**.

$$num = \sum_{0 \le i \le n-1} b_i 2^i = \sum_{0 \le i \le m-1} B_i (2^t)^i ; num^* = \sum_{0 \le i \le n-1} \beta_i 2^i = \sum_{0 \le i \le m-1} B_i' (2^t)^i.$$

t is the window size, $m = n/t$ is the number of blocks via utilizing sliding window technology.

$$token = (d_0, \ldots, d_m); token^* = (d_0', \ldots, d_m');$$
$$ciph = (I, (f_0, \ldots, f_{m-1})); ciph^* = (I', (f_0', \ldots, f_{m-1}')).$$

$(f_0, \ldots, f_{m-1})$ and $(f_0', \ldots, f_{m-1}')$ can be encoded into an integer $F_t = \sum_{0 \le i \le m-1} f_i (2^{(t+1)} - 1)^i$ and $F_t^* = \sum_{0 \le i \le m-1} f_i' (2^{(t+1)} - 1)^i$ respectively to make the ciphertext short.

From Eq. (2) we know that d_i and d_i' depend on $B_i, B_{i+1}, B_i', B_{i+1}'$ and *mkey*. Assume that l is the first different block of *num* and *num**, for $i = l+1, \ldots, m-1$, if $B_{i+1} = B_{i+1}'$ corrects, then $d_{i+1} = d_{i+1}'$ holds.

Hence, if $num = num^*$, $c_j = 0$ holds for $i = 0, \ldots, m-1$, Cmp will output 0. If $num \ne num^*$, for this i,

$$c_j = f_j - f_j' - H_3(d_{j+1}, I) + H_3(d_{j+1}, I') mod(2^{(t+1)} - 1)$$
$$= (H_3(d_{j+1}, I) + H_2(mkey, d_{j+1}) + B_j - H_3(d_{j+1}, I)) - (H_3(d_{j'+1}, I)$$
$$+ H_2(mkey, d_{j'+1}) + B_j' - H_3(d_{j+1}, I')) mod(2^{(t+1)} - 1)$$
$$= B_j - B_j' mod(2^{(t+1)} - 1)$$

For $j = 0, \ldots, m-1$, $B_j - B_j' = 0$ is the case that $num = num^*$; $B_j - B_j' \ne 0$ is the case that Cmp outputs this first non zero c_j. Specifically, if $1 \le c_j \le (2^t - 1)$, then $num > num^*$; if $2^t \le c_j \le (2^{(t+1)} - 2)$, then $num < num^*$. Hence, the PA-SCESW scheme is complete.

Theorem 4. The PA-SCESW scheme is weakly indistinguishable if H_1, H_2 and H_3 are pseudorandom functions.

Proof. Let C, C_A, and C_B represent challengers. Suppose that there exists an adversary A such that $Adv_{C,A} := |Pr(Exp_{C,A}^k = 0) - Pr(Exp_{C,A}^k = 1)| \ge \epsilon$ in the weak distinguishing game. Then, we know that Hash function is distinguishable from the random function, which is against the assumption that they are pseudorandom functions. In particular, we consider a sequence of games by challengers C, C_A, and C_B and then prove the theorem by the hybrid argument. From literature [8], we know that $|Adv_{C,A} - Adv_{C_B,A}| < \epsilon$ as long as Hash is a pseudorandom function as well as $Adv_{C_B,A} = 0$. Hence, $Adv_{C,A} < \epsilon$ and Theorem 4 is proved.

6   Performance

In this section, we first compare our schemes with SCE scheme in **Enc phase** and **Cmp phsae** in experiments, as shown in Tables 3 and 4. In **audit phase**, auditing costs of reference [15] are almost to PA-SCESW scheme, so we just evaluate the actual performance of PA-SCESW scheme in experiments. Due to the fact that reference [15] utilizes pair operations in **Enc phase**, SCESW scheme and PT-SCESW scheme use hash functions with high efficiency. We refer to reference [15] to support data integrity verification.

The experiment is conducted using C on a Ubuntu Server 15.04 with Intel Core i5 Processor 2.3 GHz. Algorithms utilize the Paring Based Cryptography (PBC). In Table 3, there exist two numbers $num_1 = (\beta_0, \ldots, \beta_{n-1})$ and $num_2 = (\gamma_0, \ldots, \gamma_{n-1})$, with L satisfying the equation $(\beta_L, \ldots, \beta_{n-1}) = (\gamma_L, \ldots, \gamma_{n-1}), \beta_{L-1} < \gamma_{L-1}$. We randomly choose n which is equivalent to 1024 bits and k which has 160 bits in experimental simulations. Experimental tests are conducted for 100 times.

Table 3. Comparison of computational cost in various schemes

	PA-SCESW scheme	SCESW scheme	SCE scheme [8]
Enc phase	$4m \cdot h + 2m \cdot E + m \cdot h'$	$4m \cdot h$	$4n \cdot h$
Cmp phase	$2(m - L + 1) \cdot h$	$2(m - L + 1) \cdot h$	$2(n - L + 2) \cdot h$
Audit phase	$(2m + 3)E + mh' + 2h + 2P$	0	0

Table 4. Comparison of storage overhead in various schemes

	Ciphertext generaation phase	Token generation phase
SCE scheme [8]	$(n + 1) \cdot k$	$k + (ln3/ln2) \cdot n$
SCESW scheme	$m \cdot k$	$k + (ln(2^{t+1} - 1)/ln(t + 1)) \cdot m$
PA-SCESW scheme	$m \cdot k$	$k + (ln(2^{t+1} - 1)/ln(t + 1)) \cdot m$

We will mainly focus on the computational and storage overhead. Due to the fact that SCESW scheme utilizes sliding window method, a comparison in computational and storage overhead between SCESW scheme and SCE scheme is made, which shows that SCESW scheme is cost-effective. Analysis can demonstrate that PA-SCESW scheme by using sliding window technology can relief the high computational and storage overhead. To largely reduce storage overhead, $(f_0, f_1, \ldots, f_{m-1})$ can be encoded into an integer

$$F_t = \sum_{0 \le i \le m-1} f_i \cdot (2^{(t+1)} - 1))^i$$

to make ciphertexts short in SCESW scheme and PA-SCESW scheme, as is shown in Table 4.

Table 3 shows the theoretical analysis of these schemes. We just only consider several time-consuming operations, such as bilinear pairing operation "P", exponentiation operation "E". We divide $Hash_i(i = 1, 2, 3, 4, 5)$ operations into two parts as well as denote $Hash_i(i = 1, 2, 3, 5)$ operation as "h" and $Hash_4$ operation as "h'" due to the fact that the $Hash$ operation "h'" is much more time-consuming than the $Hash$ operation "h". Now we give detail theoretical analysis of PA-SCESW scheme as an example.

1. In **Enc phase**, computing $ciph$ and signature σ_i for each block f_i can bring the exponentiation operation "E", $Hash_i(i = 1, 2, 3)$ operation "h" and $Hash_4$ function operation "h'". Overall, this phase costs $4m \cdot h + 2m \cdot E + m \cdot h'$ operations.
2. In **Cmp phase**, costs mainly depend on computing c_j, with computing c_j only bringing $Hash_i(i = 1, 2, 3)$ operation "h". Overall, this phase costs $2(m - L + 1) \cdot h$ operations.
3. In **Audit phase**, costs mainly depend on computing $R = (w)^r = (u^x)^r \in G_1$, $\mu = \mu' + rH_5(R) \in Z_p$ and the following verification Eq. (6). Costs can bring the exponentiation operation "E", $Hash_i(i = 1, 2, 3)$ operation "h" and $Hash_4$ function operation "h'". Overall, this phase costs $(2m + 3)E + mh' + 2h + 2P$ operations.

From Tables 3 and 4 we notice that compared with SCE scheme, our SCESW scheme can dramatically relief the computational burden and storage overhead. In Fig. 3(a), we set $n = 1024$ bits and vary the value of m from 16 to 512, then we notice that the encryption time in PA-SCESW scheme approximately increases with m. For example, when setting $m = 64$, our scheme needs 0.976 ms to generate ciphertexts and signatures. However, as the $hash_4$ operation h' is much more time-consuming than the $hash_i(i = 1, 2, 3, 5)$ operation h, the PA-SCESW scheme has much higher computational burden than other two schemes. It does not affect the user search experience because of being just a one-time cost. Consequently, our PA-SCESW scheme is still acceptable in practice, especially for users with constrained computing resources and capacities.

In Fig. 3(b), we set $n = 1024$ bits and $m = 256$, then we notice that the comparable time in PA-SCESW scheme approximately decreases with L. For example, when setting $L = 63$, our scheme needs 1.164 ms to compare ciphertexts. In Cmp phase, the PA-SCESW scheme and SCESW scheme has similar computational burden. Based on sliding window method, our PA-SCESW scheme and SCESW scheme can significantly reduce the computational overhead when these schemes are compared with SCE scheme.

In Fig. 3(c), we set $n = 1024$ bits and vary the value of m from 16 to 512, then we notice that the auditing time in PA-SCESW scheme approximately increases with m. For example, when setting $m = 64$, our scheme needs 0.872 ms to make public auditing. However, as the $hash_4$ operation h' is much more time-consuming than the $hash_5$ operation h, the PA-SCESW scheme has high computational burden to support public auditing. We send operations to the TPA and CS with almost infinite storage and computation capabilities.

Therefore, our PA-SCESW scheme is still acceptable in practice, especially for users with constrained computing resources and capacities.

To summarize, actual performance results are completely in accord with the theoretical analysis shown in Tables 3 and 4. Exploring PA-SCESW scheme mainly focus on achieving one property that is auditing. Although the $hash_4$ operation h' is a time-consuming operation, our PA-SCESW scheme is still feasible and efficient in practice applications, especially for users with constrained computing resources and capacities.

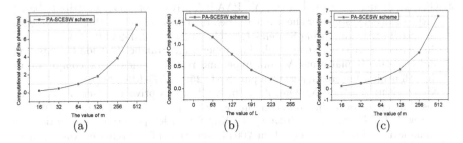

Fig. 3. Performance analysis in PA-SCESW scheme: (a) computational costs in **Enc phase**; (b) computational costs in **Cmp phase**; (c) computational costs in **Audit phase**

7   Conclusion

In this paper, we first propose a basic scheme named SCESW scheme to relief the computational and storage overhead through utilizing sliding window method. Furthermore, PA-SCESW scheme is presented for supporting public auditing as well as reducing computational and storage overhead. Then we give a detail analysis of its security. Formal security analysis proves that PA-SCESW and SCESW schemes can guarantee data security, integrity as well as weak indistinguishability in standard model. Compared with SCE scheme, SCESW scheme and PA-SCESW scheme can relief the computational and storage burden to some extent. Actual performance evaluation shows that our PA-SCESW scheme is still feasible and efficient in practice applications, especially for users with constrained computing resources and capacities.

In PA-SCESW scheme, as the $hash_4$ operation h' is much more time-consuming than the $hash_5$ operation h, the PA-SCESW scheme has relatively high computational burden to support public auditing. In our future work, we will improve PA-SCESW scheme by deducing its computational and storage overhead. Nevertheless, there is another important problem to be resolved. How to apply the PA-SCESW scheme to image retrieval field is rather a challenging task to be solved in clouding computing and artificial intelligence fields.

Acknowledgment. This work is supported by the National High Technology Research and Development Program (863 Program) (No. 2015AA016007), China Postdoctoral Science Foundation Funded Project (No. 2017M613080), the Fundamental Research Funds for the Central Universities (No. JB171504), the Key Program of NSFC (No. U1405255, No. U1135002), the Major Nature Science Foundation of China (No. 61472310, No. 61672413, No. 61370078, No. 61309016), the 111 project (No. B16037), the Shaanxi Science & Technology Coordination & Innovation Project (No. 2016TZC-G-6-3) and the Fundamental Research Funds for the Central Universities (No. BDZ011402).

References

1. Sookhak, M., Gani, A., Khan, M.K., Buyya, R.: Dynamic remote data auditing for securing big data storage in cloud computing. Inf. Sci. **380**, 101–116 (2017)
2. Guo, L., Zhang, C., Sun, J., Fang, Y.: PAAS: A privacy-preserving attribute-based authentication system for ehealth networks. In: The 32nd International Conference on Distributed Computing Systems (ICDCS 2012), pp. 224–233 (2012)
3. Buyya, R., Yeo, C.S., Venugopal, S., Broberg, J., Brandic, I.: Cloud computing and emerging it platforms: Vision, hype, and reality for delivering computing as the 5th utility. Future Gener. Comput. Syst. **25**(6), 599–616 (2009)
4. Xia, Z., Zhu, Y., Sun, X., Qin, Z., Ren, K.: Towards privacy-preserving content-based image retrieval in cloud computing. IEEE Trans. Cloud Comput. (2017)
5. Agrawal, R., Kiernan, J., Srikant, R., Xu, Y.: Order preserving encryption for numeric data. In: Proceedings of the 2004 International Conference on Management of Data (ACM SIGMOD 2004), pp. 563–574 (2004)
6. Furukawa, J.: Request-based comparable encryption. In: Crampton, J., Jajodia, S., Mayes, K. (eds.) ESORICS 2013. LNCS, vol. 8134, pp. 129–146. Springer, Heidelberg (2013). doi:10.1007/978-3-642-40203-6_8
7. Chen, P., Ye, J., Chen, X.: Efficient request-based comparable encryption scheme based on sliding window method. Soft. Comput. **20**(11), 4589–4596 (2016)
8. Furukawa, J.: Short comparable encryption. In: Gritzalis, D., Kiayias, A., Askoxylakis, I. (eds.) CANS 2014. LNCS, vol. 8813, pp. 337–352. Springer, Cham (2014). doi:10.1007/978-3-319-12280-9_22
9. Deswarte, Y., Quisquater, J.J., Saïdane, A.: Remote integrity checking. Integrity Intern. Control Inf. Syst. **VI**, 1–11 (2004)
10. Gazzoni Filho, D.L., Barreto, P.: Demonstrating data possession and uncheatable data transfer. IACR Cryptology ePrint Archive 150 (2006)
11. Ateniese, G., Burns, R., Curtmola, R., Herring, J., Kissner, L., Peterson, Z., Song, D.: Provable data possession at untrusted stores. In: ACM Conference on Computer and Communications Security (ACM 2007), pp. 598–609 (2007)
12. Wang, Q., Wang, C., Li, J., Ren, K., Lou, W.: Enabling public verifiability and data dynamics for storage security in cloud computing. In: European Symposium on Research in Computer Security, pp. 355–370 (2009)
13. Shacham, H., Waters, B.: Compact proofs of retrievability. J. Cryptology **26**(3), 442–483 (2013)
14. Juels, A., Kaliski, B.S.: Pors: proofs of retrievability for large files. In: ACM Conference on Computer and Communications Security (ACM 2007), pp. 584–597 (2007)
15. Wang, C., Wang, Q., Ren, K., Lou, W.: Privacy-preserving public auditing for data storage security in cloud computing. In: 2010 Proceedings of IEEE INFOCOM, pp. 1–9 (2010)
16. Karras, P., Nikitin, A., Saad, M., Bhatt, R., Antyukhov, D., Idreos, S.: Adaptive indexing over encrypted numeric data. In: Proceedings of the 2016 International Conference on Management of Data, pp. 171–183 (2016)
17. Koç, C.K.: Analysis of sliding window techniques for exponentiation. Comput. Math. Appl. **30**(10), 17–24 (1995)

Detecting Malicious Nodes in Medical Smartphone Networks Through Euclidean Distance-Based Behavioral Profiling

Weizhi Meng[1,2(✉)], Wenjuan Li[2,3], Yu Wang[1(✉)], and Man Ho Au[4]

[1] School of Computer Science, Guangzhou University, Guangzhou, China
`weme@dtu.dk, yuwang@gzhu.edu.cn`
[2] Department of Applied Mathematics and Computer Science,
Technical University of Denmark, Kongens Lyngby, Denmark
[3] Department of Computer Science, City University of Hong Kong,
Kowloon Tong, Hong Kong
[4] Department of Computing, The Hong Kong Polytechnic University,
Kowloon Tong, Hong Kong SAR

Abstract. With the increasing digitization of the healthcare industry, a wide range of medical devices are Internet- and inter-connected. Mobile devices (e.g., smartphones) are one common facility used in the healthcare industry to improve the quality of service and experience for both patients and healthcare personnel. The underlying network architecture to support such devices is also referred to as medical smartphone networks (MSNs). Similar to other networks, MSNs also suffer from various attacks like insider attacks (e.g., leakage of sensitive patient information by a malicious insider). In this work, we focus on MSNs and design a trust-based intrusion detection approach through Euclidean distance-based behavioral profiling to detect malicious devices (or called nodes). In the evaluation, we collaborate with healthcare organizations and implement our approach in a real simulated MSN environment. Experimental results demonstrate that our approach is promising in effectively identifying malicious MSN nodes.

Keywords: Collaborative network · Intrusion detection · Medical Smartphone Network · Trust computation and management · Insider attack · Malicious node

1 Introduction

With the rapid development of information technology (IT), healthcare domain employs many of the same infrastructure elements, applications, off-the-shelf technologies, and processes used by enterprise IT in general. In hospitals, networked medical devices can provide more effective and less expensive monitoring

---

W. Meng—The author was previously known as Yuxin Meng. The research idea was initialized when the first author has a short-term visit at Guangzhou University.

© Springer International Publishing AG 2017
S. Wen et al. (Eds.): CSS 2017, LNCS 10581, pp. 163–175, 2017.
https://doi.org/10.1007/978-3-319-69471-9_12

and treatments. One estimate points out that these networked technologies could save up to 63 billion in healthcare/medical costs over the next fifteen years, with a 15–30% reduction in hospital equipment costs [2].

However, healthcare or medical networks are more special than traditional networks in two respects [24]. First, their presented and transmitted information is significantly sensitive. The private and sensitive health data are highly valuable for hackers to make profits. Second, the complexity, number and diversity of devices, especially networked devices, that make up this infrastructure expose such networks to a broader range of security and privacy risks such as cyber attacks [25]. According to a recent survey [6], the number of information security breaches reported by healthcare providers soared 60% from 2013 to 2014, which is almost double the increase seen in other industries.

As medical industry is evolving rapidly, mobile devices have become a popular platform to carry information and speed up electronic data transfers. For instance, smartphones have been applied in various healthcare organizations, helping record patient's medical conditions and access patient's records in real-time during ward visits. As a result, an emerging medical network has been evolved, called *medical smartphone network (MSN)*, which can be considered as a special kind of wireless sensor network [21]. These devices are generally connected to the organization's wireless network and each of them can be considered as a node. McAfee report [7] indicates that Internet-enabled medical devices would expose security gaps in the integration of operational technology, consumer technology and networked information technology. Therefore, there is a need for protecting MSNs against various attacks, especially insider threats.

Contributions. Due to the importance and sensitivity of MSNs, it is crucial to identify malicious devices within such network in a fast way. In the literature, intrusion detection technologies (e.g., trust-based IDS) are often used to detect various threats. In this work, we focus on MSNs and design a trust-based intrusion detection mechanism to identify malicious MSN nodes. Trustworthiness of a node can be derived by identifying the difference between two profiles based on Euclidean distance. The contributions of our work can be summarized as below:

- To better understand MSNs, we first introduce the basic MSN features, and identify that a hierarchical infrastructure is often required in such medical network environment. We then introduce some basic requirements from health-care managers in designing security mechanisms.
- Behavioral profiling is often used to model system or network events. A behavioral profile is a collection of necessary information in order to describe basic characteristics of an object under pre-defined rules. In this work, based on the suggestions from healthcare managers, we select four mobile and network features to build behavioral profiles, and then develop a trust-based approach based on Euclidean distance to evaluate a node's trustworthiness.
- By collaborating with a healthcare center, we evaluate our approach in a real simulated MSN environment to investigate its performance. Experimental results demonstrate that our approach is feasible and promising at identifying malicious MSN nodes effectively (i.e., in a quick manner).

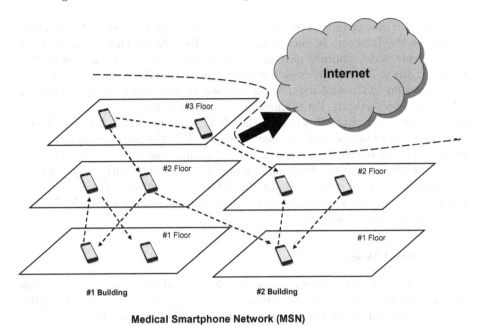

Fig. 1. The typical architecture of medical smartphone networks (MSNs).

The remaining parts of this paper are organized as follows. In Sect. 2, we introduce the background of MSNs and review related research studies on trust-based intrusion detection mechanisms. Section 3 describes our approach including how to build a behavioral profile based on the selected features, and how to compute trust based on Euclidean distance. Section 4 describes and analyzes our evaluation results. Finally, Sect. 5 concludes our paper.

2   Background and Related Work

This section introduces the background of medical smartphone networks and review relevant research work on trust-based intrusion detection.

2.1   Background of MSNs

Today's smartphone can simultaneously operate on numerous wireless network architectures. With this trend, medical smartphone networks (MSNs) have been gradually adopted in various healthcare organizations such as hospitals, clinics and healthcare centers. According to [21], most healthcare managers believe MSNs are an emerging wireless network architecture, which has its unique features in healthcare domain. A typical architecture of MSNs is depicted in Fig. 1.

The figure shows that medical smartphones are able to connect with each other and thus form an internal medical network, which can facilitate information exchange and management. Overall, a node in MSNs can connect with each other as well as the Internet. In such a way, networked phones embed the Internet into patients' lives, improve medical outcomes and lower healthcare costs [21]. However, due to the sensitive information exchanged in this environment, hackers may target on MSNs and try to compromise one node using virus, malware or other intrusion methods. For example, an attacker can lurk inside the healthcare organizations and physical access to the phones or infect them through Wi-Fi, bluetooth, etc. Once a node is compromised, then the attacker can conduct various attacks to other devices such as scanning, spoofing, denial-of-service (DoS) attacks and so on. Such insider attacks can significantly leak sensitive information and even cause the paralysis of the entire network. Therefore, it is a crucial task to identify malicious nodes in a fast manner for securing MSNs and protecting private information.

2.2   Related Work

Insider attacks are one major threat for distributed network systems, which may greatly degrade the whole network security. To discover malicious nodes in a distributed network like wireless sensor networks (WSNs) [16], trust-based intrusion detection mechanisms are widely studied [14]; however, a key challenge still remains: that is, how to evaluate the trustworthiness of a node in an active and appropriate way.

Distributed trust-based intrusion detection. Collaborative intrusion detection networks (CIDNs) [26] have been proposed and implemented, which enable an IDS node to achieve more accurate detection by collecting and communicating information with other IDS nodes.

Li *et al.* [8] identified that most distributed intrusion detection systems (DIDS) might rely on centralized fusion, or distributed fusion with unscalable communication mechanisms. Based on this, they proposed a DIDS according to the emerging decentralized location and routing infrastructure. Their approach assumes that all peers are trusted which is vulnerable to insider attacks (i.e., betrayal attacks where some nodes suddenly become malicious). To detect insider attacks, Duma *et al.* [1] proposed a P2P-based overlay for intrusion detection (Overlay IDS) that mitigated the insider threat by using a trust-aware engine for correlating alerts and an adaptive scheme for managing trust. The trust-aware correlation engine is capable of filtering out warnings sent by untrusted or low quality peers, while the adaptive trust management scheme uses past experiences of peers to predict their trustworthiness.

Later, Shaikh *et al.* [23] proposed a Group-based Trust Management Scheme (GTMS), which evaluated the trust of a group of Sensor Nodes for two topologies: intragroup topology and intergroup topology. Guo *et al.* [5] described a trust management framework to generate trust values based on Grey theory and Fuzzy sets. They computed trust values by using relation factors and weights of neighbor nodes, not just by simply taking an average value.

Challenge-based intrusion detection. Challenge-based mechanism is a special way of computing trust for IDSs, where the trustworthiness of a node depends on the received answers to the challenges. Fung *et al.* [3] proposed a HIDS collaboration framework that enables each HIDS to evaluate the trustworthiness of others based on its own experience by means of a forgetting factor. The forgetting factor can give more emphasis on the recent experience of the peer. Then, they improved their trust management model by using a Dirichlet-based model to measure the level of trustworthiness among IDS nodes according to their mutual experience [4]. This model had strong scalability properties and was robust against common insider threats. Experimental results demonstrated that the new model could improve robustness and efficiency.

To improve the performance, Li *et al.* [9] pointed out that different IDSs may have different levels of sensitivity in detecting particular types of intrusions based on their own signatures and settings. They therefore defined a notion of *intrusion sensitivity* and explore the feasibility of using this notion to evaluate the trust of an IDS node. They further designed a trust management model based on *intrusion sensitivity* to improve the robustness of CIDNs [10], and proposed a machine learning-based approach in automatically allocating the values of *intrusion sensitivity* [13]. Meng *et al.* [20] identified that challenge mechanisms would be not realistic due to some assumptions and may lead to a weak threat model in practical scenarios. They then designed an advanced collusion attack, called random poisoning attack, which enabled a malicious node to send untruthful information without decreasing its trust value at large. Several attacks can be referred to [11,12] and other related studies on improving IDSs can be referred to alert reduction [15], alert verification [18,19] and EFM [17].

Our work. As MSNs is an emerging medical network constructed by smartphones, there are few studies on the identification of malicious nodes in such environment. Motivated by this, our work proposes a trust-based intrusion detection approach based on behavioral profiling. This work is an early study, aiming to complement existing security mechanisms in healthcare domain and to stimulate more research in this field.

3   Trust Computation Based on Behavioral Profiling

This section describes the requirements from healthcare domain for designing security mechanisms and presents our proposed approach including how to construct behavioral profile and evaluate the trustworthiness of a MSN node.

3.1   Designing Security Mechanisms for MSNs

Medical network is different from a conventional network, due to its sensitivity and lack of IT experts. Thus, it has some unique requirements for designing security mechanisms [21]:

- A centralized architecture is desirable for detecting malicious nodes in MSNs, as healthcare organizations are often short of IT-trained personnel. Due to this, centralized security mechanisms can help reduce the number of potential attack vectors.
- To enable networked medical devices to operate effectively and smoothly, healthcare organizations prefer the deployed mechanisms to identify malicious nodes in a dynamic manner with fault tolerance (i.e., reducing false positives).

In total, an ideal mechanism should be able to support full-time management for inspecting traffic and applying appropriate security policies to respond to accidents. As a result, there is a need for designing appropriate security mechanisms for MSNs.

3.2   Trust-Based Intrusion Detection

As described above, a hierarchical infrastructure is preferred by healthcare domain to secure MSNs against insider attacks. Therefore, we propose a hierarchical trust-based intrusion detection mechanism to identify malicious nodes in MSNs. The high-level architecture of our mechanism with the detection flows are depicted in Fig. 2.

- Figure 2(a) presents the hierarchical trust-based intrusion detection mechanism, where the central server connects with each node in collecting behavioral data. For implementation, each node can install a lightweight IDS agent to inspect traffic and upload statistics to the central server periodically.
- Figure 2(b) illustrates the detection flows including *behavioral data collection, profile construction, statistical trust computation,* and *detection and alert.* To collect behavioral data is a key step for establishing a robust trust-based intrusion detection scheme. The data are used to build a behavioral profile (as *normal behavior*). Then, the trustworthiness of a node can be evaluated through identifying the deviations between historical profile and current profile. Finally, an alarm will be produced if the trust value of a node is lower than a pre-defined threshold.

3.3   Behavioral Profiling and Feature Selection

A behavioral profile is a collection of required information aiming to describe the characteristics of an object under pre-defined rules. For instance, it is similar to a business card that contains some basic features like name, department and business phone number. To create a stable profile, there is a need for using sensible specifications to define the behavior.

There are many basic features of smartphone users, such as phone calls (including outgoing, incoming and video), location, time, SMS, visited websites, Email address, application usage, etc. In MSNs, a balance should be made to decide what kind of data can be collected, due to its speciality and requirements

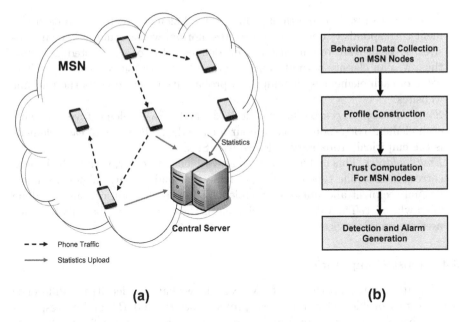

Fig. 2. (a) The high-level architecture of our mechanism; and (b) typical detection flows.

(i.e., there is a chance of leaking information to third-parties). Based on the suggestions from the collaborated healthcare organization, we choose the following features in *each day* to construct a behavioral profile.

- *Camera usage.* As medical records are extremely sensitive, camera usage should be given more attention, i.e., when the camera application is used.
- *Visited websites.* If a node is infected by malware or virus, it is very likely to open and visit certain websites to download or upload data, i.e., which websites are visited during a period of time.
- *Short Message Service.* If a node is compromised, SMS can be used for sensitive information leakage. Thus, SMS usage should be considered in practice, i.e., when the messages are sent.
- *Email address.* Similarly, sending or receiving Emails is sensitive event as well, which can be a target for phishing websites and ransomware.

To quantify behavior patterns into concrete metrics, based on the suggestions from the collaborated healthcare organizations, we devise a quantification scheme for each selected feature as below.

- *Camera usage.* This metric is defined as a 24-element vector, with each element corresponds to one hour for the day. The value of each element is the empirical probability a device uses the camera application.

- *Visited websites.* This metric is defined as a 2-element vector, with each element corresponds to one type of websites: normal website and unknown websites. A healthcare organization often defines a list of whitelisted websites; thus, we can classify normal website and unknown websites accordingly. The value of each element is the empirical probability a device visits the relevant websites.
- *Short Message Service.* This metric is defined as a 24-element vector, with each element corresponds to one hour for the day. The value of each element is the empirical probability a device uses SMS.
- *Email address.* This metric is defined as a 4-element vector, with each element corresponds to one type of email addresses: normal sender, unknown sender, normal recipient and unknown recipient. The classification can also be done via a whitelist. The value of each element is the empirical probability a device uses the email service.

3.4 Trust Computation

To evaluate the trustworthiness of a MSN node, we have to identify the difference between two profiles. Given any two profiles, like $P1$ and $P2$, and corresponding vectors $A = (a_1, a_2, ..., a_n)$ and $B = (b_1, b_2, ..., b_n)$. The Euclidean distance between the two vectors can be computed as below:

$$E(A, B) = \sqrt{\sum_{i=1}^{n}(a_i - b_i)^2} \tag{1}$$

For four sectors, the difference between two behavioral profile can be computed as below (taking the Euclidean norm of the Euclidean distance vector [22]):

$$D(P1, P2) = \sqrt{\sum_{j=1}^{4}(E_j)^2} \tag{2}$$

The resulting value is the difference of the two behavioral profiles, and has a range of $[0, 2]$. It is worth noting that a larger value indicates a more significant difference between two profiles. To tune $D(P1, P2)$ for comparing trust values, we define the trustworthiness of a node as follow.

$$t_{value}^{d} = 1 - \frac{D(P1, P2)}{2} \tag{3}$$

where t_{value}^{d} indicates the trust value of node d and $\frac{D(P1,P2)}{2}$ aims to normalize the range of $D(P1, P2)$ to $[0, 1]$. Subsequently, a node's trustworthiness can be computed using the above equation and a malicious node can be determined by setting a trust threshold. Let τ denote the trust threshold, then we can consider:

- If $t_{value}^{d} \geq \tau$, then the node is considered as a normal node.
- If $t_{value}^{d} < \tau$, then the node is regarded as a malicious (or untrusted) node.

4   Evaluation

In this section, we collaborated with a healthcare center located in South China (with around 100 personnel) to investigate the performance of our approach. Due to privacy concerns, our approach was deployed in part of a MSN, which consists of 15 nodes. A central server was implemented to collect required information from each node for computing their trust values (see Fig. 2(a)). The server was composed of an Intel(R) Core (TM)2, Quad CPU 2.66 GHz. The healthcare center defined 76 normal websites, 107 Email senders and 101 recipients based on its historical record and current settings. We mainly conduct two experiments:

- *Experiment-1.* This experiment evaluates our mechanism in a normal MSN environment, with the purpose of observing the trend of trust values and identifying an appropriate threshold.
- *Experiment-2.* This experiment aims to explore the feasibility of our mechanism under an adversary scenario, where several nodes may behave maliciously (i.e., violating normal profile).

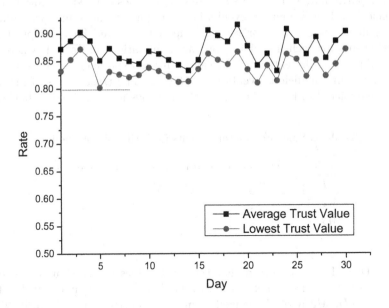

Fig. 3. The trend of trust values.

4.1   Experiment-1

In this experiment, we observe the trend of trust values in a normal MSN environment. t^d_{value} falls in the range of $[0,1]$, where a larger t^d_{value} means that a node is more credible. Ideally, t^d_{value} is expected to 1; therefore, the purpose of this experiment is to identify an appropriate threshold for detecting malicious nodes in MSNs. For computing trust values, we used half-month historical data to build a normal profile for each device. The trend of average and lowest trust value within one month is depicted in Fig. 3.

The metric of average trust value is an average value including all nodes, which can depict the overall network performance. Figure 3 shows that the trend of average trust value was generally higher than 0.83. The lowest trust value indicates the worst node's performance, which ranges from 0.81 to 0.88. As there is no update of the normal profile, the trend of trust values shows that behavioral profile is relatively stale in the deployed healthcare environment.

Overall, Fig. 3 describes that trust values can be regularly higher than 0.8 in a normal MSN environment. Therefore, we choose 0.8 as the trust threshold in our approach for the deployed environment.

4.2   Experiment-2

In this experiment, we mainly evaluate the performance of our approach in a malicious scenario, where some nodes act unusually, i.e., violating a normal profile. In particular, we randomly selected three nodes (named *M1*, *M2* and *M3*) as malicious to launch unusual events. For example, one node may visit unusual websites in a random way, or send an email to an undefined recipient. The unusual events for each malicious node are summarized in Table 1, where each node could make different unusual events. In the experiment, malicious nodes started launching malicious events from Day 31. The trust values of malicious nodes are depicted in Fig. 4. The main observations are described as below.

Table 1. Simulated unusual events for each malicious nodes.

Node	Camera	Visited websites	SMS	Email address
M1	-	-	✓	-
M2	✓	✓	-	-
M3	✓	✓	-	✓

- From Day 31, it is observed that the trust values of malicious nodes could quickly decrease and go below the threshold of 0.8 at the same day. The trust value of *M1*, *M2* and *M3* ranged from 0.68 to 0.78, from 0.56 to 0.72, and from 0.46 to 0.68, respectively.
- Table 1 states that *M1* only violated the usage of SMS, *M2* violated the usage of camera and website visit, and *M3* performed all types of unusual events except SMS. Figure 4 shows that *M3* received the lowest trust value among the three malicious nodes.

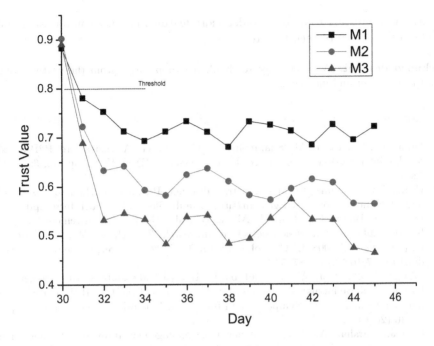

Fig. 4. The trust values of malicious nodes.

The experimental results indicate that our trust-based approach is feasible and promising to identify malicious nodes in a quick manner for MSN environments (i.e., identifying malicious nodes at the same day). In addition, it is observed that more unusual events result in a lower trust value. Our findings were also confirmed by IT administrators in the participating healthcare organization.

5 Conclusion

With more devices interconnected, medical smartphone networks (MSNs) have become an emerging architecture in various healthcare organizations. There is a great need to protect such healthcare environment against insider attacks. In this work, we focus on MSNs and propose a hierarchical trust-based intrusion detection mechanism based on behavioral profiling. Trust value is derived by identifying the difference between two profiles using Euclidean distance. By collaborating with healthcare organizations, we evaluated the proposed approach in a real simulated MSN environment to investigate its performance. Experimental results indicate that our approach is feasible and encouraging in detecting malicious MSN nodes in a quick manner.

There are many possible topics for our future work. One is to investigate how to efficiently identify a trust threshold in different network environments. It is also an interesting topic to consider more features in trust computation and exploring the effect of each feature.

Acknowledgment. We would like to thank the cooperation from the participating healthcare center and managers.

References

1. Duma, C., Karresand, M., Shahmehri, N., Caronni, G.: A trust-aware, P2P-based overlay for intrusion detection. In: Proccedings of DEXA Workshop, pp. 692–697 (2006)
2. Evans, P.C., Annunziata, M.: Industrial Internet, Pushing the Boundary of Mind and Machines. http://www.ge.com/sites/default/files/Industrial_Internet.pdf
3. Fung, C.J., Baysal, O., Zhang, J., Aib, I., Boutaba, R.: Trust management for host-based collaborative intrusion detection. In: Turck, F., Kellerer, W., Kormentzas, G. (eds.) DSOM 2008. LNCS, vol. 5273, pp. 109–122. Springer, Heidelberg (2008). doi:10.1007/978-3-540-87353-2_9
4. Fung, C.J., Zhang, J., Aib, I., Boutaba, R.: Robust and scalable trust management for collaborative intrusion detection. In: Proceedings of the 11th IFIP/IEEE International Conference on Symposium on Integrated Network Management (IM), pp. 33–40 (2009)
5. Guo, J., Marshall, A., Zhou, B.: A new trust management framework for detecting malicious and selfish behaviour for mobile ad hoc networks. In: Proceedings of the 10th IEEE International Conference on Trust, Security and Privacy in Computing and Communications (TrustCom), pp. 142–149 (2011)
6. Harries, P.: The prognosis for healthcare payers and providers: rising cybersecurity risks and costs. http://usblogs.pwc.com/cybersecurity/the-prognosis-for-healthcare-payers-and-providers-rising-cybersecurity-risks-and-costs/
7. Healey, J., Pollard, N., Woods, B.: The healthcare internet of things: rewards and risks. http://www.mcafee.com/mx/resources/reports/rp-healthcare-iot-rewards-risks.pdf
8. Li, Z., Chen, Y., Beach, A.: Towards scalable and robust distributed intrusion alert fusion with good load balancing. In: Proceedings of the 2006 SIGCOMM Workshop on Large-Scale Attack Defense (LSAD), pp. 115–122 (2006)
9. Li, W., Meng, Y., Kwok, L.F.: Enhancing trust evaluation using intrusion sensitivity in collaborative intrusion detection networks: feasibility and challenges. In: Proceedings of the 9th International Conference on Computational Intelligence and Security (CIS), pp. 518–522 (2013)
10. Li, W., Meng, W., Kwok, L.-F.: Design of intrusion sensitivity-based trust management model for collaborative intrusion detection networks. In: Zhou, J., Gal-Oz, N., Zhang, J., Gudes, E. (eds.) IFIPTM 2014. IAICT, vol. 430, pp. 61–76. Springer, Heidelberg (2014). doi:10.1007/978-3-662-43813-8_5
11. Li, W., Meng, W., Kwok, L.-F., Ip, H.H.S.: PMFA: toward passive message fingerprint attacks on challenge-based collaborative intrusion detection networks. In: Chen, J., Piuri, V., Su, C., Yung, M. (eds.) NSS 2016. LNCS, vol. 9955, pp. 433–449. Springer, Cham (2016). doi:10.1007/978-3-319-46298-1_28
12. Li, W., Meng, W., Kwok, L.-F.: SOOA: exploring special on-off attacks on challenge-based collaborative intrusion detection networks. In: Au, M.H.A., Castiglione, A., Choo, K.-K.R., Palmieri, F., Li, K.-C. (eds.) GPC 2017. LNCS, vol. 10232, pp. 402–415. Springer, Cham (2017). doi:10.1007/978-3-319-57186-7_30

13. Li, W., Meng, Y., Kwok, L.F., Ip, H.H.S.: Enhancing collaborative intrusion detection networks against insider attacks using supervised intrusion sensitivity-based trust management model. J. Netw. Comput. Appl. **77**, 135–145 (2017)
14. Meng, Y., Kwok, L.-F., Li, W.: Towards designing packet filter with a trust-based approach using Bayesian inference in network intrusion detection. In: Keromytis, A.D., Pietro, R. (eds.) SecureComm 2012. LNICSSITE, vol. 106, pp. 203–221. Springer, Heidelberg (2013). doi:10.1007/978-3-642-36883-7_13
15. Meng, Y., Kwok, L.F., Li, W.: Enhancing false alarm reduction using voted ensemble selection in intrusion detection. Int. J. Comput. Intell. Syst. **6**(4), 626–638 (2013)
16. Meng, Y., Li, W., Kwok, L.: Evaluation of detecting malicious nodes using Bayesian model in wireless intrusion detection. In: Lopez, J., Huang, X., Sandhu, R. (eds.) NSS 2013. LNCS, vol. 7873, pp. 40–53. Springer, Heidelberg (2013). doi:10.1007/978-3-642-38631-2_4
17. Meng, W., Li, W., Kwok, L.F.: EFM: enhancing the performance of signature-based network intrusion detection systems using enhanced filter mechanism. Comput. Secur. **43**, 189–204 (2014)
18. Meng, Y., Kwok, L.F.: Adaptive blacklist-based packet filter with a statistic-based approach in network intrusion detection. J. Netw. Comput. Appl. **39**, 83–92 (2014)
19. Meng, W., Li, W., Kwok, L.F.: Design of intelligent KNN-based alarm filter using knowledge-based alert verification in intrusion detection. Secur. Commun. Netw. **8**(18), 3883–3895 (2015)
20. Meng, W., Luo, X., Li, W., Li, Y.: Design and evaluation of advanced collusion attacks on collaborative intrusion detection networks in practice. In: Proceedings of the 15th IEEE International Conference on Trust, Security and Privacy in Computing and Communications (TrustCom), pp. 1061–1068 (2016)
21. Meng, W., Li, W., Xiang, Y., Choo, K.K.R.: A Bayesian inference-based detection mechanism to defend medical smartphone networks against insider attacks. J. Netw. Comput. Appl. **78**, 162–169 (2017)
22. Ruan, X., Wu, Z., Wang, H., Jajodia, S.: Profiling online social behaviors for compromised account detection. IEEE Trans. Inf. Forensics Secur. **11**(1), 176–187 (2016)
23. Shaikh, R.A., Jameel, H., d'Auriol, B.J., Lee, H., Lee, S., Song, Y.J.: Group-based trust management scheme for clustered wireless sensor networks. IEEE Trans. Parallel Distrib. Syst. **20**(11), 1698–1712 (2009)
24. Symantec. Networked medical devices: security and privacy threats, June 2015. https://www.symantec.com/content/en/us/enterprise/white_papers/b-networked _medical_devices_WP_21177186.en-us.pdf
25. Williams, P.A.H., Woodward, A.J.: Cybersecurity vulnerabilities in medical devices: a complex environment and multifaceted problem. Med. Devices Evid. Res. **8**, 305–316 (2015)
26. Wu, Y.-S., Foo, B., Mei, Y., Bagchi, S.: Collaborative intrusion detection system (CIDS): a framework for accurate and efficient IDS. In: Proceedings of the 2003 Annual Computer Security Applications Conference (ACSAC), pp. 234–244 (2003)

Two-Phase Locality-Sensitive Hashing for Privacy-Preserving Distributed Service Recommendation

Lianyong Qi[1,2(✉)], Wanchun Dou[3], and Xuyun Zhang[4]

[1] School of Information Science and Engineering,
Qufu Normal University, Jining, China
lianyongqi@gmail.com
[2] Chinese Academy of Education Big Data,
Qufu Normal University, Jining, China
[3] State Key Laboratory for Novel Software Technology,
Nanjing University, Nanjing, China
douwc@nju.edu.cn
[4] Department of Electrical and Computer Engineering,
University of Auckland, Auckland, New Zealand
xuyun.zhang@auckland.ac.nz

Abstract. With the ever-increasing volume of services registered in various web communities, it becomes a challenging task to find the web services that a target user is really interested in from the massive candidates. In this situation, Collaborative Filtering (i.e., CF) technique is introduced to alleviate the heavy burden on the service selection decisions of target users. However, present CF-based recommendation approaches often assume that the recommendation bases, i.e., historical service quality data are centralized, without considering the distributed service recommendation scenarios where data are multi-sourced. Furthermore, distributed service recommendation calls for the collaborations among multiple involved parties, during which the private information of users may be exposed. In view of these challenges, we propose a novel privacy-preserving distributed service recommendation approach based on two-phase Locality-Sensitive Hashing (LSH), named $SerRec_{two\text{-}LSH}$, in this paper. Concretely, in $SerRec_{two\text{-}LSH}$, we first look for the "similar friends" of a target user through a privacy-preserving two-phase LSH process; afterwards, we determine the services preferred by the "similar friends" of the target user, and then recommend them to the target user. Finally, through a set of experiments conducted on a real distributed service quality dataset $WS\text{-}DREAM$, we validate the feasibility of our proposal in terms of recommendation accuracy and efficiency while guaranteeing privacy-preservation.

Keywords: Distributed service recommendation · Collaborative Filtering · Privacy-preservation · Efficiency · Two-Phase Locality-Sensitive hashing

S. Wen et al. (Eds.): CSS 2017, LNCS 10581, pp. 176–188, 2017.
https://doi.org/10.1007/978-3-319-69471-9_13

1 Introduction

With the ever-increasing volume and categories of services in various web communities (e.g., *Amazon* and *IBM*), it is becoming a challenging task to find the web services that a target user is really interested in from the massive candidates [1–3]. In this situation, various light-weight service recommendation techniques, e.g., the widely adopted Collaborative Filtering (i.e., CF) is introduced to alleviate the heavy burden on the service selection decisions of target users. Generally, through CF (e.g., user-based CF[1]), a recommender system can find the "similar friends" of a target user base on the historical service quality data and then make service recommendations to the target user based on the obtained "similar friends" [4].

However, two shortcomings are present in the existing CF-based service recommendation approaches. First, present approaches often assume that the recommendation bases, i.e., historical service quality data are centralized, without considering the recommendation scenarios where service quality data are multi-sourced or distributed. Furthermore, in a distributed environment, service recommendation calls for intensive collaborations among multiple involved parties or platforms; while user privacy may be exposed during this cross-platform collaboration process.

In view of these two challenges, a novel distributed service recommendation approach based on two-phase Locality-Sensitive Hashing (LSH) [5], named $SerRec_{two\text{-}LSH}$, is put forward in this paper, to enable the privacy-preserving distributed service recommendation.

In summary, the contributions of our paper are three-fold.

(1) To the best of our knowledge, existing research work seldom considers the distributed service recommendation problems where historical service quality data are multi-sourced. We formulate this distributed service recommendation problem and clarify its significance.
(2) We introduce a two-phase Locality-Sensitive Hashing process into distributed service recommendation so as to protect the key privacy information of users, e.g., *the service quality data observed by a user, the service set ever invoked by a user*.
(3) A wide range of experiments are conducted on a distributed service quality dataset *WS-DREAM*, to validate the feasibility and advantages of our proposal. Experiment results show that our proposed $SerRec_{two\text{-}LSH}$ approach outperforms the other state-of-the-art approaches in terms of recommendation accuracy and efficiency while guaranteeing privacy-preservation.

The rest of paper is structured as follows. Related work is presented in Sect. 2. In Sect. 3, we demonstrate the research motivation of our paper. In Sect. 4, our proposed service recommendation approach, i.e., $SerRec_{two\text{-}LSH}$ is introduced in detail. In Sect. 5, we conduct a set of experiments to validate the feasibility of our proposal and finally in Sect. 6, we summarize the paper and point out the future research directions.

---

[1] Actually, CF includes user-based CF, item-based CF and Hybrid CF; however, for simplicity, only user-based CF is discussed in this paper as the rationales of these three CF variants are similar.

2 Related Work

As a classic method for information retrieval, Collaborative Filtering (i.e., CF) has become one of the most effective techniques in various recommender systems. Concretely, user-based CF and item-based CF are brought forth in work [4] and [6], respectively, for accurate service recommendation. In order to integrate the advantages of the user-based CF and item-based CF together, a hybrid CF is introduced in [7] whose experiment results indicate a better recommendation performance. As the quality of a service extremely depends on the service invocation context (e.g., service invocation time, user location, service location), time-aware CF and location-aware CF are proposed in [8] and [9], respectively. However, the above approaches only recruit the objective user-service quality data for service recommendation, without considering the target users' subjective preference which also plays an important role in the target users' service selection decisions. In view of this shortcoming, a user preference-aware CF recommendation approach is introduced in [10] to pursue more reasonable recommended results. However, the above approaches may fail to produce any recommended result when the historical service quality data are very sparse. Considering this limitation, popularity-aware CF and trust propagation-based CF are put forward in [11] and [12], respectively, to cope with the cold-start recommendation problem in the sparse-data environment.

However, the above recommendation approaches all assume that the recommendation bases, i.e., historical service quality data are centralized, without considering the distributed service recommendation scenarios as well as the resulted privacy protection problems. In order to protect user privacy, a naïve method is proposed in [13] where each user is suggested to release only a small portion of his/her observed service quality data. However, the released small portion of data can still reveal partial privacy information of a user. In view of this shortcoming, data obfuscation technique is adopted in [14] to transform the real service quality data into the obfuscated one, through which the real service quality data is hidden and protected. However, as the data recruited for service recommendation has been obfuscated, the recommendation accuracy is decreased accordingly. Considering this drawback, a "divide-merge" mechanism is taken in [15] where each piece of user-service quality data is firstly divided into several quality segments with little user privacy, and then the quality segments are employed for subsequent service recommendation. However, two shortcomings are present in this approach. First, the recommendation efficiency is reduced significantly as the "divide-merge" operations adopted in [15] are often time-consuming. Besides, this approach cannot protect some private user information, e.g., *the service intersection commonly invoked by two users*.

In view of the above challenges, a novel service recommendation approach based on two-phase LSH, i.e., $SerRec_{two\text{-}LSH}$ is put forward in this paper, to solve the privacy-preserving service recommendation problems in a distributed environment. Next, an intuitive example is provided to further demonstrate the research motivation of our paper.

3   Research Motivation

In this section, an example is presented in Fig. 1 to clarify the research motivation of our paper. As Fig. 1 shows, u_{target} (in *Amazon* platform) denotes a target user to whom a recommender system intends to recommend services; u_1 is a user in *IBM* platform; $\{ws_1, \ldots, ws_n\}$ are the candidate web services, each of which may be invoked by any user in any platform. If user u in platform pf (i.e., *Amazon* or *IBM*) has ever invoked service ws, then the service quality data of ws observed by u is recorded by pf.

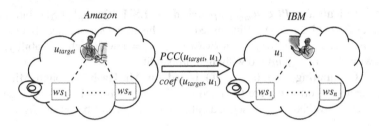

Fig. 1. Distributed service recommendation: an example.

Next, in order to find the similar friends of u_{target}, we need to first calculate the similarity between u_{target} and u_1, i.e., $Sim(u_{target}, u_1)$ by (1) according to the traditional user-based CF. Here, $PCC(u_{target}, u_1)$ ($\in[0, 1]$) denotes the Pearson Correlation Coefficient [16] between u_{target} and u_1, which can be calculated based on the historical service quality data observed by u_{target} and u_1; $coef(u_{target}, u_1)$ indicates the credibility of $PCC(u_{target}, u_1)$ and can be obtained by (2) where I_{target} and I_1 denote the service sets invoked by u_{target} and u_1, respectively.

$$Sim\big(u_{target}, u_1\big) = coef\big(u_{target}, u_1\big)*PCC\big(u_{target}, u_1\big) \tag{1}$$

$$coef\big(u_{target}, u_1\big) = \frac{|I_{target} \cap I_1|}{|I_{target} \cup I_1|} \tag{2}$$

In terms of the above analyses, we can conclude that the collaboration between *Amazon* and *IBM* is necessary in order to calculate the user similarity $Sim(u_{target}, u_1)$ in (1). While such a cross-platform collaboration process often faces a big challenge. Concretely, due to privacy concerns, *IBM* is often not willing to release its data about u_1 (e.g., *the service set ever invoked by u_1, the service quality data observed by u_1*) to *Amazon*, which impedes the collaboration between *Amazon* and *IBM* severely and renders the calculation of $Sim(u_{target}, u_1)$ in (1) infeasible.

In view of this challenge, we introduce the Locality-Sensitive Hashing (LSH) technique into cross-platform service recommendation, and develop a novel two-phase LSH-based recommendation approach, i.e., $SerRec_{two\text{-}LSH}$ to handle the privacy-preserving distributed service recommendation problems.

4   Two-Phase LSH-Based Service Recommendation Approach: *SerRec_{two-LSH}*

In this section, our proposed service recommendation approach *SerRec_{two-LSH}* is introduced, which consists of the four steps in Fig. 2. Here, $\{u_1, \ldots, u_m\}$ is the user set, u_{target} denotes a target user, $\{ws_1, \ldots, ws_n\}$ is the candidate service set, q is a quality dimension (e.g., *response time*) of web services.

Step-1:   Calculating $PCC(u_{target}, u_i)$ based on LSH. Through LSH, build user index $H(u_i)$ $(1 \leq i \leq m)$ offline based on the historical service quality observed by u_i. If $H(u_{target}) = H(u_i)$, then $PCC(u_{target}, u_i) = 1$ with high probability; otherwise, $PCC(u_{target}, u_i) = 0$ with high probability.

Step-2:   Calculating $coef(u_{target}, u_i)$ based on MinHash. Through MinHash, generate a short signature (denoted by Sig_i) for each u_i $(1 \leq i \leq m)$ based on u_i's ever-invoked service set. Calculate $coef(u_{target}, u_i)$ based on Sig_{target} and Sig_i.

Step-3:   Determining the similar friends of u_{target}. Calculate similarity $Sim(u_{target}, u_i)$ based on $PCC(u_{target}, u_i)$ derived in Sep-1 and $coef(u_{target}, u_i)$ derived in Step-2, and subsequently determine the similar friends of u_{target} based on $Sim(u_{target}, u_i)$.

Step-4:   Service recommendation. According to the similar friends of u_{target} derived in Step-3, predict the quality of services never invoked by u_{target}, and return the quality-optimal one.

Fig. 2. Four steps of *SerRec_{two-LSH}* approach

The main idea behind our proposal is: for each user u_i $(1 \leq i \leq m)$, $PCC(u_{target}, u_i)$ in (1) and $coef(u_{target}, u_i)$ in (2) can be calculated based on LSH in Step-1 and MinHash [17] (a LSH variant) in Step-2, respectively, in a privacy-preserving way; afterwards, according to the results obtained in the above two steps, $Sim(u_{target}, u_i)$ in (1) can be calculated in Step-3, based on which the similar friends of u_{target} can be determined; finally, according to the similar friends derived in Step-3, service recommendations can be made to u_{target} in Step-4. Next, we will introduce these four steps in detail.

Step-1: Calculating $PCC(u_{target}, u_i)$ based on LSH

First, we select a LSH function family $H(u_i) = \{h_1(u_i), \ldots, h_r(u_i)\}$ to build index (with little privacy information) for each user u_i $(1 \leq i \leq m)$. The LSH functions recruited here depend on the adopted "distance" type. As Pearson Correlation Coefficient (PCC) [16] is often taken as the distance measurement in various recommender systems, in this step, we utilize the LSH functions corresponding to PCC to build user indexes. Next, we introduce the concrete building process of user indexes.

For user u_i, his/her historical service quality data can be denoted by a n-dimensional vector $\overrightarrow{u_i} = (ws_1.q, \ldots, ws_n.q)$, where $ws_j.q$ represents the quality of service ws_j $(1 \leq j \leq n)$ over dimension q and $ws_j.q = 0$ if u_i has never invoked ws_j before. Then according to LSH theory [18], the LSH function for vector $\overrightarrow{u_i}$, denoted by $h(\overrightarrow{u_i})$, is shown in (3). Here, $\overrightarrow{v}$ is an n-dimensional vector $(v_1, ..., v_n)$ where v_j $(1 \leq j \leq n)$ is generated randomly and $v_j \in [-1, 1]$ holds; symbol "∘" denotes the dot product between two vectors. The rationale behind LSH is: take vector $\overrightarrow{v}$ as a hyper plane, if two vectors $\overrightarrow{u_1}$ and $\overrightarrow{u_2}$ are located on the same side of $\overrightarrow{v}$ (i.e., both $\overrightarrow{u_1} \circ \overrightarrow{v} > 0$ and $\overrightarrow{u_2} \circ \overrightarrow{v} > 0$ hold, or, both $\overrightarrow{u_1} \circ \overrightarrow{v} \leq 0$ and $\overrightarrow{u_2} \circ \overrightarrow{v} \leq 0$ hold), then $\overrightarrow{u_1}$ and $\overrightarrow{u_2}$ are similar with high probability.

$$h(\overrightarrow{u_i}) = \begin{cases} 1 & \text{if } \overrightarrow{u_i} \circ \overrightarrow{v} > 0 \\ 0 & \text{if } \overrightarrow{u_i} \circ \overrightarrow{v} \leq 0 \end{cases} \qquad (3)$$

Thus through the hash function in (3), user u_i is transformed into a binary hash value, i.e., 0 or 1. As LSH is essentially a probability-based approach [5], more hashing functions or hashing tables may lead to higher recommendation accuracy. Therefore, to make accurate service recommendation, multiple hash functions and hash tables are recruited here. Concretely, we assume that T hash tables are employed and each hash table is corresponding to r hash functions. Then for each hash table, a r-dimensional vector $H(\overrightarrow{u_i}) = (h_1(\overrightarrow{u_i}), ..., h_r(\overrightarrow{u_i}))$ is achieved, which can be regarded as the index for user u_i in the hash table. Thus for a platform (e.g., *IBM* in Fig. 1), it can release only the short user indexes with little privacy to other platforms (e.g., *Amazon* in Fig. 1), without revealing other key privacy information, e.g., *service quality data observed by a user*; therefore, user privacy is protected.

Furthermore, the user indexes can be built offline before a recommendation request arrives, as the historical service quality data used to build user indexes are already recorded by a certain platform (e.g., in Fig. 1, u_{target}'s and u_1's service quality data are recorded by *Amazon* and *IBM*, respectively). As a consequence, the recommendation efficiency can be improved considerably. Besides, for two users u_1 and u_2, if their indexes are the same in any hash table (i.e., condition in (4) holds), then u_1 and u_2 are projected into the same bucket in the hash table and hence can be regarded as similar with high probability [5].

$$\exists x, \text{satisfy } H_x(\overrightarrow{u_1}) = H_x(\overrightarrow{u_2}) \ (x \in \{1, ..., T\}) \qquad (4)$$

Next, we calculate the index for u_{target}, i.e., $H(\overrightarrow{u_{target}})$ and compare it with $H(\overrightarrow{u_i})$ $(1 \leq i \leq m)$. If $H(\overrightarrow{u_{target}}) = H(\overrightarrow{u_i})$ holds in any of the T hash tables, then we can conclude that the PCC value between u_{target} and u_i, i.e., $PCC(u_{target}, u_i) = 1$ with high probability; otherwise, $PCC(u_{target}, u_i) = 0$. Finally, we select the users u_i whose PCC $(u_{target}, u_i) = 1$ and take them as the candidates (recorded in set $Friend\_set_{PCC}$) for the similar friends of u_{target}.

Step-2: Calculating $coef(u_{target}, u_i)$ based on MinHash

For any user u_i $(1 \leq i \leq m)$, his/her ever-invoked service set can be denoted by a n-dimensional column vector $\overrightarrow{V_i} = (V_{i-1}, ..., V_{i-n})^T$ where $V_{i-j} = 1$ $(1 \leq j \leq n)$ if u_i has ever invoked service ws_j before; otherwise, $V_{i-j} = 0$. Thus we can obtain a user-service invocation matrix M in (5), where each user corresponds to a column. Next, in matrix

M, we record the position of first "1" (marked with blue circle in (5)) from the top down in each column. For example, the position value for u_1 column is "2" as u_1 has never invoked ws_1 but has ever invoked ws_2; likewise, the position value for u_2 column is "1" as u_2 has ever invoked ws_1. Thus we can obtain an m-dimensional row vector R. For example, $R = (2, 1, ..., 2)$ holds for the example in (5).

Afterwards, we randomly swap the order of all services in matrix M and then repeat the above process to generate k ($k \ll n$) row vectors $R_1, ..., R_k$. Thus a new $k*m$ matrix $M*$ in (6) is achieved, where each column $(r_{1i}, r_{2i}, ..., r_{ki})^T$ can be treated as a short user signature (denoted by set $Sig_i = \{r_{1i}, r_{2i}, ..., r_{ki}\}$) that depicts u_i's ever-invoked service set. Thus for a platform (e.g., *IBM* in Fig. 1), it can release only a short user signature of u_i, i.e., Sig_i with little privacy to other platforms (e.g., *Amazon* in Fig. 1), without revealing u_i's ever-invoked web service set; therefore, u_i's privacy is protected.

Furthermore, as the ever-invoked service set used to build a user signature is already recorded by a certain platform (considering the example in Fig. 1, u_{target}'s and u_1's ever-invoked service sets are recorded by *Amazon* and *IBM*, respectively), the user signature Sig_i ($1 \leq i \leq m$) can be generated offline before a recommendation request arrives; as a consequence, the recommendation efficiency can be improved considerably.

Next, according to the MinHash theory [17], the equation in (2) can be transformed into the equation in (7). As $k \ll n$, $|Sig_i| \ll |I_i|$ holds in (7). Thus, we can calculate $coef(u_{target}, u_i)$ by (7) in a privacy-preserving and efficient way.

$$M = \begin{matrix} ws_1 \\ ws_2 \\ \vdots \\ ws_n \end{matrix} \begin{matrix} u_1 & u_2 & \cdots & u_m \end{matrix} \begin{bmatrix} 0 & ① & \cdots & 0 \\ ① & 0 & \cdots & ① \\ \vdots & \vdots & \vdots & \vdots \\ 0 & 1 & \cdots & 1 \end{bmatrix} \quad (5)$$

$$M^* = \begin{bmatrix} R_1 \\ R_2 \\ \vdots \\ R_k \end{bmatrix} = \begin{bmatrix} r_{11} & r_{12} & \cdots & r_{1m} \\ r_{21} & r_{22} & \cdots & r_{2m} \\ & \vdots & \vdots & \\ r_{k1} & r_{k2} & \cdots & r_{km} \end{bmatrix} \quad (6)$$

$$coef(u_{target}, u_1) = \frac{|I_{target} \cap I_1|}{|I_{target} \cup I_1|} \approx \frac{|Sig_{target} \cap Sig_1|}{|Sig_{target} \cup Sig_1|} \quad (7)$$

Step-3: Determining the similar friends of u_{target}

In Step-1 and Step-2, we have obtained $PCC(u_{target}, u_i)$ and $coef(u_{target}, u_i)$ for user u_i ($1 \leq i \leq m$). Then according to (1), the similarity between u_{target} and u_i, i.e., $Sim(u_{target}, u_i)$ can be obtained. Here, we only need to calculate the similarity values between u_{target} and the users in set $Friend\_set_{PCC}$ (derived in Step-1), as those users outside $Friend\_set_{PCC}$ are not similar with u_{target} with high probability according to the nature of LSH. Next, for each $u_i \in Friend\_set_{PCC}$, we calculate $Sim(u_{target}, u_i)$ by (1); afterwards, the Top-3 users with the highest $Sim(u_{target}, u_i)$ values are considered as similar friends of u_{target} and put into a new set $Friend\_set_{coef*PCC}$.

Step-4: Service recommendation

Next, we utilize the target user's similar friends, i.e., the users in $Friend\_set_{coef*PCC}$ obtained in Step-3, to make service recommendations. Concretely, for each service ws_j never invoked by u_{target}, we predict its quality over dimension q by u_{target}, denoted by $q_{target-j}$, based on the equation in (8). Here, q_{i-j} denotes ws_j's quality over dimension q by u_i, $Sim(u_{target}, u_i)$ represents the similarity between u_{target} and u_i obtained in Step-3. Finally, we select the services with the optimal predicted quality and recommend them to the target user, so as to finish the whole service recommendation process.

$$q_{target-j} = \frac{\sum\limits_{u_i \in Friend\_set_{coef*PCC}} Sim(u_{target}, u_i)^* q_{i-j}}{\sum\limits_{u_i \in Friend\_set_{coef*PCC}} Sim(u_{target}, u_i)} \tag{8}$$

5 Experiments

In this section, we conduct a set of experiments to validate the feasibility of our proposed $SerRec_{two-LSH}$ approach. The experiments are based on a real distributed service quality (i.e., *response time* and *throughput*) dataset *WS-DREAM* [19] which collects real-world service quality evaluation results from 339 users (in different countries) on 5825 Web services. In the experiments, only a quality dimension of services, i.e., *response time* is considered and each country is recruited as an independent platform so as to simulate the distributed service recommendation scenarios.

Concretely, in order to make service quality prediction and service recommendations, $(100 - p)\%$ entries are removed from the user-service quality matrix in *WS-DREAM* (parameter $p \in (0, 100)$). Namely, we use the $p\%$ known service quality data to predict the rest $(100 - p)\%$ missing data, and compare the predicted service quality with the real service quality so as to measure the service recommendation performance. More specifically, the following two evaluation criteria are tested and compared, respectively (as user privacy can be protected well by the intrinsic nature of LSH, we will not evaluate the capability of privacy-preservation of our proposal here).

(1) *Time cost*: consumed time for generating the final recommended results.
(2) *MAE* (Mean Absolute Error, the smaller the better): average difference between the predicted service quality and the real service quality of recommended services.

Besides, we compare our proposal with another three state-of-the-art recommendation approaches, i.e., *UPCC* [20], *PPICF* [15] and *P-UIPCC* [14]. The experiments were conducted on a Lenovo laptop with 2.40 GHz processors and 12.0 GB RAM. The machine runs under Windows 10, JAVA 8 and MySQL 5.7. Each experiment was carried out 10 times and the average experiment results were adopted finally.

Concretely, the following six profiles are tested and compared in our experiments. Here, m and n denote the number of users and number of web services, respectively; T and r denote the number of LSH tables and number of hashing functions in each LSH table (see Step-1), respectively; k represents the number of MinHash functions, i.e., the number of row vectors in Eq. (6); $p\%$ denotes the density of user-service quality matrix.

Profile 1: recommendation efficiency comparison of four approaches w.r.t. *m* and *n*
In this profile, we test and compare the recommendation efficiency of four approaches. The experiment parameters are set as follows: $k = 30$, $T = 10$, $r = 8$, $p = 5$. The concrete experiment results are presented in Fig. 3.

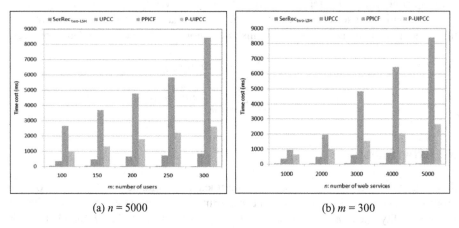

(a) $n = 5000$ (b) $m = 300$

Fig. 3. Recommendation efficiency comparison of four approaches

In Fig. 3(a), $n = 5000$ and m is varied from 100 to 300. As can be seen from Fig. 3 (a) that the time costs of *UPCC*, *PPICF* and *P-UIPCC* approaches all increase with the growth of m, this is because all the m users need to be traversed so as to find the target user's similar friends; while the time cost of our proposed $SerRec_{two-LSH}$ approach is rather small and outperforms those of the other three approaches, as most jobs (e.g., user indexes building in Step-1, user signature generation in Step-2) in our approach can be done offline. As a consequence, the recommendation efficiency is improved significantly.

In Fig. 3(b), $m = 300$ and n is varied from 1000 to 5000. The experiment results also indicate the similar variation tendency of recommendation efficiency as Fig. 3(a). The time costs of *UPCC*, *PPICF* and *P-UIPCC* approaches all increase when n grows, because all the n services should be considered in the user similarity calculation process of these three approaches. While our $SerRec_{two-LSH}$ approach outperforms the other three ones in terms of recommendation efficiency as the job of user similarity calculation is done offline in our approach. Therefore, the recommendation efficiency is improved considerably.

Profile 2: recommendation accuracy comparison of four approaches w.r.t. *m* and *n*
In this profile, we test and compare the accuracy (i.e., *MAE*, the smaller the better) values of five recommendation approaches. The concrete experiment parameters are set as follows: $k = 30$, $T = 10$, $r = 8$, $p = 5$. Experiment results are presented in Fig. 4.

In Fig. 4(a), $n = 5000$ and m is varied from 100 to 300. As Fig. 4(a) shows, the recommendation accuracy values of *PPICF* and *P-UIPCC* approaches are both low

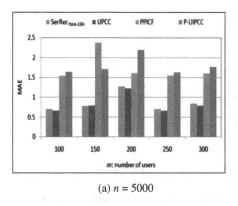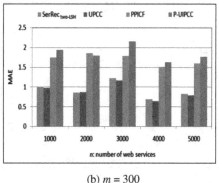

(a) $n = 5000$ (b) $m = 300$

Fig. 4. Recommendation accuracy comparison of four approaches

(i.e., *MAE* values are both high). This is because the data used to make service recommendations have been obfuscated in these two approaches so as to protect user privacy; as a consequence, the recommendation accuracy values are reduced. While due to the nature of LSH technique adopted in our proposed *SerRec*$_{two-LSH}$ approach, only the "most similar" friends of a target user could be returned for further service recommendation and hence, the recommendation accuracy of our proposal is often high (i.e., *MAE* value is low) and close to that of the benchmark approach *UPCC*. Similar experiment results can also be observed from Fig. 4(b) where $m = 300$ holds and n is varied from 1000 to 5000. The reason is the same as that in Fig. 4(a) and hence not discussed again here.

***Profile* 3: recommendation accuracy of *SerRec*$_{two-LSH}$ with respect to k**
In this profile, we test the relationship between the recommendation accuracy of our *SerRec*$_{two-LSH}$ approach and the parameter k (i.e., the number of row vectors in Eq. (6)). The experiment parameters are set as below: $m = 200, n = 3000, T = 10, r = 8, p = 5$, k is varied from 40 to 140. The concrete experiment results are shown in Fig. 5.

As Fig. 5 shows, the recommendation accuracy of *SerRec*$_{two-LSH}$ approach approximately increases (i.e., *MAE* value approximately decreases) with the growth of k; this is because the MinHash technique adopted in *SerRec*$_{two-LSH}$ approach is essentially a probability-based search technique and a larger k value often means higher search accuracy based on the MinHash theory [17].

***Profile* 4: recommendation efficiency of *SerRec*$_{two-LSH}$ with respect to k**
In this profile, we test the relationship between the recommendation efficiency of our *SerRec*$_{two-LSH}$ approach and the parameter k (i.e., the number of row vectors in Eq. (6)). The parameters are set as below: $m = 200, n = 3000, T = 10, r = 8, p = 5$, k is varied from 40 to 140. The experiment results are presented in Fig. 6.

As can be seen from Fig. 6, the relationship between time cost of *SerRec*$_{two-LSH}$ and parameter k is not so regular. This is because the k row vectors in Eq. (6) are only recruited to generate user signatures offline and not relevant to the efficiency of online similar friends search. Besides, as Fig. 6 shows, the time cost of *SerRec*$_{two-LSH}$

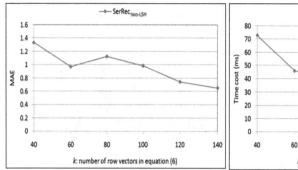
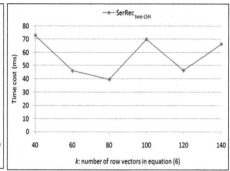

Fig. 5. Accuracy of $SerRec_{two\text{-}LSH}$ w.r.t. k **Fig. 6.** Efficiency of $SerRec_{two\text{-}LSH}$ w.r.t. k

approach is rather small as the time complexity of MinHash adopted in our approach is a constant based on the MinHash theory [17].

***Profile* 5: recommendation accuracy of $SerRec_{two-LSH}$ with respect to r**

In this profile, we test the relationship between the recommendation accuracy of our $SerRec_{two-LSH}$ approach and the parameter r (i.e., the number of hash functions in each hash table). The experiment parameters are set as follows: $m = 200$, $n = 3000$, $T = 10$, $k = 30$, $p = 5$, r is varied from 1 to 9. The experiment results are shown in Fig. 7.

As Fig. 7 shows, the recommendation accuracy increases (i.e., *MAE* decreases) with the growth of r approximately. This is because a larger r value often means a stricter filtering condition for similar friend search; as a consequence, the obtained friends of a target user are "more similar" with the target user and the recommendation accuracy is improved accordingly. Besides, when r is large (e.g., when $r = 5, 7, 9$), only the "most similar" friends of a target user are derived and recruited for service recommendation; as a consequence, the recommendation accuracy stays the same approximately.

***Profile* 6: recommendation efficiency of $SerRec_{two-LSH}$ with respect to r**

In this profile, we test the recommendation efficiency of $SerRec_{two-LSH}$ approach with respect to r. The experiment parameters are set as follows: $m = 200$, $n = 3000$, $T = 10$, $k = 30$, $p = 5$, r is varied from 1 to 10. The experiment results are presented in Fig. 8.

As Fig. 8 shows, the time cost of $SerRec_{two-LSH}$ approach approximately decreases with the growth of r. This is because a larger r value often means a stricter filtering condition for similar friend search; so only fewer similar friends of a target user are returned and recruited for service recommendation when r becomes larger. As a consequence, the time cost approximately decreases when r grows.

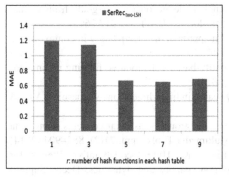

Fig. 7. Accuracy of $SerRec_{two-LSH}$ w.r.t. r

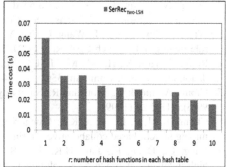

Fig. 8. Efficiency of $SerRec_{two-LSH}$ w.r.t. r

6 Conclusions

Traditional CF-based web service recommendation approaches often assume that the recommendation bases, i.e., historical service quality data are centralized, without considering the distributed service recommendation scenarios as well as the resulted privacy disclosure risk. In view of this challenge, we introduce the Locality-Sensitive Hashing (LSH) technique into distributed service recommendation and further put forward a two-phase LSH-based recommendation approach, named $SerRec_{two-LSH}$, to protect user privacy information. Concretely, first, LSH technique is recruited to protect some privacy data of users, e.g., *the historical service quality data observed by a user*; second, MinHash (a LSH variant) technique is employed to protect another type of user privacy, e.g., *the service set ever invoked by a user*. Finally, through a set of experiments conducted on a real-world distributed service quality dataset *WS-DREAM*, we validate the feasibility of our proposal in terms of service recommendation accuracy and efficiency while guaranteeing privacy-preservation.

As LSH is essentially a probability-based technique, our proposed service recommendation approach $SerRec_{two-LSH}$ may fail to generate any recommended result in certain situations. In the future, we will investigate this unexpected recommendation failure problem and further refine our work so as to improve the recommendation robustness.

Acknowledgement. This paper is partially supported by Natural Science Foundation of China (No. 61402258, 61672276), key Research and Development Project of Jiangsu Province (No. BE2015154, No. BE2016120), Open Project of State Key Laboratory for Novel Software Technology (No. KFKT2016B22).

References

1. Naim, H., Aznag, M., Quafafou, M., Durand, N.: Probabilistic approach for diversifying web services discovery and composition. In: 23rd International Conference on Web Services, pp. 73–80. IEEE, San Francisco (2016)

2. Zhang, N., Wang, J., Ma, Y.: Mining domain knowledge on service goals from textual service descriptions. IEEE Trans. Serv. Comput. doi:10.1109/TSC.2017.2693147

3. Wang, J., Zhu, Z., Liu, J., Wang, C., Xu, Y.: An approach of role updating in context-aware role mining. Int. J. Web Serv. Res. **14**(2), 24–44 (2017)

4. Rong, H., Huo, S., Hu, C., Mo, J.: User similarity-based collaborative filtering recommendation algorithm. J. Commun. **35**(2), 16–24 (2014)

5. Gionis, A., Indyk, P., Motwani, R.: Similarity search in high dimensions via hashing. VLDB **99**(6), 518–529 (1999)

6. Chung, K., Lee, D., Kim, K.J.: Categorization for grouping associative items using data mining in item-based collaborative filtering. Multimedia Tools Appl. **71**(2), 889–904 (2014)

7. Jiang, C., Duan, R., Jain, H.K., Liu, S., Liang, K.: Hybrid collaborative filtering for high-involvement products: a solution to opinion sparsity and dynamics. Decis. Support Syst. **79**, 195–208 (2015)

8. Wang, X., Zhu, J., Zheng, Z., Song, W., Shen, Y., Lyu, M.R.: A spatial-temporal QOS prediction approach for time-aware web service recommendation. ACM Trans. Web **10**(1), 1–25 (2016)

9. Yu, C., Huang, L.: A web service QOS prediction approach based on time- and location-aware collaborative filtering. Serv. Oriented Comput. Appl. **10**(2), 135–149 (2016)

10. Fletcher, K.K., Liu, X.F.: A collaborative filtering method for personalized preference-based service recommendation. In: 22nd International Conference on Web Services, pp. 400–407. IEEE, New York (2015)

11. Wang, J.H., Chen, Y.H.: A distributed hybrid recommendation framework to address the new-user cold-start problem. In: UIC-ATC-ScalCom, pp. 1686–1691. IEEE, Beijing (2015)

12. Tang, M., Dai, X., Cao, B., Liu, J.: WSWalker: a random walk method for QOS-aware web service recommendation. In: 22nd International Conference on Web Services, pp. 591–598. IEEE, New York (2015)

13. Dou, W., Zhang, X., Liu, J., Chen, J.: HireSome-II: towards privacy-aware cross-cloud service composition for big data applications. IEEE Trans. Parallel Distrib. Syst. **26**(2), 455–466 (2015)

14. Zhu, J., He, P., Zheng, Z., Lyu, M.R.: A privacy-preserving QOS prediction framework for web service recommendation. In: 22nd International Conference on Web Services, pp. 241–248. IEEE, New York (2015)

15. Li, D., Chen, C., Lv, Q., Shang, L., Zhao, Y., Lu, T., Gu, N.: An algorithm for efficient privacy-preserving item-based collaborative filtering. Future Gener. Comput. Syst. **55**, 311–320 (2016)

16. Joseph, L.R., Alan, N.W.: Thirteen ways to look at the correlation coefficient. Am. Stat. **42**(1), 59–66 (1988)

17. Broder, A.Z.: On the resemblance and containment of documents. In: Compression and Complexity of Sequences, pp. 21–29. IEEE, Salerno (1997)

18. Ioannidis, Y., et al.: Data mining and query log analysis for scalable temporal and continuous query answering (2015). http://www.optique-project.eu/

19. Zheng, Z., Zhang, Y., Lyu, M.R.: Investigating QOS of real world web services. IEEE Trans. Serv. Comput. **7**(1), 32–39 (2014)

20. Breese J.S., Heckerman, D., Kadie, C.: Empirical analysis of predictive algorithms for collaborative filtering. In: Fourteenth Conference on Uncertainty in Artificial Intelligence, pp. 43–52. IEEE, Madison (1998)

A DP Canopy *K*-Means Algorithm for Privacy Preservation of Hadoop Platform

Tao Shang[✉], Zheng Zhao, Zhenyu Guan, and Jianwei Liu

School of Electronic and Information Engineering, Beihang University,
Beijing 100083, China
shangtao@buaa.edu.cn

Abstract. *K*-means algorithm for data mining is combined with differential privacy preservation. Although it improves the security of data information, the selection of clustering number and initial center point is still blind and random. In this paper, we integrate an optimized Canopy algorithm with DP *K*-means algorithm, and apply it to Hadoop platform. Firstly, we optimize the Canopy algorithm according to the minimum and maximum principle and use the functions of the MapReduce framework to implement it. Secondly, we utilize the number and the set of center points obtained to implement the DP *K*-means algorithm on MapReduce. As a result, the improved Canopy algorithm can optimize the selection of the number of centers and clusters on Hadoop platform, so the proposed *K*-means algorithm can improve security, usability and efficiency of calculation.

Keywords: Big data · Differential privacy · Data mining · Canopy algorithm

1 Introduction

Since 2012, big data technology has grown rapidly around the world and received wide attention in global academia, industry and governments. The huge application requirement and potential value greatly contribute to the rapid development of big data technology, and promote the development of various technical aspects and system platforms. Among many technologies and systems for large data processing, the mainstreams include MapReduce that was invented by Google in 2003 and Hadoop that was launched by open-source organization Apache in 2007 [1]. Especially, Hadoop provides a distributed computing environment with open-source scalability and high reliability, which is highly efficient for a large number of data processing.

With the rapid development of big data technology, data sharing has become increasingly important, and people are more and more concerned about the privacy issues of big data. The problem of privacy preservation in data release and data mining is a hotspot in the field of information security. Until now, there exists many privacy preservation technologies in this area, such as k-anonymous, l-diversity, but they do not strictly define the attack model and the attacker's knowledge cannot be quantified. In 2006, Dwork [2] first proposed a differential privacy algorithm to fundamentally solve this problem. Differential privacy preservation [2] has many advantages. For example, it has a strictly defined privacy preservation and a reliable quantitative method.

© Springer International Publishing AG 2017
S. Wen et al. (Eds.): CSS 2017, LNCS 10581, pp. 189–198, 2017.
https://doi.org/10.1007/978-3-319-69471-9_14

In addition, it can resist a variety of new attacks. So its idea is quickly recognized by academics and widely used. As we know, cluster analysis (clustering) is an important method of data mining. K-means clustering based on partitioning is the most widely used as classical clustering algorithm. As a main direction, many scholars combine differential privacy and cluster analysis to provide valuable information while protecting data privacy as much as possible. In 2005, Blum et al. [3] achieved a differential privacy K-means algorithm in the SuLQ platform, but the query function is sensitive and does not give how to set the privacy budget. Nissim et al. [4] proposed a PK-means method to make K-means clustering satisfy differential privacy preservation, and also gave a way to calculate the sensitivity of query functions. Li et al. [5] proposed an IDP K-means algorithm in a distributed environment. It not only improves the usability of clustering methods, but also provides strong security and privacy preservation for MapReduce calculation. Although the scheme can be implemented based on a distributed environment, it is random for the selection of the number of clusters and the initial center point. It increases the number of iterations and reduces the availability of clustering results. So it is a good solution to improve the selection of a center point. As we know, the Canopy algorithm is a clustering method which was proposed by Mccallum et al. [6] to realize the clustering of high-dimension big data sets. The K-means clustering combined with the Canopy algorithm will reduce the number of iterations. However, the choice of regional radius and initial center point in the algorithm is still blind and random, which will directly affect the clustering results. Therefore, the optimization of the Canopy algorithm will benefit both clustering and privacy preservation.

In this paper, we optimize the Canopy algorithm based on the minimum and maximum principle [7], integrate the optimized Canopy algorithm with DP K-means algorithm, and design a DP Canopy K-means algorithm for privacy preservation based on big data platform. Compared with the traditional K-means algorithm, the proposed algorithm improves security, usability and efficiency of calculation.

1.1 Hadoop Platform

Hadoop [1] was developed by the Apache Software Foundation which is a popular top open-source distributed computing platform. Hadoop platform provides a distributed computing environment with open-source scalability and high reliability, which makes full use of cluster resources to store big data and perform extremely complex operations. Its distribution characteristic is embodied in the master-slave structure, which is shown in Fig. 1.

The MapReduce framework is applied to the parallel programming interface of large-scale data sets, using the idea of "divide and rule". MapReduce provides the functions of map and reduce to develop distributed applications. JobTracker is used to assign and manage tasks and TaskTracker is used to perform tasks. The diagram of MapReduce operating principle is shown in Fig. 2.

As can be seen from the above figure, the main controller is the JobTracker node which is responsible for task assignment and execution. Map and Reduce tasks are performed by the TaskTracker node. The input of Map task is a number of file blocks, and the Map task converts a file block to a set of key-value pairs. The master controller

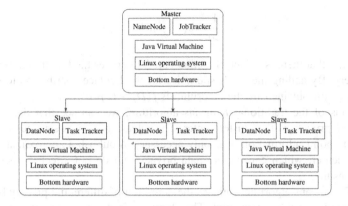

Fig. 1. Master-slave structure

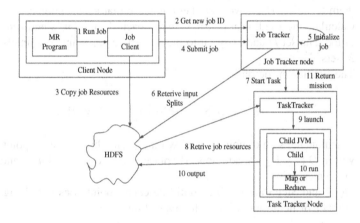

Fig. 2. MapReduce operating principle

collects a set of key-value pairs from each Map task and assigns a set of key-value pairs to the Reduce task. Application programs improve operational efficiency according to the MapReduce operating principle.

1.2 Differential Privacy Preservation Model

The key to achieving differential privacy is the noise mechanism. The commonly used noise mechanism is Laplace method and exponential method. A data set usually uses the Laplace method, while the exponential method is applicable to non-numerical results. For a data set, here we introduce the former.

The Laplace method implements ε-differential privacy preservation by adding random noise of the Laplace distribution to exact query results. When the position parameter is 0 and the Laplace distribution with a scale parameter b is $Lap(b)$, the probability density function is:

$$p(x) = \frac{1}{2b}\exp(-\frac{|x|}{b}), \; b = \Delta f/\varepsilon \tag{1}$$

Supposing that there is a query function f, $f(D)$ denotes the function in the data set D on a query. By adding the stochastic noise for the Laplace distribution to $f(D)$, the final query result obtained by the algorithm is $f(D) + Lap(b)$.

By means of the traditional K-means algorithm, we can see that the key to the disclosure of privacy is the cluster center. The release of a data set does not require detailed data point information. It is only necessary to publish a approximate value of the cluster center, which can protect data privacy and do not affect the accuracy of clustering results.

The DP K-means algorithm satisfies the definition of differential privacy by adding appropriate noise to the center point. The algorithm is described as follows:

Step1: In the data set D, randomly choose K center points $c_1, c_2, \ldots c_K$ and add them to noise. Here, we take them as the initial center points;

Step2: Calculate the Euclidean metric between each data point x_i and center point in the data set D and assign it to the nearest center point. We finally get the K sets.

The Euclidean metric is:

$$d = \sqrt{\sum_{i=1}^{n}(c - x_i)^2}, \; if \; P \; = \; P_j \tag{2}$$

Step3: Calculate the sum of points (sum) within D_i and the number of points (num) within $D_i (1 \leq i \leq K)$, add noise (Laplace noise) to sum and num and update the center point;

Step4: Step2 and Step3 are repeated until the center point does not change or the number of iterations reaches the upper limit.

The calculation of the center point deviation is:

$$D = \sum_{i=1}^{n}\left[\min_{r=1,\cdots k} distance(x_i, c_r)^2\right] \tag{3}$$

The DP K-means algorithm solves the privacy preservation of information, but there are still some shortcomings in practical application.

(1) A large number of simulation experiments show that the DP K-means algorithm is more sensitive to the selection of initial center points. Noise is added to the clustering center point after each iteration, which makes a center point increasingly deviate. When the privacy budget is below a certain value, the algorithm adds greater noise. This will result in a rapid decline in the accuracy of clustering results.

(2) There is no particular criterion for the choice of the number of clusters K, and it is not possible to determine whether K is the optimal value by experience.

(3) There is no explicit set of privacy budgets during the clustering process.

(4) It is difficult to set the sensitivity Δf for different data sets when adding noise.

In view of the above shortcomings, Dwork [8] presented the importance of privacy budgets in the DP K-means process and how to reasonably consume the privacy budget. Li [5] proposed an IDP K-means algorithm in a distributed environment. It not only improves the usability of clustering methods, but also provides strong security and privacy guarantee for MapReduce calculations. By combining the DP K-means algorithm with the Canopy algorithm, we can determine the number of clusters and reduce the number of iterations. In order to conveniently set the sensitivity, the data set is normalized when the algorithm is designed. We focus on the optimized Canopy algorithm based on the minimum and maximum principle. The improved algorithm can solve the blindness and randomness of both region radius and initial center point.

2 The Proposed Scheme

Cluster analysis algorithm will be implemented on the Hadoop platform, primarily on MapReduce. The proposed algorithm uses the optimized Canopy algorithm to get the number of clusters K, then use the DP K-means algorithm iteratively so as to get the clustering center point which satisfies differential privacy preservation. It includes two parts: (1) the optimized Canopy algorithm in MapReduce to decide the number of clusters and the initial center point. (2) the DP K-means algorithm in MapReduce to make K-means clustering satisfy differential privacy preservation.

2.1 Optimized Canopy Algorithm

The traditional Canopy algorithm is affected by the regional radiuses T_1 and T_2. When T_1 is too large, it will make a point belong to multiple Canopies. When T_2 is too large, it will reduce the number of clusters. In addition, the number of initial center points of Canopy decides the number of clustering classes K, which is usually set by experience or multiple experiments. For different data sets, the value of K is not available for reference. In order to solve the problem of the regional radius and the random selection of initial center point of Canopy, we use an optimized Canopy algorithm according to the minimum and maximum principle to improve the classification accuracy of a K-means algorithm.

The basic idea of the Canopy algorithm is that a data set is divided into several Canopies, and the distance between any two Canopy centers represents the clustering distance. In order to avoid the clustering result is local optimum, the distance between the initial center points of Canopy should be as far away as possible. Based on the above idea, we assume that the first m points are known. Then the $m + 1$ center point of Canopy should be the maximum of the minimum distance between the candidate data point and the previous m center points, which can be denoted by

$$\begin{cases} DistCollect(m+1) = \min\{d(x_{m+1}, x_r), r = 1, 2, \ldots m\} \\ Dist_{\min}(m+1) = \max\{\min[d(x_i, x_r)], i \neq 1, 2, \ldots, m, 1 \leq i \leq L\} \end{cases} \quad (4)$$

L indicates the amount of data in the data set in the current task. $DisCollect(m + 1)$ indicates the minimum distance between the $m + 1$ center point to be decided and the center point of the previous m-defined Canopy. $Dist_{min}$ indicates that the optimal x_{m+1} should be the largest of all shortest distances.

Such method avoids the setting of regional radius T_2. In addition, it gives the following rules in practical application: when the number of Canopy is small or bigger than the true value of a category, $Dist_{min}$ shows a small change. When the number of Canopy is close to or reaches the value of a category, the distance exhibits a large mutation. In order to confirm the optimal number of Canopy centers and the regional radius T_1, we introduce $Depth(i)$ indicators to represent the range of change in $Dist_{min}$. It is defined as follows:

$$Depth(i) = |Dist_{min}(i) - Dist_{min}(i-1)| + |Dist_{min}(i+1) - Dist_{min}(i)| \quad (5)$$

When i reaches the optimal clustering, $Depth(i)$ reaches the maximum value. In this case, the first i record of the center point set is the optimal initial center point, and in order that the final cluster center falls in the range of Canopy, we can set $T_1 = Dist_{min}$.

The Canopy algorithm based on the minimum and maximum principle costs too much time especially in dealing with massive data in a distributed environment. And the initial center point is not the center of the final cluster. Taking into account the above problems, we use the optimized method. Firstly, the data points in a data set that have the farthest initial distance are replaced by data points whose distance from the origin of coordinates is the nearest or farthest. The process of selecting the center point is shown in Fig. 3. Secondly, for massive data, we first obtain a local candidate center point. Then we obtain the global center point on this basis. Thirdly, in order to reduce the number of iterations, when the algorithm iterates to $\sqrt{L}$, it terminates. Here L is the size of node data.

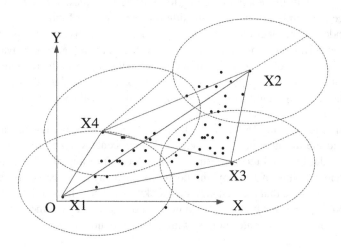

Fig. 3. Optimized Canopy algorithm

The optimized Canopy algorithm runs under a distributed computing model, which is divided into Map function and Reduce function.

Input: A data set D, a data set scale N

The data is normalized. The records in the data set are denoted as $x_i (1 \leq i \leq N)$ and the dimension is d. Each dimension of the record in the data set D is normalized to the interval $[0, 1]^d$. Then we can get a new data set D'.

For Map function:

Input: A data set D'

Output: A center point set Q

Step1: Q = null; Set the number of iterations $\sqrt{L}$; L is the total amount of data in the current Map task.

Step2: Loop on the condition of $i < \sqrt{L}$

If Q is null, find the minimum distance between the data point and the origin of coordinates by the formula 4 and save the point to the set Q.

Otherwise, find the maximum of the minimum distance between the data points in the current Map task and the data points in Q by the formula 4 and save the point to the set Q.

For Reduce function:

Input: A center point set for each node of Canopy $Q = \{Q_1, \ldots Q_n\}$

Output: A final set U of canopy center point and radius T_1

Step1: Calculate the total amount P of data for the set Q

Step2: Loop on the condition of $i < \sqrt{P}$, find the maximum of the minimum distance among the data in the data set Q by the formula 4 and save it to Q'

Step3: Calculate the total amount K of data for the set Q'

Step4: Loop on the condition of $j < K$, find the maximum of $Depth(i)$ by the formula 5 in the set Q' and output $T_1 = Dist_{\min}(i)$. Assign the first i points in Q' to the set U

After the above steps are completed, the optimized Canopy algorithm outputs the center point set U and saves it as a file. We use the Map function to calculate the distance between the node data and the data points in all canopies. We use the Euclidean metric (Formula 2) to calculate the distance. If $D \leq T_1$, the node data is marked with the corresponding Canopy. Then the algorithm outputs the final result.

2.2 DP Canopy K-Means Algorithm

In the previous section, we get the maximum of $Depth(i)$ that is the optimal clustering. On this basis, DP K-means clustering will greatly reduce the number of iterations and improve the efficiency of clustering.

Assume that the number of clusters K is known. The DP K-means algorithm based on the optimized Canopy is designed as follows:

Step1: The main task driver calculates the number of data points num_k^0 and the sum of data points $sum_k^0 (1 \leq k \leq K)$ within each Canopy. After adding noise separately to them, we get $num_{k'}^0$ and $sum_{k'}^0$. The Laplace noise is usually used. Calculate $\mu_k^0 = sum_{k'}^0 / num_{k'}^0$. μ_k^0 is the initial center point.

Step2: The master task divides all data records into M data slices on average. Meanwhile it assigns M sub-tasks to perform Map operations and assigns K sub-tasks to perform Reduce operations.

Step3: The Map function calculates and compares the distance between the marked input data point and the center point. Output the current data and its corresponding the nearest distance center point. Each record can get a $\langle key, value \rangle$ pair where key represents a cluster center identity, and value represents the attribute vector of a record.

Step4: The Reduce function receives $\langle key, value \rangle$ pair that belongs to the same center point. Calculate sum and num. Then add noise to them to get the center point μ'.

Step5: The task accepts the output μ of each Reduce node. Calculate whether the distance between the current round and the last cluster center point is less than the threshold. If the distance is less than the threshold or the number of iterations is full, the algorithm terminates. Otherwise it repeat Step3 $\sim$ Step5.

To complete the above two aspects, we get the final clustering center.

3 Scheme Analysis

3.1 Privacy Analysis

According to the nature of the differential privacy preservation algorithm, we can see that the privacy budget of the whole algorithm is:

$$\varepsilon = \sum_{t=1}^{T} \varepsilon_t \tag{6}$$

T is the total number of iterations. In terms of budget allocation, we use a strategy that consumes half of the remaining private budgets for each iteration. The privacy budget for the t th iteration is $\varepsilon_t = \varepsilon/2^t$.

In each round iteration, since the K Reducer nodes perform the operations independently, the result of each iteration is equivalent to the parallel combination of the Reduce operations. According to the nature of the differential privacy, it is necessary to satisfy the ε_t - differential privacy so that each Reducer sub-task in a distributed environment satisfies ε_t - differential privacy.

As can be seen from the definition of global sensitivity:

$$\Delta F = \max_{D,D'} \|F(D) - F(D')\|_1 \tag{7}$$

F is the query function. Data sets D and D' are identical or differ by only one record. $\| \ \|_1$ represents the sum of the absolute values of the elements of a vector.

As can be seen from the above definition, Δf_{num}, the global sensitivity of num, equals 1. If the dimension of the point is d, the global sensitivity of sum is $\Delta f_{sum} = d$. Thus the global sensitivity of the entire query sequence is $\Delta f = d + 1$.

For the calculation of the initial center point, num_k^0 and sum_k^0 add random noise $Lap(d+1)2/\varepsilon$, respectively. Meanwhile random noise $Lap(d+1)2^{t+1}/\varepsilon$ is added to num_k and sum_k at t-th iteration in the algorithm. These ensure that the DP Canopy K-means algorithm under the MapReduce framework satisfies ε-differential privacy preservation.

Compared with the traditional DP K-means algorithm, the improved calculation process of initial center point can reduce the number of iterations of the algorithm under the same privacy budget, and reduce the addition of random noise.

3.2 Scheme Complexity Analysis

The DP K-means algorithm randomly selects K data as the initial clustering centers, then iterates the execution. The whole algorithm runs until the center of gravity of a class will no longer change. The traditional DP K-means computational complexity is $O(dKt)$. d is the number of documents, K is the number of classes, and t is the number of iterations. In the case of the DP K-means optimized by the Canopy algorithm, the division of Canopies is a division of points. That is, a point may also belong to n Canopies. The cluster must be compared dKn^2t/c times, where c is the number of Canopies.

4 Conclusion

By combining the optimized Canopy algorithm with the DP K-means algorithm, we design a new algorithm and implement it in the MapReduce framework. The algorithm takes into account the factors such as the number of clusters and the selection of initial center points, so that the availability of clustering and the efficiency of cluster analysis are greatly improved.

Acknowledgment. Project supported by the National Key Research and Development Program of China (No. 2016YFC1000307) and the National Natural Science Foundation of China (No. 61571024) for valuable helps.

References

1. Hua, Y.: Understanding big data processing and programming. China Machine Press (2014)
2. Dwork, C.: Differential privacy. In: Proceedings of the 33rd International Colloquium on Automata, Languages and Programming, pp. 338–340. Springer, Berlin (2006)
3. Blum, A., Dwork, C., Mcsherry, F., et al.: Practical privacy: the SuLQ framework. In: Proceedings of the Twenty-Fourth ACM SIGMOD-SIGACT-SIGART Symposium on Principles of Database Systems, pp. 128–138 (2005)
4. Nissim, K., Raskhodnikova, S., Smith, A.: Smooth sensitivity and sampling in private data analysis. In: Proceedings of the Thirty-Ninth Annual ACM Symposium on Theory of Computing, pp. 75–84. ACM (2007)
5. Li, Y., Hao, Z., Wen, W., Xie, G.: Research on differential privacy preserving K-means clustering. Comput. Sci. **40**(3), 287–290 (2013)

HypTracker: A Hypervisor to Detect Malwares Through System Call Analysis on ARM

Dong Shen[1], Xiaojing Su[2], and Zhoujun Li[1]($^{(\boxtimes)}$)

[1] School of Computer Science and Engineering, Beihang University,
Beijing 100191, China
{dongshen,lizj}@buaa.edu.cn
[2] Key Laboratory of Microelectronics Devices and Integrated Technology,
Institute of Microelectronics, Chinese Academy of Sciences, Beijing 100029, China
suxiaojing@ime.ac.cn

Abstract. Mobile Security becomes increasingly important nowadays
due to the widely use of mobile platforms. With the appearance of ARM
virtualization extensions, using virtualization technology to protect system security has become a research hotspot. In this paper, we propose
HypTracker to detect malicious behaviours by analyzing the system call
sequences based on ARM virtualization extensions, which can intercept
the system calls at thread level transparently with Android and generate the system call sequences. We put forward a sensitive-system-call-
based feature extraction model using Relative Discrete Euclidean Distance and a greedy-like algorithm to generate the malicious behaviour
models. At runtime, a sliding-window-based detection module is used to
detect malicious behaviours. We have experimented with the samples of
DroidKungfu and the result validates the effectiveness of the proposed
methodology.

Keywords: Android · Virtualization · ARM · Hypervisor · Malware
detection

1 Introduction

Mobile platform is becoming increasingly important in modern life. People rely
more on mobile devices to handle their daily affairs, such as social activities,
mobile payments, electronic banking, internet of things [11] and so on. Hence,
personal privacy information stored on individual devices has become the target
of hacker attacks, which may have a major impact on all aspects of lives, such
as personal data disclosure or even property damage. Therefore, the security
problem on mobile platform has been a research hotspot for information security
researchers nowadays.

The existing protection technologies mainly focus on the application level
malwares. Some methods detect malicious behaviors by tracking the information
of API [6,9,14]. However, some malicious softwares bypass the detection by using
native codes to call the system functions directly. Other protection methods can

© Springer International Publishing AG 2017
S. Wen et al. (Eds.): CSS 2017, LNCS 10581, pp. 199–214, 2017.
https://doi.org/10.1007/978-3-319-69471-9_15

hook the system calls [12]. But some kernel level attacks can bypass or even shutdown the relevant protections because no software has higher privilege level than the kernel level attacks.

Virtualizaiton technology has been widely used in cloud computing platform. In addition, it has also been used for x86 platform system level security protection. In 2011, ARM proposed virtualization extensions. Subsequently, many researchers use virtualization technology to protect the system security of mobile platform [4].

Therefore, we propose HypTracker, a secure protection hypervisor based on ARM virtualization to defend the malicious behaviours by tracking the sequences of the system calls. In this paper, our contributions are as follows:

- We design a hypervisor to hook the system calls and generate the system call sequences. ARM virtualization technology is used to hook the system calls in the supervisor mode directly and save the sequences in the hypervisor. Meanwhile, the hypervisor uses different methods to get the parameters based on the instruction types.
- We propose a sensitive-system-call-based feature extraction model using Relative Discrete Euclidean Distance and a greedy-like algorithm to generate malicious behaviour models. Relative Discrete Euclidean Distance is used to calculate the similarity of two system call sequences, while the greedy-like algorithm is used to generate the malicious behaviour model.
- At runtime, HypTracker uses a sliding-window-based detection module to detect malicious behaviours. Once the system call sequence matches one of the malicious behaviour models, it represents the occurence of the malicious attack and will trigger the interception of the attack by the hypervisor.

ORGANIZATION. In the next section, we introduce the background knowledge of ARM virtualization extensions and the design of HypTracker. In Sect. 3, we present the design of interception module. The learning module and the detection module are elaborated in Sects. 4 and 5, respectively. We then present related work in Sect. 6. At last we give a conclusion in Sect. 7.

2   Overview

In this section, we will introduce the background knowledge of ARM virtualization extensions and the design of HypTracker.

2.1   Background

In 2011, ARM introduced hardware virtualization support as an optional extension in ARMv7 [1] gradually.

The virtualization extensions introduce a new non-secure privilege level called the hyp mode to hold the hypervisor. As is shown in Fig. 1, the hyp mode has a higher privilege level over the operating system (OS) kernel level (the supervisor mode). In the hyp mode, there are its own Exception Link Register (ELR_hyp), Saved Programme Status Register (SPSR_hyp) and Stack Pointer (SP_hyp). Besides, two main registers are also the significant components, i.e. Hyp Configuration Register (HCR) and Hyp Syndrome Register (HSR). HCR is used for the configuration of virtualization, such as defining whether various non-secure operations are trapped to the hyp mode. While HSR is used for recording the information of entering the hyp mode.

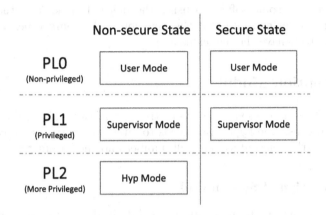

Fig. 1. The architecture of ARM processor with ARM virtualization extensions

There is a hypervisor in the hyp mode to monitor the upper mode (i.e. the supervisor mode and the user mode). The hypervisor is also called virtual machine monitor (VMM), which can intercept many types of operations with the different configurations of HCR. For instance, the hypervisor traps general exceptions such as Supervisor Call exceptions when HCR.TGE is set to 0x1. There is also a call for entering the hyp mode from the supervisor mode named Hypervisor Call (HVC). The virtualization extensions use previously unused entry (0x14 offset) in the vector table for the hypervisor traps.

The virtualization extensions also provide a non-secure PL1&0 stage-2 translation table, which is a separate page table from the non-secure PL1&0 stage-1 translation table in the supervisor mode. The translation using the non-secure PL1&0 stage-1 translation table is from Virtual Address (VA) to Intermediate Physical Address (IPA), while the translation using the non-secure PL1&0 stage-2 translation table is from IPA to Physical Address (PA). The non-secure PL1&0 stage-2 translation table can only be accessed in the hyp mode so that it can be used for protecting the memory.

2.2   Design

HypTracker is an ARM-based hypervisor, which can track the system calls sequences of the softwares to detect the malicious behaviours. Hyp-Tracker consists of three modules: **interception module, learning module**

and detection module. Comparing to other related tools, HypTracker has the following advantages:

- The hypervisor running in the hyp mode has higher privileged level than the guest OS running in the supervisor mode. Therefore, HypTracker will never be shutdown by other malwares running in the supervisor mode.
- The hypervisor hooks the system call right after the execution of swi, so that the attacks in kernel cannot hijack the control flow.
- Compared with some softwares using the method of hooking the Android API, HypTracker can intercept the malicious behaviours which use JNI or private lib to behave the malicious acts.

3   Interception Module

Interception Module is used to intercept the system call and get the sequences of the system calls. The hypervisor needs to intercept every system call, at the same time, get the relevant system call number and the parameters.

3.1   Interception of System Call

The main challenge in the interception module is the way of intercepting the system call. Although setting HCR.TGE to 0x1 can route all the system call to the hypervisor, the hypervisor needs to simulate all the system calls which makes the hypervisor more complex. Therefore, a piece of hook code is added to enter the hyp mode actively.

Original System Call Flow. After the swi instruction is issued, the Program Counter (PC) jumps to the exception vector table in the supervisor mode. The offset of the supervisor call is 0x8, running "ldr pc, __vectors_start+0x1000". This instruction then loads the value saved in the address __vectors_start+0x1000 into PC. And the value is the start address of the system call handler.

Hook. At the system boot time, the hypervisor creates a new page to place the hook code and sets the page inaccessible. Then it saves the original value at the address __vectors_start+0x1000 and replaces it with the start address of the hook code. The hook code issues an hvc instruction to get into the hypervisor. After the hypervisor returns, PC will be loaded with the original value at the address __vectors_start+0x1000. Then the program handles the system call as usual.

3.2   Parameter Acquisition

After the program is trapped into the hyp mode, the hypervisor needs to analyze the system call number and the relevant parameters.

There are two kinds of instruction sets in ARM, which are ARM and Thumb.[1] Thumb instruction set is a subset of ARM instruction set. Thumb instructions can be shorter than ARM instructions, which can save the memory of the system. In ARM, the T bit of the Current Program Status Register (CPSR) shows whether the current instruction set is Thumb. Namely, 1 means Thumb and 0 represents ARM. Figure 2 shows the format of CPSR.

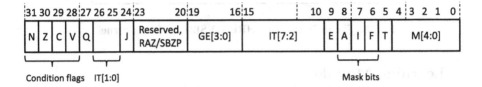

Fig. 2. The format of CPSR

Thumb uses Register 7 (R7) to save the system call number. While there are two ways to save the system call number in ARM instruction set. Two kinds of Application Binary Interface (ABI) are used in ARM: Old Application Binary Interface (OABI) and Embedded Application Binary Interface (EABI). In OABI, the system call number is a parameter of the SVC instruction. While the system call number is saved in R7 in EABI.

The parameters in ARM are passed using registers. Register 0 (R0) to Register 4 (R4) save the needed parameters. The hypervsior will get different kinds of parameters according to the system call number.

3.3   Thread-level Hook

There are many threads running in a process at the same time in Android. If the system call interception is the process-level, the unrelated running thread may affect the detection accuracy of the malicious behaviours. Therefore, the interception must be thread-level.

At the running time of thread, different threads have different stacks. The hypervisor can use the user mode Stack Pointer (SP_usr) to recognize different threads. As the definition in Linux kernel shown in Fig. 3, the PAGE_SIZE is 0x1000 and the THREAD_SIZE is 0x2000. Hence, the THREAD_MASK is ~ (THREAD_SIZE - 1) = 0xFFFFE000. The hypervisor can use SP_usr & THREAD_MASK to get the THREAD_INFO for the recognition of different threads.

---

[1] In fact, there are four kinds of instruction sets: ARM, Thumb, Jazelle, and ThumbEE. The latter two kinds of instructions sets are related to Java, which is out of our scope in this paper.

```
Linux/arch/arm/include/asm/page.h

#define PAGE_SHIFT              12
#define PAGE_SIZE               (_AC(1,UL) << PAGE_SHIFT)

Linux/arch/arm/include/asm/thread_info.h

#define THREAD_SIZE_ORDER       1
#define THREAD_SIZE             (PAGE_SIZE << THREAD_SIZE_ORDER)
```

Fig. 3. The definition of THREAD_SIZE in Linux kernel

4   Learning Module

Interception module is used to generate the system call sequence. Then it can be analyzed by the learning module and the detection module.

For one specific kind of malware, the malicious code is completely the same. However, there are many kinds of variants for one given kind of malware. The core actions are the same, but the malware maker may add or delete some unrelated instructions to perform confusion. Therefore, trapping all the system call sequences simply can't find the variants of the malware. As a result, we propose a **sensitive-system-call-based feature extraction model** in the learning module.

Next, we use the samples of **DroidKungfu** as an example to introduce the details of the learning module and detection module based on our **practical experiment results**. DroidKungfu is a typical malware modifying the system files. When the malware runs, it loads its own library to run JNI code, which releases the malicious code saved as the data.

4.1   Sensitive System Call

Among more than 300 system calls in Linux kernel, many of them are not sensitive, such as *gettid*, *close*, *sync* and so on. It is necessary to focus on the modifications of the system files because they are the main infection targets of the malicious code. Therefore, we choose the following system calls as the sensitive system calls[2].

- int *unlink*(const char **pathname*);
  This system call is used to delete the file from the system. As the application may delete its own file, the hypervisor needs to get the parameter of the system call. The *pathname* starting with "/system/" will be tagged as a sensitive system call because the application is deleting a system file.

---

[2] The choice of the sensitive system calls is based on the study of the malicious codes. Other sensitive system calls can also be added if necessary. But the performance and the complexity needs to be taken into account.

- int *chmod*(const char **path, mode_t mode*);
  This system call is used to change the permissions of a file. The parameter *path* starting with "/system/" will be recorded as a sensitive system call because the application is modifying the permissions of a system file.

- int *open*(const char **pathname*, int *flags*, [mode_t *mode*]);
  In a regular view, *open()* is a common system call. Even though the application may open a system file and read it, it doesn't mean the absolute influence to the users' systems. In fact, *write()* and *ioctl()* are more sensitive. But in the **practical experiments** we find that if the malware fails to open the system file in any cases, such as no existing file or encountering permission problems, it won't continue to call *write()* or *ioctl()*. Therefore, we define *open()* as a sensitive system call and check whether the pathname starts with "/system/".

4.2   Definition of $Seq(x)$

The sequence of the sensitive system calls only shows the accessing status to the system file from the application, which can't reveal the actual operation of the malware. The real malicious behaviours needs to be recognized by the combined utilization of the sensitive system calls and other system calls.

We represents the sensitive system call as $C(x)$, in which x represents the name of the system call. Meanwhile, a sequence centered on the sensitive system call is defined as $Seq(x)$, which contains eleven elements. The concrete definition of $Seq(x)$ with different sensitive system calls can be shown as follows:

Definition 1

$$Seq(open) \ : \ C(open), a_1, a_2, a_3, a_4, a_5, a_6, a_7, a_8, a_9, a_{10}$$
$$Seq(chmod) : \ b_5, b_4, b_3, b_2, b_1, C(chmod), a_1, a_2, a_3, a_4, a_5$$
$$Seq(unlink) : \ b_{10}, b_9, b_8, b_7, b_6, b_5, b_4, b_3, b_2, b_1, C(unlink)$$

In the sequences above, b_n and a_n represent the other system calls. The formats are different due to the semantics differences of $C(x)$. To be specific, since the system call *unlink()* is used to delete the system file, the handling of the system file will be in front of the execution of *unlink()*. While *open()* is the start operation of the system file, the system calls following it are needed. For the same reason, *chmod()* is used to modify the permissions which is in the middle of the handling process, the context of *chmod()* is required.

4.3   Feature Extraction

For a set of applications with the same kind of malicious behaviours, HypTracker needs to extract the feature based on the system call sequences. Therefore, we put forward a feature extraction algorithm to generate the feature sequence models of the malicious behaviours.

Acquisition of Seq(x). For a set of applications $apk_1, apk_2, ..., apk_n$, Hyp-Tracker runs these applications and gets the system call sequences of the apks. Then, HypTracker uses the sequences of the first two apks to generate an original model and use other sequences to optimize the model by turn.

Experiment Result. For the sequences of the first two samples of Droid-Kungfu, HypTracker can find the $Seq(x)$ with the same $C(x)$, such as $C(open["/system/lib/libbd1.so"])$. Note that the same $C(x)$ means the same sensitive system call with the totally same value of "*path/pathname*". The $Seq(open["/system/lib/libbd1.so"])$ of the two apks are as follows:

$$apk1 : C(open), close, chmod, chown32, lstat64, gettimeofday,$$
$$settimeofday, open, fstat64, read, mount$$

$$apk2 : C(open), ioctl, close, gettimeofday, settimeofday, open,$$
$$fstat64, mprotect, mprotect, read, mount$$

Calculation of Similarity. To confirm whether these two $Seq(x)$ sequences of two apks represent the same action, it is necessary to calculate the similarity of the two sequences. We use **Relative Discrete Euclidean Distance** (*RDED*) to calculate the similarity, which has the similar format as **Euclidean Distance** but different definition. *RDED* can be defined as follows:

Definition 2. For two sequences $A : a_0, a_1, a_2, ..., a_n$ and $B : b_0, b_1, b_2, ..., b_n$, the Longest Common Subsequence (LCS) can be represented as $LCS\{a_i\}$ or $LCS\{b_j\}$ as follows:

$$a_{i_0}, a_{i_1}, a_{i_2}, a_{i_3}, ..., a_{i_l} \quad 0 \le i_{m-1} < i_m \le n$$

$$b_{j_0}, b_{j_1}, b_{j_2}, b_{j_3}, ..., b_{j_l} \quad 0 \le j_{m-1} < j_m \le n$$

$$a_{i_l} = b_{j_l}$$

The **Relative Discrete Euclidean Distance** $RDED(A, B)$ is defined as:

$$RDED(A, B) = \sqrt{\sum_{k=1}^{n} DIS(a_k, B)^2}$$

$$DIS(a_k, B) = \begin{cases} ||i_m - i_{m-1}| - |j_m - j_{m-1}|| & \text{when } a_k \in LCS\{a_i\} \text{ and } k = i_m \\ 10 & \text{when } a_k \notin LCS\{a_i\} \end{cases}$$

In Definition 2, when $a_0 = b_0 = C(open)$ and $n = 10$, $RDED$ is the distance of $Seq(open)$ between two apks. In the same way, for the $Seq(unlink)$, Hyp-Tracker sets the element which is the nearest to $C(unlink)$ as b_1 in Definition 1. It can be handled as a reverse of $Seq(open)$. For the $C(chmod)$, it can be divided into two subsequences to calculate the $DIS(a_k, B)$, then HypTracker calculates the $RDED$ for them together.

HypTracker will calculate the $RDED$ for every $Seq(x)$ with the same sensitive system call and *"path/pathname"*. If two $Seq(x)$ sequences have more than one LCS, HypTracker calculates every $RDED$ for different LCSes and use the minimum $RDED$ value as the final $RDED$.

The smaller value of $RDED$ means more similar for two sequences. If the $RDED$ value is less than 25, it can be concluded that these two $Seq(x)$ sequences are similar.

Experiment Result. In the samples of DroidKungfu, the two sequences of $Seq(open["/system/lib/libbd1.so"])$ are named as seq_1 and seq_2:

$$seq_1 : C(open)_{a_0}, close_{a_1}, chmod_{a_2}, chown32_{a_3}, lstat64_{a_4}, gettimeofday_{a_5},$$
$$settimeofday_{a_6}, open_{a_7}, fstat64_{a_8}, read_{a_9}, mount_{a_{10}}$$

$$seq_2 : C(open)_{b_0}, ioctl_{b_1}, close_{b_2}, gettimeofday_{b_3}, settimeofday_{b_4}, open_{b_5},$$
$$fstat64_{b_6}, mprotect_{b_7}, mprotect_{b_8}, read_{b_9}, mount_{b_{10}}$$

The LCS is as follows:

$$LCS : C(open)_{a_0,b_0}, close_{a_1,b_2}, gettimeofday_{a_5,b_3}, settimeofday_{a_6,b_4}, open_{a_7,b_5},$$
$$fstat64_{a_8,b_6}, read_{a_9,b_9}, mount_{a_{10},b_{10}}$$

As $a_0 = b_0 = C(open)$, $a_1 = b_2 = close \in LCS$, $DIS(a_1, B) = ||1 - 0| - |2 - 0|| = 1$. While $a_2 = chmod \notin LCS$, $DIS(a_2, B) = 10$. In this way, the value of $DIS(a_k, B)$ are calculated and listed in Table 1.

Table 1. The $DIS(a_k, B)$ results for $Seq(open["/system/lib/libbd1.so"])$

Value of k	1	2	3	4	5	6	7	8	9	10
$DIS(a_k, B)$	1	10	10	10	3	0	0	0	2	0

Therefore, the $RDED(A, B) = \sqrt{\sum_{k=1}^{n} DIS(a_k, B)^2} = 17.72$. Because $RDED(A, B) < 25$, it is tagged as similar to be handled further.

Feature Extraction. After deleting the dissimilar sequences pairs, HypTracker will get the pairs of the similar sequences. HypTracker uses a **greedy-like algorithm** to get the feature sequence model, which has the following steps:

- **Step1.** HypTracker will get all $Seq(x)$ sequences with the distances less than 25 to build a sequence, named $SEQ(apk_1)$ and $SEQ(apk_2)$ for each apk respectively. Define the length of $SEQ(apk_1)$ as m and the length of $SEQ(apk_2)$ as n.

Table 2. The $RDED$ results for DroidKungfu

	0	1	2	3	4	5	6	7
0	a_{00}	$Seq(A)$	$Seq(B)$	$Seq(C)$	$Seq(D)$	$Seq(E)$	$Seq(F)$	$Seq(G)$
1	$Seq(A)$	22.52	-	-	-	-	-	-
2	$Seq(B)$	-	22.43	-	-	-	-	-
3	$Seq(C)$	-	-	22.43	-	-	-	-
4	$Seq(D)$	-	-	-	22.43	-	-	-
5	$Seq(E)$	-	-	-	-	14.14	-	-
6	$Seq(G)$	-	-	-	-	-	-	24.60
7	$Seq(F)$	-	-	-	-	-	17.72	-
8	$Seq(F)$	-	-	-	-	-	22.41	-
9	$Seq(F)$	-	-	-	-	-	22.41	-

	0	1	2	3	4	5	6	7	8	9
0	b_{00}	$Seq(H)$	$Seq(H)$	$Seq(H)$	$Seq(I)$	$Seq(H)$	$Seq(J)$	$Seq(H)$	$Seq(H)$	$Seq(K)$
1	$Seq(H)$	0	24.66	-	-	-	-	-	-	-
2	$Seq(H)$	-	20.40	17.32	-	-	-	24.90	24.52	-
3	$Seq(I)$	-	-	-	20.40	-	-	-	-	-
4	$Seq(H)$	17.38	24.78	22.65	-	24.86	-	-	-	-
5	$Seq(J)$	-	-	-	-	-	17.58	-	-	-
6	$Seq(H)$	-	-	-	-	-	-	20.40	14.28	-
7	$Seq(K)$	-	-	-	-	-	-	-	-	0

- **Step2.** HypTracker then builds a table with the size $m \times n$ and fill it with the $RDED$ values. All the entries with different sensitive system call pairs or with the value more than 25 will be represented as "-". The example table can be shown as Table 2, the entry can be named as "a_{ij}" ($1 \le i \le m, 1 \le j \le n$).
- **Step3.** HypTracker searches the table and finds the entry with the minimum value, named as a_{ij}. Then HypTracker will execute this step with the two subtable $\{a_{11}, a_{i-1j-1}\}$ and $\{a_{i+1j+1}, a_{mn}\}$ recursively until there is no any subtable.
- **Step4.** HypTracker links all the above entries and gets their $Seq(x)$ sequences. Then it gets the LCS for every $Seq(x)$ pair and links them. The final sequence is the malicious behaviour model.

Experiment Result. In the two samples of DroidKungfu, Table 2 shows the $RDED$ values for all the related system calls. $Seq(A) - Seq(K)$ mean the different kinds of sequences with different sensitive system call or different parameters. For example, $C(A)$ is $C(open["/system/lib/libc.so"])$ while $C(B)$ is $C(open["/system/lib/libstdc++.so"])$. We use "$a_{ij}$" and "$b_{mn}$" to represent these two subtable, respectively. The table is divided into two parts because (1) these two tables have no directly related system calls, (2) and at the first time to run Step 3 of the aforementioned algorithm, the value of b_{11} is 0 which is the minimum value. Therefore, the $\{a_{11}, a_{97}\}$ and $\{b_{22}, b_{79}\}$ will be used in next steps.

For the table $\{a_{11}, a_{97}\}$, the minimum value is 14.14, the value of a_{55}. Therefore, there will be two subtable needed to be handled by HypTracker as Table 3.

Table 3. The generated two subtables

	0	1	2	3	4
0		$Seq(A)$	$Seq(B)$	$Seq(C)$	$Seq(D)$
1	$Seq(A)$	22.52	-	-	-
2	$Seq(B)$	-	22.43	-	-
3	$Seq(C)$	-	-	22.43	-
4	$Seq(D)$	-	-	-	22.43

	5	6	7
5		$Seq(F)$	$Seq(G)$
6	$Seq(G)$	-	24.60
7	$Seq(F)$	17.72	-
8	$Seq(F)$	22.41	-
9	$Seq(F)$	22.41	-

Obviously, $\{a_{11}, a_{44}\}$ can be taken out successively. While in $\{a_{66}, a_{97}\}$, the minimum value is 17.72, the value of a_{76}. Then the subtable $\{a_{87}, a_{97}\}$ has no value, so the calculation is done.

Similarly, the calculation for the subtable $\{b_{22}, b_{79}\}$ is shown in Fig. 4. For every chosen $Seq(x)$ using greedy-like algorithm, HypTracker adds the $LCS(x)$ into the malicious behaviour model. As a result, the **malicious behaviour model** is as follows:

$$LCS(A), LCS(B), LCS(C), LCS(D), LCS(E), LCS(F), LCS(H),$$
$$LCS(H), LCS(I), LCS(H), LCS(J), LCS(H), LCS(K)$$

	1	2	3	4	5	6	7	8	9
1		Seq(H)	Seq(H)	Seq(I)	Seq(H)	Seq(J)	Seq(H)	Seq(H)	Seq(K)
2	Seq(H)	20.40	17.32 ③	-	-	-	24.90	24.52	-
3	Seq(I)	-	-	20.40 ⑤	-	-	-	-	-
4	Seq(H)	24.78	22.65	-	24.86 ④	-	-	-	-
5	Seq(J)	-	-	-	-	17.58 ②	-	-	-
6	Seq(H)	-	-	-	-	-	20.40	14.28	-
7	Seq(K)	-	-	-	-	-	-	-	① 0

Fig. 4. The calculation for subtable $\{b_{22}, b_{79}\}$

After the original model has been built, HypTracker then uses the system call sequences of other apks to perform the same calculation and minimize the model to get the final malicious behaviour model.

5 Detection Module

After HypTracker has learnt the malicious behaviour model of the malicious behaviour, this kind of malware can be detected by HypTracker. If there are a series of $Seq(x)$ sequences in the pending apk meeting $LCS(x) \subseteq Seq(x)$ for every $LCS(x)$ in the feature sequence model, it means that this apk has the same malicious behaviour as the model. HypTracker uses **a sliding-window-like mechanism** to perform the detection as follows:

- At initialization time, HypTracker generates a sliding window sequence with a length of 11, which has the same length as $Seq(x)$. The elements in the sliding window can be named as $e_0 - e_{10}$ as shown in Fig. 5. Among them, e_0 is the earliest element and e_{10} is the latest one. HypTracker also generates a handling queue with the same length as $Seq(x)$. Every element in the queue is consisted of the system call name $C(x)$ and the corresponding *sequence*.
- At first, the sliding window is null. When HypTracker intercepts a system call, the call will be added into the sliding window until the window reaches the full length. When HypTrakcer intercepts any system call later, the sliding window will move on to drop the earliest element and add the new system call.
- If the intercepted system call is the sensitive system call, it will be added into the queue. At same time, if this system call is $C(unlink)$, the current system call sequence in the sliding window will be saved as $Seq(unlink)$. When e_5 is $C(chmod)$ or e_0 is $C(open)$, HypTracker saves the system call sequence in the sliding window as corresponding $Seq(chmod)$ or $Seq(open)$ into the front corresponding entry whose *sequence* value is "null" in the queue.
- When the front entry of the queue is filled with $Seq(x)$, HypTracker will start the comparison with the known models of malicious behaviours. If current $LCS(x) \subseteq Seq(x)$, HypTracker will use the next $LCS(x)$ for the following comparison. If the $LCS(x)$ is the last subsequence of the model, HypTracker confirms that this apk has the related malicious behaviour and then alerts to the user. It also uses the backups to recover the related system files.

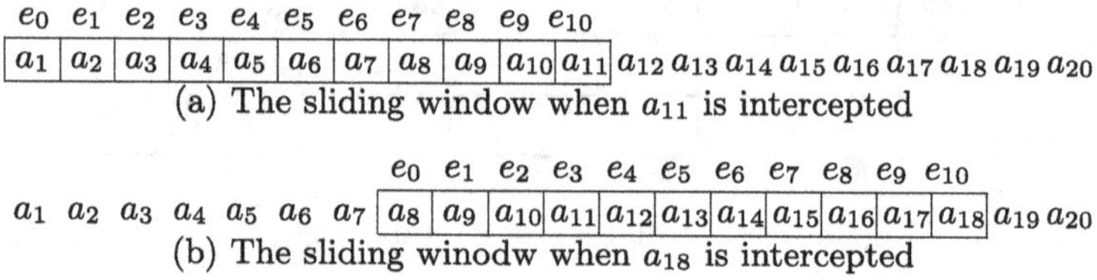

$$e_0 \quad e_1 \quad e_2 \quad e_3 \quad e_4 \quad e_5 \quad e_6 \quad e_7 \quad e_8 \quad e_9 \quad e_{10}$$

| a_1 | a_2 | a_3 | a_4 | a_5 | a_6 | a_7 | a_8 | a_9 | a_{10} | a_{11} | a_{12} a_{13} a_{14} a_{15} a_{16} a_{17} a_{18} a_{19} a_{20} |

(a) The sliding window when a_{11} is intercepted

$$e_0 \quad e_1 \quad e_2 \quad e_3 \quad e_4 \quad e_5 \quad e_6 \quad e_7 \quad e_8 \quad e_9 \quad e_{10}$$

a_1 a_2 a_3 a_4 a_5 a_6 a_7 | a_8 | a_9 | a_{10} | a_{11} | a_{12} | a_{13} | a_{14} | a_{15} | a_{16} | a_{17} | a_{18} | a_{19} a_{20}

(b) The sliding winodw when a_{18} is intercepted

Fig. 5. The samples of sliding window

Experiment Result. We use a system call sequence fragment of Droid-Kungfu as an example, which has been shown in Table 4.

After the learning of HypTracker, there are a lot of malicious behaviour models in the database. We use the following three malicious behaviour models

Table 4. An actual example sequence of DroidKungfu

a_1	a_2	a_3	a_4	a_5	a_6	a_7
settimeofday	lstat64	stat64	C(open)	ioctl	close	stat64
a_8	a_9	a_{10}	a_{11}	a_{12}	a_{13}	a_{14}
C(open)	ioctl	close	C(unlink)	sync	sync	open
a_{15}	a_{16}	a_{17}	a_{18}	a_{19}	a_{20}	a_{21}
C(open)	close	C(chmod)	chown32	lstat64	stat64	C(open)
a_{22}	a_{23}	a_{24}	a_{25}	a_{26}	a_{27}	a_{28}
ioctl	close	stat64	open	ioctl	close	gettimeofday
a_{29}	a_{30}	a_{31}	a_{32}	a_{33}	a_{34}	a_{35}
settimeofday	open	fstat64	read	mount	close	unlink

as an example[3]:

$model1 : LCS(open), LCS(open), LCS(open), LCS(open), LCS(unlink)$

$model2 : LCS(open), LCS(unlink), LCS(chmod), LCS(open), LCS(open)$

$model3 : LCS(open), LCS(unlink), LCS(open), LCS(chmod), LCS(open)$

At first, HypTracker intercepts *settimeofday* and saves it into e_{10}. When HypTracker intercepts a_4, it will add $C(open)$ into the queue. Then HypTracker also intercepts a_8 and adds it into the queue. When e_{10} equals a_{11} as Fig. 5(a), it is $C(unlink)$ and e_0 is a_1. Therefore, HypTracker saves $C(unlink)$ and the sequence $a_1 - a_{11}$ as $Seq(unlink)$ into the queue as Fig. 6(a). When HypTracker intercepts a_{14} and saves it into e_{10}, e_0 is $C(open)$. Therefore, HypTracker saves the current sequence in the sliding window into the first $C(open)$ entry of the queue. Then HypTracker uses $Seq(open)$ to compare with the malicious models. Suppose all the three models satisfy $LCS(open) \subseteq Seq(open)$, then HypTracker will prepare to compare the second elements of the models.

When HypTracker intercept a_{18}, e_0 becomes a_8 as shown in Fig. 5(b). HypTracker then saves the current sequence in the sliding window and performs the comparison with the malicious model. Suppose the second $LCS(open)$ is the subset of $Seq(open)$, then HypTracker will compare the third element in model 1 next time. As shown in Fig. 6(b), the $Seq(unlink)$ has been saved before. Therefore, HypTracker also compares the $Seq(unlink)$ with the models.

Using this method, HypTracker will accomplish the comparisons. When HypTracker intercepts a_{35}, it will compare the $Seq(open)$ with the models. The third model has reached the last LCS, HypTracker will tell the user that the third kind of malicious behaviour exists in this apk and then recover the related system files automatically.

---

[3] For simplicity, we hide the parameters of the system calls and suppose the parameters are the same. But in practical, the files needed to be opened in different malicious behaviours are different as a general rule.

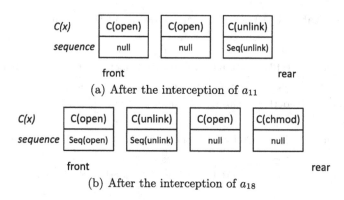

(a) After the interception of a_{11}

(b) After the interception of a_{18}

Fig. 6. The queue of the example

6   Related Work

The virtualization extensions on ARM is a new introduced technology. Nowadays many researchers use this technology to protect the mobile systems. DroidVisor [10] uses virtualization extensions to detect rootkit through detecting the hidden modules and hidden processes. Horsch [3] built a framework tracking the control flow to protect the programs. It used page fault to intercept the control flow. This framework can intercept not only the system call sequence but also any control flow, but they didn't give out any special modules to detect the malicious behaviours. H-Binder [7] is proposed to protect Binder transaction data in the kernel using virtualizaiton extensions. Generally speaking, different researchers use the virtualization extensions on ARM to protect the system security in different ways. And there are many potential usages of the virtualization extensions on ARM to be discovered.

In x86 platforms, there were many researchers using system call features to detect the malwares. SCSdroid [5] was proposed to detect repackage malicious applications using the system call sequences. It gave a way to train the case and perform the detection. Ham et al. [13] used the called number of system calls to build a pattern for malicious attacks. Wahanggara et al. [8] used Support Vector Machine (SVM) method to analyze the system call to detect malwares. Amamra et al. [2] used a system call filtering method to detect the malwares which is similar with our method. They ignored the useless system calls and also used the sliding window to analyze the model. But HypTrakcer can use an easier approach to analyze the permission-related malwares which can prove the performance distinctly. Meanwhile, all these methods are run in the supervisor mode which have the same privileged level as some kernel attacks. Hence these methods may not work or the interception of the system call may be effected due to the disturbing of the kernel attacks.

7 Conclusion

We have proposed HypTracker which can analyze the system call sequences to detect the malicious behaviours based on ARM virtualization extensions. HypTracker can intercept the system calls at the thread level and analyze the sequences. It can learn and extract the malicious behaviour models of the malwares families using Relative Discrete Euclidean Distance and the greedy-like algorithm proposed in our paper. At runtime, HypTracker can use a sliding-window-like mechanism to detect the malicious behaviours. We have implemented the experiment on the samples of DroidKungfu to verify the learning module and detection module. Our future work is to optimize the model and put forward a new method to detect the unknown malwares based on the abnormal system call sequences.

Acknowledgment. This research work is supported in part by the National High Technology Research and Development Program of China (No. 2015AA016004), and the National Natural Science Foundation of China (Grand Nos. U1636211, 61672081, 61602237, 61370126).

References

1. Architecture Reference Manual (ARMv7-A and ARMv7-R edition). ARM DDI C (2008)
2. Amamra, A., Robert, J., Talhi, C.: Enhancing malware detection for android systems using a system call filtering and abstraction process. Secur. Commun. Netw. **8**(7), 1179–1192 (2015)
3. Horsch, J., Wessel, S.: Transparent page-based kernel and user space execution tracing from a custom minimal ARM hypervsior. In: The IEEE International Conference on Trust, Security and Privacy in Computing and Communications, pp. 408–417 (2015)
4. Li, Z., Shen, D., Su, X., Ma, J.: Security technology based on arm virtualization extension. J. Softw. **28**(9), 2–20 (2016)
5. Lin, Y.D., Lai, Y.C., Chen, C.H., Tsai, H.C.: Identifying android malicious repackaged applications by thread-grained system call sequences. Comput. Secur. **39**(39), 340–350 (2013)
6. Peiravian, N., Zhu, X.: Machine learning for android malware detection using permission and API calls. In: IEEE International Conference on TOOLS with Artificial Intelligence, pp. 300–305 (2013)
7. Shen, D., Zhang, Z., Ding, X., Li, Z., Deng, R.: H-Binder: a hardened binder framework on Android systems. In: Deng, R., Weng, J., Ren, K., Yegneswaran, V. (eds.) SecureComm 2016. LNICSSITE, vol. 198, pp. 24–43. Springer, Cham (2017). doi:10.1007/978-3-319-59608-2_2
8. Wahanggara, V., Prayudi, Y.: Malware detection through call system on android Smartphone using vector machine method. In: International Conference on Cyber Security, pp. 62–67 (2015)
9. Wu, D.J., Mao, C.H., Lee, H.M., Wu, K.P.: DroidMat: Android malware detection through manifest and API calls tracing. In: Information Security, pp. 62–69 (2012)

10. Yang, Y., Qian, Z., Huang, H.: A lightweight monitor for android kernel protection. Comput. Eng. **40**(4), 48–52 (2014)
11. Yao, X., Han, X., Du, X., Zhou, X.: A lightweight multicast authentication mechanism for small scale iot applications. IEEE Sens. J. **13**(10), 3693–3701 (2013)
12. You, J.H., Lee, H.W.: Detection of malicious android mobile applications based on aggregated system call events. Int. J. Comput. Commun. Eng. **3**(2), 149–154 (2014)
13. You, J.H., Moon, D., Lee, H.W., Lim, J.D., Kim, J.N.: Android mobile application system call event pattern analysis for determination of malicious attack. Int. J. Secur. Appl. **8**(1), 231–246 (2014)
14. Zhang, M., Duan, Y., Yin, H., Zhao, Z.: Semantics-aware android malware classification using weighted contextual API dependency graphs, pp. 1105–1116 (2014)

A Fibonacci Based Batch Auditing Protocol for Cloud Data

Jian Shen[1,2,3,4(✉)], Jun Shen[3], Chen Wang[3], and Anxi Wang[3]

[1] Jiangsu Engineering Center of Network Monitoring, Nanjing, China
s_shenjian@126.com
[2] Jiangsu Collaborative Innovation Center on Atmospheric Environment
and Equipment Technology, Nanjing, China
[3] School of Computer and Software, Nanjing University of Information Science
and Technology, Nanjing, China
sj310310@qq.com
[4] State Key Laboratory of Information Security,
Institute of Information Engineering,
Chinese Academy of Sciences, Beijing, China

Abstract. As cloud storage is developing fast with time going by, the design of auditing protocols has caught a large number of researchers' eyes. However, though most of the existing auditing protocols have considered batch auditing to save resources in the auditor side, the design of methods to locate the specific positions of the corrupted data blocks is ignored. In this paper, we propose a novel batch auditing protocol based on the Fibonacci sequence to save resources in the cloud, which is an extension of our previous work. Experimental results and numerical analysis indicate that the proposed scheme is efficient.

Keywords: Cloud storage · Auditing protocols · Batch auditing · The fibonacci sequence

1 Introduction

Nowadays, cloud storage has been accepted by more and more individuals and corporations for its on-demand outsourcing function, ubiquitous network access and location-independent resources [1–5]. However, by using cloud storage, data owners (DOs) longer hold the data locally and may suffer from the worries about the security of the outsourced cloud data, for various internal and external security attacks in the cloud. To be more specific, on the one hand, malicious network attacks, which are external and familiar to the Internet users, threaten cloud data [6–8]. Hackers might retrieve and steal cloud users' data or even corrupt and delete the data, destroying its confidentiality, integrity, and availability. On the other hand, the outsourced data might suffer from cloud service providers' (CSPs') illegal behaviors. In particular, a CSP may secretly delete some data in its storage cycle without authorization from the owners of these data to save space for other clients' data. On top of this, a CSP might attempt to obtain the specific content of the data outsourced in the cloud.

© Springer International Publishing AG 2017
S. Wen et al. (Eds.): CSS 2017, LNCS 10581, pp. 215–222, 2017.
https://doi.org/10.1007/978-3-319-69471-9_16

Hence, a large number of researchers have devoted themselves to the design of auditing protocols to ensure the completeness and correctness of the outsourced cloud data. At the very beginning, researchers considered auditing protocols as the private one [9–11], in which the auditing tasks were conducted by DOs themselves. To be more flexible, the public auditing was proposed [12–15], in which a trusted third party auditor (TPA) is introduced in the verification system to audit the cloud data. With the proposal of public auditing, the burden on the DO side, especially the computational burden, can be relieved substantially. However, once the auditing tasks are delegated to the TPA, the security of the data and the DOs' information may be under threatens. To be more secure, the auditing protocols were designed to be privacy-preserving using technologies like random masking and index hash table by some researchers later. It is comprehensive that some data outsourced in the cloud may be altered from time to time to keep up with the times. In order to make the auditing protocols more practical, dynamic operations were supported by more and more protocols afterwards [16–20]. Besides, it is possible that sometimes more than one auditing tasks may be deputed to the TPA, therefore, researchers have designed auditing protocols to support batch auditing to save more computational and communication cost. Every little make a mickle, much resources can be saved by batch auditing.

However, though most of the existing protocols have considered public auditing, privacy preserving, dynamic support, batch auditing and other additional functions, researchers ignored the design of the details of batch auditing. Specifically, most auditing protocols supporting batch auditing for multiple data blocks from one/more files or one/more DOs do not consider how to deal with the situation where one/more data blocks are corrupted. In another word, once the batch auditing fails, which means that one or more data blocks are no longer correct or integrated, many researchers have not considered how to locate the specific positions of these corrupted blocks. Therefore, in this paper, we design a novel batch auditing protocol to solve the mentioned problem above, which makes it possible to make sure which file of whom the corrupted blocks belong to.

The remainder of this paper is organized as follows. Section 2 introduces some related works. Section 3 presents the system model. Section 4 describes the detailed batch auditing protocol proposed in this paper. Section 5 displays the experimental results and numerical analysis. The conclusion is drawn in Sect. 6.

2   Related Works

Auditing protocols for the outsourced cloud data have been studied by many researchers in recent years. So far, a large number of the corresponding protocols have been proposed.

Specifically, the auditing protocols are divided into the private one and the public one. In the model of private auditing protocols, entities participated in are the DO and the CSP merely. Only the DO possesses the private key, and executes all the auditing process. However, these solutions increase the burden on DOs, who are not equipped with enough computing resources and professional auditing knowledges. To remove the above doubts, the TPA is introduced into the whole system. In 2007, Ateniese *et al.* [21]

first proposed the idea of public auditing, which is widely accepted by researchers. After that, more and more auditing protocols are designed based on the mechanism of "challenge -proof -verify". In 2013, Wang *et al.* [12] pointed out that the proposed scheme with public auditability in [21] might leak the information of the data under verification. As a result, the auditing protocol in [12] is designed to be privacy-preserving realized by the combination of homomorphic linear authenticator (HLA) and random masking technique. Moreover, the protocol is extended to support multi users by Wang *et al.* In 2008, Ateniese *et al.* [22] first proposed a partially dynamic provable data possession (PDP) protocol, which represented an important step forward towards substantially more practical PDP technique. Inspired by Ateniese's work, Erway *et al.* [16] extended auditing protocol to support fully dynamic storage with the employment of skip list, which still has much for improvement in efficiency and privacy.

3 The System Model

In this section, the system model of the proposed protocol is introduced. As is described in Fig. 1, the whole model contains three primary entities: the CSP, the TPA and the DO.

The CSP is an entity providing cloud clients with countless cloud resources and various cloud services. In our protocol, the CSP is responsible for the storage of the outsourced cloud data, which relies on the storage service of the cloud. The TPA is a trusted third party equipped with professional auditing knowledges. The DO are cloud clients who have outsourced their data to the cloud for benefit but are worried about the security of these data. Hence, DOs employ the TPA to check the integrity and correctness of their cloud data. In our protocol, more than one DO delegate the auditing tasks to one TPA, which are picked from DO_1 to DO_x in Fig. 1. Besides, each DO has y files, and the data files to be verified are chosen from them. In addition, there are z data blocks in every file, and the blocks to be checked are chosen randomly from the chosen

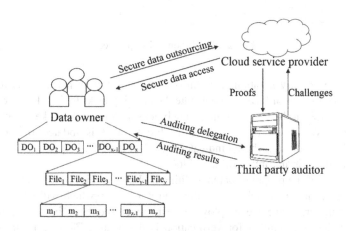

Fig. 1. The system model.

files. In another word, the auditing tasks delegated to the TPA may be several data blocks from different files belonged to different DOs.

4   The Proposed Batch Auditing Protocol

In this section, we will present the high descriptions of the proposed batch auditing protocol. Note that this protocol is an extension of our previous work [5], which aims to locate the position of the corrupted data blocks. As for the details for verification and the equations for auditing, the readers can refer to our previous work [5].

As is shown in Fig. 2, the Fibonacci sequence is listed. What is known to us all is that the Fibonacci sequence is a list of numbers intimately connected with the golden ratio. Specifically, when the number in the sequence is large enough, the ratio of the last two number is close to $(\sqrt{5}-1)/2$, which approximately equals 0.618 generally. In Fig. 2, it is clear that each number in the right is the sum of the two preceding ones, except for the first two numbers "1" and "1". Mathematically, $F(n) = F(n-1) + F(n-2)$, where $n > 2$. The division of the Fibonacci sequence involves addition and subtraction merely, and that of the dichotomy of a sequence involves division operation. For the fact that division costs more than addition and subtraction, the efficiency of the Fibonacci sequence is higher theoretically. Inspired by this fantastic sequence, we design the batch auditing protocol aiming at locating the positions of the corrupted data blocks.

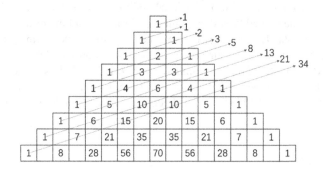

Fig. 2. The Fibonacci sequence.

First, some primary notations used in our protocol will be listed in the following. We denote the number of DOs who delegate the auditing tasks to the TPA is x. Besides, each DO has y files to be verified, and z data blocks are randomly picked from each file to be checked. What's more, the index of each data block is updated to "i, j, k" in the process of batch auditing, where i indicates the ID of the DO, j represents the ID of file and k shows the original index of each block.

The process of the proposed batch auditing is shown in Fig. 3. It is obvious that the total number of the data blocks for verification is $x * y * z$, which will not always be a Fibonacci number. Since we employ the Fibonacci sequence in our protocol, we assume that the total number for verification is the nearest Fibonacci number larger

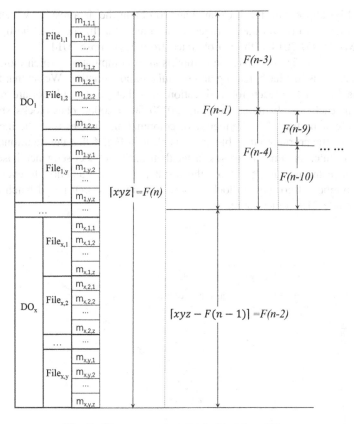

Fig. 3. The proposed method of batch auditing.

than $x * y * z$. Mathematically, it is $\lceil xyz \rceil = F(n)$, where $F(n)$ is a Fibonacci number. Since a Fibonacci number satisfies $F(n) = F(n-1) + F(n-2)$, all the blocks are divided into two parts. There are $F(n-1)$ blocks in the first part, and $\lceil xyz - F(n-1) \rceil = F(n-2)$ in the second part. As is shown in Fig. 3, we suppose that the corrupted data block is in the first part, the TPA will audit the first $F(n-1)$ blocks. If the corrupted block is in the second part, the TPA will audit $xyz - F(n-1)$ blocks, instead of $F(n-2)$ blocks. Then, the TPA will continue to audit the next part of blocks, which is shown as the $F(n-4)$ blocks' part in Fig. 3, until the TPA find the corrupted data block. As for the location of this block, its index indicates the information, which will expose the DO's ID, the file's ID and the block's sequence number.

5 Performance Analysis

In this part, we will analysis the performance of our batch auditing protocol based on the Fibonacci sequence. We conduct the experiments on a desktop running Windows 7 with a 2.50 GHz Intel Core i5-2450 M CPU and 12 GB of memory. The codes were written in MyEclipse with the Java language to obtain the data results, which are the results of 50 runs to obtain the averages as the final data. In addition, the figures are drawn in MATLAB 2014 with data obtained from MyEclipse 2014.

As is shown in Fig. 4, this is the comparison of computation, which indicates the times of operations like hash, pairing and modular exponentiation. We set that there are 20 DOs having 20 files each for verification, and that 50 data blocks are randomly picked from each file. In total, there are 20*20*50 = 20000 data blocks should be audited at the same time. The frequency of computation changes with the increase of the number of the corrupted data blocks. It is clear in Fig. 4 that the traditional binary search based batch auditing increases faster than the Fibonacci sequence based batch auditing. Since the unit is "*10 ^ 5", the result is not obvious enough, even though when the number of corrupted blocks is 450 the binary search based batch auditing should compute 2192 times more.

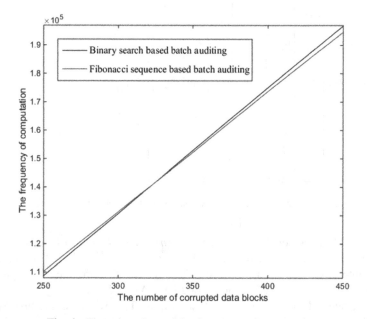

Fig. 4. The comparison of the frequency of computation.

In Table 1, we present the time for each operation. As for the detailed auditing process and verification equations, please refer to our previous work [5]. According to Eq. (10) (11) (12) in [5], we can conclude that there are $(3\,EXP + 1\,Hash + 2\,NumberMUL + 1\,PointMUL + 2\,Pairing)$ in each computation. Therefore, when the number of the corrupted blocks is 450, the extra time of the traditional batch auditing will be:

$$2192*(3 * 0.003707 + 1 * 0.000013 * 2 * 0.000003 + 1 * 0.000069 + 2 * 0.007834)$$
$$= 58.872736 \text{ s}$$

Table 1. The time cost for each basic operation.

Operations	Time(s)
Hash	0.000013
Modular exponentiation	0.003707
Number multiplication	0.000003
Point multiplication	0.000069
Pairing	0.007834

The result indicates that when (450/20000) = 2% data blocks are corrupted the proposed batch auditing can save at least 1 min. Therefore, when there are more corrupted data blocks, the advantages of our protocol will be more obvious.

6 Conclusion

In this paper, we proposed a Fibonacci based batch auditing protocol, which is based on our previous work [5]. The proposed protocol employs the Fibonacci sequence, which can efficiently locate the position of the corrupted data blocks. Experimental results and numerical analysis show the efficiency of the protocol.

Acknowledgements. This work is supported by the National Science Foundation of China under Grant No. 61672295, No. 61300237 and No. U1405254, the State Key Laboratory of Information Security under Grant No. 2017-MS-10, the 2015 Project of six personnel in Jiangsu Province under Grant No. R2015L06, the CICAEET fund, and the PAPD fund.

References

1. Mell, P., Grance, T.: The NIST definition of cloud computing. Commun. ACM **53**(6), 50 (2011)
2. Yang, K., Jia, X.: Data storage auditing service in cloud computing: challenges, methods and opportunities. World Wide Web Internet Web Inf. Syst. **15**(4), 409–428 (2011)
3. Xia, Z., Wang, X., Sun, X., Wang, Q.: A secure and dynamic multi-keyword ranked search scheme over encrypted cloud data. IEEE Trans. Parallel Distrib. Syst. **27**(2), 340–352 (2015)
4. Fu, Z., Sun, X., Liu, Q., Zhou, L., Shu, J.: Achieving efficient cloud search services: multi-keyword ranked search over encrypted cloud data supporting parallel computing. IEICE Trans. Commun. **98**(1), 190–200 (2015)
5. Shen, J., Shen, J., Chen, X., Huang, X., Susilo, W.: An efficient public auditing protocol with novel dynamic structure for cloud data. IEEE Trans. Inf. Forensics Secur. **12**(10), 2402–2415 (2017)
6. Khorshed, M.T., Ali, A.B.M.S., Wasimi, S.A.: A survey on gaps, threat remediation challenges and some thoughts for proactive attack detection in cloud computing. Future Gener. Comput. Syst. **28**(6), 833–851 (2012)
7. Liu, Q., Cai, W., Shen, J., Fu, Z., Liu, X., Linge, N.: A speculative approach to spatial-temporal efficiency with multi-objective optimization in a heterogeneous cloud environment. Secur. Commun. Netw. **9**(17), 4002–4012 (2016)

8. Soares, L.F.B., Fernandes, D.A.B., Gomes, J.V., Freire, M.M., Inácio, P.R.M.: Cloud security: state of the art. In: Nepal, S., Pathan, M. (eds.) Security, Privacy and Trust in Cloud Systems. Springer, Heidelberg (2014). doi:10.1007/978-3-642-38586-5_1

9. Fu, Z., Huang, F., Sun, X., Vasilakos, A.V., Yang, C.: Enabling semantic search based on conceptual graphs over encrypted outsourced data. IEEE Trans. Serv. Comput. (2017). doi:10.1109/TSC.2016.2622697

10. Chen, B., Shu, H., Coatrieux, G., Chen, G., Sun, X., Coatrieux, J.: Color image analysis by quaternion-type moments. J. Math. Imaging Vis. 51(1), 124–144 (2015)

11. Sebé, F., Domingoferrer, J., Martnezballest, A., Deswarte, Y., Quisquater, J.J.: Efficient remote data possession checking in critical information infrastructures. IEEE Trans. Knowl. Data Eng. 20(8), 1034–1038 (2008)

12. Wang, C., Chow, S.S.M., Wang, Q., Ren, K., Lou, W.: Privacy-preserving public auditing for secure cloud storage. IEEE Trans. Comput. 2009(2), 362–375 (2013)

13. Worku, S.G., Xu, C., Zhao, J., He, X.: Secure and efficient privacy-preserving public auditing scheme for cloud storage ⋆. Comput. Electr. Eng. 40(5), 1703–1713 (2014)

14. Shen, J., Tan, H., Wang, J., Wang, J., Lee, S.: A novel routing protocol providing good transmission reliability in underwater sensor networks. J. Internet Technol. 16(1), 171–178 (2015)

15. Yu, J., Ren, K., Wang, C.: Enabling cloud storage auditing with verifiable outsourcing of key updates. IEEE Trans. Inf. Forensics Secur. 11(6), 1362–1375 (2016)

16. Erway, C.C., Papamanthou, C., Tamassia, R.: Dynamic provable data possession. ACM Trans. Inf. Syst. Secur. 17(4), 213–222 (2009)

17. Kong, Y., Zhang, M., Ye, D.: A belief propagation-based method for task allocation in open and dynamic cloud environments. Knowl. Based Syst. 115, 123–132 (2016)

18. Shen, J., Liu, D., Shen, J., Liu, Q., Sun, X.: A secure cloud-assisted urban data sharing framework for ubiquitous-cities. Perv. Mobile Comput. (2017). doi:10.1016/j.pmcj

19. Ren, Y., Shen, J., Wang, J., Han, J., Lee, S.: Mutual verifiable provable data auditing in public cloud storage. J. Internet Technol. 16(2), 317–323 (2015)

20. Jin, H., Jiang, H., Zhou, K.: Dynamic and public auditing with fair arbitration for cloud data. IEEE Trans. Cloud Comput. (2016). doi:10.1109/TCC.2016.2525998

21. Ateniese, G., Burns, R., Curtmola, R., Herring, J., Kissner, L., Peterson, Z.: Provable data possession at untrusted stores. In: ACM Conference on Computer and Communications Security, vol. 14, pp. 598–609 (2007)

22. Ateniese, G., Pietro, R.D., Mancini, L.V., Tsudik, G.: Scalable and efficient provable data possession. In: The 4th International Conference on Security and Privacy in Communication Networks, pp. 1–10 (2008)

A WeChat User Geolocating Algorithm Based on the Relation Between Reported and Actual Distance

Wenqi Shi[1], Xiangyang Luo[1(✉)], Fan Zhao[1], Ziru Peng[1],
and Yong Gan[2]

[1] State Key Laboratory of Mathematical Engineering and Advanced Computing,
Zhengzhou Science and Technology Institute, Zhengzhou, China
{shiwenqi2997,luoxy_ieu}@sina.com,
zhaofan_123@yeah.net, Peng_Ziru@outlook.com
[2] School of Computer and Communication Engineering,
Zhengzhou University of Light Industry, Zhengzhou, China
ganyong@zzuli.edu.cn

Abstract. The accuracy of existing geolocation methods for WeChat users depends on the stable correspondence between reported distance and actual distance. In view of the difficulty to pinpoint users' location in real-world due to WeChat location protection strategy, a WeChat User geolocating Algorithm based on reported and actual distance relation analysis is proposed. Firstly, statistical characteristics of the relation between reported distance and actual distance are obtained based on collected data. Secondly, optimization parameters are selected based on these characteristics to determine the space where the target user is located. Finally, stepwise strategies are taken to improve the accuracy rate of space partition. Experimental results show that, on the premise that target users can be discovered, the proposed algorithm could achieve higher accuracy compared with the classical space partition based algorithm and the heuristic number theory based algorithm. The highest geolocating accuracy is within 10 m and 56% of geolocation results are within 60 m.

Keywords: Location based social networks · Statistical characteristics · Optimization parameters · Stepwise strategies · WeChat user geolocating

1 Introduction

With the rapid popularization of mobile Internet and the wide application of smart mobile devices, mobile social networks have gained enormous momentum, such as WeChat, Twitter and Momo, which provide a more convenient way for people to communicate with each other [1–3]. Meanwhile, it provides convenience for malicious users to engage in illegal activities such as fraud. WeChat is one of the largest mobile social networks in China, which has a wide range of users around the world. For the advantage that mobile social network applications can access to the location of devices conveniently, a wide variety of Location-Based Social Networks (LBSNs) and particular Location-Based Services (LBSs) sprang up [4, 5], which make it possible to

© Springer International Publishing AG 2017
S. Wen et al. (Eds.): CSS 2017, LNCS 10581, pp. 223–235, 2017.
https://doi.org/10.1007/978-3-319-69471-9_17

geolocate social network users. Carrying out the research of geolocating technology for mobile social network users is significative to pinpoint the location of malicious user and raise awareness of location privacy protection for ordinary users, meanwhile, help service providers afford more secure services to users [6]. The paper is focusing on WeChat, one of the most popular social network applications in China, to explore whether the existing privacy protection strategies of WeChat can protect users' location privacy effectively. The existing geolocation methods for WeChat users can be divided into two categories: number theory based geolocation algorithm and successive approximation based geolocation algorithm.

Number theory based geolocation algorithm abstract the relation between reported distance and actual distance as an ideal mathematical model. By setting probes equidistantly with certain rules in the region where the target user is located, reported distances of the target user collected from probes are constraint solved, thereby the location of the target user is pinpointed. Paper [7] has proposed one-dimension adversarial method firstly to detect the target user's location along a line, and further extended the method to two-dimensional space. What's more, the method is proved theoretically that it can get high positioning accuracy under ideal conditions. Paper [8] analyzed the influence of noise on the reported distance based on hypothesis and a heuristic number theory approach was proposed, what reduced the influence of noise on geolocating procedures to a certain extent. Paper [9] pointed out that the existence of noise makes geolocating errors of number theory-based algorithm increases as the actual distance between probes and the target user increases. In addition, placement strategies for the first probe was proposed to improve the practicality of the number theory based geolocation algorithm. Number theory based geolocation algorithm has high geolocation accuracy in theory, but in practical, as there is no stable relation between reported distance and actual distance, the gap between actual results and theoretical precision is large and the theoretical precision is hard to achieve.

Successive approximation based geolocation algorithm firstly determines the target user's location within a certain region. Then the region is divided into several sub-regions by collecting target users' reported distance from different positions. By determining which sub-region the target user is located, the size of potential region is reduced. Constantly repeating the procedure to approach the real location of the target user. Paper [10] geolocated WeChat user based on the improved triangle geolocation algorithm which utilizes the band-like reported distance characteristic of WeChat. The center of the intersection of rings determined by several probes was taken as the location of the target user. In order to break the minimum reported distance limit of WeChat, Paper [11] has proposed a geolocation algorithm based on space partition. The algorithm first determines the target user within the minimum reported distance, and then partition the space determined by the minimum reported distance until the threshold is achieved.

Space partition based geolocation algorithm is less time consuming and easy to implement. As shown in paper [11], the algorithm is able to geolocate 50% of users in less than 40 m, and the average positioning accuracy is about 51 m. However, actual tests show that there is no stable correspondence between reported distance and actual distance affected by the update of location protection strategy of WeChat, and the algorithm is difficult to geolocate target users with high precision in current conditions.

To analyze the correspondence between reported distance and actual distance, furthermore, improve the geolocating accuracy for WeChat users in actual environment, a geolocating algorithm based on optimization parameters selection of space partition is proposed.

In this paper, we improve space partition based geolocation algorithm by selecting optimization parameters based on statistical characteristics of the relation between reported distance and actual distance, and stepwise strategies are proposed to improve the accuracy rate of space partition. Experimental results show that, if the target user can be discovered, the proposed algorithm can geolocate WeChat users with higher accuracy compared with the classical space partition based algorithm and the heuristic number theory based algorithm, and the highest geolocating accuracy is within 10 m.

2 Problem Statement

In this Section, Location-based Social Discovery (LBSD) services and location protection strategies of WeChat are introduced. Then theory and shortcomings of the classical space partition based geolocation algorithm are discussed.

2.1 LBSD Services and Location Protection Strategies of WeChat

LBSD is an important kind of LBS, which provides the service for users to find other users close to their geographical location, and the relative distance between them are reported [12, 13]. "*People Nearby*" function in WeChat is a typical LSBD service. By querying "*People Nearby*", users can find users with geographic proximity and get the relative distance between them, meanwhile, leave a record in the querying position.

To defend against the traditional triangle geolocating attack and protect users' location privacy, most LBSD services of social network applications such as WeChat report relative distance between users in concentric bands. WeChat report relative distance between users in bands of 100 m instead of exact distance, until the report distance is 1000 m, and then in bands of 1000 m. By setting the minimum reported distance, users cannot obtain accurate distance to other users directly. What's more, the uncertainty of the corresponding relation between reported distance and actual distance is increased. In other words, it's difficult to determine the position of users within a circular region accurately even the reported distance of the user is known.

2.2 Analysis of Original Space Partition Based Geolocation Algorithm

Space partition based geolocation algorithm is designed to break the minimum reported distance limit of LBSD services and further enhance the localization accuracy. Implementation of the algorithm should meet the following prerequisites:

- Reported distance of the target user getting from the initial probe is the minimum reported distance, that is 100 m for WeChat;

- Each probe reports the relative distance to the target user in bands of K and the relation between reported relative distance W_d and actual distance d can be formalized as follows:

$$W_d = \left(\left\lfloor \frac{d}{K} \right\rfloor + 1 \right) * K \tag{1}$$

Where $K = 100$ when $d < 1000$, and $K = 1000$ when $d \geq 1000$.
The illustration of space partition based geolocation algorithm is shown in Fig. 1.

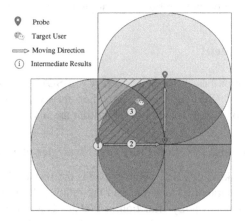

Fig. 1. Illustration of space partition based geolocation algorithm

The algorithm is based on the idea of successive approximation. For the simplicity of problem presentation, the algorithm consider the minimum distance limit as the box rather than the circle. Firstly, the location of probes is dynamically changed until the target user occurs with the minimum reported distance in query results list of the probe. So the potential area where the target user is located is determined as a box with 200 m in length, and current position of the probe is taken as intermediate geolocation result. Secondly, the position of the probe is shifted relative to the last intermediate result, consequently, the range determined by the minimum reported distance covers half of the potential area. Thirdly, the half region that the target user is located is determined by judging whether the reported distance of the target user getting from the shifted probe changes. If it changes, it is derived that the target user is in the un-overlapped half. Otherwise, the target user is located in overlapped half. In this way, the potential area is reduced to half after each round check. Modifying intermediate result to make it in the center of current potential area. Repeating this partition for multiple rounds until the expected accuracy is achieved and taking the last intermediate result as the location of the target user.

The space partition based geolocation algorithm takes the region determined by the minimum reported distance as the target space, and decide the sub-space that contains the target by checking whether the reported distance of the target user is increasing after shifting the probe. The location accuracy of the algorithm depends on the strict correspondence between reported distance and actual distance, that is formula (1). The algorithm will achieve high accuracy if the correspondence is satisfied. However, actual test shows that there is no strict correspondence between reported distance and actual distance. The situation that the reported relative distance shows 200 m or bigger is frequent even though the actual distance between two users is less than 100 m. In such conditions, the algorithm will identify the target user's location in wrong half space, which will lead to misjudgment and enlarge the geolocation error.

3 WeChat Users Geolocation Algorithm Based on Optimization Parameters Selection of Space Partition

The update of privacy protection policy can be taken as a possible reason for the fact that there is no strict correspondence between reported distance and actual distance in "*People Nearby*" function of WeChat. In this paper, we only consider the region within reported distance of 1000 m. By analyzing the relation between reported distance and actual distance, optimal parameters that decrease the probability of misjudgment are selected. In addition, stepwise strategies are adopted to improve the accuracy rate of space partition.

Assuming that the algorithm take Wp_i as the target reported distance, which means that the algorithm starts to geolocate the target user when the reported distance of the target user is Wp_i in the query results list of probes. For the simplicity of problem presentation, we consider the area determined by Wp_i as a box rather than a circle, which centered on the current probe and take $2D$ as the edge length. Taking R as effective actual distance determined by Wp_i. When the actual distance is less than R, the probability that the reported distance of the target user is not greater than Wp_i is higher compared with the probability that the reported distance is greater than Wp_i. The framework of WeChat users geolocating algorithm based on optimization parameter selection of space partition is shown in Fig. 2 and the main steps are as follows.

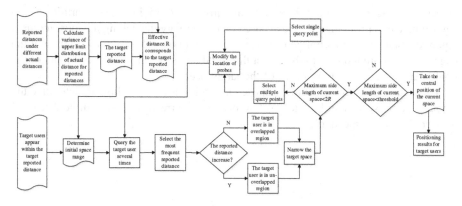

Fig. 2. Framework of WeChat users geolocating algorithm based on optimization parameter selection of space partition

3.1 Data Collecting

Recording the reported distance under different actual distances by dynamically adjusting the location of WeChat users. The target reported distance Wp_i and the corresponding effective value R are obtained based on statistical analysis on collected actual distance/reported distance data pairs.

3.2 Initial Space Determination

Modifying the location of probes until the target user is within the target reported distance of one probe. Utilizing statistical characteristics of the relation between reported distance and actual distance to determine the maximum possible actual distance D between the probe and the target user, according to the statistical analysis on probability distribution of the actual distance upper limit corresponding to reported distances. Thereby determining the initial space.

3.3 Narrow Initial Space

Firstly, multiple query points are selected on one side of the current target space and the distance between adjacent query points is R. Secondly, setting the location of probes in these points so that the union of areas determined by all probes with $2R$ length can cover half of the initial space. Thirdly, querying the target user several times at each point. The most frequent reported distance is taken as the reported distance of the target user.

If and only if reported distances obtained by all query points are increased, the location of the target user is judged in the un-overlapped region, otherwise the target user is determined in the overlapped region. Repeating this process until the length of larger edge of current target space is less than $2R$, so that the current target space can be divided into two equal regions by shifting the probe only one time.

3.4 Geolocate the Target User

Selecting a single query point in each round, just as the original space partition based algorithm, and partitioning the space based on the strategy that taking the most frequent reported distance as the reported distance of the target user. Iterating this step until the edges of target are reduced to the preset threshold and selecting the central point of the final area as the geolocating result of the target user.

Particularly, key points of the proposed algorithm are below: how to determine the range of target space and how to position the space correctly, which will be discussed in Sect. 4 and 5 respectively.

4 Determining Target Space Based on Statistical Characteristics of Reported Distance

How to determine the target reported distance and the corresponding geographical spatial scope is the first problem to be solved when geolocating a WeChat user. In this paper, we study the relation between reported distance and actual distance by analyzing the statistical characteristics of the actual distance upper limit corresponding to each reported distance (from 100 m to 900 m), and determine the target space range based on the characteristics.

4.1 Selection of Target Reported Distance

The selection of the target reported distance should follow principles below:

- The upper limit of actual distance corresponding to the target reported distance is relatively stable.
- Selecting the smaller reported distance under the same condition.

The target reported distance affects the scale of initial space range directly. The more stable the interval of actual distance corresponding to the target reported distance is, the easier to determine initial space range. We take the variance of upper limit distribution of actual distance as the measure and the reported distance with the minimum variance is taken as the target reported distance, what makes it easier to determine the target space range and reduce the possibility of misjudgment on the geolocation procedure. Selecting the smaller reported distance if there are more than one reported distance with the minimum variance, which can reduce the range of initial space as well as the positioning error caused by miscarriage of justice. The paper does not consider the lower limit distribution of actual distance corresponding to the target reported distance and take the target space as the box rather than a concentric ring, which can reduce the complexity to determine the initial space range and increase the possibility that the user's location is covered by the determined space.

4.2 Determination of Target Space Range

Calculating the value D that makes cumulative probability of the actual distance upper limit distribution for Wp_i up to P, that is:

$$P_i(d \leq D) = P \qquad (2)$$

Where d is the actual distance. The space where the target user is located is determined as a box centered on the probe, with $2D$ as the side length. The probability that the determined area covering the target user is more than P when the target user is within the target reported distance of the probe.

Determining the value of D according to cumulative probability instead of the maximum value, which can make the target space cover the location of target user with high probability (if P is big enough) as well as narrow the target space to reduce time consumption.

5   Partitioning Target Space Based on Stepwise Strategies

For the fact that value D is selected to make the determined target area cover the target user's location with high probability, the reported distance is very likely to be bigger than Wp_i even the actual distance is smaller than D. The paper delimits effective space range of the target reported distance and proposes stepwise strategies to improve the accuracy rate of space partition.

5.1   Delimiting Effective Space of Target Reported Distance

Taking a smaller value R than D as the effective distance relative to Wp_i, meanwhile, as the distance between adjacent query points in each round partition. When the actual distance is less than R, the probability that the reported distance of the target user is not greater than Wp_i is higher compared with the probability that the reported distance is greater than Wp_i, and the effective space bounded by $2R$ is determined. When a probe is shifted by R in one dimension of the space, the probability that reported distances of users within the overlapped area are no more than Wp_i is higher.

5.2   Improving the Accuracy of Space Partition by Stepwise Strategies

The effective space with the length of $2R$ cannot cover half of the initial target space as R is smaller than D. To improve the accuracy of judgment, multiple query points are selected on one side of the current space.

The selection of query points need to meet following conditions:

- The union region of effective spaces defined by all query points can cover half of the current target area.
- Users in the overlapped region have a lower probability that reported distance getting from at least one query point is larger than Wp_i.
- Users in the un-overlapped region have a higher probability that reported distances getting from all query points are larger than Wp_i.

The paper selects query points with intervals of R, and set probes in these points. The diagram of query point selection is shown in Fig. 3.

Setting probes at the location of query points and the actual distance between adjacent probes is R. If the target user is in the overlapped region, there are at least one probe which actual distance to the target user is less than R. So reported distances getting from these probes are more likely to be Wp_i. Each probe queries the target user repeatedly. For at least one probe, it will obtain more reported distances that are no more than Wp_i with high probability. Taking the most frequent reported distance as the reported distance of the target user, and determining which half region the target user is located according to the reported distance obtained by probes, which can reduce the rate of misjudgment in probability.

Repeating the above process until the larger edge of current target space is less than $2R$, so that the region determined by the length of the $2R$ can cover half of the current target space. Then the original algorithm can be employed to geolocate the target user.

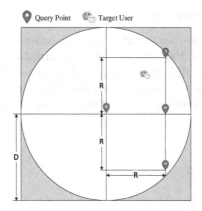

Fig. 3. The diagram of query point selection

6 Experimental Results and Analysis

To verify the effectiveness of the proposed algorithm, we implement real-world geolocating experiments using multiple mobile phones running ten different WeChat accounts. Mock GPS is used to fake geographic locations of probes and target users. The parameters of the proposed algorithm are determined by statistical analysis of reported distances and the comparison with the original space partition based algorithm and the heuristic number theory based algorithm [8] are given.

6.1 Experiments Settings

In terms of parameters determination, the geographic locations of WeChat accounts are faked by the same application, and statistical analysis on the relation between actual distances and reported distances is maked. Setting the location of user A firstly and user A leave a record in the position by using *"People Nearby"* function. Then, dynamically changing the location of user B to make the actual distance between user A and B enlarges in increments of 10 m. Reported distances of user A under different actual distances getting from user B are recorded.

In terms of geolocation, the experiment is compared with the original space partition based algorithm and the heuristic number theory based algorithm. We select a geographical area of size 1000 m*1000 m as our test field, and 50 target users are located within the region using the fake location application with known GPS coordinates. The proposed algorithm and the original space partition based algorithm query over the target area at particular intervals (100 m for space partition based algorithm and Wp_i for the proposed algorithm) until the target user is presented in the respective target reported distance list. Then geolocating the target user with the threshold for partition is 5 m. Experiment setting of the heuristic number theory based algorithm is in accordance to paper [8].

6.2   Parameters Determination

Taking it as one round test when the actual distance between user A and B is changed from 0 m to 1000 m, and 100 rounds of test are carried out. The maximum actual distance corresponding to Wp_i in each round test is defined as the upper limit of the actual distance, so that each reported distance has 100 sets of records. The variance of actual distance upper limit for each reported distance is calculated, as shown in Fig. 4.

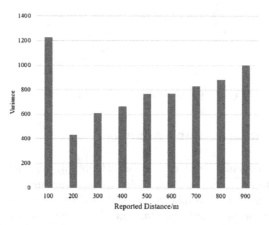

Fig. 4. The variance of actual distance upper limit for each reported distance

The figure shows that variances for each reported distance are fairly large, and variances have an increasing tendency with the increases of reported distance. Taking 200 m as the target reported distance as it has smaller variance. It is worth noting that the variance of 100 m reported distance is abnormally large. The abnormal phenomenon is caused by the frequent appearance of following situation: even two users are geographically close to each other, the reported distance of user A getting from user B is 200 m or bigger, rather than 100 m. The reason for this may be that WeChat thought it privacy- threating if report relative distance with 100 m when the actual distance between users is short, for the location of users can be determined within a smaller area. So the reported distance of 100 m will be avoided deliberately.

The probability distribution is shown in Fig. 5. It is observed that the upper actual distance of 200 m reported distance obey the normal distribution approximately, and the upper value has the maximum probability in about 170 m. The probability that reported distance changes to 300 m is pretty high when the actual distance between users is about 170 m. Based on the strategy of parameters selection, calculating the value that makes cumulative probability of the upper limit probability distribution for the target reported distance up to 95% and 50% respectively and corresponding actual distances value are taken as the initial target space range D and the effective distance R. In this way, the probability that the determined target space cover the location of target users is greater than 95%, and the determined effective space range meets the constraints. The obtained parameters are 225 and 173 for D and R.

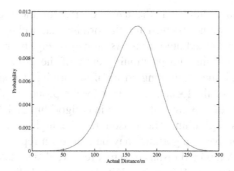

Fig. 5. Probability distribution of the upper limit of the actual distance for the target reported distance

6.3 Comparison of Experimental Results

In the experiment that geolocating 50 target users, the original space partition based algorithm discover 46 target users within the minimum reported distance successfully, and 46 positioning results are obtained. Nevertheless, all target users appear in the list of 200 m reported distance. The reason for the fact that 4 target users are failed to be determined within the minimum reported distance is that the existence of noise makes the probe obtain 200 m reported distance of target users, even the actual distance between target users and the probe is less than the minimum reported distance. The error distribution of the positioning results is shown in Fig. 6.

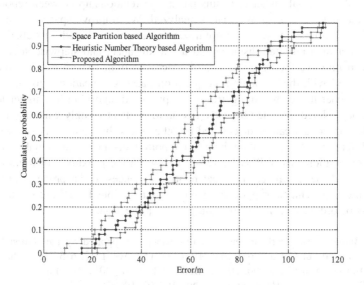

Fig. 6. Geolocation error comparison

Experimental results show that the average error of the proposed algorithm is 56.5 m, which is lower than 68.9 m for the original algorithm and 63.1 m for the heuristic number theory based algorithm. As shown in Fig. 6, under the same experimental conditions, the minimum positioning error of the proposed algorithm is less than 20 m, however, all the positioning errors of the original algorithm are higher than 20 m. Moreover, 56% of the localization error for the proposed algorithm is less than 60 m, which is higher than 34.8% of the original algorithm and 42% of the heuristic number theory based algorithm. The reason for the high geolocating error of the original space partition based algorithm may be that, even reported distances of target users are the minimum reported distance, actual relative distances between target users and the probe are greater than 100 m. The initial space is failed to cover the location of target users, what's more, frequently misjudge during space partition enlarges the deviation between positioning results and actual location of target users. For the heuristic number theory based algorithm, the unstable relationship between reported distance and actual distance make it hard to get accurate coordinates of target users. It is obvious to see from Fig. 6 that the proposed algorithm can geolocate WeChat users accurately in practical environment. The factors which may affect the geolocating accuracy includes: errors of fake location applications, low-probability misjudgment of space partition, the time of users' location is cached in WeChat server, and so on.

7 Conclusion

LBSD services of mobile social networks report the relative distance of nearby users in concentric bands. However, there is no strict correspondence between the reported distance and the actual distance. In this paper, the relationship between reported distance and actual distance of WeChat is analyzed. We improve space partition based geolocation algorithm by selecting optimization parameters based on statistical characteristics between reported distance and actual distance, and stepwise strategies are proposed to improve the accuracy rate of space partition. Experimental results show that, compared with the original space partition based geolocation algorithm and the heuristic number theory based algorithm, the proposed algorithm has higher localization accuracy. Noted that the proposed algorithm is effective only when the user uses the LBSD service and can be discovered by other users. In future work, we will focus on the difference of the relation between reported distance and actual distance in different orientations, as well as the relation between the proximity of users in query results list and the difference of actual relative distances to the probe. The research hopes to provide technical support for geolocating malicious LBSN users and raise the awareness of ordinary users for location privacy protection.

Acknowledgment. The work presented in this paper is supported by the National Natural Science Foundation of China (No. U1636219, 61379151, 61401512, 61572052), the National Key R&D Program of China (No. 2016YFB0801303, 2016QY01W0105) and the Key Technologies R&D Program of Henan Province (No. 162102210032).

References

1. Kwak, H., Lee, C., Park, H., Moon, S.: What is Twitter, a social network or a news media? In: Proceedings of the International Conference on World Wide Web, pp. 591–600. ACM, Raleigh (2010)
2. Nemelka, C.L., Ballard, C.L., Liu, K., Xue, M., Ross, K.W.: You can yak but you can't hide. In: Proceedings of the ACM Conference on Online Social Networks, p. 99. ACM, Stanford (2015)
3. Wang, G., Wang, B., Wang, T., Nika, A., Zheng, H., Zhao, B.Y.: Whispers in the dark: analysis of an anonymous social network. In: Proceedings of the Internet Measurement Conference, pp. 137–150. ACM, Vancouver (2014)
4. Zheng, Y.: Location-based social networks: users. In: Zheng, Y., Zhou, X. (eds.) Computing with Spatial Trajectories, pp. 243–276. Springer, New York (2011). doi:10.1007/978-1-4614-1629-6_8
5. Hoang, N.P., Asano, Y., Yoshikawa, M.: Your neighbors are my spies: location and other privacy concerns in dating apps. In: Proceedings of the 18th International Conference on Advanced Communication Technology, pp. 715–721. IEEE, PyeongChang (2016)
6. Shokri, R., Theodorakopoulos, G., Papadimitratos, P., Kazemi, E., Hubaux, J.: Hiding in the mobile crowd: location privacy through collaboration. IEEE Trans. Dependable Secure Comput. 11(3), 266–279 (2014)
7. Xue, M., Liu, Y., Ross, K.W., Qian, H.: I know where you are: thwarting privacy protection in location-based social discovery services. In: Proceedings of the IEEE Conference on Computer Communications Workshops, pp. 179–184. IEEE, Hong Kong (2015)
8. Peng, J., Meng, Y., Xue, M., Hei, X., Ross, K.W.: Attacks and defenses in location-based social networks: a heuristic number theory approach. In: Proceedings of the International Symposium on Security and Privacy in Social Networks and Big Data, pp. 64–71. IEEE, Hangzhou (2015)
9. Cheng, H., Mao, S., Xue, M., Hei, X.: On the impact of location errors on localization attacks in location-based social network services. In: Wang, G., Ray, I., Alcaraz Calero, J. M., Thampi, S.M. (eds.) SpaCCS 2016. LNCS, vol. 10066, pp. 343–357. Springer, Cham (2016). doi:10.1007/978-3-319-49148-6_29
10. Ding, Y., Peddinti, S.T., Ross, K.W.: Stalking Beijing from Timbuktu: a generic measurement approach for exploiting location-based social discovery. In: Proceedings of the 4th ACM Workshop on Security and Privacy in Smartphones & Mobile Devices, pp. 75–80. ACM, Scottsdale (2014)
11. Li, M., Zhu, H., Gao, Z., Chen, S., Ren, K., Yu, L., Hu, S.: All your location are belong to us: breaking mobile social networks for automated user location tracking. In: Proceedings of the 15th ACM international symposium on Mobile ad hoc networking and computing, pp. 43–52. ACM, Philadelphia (2014)
12. Polakis, I., Argyros, G., Petsios, T., Sivakorn, S., Keromytis, A.D.: Where's Wally? Precise user discovery attacks in location proximity services. In: Proceedings of the 22nd ACM SIGSAC Conference on Computer and Communications Security, pp. 817–828. ACM, Denver (2015)
13. Wang, R., Xue, M., Liu, K., Qian, H.: Data-driven privacy analytics: a WeChat case study in location-based social networks. In: Xu, K., Zhu, H. (eds.) WASA 2015. LNCS, vol. 9204, pp. 561–570. Springer, Cham (2015). doi:10.1007/978-3-319-21837-3_55

An Online Approach to Defeating Return-Oriented-Programming Attacks

Donghai Tian[1,2(✉)], Xiaoqi Jia[2], Li Zhan[1], Changzhen Hu[1], and Jingfeng Xue[1]

[1] Beijing Key Laboratory of Software Security Engineering Technique,
Beijing Institute of Technology, Beijing 100081, China
donghaitad@gmail.com
[2] Key Laboratory of Network Assessment Technology,
Institute of Information Engineering, Chinese Academy of Sciences,
Beijing 100093, China

Abstract. Return-oriented programming (ROP) attacks become very popular in recent years, as these attacks can bypass traditional defense mechanisms such as data execution prevention (DEP) effectively. Previous solutions suffer from limitations in that: (1) Some methods need to modify the target programs; (2) Some methods introduce considerable performance cost; (3) Almost all methods could not provide an online protection for the target processes. In this paper, we present OnDrop, an on-the-fly ROP protection system by using the OS internal facilities. Our system is compatible with the existing programs, and its protection layer can be added on demand. The experiments show that OnDrop can detect ROP attacks effectively with a little performance overhead.

Keywords: Return-oriented programming · On-the-fly · Protection

1 Introduction

As more and more software vulnerabilities are exposed to the public, runtime attacks on software (and IOT [1]) become very popular in recent years. Even some beginners can make use of the public exploitation tools [2] to attack the target programs. Once the program vulnerabilities (e.g., buffer overflow) are exploited by attackers, they can subvert the execution of the target programs.

To defend against the runtime attacks on software, some security mechanisms have been proposed. For instance, data execution prevention (DEP) is an effective approach to defeating code-injection attacks. Since the DEP mechanisms have been widely deployed in the commodity operating systems, it is very difficult for attackers to inject code into the target programs. Recently, Return-Oriented-Programming (ROP) is introduced to bypass the DEP mechanisms. This technique refines the traditional return-to-libc attacks and utilizes the ROP chains located in the program code or libraries to launch attacks. Previous studies [3] show that ROP attacks can perform arbitrary computation without executing any injected code.

© Springer International Publishing AG 2017
S. Wen et al. (Eds.): CSS 2017, LNCS 10581, pp. 236–247, 2017.
https://doi.org/10.1007/978-3-319-69471-9_18

Several solutions to defeat ROP attacks have been proposed by researchers. In general, these methods can be divided into two categories: instrumentation-based method and compiler-based method. The first method utilizes the dynamic binary instrumentation framework (e.g., Pin [4]) to instrument the call and ret instructions in the target program. In this way, the abnormal return instructions can be identified from the instruction stream for ROP detection. Unfortunately, this method imposes considerable performance overhead. For the compiler-based method, it exploits the compiler extension to rewrite the source code or binary code statically so that the control transfer targets can be checked before running the execution transfer instructions. Since the compiler-based solution requires accessing the source code or debug information of the programs, it may be limited to protect the commercial programs. Moreover, both of these two methods cannot protect the existing running programs (e.g., massively multiplayer online games) which cannot afford to restart.

To deal with the above problems, in this paper, we present the design and implementation of OnDrop, an on-the-fly ROP protection system based on the OS internal facilities. Compared with the previous solutions, OnDrop offers the protected program an easy deployment, and it can protect the running program dynamically.

The basic idea of our approach is to trap the target program's return operations and then check whether the return targets are valid. To this end, we exploit the static binary analysis to identify the return instructions. Then, we make use of the online patching to replace the return instructions with trap instructions so that the OS kernel can trap the return operations inside the target program. Furthermore, to intercept the return operations in the libraries, we utilize the memory isolation technique to isolate the program code from libraries and then enforce their interactions. We have implemented a prototype of OnDrop based on Linux. Most of our system functionalities are performed at the kernel layer.

In summary, we make the following contributions:

- We propose an on-the-fly ROP detection approach, which can secure the running program with transparency and continuity.
- We leverage the static binary analysis, online patching and memory isolation techniques to achieve the on-the-fly ROP defense.
- We design and implement a prototype of OnDrop based on Linux. The evaluations show that our system can detect ROP attacks effectively.

2   Overview of Our Approach

Different from previous ROP solutions, our approach utilizes the OS internal facilities to defend against ROP exploits. In basic, the key point of our approach is to trap the return operations and then check the return targets in the protected programs. For this purpose, we first utilize static analysis to identify the return instructions inside the target program offline. Then, we leverage the online patching technique to replace the return instruction with trap instructions. Since the target program may invoke library functions to finish its tasks, we need to intercept the return operations inside the libraries. To this end, we exploit the memory management subsystem in the kernel to set different access rights in the page tables for the program code and libraries. By doing so, the execution transfer between the program and libraries could be intercepted by the kernel. Then, we can verify whether the execution transfer target is valid. Moreover, to locate the ROP gadgets located in the libraries, we leverage the hardware debug feature that can record the recent branches. In this way, our system could capture the abnormal execution transfer inside the libraries.

3   System Design

We have developed OnDrop, a prototype based on Linux system to demonstrate our approach. As Fig. 1 shows, there are four components in the architecture, which include Disassembler, Online Patcher, Enforcer, and Memory Protector. The Disassembler, the only user-level component, is responsible for offline identification. The Online Patcher is used to replace the return instructions inside the target program with trap instructions on-the-fly. The role of the Memory Protector is to isolate the program core code from dynamic libraries by utilizing the memory isolation technique. The Enforcer is aimed at enforcing the target program's return operations.

In general, the workflow of OnDrop can be summarized as follows: First, the Disassembler identifies the return instructions offline. Then, the Online Patcher performs dynamic patching by leveraging the offline and online information. After that, the Memory Protector isolates the target program's core code from its dynamic libraries by setting different access permissions on the page tables. In this way, the OS kernel is able to intercept the target process' return operations. Accordingly, the Enforcer can check each return target to ensure it is valid. If not, the Enforcer will terminate the process by sending the SIGKILL signal.

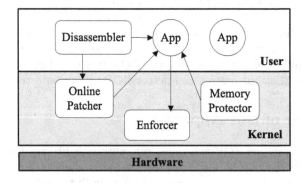

Fig. 1. The OnDrop architecture.

3.1   Offline Analysis

The purpose of offline analysis is to identify the return instructions in the target program. To this end, we make use of the objdump tool to disassemble the binary code and then obtain the offsets of the return instructions within the executable. By adding the offsets and the base address of the program code, we can calculate the specific locations of the return instructions. Please note the base address of the executable cannot be inferred offline if the Address Space Layout Randomization (ASLR) scheme is deployed by the target OS. Instead, we need to make use of the runtime information to get the base address.

3.2   Online Patching

The basic method of online patching is to replace the return instructions with trap instructions in the target program. In the x86 platform, we use the INT 3 instruction as the trap instruction. By doing so, the OS kernel can intercept the target application's execution when the INT 3 instruction gets executed. Since the program code regions are not writable by default, we should change the memory permissions before carrying out online patching. To this end, we need to traverse the page tables to reset the page permissions. To ensure all the return instructions are fully patched by our system, we need to consider one special situation: some return instructions are not yet loaded into physical memory due to on-demand loading scheme employed by modern operating systems. To deal with this case, our system does not replace the return instructions until the corresponding page faults are triggered due to a reference to a page that belongs to the target code address space but is not allocated yet. Moreover, to ensure the patched pages will not be discarded when no free pages are available, we should turn on the Dirty bits in the page table entries.

Although online patching can be applied to most programs, this technique has some side effects for the code modification. As a result, some special programs may stop running when they find their code is modified. To address this problem, we leverage the split TLB architecture to hide our modified code.

In x86 processors, Translation Lookaside Buffer (TLB) is used to speed up memory address translation. For each memory access, TLB is searched first. If the address translation was not found, the associated page tables need to be accessed. There are two different types of TLB for instructions and data, which are called ITLB and DTLB. Specially, ITLB holds virtual address to physical address translations for instructions, while DTLB holds virtual address to physical address translations for data.

In general, the contents in ITLB and DTLB are kept synchronized. However, there is no hardware requirement that the synchronization must be always done. This observation enables us to split code and data view on the same memory page by desynchronizing the ITLB and DTLB. In other words, we can somehow main two different virtual to physical translations in ITLB and DTLB for the code and data view respectively.

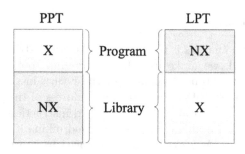

Fig. 2. Memory isolation mechanism.

Figure 2 shows our desynchronization mechanism for ITLB and DTLB. Initially, the page table is set to map the original code with read but non-executable permission. As a result, the original code can be read directly. Nevertheless, code access to the original code region will cause a page fault. Then, in the page fault handler, we should change the memory mapping to the modified code and mark the corresponding page executable. By doing so, the virtual to physical translation and its related permission will be loaded into the ITLB.

To prevent the ITLB entry from being populated to the DTLB, we need to restore the memory mapping to the original code. By setting the TF of the EFLAGS register, the OS kernel can regain the execution control after one instruction in the modified code gets executed. Then, we hook the debug exception handler in the kernel to restore the memory mapping back to the page table entry. As long as the TLB entries are not evicted, more page faults will not be generated for the later code and data access.

3.3   Memory Isolation

In addition to intercepting the return instructions inside the program code section, we also need to trap the return instructions in the libraries. To this end, a straightforward method is also to perform online patching for these libraries. However, doing so may affect the other programs' execution because the dynamic libraries are usually shared with many other processes. Instead, we utilize the memory isolation mechanism to isolate the libraries from the target process' address space.

Specifically, we exploit the memory management subsystem in the OS kernel to maintain two mutually exclusive page tables for the target process and libraries. These two page tables have exactly the same memory mapping but with different access permissions. In this way, the control flow transition between the target process and libraries (e.g., the program invokes a library function) will be intercepted by the OS kernel.

Before setting the memory permissions, we should first locate the specific memory area where the program code and libraries are located. To obtain this information, we need to analyze the corresponding kernel data structures.

In Linux, the OS kernel utilizes the VMA (Virtual Memory Area) structures to maintain the memory mapping information. Specifically, these data structures record the start and end of memory regions as well as the mapped file information (e.g., file name). In addition, all the VMA structures are linked together and the list header is stored in the process descriptor. Therefore, the program code and library memory areas can be extracted by analyzing the process descriptor.

After getting the memory mapping information, we can traverse the page tables to set the page permissions, which is shown in Fig. 3. For the original page table, which we call PPT (Program Page Table), we set the pages containing the program code to executable (X), and pages containing library code to non-executable. For the other page table, which we call LPT (Library Page Table), the pages that contain the program and library code are set to the opposite permissions. By doing so, when the program attempts to make a library call, it will cause a page fault. Then, we hook the page fault handler in the kernel to switch the active page table from PPT to LPT so that the library code can get executed after the execution is transferred to the target process. Later on, when the library finishes its operations and returns to the program caller, a page fault will reoccur. Similarly, the active page table should be switched from LPT to PPT so that the normal execution can be continued.

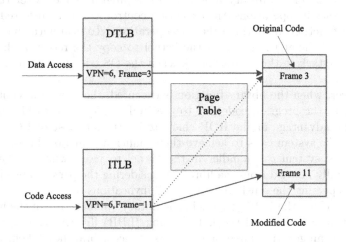

Fig. 3. Desynchronizing ITLB and DTLB.

3.4 Enforcement

The role of the enforcement component is to monitor the target program's return operations and then perform security checks for the return targets. Thanks to our online patching, whenever the target program executes a RET instruction (Actually, the INT 3 instruction gets executed), the execution is trapped into the OS kernel. To ensure the operation is carried out by our protected process, the

Enforcer checks whether the current process id is the same as our protected one. If it is, our enforcement component will verify the return target that is stored on the stack. If the target address is the one next to a call instruction, we will emulate the return operation to let the execution continue. For this purpose, we should first fetch the return address from the stack and put it to the EIP register. Then, we add 4 bytes value to the ESP register. After the execution is returned to the userland, the target program will execute the instruction, whose location is the target address.

On the other hand, when the program tries to invoke a library function, it will trigger a page fault due to our memory isolation. Then, the Enforcer has a chance to store a copy of the pushed return address in a shadow stack for later check. Once the library function finishes its operations and tries to return its execution to the program, the Enforcer will check if the return address on the top of the stack equals to the return address stored on the shadow stack. If not match, it indicates the return address may be corrupted.

Sometimes, we need to handle one special exception due to the OS signal handling mechanism. Specifically, when a signal is received, the OS kernel will help the program to invoke the signal handler located in the user space without using a call instruction. As a result, the execution control may be transferred from the middle of the library function to the program code. After the signal handler finishes its operations, the execution control will be transferred back to the library function to continue the rest operations. To deal with this case, we hook the send_signal() function in the kernel to copy the return address from the program stack to the shadow stack when the OS tries to send a signal to a process.

Moreover, when the library function is executed, the execution control may not return to the program code due to the ROP exploits. To tackle this issue, we take the advantage of the ROP characteristics that most of ROP exploits need to invoke system calls to achieve their malicious functionalities. Thus, we can hook the system call handler in the kernel to judge whether the system call is normally invoked from the library. Considering the performance issue, we focus on inspecting the sensitive system call invocations (e.g., execv(), mmap(), write()). To locate the ROP gadgets in the library, we make use of the hardware debug feature called Last Branch Recording (LBR) [5]. By reading the LBR registers, we can get the sources and targets of recent branches. Then, we check whether the branches contain the ROP gadgets, which can be extracted offline. If one of the recent branches contains the gadget, the target process may be attacked. Accordingly, the process should be re-started or terminated.

4   Evaluation

In this section, we evaluate both the detection effectiveness and the performance of OnDrop. All the experiments are carried out on a Dell PowerEdge T410 workstation with a 2.13G Intel Xeon E5606 CPU and 4 GB memory.

4.1   Effectiveness

We evaluate the effectiveness of OnDrop for ROP detection with two synthetic examples and two real-world examples. In our first test, we develop a vulnerable program to read certain data from a file. The data is stored in the heap memory area whose permissions are set executable. Since the program does not perform boundary check when it stores the data, we can launch a ROP attack by manipulating the file. In the second test, we develop a small program that contains a stack buffer overflow vulnerability. Then, we utilize the ROPEME tool [6] to extract usable ROP gadgets from the program code and libraries. With the gadget information, we craft a ROP exploit to start a shell.

In the third test, we use a realistic vulnerable program: a Linux Hex Editor (htediter). From the exploitDB web site [7], we download the corresponding ROP payload and then utilize it to attack the Editor. In the final test, we use ProFtpd (version 1.3.0) as the attack target. We exploit the stack overflow vulnerability of the program to launch the ROP attack.

With our protection mechanism enabled, OnDrop detects all these ROP attacks successfully by identifying the invalid return operations and abnormal system call invocations.

4.2   Performance Overhead

To evaluate the performance cost of our protection mechanism, we perform a set of benchmarks to compare the performance of a system protected by API-defender with the native system that does not have our protection.

To test the micro-benchmark, we measure the overhead of invoking a library function by a target program. Specifically, we develop a C program that invokes the strcpy function to copy 1000 bytes to a heap buffer. Then, we utilize the rdtsc instruction to measure the whole execution time of this function. In our protection environment, the strcpy function takes about $0.652\,\mu s$ to finish the task, while in the native environment it only needs $0.169\,\mu s$ to complete the operations. The main cause for this overhead is that OnDrop needs to switch the active page tables for the memory isolation.

To test the application-level cost, we apply OnDrop to protect a running Aapche web server. In particular, OnDrop first performs online patching on the code section of this web server. Then, it isolates the related libraries from the code section by setting different memory permissions. After that, we utilize ApacheBench to measure the average response time. In our test, the Apache serves a 112 KB html webpage, and the ApacheBench is configured to set up 6 concurrent clients with each one generating 30 requests. To calculate the average performance overhead, we run this benchmark 10 times. Similarly, we apply OnDrop to protect the other web servers: Lighttpd and Nginx. An ab tool is adopted to measure the request throughput of these servers, both of which are configured to serve a 72 KB php webpage. In addition, our system is applied to protect a running Proftpd ftp server. To measure the performance of the protected Proftpd, we utilize a ftp client to download a 36.7 MB file from the

Table 1. Application-level overhead

Benchmark	Native performance	OnDrop performance	Add-on overhead
Kernel decompression	32785 ms	37172 ms	13.38%
Proftpd transfer rate	3227 Kb/s	2956 Kb/s	9.17%
Apache response time	53.26 ms	58.73 ms	10.27%
Lighttpd request throughput	8735.36 #/s	7826.86 #/s	11.61%
Nginx request throughput	9813.52 #/s	8972.35 #/s	9.38%

ftp server. By recording the start and end time, we can calculate the ftp transfer rate. Finally, we test the tar tool to decompress Linux 2.6.24 kernel gzipped tarball with our protection enabled.

The result of these application level benchmarks is shown in Table 1. We can see that the performance cost introduced by OnDrop is relatively small. Generally, the performance cost relies on the frequency of library calls and our enforcement on the return instructions. If the protected application includes a lot of library invocation and return instructions, the add-on cost introduced by OnDrop will be a little bit higher. In these application benchmarks, the maximum performance overhead added by our protection is the kernel decompression. The major reason is due to the frequent interaction with the libraries.

5   Related Work

5.1   Instrumentation-Based Methods

Basically, these approaches leverage the dynamic binary frameworks [4] to identify ROP attacks. ROPDefender [8] instruments the call and ret instructions to manipulate the shadow stack in the memory so that the stack's first-in-last-out rule can be enforced. DROP [9] exploits the ROP's intrinsic feature that the ret instructions are frequently used in the malicious instruction stream to detect ROP exploits. Similarly, Han [10] proposes an improved method that combines static instrument and dynamic runtime checking for ROP defense. Although these approaches can well defend against ROP attacks, they may introduce significant performance overhead.

5.2   Compiler-Based Methods

In general, these methods depend on the compiler techniques to rewrite the target program for ROP defense. Abadi et al. [11] propose a very famous technique (called CFI) to defeat the code reuse attack. This technique enforces the control flow integrity for the target program by using software rewriting. However, this technique can only work in the function level. To address this problem, Control Flow Locking (CFL) [12] is introduced to lock the abnormal control flow transfer by recompiling the source code. G-Free [13] applies the compiler techniques to eliminate the available ROP gadgets inside a binary code. Recently, some binary rewriting techniques [14,15] are applied to achieve the CFI protections. The major limitation of these approaches is the compatibility issue such that some other security mechanisms (e.g., Integrity Measurement Architecture) could not be applied.

5.3 ASLR-Based Methods

Address Space Layout Randomization (ASLR) is an effective technique to defend against ROP attacks. There are two different methods to achieve ASLR: address-space randomization [16,17] and instruction set randomization [18,19]. The first one either randomizes the base addresses of code segments or reorders the basic blocks in each binary code section. The second one uses a private (or secret) machine instruction set for executing the target program so that it is very difficult for attackers to craft ROP exploits. Since applying ASLR requires to be supported by the executable and shared libraries, it may not be deployed in the legacy systems. Recently, some function-level randomization and control-block randomization techniques [17,20] are proposed. Unfortunately, all these methods could be bypassed if the code information is leaked [21].

5.4 Hardware-Based Solutions

In basic, these methods rely on special hardware features. CFIMon [22] leverages the Performance Monitoring Units (PMU) to collect and analyze runtime traces to detect the invalid control flow transfer in the target program. KBouncer [23] and ROPecker [24] utilize the Last Branch Recording (LBR) to check the presence of a sufficiently long chain of gadgets for ROP detection. HyperCropII [25] makes use of the hardware assisted virtualization technology to defeat ROP attacks. Recently, FlowGuard [26] leverages a new hardware feature (i.e., Intel Processor Trace) for CFI enforcement. All these approaches are limited to protect the existing running programs on-the-fly.

6 Conclusion

In this paper, we present OnDrop, an online return-oriented-programming attack detection system. We exploit the binary analysis, memory isolation and online patching techniques, which allows us to protect the running program on-the-fly. Moreover, our system does not require any modifications to the target programs, and the ROP protection mechanism can be loaded on demand. Our evaluations show that OnDrop can defend against ROP attacks effectively with a little performance cost.

Acknowledgments. This work was supported in part by National Natural Science Foundation of China (NSFC) under Grant No. 61602035, the National Key Research and Development Program of China under Grant No. 2016YFB0800700, the Open Found of Key Laboratory of Network Assessment Technology, Institute of Information Engineering, Chinese Academy of Sciences.

References

1. Yao, X., Han, X., Du, X., Zhou, X.: A lightweight multicast authentication mechanism for small scale IoT applications. IEEE Sens. J. **13**, 3693–3701 (2013)
2. Metasploit (2014). http://www.metasploit.com/
3. Shacham, H.: The geometry of innocent flesh on the bone. In: ACM Conference on Computer and Communications Security, CCS 2007, Alexandria, Virginia, USA, pp. 552–561, October 2007
4. Luk, C.K., Cohn, R., Muth, R., Patil, H., Klauser, A., Lowney, G., Wallace, S., Reddi, V.J., Hazelwood, K.: Pin: building customized program analysis tools with dynamic instrumentation. In: Proceedings of the ACM SIGPLAN Conference on Programming Language Design and Implementation (PLDI), vol. 40(6), pp. 190–200 (2005)
5. Intel corp. intel 64 and ia-32 architectures software developer's manuals (2014). http://www.intel.com/Assets/PDF/manual/253669.pdf
6. Longld. payload already inside: Data resue for ROP exploits (2010). https://media.blackhat.com/bh-us-10/whitepapers/Le/BlackHat-USA-2010-Le-Paper-Payload-already-inside-data-reuse-for-ROP-exploits-wp.pdf
7. The exploit database (2014). http://www.exploit-db.com/
8. Davi, L., Sadeghi, A.R., Winandy, M.: Ropdefender: a detection tool to defend against return-oriented programming attacks. In: ACM Symposium on Information, Computer and Communications Security, ASIACCS 2011, Hong Kong, China, pp. 40–51, March 2011. doi:10.1145/1966913.1966920
9. Chen, P., Xiao, H., Shen, X., Yin, X., Mao, B., Xie, L.: DROP: detecting return-oriented programming malicious code. In: Prakash, A., Sen Gupta, I. (eds.) ICISS 2009. LNCS, vol. 5905, pp. 163–177. Springer, Heidelberg (2009). doi:10.1007/978-3-642-10772-6_13
10. Han, H., Mao, B., Xie, L.: Dynamic runtime detection system for return-oriented programming attack. Comput. Eng. **38**(4), 122–125 (2012)
11. Abadi, M., Budiu, M., Erlingsson, I., Ligatti, J.: Control-flow integrity. In: ACM Conference on Computer and Communications Security, CCS 2005, Alexandria, VA, USA, pp. 340–353, November 2005. doi:10.1145/1102120.1102165
12. Bletsch, T., Jiang, X., Freeh, V.: Mitigating code-reuse attacks with control-flow locking. In: Twenty-Seventh Computer Security Applications Conference, ACSAC 2011, Orlando, FL, USA, pp. 353–362, 5–9 December 2011. doi:10.1145/2076732.2076783
13. Onarlioglu, K., Bilge, L., Lanzi, A., Balzarotti, D., Kirda, E.: G-free: defeating return-oriented programming through gadget-less binaries. In: Proceedings of the 26th Annual Computer Security Applications Conference (ACSAC), pp. 49–58 (2010)
14. Zhang, C., Wei, T., Chen, Z., Duan, L., Szekeres, L., Mccamant, S., Song, D., Zou, W.: Practical control flow integrity and randomization for binary executables. In: 34th IEEE Symposium on Security & Privacy, Oakland, pp. 559–573 (2013). doi:10.1109/sp.2013.44
15. Zhang, M., Sekar, R.: Control flow integrity for cots binaries. In: USENIX Conference on Security, pp. 337–352 (2013). doi:10.1145/2818000.2818016
16. Bhatkar, S., Sekar, R., Duvarney, D.C.: Efficient techniques for comprehensive protection from memory error exploits. In: Proceedings of the 14th USENIX Security Symposium, p. 17 (2005)

17. Wartell, R., Mohan, V., Hamlen, K.W., Lin, Z.: Binary stirring: self-randomizing instruction addresses of legacy x86 binary code. In: Proceedings of the 19th ACM Conference on Computer and Communications Security (CCS), pp. 157–168 (2012). doi:10.1145/2382196.2382216
18. Barrantes, E.G., Ackley, D.H., Palmer, T.S., Stefanovic, D., Zovi, D.D.: Randomized instruction set emulation to disrupt binary code injection attacks. In: ACM Conference on Computer and Communications Security, CCS 2003, Washington, DC, USA, pp. 281–289, October 2003
19. Kc, G.S., Keromytis, A.D., Prevelakis, V.: Countering code-injection attacks with instruction-set randomization. In: ACM Conference on Computer and Communications Security, pp. 272–280 (2003)
20. Backes, M., Rnberger, S.: Oxymoron: making fine-grained memory randomization practical by allowing code sharing. In: Proceedings of the 23rd USENIX Security Symposium, pp. 433–447 (2014)
21. Oikonomopoulos, A., Athanasopoulos, E., Bos, H., Giuffrida, C.: Poking holes in information hiding. In: Proceedings of the 25th USENIX Security Symposium (2016)
22. Xia, Y., Liu, Y., Chen, H., Zang, B.: Cfimon: detecting violation of control flow integrity using performance counters. In: Proceedings of the 42nd Annual IEEE/IFIP International Conference on Dependable Systems and Networks (DSN), pp. 1–12 (2012). doi:10.1109/dsn.2012.6263958
23. Pappas, V., Polychronakis, M., Keromytis, A.D.: Transparent ROP exploit mitigation using indirect branch tracing. In: Proceedings of the 22nd USENIX Security Symposium, pp. 447–462 (2013)
24. Cheng, Y., Zhou, Z., Yu, M., Ding, X., Deng, R.H.: Ropecker: a generic and practical approach for defending against rop attacks. In: Proceedings of the 21st Annual Network and Distributed System Security Symposium (NDSS) (2014). doi:10.14722/ndss.2014.23156
25. Jia, X., Wang, R., Jiang, J., Zhang, S., Liu, P.: Defending return-oriented programming based on virtualization techniques. Secur. Commun. Netw. (SCN) 6(10), 1236–1249 (2013)
26. Yutao, L., Peitao, S., Xinran, W., Haibo, C., Binyu, Z., Haibing, G.: Transparent and efficient CFI enforcement with intel processor trace. In: IEEE Symposium on High Performance Computer Architecture (2017). doi:10.1109/hpca.2017.18

An Efficient and Provably Secure Pairing-Free Certificateless Signature Scheme Based on Variant of RSA

Liangliang Wang[1,2], Mi Wen[1(✉)], Kefei Chen[3,4], Zhongqin Bi[1], and Yu Long[5]

[1] Shanghai University of Electric Power, Shanghai 200090, China
miwen@shiep.edu.cn
[2] Xihua University, Chengdu 610039, China
[3] Hangzhou Normal University, Hangzhou 310036, China
[4] Westone Cryptologic Research Center, Beijing 100070, China
[5] Shanghai Jiao Tong University, Shanghai 200240, China

Abstract. Through the application of certificateless signature, certificate management in traditional signatures can be simplified. Furthermore, the key escrow problem in identity-based signatures can be solved as well. As history has shown, there has not been a general pairing-free certificateless signature scheme which is mainly designed with modular exponentiation and modular multiplication that can possess resistance to Type I and Type II adversaries so far. Therefore, a new hard mathematic problem is firstly defined in this paper, which is called variant of RSA problem. In the next step, a new general pairing-free certificateless signature scheme is proposed based on the newly defined variant of RSA problem and the well known discrete logarithm problem. Fortunately, the proposed scheme is also the first RSA-based certificateless signature scheme that can possess resistance to Type I and Type II adversaries. In addition, a formal security proof is provided to demonstrate that, under adaptively chosen message attacks, the proposed scheme is provably secure against Type I and Type II adversaries in the random oracle model. When compared with other known pairing-free certificateless signature schemes of the same type, the computation cost of our scheme is slightly higher, however, a higher security level can be achieved.

Keywords: Certificateless public key signature · RSA · Discrete logarithm · Random oracle model

This work was partially supported by the National Natural Science Foundation of China (No. 61572311, No. 61472114 and No. 61572318), the Fund of Lab of Security Insurance of Cyberspace, Sichuan Province, the DawnProgram of Shanghai Education Commission (No. 16SG47), the Project of Shanghai Science and Technology Committee (No. 15110500700), the Open Project of Key Laboratory of Cryptologic Technology and Information Security, Ministry of Education, Shandong University.

© Springer International Publishing AG 2017
S. Wen et al. (Eds.): CSS 2017, LNCS 10581, pp. 248–266, 2017.
https://doi.org/10.1007/978-3-319-69471-9_19

1 Introduction

The concept of asymmetric cryptography which is also named public key cryptography (PKC) was introduced by Diffie and Hellman [1], which opens up a new era for cryptography that it solves the key distribution problem in symmetric cryptography. In original PKC, a legitimate user's public key is randomly generated, which is linked to the user by means of a digital certificate. The digital certificate refers to a digital signature on the public key and its generation is completed by certificate authority (CA) which is considered to be full trusted. Anyone who wants to employ the public key to encrypt messages or verify signatures must obtain corresponding authorized digital certificate and provide valid public key authentication, so as to manifest that the public key can be trusted. Moreover, a significant mechanism named public key infrastructure (PKI) is adopted to manage users' digital certificates. But in practice, the requirement of digital certificates brings various certificate management problems and the public key authentication needs to consume a tremendous amount of storage, computing and communication resource.

The concept of identity-based public key cryptography (ID-PKC) was introduced by Shamir [2], so as to facilitate the management procedure of digital certificates. In this new cryptography, a user's publicly known unique identity mark serves as the user's public key and there is not need to provide the corresponding public key certificate to authenticate the user's public key. However, a new problem occurs in ID-PKC, namely, a key generation center (KGC) which is considered to be full trusted can forge signatures and decrypt ciphertexts for any user through the use of a master secret key, by which each user's private key is able to be produced. This troubling problem is the alleged key escrow problem. Therefore, the KGC is not allowed to be a malicious one, which should be completely trusted in ID-PKC.

For the purpose of avoiding the shortcoming brought by the fully trusted KGC, the concept of certificateless public key cryptography (CL-PKC) was introduced by Al-Riyami and Paterson [3], which eliminates the application of certificates in original PKC and provides a good solution for the key escrow problem in ID-PKC. In the newly proposed CL-PKC, the generation of a user's private key is no longer completed by the KGC solely, it is based on a so-called partial private key generated by the KGC and a secret value selected privately by the user himself/herself. In this case, the key escrow event does not happen in CL-PKC. The reason is that the KGC is considered to be semi-trusted that it cannot obtain the user's full private key by itself. It is necessary to note that this system is not purely ID-based, because the public key in this system is no longer just the user's identity mark and there should be accessional public keys for the user, and public keys in this system are not required to be explicitly certified. Moreover, two kinds of attackers for this system were also defined by Al-Riyami and Paterson, they are Type I and Type II adversaries. The former stands for a malicious third party who is not permitted to control the master secret key but is able to perform public keys replacement and the latter stands for a malicious KGC who is not permitted to replace public key but is able to possess the master secret key.

1.1 Motivations

After a detailed certificateless public key signature (CL-PKS) scheme [3] was first presented, a lot of other work [4–24] concerning CL-PKS was proposed subsequently. These CL-PKS schemes can be mainly divided into three types, including pairing-based CL-PKS schemes (mainly designed with bilinear pairings), elliptic curve cryptography (ECC)-based pairing-free CL-PKS schemes (mainly designed with point scalar multiplication) and general pairing-free CL-PKS schemes (mainly designed with modular exponentiation and modular multiplication). And then, our motivations are shown from the following three perspectives.

- **Security.** For all CL-PKS schemes, a great deal of work regarding cryptanalysis of CL-PKS schemes has demonstrated that the majority of schemes cannot achieve claimed and expected security levels. Therefore, it is quite necessary to continue to construct provably secure CL-PKS schemes under formal security models.
- **Practicability.** History has shown that bilinear pairings operations are very expensive. Therefore, in some resource-limited equipments, pairing-based CL-PKS schemes cannot be practicably implemented, such as smart cards, mobile phones and PDAs. Hence, it is also quite imperative to construct efficient CL-PKS schemes without bilinear pairings.
- **Filling in gaps.** According to our survey on the three types of CL-PKS schemes, work concerning general pairing-free CL-PKS schemes is found to be the least. As far as we know, there has not been a general pairing-free CL-PKS scheme which is secure against both Type I and Type II adversaries up to now. Therefore, it is extremely urgent to construct a provably secure general pairing-free CL-PKS scheme that can possess resistance to the two adversaries. In addition, the first RSA-based CL-PKS scheme [23] has been broken by He et al. [24]. Therefore, constructing the first provably secure RSA-based CL-PKS scheme also always attracts us.

According to the considerations above all, constructing a provably secure general pairing-free CL-PKS schemes that can possess resistance to Type I and Type II adversaries and a RSA-based CL-PKS scheme with provable security that is secure against both Type I and Type II adversaries remains to be open problems.

1.2 Our Contributions

In this paper, existing main three types of CL-PKS schemes are investigated and general pairing-free CL-PKS schemes are mainly studied. Our contributions to this paper are detailed as follows.

- Based on RSA, a new hard mathematic problem called variant of RSA (VRSA) problem is defined. Briefly, the VRSA problem can be described as: giving two parameters of RSA problem e and n and two integers a and z, try to find a pair of integers (d, u) such that $u^e = ad^z \bmod n$.
- A detailed proof is provided to indicate that the hardness of breaking VRSA problem is equivalent to that of breaking RSA problem.
- Based on the newly defined VRSA problem and the well known discrete logarithm problem (DLP), a new pairing-free CL-PKS scheme is proposed. Besides, a detailed and strict formal security proof is provided to demonstrate that the newly proposed CL-PKS scheme is provably secure against both Type I and Type II adversaries in the random oracle model (ROM).
- As far as we know, the newly proposed scheme is the first general pairing-free CL-PKS scheme with provable security that achieves both Type I and Type II adversaries resistance and it is also the first RSA-based CL-PKS scheme that can possess resistance to Type I and Type II adversaries, fortunately.
- Tables 1 and 2 show the comparisons of several general pairing-free CL-PKS schemes. When compared with other existing pairing-free CL-PKS schemes [22,23] of the same type, namely, general pairing-free CL-PKS schemes, the computation cost of our scheme is slightly higher, but the scheme can achieve a higher security level.

1.3 Related Work

For pairing-based CL-PKS schemes, the first CL-PKS scheme was proposed by Al-Riyami and Paterson [3]. Soon after, an attack was proposed by Huang et al. [4] to indicate that Al-Riyami and Paterson's scheme is insecure against Type I adversary. In the forthcoming pairing-based CL-PKS schemes [5–8,13,14], most of them were found to be insecure against Type I adversary, where a security proof was not provided by Li et al. [5] for their scheme; Gorantla and Saxena's scheme [6], Yap et al.'s scheme [7] and Yum and Lee's scheme [8] were indicated to be insecure against Type I adversary, sequentially by work [9–12] of cryptanalysis. In 2006, a formal security model was first definited by Zhang et al. [13] for CL-PKS schemes, in which, Type I and Type II adversaries were defined. In 2007, Huang et al. [14] visited CL-PKS again with potential adversaries being divided into three kinds, such as Normal, Strong and Super adversaries. In this paper, Zhang et al.'s adversary model is followed to construct our scheme and it is slightly weakened by us. The difference will be detailed in the following part of security model.

For ECC-based pairing-free CL-PKS schemes, several schemes have weaknesses in security. He et al.'s scheme [15] was respectively demonstrated to be insecure against Type II adversary by Tian and huang [16] and Tsai et al. [17]. It was shown by Yeh et al. [19] that Gong and Li's scheme [18] could not satisfy the security requirements that Gong and Li claimed. In addition, some other ECC-based pairing-free CL-PKS schemes [20,21] were proposed to focus on the practicability and efficiency.

For general pairing-free CL-PKS schemes, they seem to be rare throughout history. In 2009, a DLP-based scheme was proposed by Harn et al. [22]. However, their security model was found to be informally defined and their security proof was performed informally as well. In 2012, a RSA-based scheme was proposed by Zhang and Mao [23], which was then pointed out to be insecure against Type I adversary by He et al. [24].

1.4 Roadmap

The remaining part of this paper is organized as follows. Some preliminaries regarding complexity assumptions and CL-PKS are introduced and a new hard mathematic problem called variant of RSA problem is defined in Sect. 2. In Sect. 3, a new pairing-free CL-PKS scheme based on the newly defined variant of RSA problem and the well known DLP is presented. A formal security proof for this scheme and a performance comparison are presented in Sect. 4. Finally, this paper is concluded in Sect. 5.

2 Preliminaries

We first review some fundamental complexity assumptions about discrete logarithm and RSA in this section, then we define a new hard mathematic problem based on RSA and we call it variant of RSA (VRSA) problem. After giving the hardness proof of the VRSA problem, we continue to introduce some definitions about CL-PKS related to our proposal, such as syntax and security model.

2.1 Complexity Assumptions

Definition 1 (DLP). *A polynomial-time adversary $\mathcal{A}$ tries to find an integer α such that $g^\alpha = \beta \bmod p$ for given (p, g, β), where p is a prime, g is a generator of Z_p^* and $\beta \in Z_p^*$.*

Definition 2 (DL Assumption). *A polynomial-time adversary $\mathcal{A}$' success probability of obtaining the solution to DLP is defined as*

$$Succ_{\mathcal{A}}^{DLP} = Pr[\mathcal{A}(p, g, \beta) \to \alpha],$$

We claim that the DL assumption holds if $Succ_{\mathcal{A}}^{DLP}$ is negligible.

Definition 3 (RSA Problem). *A polynomial-time adversary $\mathcal{A}$ tries to find an integer u such that $u^e = c \bmod n$ for given (n, e, c), where n is a positive integer and it is the product of two distinct odd primes p and q, e is a positive integer such that $gcd(e, (p-1)(q-1)) = 1$ and c is an integer.*

Definition 4 (RSA Assumption). *A polynomial-time adversary $\mathcal{A}$' success probability of obtaining the solution to RSA problem is defined as*

$$Succ_{\mathcal{A}}^{RSA} = Pr[\mathcal{A}(n, e, c) \to u],$$

We claim that the RSA assumption holds if $Succ_{\mathcal{A}}^{RSA}$ is negligible.

Definition 5 (VRSA Problem). *A polynomial-time adversary $\mathcal{A}$ tries to find a pair of integers (d, u) such that $u^e = ad^z \bmod n$ for given (n, e, a, z), where n is a positive integer and it is the product of two distinct odd primes p and q, e is a positive integer such that $gcd\,(e, (p - 1)(q - 1)) = 1$ and a and z are two integers.*

Definition 6 (VRSA Assumption). *A polynomial-time adversary $\mathcal{A}$' success probability of obtaining the solution to VRSA problem is defined as*

$$Succ_{\mathcal{A}}^{VRSA} = Pr[\mathcal{A}(n, e, a, z) \to (d, u)],$$

We claim that the VRSA assumption holds if $Succ_{\mathcal{A}}^{VRSA}$ is negligible.

Theorem 1. *A polynomial-time adversary $\mathcal{B}$ can solve the VRSA problem with a non-negligible probability if and only if there is a polynomial-time adversary $\mathcal{A}$ that can solve the RSA problem with a non-negligible probability.*

Proof (Theorem 1). The *Theorem 1* can be obtained if the following two lemmas can be obtained.

Lemma 1. *A polynomial-time adversary $\mathcal{B}$ can solve the VRSA problem with a non-negligible probability if there is a polynomial-time adversary $\mathcal{A}$ that can solve the RSA problem with a non-negligible probability.*

Proof (Lemma 1). We suppose a polynomial-time adversary $\mathcal{A}$ is able to solve the RSA problem with a non-negligible probability ϵ, then our goal is to show there is a polynomial-time algorithm $\mathcal{B}$ that is able to solve the VRSA problem with a non-negligible probability by using the capabilities of $\mathcal{A}$. In the following, $\mathcal{B}$ simulates a real environment of RSA and provide the service of breaking RSA problem for $\mathcal{A}$.

Firstly, $\mathcal{B}$ is given a random VRSA instance (n, e, a, z), then it chooses an integer d and aims to output u such that $u^e = ad^z \bmod n$. When $\mathcal{A}$ requires a service of breaking RSA problem on $(n' = n, e' = e, c' = ad^z)$, $\mathcal{B}$ returns an integer u such that $u^{e'} = c' \bmod n$, that is, $u^e = ad^z \bmod n$. Therefore, $\mathcal{B}$ can output (d, u) as the solution of the given VRSA instance with a non-negligible probability ϵ. $\square$

Lemma 2. *A polynomial-time adversary $\mathcal{B}$ can solve the RSA problem with a non-negligible probability if there exists a polynomial-time adversary $\mathcal{A}$ that can solve the VRSA problem with a non-negligible probability.*

Proof (Lemma 2). We suppose a polynomial-time adversary $\mathcal{A}$ is able to solve the VRSA problem with a non-negligible probability ϵ, then our goal is to show there is a polynomial-time algorithm $\mathcal{B}$ that is able to solve the RSA problem with a non-negligible probability by using the capabilities of $\mathcal{A}$. In the following, $\mathcal{B}$ simulates a real environment of VRSA and provide the service of breaking VRSA problem for $\mathcal{A}$.

Firstly, $\mathcal{B}$ is given a random RSA instance (n, e, c), and it aims to output u such that $u^e = c \bmod n$. When $\mathcal{A}$ requires a service of breaking VRSA problem on $(n' = n, e' = e, a' = c, z' = -e)$, $\mathcal{B}$ returns an integer (d, u) such that $u^{e'} = a'd^{z'} \bmod n$, that is, $u^e = cd^{-e} \bmod n$. Therefore, $\mathcal{B}$ can output du as the solution of the given RSA instance with a non-negligible probability ϵ.   □

From the above two lemmas, we can conclude the *Theorem* 1 which we aims to obtain. We can also specify another meaning of this theorem that the hardness of breaking VRSA problem is equivalent to the hardness of breaking RSA problem.   □

2.2   Syntax of CL-PKS

Definition 7 (CL-PKS). *A CL-PKS scheme consists of the following seven probabilistic polynomial-time algorithms:*

- Setup: This probabilistic algorithm accepts a security parameter λ, produces a master secret key *masterkey* and system parameters *params*.
- PartialPrivateKeyExtract: This deterministic algorithm accepts a user's identity ID, the master secret key *masterkey* and system parameters *params*, produces the user ID's partial private key PS_{ID}.
- SetSecretValue: This probabilistic algorithm accepts a user's identity ID and the system parameters *params*, produces the user ID's secret value s_{ID}.
- SetPrivateKey: This probabilistic algorithm accepts the system parameters *params*, a user ID's partial private key PS_{ID} and secret value s_{ID}, produces the user ID's full private key SK_{ID}.
- SetPublicKey: This deterministic algorithm accepts the system parameters *params* and a user ID's secret value s_{ID}, produces the user ID's public key PK_{ID}.
- Sign: This probabilistic algorithm accepts a user's identity ID, the system parameters *params*, a message m and the user ID's full private key SK_{ID}, produces a certificateless signature σ associated with the identity ID and the message m.
- Verify: This deterministic algorithm accepts a user's identity ID, the system parameters *params*, a message-and-signature pair (m, σ), and the user ID's public key PK_{ID}, produces a bit 1 or 0. The signature σ is consider to be valid if and only if this algorithm produces 1, 0 implies the signature σ cannot be accepted.

2.3   Security Model of CL-PKS

Two kinds of adversaries about CL-PKS are introduced in [13], we consider the similar attack model in this paper. But the security model considered here has a little difference with the original model, it is that we slightly weaken Type I adversary's capabilities, namely, the Type I adversary in our model is not permitted to submit a query of the form (*identity, message*) to signing orale, where *identity* is a target identity for which the Type I adversary aims to forge a signature and *message* may be any message. We will specify the difference again in the following description of Type I adversary's capabilities. The reason why we make this change is that we should make a cryptography scheme pass a formal security proof feasibly under a formal security model to provide reliable security for the scheme. We denote Type I and Type II adversaries by $\mathcal{A}_I$ and $\mathcal{A}_{II}$. And the following two interaction games between the adversaries and a challenger $\mathcal{B}$ are defined, so as to represent adversaries' capabilities.

$\mathcal{A}_I$: This kind of adversary is consider to be a malicious third party who is not permitted to control the master secret key but is able to perform public keys replacement for all users.

$\mathcal{A}_{II}$: This kind of adversary is consider to be a malicious untrusted KGC who is not permitted to replace any user's public key but is able to possess the master secret key of system.

Game I. This game is played by both $\mathcal{A}_I$ and $\mathcal{B}$.

- **Setup:** On receiving a security parameter λ, the challenger $\mathcal{B}$ runs the predefined Setup to generate a master secret key *masterkey* and system parameters *params*, then $\mathcal{B}$ returns *params* to $\mathcal{A}_I$ and keeps *masterkey* in secret.
- **Partial private key queries:** On receiving a user's identity ID, $\mathcal{B}$ runs the predefined PartialPrivateKeyExtract to generate a partial private key PS_{ID} for the user ID and returns PS_{ID} to $\mathcal{A}_I$.
- **Private key queries:** On receiving a user's identity ID, $\mathcal{B}$ first runs the PartialPrivateKeyExtract and SetSecretValue algorithms to generate a partial private key PS_{ID} and a secret value s_{ID}, then $\mathcal{B}$ continues to run the predefined SetPrivateKey to generate the user ID's full private key SK_{ID} and returns SK_{ID} to $\mathcal{A}_I$.
- **Public key queries:** On receiving a user's identity ID, $\mathcal{B}$ first runs the predefined SetSecretValue to generate a secret value s_{ID}, then $\mathcal{B}$ continues to run the SetPublicKey algorithm to generate the user ID's public key PK_{ID} and returns PK_{ID} to $\mathcal{A}_I$.
- **Public key replacement:** For any user ID, $\mathcal{A}_I$ can generate a new public key $\widetilde{PK_{ID}}$ by choosing a new secret value $\widetilde{s_{ID}}$. Then the public key replacement can be performed as $PK_{ID} = \widetilde{PK_{ID}}$, where PK_{ID} is the user ID's original public key.
- **Signing queries:** On receiving a user's identity ID and a message m, $\mathcal{B}$ runs the predefined Sign to generate a certificateless signature σ and returns σ to $\mathcal{A}_I$. Note that if the original PK_{ID} has been replaced with the new $\widetilde{PK_{ID}}$, then $\mathcal{B}$ cannot obtain the correct $\widetilde{SK_{ID}}$ and this can make some errors of the **Signing queries** oracle's responds. Therefore, we assume that $\mathcal{A}_I$ submits the newly chosen $\widetilde{s_{ID}}$ to the **Signing queries** oracle to correct the **Signing queries** oracle's responds when the public key replacement event happens.
- **Output:** After all the queries, $\mathcal{A}_I$ outputs a message-and-signature pair $(\widehat{m}, \widehat{\sigma})$ associated with $PK_{\widehat{ID}}$ for a target identity $\widehat{ID}$.

(1) $\mathcal{A}_I$ has never make queries to the **Private key queries** oracle on $\widehat{ID}$.
(2) $\mathcal{A}_I$ has never make queries to both the **Partial private key queries** and **Public key replacement** oracles on $\widehat{ID}$.
(3) $\mathcal{A}_I$ has never make queries to the **Signing queries** oracle on $\widehat{ID}$. Here it is necessary to emphasize that we slightly weaken Type I adversary's capabilities when compared with the original security model [13]. That is, the Type I adversary in our model is not permitted to issue a query on $(\widehat{ID}, m)$ to the **Signing queries** oracle, while in the security model defined in [13] only $(\widehat{ID}, \widehat{m})$ cannot be submitted to the **Signing queries** oracle and any $(\widehat{ID}, m)$ where $m \neq \widehat{m}$ is allowed to be submitted to the **Signing queries** oracle.
(4) $\mathsf{Verify}(params, PK_{\widehat{ID}}, \widehat{m}, \widehat{ID}, \widehat{\sigma}) = 1$. Note that the public key $PK_{\widehat{ID}}$ here may have been replaced, it means the signature can pass the verification even the public keys replacement event happens.

Definition 8. *A CL-PKS scheme is existentially unforgeable under Type I adaptively chosen message attacks (EUF-CMA), if $Succ_{\mathcal{A}_I}^{EUF\text{-}CMA}$ is negligible, where $Succ_{\mathcal{A}_I}^{EUF\text{-}CMA}$ denotes $\mathcal{A}_I$'s success probability to win* **Game I**.

Game II. This game is played by both $\mathcal{A}_{II}$ and $\mathcal{B}$.

- **Setup:** On receiving a security parameter λ, the challenger $\mathcal{B}$ runs the predefined Setup to generate a master secret key *masterkey* and system parameters *params*, then $\mathcal{B}$ returns *masterkey* and *params* to $\mathcal{A}_{II}$.
- **Private key queries:** On receiving a user's identity ID, $\mathcal{B}$ first runs the PartialPrivateKeyExtract and SetSecretValue algorithms to generate a partial private key PS_{ID} and a secret value s_{ID}, then $\mathcal{B}$ continues to run the predefined SetPrivateKey to generate the user ID's full private key SK_{ID} and returns SK_{ID} to $\mathcal{A}_{II}$.
- **Public key queries:** On receiving a user's identity ID, $\mathcal{B}$ first runs the predefined SetSecretValue to generate a secret value s_{ID}, then $\mathcal{B}$ continues to run the SetPublicKey algorithm to generate the user ID's public key PK_{ID} and returns PK_{ID} to $\mathcal{A}_{II}$.
- **Signing queries:** On receiving a user's identity ID and a message m, $\mathcal{B}$ runs the Sign algorithm to generate a signature σ and returns σ to $\mathcal{A}_{II}$.
- **Output:** After all the queries, $\mathcal{A}_{II}$ outputs a message-and-signature pair $(\widehat{m}, \widehat{\sigma})$ associated with $PK_{\widehat{ID}}$ for a target identity $\widehat{ID}$. The identity $\widehat{ID}$ must satisfy the following requirements:
  (1) $\mathcal{A}_{II}$ has never make queries to the **Private key queries** oracle on $\widehat{ID}$.
  (2) $\mathcal{A}_{II}$ has never make queries to the **Signing queries** oracle on $(\widehat{ID}, \widehat{m})$. Note that here we following the original model without making any change. Queries of the form $(\widehat{ID}, m)$ for all $m \neq \widehat{m}$ are allowed to be submitted to the **Signing queries** oracle.
  (3) $\mathsf{Verify}(params, PK_{\widehat{ID}}, \widehat{m}, \widehat{ID}, \widehat{\sigma}) = 1$.

Definition 9. *A CL-PKS scheme is existentially unforgeable under Type II adaptively chosen message attacks (EUF-CMA), if $Succ_{\mathcal{A}_{II}}^{EUF\text{-}CMA}$ is negligible, where $Succ_{\mathcal{A}_{II}}^{EUF\text{-}CMA}$ denotes $\mathcal{A}_{II}$'s success probability to win **Game II**.*

3   Proposed CL-PKS Scheme

In this section, following the definitions of CL-PKS, we propose a detailed pairing-free CL-PKS scheme based on the newly defined VRSA problem and DLP. Seven polynomial-time algorithms are included in the proposed scheme and they are constructed as below.

- Setup: Given a security parameter λ,
  (1) Pick two random large primes p and q, assign $\varphi(n) = (p-1)(q-1)$ and $n = pq$ and keep p, q and $\varphi(n)$ in secret.
  (2) Pick two random large primes p' and q' such that $p' \neq p$, $q' \neq q$, $q'|p'-1$ and $g^{q'} = 1 \bmod p'$, where $g \in Z_{p'}^*$ and $g \neq 1$.
  (3) Pick a random integer e such that $1 < e < \varphi(n)$ and $gcd(e, \varphi(n)) = 1$. Obtain the master secret key $masterkey = s$ from the equation $es = 1 \bmod \varphi(n)$ and keep s in secret.
  (4) Define three cryptographic hash functions as $H_1 : \{0,1\}^* \rightarrow Z_n^*$, $H_2 : \{0,1\}^* \rightarrow \{0,1\}^{\frac{|n|}{4}}$ and $H_3 : \{0,1\}^* \times \{0,1\}^* \times Z_{p'}^* \rightarrow Z_{q'}^*$, define the system parameters as $params = (p', q', n, e, g, H_1, H_2, H_3)$ and publish them.
- PartialPrivateKeyExtract: Given a user's identity ID and the master secret key s,
  (1) Calculate $PS_{ID} = H_1(ID)^s \bmod n$ by using the master secret key s and hash function H_1
  (2) Return PS_{ID} as the user ID's partial private key. The user ID can obtain PS_{ID} through a secure channel.
- SetSecretValue: Given a user's identity ID, randomly select $x \in Z_{q'}^*$ as the user ID's secret value and assign $s_{ID} = x$.
- SetPrivateKey: Given a user ID's partial private key PS_{ID} and secret value s_{ID}, use PS_{ID} and s_{ID} to comprise a full private key $SK_{ID} = (PS_{ID}, s_{ID})$ for the user ID.
- SetPublicKey: Given a user ID's secret value s_{ID}, use s_{ID} to compute $PK_{ID} = g^x \bmod p'$ and return PK_{ID} as the use ID's public key.
- Sign: Given a user's identity ID, a message m and the full private key SK_{ID} associated with the user ID,
  (1) Randomly select $l \in Z_n^*$ and compute $d = l^e \bmod n$. Use the hash function H_2 and PS_{ID} to compute $u = PS_{ID}l^{H_2(m)} \bmod n$.
  (2) Pick random $k \in Z_{q'}^*$ and calculate $r = g^k \bmod p'$. Continue to calculate $h = H_3(m, ID, r)$ by using the hash function H_3 and assign $v = k - xh \bmod q'$ by using the master secret key x.
  (3) Return (d, u, r, h, v) as the certificateless signature σ associated with the message m.

– Verify : Given a user's identity ID, a message-and-signature pair (m, σ) and the user ID's public key PK_{ID},

(1) First check whether the equation $u^e = H_1(ID)d^{H_2(m)} \mod n$ holds or not, if yes, continue to perform the next checking.

(2) And then compute $r' = g^v PK_{ID}{}^h \mod p'$ and $h' = H_3(m, ID, r')$, continue to check whether $h = h'$ holds or not, if yes, return 1 to mean the signature σ is consider to be accepted.

4   Analysis of Our CL-PKS Scheme

4.1   Correctness Analysis

The following calculations are used to shown the correctness of the proposed CL-PKS scheme.

$$
\begin{aligned}
u^e &= (PS_{ID}l^{H_2(m)})^e \mod n \\
&= (H_1(ID)^s l^{H_2(m)})^e \mod n \\
&= H_1(ID)^{se} l^{H_2(m)e} \mod n \\
&= H_1(ID)d^{H_2(m)} \mod n
\end{aligned}
$$

$$
\begin{aligned}
r &= g^k \mod p' \\
&= g^k g^{-xh} g^{xh} \mod p' \\
&= g^{k-xh}(g^x)^h \mod p' \\
&= g^{k-xh} PK_{ID}{}^h \mod p' \\
&= g^v PK_{ID}{}^h \mod p'
\end{aligned}
$$

4.2   Security Proof

Based on the newly defined VRSA problem and the well known DLP, we give a detailed and strict security proof for the proposed scheme in this section.

Theorem 2. *Under the hardness assumptions of VRSA problem and DLP, the newly proposed CL-PKS scheme is able to achieve existentially unforgeable against adaptively chosen message attacks in the ROM.*

The *Theorem* 2 can be concluded from the following *Lemmas* 3 and 4 and the two lemmas are shown in detail as below.

Lemma 3. *In **Game I**, suppose a polynomial-time Type I adversary $\mathcal{A}_I$ issues $(q_{H_1}, q_{H_2}, q_{H_3}, q_{pub}, q_{par}, q_{pri}, q_{pubr}, q_{sig})$ queries to the the corresponding H_1 queries, H_2 queries, H_3 queries, **Public key queries**, **Partial private key queries**, **Private key queries**, **Public key replacement** and **Signing queries** oracles and runs in time t to output a correct signature with success* *probability ε, then there is an algorithm $\mathcal{B}$ that can solve the VRSA problem with success probability*

$$\varepsilon' > (\varepsilon - \frac{2}{2^\lambda}) \times (1 - \frac{1}{q_{H_1}})^{q_{par}+q_{pri}+q_{sig}} \times (1 - \frac{1}{q_{H_3}})^{q_{sig}} \times \frac{1}{q_{H_1}q_{H_2}},$$

within time

$$t' < t + (q_{pub} + q_{pri} + q_{pubr} + 4q_{Sig})t_e + 2q_{Sig}t_m,$$

where t_e denotes the time required to calculate a modular exponentiation and t_m denotes the time required to calculate a modular multiplication.

Proof. (Lemma 3). The goal of this proof is to show there is an algorithm $\mathcal{B}$ that can solve the VRSA problem by using $\mathcal{A}_I$'s attack capabilities. First, $\mathcal{B}$ is given a random VRSA problem instance (n, e, a, z) and initializes $\mathcal{A}_I$ with the system parameters $(p', q', n, e, g, H_1, H_2, H_3)$. Then $\mathcal{B}$ responds to $\mathcal{A}_I$'s oracle queries and simulate oracles of the proposed CL-PKS scheme as follows.

– H_1 **queries:** $\mathcal{A}_I$ can issue queries to this oracle on an identity ID_i and $\mathcal{B}$ answers $\mathcal{A}_I$'s queries through a list L_1 which is in the form of (ID_i, h_{1i}, t_i). Once $\mathcal{B}$ receives a H_1 query on ID_i, $\mathcal{B}$ first check if L_1 contains ID_i. If yes, $\mathcal{B}$ returns the predefined h_{1i} to $\mathcal{A}_I$. Otherwise, $\mathcal{B}$ randomly selects $c \in [1, q_{H_1}]$.
  (1) If $i = c$, $\mathcal{B}$ assigns $ID_i = ID^*$, returns a to $\mathcal{A}_I$ and add an element $(ID_i, a, \perp)$ to the list L_1.
  (2) Otherwise, $\mathcal{B}$ randomly selects $t_i \in Z_n^*$ and computes $h_{1i} = t_i{}^e$, then returns h_{1i} to $\mathcal{A}_I$ and inserts a tuple (ID_i, h_{1i}, t_i) in the list L_1.
– H_2 **queries:** $\mathcal{A}_I$ is able to make queries to this oracle on a message m_i and $\mathcal{B}$ maintains a list L_2 of the form (m_i, h_{2i}) to answer $\mathcal{A}_I$'s queries. Once $\mathcal{B}$ receives a H_2 query on a message m_i, $\mathcal{B}$ first check if the list L_2 contains m_i. If yes, $\mathcal{B}$ returns the predefined h_{2i} to $\mathcal{A}_I$. Otherwise, $\mathcal{B}$ randomly selects $f \in [1, q_{H_2}]$.
  (1) If $i = f$, $\mathcal{B}$ sets $m_i = m^*$, then returns z to $\mathcal{A}_I$ and inserts a tuple (m_i, z) in the list L_2.
  (2) Otherwise, $\mathcal{B}$ first randomly selects $h_{2i} \in \{0, 1\}^{\frac{|n|}{4}}$, then returns h_{2i} to $\mathcal{A}_I$ and inserts a tuple (m_i, h_{2i}) in the list L_2.
– H_3 **queries:** $\mathcal{A}_I$ can issue queries to this oracle on a tuple (m_i, ID_i, r_i) and $\mathcal{B}$ answers $\mathcal{A}_I$'s queries through a list L_3 which is in the form of (m_i, ID_i, r_i, h_{3i}). Once $\mathcal{B}$ receives a H_3 query on a tuple (m_i, ID_i, r_i), $\mathcal{B}$ first check if the list L_3 contains (m_i, ID_i, r_i). If yes, $\mathcal{B}$ returns the predefined h_{3i} to $\mathcal{A}_I$. Otherwise, $\mathcal{B}$ randomly selects $h_{3i} \in Z_{q'}^*$, returns h_{3i} to $\mathcal{A}_I$ and inserts a tuple (m_i, ID_i, r_i, h_{3i}) in the list L_3.
– **Partial private key queries:** Once $\mathcal{B}$ receives a query on ID_i,
  (1) If $ID_i = ID^*$, $\mathcal{B}$ ends this game and outputs "fault".
  (2) Otherwise, $\mathcal{B}$ recovers the predefined (ID_i, h_{1i}, t_i) from the list L_1 and returns t_i to $\mathcal{A}_I$. If the tuple (ID_i, h_{1i}, t_i) has not been defined in L_1, $\mathcal{B}$ issue a new H_1 query on ID_i to get a new t_i, then $\mathcal{B}$ returns t_i to $\mathcal{A}_I$ and add an element (ID_i, h_{1i}, t_i) to the list L_1.

- **Public key queries:** $\mathcal{A}_I$ can issue queries to this oracle on an identity ID_i and $\mathcal{B}$ maintains a list L_{pub} of the form $(ID_i, PK_{ID_i}, s_{ID_i})$ to answer $\mathcal{A}_I$'s queries. Once $\mathcal{B}$ receives a query on an identity ID_i, $\mathcal{B}$ first check if L_{pub} contains ID_i. If yes, $\mathcal{B}$ returns the predefined PK_{ID_i} to $\mathcal{A}_I$. Otherwise, $\mathcal{B}$ randomly selects $j_i \in Z_{q'}^*$ and computes $PK_{ID_i} = g^{j_i} \bmod p'$, here we implicitly assign $s_{ID_i} = j_i$. Then $\mathcal{B}$ returns PK_{ID_i} to $\mathcal{A}_I$ and saves $(ID_i, PK_{ID_i}, s_{ID_i})$ in the list L_{pub}.
- **Private key queries:** Once $\mathcal{B}$ receives a query on ID_i,
  (1) If $ID_i = ID^*$, $\mathcal{B}$ ends this game and outputs "fault".
  (2) Otherwise, $\mathcal{B}$ recovers (ID_i, h_{1i}, t_i) and $(ID_i, PK_{ID_i}, s_{ID_i})$ from the lists L_1 and L_{pub} and returns (t_i, s_{ID_i}) to $\mathcal{A}_I$. If the tuples (ID_i, h_{1i}, t_i) and $(ID_i, PK_{ID_i}, s_{ID_i})$ have not been defined in the lists L_1 and L_{pub}, $\mathcal{B}$ issue a H_1 query and a public key query on ID_i to get a new t_i and a new s_{ID_i}, then $\mathcal{B}$ returns (t_i, s_{ID_i}) to $\mathcal{A}_I$ and saves (ID_i, h_{1i}, t_i) and $(ID_i, PK_{ID_i}, s_{ID_i})$ in the lists L_1 and L_{pub}, respectively.
- **Public key replacement:** Once $\mathcal{B}$ receives a query on $(ID_i, \widetilde{PK_{ID_i}})$,
  (1) If there is a tuple $(ID_i, PK_{ID_i}, s_{ID_i})$ has been defined in the list L_{pub}, then $\mathcal{B}$ assigns $PK_{ID_i} = \widetilde{PK_{ID_i}}$ and saves $(ID_i, \widetilde{PK_{ID_i}}, \perp)$ in the list L_{pub}.
  (2) Otherwise, $\mathcal{B}$ issues a public key query on ID_i to get a new PK_{ID_i}. Then $\mathcal{B}$ assigns $PK_{ID_i} = \widetilde{PK_{ID_i}}$ and saves $(ID_i, \widetilde{PK_{ID_i}}, \perp)$ in the list L_{pub}.
- **Signing queries:** Once $\mathcal{B}$ receives a signing query on a tuple (m_i, ID_i),
  (1) If $ID_i = ID^*$, $\mathcal{B}$ ends this game and outputs "fault".
  (2) Otherwise, $\mathcal{B}$ randomly selects $l_i \in Z_n^*$ and computes $d_i = l_i^e \bmod n$. Then $\mathcal{B}$ recovers (ID_i, h_{1i}, t_i), (m_i, h_{2i}) and $(ID_i, PK_{ID_i}, s_{ID_i})$ from the lists L_1, L_2 and L_{pub}, randomly selects $h_{3i} \in Z_{q'}^*$ and $v_i \in Z_{q'}^*$, computes $u_i = t_i l_i^{h_{2i}} \bmod n$ and $r_i = g^{v_i} PK_{ID_i}^{h_{3i}} \bmod p'$. Thus the tuple $(d_i, u_i, r_i, h_{3i}, v_i)$ comprises a correct certificateless signature σ_i associated with (m_i, ID_i), $\mathcal{B}$ returns σ_i to the adversary $\mathcal{A}_I$ and add an element (m_i, ID_i, r_i, h_{i3}) to the list L_3 ($\mathcal{B}$ stops this simulation and outputs "fault", if the tuple (m_i, ID_i, r_i, h_{i3}) has already been defined in L_3). It is important to note that the signing simulation can be performed well by $\mathcal{B}$ even without possessing s_{ID_i} with respect to PK_{ID_i}, therefore if the original PK_{ID_i} has been replaced with $\widetilde{PK_{ID_i}}$, $\mathcal{B}$ can still perform the simulation as the above process.

Finally, $\mathcal{A}_I$ stops to issue queries and outputs a forgery $(\widehat{d}, \widehat{u}, \widehat{r}, \widehat{h}, \widehat{v})$ with respect to $(\widehat{ID}, \widehat{m})$. If $\widehat{ID} \neq ID^*$ or $\widehat{m} \neq m^*$, $\mathcal{B}$ ends and outputs "fault". Otherwise, the signature should satisfy

$$\widehat{u}^e = H_1(ID^*)\widehat{d}^{H_2(m^*)} \bmod n,$$

From the above simulations, $\mathcal{B}$ can obtain

$$\widehat{u}^e = a\widehat{d}^z \bmod n,$$

Therefore, $\mathcal{B}$ can output $(\widehat{d}, \widehat{u})$ as the solution to the given VRSA instance.

In the following, we will give a detailed probability analysis of the success probability of $\mathcal{B}$ in **Game I**. Thus we only need to find all the errors happened during the simulations. Since both H_2 and H_3 are considered to be random oracles, $\mathcal{A}_I$ may produce a correct signature without issuing the $H_2(\widehat{m})$ query or $H_3(\widehat{m}, \widehat{ID}, \widehat{r})$ query with a probability which is at most $2/2^\lambda$. We can easily find that in the whole simulations, the error event that $\mathcal{B}$ outputs "fault" happens several times. In the **Partial private key queries** simulation, the error event does not occur with probability $(1 - 1/q_{H_1})^{q_{par}}$. In the **Private key queries** simulation, the error event does not occur with probability $(1 - 1/q_{H_1})^{q_{pri}}$. In the **Signing queries** simulation, the error event does not occur with probability $(1 - 1/q_{H_1})^{q_{sig}}(1 - 1/q_{H_3})^{q_{sig}}$. Similarly, the error event does not happen in the VRSA problem computation with probability $(1/q_{H_1})(1/q_{H_2})$. From what has been discussed above, we can obtain the success probability of $\mathcal{B}$ in **Game I** is at least

$$(\varepsilon - \frac{2}{2^\lambda}) \times (1 - \frac{1}{q_{H_1}})^{q_{par}+q_{pri}+q_{sig}} \times (1 - \frac{1}{q_{H_3}})^{q_{sig}} \times \frac{1}{q_{H_1}q_{H_2}},$$

We can also obtain the time required to run this game is at most

$$t + (q_{pub} + q_{pri} + q_{pubr} + 4q_{Sig})t_e + 2q_{Sig}t_m.$$

Lemma 4. *In **Game II**, suppose a polynomial-time Type II adversary $\mathcal{A}_{II}$ issues $(q_{H_3}, q_{pub}, q_{pri}, q_{sig})$ queries to the corresponding H_3 **queries**, **Public key queries**, **Private key queries** and **Signing queries** oracles and runs in time t to output a correct signature with success probability ε, then there is an algorithm $\mathcal{B}$ that can solve the DLP with success probability*

$$\varepsilon' > (\varepsilon - \frac{2}{2^\lambda}) \times (1 - \frac{1}{q_{pub}})^{q_{pri}} \times (1 - \frac{1}{q_{H_2}})^{q_{sig}} \times (1 - \frac{1}{q_{H_3}})^{q_{sig}} \times \frac{1}{q_{pub}},$$

within time

$$t' < t + (q_{pub} + q_{pri} + 4q_{Sig} + 1)t_e + (q_{pri} + 2q_{Sig})t_m,$$

where t_e denotes the time required to calculate a modular exponentiation and t_m denotes the time required to calculate a modular multiplication.

Proof (Lemma 4). The goal of this proof is to show there is an algorithm $\mathcal{B}$ that can solve the DLP by using $\mathcal{A}_{II}$'s attack capabilities. First, $\mathcal{B}$ is given a random DLP instance (p', g, β) and initializes $\mathcal{A}_{II}$ with the master secret key s and system parameters $(p', q', n, e, g, H_1, H_2, H_3)$. It is necessary to note that $\mathcal{A}_{II}$ represents a malicious KGC who has ability to get the partial private key as $PS_{ID} = H_1(ID)^s \bmod n$ which can also be computed by $\mathcal{B}$, thereby the hash function H_1 and the PartialPrivateKeyExtract algorithm are not required to simulate in this case. Then $\mathcal{B}$ responds to $\mathcal{A}_{II}$'s oracle queries and simulate oracles of the proposed CL-PKS scheme as follows.

- **Public key queries:** $\mathcal{A}_{II}$ can issue queries to this oracle on an identity ID_i. $\mathcal{B}$ answers $\mathcal{A}_I$'s queries through a list L_{pub} which is in the form of $(ID_i, PK_{ID_i}, s_{ID_i})$. Once $\mathcal{B}$ receives a query on an identity ID_i, $\mathcal{B}$ first check if L_{pub} contains ID_i. If yes, $\mathcal{B}$ returns the predefined PK_{ID_i} to $\mathcal{A}_{II}$. Otherwise, $\mathcal{B}$ randomly selects $c \in [1, q_{pub}]$.
  (1) If $i = c$, $\mathcal{B}$ assigns $ID_i = ID^*$, $\mathcal{B}$ sets $PK_{ID_i} = \beta$, returns β to $\mathcal{A}_{II}$ and add an element $(ID_i, \beta, \perp)$ to the list L_{pub}.
  (2) Otherwise, $\mathcal{B}$ first randomly selects $j_i \in Z_{q'}^*$ and computes $PK_{ID_i} = g^{j_i} \bmod p'$, here it implies that $s_{ID_i} = j_i$. Then $\mathcal{B}$ returns PK_{ID_i} to $\mathcal{A}_{II}$ and add an element (ID_i, PK_{ID_i}, j_i) to the list L_{pub}.

- **H_2 queries:** $\mathcal{A}_{II}$ can issue queries to this oracle on a message m_i. $\mathcal{B}$ maintains a list L_2 of the form (m_i, h_{2i}) to answer $\mathcal{A}_{II}$'s queries. Once $\mathcal{B}$ receives a H_2 query on a message m_i, $\mathcal{B}$ first check if the list L_2 contains m_i. If yes, $\mathcal{B}$ returns the predefined h_{2i} to $\mathcal{A}_{II}$. Otherwise, $\mathcal{B}$ randomly selects $f \in [1, q_{H_2}]$. If $i = f$, $\mathcal{B}$ sets $m_i = m^*$. For all messages submitted to this oracle in the case that the list L_2 does not contain m_i, $\mathcal{B}$ randomly selects $h_{2i} \in \{0,1\}^{\frac{|n|}{4}}$, returns h_{2i} to $\mathcal{A}_{II}$ and inserts a tuple (m_i, h_{2i}) in the list L_2.

- **H_3 queries:** $\mathcal{A}_{II}$ can issue queries to the oracle on a tuple (m_i, ID_i, r_i), $\mathcal{B}$ answers $\mathcal{A}_I$'s queries through a list L_3 which is in the form of (m_i, ID_i, r_i, h_{3i}). Once $\mathcal{B}$ receives a H_3 query on a tuple (m_i, ID_i, r_i), $\mathcal{B}$ first check if the list L_3 contains (m_i, ID_i, r_i). If yes, $\mathcal{B}$ returns the predefined h_{3i} to $\mathcal{A}_{II}$. Otherwise, $\mathcal{B}$ randomly selects $h_{3i} \in Z_{q'}^*$, returns h_{3i} to $\mathcal{A}_{II}$ and inserts a tuple (m_i, ID_i, r_i, h_{3i}) in the list L_3.

- **Private key queries:** Once $\mathcal{B}$ receives a query on ID_i,
  (1) If $ID_i = ID^*$, $\mathcal{B}$ ends this game and outputs "fault".
  (2) Otherwise, $\mathcal{B}$ recovers the predefined $(ID_i, PK_{ID_i}, s_{ID_i})$ from the list L_{pub} and returns (PS_{ID_i}, s_{ID_i}) to $\mathcal{A}_{II}$. If the tuples $(ID_i, PK_{ID_i}, s_{ID_i})$ has not been defined in the list L_{pub}, $\mathcal{B}$ issue a public key query on ID_i to get a new s_{ID_i}, then $\mathcal{B}$ returns (PS_{ID_i}, s_{ID_i}) to $\mathcal{A}_{II}$ and saves $(ID_i, PK_{ID_i}, s_{ID_i})$ in the list L_{pub}.

- **Signing queries:** Once $\mathcal{B}$ receives a signing query on a tuple (m_i, ID_i),
  (1) If $ID_i \neq ID^*$, $\mathcal{B}$ returns a certificateless signature σ_i with respect to m_i by the private key returned to $\mathcal{A}_{II}$, then $\mathcal{B}$ returns σ_i to $\mathcal{A}_{II}$.
  (2) Otherwise,
    (a) If $m_i = m^*$, $\mathcal{B}$ ends this game and outputs "fault".
    (b) Otherwise, $\mathcal{B}$ randomly selects $l_i \in Z_n^*$ and computes $d_i = l_i^e \bmod n$. Then $\mathcal{B}$ recovers the predefined (m_i, h_{2i}) and $(ID_i, PK_{ID_i}, s_{ID_i})$ from the lists L_2 and L_{pub}, randomly selects $h_{3i} \in Z_{q'}^*$ and $v_i \in Z_{q'}^*$, computes $u_i = PS_{ID_i} l_i^{h_{2i}} \bmod n$ and $r_i = g^{v_i} PK_{ID_i}^{h_{3i}} \bmod p'$. Thus the tuple $(d_i, u_i, r_i, h_{3i}, v_i)$ comprises a correct certificateless signature σ_i with respect to (ID_i, m_i), $\mathcal{B}$ returns σ_i to $\mathcal{A}_{II}$ and add an element (m_i, ID_i, r_i, h_{3i}) to the list L_3 ($\mathcal{B}$ stops this simulation and outputs "fault", if the tuple (m_i, ID_i, r_i, h_{3i}) has already been defined in the list L_3).

Finally, $\mathcal{A}_{II}$ stops to issue queries and outputs a correct signature tuple $(\widehat{d}, \widehat{u}, \widehat{r}, \widehat{h}, \widehat{v})$ with respect to $(\widehat{ID}, \widehat{m})$. If $\widehat{ID} \neq ID^*$, $\mathcal{B}$ ends and outputs "fault". Otherwise, by replays of $\mathcal{B}$ with the same random tape but different choices of the oracle H_3, according to the forking lemma [25], $\mathcal{B}$ obtains another correct signature $(\widehat{d}, \widehat{u}, \widehat{r}, \widehat{h}', \widehat{v}')$. Thus the two correct signatures should satisfy

$$g^{\widehat{v}} PK_{ID^*}{}^{\widehat{h}} = \widehat{r} \bmod p',$$
$$g^{\widehat{v}'} PK_{ID^*}{}^{\widehat{h}'} = \widehat{r} \bmod p',$$

From the above two equations, $\mathcal{B}$ can obtain

$$\log_g PK_{ID^*} = \frac{\widehat{v} - \widehat{v}'}{\widehat{h}' - \widehat{h}},$$

That is

$$\log_g \beta = \frac{\widehat{v} - \widehat{v}'}{\widehat{h}' - \widehat{h}},$$

Therefore, $\mathcal{B}$ can output $\frac{\widehat{v} - \widehat{v}'}{\widehat{h}' - \widehat{h}}$ as the solution to the given DLP instance.

Next, we will give a similar probability analysis for the success probability of $\mathcal{B}$ in **Game II** as in *Lemma 3*. $\mathcal{A}_{II}$ may produce a correct signature without issuing the $H_2(\widehat{m})$ query or $H_3(\widehat{m}, \widehat{ID}, \widehat{r})$ query with a probability which is at most $2/2^\lambda$. In the **Private key queries** simulation, the error event that $\mathcal{B}$ outputs "fault" does not happen with probability $(1 - 1/q_{pub})^{q_{pri}}$. In the **Signing queries** simulation, the error event does not happen with probability $(1 - 1/q_{H_2})^{q_{sig}}(1 - 1/q_{H_3})^{q_{sig}}$. In the same way, the error event does not happen in the DLP computation with probability $1/q_{pub}$. From what has been discussed above, we can obtain the success probability of $\mathcal{B}$ in **Game II** is at least

$$(\varepsilon - \frac{2}{2^\lambda}) \times (1 - \frac{1}{q_{pub}})^{q_{pri}} \times (1 - \frac{1}{q_{H_2}})^{q_{sig}} \times (1 - \frac{1}{q_{H_3}})^{q_{sig}} \times \frac{1}{q_{pub}},$$

We can also obtain the time required to run this game is at most

$$t + (q_{pub} + q_{pri} + 4q_{Sig} + 1)t_e + (q_{pri} + 2q_{Sig})t_m.$$

4.3 Comparison

Tables 1 and 2 show the comparisons of several general pairing-free CL-PKS schemes. For the computation cost, seven modular exponentiation operations and four modular multiplication operations are required in our scheme, while six modular exponentiation operations and four modular multiplication operations are required in the scheme proposed by Harn et al. and seven modular exponentiation operations and three modular multiplication operations are needed in Zhang and Mao's scheme, when compared with other existing pairing-free CL-PKS schemes [22, 23] of the same type, namely, general pairing-free CL-PKS

Table 1. Performance comparison of general pairing-free CL-PKS schemes

Scheme	Signing cost	Verification cost	Sum
HRL [22]	$t_e + 2t_m$	$5t_e + 2t_m$	$6t_e + 4t_m$
ZM [23]	$3t_e + t_m$	$4t_e + 2t_m$	$7t_e + 3t_m$
Ours	$t_e + 2t_m$	$t_e + 2t_m$	$7t_e + 4t_m$

t_e: the time required to calculate a modular exponentiation; t_m: the time required to calculate a modular multiplication

Table 2. Security comparison of general pairing-free CL-PKS schemes

Scheme	Type I Resist.	Type II Resist.	Assumption
HRL [22]	No Formal Proof	No Formal Proof	DLP
ZM [23]	√	×	RSA
Ours	√	√	VRSA+DLP

Type I Resist.: Type I Adversary Resistance; Type II Resist.: Type II Adversary Resistance.

schemes. Therefore, the computation cost of our scheme is slightly higher, but the scheme can achieve a higher security level. The reason is that Harn et al. did not provide a formal security proof for the scheme they proposed under a formal security model and Zhang and Mao's scheme has been demonstrated to be insecure against Type I adversary by He et al. [24].

5   Conclusion

We have surveyed the known main three types of CL-PKS schemes and mainly studied general pairing-free CL-PKS schemes in this paper. We briefly conclude our paper as the following points.

- We have defined a new hard mathematic problem called VRSA problem based on RSA and the hardness of breaking VRSA problem has been proven to be equivalent to the hardness of breaking RSA problem. The VRSA problem can be briefly described as: giving two parameters of RSA problem e and n and two integers a and z, try to find a pair of integers (d, u) such that $u^e = ad^z \mod n$.
- We have proposed a new pairing-free CL-PKS scheme based on the newly defined VRSA problem and the well known DLP. Besides, we also have shown a detailed and strict formal security proof to demonstrate that this scheme is secure against Type I and Type II adversaries under adaptively chosen message attacks in the ROM.
- Fortunately, our newly proposed scheme is the first general pairing-free CL-PKS scheme with provable security that achieves both Type I and Type II adversaries resistance and it is also the first RSA-based CL-PKS scheme that can possess resistance to Type I and Type II adversaries.

- We have analyzed the performance and security levels of our scheme, when compared with other known general pairing-free CL-PKS schemes [22,23] which are same type with our scheme, our scheme enjoys a slightly higher computation cost but achieves a higher security level.

Acknowledgment. The authors are grateful to the reviewers for their comments to improve the quality of this paper.

References

1. Diffie, W., Hellman, M.E.: New directions in cryptography. IEEE Trans. Inform. Theory **22**(6), 644–654 (1976)
2. Shamir, A.: Identity-based cryptosystems and signature schemes. In: Blakley, G.R., Chaum, D. (eds.) CRYPTO 1984. LNCS, vol. 196, pp. 47–53. Springer, Heidelberg (1985). doi:10.1007/3-540-39568-7_5
3. Al-Riyami, S.S., Paterson, K.G.: Certificateless public key cryptography. In: Laih, C.-S. (ed.) ASIACRYPT 2003. LNCS, vol. 2894, pp. 452–473. Springer, Heidelberg (2003). doi:10.1007/978-3-540-40061-5_29
4. Huang, X., Susilo, W., Mu, Y., Zhang, F.: On the security of certificateless signature schemes from asiacrypt 2003. In: Desmedt, Y.G., Wang, H., Mu, Y., Li, Y. (eds.) CANS 2005. LNCS, vol. 3810, pp. 13–25. Springer, Heidelberg (2005). doi:10.1007/11599371_2
5. Li, X.-X., Chen, K.-F., Sun, L.: Certificateless signature and proxy signature schemes from bilinear pairings. Lith. Math. J. **45**(1), 76–83 (2005)
6. Gorantla, M.C., Saxena, A.: An efficient certificateless signature scheme. In: Hao, Y., Liu, J., Wang, Y.-P., Cheung, Y., Yin, H., Jiao, L., Ma, J., Jiao, Y.-C. (eds.) CIS 2005. LNCS, vol. 3802, pp. 110–116. Springer, Heidelberg (2005). doi:10.1007/11596981_16
7. Yap, W.-S., Heng, S.-H., Goi, B.-M.: An efficient certificateless signature scheme. In: Zhou, X., et al. (eds.) EUC 2006. LNCS, vol. 4097, pp. 322–331. Springer, Heidelberg (2006). doi:10.1007/11807964_33
8. Yum, D.H., Lee, P.J.: Generic construction of certificateless signature. In: Wang, H., Pieprzyk, J., Varadharajan, V. (eds.) ACISP 2004. LNCS, vol. 3108, pp. 200–211. Springer, Heidelberg (2004). doi:10.1007/978-3-540-27800-9_18
9. Cao, X., Paterson, K.G., Kou, W.: An attack on a certificateless signature scheme, IACR Cryptology ePrint Archive 2006, 367 (2006)
10. Park, J.H.: An attack on the certificateless signature scheme from euc workshops 2006. IACR Cryptology ePrint Archive 2006, 442 (2006)
11. Zhang, J., Mao, J.: Security analysis of two signature schemes and their improved schemes. In: Gervasi, O., Gavrilova, M.L. (eds.) ICCSA 2007. LNCS, vol. 4705, pp. 589–602. Springer, Heidelberg (2007). doi:10.1007/978-3-540-74472-6_48
12. Hu, B.C., Wong, D.S., Zhang, Z., Deng, X.: Key replacement attack against a generic construction of certificateless signature. In: Batten, L.M., Safavi-Naini, R. (eds.) ACISP 2006. LNCS, vol. 4058, pp. 235–246. Springer, Heidelberg (2006). doi:10.1007/11780656_20
13. Zhang, Z., Wong, D.S., Xu, J., Feng, D.: Certificateless public-key signature: security model and efficient construction. In: Zhou, J., Yung, M., Bao, F. (eds.) ACNS 2006. LNCS, vol. 3989, pp. 293–308. Springer, Heidelberg (2006). doi:10.1007/11767480_20

14. Huang, X., Mu, Y., Susilo, W., Wong, D.S., Wu, W.: Certificateless signature revisited. In: Pieprzyk, J., Ghodosi, H., Dawson, E. (eds.) ACISP 2007. LNCS, vol. 4586, pp. 308–322. Springer, Heidelberg (2007). doi:10.1007/978-3-540-73458-1_23

15. He, D., Chen, J., Zhang, R.: An efficient and provably-secure certificateless signature scheme without bilinear pairings. Int. J. Commun. Syst. **25**(11), 1432–1442 (2012)

16. Tian, M., Huang, L.: Cryptanalysis of a certificateless signature scheme without pairings. Int. J. Commun. Syst. **26**(11), 1375–1381 (2013)

17. Tsai, J.-L., Lo, N.-W., Wu, T.-C.: Weaknesses and improvements of an efficient certificateless signature scheme without using bilinear pairings. Int. J. Commun. Syst. **27**(7), 1083–1090 (2014)

18. Gong, P., Li, P.: Further improvement of a certificateless signature scheme without pairing. Int. J. Commun. Syst. **27**(10), 2083–2091 (2014)

19. Yeh, K.-H., Tsai, K.-Y., Kuo, R.-Z., Wu, T.-C.: Robust certificateless signature scheme without bilinear pairings. In: 2013 International Conference on IT Convergence and Security (ICITCS), pp. 1–4. IEEE (2013)

20. Yeh, K.-H., Tsai, K.-Y., Fan, C.-Y.: An efficient certificateless signature scheme without bilinear pairings. Multimedia Tools Appl., 1–12 (2014)

21. Liu, W., Xie, Q., Wang, S., Han, L., Hu, B.: Pairing-free certificateless signature with security proof. J. Comput. Netw. Commun. **2014**, 6 (2014)

22. Harn, L., Ren, J., Lin, C.: Design of dl-based certificateless digital signatures. J. Syst. Softw. **82**(5), 789–793 (2009)

23. Zhang, J., Mao, J.: An efficient rsa-based certificateless signature scheme. J. Syst. Softw. **85**(3), 638–642 (2012)

24. He, D., Khan, M.K., Wu, S.: On the security of a rsa-based certificateless signature scheme. IJ Network Secur. **16**(1), 78–80 (2014)

25. Pointcheval, D., Stern, J.: Security proofs for signature schemes. In: Maurer, U. (ed.) EUROCRYPT 1996. LNCS, vol. 1070, pp. 387–398. Springer, Heidelberg (1996). doi:10.1007/3-540-68339-9_33

A Privacy-Preserving Framework for Collaborative Intrusion Detection Networks Through Fog Computing

Yu Wang[1], Lin Xie[3], Wenjuan Li[2,3], Weizhi Meng[2(✉)], and Jin Li[1]

[1] School of Computer Science, Guangzhou University, Guangzhou, China
yuwang@gzhu.edu.cn
[2] Department of Applied Mathematics and Computer Science,
Technical University of Denmark, Lyngby, Denmark
weme@dtu.dk
[3] Department of Computer Science, City University of Hong Kong,
Kowloon Tong, Hong Kong

Abstract. Nowadays, cyber threats (e.g., intrusions) are distributed across various networks with the dispersed networking resources. Intrusion detection systems (IDSs) have already become an essential solution to defend against a large amount of attacks. With the development of cloud computing, a modern IDS is able to implement more complicated detection algorithms by offloading the expensive operations such as the process of signature matching to the cloud (i.e., utilizing computing resources from the cloud). However, during the detection process, no party wants to disclose their own data especially sensitive information to others for privacy concerns, even to the cloud side. For this sake, privacy-preserving technology has been applied to IDSs, while it still lacks of proper solutions for a collaborative intrusion detection network (CIDN) due to geographical distribution. A CIDN enables a set of dispersed IDS nodes to exchange required information. With the advent of fog computing, in this paper, we propose a privacy-preserving framework for collaborative networks based on fog devices. Our study shows that the proposed framework can help reduce the workload on cloud's side.

Keywords: Collaborate network · Privacy preserving · Intrusion detection · Cloud environment · Fog computing

1 Introduction

Cyber threats (e.g., virus, denial-of-service (DoS) attack) are a big issue for current computer networks. To defend against various cyber attacks, intrusion detection systems (IDSs) have been widely deployed in organizations. Based on the detection approaches, an IDS can be roughly classified as signature-based

---

W. Meng—The author was previously known as Yuxin Meng.

S. Wen et al. (Eds.): CSS 2017, LNCS 10581, pp. 267–279, 2017.
https://doi.org/10.1007/978-3-319-69471-9_20

IDS and anomaly-based IDS [31]. The former (e.g., Snort [28]) detects an intrusion through comparing the packet payload with stored signatures (i.e., which describes a known attack or exploit), while the latter uses a pre-defined threshold and identifies an anomaly by comparing current profile with normal profile (i.e., which describes normal status of a network or system). Additionally, an IDS can be categorized as network-based IDS (NIDS) and host-based IDS (HIDS) in terms of the deployed locations.

With the increasing traffic volumes, it is hard for a traditional IDS to handle large incoming traffic. For example, the processing burden of a signature-based IDS is at least linear to the size of an input string [4]. With the development of cloud environment, an IDS can reduce its burden by offloading expensive operations to such computing infrastructures. For instance, Alharkan and Martin [1] proposed *IDSaaS* in Amazon EC2 cloud, which could monitor and record malicious network behaviors between virtual machines and users within a Virtual Private Cloud. Yassin et al. [33] proposed *CBIDS*, a Cloud-based Intrusion Detection Service Framework (CBIDS) to monitor different layers' traffic and detect unexpected activities from different points of a network.

In practical usage, an IDS should upload its traffic to the cloud side for inspection, which leads to threaten users' privacy. For example, cloud service provider may passively monitor users' log information to improve some of their services, but users may not want their log information to be monitored. As a result, privacy-preserving technology is widely applied to current IDSs. As an example, Park et al. [26] proposed *PPIDS*, a privacy preserving method for IDSs by applying cryptographic approaches to log files without a trusted third party (TTP). This system can encrypt the audit log file and identify intrusions over encrypted data.

Motivations. However, current cloud-based IDS is not suitable for a distributed IDS infrastructure due to its geographical distribution. Collaborative intrusion detection networks (CIDNs) enable a set of IDS nodes to collect and exchange information with each other [32]. If all data is uploaded to a cloud server for computation, it would consume considerable communication and computing resources, which makes a negative impact on the quality of service (QoS) (i.e., dealing with many redundant data). To further mitigate this issue, fog computing is a paradigm extending cloud computing and its services to the edge of the network (i.e., proximity to end-users/nodes), which can support for mobility, heterogeneity, interoperability and pre-processing.

Contributions. As fog computing can provide a computing and storage platform physically closer to the end nodes and users, provisioning a new breed of applications and services with the cloud layer, it well complements the application of cloud computing. In this paper, we thus propose a privacy-preserving framework for CIDNs based on fog devices. The contributions of our work can be summarized as below:

– We introduce the background of collaborative intrusion detection environments including its major components and propose a privacy-preserving

framework for CIDNs based on fog computing. The fog computing can provide storage, computing and networking services between an IDS and a cloud. With the equipped resource, fog devices could loose the workload of a cloud server.
- As a study, we apply Rabin fingerprint algorithm to our proposed framework, and evaluate our approach in a simulated environment. The experimental results show that our framework can help reduce the workload of a central server on the cloud.

Organization. The rest of this paper is organized as follows. In Sect. 2, we introduce the background of collaborative intrusion detection networks. Section 3 describes our proposed privacy-preserving framework and Sect. 4 shows a study and performance results. Section 5 introduces related work and Sect. 6 concludes our paper.

2   Background of CIDNs

This section briefly introduces the background of collaborative intrusion detection networks (CIDNs). As a CIDN is vulnerable to insider attacks, trust computation and evaluation is essential within such network [18,20,25]. This section takes challenge-based CIDNs as an example, describing its major components and explaining how it works.

Major components. In addition to a detection engine, each node in a CIDN usually contains several components including *trust management component, collaboration component* and *P2P communication.*

- *Trust management component.* This component aims to evaluate the trustworthiness of other nodes. Regarding challenge-based CIDNs, the trustworthiness of target nodes is mainly computed by evaluating the received feedback. Each node can send out either normal requests or challenges for alert ranking (consultation). To protect challenges, it is worth noting that challenges should be sent out in a random manner and in a way that makes them difficult to be distinguished from a normal alarm ranking request.
- *Collaboration component.* This component is mainly responsible for assisting a node to evaluate the trustworthiness of others by sending out *normal requests* or *challenges*, and receiving the relevant *feedback*. If a tested IDS node receives a request or challenge, this component will help send back its feedback. As shown in Fig. 1, if node A sends a *request/challenge* to node B, then node B will send back relevant feedback.
- *P2P communication.* This component is responsible for connecting with other IDS nodes and providing network organization, management and communication among IDS nodes.

Network Interactions. In a CIDN, each IDS node can choose its partners or collaborators based on its own policies and experience. These IDS nodes can be

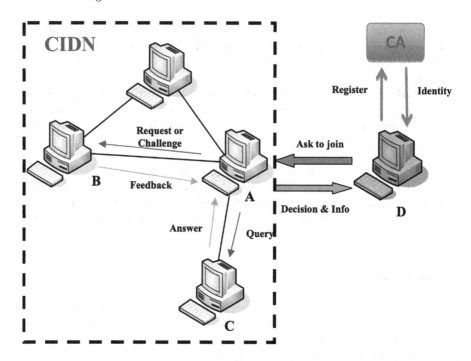

Fig. 1. The high-level architecture of a typical challenge-based CIDN.

associated if they have a collaborative relationship. Each node can maintain a list of their collaborated nodes, called *partner list* (or *acquaintance list*). Such list is customizable and stores information of other nodes (e.g., public keys and their current trust values). Before a node asks for joining the network, it has to register to a trusted certificate authority (*CA*) and obtain its unique proof of identity (e.g., a public key and a private key). As shown in Fig. 1, if node *D* wants to join the network, it needs to send an application to a network node, say node *A*. Then, node *A* makes a decision and sends back an initial *partner list*, if node *D* is accepted.

CIDNs allow IDS nodes exchanging required messages in-between to enhance their performance. There are two major types of messages for interactions.

- *Challenges.* A challenge contains a set of IDS alarms asking for labeling their severity. A testing node can send a challenge to other tested nodes and obtain the relevant feedback. As the testing node knows the severity of the alarms, it can use the received feedback to derive a trust value (e.g., satisfaction level) for the tested node.
- *Normal requests.* A normal request is sent by a node for alarm aggregation. Other IDS nodes should send back alarm ranking information as their feedback. Alarm aggregation is an important feature for CIDNs, which can help improve the detection performance, and it usually considers the feedback from trusted nodes.

3   Our Approach

This section introduces the concept of fog computing and details our proposed privacy-preserving framework for collaborative intrusion detection.

3.1   Fog Computing

Fog computing is proposed by Cisco, which aims to help ease the burden of the IoT server and safeguard the QoS [3]. As cloud computing does not need the enterprise and the end user to know specification or many details, it bliss becomes a problem for latency-sensitive applications, which require nodes in the vicinity to meet their delay requirements. For this sake, fog computing is proposed, which enables a new set of applications and services. There is a fruitful interplay between the cloud layer and the fog layer, particularly in the aspects of data management and analytic.

The main idea of fog computing is to provide storage, computing and various networking services between the environmental devices and the cloud side. For this sake, fog devices are often close to end devices, and provide a certain amount of storage and computation resource. With these resources, fog devices can process the collected data locally, in order to ease the burden of the cloud side (e.g., a central server). For example, the fog devices can perform some specific operations on the received data and send the results to the central server. In this case, the volume of data sent to the server could be reduced to a large extend.

3.2   Our Proposed Framework

Due to the features of fog computing, it is suitable for distributed intrusion detection architectures. Figure 2 depicts our proposed privacy-preserving framework for CIDNs based on fog devices. There are totally three layers:

- *CIDN layer.* This is the normal collaborative network layer, where different IDS nodes can improve their detection performance by exchanging required information with each other. Some expensive operations (e.g., signature matching) and sensitive information (e.g., logs) could be offloaded to the cloud side (cloud layer).
- *Cloud layer.* The cloud environment can provide sufficient computation resources for the CIDN layer, so that data owners can ease the computational burden. However, cloud side cannot ensure an instant reply or return of the computational results, depending on the geographical locations.
- *Fog layer.* The fog layer often embodies software modules and embedded operating systems. This layer is able to analyze gathered data obtained from the CIDN layer and thus make decisions locally. Local decision making is an important way to reduce latency, and thus to provide quick responses to unusual behaviors.

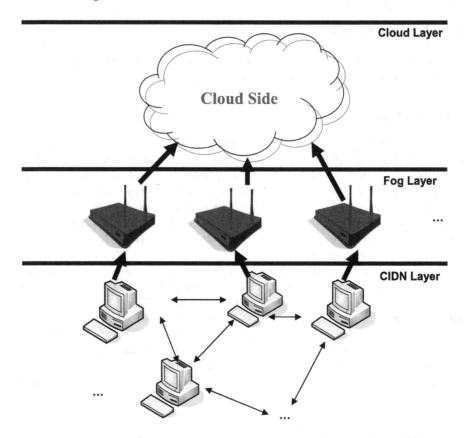

Fig. 2. Our privacy-preserving framework for CIDNs using fog devices.

4   Study and Evaluation

In this section, we detail the threat model, present a study of applying Rabin fingerprint algorithm to our framework, and illustrates performance results.

4.1   Threat Model

This work adopts the *curious-but-honest model* for a cloud provider [5]. That is, the cloud provider is trustful to follow the agreed protocol and perform intrusion inspection (i.e., analyzing network traffic for an organization); however, the cloud provider attempts to monitor, store, and learn the information about the sensitive (or private) data from the examined traffic, or attempt to discover anything they are interested in.

4.2   Fingerprint Computation for Signature-Based IDS

To facilitate comparison with [17], we conduct a study by applying *Rabin fingerprint algorithm* [27] to our framework. Rabin fingerprints can be computed using polynomial modulus operations with fast XOR, shift and table look-up operations. It has two merits: (1) one way; and (2) fast computation. For a signature-based IDSs, these fingerprints can be applied to the process of signature matching for the real-time requirement. More formally, for a binary string, given a sliding window and an irreducible polynomial $p(x)$, the fingerprint of each k-bit gram can be computed as below:

$$f(x) = m_k + m_{k-1}x + m_{k-2}x^2 + ... + m_1x^{k-1} mod \ p(x) \qquad (1)$$

Based on Eq. (1), we can generate fingerprints for both IDS signatures and transmitted network packets, and the cloud side can raise an alarm if any packet fingerprint matches the signature fingerprints. However, our previous work [17] indicated that the above straightforward approach has a privacy concern if there is a match between two fingerprints from signatures and packet payloads. For example, the cloud provider can still learn some useful information (i.e., which part of a signature did match), as the signatures may be known.

To resolve this issue, we can perturb fingerprints before sending them to the cloud provider. Note that for the exact matching, it is hard to completely prevent the cloud provider from successfully launching brute-force attacks, but we can still reduce the possibility of cracking.

As a study, we employ a simple approach; that is, the data owner can select a secret s with a length of l_s and use this secret to perturb the original fingerprints. This approach enables the data owner to decide the length of l_s so that the cloud provider still needs to guess the secret and its length. The equation can be presented as below:

$$f'(x) = f(x) \oplus s \ (0 < l_s < |f(x)|) \qquad (2)$$

4.3   Performance Results

To investigate the performance, we simulated a cloud environment based on iCanCloud[1], which can simulate instance types provided by Amazon. The simulated CIDN consists of 10 nodes. The implementation of Rabin fingerprint is based on cyclic redundancy code and all grams are in 8-byte. The fingerprints are in 128-bit with 129-bit irreducible polynomials, and we set the length (l_s) of the secret s to 64-bit (half length of the fingerprints).

Fog devices can help perform signature matching for the transmitted traffic from the CIDN layer to the cloud layer, and send the alarms/records to the cloud side. The reduced workload of the central server on cloud's side is shown in Fig. 3. It is observed that with more traffic processed by fog devices, the workload of the central server (in the cloud environment) can be greatly reduced. It is worth noting that the central server still needs to aggregate IDS alarms and correlate information. Overall, our results demonstrate that our proposed framework can help reduce the burden of the central server on cloud's side.

---

[1] http://icancloudsim.org/Home.html.

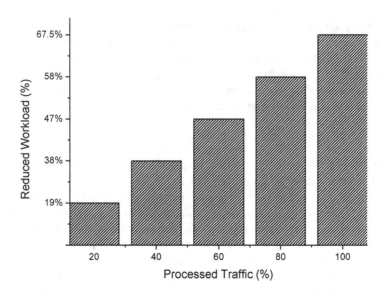

Fig. 3. Performance result of reduced workload vs. processed traffic on fog devices.

Security discussion. In current IDS scenario, we consider signatures are sensitive as well, and we can use Eq. (2) to perturb the fingerprints. According to [17], assume that there are matches between signature fingerprints and payload fingerprints. Given the secret length l_s (assuming that the length of l_s is random with uniformly distribution) and the fingerprint length l_p, thus, the cloud provider has no more than $\frac{1}{2^{l_s} \times 2^{l_p}}$ $(0 < l_s < l_p)$ probability of inferring the sensitive information. If there is no match, then the cloud provider should brute force to reverse the Rabin fingerprinting calculation. This brute-force attack is difficult for a polynomial-time adversary [27].

5   Related Work

This section introduces related work about distributed intrusion detection systems, challenge-based CIDNs and privacy-preserving IDSs.

Distributed trust-based intrusion detection. Collaborative intrusion detection networks (CIDNs) [32] can enable an IDS node to achieve better detection performance by collecting and communicating information with other IDS nodes.

Li *et al.* [11] identified that most distributed intrusion detection systems (DIDS) might rely on centralized fusion, or distributed fusion with unscalable communication mechanisms. Based on this, they proposed a DIDS according to the emerging decentralized location and routing infrastructure. Their approach assumes that all peers are trusted which is vulnerable to insider attacks (i.e., betrayal attacks where some nodes suddenly become malicious). To detect insider attacks, Duma *et al.* [6] proposed a P2P-based overlay for intrusion detection (Overlay IDS) that mitigated the insider threat by using a trust-aware engine for correlating alerts and an adaptive scheme for managing trust. The trust-aware correlation engine is capable of filtering out warnings sent by untrusted or low quality peers, while the adaptive trust management scheme uses past experiences of peers to predict their trustworthiness.

Similarly, Shaikh et al. [30] proposed a Group-based Trust Management Scheme (GTMS), which evaluated the trust of a group of Sensor Nodes for two topologies: intragroup topology and intergroup topology. Guo et al. [9] described a trust management framework to generate trust values based on Grey theory and Fuzzy sets. They computed trust values by using relation factors and weights of neighbor nodes, not just by simply taking an average value.

Challenge-based intrusion detection. Challenge-based mechanism is a special way of computing trust for IDSs, where the trustworthiness of a node depends on the received answers to the challenges. Fung et al. [7] proposed a HIDS collaboration framework that enables each HIDS to evaluate the trustworthiness of others based on its own experience by means of a forgetting factor. The forgetting factor can give more emphasis on the recent experience of the peer. Then, they improved their trust management model by using a Dirichlet-based model to measure the level of trustworthiness among IDS nodes according to their mutual experience [8]. This model had strong scalability properties and was robust against common insider threats. Experimental results demonstrated that the new model could improve robustness and efficiency.

To further enhance the performance of CIDNs, Li et al. [12] identified that different IDSs may have distinct levels of sensitivity in detecting particular types of threats based on their own signatures and profiles. They thus defined a concept of *intrusion sensitivity* and explored its feasibility on evaluating the trust of an IDS node. They further designed a trust management model based on *intrusion sensitivity* to improve the robustness of CIDNs [13], and proposed a machine learning-based approach in automatically allocating the values of *intrusion sensitivity* [16].

On the other hand, Li et al. [14] proposed a novel type of collusion attack, called passive message fingerprint attack (PMFA), which can collect messages and identify normal requests in a passive way. In the evaluation, their results demonstrated that under PMFA, malicious nodes can send malicious responses to normal requests while maintaining their trust values. A special On-Off attack (called SOOA) was also developed by them, which could keep responding normally to one node while acting abnormally to another node [15]. As a result, there is still a need to enhance the security of CIDN frameworks [24], i.e., considering behavior profile [29]. Other related studies on improving IDSs can be referred to alert reduction [19], alert verification [22,23] and EFM [21].

IDS and privacy-preserving techniques. A number of privacy-preserving schemes are developed for protecting data privacy during data sharing and intrusion detection. For example, Park et al. [26] proposed *PPIDS*, a privacy preserving approach for an IDS through applying cryptographic methods to log files without a trusted third party (TTP). Thanks to the use of cryptographic methods, *PPIDS* could prevent users' log information from being monitored and misused. In addition, their approach could provide anonymity (encryption of ID), pseudonymity (encryption of quasi-identifier such as IP address), confidentiality of data, and unobservability. One major issue is that *PPIDS* could lower the performance due to encryptions when log information was stored in SQL table and it could not provide perfect unlinkability.

Regarding the integration of a trusted third party, Benali *et al.* [2] identified and discussed some privacy issues. For example, when several organizations decided to collaborate in identifying intrusive activities, every organization resource manager was requested to send the events log to a central unit. As a result, such central unit was supposed to act as a trusted entity. Indeed, when the analyzer received the event from the participant, a large amount of private information regarding resources and IP addresses would be communicated. In addition, it could be embarrassing for a participant to be pointed out by the third party as a particular weak participant.

Zhou *et al.* [35] proposed a framework to detect Sybil attacks, while preserving the privacy of users in vehicular ad hoc networks. The framework could distribute the responsibility of detecting Sybil attacks to semi-trusted third parties. Kerschbaum and Oertel [10] presented a provably secure pattern matching algorithm that could be used for distributed anomaly detection. Their algorithm implemented pattern matching that could be used as the building block for anomaly detection. The experiments indicated that their algorithm was acceptable in RFID anti-counterfeiting. Later, Zhang *et al.* [34] designed a 'semi-centralized' architecture, which used secure multiparty computation (SMC) protocol to conduct a privacy-preserving Principal Component Analysis (PCA), and maintain its scalability and accuracy for anomaly detection. In the evaluation, they showed that none of the participant could learn the private information of other participants during the computation progress.

6   Conclusion

Intrusion detection systems are an important solution to defend against cyber attacks. With the help of cloud computing, a modern IDS is able to deploy advanced detection algorithms by offloading the expensive operations like the process of signature matching to the cloud side. However, during the detection, no party wants to disclose their own data especially sensitive data to others. For this sake, privacy-preserving intrusion detection technology has received much attention, while most current approaches are not suitable for collaborative intrusion detection networks (CIDNs) due to its geographical distribution. With the advent of fog computing, in this paper, we propose a privacy-preserving framework for CIDNs based on fog devices. In our study, we apply Rabin fingerprint algorithm to our framework, and found that our approach can greatly reduce the workload of the central server on cloud's side.

This is an early study in this direction, and there are many topics for our future work. One is to apply our proposed framework to a real network environment and investigate the detection performance. It is also an interesting topic to analyze accuracy, privacy and efficiency of the proposed framework for an anomaly-based IDS.

Acknowledgment. This work was partially supported by National Natural Science Foundation of China (No. 61472091), Natural Science Foundation of Guangdong Province for Distinguished Young Scholars (2014A030306020), Science and Technology Planning Project of Guangdong Province, China (2015B010129015) and the Innovation Team Project of Guangdong Universities (No. 2015KCXTD014).

References

1. Alharkan, T., Martin, P.: IDSaaS: intrusion detection system as a service in public clouds. In: Proceedings of the 12th IEEE/ACM International Symposium on Cluster, Cloud and Grid Computing (CCGrid), pp. 686–687 (2012)
2. Benali, F., Bennani, N., Gianini, G., Cimato, S.: A distributed and privacy-preserving method for network intrusion detection. In: Meersman, R., Dillon, T., Herrero, P. (eds.) OTM 2010. LNCS, vol. 6427, pp. 861–875. Springer, Heidelberg (2010). doi:10.1007/978-3-642-16949-6_13
3. Bonomi, F., Milito, R., Zhu, J., Addepalli, S.: Fog computing and its role in the internet of things. In: Proceedings of the First Edition of the MCC Workshop on Mobile Cloud Computing (MCC), pp. 13–16 (2012)
4. Dreger, H., Feldmann, A., Paxson, V., Sommer, R.: Operational experiences with high-volume network intrusion detection. In: Proceedings of the 11th ACM Conference on Computer and Communications Security (CCS), pp. 2–11 (2004)
5. di Vimercati, S.D.C., Foresti, S., Jajodia, S., Paraboschi, S., Samarati, P.: Over-encryption: management of access control evolution on outsourced data. In: Proceedings of the 33rd International Conference on Very Large Data Bases (VLDB), pp. 123–134 (2007)
6. Duma, C., Karresand, M., Shahmehri, N., Caronni, G.: A trust-aware, P2P-based overlay for intrusion detection. In: Proccedings of DEXA Workshop, pp. 692–697 (2006)
7. Fung, C.J., Baysal, O., Zhang, J., Aib, I., Boutaba, R.: Trust management for host-based collaborative intrusion detection. In: Turck, F., Kellerer, W., Kormentzas, G. (eds.) DSOM 2008. LNCS, vol. 5273, pp. 109–122. Springer, Heidelberg (2008). doi:10.1007/978-3-540-87353-2_9
8. Fung, C.J., Zhang, J., Aib, I., Boutaba, R.: Robust and scalable trust management for collaborative intrusion detection. In: Proceedings of the 11th IFIP/IEEE International Conference on Symposium on Integrated Network Management (IM), pp. 33–40 (2009)
9. Guo, J., Marshall, A., Zhou, B.: A new trust management framework for detecting malicious and selfish behaviour for mobile ad hoc networks. In: Proceedings of the 10th IEEE International Conference on Trust, Security and Privacy in Computing and Communications (TrustCom), pp. 142–149 (2011)
10. Kerschbaum, F., Oertel, N.: Privacy-preserving pattern matching for anomaly detection in RFID anti-counterfeiting. In: Ors Yalcin, S.B. (ed.) RFIDSec 2010. LNCS, vol. 6370, pp. 124–137. Springer, Heidelberg (2010). doi:10.1007/978-3-642-16822-2_12
11. Li, Z., Chen, Y., Beach, A.: Towards scalable and robust distributed intrusion alert fusion with good load balancing. In: Proceedings of the 2006 SIGCOMM Workshop on Large-Scale Attack Defense (LSAD), pp. 115–122 (2006)

12. Li, W., Meng, Y., Kwok, L.F.: Enhancing trust evaluation using intrusion sensitivity in collaborative intrusion detection networks: feasibility and challenges. In: Proceedings of the 9th International Conference on Computational Intelligence and Security (CIS), pp. 518–522 (2013)

13. Li, W., Meng, W., Kwok, L.-F.: Design of intrusion sensitivity-based trust management model for collaborative intrusion detection networks. In: Zhou, J., Gal-Oz, N., Zhang, J., Gudes, E. (eds.) IFIPTM 2014. IAICT, vol. 430, pp. 61–76. Springer, Heidelberg (2014). doi:10.1007/978-3-662-43813-8_5

14. Li, W., Meng, W., Kwok, L.-F., Ip, H.H.S.: PMFA: toward passive message fingerprint attacks on challenge-based collaborative intrusion detection networks. In: Chen, J., Piuri, V., Su, C., Yung, M. (eds.) NSS 2016. LNCS, vol. 9955, pp. 433–449. Springer, Cham (2016). doi:10.1007/978-3-319-46298-1_28

15. Li, W., Meng, W., Kwok, L.-F.: SOOA: exploring special on-off attacks on challenge-based collaborative intrusion detection networks. In: Au, M.H.A., Castiglione, A., Choo, K.-K.R., Palmieri, F., Li, K.-C. (eds.) GPC 2017. LNCS, vol. 10232, pp. 402–415. Springer, Cham (2017). doi:10.1007/978-3-319-57186-7_30

16. Li, W., Meng, Y., Kwok, L.F., Ip, H.H.S.: Enhancing collaborative intrusion detection networks against insider attacks using supervised intrusion sensitivity-based trust management model. J. Netw. Comput. Appl. **77**, 135–145 (2017)

17. Meng, Y., Li, W., Kwok, L.F., Xiang, Y.: Towards designing privacy-preserving signature-based IDS as a service: a study and practice. In: Proceedings of the 5th IEEE International Conference on Intelligent Networking and Collaborative Systems (INCoS), pp. 181–188 (2013)

18. Meng, Y., Kwok, L.-F., Li, W.: Towards designing packet filter with a trust-based approach using bayesian inference in network intrusion detection. In: Keromytis, A.D., Pietro, R. (eds.) SecureComm 2012. LNICSSITE, vol. 106, pp. 203–221. Springer, Heidelberg (2013). doi:10.1007/978-3-642-36883-7_13

19. Meng, Y., Kwok, L.F., Li, W.: Enhancing false alarm reduction using voted ensemble selection in intrusion detection. Int. J. Comput. Intell. Syst. **6**(4), 626–638 (2013)

20. Meng, Y., Li, W., Kwok, L.: Evaluation of detecting malicious nodes using bayesian model in wireless intrusion detection. In: Lopez, J., Huang, X., Sandhu, R. (eds.) NSS 2013. LNCS, vol. 7873, pp. 40–53. Springer, Heidelberg (2013). doi:10.1007/978-3-642-38631-2_4

21. Meng, W., Li, W., Kwok, L.F.: EFM: enhancing the performance of signature-based network intrusion detection systems using enhanced filter mechanism. Comput. Secur. **43**, 189–204 (2014)

22. Meng, Y., Kwok, L.F.: Adaptive blacklist-based packet filter with a statistic-based approach in network intrusion detection. J. Netw. Comput. Appl. **39**, 83–92 (2014)

23. Meng, W., Li, W., Kwok, L.F.: Design of intelligent KNN-based alarm filter using knowledge-based alert verification in intrusion detection. Secur. Commun. Netw. **8**(18), 3883–3895 (2015)

24. Meng, W., Luo, X., Li, W., Li, Y.: Design and evaluation of advanced collusion attacks on collaborative intrusion detection networks in practice. In: Proceedings of the 15th IEEE International Conference on Trust, Security and Privacy in Computing and Communications (TrustCom), pp. 1061–1068 (2016)

25. Meng, W., Li, W., Xiang, Y., Choo, K.K.R.: A Bayesian inference-based detection mechanism to defend medical smartphone networks against insider attacks. J. Netw. Comput. Appl. **78**, 162–169 (2017)

26. Park, H.-A., Lee, D.H., Lim, J., Cho, S.H.: PPIDS: privacy preserving intrusion detection system. In: Yang, C.C., Zeng, D., Chau, M., Chang, K., Yang, Q., Cheng, X., Wang, J., Wang, F.-Y., Chen, H. (eds.) PAISI 2007. LNCS, vol. 4430, pp. 269–274. Springer, Heidelberg (2007). doi:10.1007/978-3-540-71549-8_27

27. Rabin, M.O.: Fingerprinting by Random Polynomials. Center for Research in Computing Technology, Harvard University. Technical Report TR-CSE-03-01 (1981)

28. Roesch, M.: Snort: lightweight intrusion detection for networks. In: Proceedings of the 1999 Usenix Lisa Conference, pp. 229–238 (1999)

29. Ruan, X., Wu, Z., Wang, H., Jajodia, S.: Profiling online social behaviors for compromised account detection. IEEE Trans. Inf. Forensics Secur. 11(1), 176–187 (2016)

30. Shaikh, R.A., Jameel, H., d'Auriol, B.J., Lee, H., Lee, S., Song, Y.J.: Group-based trust management scheme for clustered wireless sensor networks. IEEE Trans. Parallel Distrib. Syst. 20(11), 1698–1712 (2009)

31. Scarfone, K., Mell, P.: Guide to Intrusion Detection and Prevention Systems (IDPS). NIST Special Publication 800–94, February 2007

32. Wu, Y.-S., Foo, B., Mei, Y., Bagchi, S.: Collaborative Intrusion Detection System (CIDS): a framework for accurate and efficient IDS. In: Proceedings of the 2003 Annual Computer Security Applications Conference (ACSAC), pp. 234–244 (2003)

33. Yassin, W., Udzir, N.I., Muda, Z., Abdullah, A., Abdullah, M.T.: A Cloud-based Intrusion Detection Service framework. In: Proceedings of the 2012 International Conference on Cyber Security, Cyber Warfare and Digital Forensic, pp. 213–218 (2012)

34. Zhang, P., Huang, X., Sun, X., Wang, H., Ma, Y.: Privacy-Preserving Anomaly Detection across Multi-Domain Networks. In: Proceedings of the 9th International Conference on Fuzzy Systems and Knowledge Discovery (FSKD), pp. 1066–1070 (2012)

35. Zhou, T., Choudhury, R.R., Ning, P., Chakrabarty, K.: Privacy-preserving detection of sybil attacks in vehicular ad hoc networks. In: Proceedings of the Fourth Annual International Conference on Mobile and Ubiquitous Systems: Networking & Services (MobiQuitous), pp. 1–8 (2007)

Predicting Vulnerable Software Components Using Software Network Graph

Shengjun Wei[1($\boxtimes$)], Xiaojiang Du[2], Changzhen Hu[1], and Chun Shan[1]

[1] Beijing Key Laboratory of Software Security Engineering Technique,
Beijing Institute of Technology, Beijing 100081, China
{sjwei, chzhoo, sherryshan}@bit. edu. cn
[2] Department of Computer and Information Sciences, Temple University,
Philadelphia, PA 19122, USA
dxj@ieee.org

Abstract. Vulnerability Prediction Models (VPMs) are used to predict vulnerability-prone modules and now many software security metrics have been proposed. In this paper, we predict vulnerability-prone components. Based on software network graph we define component cohesion and coupling metrics which are used as security metrics to build the VPM. To validate the prediction performance, we conduct an empirical study on Firefox 3.6. We compare the results with other works', it shows that our model has a good performance in the accuracy, precision, and recall, and indicate that the proposed metrics are also effective in vulnerability prediction.

Keywords: Software security · Vulnerability prediction · Component cohesion and coupling · Software network

1 Introduction

With rapid development of information technology, Information security issues are becoming increasingly prominent. Among these issues, software vulnerability and software security are the core points, which have been studied in several papers (e.g., [1–11]) from multiple perspectives. If a single software vulnerability is utilized by a hostile attacker, severe damage will be caused to an organization. Software developer are unlikely to find all vulnerabilities in a software product because of the limited time and budget. If those vulnerability-prone modules can be predicted, testing and inspection efforts will be prioritized on these modules, more security vulnerabilities would be found.

"High Cohesion and Low Coupling" are thought as marks of high quality software, which are always the ultimate goal pursued by a software developer [12]. High complexity and coupling and low cohesion can lead to the difficulty of software understanding, developing, testing and maintaining, and so may introduce vulnerabilities into software systems [13, 14]. Many software security metrics including complexity, cohesion and coupling metrics have been proposed to predict vulnerabilities, the correlations between the metrics and vulnerabilities are generalized [14–18]. Paper [18] discovers that the sole classic nine code complexity metrics have weak correlation with

© Springer International Publishing AG 2017
S. Wen et al. (Eds.): CSS 2017, LNCS 10581, pp. 280–290, 2017.
https://doi.org/10.1007/978-3-319-69471-9_21

security problems for Mozilla JavaScript Engine, and paper [16] believes that univariate analysis with only one of the complexity, coupling and cohesion metrics is not effective to identify vulnerability-prone modules under many situations, and multivariate interactions should be taken into account. In this paper, we conduct vulnerability prediction research at component level. We use component cohesion and coupling metrics simultaneously which are defined based on software network graph to build prediction models. To validate the efficiency of the model, experiments are carried out targeting an open source software Firefox based on their public vulnerabilities.

The rest of this paper is organized as follows: Sect. 2 provides related work. Section 3 introduces metrics we collect for this study. Section 4 describes the case study design and evaluation criteria. Section 5 provides the results and discusses our findings and limitations and Sect. 6 summarizes our study.

2 Related Work

The code metrics which include code complexity and developing process metrics which include code churn, developer's experience and the development team's organizational structure, etc. are firstly used to build Defect Prediction Models (DPMs) to predict potential defect-proneness of program modules [19–21], and then by reference, these metrics are used to build VPMs because of regarding software security vulnerabilities as special defects.

Shin et al. [18, 22] study the correlations between nine classic code complexity metrics and security vulnerabilities at function level targeting JavaScript Engine, the experimental results show that the correlations are weak, the models have high false negative rate. Later, they take the code complexity metrics, the dependency network complexity metrics and execution complexity metrics into account together, the granularity is at file-level, the experimental results show that the false negative rate decreases [23]. Later on, they use the complexity, code churn and past fault history metrics, as well as the complexity, code churn, and developer activity (CCD) metrics, they conduct experiments on Mozilla Firefox web browser and the Red Hat Enterprise Linux kernel at file level, the recalls are over 80% and the false positives are also over 20% [15, 24].

Zimmermann et al. [25] adopt the churn, coverage, dependency measures, and organizational structure of the company metrics, they perform their analysis at binary level, conduct experiment targeting windows vista, they observe that classical metrics predict vulnerabilities with a high precision but low recall values. However, the dependencies predict vulnerabilities with a lower precision but higher recall.

Nguyen et al. [26] propose code metrics based on dependency graphs, they conduct a prediction model which targets the JavaScript Engine at component level. They obtain a good accuracy but a very low recall rate.

Chowdhury et al. [27] carry on researches on the classical object-oriented architecture metrics which are class complexity, coupling and cohesion metrics, they perform their analysis at file level, evaluate the model on Mozilla Firefox and achieve a means recall of 74.22%.

Neuhaus et al. [28] discover a correlation between import/function calls and vulnerabilities, they use them to build a classifier at file level. Their experiment targeting on the Mozilla Firefox show that a recall of 45% and a precision of 70% can be achieved.

Scandariato et al. [29] treat a source code file as a textfile, with the help of text mining, they build a classifier. The features are a set of words mined out from the code file text. In following research [30], they compare the performance of software metrics and text mining based on the same vulnerability database built by themselves, they discover that text mining models had higher recall than software metrics. Jimenez et al. [31] also compare the performance of software metrics, text mining and includes and function calls, in the context of the Linux kernel, they find that models based on code metrics perform poorly.

3 Metrics

A software network graph describes the architecture of a software system, at different granularities, the nodes of which could be component, package, class, method, and data etc., and the edges of which are dependencies among the nodes.

A software system can be regarded as a set of components and dependencies among these components. The members of a component are data items and executable codes. The relations between data item and executable code are data write and data read, and relations between executable codes are function call and function return.

We firstly construct the software network graph at method and data granularities, then the software network graph at component granularity is obtained by treating all the methods and data belonging to a component as a whole, as well as retaining all edges between two components.

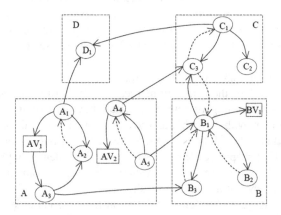

Fig. 1. Software network graph

3.1   Software Network Graph

Definition 1. The Software Network Graph of a software system is a direct graph $G_{SN}(V^d, V^m, E^c, E^r, E^d)$, where: V^d: is a set of data nodes; V^m: is a set of function nodes; $E^c \subseteq V^m \times V^m$: is a set of call-edges; $E^r \subseteq V^m \times V^m$: is a set of return-edges; $E^d \subseteq V^d \times V^m$: is a set of data-edges, including data write and data read.

As shown in Fig. 1, it is a software network graph of a software system. This system has four components: A, B, C, and D, which are represented by four big dashed quadrangles. In every component, there are some functions which are represented by elliptical nodes and data items which are represented by rectangular nodes. The solid

Table 1. Cohesion and coupling metrics based on software network graph

Cohesion metrics	Description and rationale
AveDegofIntNod	The degree of a node is the number of all the edges connected in or out the node. The AveDegofIntNod is the average degree of all the nodes in a component. the larger the value, the stronger the dependency between the nodes, and the more important the component
AveCltCoeofIntNod	The definition of clustering coefficient C_i of a node v_i: Suppose node v_i has k_i adjacent nodes and there have M_i edges among these k_i adjacent nodes, but the possible maximal number of edges among these k_i adjacent nodes is $k_i(k_i - 1)$, so $C_i = M_i/[k_i(k_i - 1)]$. AveCltCoeofIntNod is the average clustering coefficient of all the nodes in a component. AveCltCoeofIntNod reflects the cohesion of elements in a component. The larger the value, the higher the cohesion
Maxz-ValofIntNod	We define the z-value of a node v_i is z_i: $z_i = (k_i - \bar{k}_C)/\sigma_{k_C}$, where, k_i is the degree of node v_i in the component, $\bar{k}_C$ and σ_{k_C} are the average degree and standard deviation of degrees of all nodes in the component respectively. Maxz-ValofIntNod is the maximal z-value in the component. z_i reflects the connection strength between v_i and the other nodes. The larger the value, the higher the node cohesion
Coupling metrics	Description and rationale
DegofCom	DegofCom is the degree of a component node: the number of edges connected in or out the component. The larger the value, the higher the coupling
ClsCoeofCom	ClsCoeofCom is the clustering coefficient of a component node. The larger the value, the higher the coupling
BetofCom	BetofCom is the betweenness of a component node. There has a shortest path between any two reachable nodes in the graph. The betweenness of a node is the number of the shortest paths across the node. The larger the value, the higher the coupling
z-ValofCom	The z-ValofCom is the z-value of a component. The z-value of a component c is $z_C = (k - \bar{k})/\sigma_k$, where, k is the degree of component c, $\bar{k}$ is the average degree of all components, and σ_k is the standard deviation of the degrees of all components. The larger the value, the higher the coupling

line represents both data-edge and call-edge regarding to the source and the target. The dash line represents the return-edge.

3.2 Metrics

We perform our analysis aiming at a component. The high cohesion of members in a component and low coupling between components indicate a high quality for a software, we adopt component cohesion and coupling metrics to build a classifier. We define the component cohesion metrics and coupling metrics based on the software network graph described in Sect. 3.1, as shown in Table 1. The component cohesion is the dependency among members in a component, the component coupling is the dependency between components.

4 Case Studies

We perform an empirical case study on Mozilla Firefox 3.6. According to the security advisories for Firefox 3.6 [32], Firefox 3.6 contains 36 releases (main and minor) which are reported owning security advisories. Firefox 3.6 has 8,571 C/C++ files which are combined into 6,025 components. We assume that the same vulnerability exists in all previous revisions.

4.1 Vulnerability Data Collection

The discovered vulnerabilities in Mozilla Firefox are reported as Mozilla Foundation Security Advisories (MFSAs) [32]. For Firefox 3.6, there are 124 MFSAs, in which bug IDs are included for the bug reports in the bug database. From these bug reports, the files that are fixed to mitigate vulnerabilities can be identified. Among those bug reports linked from MFSAs for Firefox 3.6, if there exists a bug report that has bug patches for the file, the file is considered vulnerable. As a file is contained in a component, whether a component is vulnerable or not is determined.

There are three steps for collecting vulnerabilities data:

(1) Searching vulnerabilities from MFSA,
(2) For every vulnerability obtained by step (1), found out the corresponding bug links in Bugzilla,
(3) For every bug obtained by step (2), found out the patched files for fixing the bug, then plus 1 to the vulnerability number of the files.

We develop a crawler tool for collecting vulnerability data, this tool are working with 4 loops, as shown in Fig. 2. The tool's run results show that among the 6,025 components of Firefox 3.6, there are 212 vulnerable components (3.5% of the total components).

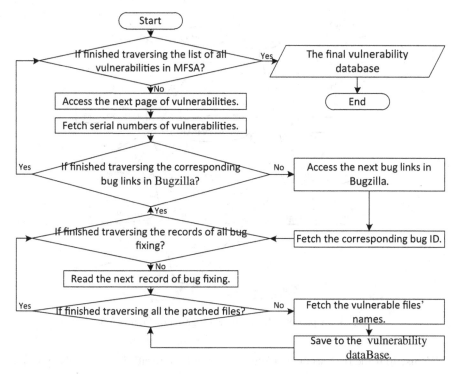

Fig. 2. Flowchart of the crawler tool

4.2 Data Collection

Doxygen is an open source tool for code analysis [33]. We develop a software network graph generation tool based on the Doxygen. We design the required functions. We analyze code structure, extract the private and static members of a component, fetch dependency information for these members, generate the network graph finally, and then compute the metric values associated with the nodes and edges based on the network graph.

Figure 3 is a part of the software network graph of Firefox 3.6, it shows the dependencies between component nsJsWinProfile and component nsWinProfile, as well as the dependencies between component nsJsWinProfile and component nsSoftware UpdateRun.

4.3 Prediction Performance Measures

To compare our results with [26], we select the five same machine learning techniques with [26] which are Bayesian Network (BN), Naïve Bayes (NB), Neural Network (NN), Random Forest (RF), and Support Vector Machine (SVM).

In our experiment, we set the threshold at 0.5. That is, a component is classified as vulnerable when its estimated probability of vulnerability is over 0.5. Otherwise, a component is classified as neutral.

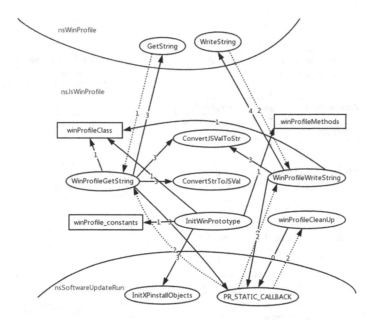

Fig. 3. A part of software network graph of Firefox 3.6

We use four metrics: accuracy (Acc), precision (Pr), recall (Re), and false positive (FP) rate to evaluate the performances of our models. For the two-class problem (vulnerable or neutral), these performance measures are explained using a confusion matrix, shown in Table 2.

Table 2. Confusion matrix

Actual	Predicted as	
	Neutral	Vulnerable
Neutral	TN = True Negative	FP = False Positives
Vulnerable	FN = False Negatives	TP = True Positives

The four prediction performance measures are defined in the following formula:

$$Acc = (TP + TN)/(TP + FP + TN + FN) \tag{1}$$

$$Pr = TP/(TP + FP) \tag{2}$$

$$FP = FP/(FP + TN) \tag{3}$$

$$Re = TP/(TP + FN) \tag{4}$$

5   Results and Discussions

5.1   Predictive Power

Before using machine learning techniques to build the VPMs, we employ the Wilcoxon rank sum test to evaluate the discriminative power of the metrics. The null hypothesis is that there is no statistically significant difference between the metric values for vulnerable components and neutral components. The results show that the measures of all seven metrics for the vulnerable components and the neutral components in Firefox 3.6 are significantly different at the 0.05 significance level.

We choose Weka [34] to implement the five machine learning techniques introduced in Sect. 4.3. The parameters in the models are initialized with the default settings. The source code of Firefox 3.6 contains 6,025 components, among which, 212 are vulnerable (less than 3.5%). Such a dataset is heavily imbalanced. We use undersampling to balance the dataset. With undersampling, all the vulnerable components in the dataset are retained, while only a subset of the neutral components is selected. The sample of neutral components is randomly chosen that the number of vulnerable components matches the number of neutral components. The dataset has 424 items, each is 50%. To some degree, undersampling provides better results than using the unbalanced data. We split the dataset into 10 folds of equal size randomly for 10×10 cross validation and use one fold for testing and the other 9 folds for training, rotating each fold as the test fold. The entire process is then repeated 10 times and the results are averaged. Table 3 shows the Acc, Pr, FP, and Re in the experiments.

Table 3. Prediction results in our experiments

Technique	Acc (%)	Pr (%)	FP (%)	Re (%)
BN	85.99	84.35	16.79	88.77
NB	85.47	84.24	16.32	87.26
NN	87.92	91.75	8.020	83.87
RF	88.73	87.80	13.11	90.57
SVM	87.03	84.56	16.60	90.66
Average	87.03	86.54	14.17	88.23

5.2   Discussion

From Table 3, we can make some conclusions as follows.

- From the experimental results, five techniques have similar performance, but NN has the best level at Pr and FP, which are over 90% and below 10% respectively. From the average value of five results, Acc, Pr, and Re are all over 85%, and FN is 14.17%. That is, among all the 424 components, 87.03% are classified correctly, and among the components classified as vulnerable, 86.54% are actual vulnerable ones. Among all the 212 vulnerable component, 88.23% can be classified correctly. Among all the normal components, 14.17% are classified falsely. These results

Table 4. Results comparison with others'

	Our results	Results of [26]
Acc	0.8703	0.8461
Pr	0.8654	0.6801
FP	0.1417	0.0870
Re	0.8823	0.5953

indicate that the proposed metrics are effective for vulnerable components prediction.

- Compared with the results of [26], there is an increase in the FP (still below 15%), but the Pr and Re are improved obviously, as shown in Table 4. Pr is increased by 27.2%, Re is increased by 48.2%, up to 50%, and Acc is also increased simultaneously. Figure 4 shows the results comparison with a histogram. We believe this is worthwhile under the circumstance of a little loss of the FP.
- A security vulnerability can cause severe damage to an organization, we think we should pay more attentions on the Recall rate, but relax FP rate within a rational scope. We believe that it is more important to identify the vulnerable components, even at the expense of incorrectly predicting some non-vulnerable components as vulnerability-prone. On the other hand, our FP rate of 14.17% is still below 15%.

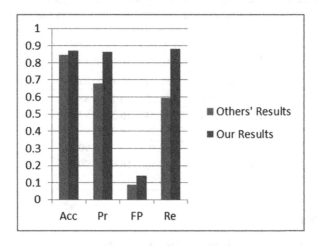

Fig. 4. Comparison of our results with others' results in [26]

5.3 Threats to Validity

We collect vulnerability data from the published security advisories, the unpublished security advisories and vulnerabilities would be missed. The assumption of the same vulnerability existing in all previous revisions is not correct complete. Therefore, the quality of vulnerability data may be impacted. However, we believe the overall comparative tendency is correct.

6   Summary and Future Work

"High Cohesion and Low Coupling" are thought as marks of high quality software, we use cohesion and coupling metrics to predict vulnerability-proneness. We define the component cohesion and coupling metrics based on a software network graph. We conduct experiments to validate the efficiency of these metrics and compare the results with other works. We discover that the proposed metrics are effective, and the accuracy, precision, and recall rate are improved according to the comparison with other works. In our future work, we will conduct more experiments targeting on more projects and make more comparison with other different works.

Acknowledgments. This work was supported by National Natural Science Foundation of China (NSFC) (Grant No. U1636115).

References

1. Liang, S., Du, X.: Permission-combination-based scheme for android mobile malware detection. In: Proceedings of the IEEE ICC 2014, Sydney, Australia (2014)
2. Du, X., Rozenblit, M., Shayman, M.: Implementation and performance analysis of SNMP on a TLS/TCP base. In: 7th IFIP/IEEE International Symposium on Integrated Network Management, Seattle, WA, pp. 453–466 (2001)
3. Xiao, Y., Chen, H., Du, X., Guizani, M.: Stream-based cipher feedback mode in wireless error channel. IEEE Trans. Wireless Commun. **8**(2), 662–666 (2009)
4. Yao, X., Han, X., Du, X., Zhou, X.: A lightweight multicast authentication mechanism for small scale IoT applications. IEEE Sens. J. **13**(10), 3693–3701 (2013)
5. Cheng, Y., Fu, X., Du, X., Luo, B., Guizani, M.: A lightweight live memory forensic approach based on hardware virtualization, vol. 379, pp. 23–41. Elsevier Information Sciences (2017)
6. Fu, X., Graham, B., Bettati, R., Zhao, W.: On countermeasures to traffic analysis attacks. In: 4th IEEE SMC Information Assurance Workshop (2003)
7. Ling, Z., Luo, J., Yu, W., Fu, X., Xuan, D., Jia, W.: A new cell counting based attack against tor. IEEE/ACM Trans. Network. (ToN) **20**(4), 1245–1261 (2012)
8. Yue, Q., Ling, Z., Fu, X., Liu, B., Ren, K., Zhao, W.: Blind recognition of touched keys on mobile devices. In: 21st ACM Conference on Computer and Communications Security, Scottsdale, Arizona, USA (2014)
9. Qian, Y., Moayeri, N.: Design of secure and application-oriented VANETs. In: Proceedings of IEEE VTC2008-Spring, Singapore (2008)
10. Zhou, J., Hu, R., Qian, Y.: Scalable distributed communication architectures to support advanced metering infrastructure in smart grid. IEEE Trans. Parallel Distrib. Syst. **23**(9), 1632–1642 (2012)
11. Wei, L., Hu, R., Qian, Y., Wu, G.: Enabling device-to-device communications underlaying cellular networks: challenges and research aspects. IEEE Commun. **52**(6), 90–96 (2014)
12. Taube-Schock, C., Walker, R.J., Witten, I.H.: Can we avoid high coupling? In: Mezini, M. (ed.) ECOOP 2011. LNCS, vol. 6813, pp. 204–228. Springer, Heidelberg (2011). doi:10. 1007/978-3-642-22655-7_10
13. Viega, J., Mcgraw, G.: Building Secure Software. Addison-Wesley, Boston (2002)

14. Morrison, P., Herzig, K., Murphy, B., Williams, L.: Challenges with applying vulnerability prediction models. In: Proceedings of the 2015 Symposium and Bootcamp on the Science of Security. ACM-Association for Computing Machinery (2015)

15. Shin, Y., Meneely, A., Williams, L., Osborne, J.A.: Evaluating complexity, code churn, and developer activity metrics as indicators of software vulnerabilities. IEEE Trans. Softw. Eng. **37**(6), 772–787 (2011)

16. Chowdhury, I., Zulkernine, M.: Using complexity, coupling, and cohesion metrics as early indicators of vulnerabilities. J. Syst. Archit. **57**(3), 294–313 (2011)

17. Zimmermann, T., Nagappan, N., Williams, L.: Searching for a needle in a haystack: predicting security vulnerabilities for windows vista. In: Software Testing, Verification and Validation (ICST), pp. 421–428. IEEE (2010)

18. Shin, Y., Williams, L.: Is complexity really the enemy of software security? In: Proceedings of the ACM Workshop Quality Protection, pp. 47–50 (2008)

19. Fenton, N., Krause, P., Neil, M.: A probabilistic model for software defect prediction. IEEE Trans. Softw. Eng. **2143**, 444–453 (2001)

20. Emam, K., Melo, W., Machado, J.C.: The prediction of faulty classes using object-oriented design metrics. J. Syst. Softw. **56**, 63–75 (2001)

21. Succi, G., Pedrycz, W., Stefanovic, M., Miller, J.: Practical assessment of the models for identification of defect-prone classes in object-oriented commercial systems using design metrics. J. Syst. Softw. **65**, 1–12 (2003)

22. Shin, Y., Williams, L.: An empirical model to predict security vulnerabilities using code complexity metrics. In: Proceedings of the International Symposium Empirical Software Engineering and Measurement, pp. 315–317 (2008)

23. Shin, Y., Williams, L.: An initial study on the use of execution complexity metrics as indicators of software vulnerabilities. In: SESS 2011, Waikiki, Honolulu, HI, USA (2011)

24. Shin, Y., Williams, L.: Can traditional fault prediction models be used for vulnerability prediction? Empir. Softw. Eng. **18**, 25–59 (2013)

25. Zimmermann, T., Nagappan, N., Williams, L.: Searching for a needle in a haystack: predicting security vulnerabilities for windows vista. In: Third International Conference on Software Testing, Verification and Validation (ICST), pp. 421–428. IEEE (2010)

26. Nguyen, V.H., Tran, L.M.S.: Predicting vulnerable software components with dependency graphs. In: MetriSec2010, Bolzano-Bozen, Italy (2010)

27. Chowdhury, I., Zulkernine, M.: Using complexity, coupling, and cohesion metrics as early indicators of vulnerabilities. J. Syst. Architect. **57**, 294–313 (2011)

28. Neuhaus S., Zimmermann T., Holler C., Zeller A.: Predicting vulnerable software components. In: CCS'07, pp. 529–540 (2007)

29. Scandariato, R., Walden, J., Hovsepyan, A., Joosen, W.: Predicting vulnerable software components via text mining. IEEE Trans. Softw. Eng. **40**(10), 993–1006 (2014)

30. Walden, J., Stuckman, J., Scandariato, R.: Predicting vulnerable components: software metrics vs text mining. In: IEEE 25th International Symposium on Software Reliability Engineering, pp. 23–33 (2014)

31. Jimenez, M., Papadakis, M., Traon, Y.L.: Vulnerability prediction models: a case study on the linux kernel. In: IEEE International Working Conference on Source Code Analysis and Manipulation (SCAM), pp. 1–10 (2016)

32. Mozilla Foundation Security Advisories. https://www.mozilla.org/en-US/security/known-vulnerabilities/. Accessed July 2017

33. Doxygen. http://www.doxygen.org. Accessed July 2017

34. WeKa. http://www.cs.waikato.ac.nz/ml/weka/. Accessed July 2017

My Smartphone Knows Your Health Data: Exploiting Android-Based Deception Attacks Against Smartbands

Jun Xie, Sha Wu, Yansong Li, Jun Guo, Wen Sun, and Jiajia Liu$^{(\boxtimes)}$

School of Cyber Engineering, Xidian University, Xi'an, China
liujiajia@xidian.edu.cn

Abstract. Although a number of vulnerabilities have been reported for smart wearables and lots of efforts have been taken to strengthen their security, wearable devices face still significant threats of privacy leakage due to their own inherent characteristics. Towards this end, we re-investigate in this paper the security concerns of smartbands. In particular, we first introduce our detailed methodology for security analysis, including log analysis, Hook technology, and Android reverse engineering. Then, we apply it to popular commercial smartbands of three different brands the concrete information of which is omitted, identify their common vulnerabilities, and develop accordingly a fake Android application (App) utilizing the identified loopholes, given the protection measures of shelling, obfuscation, as well as forcible pairing and resetting. By installing the fake App, we are able to conduct deception attacks against the targeted smartbands, succeeding to remotely activate/deactivate shaking function, to adjust/modify time (including value and format), and to obtain the smartband owner's sensitive/health data. During our deception attacks, no cooperation from the smartband owner is required, neither the pairing process between the targeted smartbands and our fake App.

Keywords: Commercial smartband · Wearable devices · Privacy leakage · Android APP

1 Introduction

Due to their own inherent characteristics, wearable devices, such as smartglasses, smartbands, etc., face significant risks of privacy leakage. In particular, first, wearable devices usually have limited computational capacity and memory. In order to guarantee the battery life or power supply time, most functions operate intermittently but not continuously, which brings up the chance of malicious attacks. Second, most wearable devices use TinyOS or LiteOS, in which the system's security policies and algorithms cannot be sufficiently complicated. Third, smart wearables interact with Android/iOS applications (Apps) or other devices through wireless communication, providing convenience for grabbing data and

© Springer International Publishing AG 2017
S. Wen et al. (Eds.): CSS 2017, LNCS 10581, pp. 291–306, 2017.
https://doi.org/10.1007/978-3-319-69471-9_22

consequently leading to security concerns. Fourth, the majority of wearable devices connect with the Internet via the smartphone Apps so as to synchronize and update data in the cloud, and any vulnerability inside may result in potential privacy unveiling.

According to the latest Cisco Visual Networking Index [2], the total number of smartphones is predicted to beyond 50% of global devices by 2021. The malware, i.e., any software used to disrupt a system, to gather sensitive information, to display unwanted advertisements or to do other abnormal actions, will inevitably become a major threat to the privacy of wearable devices among various applications in all aspects of life. As illustrated in Fig. 1, hackers usually apply reverse-engineering towards the official Apps, find out the loopholes, and develop accordingly fake Apps with functions similar to that of the official Apps, thus establishing malicious attacks. In this paper, we focus on the security concerns caused by the interaction between smartbands and smartphone Apps. Since Android is the most popular and pervasive mobile device operating system, we focus on Android platform.

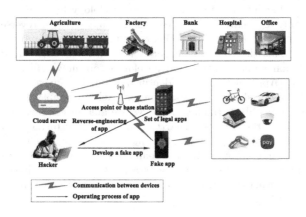

Fig. 1. Illustration of Android-based attacks.

There has been some pioneering works studying the privacy leakage of wearable devices. Embedded sensors on wearable devices can be utilized to capture the motion information of users and have the possibility of leaking their sensitive information [7,9,11]. Sensor data of smartwatches was also reported for leaking information about what the user is typing on a regular keyboard under the condition that the smartwatch is only on the left hand [14]. Later, a similar work was conducted which exploited sensors in smartwatches to infer user's highly sensitive information by devising a data training based system [6]. Wang et al. showed that the sensors embedded in wrist-worn wearable devices such as smartwatches and fitness trackers, can be utilized to discriminate mm-level distances of the user's fine-grained hand movements during key-entry activities [13]. Pan et al. showed that it is possible to recover passwords input by a Bluetooth mouse and an onscreen keyboard through capturing Bluetooth communication packets [8]. It was further reported in [10,12] that, adversaries can obtain the readings of sensors in wearable devices via sniffing Bluetooth communications and analyzing the data packets.

Given the above pioneering works and lots of efforts from the industry to further strengthen the security of smart wearables, wearable devices face still significant threats of privacy leakage due to their own inherent characteristics. Towards this end, we re-investigate in this paper the security concerns of smartbands, and present Android-based deception attacks against popular commercial smartbands of three different brands. To the best of our knowledge, the work most close to ours is [5], in which the authors proposed the fake App based attack on a commercial smartband. The major differences between our work and [5] are summarized as follows:

– First, it is noticed that one prerequisite of the attack in [5] is the successful pairing process between the attacking smartphone and the targeted smartband; while in our deception attacks no cooperation from the smartband owner is required, neither the pairing process between the targeted smartbands and our fake App. What's more, all the three different smartbands selected in our work, adopt the latest protection technology of forcible pairing and resetting, where any forcible pairing between the device and non-official app will directly result in resetting of whole smartband system. Therefore, the attacking scheme in [5] cannot be applied here.
– Another major difference is that, the attack scheme in [5] can only obtain user privacy information of the targeted smartband; while by installing our fake App, as long as the targeted smartband is located within the communication range, we are able to remotely activate/deactivate shaking function, to adjust/modify time (including value and format), in addition to obtain the smartband owner's sensitive/health data.
– Finally, our Android based deception attacks are developed after successfully identifying the common vulnerabilities of current mainstream smartbands, and can be efficiently conducted towards three different commercial smartbands, rather than one single type.

Our concrete contributions in this paper are manifold. We study security concerns of smartbands from the perspective of corresponding official Apps using methodologies including log analysis, hook technology and Android reverse engineering. Exploiting the vulnerabilities found in the App, we develop a fake App which can implement deception attacks against three different smartbands successfully (obtain user data or control the smartband). Our deception attacks need neither the cooperation of the smartband owner nor the pairing process between the smartband and the fake App.

The rest of the paper is organized as follows: Sect. 2 introduces vulnerabilities, common attacks and countermeasures of Android Apps. Section 3 describes our detailed methodology for security analysis, including log analysis, Hook technology, and Android reverse engineering. Extensive experimental results are provided in Sect. 4 and suggestion are presented in Sect. 5. Finally, we conclude the whole paper in Sect. 6.

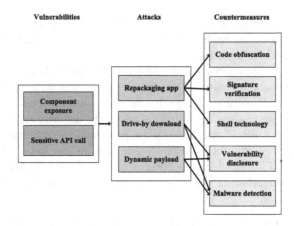

Fig. 2. Vulnerabilities, common attacks and countermeasures of Android Apps.

2 Vulnerabilities, Attacks and Countermeasures for Android Apps

(1) App Vulnerabilities

The vulnerabilities of Android Apps generally can be classified as two categories: component exposure and sensitive application program interface (API) call. Component exposure of Android Apps means that functions realized by the component can be maliciously called by attackers or injected with malicious data, thus affecting the normal operations of the application. The relaxed permission management of sensitive API call also makes it possible that the hackers can access the API and call it to facilitate malicious behaviors.

(2) App Attacks

Repackaging App: Repackaging is a process of decompiling a popular App, inserting malicious code, recompiling the App and distributing it to App markets, which accounts for the majority of Android App's hacking. By using hacking tools and techniques, repackaging attacks can be successfully implemented against mission critical Android mobile applications [15]. The repackaged App with malicious payload may send premium SMS messages stealthily, steal personal data, or purchase apps without user's awareness [1,4,16]. This kind of hacking is mainly due to the fact that Android Apps are usually written in Java language (although some have "native" C calls) and it is easy to reversely analyze the App with existing reverse-engineering tools. There are many reverse-engineering tools, such as apktool, dex2jar, etc.

Drive-by Download: Drive-by download is a kind of attack that forces users to automatically download and install malware by redirecting them to malicious URLs. A drive-by download usually exploit an App that is out of date or has a security flaw. Since the job of the downloaded code is only to contact another computer where it can pull down the rest of the code on the smartphone, it is often very small so that user probably wouldn't notice it. For example, a file sharing program might include a spyware program that tracks and reports user information for targeted marketing purposes. An associated adware program can then generate pop-up advertisements using that information.

Dynamic Payload: Malicious payload can be embedded into an App as an executable apk/jar. The App will decrypt the payload once it is installed. Usually, the embedded APK disguises as an important update so as to coax user install it.

(3) Countermeasures

Code Obfuscation: Code obfuscation techniques transform a program so that it is difficult to understand while its functionality is identical to that of the original. However, code obfuscation only increases the difficulty in reading source code, it cannot play an efficient part in defense. Code obfuscation usually can be divided into three kinds: layout obfuscation, data obfuscation and control obfuscation. Layout obfuscation alters the information unnecessary to the execution of the program, such as identifier names and comments. Data obfuscation changes the storage, the organization structure and the order of the data in a program. Control obfuscation disguises the real control flow in a program.

Signature Verification: It's necessary to sign the new APK generated from the modified bytecode file before redistributing it to the App store. When installing an APK, Android system will verify its digital signature information and check its integrity according to this. If the signature of an APK is different from the original APK, the software has been tampered. Thus, the system will stop its running.

Shell Technology: Shell protection is a kind of code encryption technology. In fact, shell technology means using special algorithms to compress the resources of the executable file. The compressed file can run independently and its decompression process is hidden completely in the memory. The shell program is executed before the execution of the original program, so it can obtain the control right and decrypt as well as restore the program. After the program being restored, the shell program will return the control right to the original program and the original code will be executed. Adding a shell to the protected software makes it difficult for the software to be cracked. Shell technology and code obfuscation mentioned above are the most popular techniques applied in anti-decompilation.

Vulnerability Disclosure: The vulnerabilities of Android Apps not only threaten the stability of the running process and security of privacy information, but also threaten the security of the whole system because of exposing the critical function. The vulnerability disclosure techniques aim to discover the potential vulnerabilities of Android App so as to restore the vulnerabilities and protect the operation of the application. According to the difference in analyzed objects, the techniques of vulnerability disclosure can be classified as source code based techniques and target code based techniques.

Malware Detection: Malware detection can find out those Apps with malicious code. Usually the malware detection techniques are divided into two kinds: static detection techniques and dynamic detection techniques. Static detection techniques analyze code without actually running it, hence their execution speeds are quick and this method is simple as well as efficient. Dynamic detection techniques monitor the executed code and inspect its interaction with the system, extracting the critical data of App operation process as characteristic. Malware detection plays an important role in the protection of Android Apps. Hu *et al.* propose a new system named MIGDroid that leverages method invocation graph based static analysis to detect repackaged Android Apps [3].

Figure 2 intuitively depicts the vulnerabilities, common attacks and corresponding countermeasures of Android Apps.

Table 1. Instructions found in the decompiled code

Instructions	Function	Returned value type	Remarks
110, 1, 15, 1, −113	Read battery power	Byte array	The 3rd digit of returned byte array multiplied by 5 is current battery power
110, 1, 21, m, d, y, h, m, s	Set date and time	0 or 1	m, d and y represent date; h, m, and s represent time
110, 1, 4, 1, −113	Read motion data	Byte array	The 12th and the 18th digit of returned byte array represent the calories burned and the step number
...	...	...	...

3   Empirical Study on Commercial Smartbands of Three Different Brands

3.1   General Protocol Stack for Smartbands

The structure of general communication protocol stack for smartbands is shown as Fig. 3. Our research concentrates on the UART Profile layer, which lay above the BLE Stack. The UART profile is realized at the smartband end. There are two kinds of characteristics in the UART Profile layer, one kind is write characteristic and another is read characteristic. Every time the smartphone wants to interact with the smartband, it first sends operation code to the receive interface of the smartband through write characteristic. If the smartband can parse the operation code, then it will execute the corresponding operations. Finally, a value will be returned to the smartphone through the read characteristic of the smartband to notify the smartphone that the operation is executed successfully or not. Since we only implement our attacks on the UART Profile layer, we can

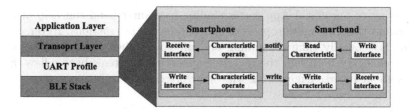

Fig. 3. Communication protocol stack of the smartband.

bypass the authentication between the smartband and the smartphone as well as the operations related to the cloud server.

3.2   Methodologies

By the description of the protocol stack of the smartband, we can know the key point of our attacks is to get the instructions (write, read, and notify instructions) of the interaction between the smartband and the smartphone. Only when specific instruction is wrote to relevant characteristic can attacker obtain the sensitive/health data contained in the smartband or control the smartband. There are three methods we use to obtain the instructions: log analysis, hook technology and Android reverse engineering.

(1) Log Analysis
Find the process of the official App installed on the smartphone using specific software tool, then dynamically get the corresponding log files through the process. By analyzing the log files, we can obtain the instructions sent from the App to the smartband and the returned results sent from the smartband to the App. Figure 4 gives the instruction we obtained through this method. However, for some smartbands, the log files of their official Apps are processed with security precautions, hence, the method fails under this situation.

(2) Hook Technology
Hook is a message processing mechanism as well as a program segment to process message. Hook mechanism allows application to capture message and to get its control rights before the message is transmitted to target address. The specific Xposed module application installed on the smartphone can monitor the instructions of the interaction between the official App and the smartband, as shown in Fig. 4. However, the instructions of some smartbands have a timestamp, namely, the instruction sent to implement the same function every time is different. So this method is not applicable to these smartbands.

(3) Android Reverse Engineering
Apply shell removal, decompilation, program understanding and other computer technologies to an executable App, then analyze the structure, flow, algorithms and code of the program, finally infer the App's source code, design principle and so on, this process is called Android reverse engineering. Applying reverse

engineering to an official App corresponding to a smartband can help attacker understand their interaction process and obtain the instructions. Reverse engineering is generally time consuming and difficult. When the log analysis and Hook technology both fail, the reverse engineering can remedy this flaw. Some details about reverse engineering will be involved in following contents.

3.3   Deception Attacks Based on Reverse Engineering

Since Android reverse engineering is complicated, it's necessary to introduce the process in detail. In the following, we first describe the overall attack idea, then the attack process is depicted, finally we illustrate the attack route.

(1) Overall Attack Procedure

- Be familiar with the interfaces, operations and functions of the official App matched with the smartband. This step provides convenience for the analysis of the decompiled code.
- Get the targeted APK and check the type and the version number of its shell by using AndroidKiller. Then remove its shell with proper program and software tools.
- Decompile the APK file whose shell has been removed and analyze the decompiled code, locating the function we want to emulate.
- Develop an App according to the parameters and instructions found in the previous step, which can read data or modify some settings of the smartband.

(2) Detailed Attacking Procedures

Figure 4 shows the process of cracking an App, of which the most challenging thing is to apply reverse engineering to the App. In the reverse engineering stage, the first step is to remove the shell from the APK file. Since we don't need to repackage the App, we can bypass the signature verification. Then we make an analysis of the code derived from the decompilation of the APK file. After reverse engineering, we develop a fake App in light of the instructions or methods found in the decompiled code. In the following, some details of the attack process are introduced.

Shell Removal: We use AndroidKiller to check the shell type of the APK, then we remove the shell manually using IDA Pro. The key idea of this procedure is to set a breakpoint on the *dvmDexFileOpenPartial()* function and dump the *.dex* file in the memory.

Decompiled Code Analysis: After the step above, we begin to analyze the logic of the code. The analyzing process is depicted in Fig. 4. First, be sure to get familiar with the interfaces of the official App and understand its functions along with operations. Second, find program entry of the project. In our experiment, the program entry is *WelcomeActivity*. Third, track the code according to the implementation of the function we interested in. Fourth, locate the targeted function and finally find out the parameters and instructions which are necessary for the function to be realized. Table 1 presents the information of instructions we found in the decompiled code and the instructions are represented by byte arrays. When the App sends an instruction to the smartband it will receive the returned value later, according to which the App can obtain the data contained in the smartband or the results indicating whether the instruction is executed successfully or not. A challenge in this process is that there are many errors in the decompiled code resulting from the security reinforcement techniques of the App. Apparently, we cannot trust the code completely and need to avoid code traps.

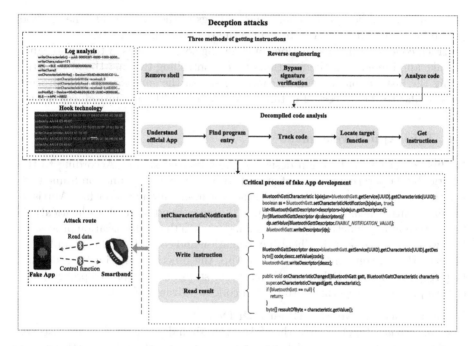

Fig. 4. Illustration of deception attacks, where the focus is the process of reverse engineering of the official App and the development of fake App. Fake App aims to read data and modify some settings of the smartband.

(3) Attack Route
Obtain Sensitive/Health Data

- Since the resource files of an APK cannot be obfuscated, we first locate the activity of data synchronization and then find the corresponding XML file according to the button icon in the resource files where the button is used to synchronize data to App. Analyze the click event triggered by the button.
- By analyzing the click event, we find that App needs to interact with cloud server so as to obtain the authentication and then connect with smartband

using the authentication. We use a counterfeit authentication scheme to address this problem.

- The usage of counterfeit authentication scheme makes us avoid the operations related to the cloud server, so we locate the *SynDataActivity.class* directly, neglecting the code about cloud.
- Analyze *SynDataActivity.class* and find out the instructions about data synchronization. The instructions are significantly important, because they are the keys to obtain the data contained in the smartband.

Control Smartband

- Locate the method of changing some settings of the smartband. The method can be applied in fake App to realize the relevant functionality.
- Track code, find the instructions of changing some settings of the smartband. Fake app implements the functionality of controlling the smartband via writing the instructions to related characteristic of the smartband. This process is similar to the process of obtaining sensitive/health data introduced above.

3.4   Fake App Development

We first describe the function design of the fake App simply. According to the function and operating process of official App, we design the function framework and the call relations among modules. Since the main function of the fake App is to obtain sensitive/health data and control the smartband without authentication, the corresponding functional module should weaken the authentication process so that we can get the sensitive/health information and control the smartband more directly. Hence, compared with official App, the functions and interfaces of the fake App are simpler. Below are the concrete steps of development process, and critical procedures together with related code are given in Fig. 4.

Step 1: Discover Nearby Bluetooth Devices
The most basic functionality this fake App should implement is to discover nearby Bluetooth devices which hasn't pair with any other Bluetooth devices and add them to the list. This step is executed when the user taps the scan button. Android system provide a *BluetoothAdapter* class, of which the *bluetoothAdapter.startLeScan(callback)* method can be used to scan peripheral Bluetooth devices. After the scanning procedure, device information will be placed in *deviceList*.

Step 2: Connect the Smartband to the Smartphone
Bluetooth connections operate like any other communicating connections. There is a server and a client, which communicate via RFCOMM sockets. On Android, RFCOMM sockets are represented as a *BluetoothSocket* object. Fortunately, most of the technical code for servers is handled by the Android SDK and available through the Bluetooth API. We obtain the RFCOMM socket from the desired *BluetoothDevice* by calling the method *createRfcommSocketToServiceRecord()*, using a 128-bit UUID which is similar to a port number.

Step 3: Open the *setCharacteristicNotification* of Related Character-istic

If the value of *BluetoothGatt.GATT_SUCCESS* is true, then use *BluetoothGATT* to set the value of related characteristic A to true in the method *onServicesDiscovered()*.

Step 4: Write the Instruction to the Related Characteristic

Write the instruction to the related characteristic B in the method *onServicesDiscovered()*, triggering the method *onCharacteristicChanged()*.

Step 5: Read the Returned Results through Characteristic

The characteristic A gives the result to the App by notification while the result is the executed result of the instruction written to characteristic B. At the same time the result is a condition whether to execute next instruction.

Fig. 5. Fake App (right) shows the same motion data as that of official App (left).

4   Experiments and Results

4.1   Tools and Environment

Our experiments setup consists of five devices, three commercial smartbands, a smartphone and a computer. In this paper, the brands of the smartbands are made anonymous and we only introduce partial parameters of their hardware. Their MCU adopts W25Q80BV, STM32L151CBU6 and nRF51822 chip respectively. The brand of the smartphone is Lenovo and its model is K30-T, besides, its Android version is 4.4.4. The computer's OS is Windows7.

The software tool of shell removal is IDA pro v6.6. In order to reverse engineer on the official APK file, we apply Android Killer v1.3.1.0 to it. Log analysis also uses Android Killer v1.3.1.0. The fake App development uses Android Studio v2.2. Table 2 shows the information about experimental tools and environment.

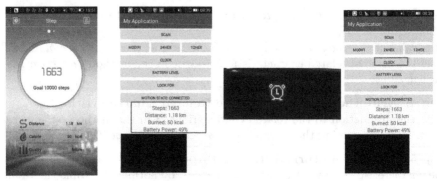

(a) Fake App (right) shows the same motion(b) Fake App (right) can set an alarm for
data as official App (left).   the smartband.

Fig. 6. Fake App (right) shows the same motion data as official App (left) does and
can set an alarm for the smartband.

Table 2. Experimental tools and environments

Experiment equipments or software tools	Model or configuration
Smartband 1	MCU: W25Q80BV
Smartband 2	MCU: STM32L151CBU6
Smartband 3	MCU: nRF51822
Smartphone	Lenovo K30-T, Android 4.4.4
Computer	Windows7
IDA pro	v6.6
Android Killer	v1.3.1.0
Android Studio	v2.2

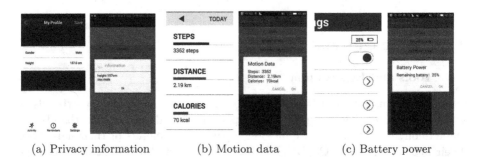

(a) Privacy information   (b) Motion data   (c) Battery power

Fig. 7. Fake App (right) shows the same privacy information, motion data and battery
power as official App (left).

4.2   Experimental Results

We adopt log analysis to conduct research on the first smartband. According to the instructions we find, we can obtain the motion data of user from the smartband. The results are shown in Fig. 5.

For the second smartband, we use Hook technology to find its instructions. Figure 6a shows that the fake App can get motion data (step number, distance,

(a) Fake App synchronizes the local time of the smartphone to the smartband.

(b) Fake App sets an alarm for the smartband.

Fig. 8. Fake App synchronizes the local time of the smartphone to the smartband and sets an alarm for the smartband.

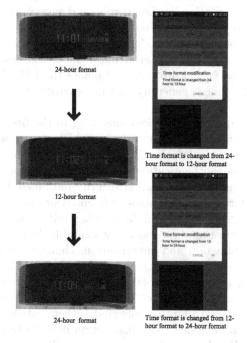

Fig. 9. The time format of the smartband changes between 12-hour format and 24-hour format.

calories burned) contained in the smartband and Fig. 6b shows that fake App can set an alarm for the smartband. Besides, the fake App can shake the smartband so as to realize search function. Unfortunately, the search function can not be shown in figures.

We apply reverse engineering to the third smartband. From Fig. 7 we can see that the fake App obtains the same data from the smartband as the official App does. Figure 7a, b and c respectively show that the fake App can get the privacy information (gender and height) of user, motion data (step number, distance, calories burned) and battery power from the smartband. Figure 8a shows that the fake App can synchronize the local time of the smartphone to the smartband and Fig. 8b shows that the fake App can set an alarm for the smartband. Figure 9 shows that the fake App can change the time format of the smartband between 12-hour format and 24-hour format.

Our attacks work on the smartbands effectively. The deception attacks in this paper result from the vulnerability that the smartband and smartphone do not authenticate each other at every connection time, so that the smartband cannot differentiate legal user's smartphone from hacker's one.

5   Suggestions

Bluetooth protocol has three security modes. First mode, Bluetooth devices communicate without any security mechanisms. Second mode, devices perform the operations of authorization, authentication and encryption after the L2CAP communication link is established. This mode generally improves security issues in the high-layer protocols. Third mode, devices need to perform link-layer security mechanism before communication, namely, the operations of authorization, authentication and encryption are executed before the L2CAP communication link is established. This mode generally provides security guarantee in the underlying protocols.

Some companies allow their devices operating in the first mode, inevitably leading to information leakage. Currently many Bluetooth devices operate in the second mode, however, information leakage will also happens due to the imperfect authorization, authentication and encryption mechanisms of high-layer protocols. The third mode has the highest security but raises the costs of devices, hence it is suitable for high-end or high-confidential products.

We give some suggestions to avoid data leakage with emphasis on the second mode. The key to preventing data leakage of wearable devices is to enhance the authorization, authentication and encryption mechanisms of high-layer protocols. For encryption mechanism, companies can design ultra-lightweight encryption algorithms applicable for wearable devices based on the widely used encryption algorithm SMS4 in the Internet of Things. Due to the hardware limitation of wearables, its impossible to adopt complicated authentication mechanism. However, a timestamp can be added to an instruction in order to make the instruction vary with time. Besides, an instruction counter (IC) can be added to device and a property that records the execution order can be added to instruction.

Only if the property value is equal to the value of IC plus one does the device execute the instruction. Timestamp and IC can accomplish the authentication of user identity, because the instructions captured by illegal user will make a big difference owing to different time and operating sequence.

The security of authorization, authentication and encryption mechanism is also of great importance. Software developers can use commercial security reinforcement tools to reinforce their official App, and pay attention to upgrading the security reinforcement tools in time. At the same time, code obfuscation can be used to obfuscate the source code and signature verification can be used to prevent malicious code injection.

6   Conclusions

In this paper, we have investigated the vulnerabilities of three popular brands of commercial smartbands. A general methodology for security analysis was presented with special emphasis on Android reverse engineering, for which detailed procedures were provided. Based on the identified common loopholes, a fake Android App was developed to successfully conduct deception attacks against the targeted three smartbands. Extensive experiments have been conducted and the results corroborated that our fake App is able to obtain the sensitive/health data of the smartband owner as well as to remotely activate/deactivate some key functions of smartband.

References

1. Chen, K., Wang, P., Lee, Y., Wang, X., Zhang, N., Huang, H., Zou, W., Liu, P.: Finding unknown malice in 10 seconds: mass vetting for new threats at the google-play scale. In: USENIX Security, pp. 659–674 (2015)
2. Cisco: Cisco Visual Networking Index: Global Mobile Data Traffic Forecast Update, 2016–2021 White Paper (2017)
3. Hu, W., Tao, J., Ma, X., Zhou, W., Zhao, S., Han, T.: MIGDroid: detecting app-repackaging android malware via method invocation graph. In: IEEE International Conference on Computer Communication and Networks (ICCCN), pp. 1–7 (2014)
4. Huang, H., Zhu, S., Liu, P., Wu, D.: A framework for evaluating mobile app repackaging detection algorithms. In: Huth, M., Asokan, N., Čapkun, S., Flechais, I., Coles-Kemp, L. (eds.) Trust 2013. LNCS, vol. 7904, pp. 169–186. Springer, Heidelberg (2013). doi:10.1007/978-3-642-38908-5_13
5. Lee, M., Lee, K., Shim, J., Cho, S., Choi, J.: Security threat on wearable services: empirical study using a commercial smartband. In: IEEE International Conference on Consumer Electronics-Asia (ICCE-Asia), pp. 1–5 (2016)
6. Liu, X., Zhou, Z., Diao, W., Li, Z., Zhang, K.: When good becomes evil: keystore inference with smartwatch. In: ACM CCS, pp. 1273–1285 (2015)
7. Miluzzo, E., Varshavsky, A., Balakrishnan, S., Choudhury, R.R.: Tapprints: your finger taps have fingerprints. In: ACM MobiSys, pp. 323–336 (2012)
8. Pan, X., Ling, Z., Pingley, A., Yu, W., Zhang, N., Fu, X.: How privacy leaks from bluetooth mouse? In: ACM CCS, pp. 1013–1015 (2012)

9. Ren, Y., Chen, Y., Chuah, M.C., Yang, J.: User verification leveraging gait recognition for smartphone enabled mobile healthcare systems. IEEE Trans. Mobile Comput. **14**(9), 1961–1974 (2014)

10. Ryan, M.: Bluetooth: with low energy comes low security. In: USENIX WOOT, p. 4 (2013)

11. Sherman, M., Clark, G., Yang, Y., Sugrim, S., Modig, A., Lindqvist, J., Oulasvirta, A., Roos, T.: User-generated free-form gestures for authentication: security and memorability. In: ACM Mobisys, pp. 176–189 (2014)

12. Spill, D., Bittau, A.: Bluesniff: eve meets alice and bluetooth. In: USENIX WOOT, pp. 1–10 (2007)

13. Wang, C., Guo, X., Wang, Y., Chen, Y., Liu, B.: Friend or foe? Your wearable devices reveal your personal PIN. In: ACM ASIA CCS, pp. 189–200 (2016)

14. Wang, H., Lai, T.T.T., Choudhury, R.R.: Mole: motion leaks through smartwatch sensors. In: ACM MobiCom, pp. 155–166 (2015)

15. Zheng, X., Pan, L., Yilmaz, E.: Security analysis of modern mission critical android mobile applications. In: ACM ACSW (2017)

16. Zhou, W., Zhou, Y., Jiang, X., Ning, P.: Detecting repackaged smartphone applications in third-party android marketplaces. In: ACM CODASPY, pp. 317–326 (2012)

A Novel Image Encryption Scheme Using Josephus Permutation and Image Filtering

Binxuan Xu, Zhongyun Hua, and Hejiao Huang[(✉)]

School of Computer Science and Technology, Harbin Institute of Technology
Shenzhen Graduate School, Shenzhen 518055, China
huanghejiao@hit.edu.cn

Abstract. To efficiently protect digital images, this paper proposes a novel image encryption scheme using the concepts of Josephus permutation and image filtering. It adopts the well-known architecture of confusion and diffusion. The Josephus permutation is designed to achieve the confusion property by fast separating adjacent pixels into different rows and columns, while the image filtering is to obtain the diffusion property by spreading tiny change in plain-image to the whole cipher-image. Simulation results demonstrate that the proposed image encryption scheme can encrypt different kinds of images into noise-like cipher-images. Security analysis shows that it has high security level and can outperform several other image encryption schemes.

Keywords: Image encryption · Image filtering · Josephus permutation · Security analysis

1 Introduction

Nowadays, more and more digital data are produced by various digital devices and transmitted through all kinds of networks. A large portion of these digital data is represented by image format, because image can display information in a visualized way. Thus, image security attracts increasing attentions [1–3]. Among all kinds of image security technologies, image encryption is an efficient way that transforms digital images into unrecognized formats. Only with the correct key, can one recover the original image information [4–6].

One strategy of encrypting images is to treat digital images as data sequences, and then encrypt them using traditional data encryption technologies, such as the Advanced Encryption Standard (AES) [7]. However, every pixel of digital images may be represented by 8 or more bits. Treating image as data sequence can't sufficiently utilize the property of image pixel, and thus may result in low encryption efficiency. To address this problem, many image encryption algorithms considering image properties have been developed [4,8]. Among all these image encryption technologies, the chaos-based encryption is one of the most popular technologies, because chaotic systems have many inner properties that are similar with encryption. In [9], Zhou *et al.* developed a novel image encryption using the combination of chaotic systems. In [10], an image encryption

© Springer International Publishing AG 2017
S. Wen et al. (Eds.): CSS 2017, LNCS 10581, pp. 307–319, 2017.
https://doi.org/10.1007/978-3-319-69471-9_23

algorithm using a two-dimensional chaotic system was designed. For these chaos-based image encryption algorithms, their security performance are highly dependent on the chaos performance of the used chaotic systems. Because chaotic systems have unstable properties when implemented in digital platforms, their developed image encryption algorithms can't obtain stable high security [11,12]. Thus, it is desirable to develop image encryption schemes with high security levels using other technologies.

This paper proposes a new image encryption scheme using Josephus permutation and image filtering. It strictly follows the structure of confusion and diffusion. The Josephus permutation, derived from the theory of Josephus problem [13], can achieve the confusion property by first selecting a set of pixels in image, and then shuffling these pixels into different rows and columns. With a random mask generated from secure key, the image filtering can randomly change a pixel value using its adjacent pixels, and thus can obtain confusion property. After two rounds of Josephus permutation and image filtering, a natural image can be encrypted into a random-like one. Simulation results prove the efficiency of the proposed encryption scheme in encrypting different images. Security analysis demonstrates that it can protect digital images with high security levels.

The rest of this paper is organized as follows. Section 2 presents the proposed image encryption scheme. Section 3 simulates it using different kinds of images and discusses its properties. Section 4 analyzes its security from different aspects and Sect. 5 concludes this paper.

2   Proposed Encryption Scheme

This section introduces the proposed image encryption scheme. Its structure is shown in Fig. 1. As can be seen, the secure key is to generate parameters for the Josephus permutation and image filtering. The Josephus permutation, derived from the well-known Josephus problem [13], is to randomly separate image pixels to different rows and columns, while the image filtering is used to randomly change image pixel values. After two rounds of Josephus permutation and image filtering, a meaningful image can be encrypted as a random-like cipher-image. The rest of this section will present each of these operations in detail.

2.1   Parameter Generation

The secure key $\mathbf{K}$ is of length 256 bits and it consists of four parts, $\mathbf{K} = \{\mathbf{f}_1, \mathbf{f}_2, \mathbf{s}_1, \mathbf{s}_2\}$. Among the four parts, $\mathbf{f}_1$ and $\mathbf{f}_2$ are original initial components, while $\mathbf{s}_1$ and $\mathbf{s}_2$ are distribution parameters to enlarge the key space. Each of them is of length 64 bits. The two sub-keys, $\mathbf{k}_1$ and $\mathbf{k}_2$ for the two encryption rounds can be generated by the equations

$$\mathbf{k}_i = \mathbf{f}_i \oplus \mathbf{s}_i, \tag{1}$$

where $i \in \{1, 2\}$. The sub-key also has the length of 64 bits and it generates parameters for the Josephus permutation and image filtering.

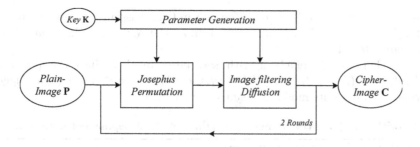

Fig. 1. Structure of the proposed image encryption scheme.

2.2   Josephus Permutation

As high adjacent correlations may exist in natural images, an image encryption scheme should have the ability to decorrelate these correlations. To achieve this property, We designed a Josephus permutation in our encryption scheme according to the Josephus problem [13]. It can randomly select pixels from an image and permutate them to different rows and columns.

Suppose the image to be encrypted is of size $M \times N$, a set of parameters is first generated using the 64-bit sub-key $\mathbf{k}$,

$$
\begin{aligned}
MP &= (\text{bi2de}(\mathbf{k}(1:8)) \mod M) + 1 \\
NP &= (\text{bi2de}(\mathbf{k}(9:16)) \mod N) + 1 \\
CP &= (\text{bi2de}(\mathbf{k}(25:32)) \mod N) + 1 \\
MStep &= \text{bi2de}(\mathbf{k}(17:20) + 1 \\
NStep &= \text{bi2de}(\mathbf{k}(21:24) + 1 \\
CStep &= \text{bi2de}(\mathbf{k}(33:36) + 1
\end{aligned}
\tag{2}
$$

where $[MP, NP]$ is the initial pixel position, $MStep$ is the row skipped step and $NStep$ is the column skipped step, CP denotes the column position that the first selected pixel will move to, and $CStep$ is the skipped step of CP. The whole procedure of the Josephus permutation can be described as follows,

Step 1: Initialize an M-dimensional vector $\mathbf{A}$ and two N-dimensional vectors $\mathbf{B}$ and $\mathbf{C}$, and assign $\mathbf{A}(i) = i$, $\mathbf{B}(j) = \mathbf{C}(j) = j$;

Step 2: A set of N pixels is selected as follows: (1) set MP as their row positions, remove MP from $\mathbf{A}$, cyclic skip $MStep$ in $\mathbf{A}$, and assign the next number to MP; (2) set the column position of first pixel as NP, and remove NP from $\mathbf{B}$; (3) starting from the previously removed number, cyclic skip $NStep$ cells in $\mathbf{B}$ and assign the next number to the column position of second pixel; (4) repeat the operation (3) until all the column positions of N pixels are determined; (5) assign the last selected column position to NP;

Step 3: Repeat *Step 2* until M sets of N pixels are recorded;

Step 4: Initialize an N-dimensional vector $\mathbf{CI}$ and assign it as follows: (1) set $\mathbf{CI}(1) = CP$ and remove CP from $\mathbf{C}$; (2) starting from the previously removed number, cyclic skip $CStep$ cells in $\mathbf{C}$ and assign the next number to $\mathbf{CI}(2)$; (3) repeat the operation (2) until all the N numbers in $\mathbf{C}$ have been assigned to $\mathbf{CI}$;

Step 5: For the N pixels in i-th set, permute them into the positions $\{(i, \mathbf{CI}(1)), (i+1, \mathbf{CI}(2)), \cdots, (i+N, \mathbf{CI}(N))\}$. Note that if $i+j$ is bigger than M, we use its modulus result to M instead.

Algorithm 1 shows the detailed procedure of the Josephus permutation.

Algorithm 1. Josephus permutation

Input: The plain-image $\mathbf{P}$ with size of $M \times N$, parameters $MP, NP, CP, MStep, NStep$, and $CStep$ calculated by Eq. (2).

Output: The permutation result $\mathbf{I}$.

1: $\mathbf{A}$=1:M; $\mathbf{B}$=1:N; $\mathbf{C}$=1:N;
2: Set $\mathbf{CI} \in \mathbb{N}^{1 \times N}$, $NP\_new = NP$.
3: **for** $k = 1$ to N **do**
4:     $\mathbf{CI}(k) = \mathbf{C}(CP)$;
5:     $\mathbf{C}(CP) = [\,]$;
6:     $CP = ((CP - 2 + CStep) \mod (N - k)) + 1$;
7:     $CStep = CStep + 1$;
8: **end for**
9: **for** $i = 1$ to M **do**
10:     $row = \mathbf{A}(MP)$;
11:     $\mathbf{A}(MP) = [\,]$;
12:     $NP = NP\_new$;
13:     $\mathbf{B} = 1 : N$;
14:     **for** $j = 1$ to N **do**
15:         $column = \mathbf{B}(NP)$;
16:         $\mathbf{I}(((i+j-2) \mod M) + 1, CI(j)) =$
17:         $\mathbf{P}(row, column)$;
18:         $NP\_new = \mathbf{B}(NP)$;
19:         $\mathbf{B}(NP) = [\,]$;
20:         $NP = (NP - 2 + NStep) \mod (N - j) + 1$;
21:         $NStep = NStep + 1$;
22:     **end for**
23:     $MP = (MP - 2 + MStep) \mod (M - i) + 1$;
24:     $MStep = MStep + 1$;
25: **end for**

2.3 Image Filtering

An image encryption algorithm should have the diffusion property, which means that slight change in plain-image can cause the change of all the pixels in cipher-image. To obtain this property, we use the concept of image filtering to randomly change pixel values in our image encryption algorithm. The image filtering is widely used in image processing, such as image denoising and edge detection. It does convolution operation using a mask with adjacent pixels. By this way, the current pixel can be affected by its adjacent pixels.

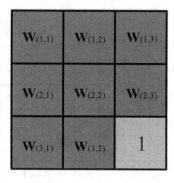

Fig. 2. The mask of image filtering.

Figure 2 shows an example of the mask **W** used in our experiment. As can be seen, it is of size 3×3 and its lower right position $\mathbf{W}(3,3)$ corresponds to the current pixel. To recover the current pixel value, the weight coefficient $\mathbf{W}(3,3)$ is set as one and other weight coefficients are integers determined by the sub-key **k**, which is defined as

$$WV(i) = \text{bi2de}(\mathbf{k}_i((8i - 7) : 8i))$$
$$[WS, IX] = \text{sort}(WV)$$
$$w_i = WV(i) + \text{find}(IX == i)$$

Using the mask presented in Fig. 2, we can perform the image filtering to the permutation result. First, initialize the result **C** using the permutation result. Then, update the pixel value of **C** using the following equation,

$$\mathbf{C}(x,y) = \sum_{i,j \in \{1,2,3\}} \mathbf{W}(i,j)\mathbf{C}(x - i + 1, y - j + 1) \quad \text{mod} \quad F, \qquad (3)$$

where F is number of allowed pixel value in the original image, e.g. $F = 256$ if every pixel is represented by 8 bits.

Using the same mask **W**, the inverse filtering operation in the decryption process is defined as

$$\mathbf{C}(x,y) = (\mathbf{C}(x,y) -$$
$$\sum_{i,j \in \{1,2,3\} \cap i,j \neq (1,1)} \mathbf{W}(i,j)\mathbf{C}(x - i + 1, y - j + 1)) \quad \text{mod} \quad F \qquad (4)$$

Note that the operation order in the decryption process is opposite to that in the encryption process.

For these border pixels in the left two columns and top two rows, they don't have or have insufficient left and top adjacent pixels. To address this problem, when processing these border pixels, we use the right and bottom pixels to extend the images, which is demonstrated as Fig. 3. It is noticed that this won't enlarge the size of encrypted image, because we don't need to store these extended pixels.

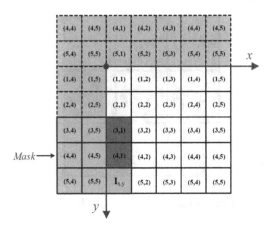

Fig. 3. Demonstration of extending image.

After two rounds of Josephus permutation and image filtering, a plain-image can be encrypted into cipher-image with high security level.

3 Simulations Results

This section simulates the proposed image encryption scheme in software environment. The test images are selected from USC-SIPI[1] and CVonline[2] image databases.

3.1 Simulation Results

An universal image encryption algorithm should have the ability to process different kinds of images. Figure 4 shows the simulation results of the proposed image encryption scheme for binary, grayscale and color images. As can be seen that the proposed encryption scheme can encrypt these digital images into noise-like images with uniform distribution. One can't obtain any information about the original images from the visual effects or from their pixel distributions. Using the corresponding key, the decryption process can completely recover the original images.

3.2 Discussion

As the architecture of confusion and diffusion is followed, the used Josephus permutation has high efficiency of separating pixels and the image filtering can randomly change pixel values, the proposed image encryption scheme can achieve

---

[1] http://sipi.usc.edu/database/.
[2] http://homepages.inf.ed.ac.uk/rbf/CVonline/Imagedbase.htm.

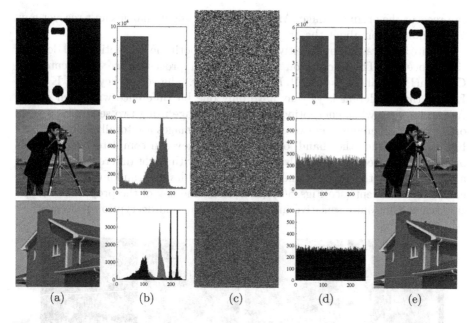

Fig. 4. Simulation results of the proposed image encryption scheme. (a) The plain-images of the binary, grayscale and color images; (b) histograms of (a); (c) encrypted results of (a); (d) histograms of (c); (e) decrypted results of (c).

the following advantages. (1) It can achieve the confusion and diffusion properties. (2) It can resist many commonly used security attacks, such as the brute-force attack, differential attack; This will be verified by experimental results in Sect. 4; (3) It has high encryption speed, because only two encryption rounds are performed and the Josephus permutation has a linear computation complexity.

4   Security Analysis

A high efficient image encryption algorithm should have high security level. That is to say, its encrypted cipher-images are expected to resist the commonly used security attacks. The proposed image encryption scheme has strong ability of resisting these attacks. This section analyzes the security performance of the proposed scheme and compares it with schemes in [14] and [15].

4.1   Key Sensitivity

First of all, an encryption algorithm should have secure key. The key security includes two parts. First, the length of key should be large enough to resist brute-force attack. Our encryption scheme has the secure key with length of 256 bits, which has a proper length of resisting brute-force attack. Besides, the secure key should be extremely sensitive, which means that only the correct key can recover the original image. Another key with slight change can't recover any useful information about the original image.

Figure 5 shows the key sensitivity analysis in both the encryption and decryption processes. The encryption and decryption processes are represented as $C = En(P, K)$ and $C = En(P, K)$, respectively. The secure keys K_1, K_2 and K_3 are three different keys that have only one bit difference with each other. As can be seen, when encrypting an identical image using two secure keys with only one bit difference, the two obtained cipher-images are totally different (see Fig. 5(d)). On the other hand, only the correct key can completely recover the original image (see Fig. 5(e)). Using secure keys with slight difference to decrypt a cipher-image, the two obtained decrypted results are random-like, and also completely different (see Figs. 5(f)–(h)). Thus, the key of the proposed encryption scheme are quite sensitive in both encryption and decryption processes.

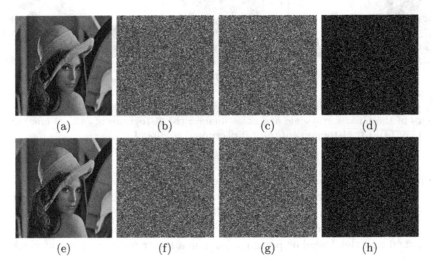

Fig. 5. Key sensitivity analysis. (a) Plain-image P; (b) cipher-image $C_1 = En(P, K_1)$; (c) cipher-image $C_2 = En(P, K_2)$; (d) the difference between C_1 and C_2, $|C_1 - C_2|$; (e) decrypted image $D_1 = De(C_1, K_1)$; (f) decrypted image $D_2 = De(C_1, K_2)$; (g) decrypted image $D_3 = De(C_1, K_3)$; (f) the difference between D_2 and D_3, $|D_2 - D_3|$.

4.2   Local Shannon Entropy

To resist statistic attack, an ideal cipher-image is expected to have uniform distribution. The local Shannon entropy is designed to test the randomness of a block data from local view and it can provide a quantitative description to the randomness of cipher-image [16]. Mathematically, the calculation procedure of local Shannon entropy is defined as

$$\overline{H_{k,T_B}} = \sum_{i=1}^{k} \frac{H(S_i)}{k}, \tag{5}$$

where k is the number of image block, T_B denotes the number of pixels in each image block, $S_1 \sim S_k$ indicates the randomly selected image blocks and $H(S_i)$ is S_i's information entropy, which is defined as

$$H(S_i) = -\sum_{j=1}^{L} Pr(s_j) \log_2 Pr(s_j),\qquad(6)$$

where L is the number of allowed values and s_j represents the j-th possible pixel value in image block S_i, and $Pr(s_j)$ is the probability of s_j.

Table 1. Local Shannon entropy values of several image encryption schemes. $\alpha = 0.05$, $k = 30$, $T_B = 1936$.

File name	Ref. [14]	Ref. [15]	Proposed
6.1.01	7.90153079	7.90625727	7.90212377
6.1.02	7.90302019	7.89802040	7.90253124
6.1.03	7.90157342	7.90364200	7.90264621
6.1.04	7.90393573	7.90203689	7.90220704
motion01.512	7.90397726	7.89959521	7.90219051
motion02.512	7.90304833	7.90257791	7.90270603
motion03.512	7.90241218	7.90466502	7.90243374
motion04.512	7.90339060	7.89972857	7.90230303
5.3.01	7.90085003	7.89893143	7.90232586
5.3.02	7.90465776	7.89797578	7.90279932
Pass rate	2/10	2/10	10/10

According to the recommendation in [16], our experiments set the significance level $\alpha = 0.5$, $k = 30$, and $T_B = 1936$. Then the local Shannon entropy is expected to fall into the interval $(h^*_{left}, h^*_{right}) = (7.901901305, 7.903037329)$ to pass the test for 8-bit grayscale image. Table 1 lists the local Shannon result of cipher-images generated by different image encryption schemes. As one can see that all the ten cipher-images generated by our proposed image encryption scheme can pass the local Shannon entropy. On the other hand, not all the cipher-images generated by [14] and [15] can pass the test. As a consequence, our proposed image encryption algorithm can generate cipher-images with high randomness.

4.3   Differential Attack

The differential attack is a widely used and efficient security attack. By observing how the difference in plaintext affects the change in ciphertexts, it aims to build the relationship between plaintext and ciphertext, and uses the built relationship to recover the original information without secure key. The success of differential attack can even totally recover the original data. Worse yet, it can recover the secure key or equivalent key. An encryption algorithm with diffusion property can efficiently resist the differential attack. The diffusion property means that little change in plaintext can spread to the whole ciphertext. Figure 6 demonstrates the visualized effect of diffusion property of our image encryption algorithm. When using the same secure key to encrypt two plain-images with only one bit difference, the two obtained cipher-images are totally different and their difference can be seen in Fig. 6(f). This means that the proposed encryption scheme has good diffusion property.

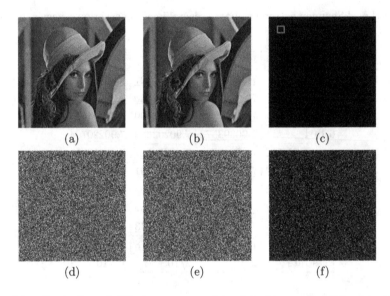

Fig. 6. Visualized effect of diffusion property. (a) original image P_1; (b) original image P_2, which has one bit difference with P_1; (c) difference between P_1 and P_2, $|P_1 - P_2|$; (d) encrypted image $C_1 = En(P_1, K_1)$; (e) encrypted image $C_2 = En(P_2, K_1)$; (f) difference between C_1 and C_2, $|C_1 - C_2|$.

The number of pixel change rate (NPCR) and unified averaged changed intensity (UACI) can provide a quantitative description about the ability of resisting differential attack. Suppose C_1 and C_2 are two cipher-images encrypted from two plain-images with only one bit difference, the NPCR between C_1 and C_2 can be defined as

$$NPCR(C_1, C_2) = \sum_{i=1}^{M} \sum_{j=1}^{N} \frac{D(i,j)}{G} \times 100\%, \tag{7}$$

where M, N are the height and width of the images, respectively, G denotes the total number pixels in an image, and D represents the difference between C_1 and C_2 and can be obtained by

$$\mathbf{D}(i,j) = \begin{cases} 0, & \text{if } \mathbf{C}_1(i,j) = \mathbf{C}_2(i,j), \\ 1, & \text{if } \mathbf{C}_1(i,j) \neq \mathbf{C}_2(i,j). \end{cases}$$

The UACI is mathematically defined as

$$UACI(\mathbf{C}_1, \mathbf{C}_2) = \sum_{i=1}^{M} \sum_{j=1}^{N} \frac{|\mathbf{C}_1(i,j) - \mathbf{C}_2(i,j)|}{T \times G} \times 100\%,$$

where T is the largest allowed pixel value.

Recently, strict critical values were developed in [17]. Firstly, an interval $(\mathcal{U}_\alpha^{*-}, \mathcal{U}_\alpha^{*+})$ for NPCR and a threshold $\mathcal{N}_\alpha^*$ for UACI were calculated, where α is the significance level. The obtained NPCR value falls into $(\mathcal{U}_\alpha^{*-}, \mathcal{U}_\alpha^{*+})$ and the UACI value is bigger than $\mathcal{N}_\alpha^*$ are considered to pass the corresponding test. According to the setting in [17], our experiments set $\alpha = 0.05$. Then for size of 256×256, $\mathcal{N}_\alpha^* = 99.5693\%$ and $(\mathcal{U}_\alpha^{*-}, \mathcal{U}_\alpha^{*+}) = (33.2824\%, 33.6447\%)$. For the size of 512×512, $\mathcal{N}_\alpha^* = 99.5893\%$ and $(\mathcal{U}_\alpha^{*-}, \mathcal{U}_\alpha^{*+}) = (33.3730\%, 33.5541\%)$. For the size of 1024×1024, $\mathcal{N}_\alpha^* = 99.5994\%$ and $(\mathcal{U}_\alpha^{*-}, \mathcal{U}_\alpha^{*+}) = (33.4183\%, 33.5088\%)$.

Table 2. NPCR results of several image encryption schemes with different images.

File name	Ref. [14]	Ref. [15]	Proposed
6.1.01	97.6165%	99.6051%	99.6322%
6.1.02	98.6066%	99.6087%	99.6017%
6.1.03	93.6384%	99.6065%	99.6002%
6.1.04	93.6402%	99.6057%	99.6200%
motion01.512	95.6271%	99.6091%	99.6181%
motion02.512	95.6280%	99.6085%	99.5922%
motion03.512	85.6641%	99.6114%	99.6017%
motion04.512	91.6419%	99.6099%	99.6192%
5.3.01	91.6390%	99.6083%	99.6109%
5.3.02	95.6293%	99.5809%	99.6171%
Pass rate	0/10	10/10	10/10

Tables 2 and 3 list the NPCR and UACI results of several image encryption schemes with different sizes of images. One can see that the image encryption in [14] can't pass most of the test images for both the NPCR and UACI tests, and the scheme in [15] fails one test in the UACI test. On the other hand, our proposed scheme can pass all the tests in both NPCR and UACI. As a result, our proposed image encryption scheme can achieve a strong ability of resisting differential attack.

Table 3. UACI results of several image encryption schemes with different images.

File name	Ref. [14]	Ref. [15]	Proposed
6.1.01	32.8546%	33.4473%	33.4799%
6.1.02	33.4571%	33.4697%	33.5830%
6.1.03	31.4938%	33.4356%	33.5983%
6.1.04	31.5274%	33.4731%	33.4297%
motion01.512	32.1218%	33.4901%	33.4531%
motion02.512	32.1020%	33.4684%	33.4457%
motion03.512	28.7945%	33.4603%	33.5269%
motion04.512	30.7904%	33.4740%	33.4532%
5.3.01	30.7987%	33.4460%	33.4941%
5.3.02	32.1332%	33.4104%	33.4768%
Pass rate	1/10	9/10	10/10

5   Conclusion

This paper introduced a new image encryption scheme according to Josephus permutation and image filtering. The Josephus permutation can break the high correlations between adjacent pixels by fast shuffling image pixels into different rows and columns. The image filtering using a random mask can efficiently spread the slight change of plain-image to the whole pixels of cipher-images. We provided the simulation results of the proposed image encryption scheme using different images. The security analysis was performed from the security key analysis, local Shannon entropy and differential attack analysis. The results show that, compared with several other image encryption schemes, the proposed scheme can encrypt images into cipher-images with higher security levels.

Acknowledgement. This work was financially supported by National Natural Science Foundation of China with Grant No. 61701137, No. 11371004 and No. 61672195, National Key Research and Development Program of China with Grant No. 2016YFB0800804 and No. 2017YFB0803002, and Shenzhen Science and Technology Plan with Grant No. JCYJ20170307150704051, No. JCYJ20160318094336513, No. JCYJ20160318094101317 and No. KQCX20150326141251370.

References

1. Jain, Y., Bansal, R., Sharma, G., Kumar, B., Gupta, S.: Image encryption schemes: a complete survey. Int. J. Sig. Process. Image Process. Patt. Recogn. 9(7), 157–192 (2016)
2. Zhang, L.Y., Liu, Y., Pareschi, F., Zhang, Y., Wong, K.W., Rovatti, R., Setti, G.: On the security of a class of diffusion mechanisms for image encryption. IEEE Trans. Cybern. **PP**, 1–13 (2017)

3. Hua, Z., Wang, Y., Zhou, Y.: Image cipher using a new interactive two-dimensional chaotic map. In: 2015 IEEE International Conference on Systems, Man, and Cybernetics (SMC), pp. 1804–1808. IEEE (2015)
4. Chai, X., Chen, Y., Broyde, L.: A novel chaos-based image encryption algorithm using DNA sequence operations. Opt. Lasers Eng. **88**, 197–213 (2017)
5. Hua, Z., Zhou, Y.: Design of image cipher using block-based scrambling and image filtering. Inf. Sci. **396**, 97–113 (2017)
6. Chen, J., Zhu, Z.L., Zhang, L.B., Zhang, Y., Yang, B.Q.: Exploiting self-adaptive permutation-diffusion and dna random encoding for secure and efficient image encryption. Sig. Process. **142**, 340–353 (2018)
7. FIPS PUB 197: Advanced encryption standard (AES) (2001)
8. Ye, G., Huang, X.: An efficient symmetric image encryption algorithm based on an intertwining logistic map. Neurocomputing **251**, 45–53 (2017)
9. Zhou, Y., Bao, L., Chen, C.P.: A new 1D chaotic system for image encryption. Sig. Process. **97**, 172–182 (2014)
10. Hua, Z., Zhou, Y.: Image encryption using 2D Logistic-adjusted-Sine map. Inf. Sci. **339**, 237–253 (2016)
11. Arroyo, D., Rhouma, R., Alvarez, G., Li, S., Fernandez, V.: On the security of a new image encryption scheme based on chaotic map lattices. Chaos Interdisc. J. Nonlinear Sci. **18**(3), 033112 (2008)
12. Ping, P., Xu, F., Wang, Z.J.: Image encryption based on non-affine and balanced cellular automata. Sig. Process. **105**, 419–429 (2014)
13. Halbeisen, L., Hungerbühler, N.: The josephus problem. J. de théorie des nombres de Bordeaux **9**(2), 303–318 (1997)
14. Xu, L., Li, Z., Li, J., Hua, W.: A novel bit-level image encryption algorithm based on chaotic maps. Opt. Lasers Eng. **78**, 17–25 (2016)
15. Wang, X., Wang, Q., Zhang, Y.: A fast image algorithm based on rows and columns switch. Nonlinear Dyn. **79**(2), 1141–1149 (2015)
16. Wu, Y., Zhou, Y., Saveriades, G., Agaian, S., Noonan, J.P., Natarajan, P.: Local shannon entropy measure with statistical tests for image randomness. Inf. Sci. **222**, 323–342 (2013)
17. Wu, Y., Noonan, J.P., Agaian, S.: NPCR and UACI randomness tests for image encryption. Cyber J. Multi. J. Sci. Technol. J. Sel. Areas Telecommun. (JSAT), 31–38 (2011)

Modeling and Hopf Bifurcation Analysis of Benign Worms with Quarantine Strategy

Yu Yao[1,2(✉)], Qiang Fu[1,2(✉)], Chuan Sheng[1,2], and Wei Yang[1,3]

[1] Key Laboratory of Medical Image Computing of Ministry of Education,
Northeastern University, Shenyang 110004, China
yaoyu@mail.neu.edu.cn, qiang.fu@outlook.com
[2] College of Compute Science and Engineering, Northeastern University,
Shenyang 110819, China
[3] Software College, Northeastern University, Shenyang 110819, China

Abstract. Since the Morris worm occurred in 1988, malwares have threatened the network persistently. With rapid development of the Internet, network security issues become increasingly serious. Recently, the benign worms become a new active countermeasure to deal with the worm threat. In this paper, we propose a compositive-hybrid benign worm propagation model with quarantine strategy. Usually, quarantine strategy will lead to a time delay, and the worm propagation system will be unstable and out of control with the time delay increases. Then the existence condition and the stability of the positive equilibrium are derived. Through our derivation and analysis, the threshold τ_0 of Hopf bifurcation is obtained. The system will be stable when time delay $\tau < \tau_0$. In addition, numerical experiments are performed and the effect of benign worms is displayed by comparing with the model that do not include benign worms. Furthermore, simulation experiments are carried out to verify our conclusions.

Keywords: Worm propagation model · Benign worms · Hopf bifurcation · Time delay

1 Introduction

Nowadays, the Internet has penetrated into people's life, work, and study, the network security is closely related to social stability and economic prosperity. However, since the Morris worm occurred in 1988, malwares have threatened the network persistently. With the development of malware such as virus, worms and Botnet, the malware is becoming more and more harmful. The worm, as a kind of malware, is a self-replicating and self-propagating piece of code that spreads via networks. Just like the Code Red worm [1–3] and Slammer worm [4], they can infect thousands of hosts in several hours and cause remarkable disruption to economic, transportation and government instructions. Therefore, it is significant to derive methods to counter against worms. There are many models to describe the spread of worms [5–7], however, these models can only give an early warning about the appearance of a worm. The common models usually

© Springer International Publishing AG 2017
S. Wen et al. (Eds.): CSS 2017, LNCS 10581, pp. 320–336, 2017.
https://doi.org/10.1007/978-3-319-69471-9_24

counter against a worm passively, then is there a method that can suppress a worm actively?

Fortunately, a benign worm can counter against a worm actively in spite of some legal issues and disputes on network traffic. In this paper, we aim to propose a worm propagation model with benign worms. Alun et al. [8] point out that the self-replicating and propagation behaviors of the worms are similar to biological viruses. Therefore, some traditional models of infectious diseases have been used to reveal the propagation of worms when the Red code worms broke out in 2001 [9]. The simple epidemic model (SEM) is the most basic network worm propagation model [10]. In order to study the propagation of worms among mobile phones, the SIS model [11] is proposed by Martin et al. Compared with the simple epidemic model, the Kermack-Mckendrick model assume that some infectious hosts can recover by patching [12]. Then many mathematical models based on the K-M model have been applied to study the spread of network worms. Such as the Two-factor model, Zou et al. [19] consider the dynamic external factor and the slower propagation speed. Zhou et al. [13] also model active benign worms and hybrid benign worms based on the Two-factor model. They find that the hybrid benign worm compositive-hybrid benign worm has better effect of suppressing a worm. In addition, some researches show that spread dynamic system of worm model will be unstable and bifurcation will occur. Dong et al. [14] propose a computer virus model with time delay, they regard the time delay as bifurcating parameter to study the dynamical behaviors that include local Hopf bifurcation and local asymptotical stability. Later Yao et al. [15] obtain the threshold of time delay when Hopf bifurcation occurs by considering the intrusion detection system (IDS).

However, there is still lack of a complete analysis about bifurcation in benign worm model with time delay. Zhou et al. [13] do not consider that a bad-worm may infect a benign worm in a certain probability in their paper. Based on their works, we propose a benign worm model with time delay. Then we derive the model and simulate the model. Through our analysis, we show that the system if stable when time delay is less than the threshold, and when time delay is equal or larger than the threshold, Hopf bifurcation will occur. Furthermore, we compare our model with which do not include a benign worm. We believe our model with benign worms can provide an additional measure to suppress worm spread in networks.

The rest of the paper is organized as follows. In Sect. 2, we present the SUIDQR model with benign worms. Section 3 analyzes the stability of equilibrium and the threshold of Hopf bifurcation. In Sect. 4, we carry out the numerical analysis of our model. Section 5 gives the simulation experiments and the simulation results match with the numerical results very well. Finally, we give the conclusions in Sect. 6.

2 Model Formulation

By applying the ideal combating poison with poison, Castaneday et al. [16] propose to counter against the worms with benign worms. The benign worms can apply patches and fix the infected hosts. Castaneday et al. [16] classify the benign worms into four types: a passive benign worm, an active benign worm, a hybrid benign worm and an IDS-based benign worm. The passive benign worms wait on a host for attacks from the original worms. The active benign worms can scan the IP address and counter against the original worms. The hybrid benign worms combine the functions of both passive and active benign worms. And the IDS-based benign worm can identify the original worm through the IDS sensors. Moreover, Zhou et al. [13] classify hybrid benign worms into three sub types: a patching-hybrid benign worm, a predatorial-hybrid benign worm and a compositive-hybrid benign worm.

In this paper, we mainly model the compositive-hybrid benign worm. It can patch the hosts, and "compromise" the infectious hosts, it also has the feature of the passive benign worms. In addition, we consider worms exploiting zero-day vulnerabilities and quarantine strategies. There are not effective and safe patches when the zero-day vulnerabilities appear. So we propose quarantine strategy to control the worm propagation. As we know, people may immunize their computers with counter measures in infectious hosts, which may take a period of time. Thus, the infectious hosts will go through a temporary state before removed, and we assume that the hosts are delayed state. According to our descriptions, we give an SUIDQR worm propagation model. We assume all the hosts change over the time among the following six states: Susceptible state (S), Benignly Infectious state (U), Infectious state (I), Delayed state (D), Quarantined state (Q), and Removed state (R). Let $S(t)$, $U(t)$, $I(t)$, $D(t)$, $Q(t)$ and $R(t)$ denote the number of susceptible, benignly infectious, infectious, delayed, quarantined and removed hosts at time t, respectively. The susceptible hosts change to the infectious hosts with the infection rate β, the rate μ_1 is the infection rate of the benign worm, μ_2 is the success rate of the worm infect the benign worm, and μ_3 is the passively infection rate of the benign worm, because the worm and the benign worm can attack each other in the process of worm propagation. More parameters are listed in Table 1, and the state transition diagram is given in Fig. 1 as follow.

It is worth noting that the worm and the benign worm can attack each other in this model. At time t the success rate of that the worm infect the benign worm is μ_2, then the number of benignly infectious hosts which is infected by infectious hosts is $\mu_2 \beta I(t) U(t)$. Meanwhile, the benign worm can defense the worms passively. When the worms are attacking the benignly infectious hosts at time t, there are $\mu_3 \beta I(t) U(t)$ infectious hosts that can be changed to benignly infectious hosts. Thus, we can express the model with the following equations.

$$\begin{cases} \frac{dS(t)}{dt} = \alpha R(t) - \beta I(t)S(t) - \mu_1(t)U(t)S(t), \\ \frac{dU(t)}{dt} = \mu_1 U(t)S(t) + (\mu_1 + \mu_3\beta)I(t)U(t) - \mu_2\beta I(t)U(t) - \varphi_2 U(t), \\ \frac{dI(t)}{dt} = \beta I(t)S(t) + \mu_2\beta I(t)U(t) - \theta I(t) - \varphi_1 I(t) - (\mu_1 + \mu_3\beta)I(t)U(t), \\ \frac{dD(t)}{dt} = \theta I(t) - \theta I(t - \tau), \\ \frac{dQ(t)}{dt} = \theta I(t - \tau) - \gamma Q(t), \\ \frac{dR(t)}{dt} = \varphi_1 I(t) + \varphi_2 U(t) + \gamma Q(t) - \alpha R(t). \end{cases} \tag{1}$$

Table 1. Parameters and their meanings in this paper

Parameters	Explanation
$S(t)$	The number of susceptible hosts at time t
$U(t)$	The number of benignly infectious hosts at time t
$I(t)$	The number of infectious hosts at time t
$D(t)$	The number of delayed hosts at time t
$Q(t)$	The number of quarantined hosts at time t
$R(t)$	The number of removed hosts at time t
N	Total number of hosts in the network
β	The infection rate of the worm
α	The rate at which the removed hosts lose immunity
θ	The quarantine rate of infectious hosts
φ_1	The recovered rate of infectious hosts
φ_2	The recovered rate of benignly infectious hosts
μ_1	The infection rate of the benign worm
μ_2	The success rate of a worm infect the benign worm
μ_3	The passively infection rate of the benign worm
τ	The time delay
γ	The immune rate of quarantined hosts

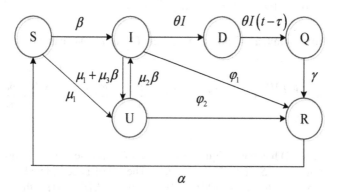

Fig. 1. State transition diagram of the SUIDQR model

The population size is set N, which can be set to unity

$$N = S(t) + U(t) + I(t) + D(t) + Q(t) + R(t). \tag{2}$$

3   Stability of Equilibrium and Bifurcation Analysis

System (1) has a unique positive equilibrium point $E^* = (S^*, U^*, I^*, D^*, Q^*, R^*)$, where

$$S^* = \frac{\varphi_2 + (\mu_2\beta - \mu_1 - \mu_3\beta)I^*}{\mu_1}, U^* = \frac{(\varphi_1 + \theta - \beta S)I^*}{\mu_1 S^* - \varphi_2}, D^* = 0, Q^* = \frac{\theta}{\gamma}I^*,$$
$$R^* = \left[\varphi_1 + \theta + \frac{\varphi_2(\varphi_1 + \theta - \beta S^*)}{\mu_1 S^* - \varphi_2}\right]\frac{I^*}{\alpha}.$$

Proof. When system (1) is stable, all the derivatives on the left of equal sign of the system are set to zero, which implies that the system becomes stable, we can obtain:

$$\begin{cases} \alpha R(t) - \beta I(t)S(t) - \mu_1 U(t)S(t) = 0, \\ \mu_1 U(t)S(t) + (\mu_1 + \mu_3\beta)I(t)U(t) - \mu_2\beta I(t)U(t) - \varphi_2 U(t) = 0, \\ \beta I(t)S(t) + \mu_2\beta I(t)U(t) - \theta I(t) - \varphi_1 I(t) - (\mu_1 + \mu_3\beta)I(t)U(t) = 0, \\ \theta I(t) - \theta I(t - \tau) = 0, \\ \theta I(t - \tau) - \gamma Q(t) = 0, \\ \varphi_1 I(t) + \varphi_2 U(t) + \gamma Q(t) - \alpha R(t) = 0. \end{cases} \quad (3)$$

Then we can derive

$$S^* = \frac{\varphi_2 + (\mu_2\beta - \mu_1 - \mu_3\beta)I^*}{\mu_1}, U^* = \frac{(\varphi_1 + \theta - \beta S)I^*}{\mu_1 S^* - \varphi_2}, Q^* = \frac{\theta}{\gamma}I^*,$$
$$R^* = \left[\varphi_1 + \theta + \frac{\varphi_2(\varphi_1 + \theta - \beta S^*)}{\mu_1 S^* - \varphi_2}\right]\frac{I^*}{\alpha}.$$

Since the total number of hosts in system (3) is N, we can get the following equation of I,

$$\frac{\varphi_2 + (\mu_2\beta - \mu_1 - \mu_3\beta)I^*}{\mu_1} + I^* + \frac{\theta}{\gamma}I^* + \frac{\varphi_1}{\alpha}I^* + \frac{\theta}{\alpha}I^* + \frac{\varphi_2 + \alpha(\varphi_1 + \theta - \beta S^*)}{\alpha}\frac{I^*}{\mu_1 S^* - \varphi_2} = N. \quad (4)$$

Obviously, Eq. (4) has one unique positive root I^*, and there is one unique positive equilibrium point $E^* = (S^*, U^*, I^*, D^*, Q^*, R^*)$. The proof is completed.

According to (2), $Q(t) = N - S(t) - U(t) - I(t) - D(t) - R(t)$, thus system (1) can be simplified to

$$\begin{cases} \frac{dS(t)}{dt} = \alpha R(t) - \beta(t)I(t)S(t) - \mu_1(t)U(t)S(t) \\ \frac{dU(t)}{dt} = \mu_1 U(t)S(t) + (\mu_1 + \mu_3\beta)I(t)U(t) - \mu_2\beta_1 I(t)U(t) - \varphi_2 U(t) \\ \frac{dI(t)}{dt} = \beta I(t)S(t) + \mu_2\beta_1 I(t)U(t) - \theta I(t) - \varphi_1 I(t) - (\mu_1 + \mu_3\beta_1)I(t)U(t) \\ \frac{dD(t)}{dt} = \theta I(t) - \theta I(t - \tau) \\ \frac{dR(t)}{dt} = \varphi_1 I(t) + \varphi_2 U(t) + \gamma[N - (S(t) + I(t) + R(t) + U(t) + D(t))] - \alpha R(t) \end{cases} \quad (5)$$

The Jacobi matrix of system (5) about $E^* = (S^*, U^*, I^*, D^*, Q^*, R^*)$ is given by

$$J(E^*) = \begin{pmatrix} c_1 & c_5 & \beta_1 & 0 & \alpha \\ c_4 & -c_5+c_2-\varphi_2 & c_3 & 0 & 0 \\ c_6 & -c_2 & c_7-\theta_1-\varphi_1-c_3 & 0 & 0 \\ 0 & 0 & \theta_1-\theta_1 e^{-\lambda\tau} & 0 & 0 \\ -\gamma & \varphi_2-\gamma & \varphi_1-\gamma & -\gamma & -\gamma-\alpha \end{pmatrix}, \quad (6)$$

where

$$c_1 = -\beta I^* - \mu_1 U^*, c_2 = (\mu_1+\mu_3\beta)I^* - \mu_2\beta I^*, c_3 = (\mu_1+\mu_3\beta)U^* - \mu_2\beta U^*$$
$$c_4 = \mu_1 U^*, c_5 = -\mu_1 S^*, c_6 = \beta I^*, c_7 = \beta_1 S^*$$

The characteristic equation of that matrix (6) can be obtained by

$$P(\lambda) + Q(\lambda)e^{-\lambda\tau} = 0. \quad (7)$$

The expression of $P(\lambda)$, $Q(\lambda)$ are

$$P(\lambda) = \lambda^5 + p_4\lambda^4 + p_3\lambda^3 + p_2\lambda^2 + p_1\lambda + p_0, \quad Q(\lambda) = q_0,$$

where

$p_4 = c_5 - c_2 + \varphi_2 - c_1 + \gamma + \alpha - c_7 + \theta + c_3,$

$$p_3 = \begin{pmatrix} -c_5c_1+c_2c_1-\varphi_2c_1-c_1\gamma+c_5\alpha+c_5\gamma-c_2\gamma+\varphi_2\gamma-c_1\alpha-c_2\alpha+\varphi_2\alpha \\ -c_5c_7+c_2c_7-\varphi_2c_7+c_1c_7-c_7\gamma-\alpha c_7+c_5\theta-c_2\theta+\varphi_2\theta-c_1\theta \\ +\gamma\theta+\alpha\theta+c_5c_3-c_2c_3+\varphi_2c_3-c_1c_3+\gamma c_3+\alpha c_3 \\ +\gamma\varphi_1+\alpha\varphi_1-c_1\varphi_1+c_5\varphi_1-c_2\varphi_1+\varphi_2\varphi_1 \end{pmatrix},$$

$$p_2 = \begin{pmatrix} c_5c_1c_7-c_2c_1c_7+\varphi_2c_1c_7+c_1c_7\gamma+c_2\alpha c_7-\varphi_2\alpha c_7-c_5c_7\gamma \\ +c_1c_7\alpha-c_5c_1\alpha+c_2c_1\alpha-\varphi_2c_1\alpha-c_5c_1\gamma+c_2c_1\gamma-\varphi_2c_1\gamma-c_5c_1\theta \\ +c_2c_1\theta-\varphi_2c_1\theta-c_1\theta\gamma-c_2\alpha\theta+\varphi_2\alpha\theta+c_5\gamma\theta-c_2\gamma\theta \\ +\varphi_2\gamma\theta+c_5\alpha\theta-c_1\alpha\theta-c_5c_1c_3+c_2c_1c_3-\varphi_2c_1c_3-c_1c_3\gamma-c_1\alpha c_3 \\ +c_5\gamma c_3-c_2\gamma c_3+\varphi_2\gamma c_3+c_5\alpha c_3-c_2\alpha c_3+\varphi_2\alpha c_3 \\ +\gamma\varphi_2\varphi_1+\alpha\varphi_2\varphi_1-c_1\varphi_1\varphi_2-\gamma c_1\varphi_1-\alpha c_1\varphi_1+c_2c_7\gamma-\varphi_2c_7\gamma-c_5\alpha c_7 \\ +\gamma c_5\varphi_1+\alpha c_5\varphi_1-c_5c_1\varphi_1-\gamma c_2\varphi_1-\alpha c_2\varphi_1+c_2c_1\varphi_1 \end{pmatrix}, \quad (8)$$

$$p_1 = \begin{pmatrix} +c_5c_1c_7\gamma-c_2c_1c_7\gamma+\varphi_2c_1c_7\gamma+c_5c_1c_7\alpha-c_2c_1c_7\alpha+\varphi_2c_1c_7\alpha \\ -c_5c_1\theta\gamma+c_2c_1\theta\gamma\lambda-\varphi_2c_1\theta\gamma\lambda-c_5c_1\alpha\theta+c_2c_1\alpha\theta-\varphi_2c_1\alpha\theta \\ -c_5c_1c_3\gamma+c_2c_1c_3\gamma-\varphi_2c_1c_3\gamma-c_5c_1\alpha c_3+c_2c_1\alpha c_3-\varphi_2c_1\alpha c_3 \\ ++\gamma\varphi_1+\alpha\varphi_1-c_1\varphi_1+c_5\varphi_1-c_2\varphi_1+\varphi_2\varphi_1 \end{pmatrix},$$

$p_0 = c_2c_4\alpha\gamma\theta,$

$q_0 = -c_2c_4\alpha\gamma\theta.$

Lemma 1. If the condition is satisfied as (H_1), the positive equilibrium $E^* = (S^*, U^*, I^*, D^*, Q^*, R^*)$ is locally asymptotically stable without time delay.

$$(H_1): \ p_4 > 0, d_1 > 0, p_1 > 0, p_2 d_1 - p_4^2 p_1 > 0, \tag{9}$$

where $d_1 = p_3 p_4 - p_2$.

Proof. When $\tau = 0$, the Eq. (7) simplifies to

$$\lambda^5 + p_4 \lambda^4 + p_3 \lambda^3 + p_2 \lambda^2 + p_1 \lambda + p_0 + q_0 = 0. \tag{10}$$

According to Routh-Hurwitz criterion, all the roots of Eq. (10) have negative real parts. Hence, we can deduce that the positive equilibrium $E^* = (S^*, U^*, I^*, D^*, Q^*, R^*)$ is locally asymptotically stable without time delay. The proof is completed.

For Eq. (7), the root is $\lambda = i\omega$, we substitute it into Eq. (7). After separating the real and imaginary parts, we can obtain two equations:

$$p_4 \omega^4 - p_2 \omega^2 + p_0 + q_0 \cos(\omega\tau) = 0. \tag{11}$$

$$\omega^5 - p_3 \omega^3 + p_1 \omega - q_0 \sin(\omega\tau) = 0. \tag{12}$$

Uniting Eqs. (11) and (12), then we can obtain:

$$q_0^2 = (p_4 \omega^4 - p_2 \omega^2 + p_0)^2 + (\omega^5 - p_3 \omega^3 + p_1 \omega)^2. \tag{13}$$

which implies

$$\begin{aligned} \omega^{10} + p_4^2 \omega^8 - 2p_3 \omega^8 + 2p_1 \omega^6 + p_3^2 \omega^6 - 2p_2 p_4 \omega^6 \\ + p_2^2 \omega^4 - 2p_1 p_3 \omega^4 + 2p_0 p_4 \omega^4 + p_1^2 \omega^2 - 2p_0 p_2 \omega^2 + p_0^2 - q_0^2 = 0 \end{aligned}\ ,$$

since $p_0^2 - q_0^2 = 0$, that is

$$\omega^8 + D_3 \omega^6 + D_2 \omega^4 + D_1 \omega^2 + D_0 = 0, \tag{14}$$

where

$$\begin{aligned} D_3 &= p_4^2 - 2p_3, \\ D_2 &= p_3^2 + 2p_1 - 2p_2 p_4, \\ D_1 &= p_2^2 + 2p_0 p_4 - 2p_1 p_3, \\ D_0 &= p_1^2 - 2p_0 p_2. \end{aligned} \tag{15}$$

Let $z = w^2$, then the Eq. (17) can be turned into:

$$h(z) = z^4 + D_3 z^3 + D_2 z^2 + D_1 z + D_0 \tag{16}$$

Yang et al. [17] concluded the following results on the distribution of roots of Eq. (16). Denote

$$m = \tfrac{1}{2}D_2 - \tfrac{3}{16}D_3^2, \; n = \tfrac{1}{32}D_3^3 - \tfrac{1}{8}D_3D_2 + D_1, \; \Delta = \left(\tfrac{n}{2}\right)^2 + \left(\tfrac{m}{3}\right)^3, \; \sigma = \tfrac{-1+\sqrt{3}i}{2},$$

$$y_1 = \sqrt[3]{-\tfrac{n}{2} + \sqrt{\Delta}} + \sqrt[3]{-\tfrac{n}{2} - \sqrt{\Delta}}, \; y_2 = \sqrt[3]{-\tfrac{n}{2} + \sqrt{\Delta}}\sigma + \sqrt[3]{-\tfrac{n}{2} - \sqrt{\Delta}}\sigma^2,$$

$$y_3 = \sqrt[3]{-\tfrac{n}{2} + \sqrt{\Delta}}\sigma^2 + \sqrt[3]{-\tfrac{n}{2} - \sqrt{\Delta}}\sigma, \; z_i = y_i - \tfrac{3D_3}{4}, \; (i = 1, 2, 3).$$

$$(17)$$

Lemma 2. For the polynomial Eq. (16)

(1) if $D_0 < 0$, then Eq. (16) has at least one positive root,
(2) if $D_0 \geq 0$, and $\Delta \geq 0$, then Eq. (16) has positive roots if and only if $z_1 > 0$ and $h(z_1) < 0$,
(3) if $D_0 \geq 0$, and $\Delta < 0$, then Eq. (16) has positive roots if and only if there exists at least one $z^* \in (z_1, z_2, z_3)$, such $z^* > 0$ and $h(z^*) \leq 0$.

Lemma 3. Supposing that (H_1): $p_4 > 0, d_1 > 0, p_1 > 0, p_2 d_1 - p_4^2 p_1 > 0$ is satisfied.

(1) If one of following conditions holds: (a) $D_0 < 0$; (b) $D_0 \geq 0, \Delta \geq 0, z_1 > 0$ and $h(z_1) < 0$; (c) $D_0 \geq 0, \Delta < 0$ and there exists at least $z^* \in (z_1, z_{,2} z_3)$ such that $z^* > 0$ and $h(z^*) \leq 0$, then all roots of Eq. (7) have negative real parts when $\tau \in [0, \tau_0)$, τ_0 is a certain positive constant.
(2) If the conditions (a)–(c) are not satisfied, all roots of Eq. (11) have negative real parts for all $\tau_0 \geq 0$.

Proof. When $\tau_0 = 0$, Eq. (7) becomes

$$\lambda^5 + p_4\lambda^4 + p_3\lambda^3 + p_2\lambda^2 + p_1\lambda + p_0 + q_0 = 0.$$

By the Routh-Hurwitz criterion, all roots of Eq. (10) have negative real parts if and only if $p_4 > 0, d_1 > 0, p_1 > 0, p_2 d_1 - p_4^2 p_1 > 0$.

From Lemma 2, we know that if conditions (a)–(c) are not satisfied, then Eq. (7) has no roots with zero real part for all $\tau_0 \geq 0$; when $\tau \geq \tau_k^{(j)}(k = 1, 2, 3, 4, j \geq 1)$, if one of the conditions (a)–(c) holds, Eq. (11) has no roots with zero real part and τ_0 is the minimum value of τ, so Eq. (7) has purely imaginary roots [20].

When conditions (a)–(c) of Lemma 3 are not satisfied, $h(z)$ always has no positive roots. Therefore, Eq. (11) has no purely imaginary roots for any $\tau > 0$, which implies that the positive equilibrium $E^* = (S^*, U^*, I^*, D^*, Q^*, R^*)$ of system (1) is absolutely stable.

Lemma 4. From the discussions above, we assume that (H_1) are satisfied, (a) $D_0 \geq 0, \Delta \geq 0, z_1 > 0$ or $h(z_1) > 0$; (b) $D_0 \geq 0, \Delta < 0$ and there is no $z^* \in (z_1, z_{,2} z_3)$ such that $z^* > 0$ and $h(z^*) \leq 0$. Then the positive equilibrium $E^* = (S^*, U^*, I^*, D^*, Q^*, R^*)$ of system (1) is absolutely stable. Namely, $E^* = (S^*, U^*, I^*, D^*, Q^*, R^*)$ is asymptotically stable for any $\tau \geq 0$.

(H_2): (a) $D_0 \geq 0, \Delta \geq 0, z_1 > 0$ or $h(z_1) > 0$; (b) $D_0 \geq 0, \Delta < 0$ and there is no $z^* \in (z_1, z_2, z_3)$ such that $z^* > 0$ and $h(z^*) \leq 0$.

From previous lemmas, we know that Eq. (16) has at least a positive root w_0 which also means Eq. (7) has a pair of purely imaginary roots $\pm i w_0$. By uniting the Eqs. (11) and (12), we can get the corresponding $\tau_k > 0$.

$$\tau_k = \frac{1}{\omega_0} \arccos\left(\frac{p_2\omega_0^2 - p_4\omega_0^4 - p_0}{q_0}\right) + \frac{2k\pi}{\omega_0}. \tag{18}$$

Let $\lambda(\tau) = v(\tau) + i\omega(\tau)$ be the root of Eq. (7). It is satisfied that $v(\tau_k) = 0$, $\omega(\tau_k) = \omega_0$ when $\tau = \tau_k$.

Lemma 5. Supposing $h'(z_0) \neq 0$. If $\tau = \tau_0$, $\pm i\omega_0$ is a pair of purely imaginary roots of Eq. (7). If the conditions in Lemma 3 (1) are satisfied,

$$\frac{d\,\mathrm{Re}\,\lambda(\tau_0)}{d\tau} > 0.$$

This means that there exists at least one eigenvalue with positive real part when $\tau > \tau_k$. Differentiating on both sides of Eq. (7) with respect to τ, we can obtain:

$$\left(\frac{d\lambda}{d\tau}\right)^{-1} = \frac{(5\lambda^4 + 4p_4\lambda^3 + 3p_3\lambda^2 + 2p_2\lambda + p_1) - q_0\tau e^{-\lambda\tau}}{q_0\lambda e^{-\lambda\tau}}$$
$$= \frac{(5\lambda^4 + 4p_4\lambda^3 + 3p_3\lambda^2 + 2p_2\lambda + p_1)e^{\lambda\tau}}{q_0\lambda} - \frac{\tau}{\lambda}. \tag{19}$$

Uniting Eqs. (11) and (12), we can obtain:

$$\mathrm{sgn}\left[\frac{d\,\mathrm{Re}\,\lambda}{d\tau}\right]_{\tau=\tau_k} = \mathrm{sgn}\left[\mathrm{Re}\left(\frac{d\lambda}{d\tau}\right)^{-1}\right]_{\lambda=i\omega_0}$$
$$= \mathrm{sgn}\left[\mathrm{Re}\left(\frac{(5\lambda^4 + 4p_4\lambda^3 + 3p_3\lambda^2 + 2p_2\lambda + p_1)e^{\lambda\tau}}{q_0\lambda} - \frac{\tau}{\lambda}\right)\right]_{\lambda=i\omega_0}$$
$$= \mathrm{sgn}\frac{\omega_0^2}{q_0^2\omega_0^2}[4\omega_0^6 + (3p_3^2 - 6p_3)\omega_0^4 + (2p_3^2 + 4p_1 - 4p_2p_4)\omega_0^2 + (p_2^2 + 2p_0p_4 - 2p_1p_3)]$$
$$= \mathrm{sgn}\frac{\omega_0^2}{q_0^2\omega_0^2} = \mathrm{sgn}\frac{\omega_0^2}{q_0^2\omega_0^2}\{h'(\omega_0^2)\} = \mathrm{sgn}\{h'(\omega_0^2)\}$$

Then it follows Lemma 4 that $h'(w_0^2) \neq 0$. Therefore,

$$\frac{d(\mathrm{Re}\,\lambda)}{d\tau}\bigg|_{\tau=\tau_k} > 0. \tag{20}$$

According to Routh's theorem [18], as τ continuously varies from a value less than τ_k to one greater than τ_k, the root of characteristic Eq. (11) crosses from left to right on the imaginary axis. Thus, the transverse condition holds and the conditions for Hopf bifurcation are satisfied at $\tau = \tau_k$ according to Hopf bifurcation theorem.

Lemma 6. Supposing that the conditions (H_1) are satisfied.

(1) When $\tau < \tau_0$, the positive equilibrium $E^* = (S^*, U^*, I^*, D^*, Q^*, R^*)$ of system (2) is locally asymptotically stable, and unstable when $\tau \geq \tau_0$.

(2) When system (5) satisfies (H_2), the system undergoes a Hopf bifurcation at the positive equilibrium $E^* = (S^*, U^*, I^*, D^*, Q^*, R^*)$ when time delay $\tau = \tau_0$.

This implies that when time delay $\tau < \tau_0$, the system will stabilize at its infection equilibrium point, which is beneficial for us to implement a containment strategy; when the delay $\tau \geq \tau_0$, the system will be unstable and worms cannot be effectively controlled.

4   Numerical Analysis

In order to verify the theorems propose in Sect. 3, we make numerical experiments in this section. The total number N of hosts is assumed 500000, and the worm's average scan rate is $\eta = 4000$ per second. So the worm's infection rate can be calculated as $\beta = \eta N / 2^{32} = 0.465$. It means that 0.465 host of all hosts can be scanned by an infectious host. In order to reduce the network congestion, we set the benign worm's average scan rate $\eta_1 = 155$ per second. Then the benign worm's infection rate is $\mu_1 = 0.018$. Since the benign worms and the worms can attack each other, we assume the success rate of a worm infect the benign worm is $\mu_2 = 0.025$, and the passively infection rate of the benign worm is $\mu_3 = 0.2$. The quarantine rate of infectious hosts is $\theta = 0.046$, the immune rate of quarantined hosts is $\gamma = 0.2$, and the rate at which the removed hosts lose immunity is $\alpha = 0.062$. At the beginning, the number of infectious hosts and benignly infectious hosts is 50 and 40, respectively. Other hosts are susceptible.

Based on the parameters above, Fig. 2 shows the curves of six kind of hosts when $\tau = 50 < \tau_0$. We can find that the curves of every state hosts will be stable when $t = 1000$ which implies E^* is locally asymptotically stable. Clearly the benign worm can restrain the worm propagation effectively. In Fig. 3, it shows that the numbers of every kind of hosts when $\tau = 200 > \tau_0$. It is clearly to see that the number of every six kinds of hosts will outburst after a short period of peace and repeat again and again. And it is interesting to find that the number of benignly infectious hosts is quite small when $\tau = 200 > \tau_0$. That is because the quarantine strategy is just direct at the infectious hosts, and the number of delayed hosts can be very large.

In order to contrast our model with that do not contain benign worms, we remove the benign worm in the model, and make numerical experiments. The parameters are same in both models. In Fig. 4, the blue lines represents the infectious hosts in SUIDQR model with benign worms, and the red lines represents the infectious hosts in which without benign worms. Obviously, the benign worms can restrain the worm propagation effectively. For the SUIDQR model, the number of infectious hosts is much less than that without benign worms when the systems reach stability.

Figure 5 shows the number of infectious hosts with different time delay $\tau = 50$, $\tau = 100$, $\tau = 150$, and $\tau = 200$. In Fig. 5, we can find that the curve will begin to

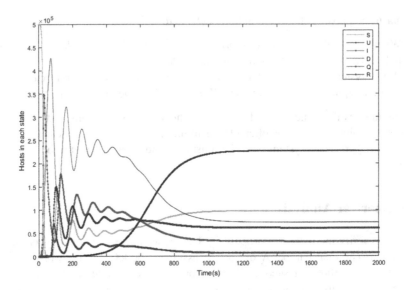

Fig. 2. The worm propagation of the six kinds hosts results with $\tau < \tau_0$

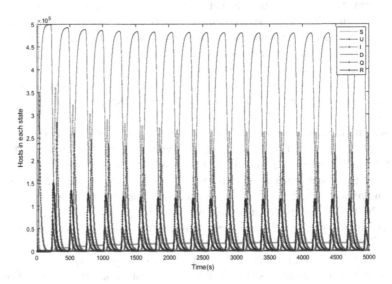

Fig. 3. The worm propagation of the five kinds hosts results with $\tau > \tau_0$

oscillate with the increase of time delay. And the infecting process becomes unstable with time delay exceeds the threshold τ_0 which meets our conclusions. Figures 6 and 7 are the projection of the phase portrait of system (1) in (S, I, R) space when $\tau = 50$ and $\tau = 200$. From Fig. 5 we can find that the curve converges to a fixed point which means the system is stable when $\tau = 50 < \tau_0$, and the curve in Fig. 6 radiates to a limit cycle which means the system is unstable when $\tau = 200 > \tau_0$. Figure 8 gives the

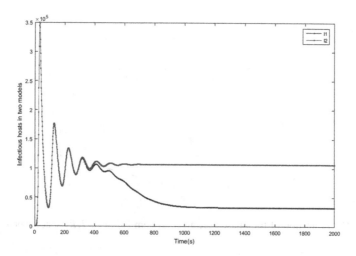

Fig. 4. Comparison of infectious hosts with and without benign worms (Color figure online)

bifurcation diagram of system (1). It is clearly that the Hopf bifurcation occurs at $\tau = \tau_0 = 178$, and this is similar the results of our theoretical derivation. In Fig. 9, the bifurcation diagram of the system without benign worms is given. The threshold of is smaller than the model with benign worms, it illustrates that the model with benign worms is easier to get stable.

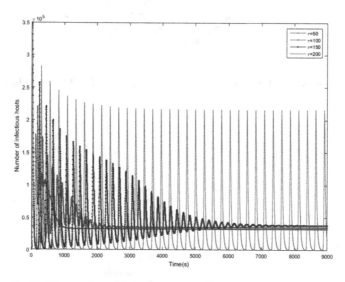

Fig. 5. The number of infectious hosts $I(t)$ with different values of τ

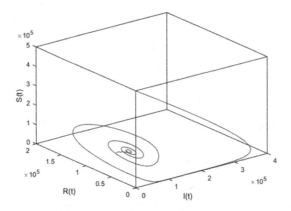

Fig. 6. The projection of the phase portrait of system (1) in (S, I, R)-space when $\tau = 50$

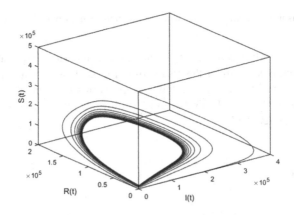

Fig. 7. The projection of the phase portrait of system (1) in (S, I, R)-space when $\tau = 200$

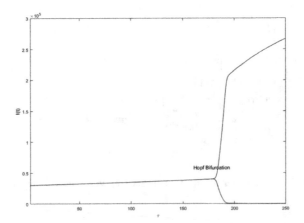

Fig. 8. Bifurcation diagram of system (1) with benign worms

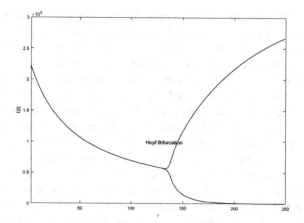

Fig. 9. Bifurcation diagram of system (1) without benign worms

5 Simulation Experiments

In this section, we simulate the actual behavior of worm propagation and verify the correctness of our numerical simulation and theoretical analysis above. The discrete-time simulation is an expanded version of Zou's [19] program. There are

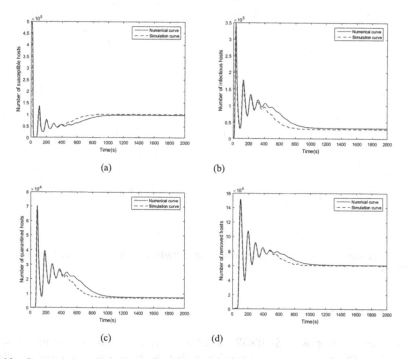

Fig. 10. Comparisons between numerical and simulation curves of system (1) when $\tau = 50 < \tau_0,$

500000 hosts in our simulation experiments. At the beginning, 50 hosts are chosen to be infectious and 40 hosts are chosen to be benignly infectious, other hosts are set to be susceptible. The parameters are same with the numerical simulation, the implement of transition rates of the propagation model depends on probability.

Figure 10 shows that the comparisons between numerical and simulation curves of susceptible, infectious, quarantined and removed hosts when $\tau = 50 < \tau_0$. The blue solid curves and red dashed curves represent the numerical and simulation results, and (a), (b), (c), and (d) corresponds to the susceptible, infectious, quarantined and removed hosts, respectively. Figure 11 is the comparisons when $\tau = 200 > \tau_0$. From Figs. 10 and 11, we can see that the numerical curves and the simulation curves are very well matched. As it is expected, there exists little difference in two kinds of curves because of the high precision of numerical experiment. The number of hosts in numerical experiments can be integer or decimal, but in simulation experiments, the number must be integer. However, the little difference does not affect our conclusions.

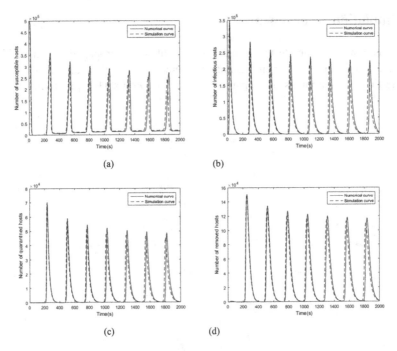

Fig. 11. Comparisons between numerical and simulation curves of system (1) when $\tau = 200 > \tau_0$.

6 Conclusions

In this paper, we propose a SUIDQR model with benign worms to restrain the worm propagation. The numerical simulation show that the benign worms have significant effects to restrain the worm propagation. In addition, we analyze the stability of the positive equilibrium of the system (1). Furthermore, the threshold value of Hopf bifurcation is obtained. Through our theoretical analysis, the following conclusions which verified by numerical and simulation experiments can be derived.

(1) The critical time delay τ_0 in which Hopf bifurcation appears can be obtained.

$$\tau_k = \frac{1}{\omega_0} \arccos\left(\frac{p_2\omega_0^2 - p_4\omega_0^4 - p_0}{q_0}\right) + \frac{2k\pi}{\omega_0}$$

(2) When time delay $\tau < \tau_0$, the worm propagation system is stable. It is useful to implement a containment strategy, and the worms can be reduced to a low extent at the infection equilibrium point.
(3) When time delay $\tau \geq \tau_0$, the worm propagation system will be unstable, and the system is out of control. Therefore, the time delay should be controlled in the range of $\tau < \tau_0$.
(4) The benign worm can diminish the infectious hosts effectively. The threshold τ_0 is larger after adding benign worms. In this way, people have more time to deal with the worm propagation and the system is easier to be stable and controllable.

We propose a benign worm propagation model SUIDQR with quarantine strategy. This model can be used for Internet worms, such as Code red worms, Slammer worms and so on. Our study show that the benign worm can restrain the worm propagation effectively. However, there are still some controversies on benign worms. So it is needed to consider more impact factors to worm propagation in our future work.

Acknowledgments. This paper is supported by Program for Fundamental Research Funds of the Central Universities under Grant no. N150402006 and N161704005.

References

1. Moore, D., Shannon, C., Claffy, K.: Code-Red: a case study on the spread and victims of an internet worm. In: ACM SIGCOMM Workshop on Internet Measurement 2002, pp. 273–284, Marseille, France, November 2002. doi:10.1145/637201.637244
2. EEye Digital Security. Code Red worm (2001). http://www.eeye.com/html/research/advisories/al20010717.html
3. eEye Digital Security, ANALYSIS: CodeRed II Worm. http://www.eeye.com/html/Research/Advisories/AL20010804.html
4. Moore, D., Paxson, V., Savage, S., Shannon, C., Staniford, S., Weaver, N.: Inside the slammer worm. IEEE Mag. Secur. Privacy 1(4), 33–39 (2003). doi:10.1109/MSECP.2003.1219056
5. Weaver, N., Staniford, S., Paxson, V.: Very fast containment of scanning worms. In: Conference on Usenix Security Symposium, vol. 13, p. 3. USENIX Association (2004). doi: https://doi.org/10.1007/978-0-387-44599-1_6
6. Schechter, S.E., Jung, J., Berger, A.W.: Fast detection of scanning worm infections. In: Jonsson, E., Valdes, A., Almgren, M. (eds.) RAID 2004. LNCS, vol. 3224, pp. 59–81. Springer, Heidelberg (2004). doi:10.1007/978-3-540-30143-1_4

7. Kim, H.A., Karp, B.: Autograph: toward automated, distributed worm signature detection. In: USENIX Security Symposium, August 9–13, 2004, San Diego, CA, USA, pp. 271–286. DBLP (2004)

8. Lloyd, A.L., May, R.M.: Epidemiology. How viruses spread among computers and people. Science 292(5520), 1316 (2001). doi:10.1126/science.1061076

9. Staniford, S., Paxson, V., Weaver, N.: How to own the internet in your spare time. In: USENIX Security Symposium, (pp. 149–167). USENIX Association (2002)

10. Streftaris, G., Gibson, G.J.: Statistical inference for stochastic epidemic models. In: Proceedings of the 17th International Workshop on Statistical Modeling, Chania, UK, pp. 609–616 (2002)

11. Martin, J.C., Burge III, L.L., Gill, J.I., Washington, A.N., Alfred, M.: Modelling the spread of mobile malware. Int. J. Comput. Aided Eng. Technol. 2(1), 3–14 (2010). doi:10.1504/IJCAET.2010.029592

12. Frauenthal, J.C.: Mathematical Modeling in Epidemiology, pp. 115–123. Springer, New York (1980)

13. Zhou, H., Wen, Y., Zhao, H.: Modeling and analysis of active benign worms and hybrid benign worms containing the spread of worms. In: International Conference on Networking, p. 65. IEEE (2007). doi:http://doi.ieeecomputersociety.org/10.1109/ICN.2007.58

14. Dong, T., Liao, X., Li, H.: Stability and Hopf bifurcation in a computer virus model with multistate antivirus. Abstract Appl. Anal. 2012(2), 374–388 (2012). doi:10.1155/2012/841987

15. Yao, Y., Xie, X.W., Guo, H., et al.: Hopf bifurcation in an Internet worm propagation model with time delay in quarantine. Math. Comput. Model. 57(11–12), 2635–2646 (2013). doi:10.1016/j.mcm.2011.06.044

16. Castaneda, F., Sezer, E.C., Xu, J.: WORM vs. WORM: preliminary study of an active counter-attack mechanism. In: ACM Workshop on Rapid Malcode, Worm 2004, Washington, DC, USA, pp. 83–93, October 2004. doi:10.1145/1029618.1029631

17. Yang, Y., Fang, Y., Li, L.Y.: The analysis of propagation model for internet worm based on active vaccination. IEEE (2008). doi:10.1109/ICNC.2008.431

18. Hassard, B., Kazarino, D., Wan, Y.: Theory and Application of Hopf Bifurcation. Cambridge University Press, Cambridge (1981)

19. Zou, C.C., Gong, W., Towsley, D.: Worm propagation modeling and analysis under dynamic quarantine defense. In: ACM Workshop on Rapid Malcode, vol. 23, pp. 51–60. ACM (2003) doi:10.1145/948187.948197

20. Zhang, J.F., Li, W.T., Yan, X.P.: Hopf bifurcation and stability of periodic solutions in a delayed eco-epidemiological system. Appl. Math. Comput. 198(2), 865–876 (2008). doi:10.1016/j.amc.2007.09.045

Accountable Multi-authority Ciphertext-Policy Attribute-Based Encryption Without Key Escrow and Key Abuse

Gang Yu[1,2](✉), Xiaoxiao Ma[3](✉), Zhenfu Cao[2](✉), Weihua Zhu[1],
and Junjie Zeng[1]

[1] State Key Laboratory of Mathematical Engineering and Advanced Computing,
Information Science and Technology Institute, Zhengzhou 450001, China
gyu1010@126.com, weihua1_2001@163.com, zengjj_lab@163.com
[2] Shanghai Key Lab for Trustworthy Computing, East China Normal University,
Shanghai 200062, China
zfcao@sei.ecnu.edu.cn
[3] Zheng Zhou Vocational University of Information and Technology,
Zhengzhou 450046, China
mxx1010@126.com

Abstract. Ciphertext-policy attribute-based encryption (CP-ABE) is a promising public key encryption primitive enabling fine-grained access control on shared data in public cloud. However, two quite challenging issues, the prevention of key escrow and key abuse, still exist in CP-ABE system. In this paper, we propose a multi-authority CP-ABE scheme without key escrow and key abuse. To prevent key escrow, multiple authorities are employed to perform the same procedure of key generation for an attribute. Thus, no individual authority or colluded authorities that manage no common attribute can decrypt any ciphertext, and it can also resist collusion attack from curious authority with the help of dishonest users. To prevent key abuse of dishonest users, user's global identifier along with a signature is embedded into the secret key. Thus, any third party can learn the identity from a shared secret key and publicly verify its validity. An advantage of simultaneously preventing key escrow and key abuse is that the proposed scheme can achieve accountability, i.e. an auditor can publicly audit a user or authorities abuse the secret key. At last, the proposed scheme is fully secure in the random oracle model, and due to a key aggregate algorithm its efficiency is comparable to the decentralizing CP-ABE scheme [18] on which it is based.

Keywords: Attribute-based encryption · Multi-authority · Key escrow · Key abuse · Traceability · Accountability

© Springer International Publishing AG 2017
S. Wen et al. (Eds.): CSS 2017, LNCS 10581, pp. 337–351, 2017.
https://doi.org/10.1007/978-3-319-69471-9_25

1   Introduction

With the rapid development of cloud computing and Internet, more and more enterprises and individuals are willing to outsource data or applications to cloud storage servers to enjoy scalable services on-demand. Although cloud storage provides an ease of accessibility, it also raises concerns about data security and access control.

Attribute-based encryption (ABE) is a promising one-to-many encryption primitive with fine-grained access control. It usually has two classifications: key policy attribute-based encryption (KP-ABE) and ciphertext policy attribute-based encryption (CP-ABE). In CP-ABE, attributes of a user are specified in the secret key and access policy defined over some attributes is assigned in the ciphertext. In KP-ABE, the situation is reversed.

In CP-ABE access control system, a user can decrypt a ciphertext if and only if his/her attributes satisfy the access policy specified by the ciphertext, and the secret key is defined over a set of attributes that may be owned by multiple users. No user-specific information is specified in secret keys and ciphertexts. Thus, the secret keys are non-traceable, i.e. given a secret key it is hard to find out its owner due to the fact that the secret key may belong to multiple users. Consequently, a dishonest user dares to share its secret key among users without any risk of being caught.

In a single authority ABE system, all the secret keys are issued by the authority. The authority is able to generate and (re-)distribute secret keys associated with arbitrary set of attributes to unauthorized users without being detected. Even worse, the authority can illegally decrypt arbitrary ciphertext directly using its master key.

Thus, there are two challenging issues: (1) illegal key sharing among users and illegal key distribution by the authority (also called the key abuse problem) (2) illegal ciphertext decryption by the authority (also called the key escrow problem). To securely deploy an ABE access control system, both the misbehavior of dishonest users and curious authority should be prevented.

1.1   Related Works

Sahai and Waters [1] introduced the notion of ABE, and since then many ABE schemes [2–13] have been proposed aiming at better expressiveness, efficiency or security. These schemes [2–13] are single authority ABE that assume there is a central authority who issues secret keys for all users. However, in some applications, data owner may want to share data according to a policy written over attributes issued across different trust domains. A single-authority ABE system will not be appropriate in this scenario.

Multi-authority ABE helps alleviate the extent of trust on authority. In a single authority ABE system [1–13], the authority can directly decrypt all the ciphertexts. In multi-authority ABE schemes [14,15], a central authority can decrypt all ciphertexts. Schemes [16–18, 20–24] do not require such a central authority, and no individual authority can decrypt all ciphertexts, but individual authority can decrypt ciphertexts that the associated access policy can be satisfied by attributes that under its domain. To prevent individual authority from decrypting any ciphertext, scheme [19] introduced multiple central authorities (CAs) besides multiple attribute authorities (AAs). However, in the scheme [19] AA should register itself to the CAs which will need troublesome authenticated interaction and it cannot resist collusion attack from dishonest user and AA, i.e. with the help of a corrupted user AA can decrypt all cipher-texts that the associated access policy can be satisfied by attributes under its domain. In 2015, Zhang et al. [25] proposed a two-authority ABE scheme without key escrow where neither of the two authorities can decrypt the ciphertext even with the help of corrupted users. However, one of the two authorities in [25] manages all attributes, and so the scheme [25] is not suitable for applications across different trust domains.

To prevent illegal key sharing among users, Li et al. [26] gave an accountable ABE supporting AND gate with wildcards access policy. For a better expressiveness, Ning et al. [27] gave a white-box traceable CP-ABE supporting flexible attributes. But scheme [27] can't achieve accountability because nobody can prove whether a leaked key is shared by a malicious user or illegally generated by the authority. In 2015, Ning et al. [28] proposed an accountable ABE with white-box traceability and public auditing. However, schemes [26,28] can't resist key escrow.

1.2   Our Technique

To solve the key escrow problem in CP-ABE system, multiple authorities are employed to reduce the degree of trust. Concretely, different authorities that have different master keys perform the same procedure of key generation for an attribute. As illustrated in Fig. 1, there are n authority sets in the system, denoted by $\mathbb{A}_1, \mathbb{A}_2, ..., \mathbb{A}_n$. Each authority $A_{i,j} \in \mathbb{A}_i$ manages a different domain of attributes, and all the authorities $A_{i,j}$ in set $\mathbb{A}_i$ manage the attribute universe $\mathbb{U}$. Let $\mathcal{T}_i : \mathbb{U} \to \mathbb{A}_i, i = 1, ..., n$ be maps from an attribute $at \in \mathbb{U}$ to an

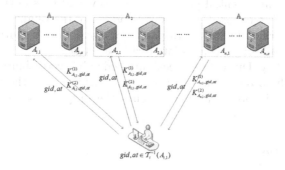

Fig. 1. Process of key generation in MCP-AABE

authority $A_{i,j} \in \mathbb{A}_i$. Let $\mathcal{T}_i^{-1}(A_{i,j}) = \{at \in \mathbb{U} : \mathcal{T}_i(at) = A_{i,j}\}$, then there is $\bigcup_{A_{i,j} \in \mathbb{A}_i} \mathcal{T}_i^{-1}(A_{i,j}) = \mathbb{U}$. When a user with identity gid and attribute set $S \in \mathbb{U}$ joins the system, for each attribute $at \in S$ the user submits the identity gid and attribute at to authorities $A_{i,j} \in \mathbb{A}_i, i = 1, ..., n$, where $\mathcal{T}_i(at) = A_{i,j}$ (takes $A_{i,1}, i = 1, ..., n$ for example in Fig. 1). For $i = 1, ..., n$, $A_{i,1}$ verifies the correctness of gid, at, and generates the corresponding secret key $K_{A_{i,1},gid,at}, i = 1, ..., n$ for user.

To improve efficiency, each authority independently issue secret key for users and no coordination between authorities is required. Secondly, to decrease the size of secret key, a simple key aggregate algorithm is proposed and each user can aggregate the received n secret keys from n different authorities into one aggregate secret key.

1.3   Our Contributions

This paper deals with both the key escrow and key abuse issues in CP-ABE system, and we propose an accountable multi-authority CP-ABE without key escrow and key abuse, denoted by MCP-AABE. The main features of the proposed MCP-AABE scheme can be summarized as follows.

- **High efficiency:** Although there are n attribute authority sets, each authority can independently issue secret keys for users, and no global coordination other than the generation of an initial set of common reference parameters is required. Due to a key aggregate algorithm, both the key/ciphertext size and encryption/decryption cost of the proposed MCP-AABE scheme are comparable to the decentralizing CP-ABE scheme [18].
- **Without key escrow:** The proposed MCP-AABE scheme can be proved to prevent the misbehavior of authorities. No individual authority can decrypt any ciphertext independently; no individual authority even with the help of corrupted users can decrypt ciphertexts not intended for the corrupted users; colluded authorities can't decrypt any ciphertext if they have no common attribute under their domains of attributes.
- **Without key abuse:** The identity gid, which is indispensable for decryption, is regarded as an essential part of a secret key, and thus anybody can trace the identity of an exposed secret key. In addition, the validity of identity can be publicly verified by any third party because a short signature of identity signed by n authorities is associated with secret key.
- **Accountability:** Due to the traceability and public verifiability of an exposed secret key, the owner of a secret key can't deny due to the effective resistance of misbehavior of authority. Thus the proposed scheme can achieve accountability.

1.4   Organization

In Sect. 2, we review the related preliminaries. In Sect. 3, we give the definition and security models. In Sect. 4, we give a concrete construction. And then, we give the security analysis and property comparison with other works in Sect. 5. Finally, the paper is concluded in Sect. 6.

2   Preliminaries

Let $\mathbb{G}, \mathbb{G}_T$ denote two cyclic groups of order $N = p_1 p_2 p_3$, where p_1, p_2, p_3 are three distinct primes; for $i = 1, 2, 3$, let $\mathbb{G}_{p_i}$ denote the subgroup of order p_i in $\mathbb{G}$ and g_i denote a random generator of $\mathbb{G}_{p_i}$.

Definition 1. *A bilinear pairings e is a map such that: (1) Bilinearity: $\forall g, h \in \mathbb{G}$ and $a, b \in \mathbb{Z}_p$, we have $e(g^a, h^b) = e(g, h)^{ab}$; (2) Non-degeneracy: $\exists g \in \mathbb{G}$ such that $e(g, g)$ has order N in $\mathbb{G}_T$. (3) Computability: e can be efficiently computed.*

The subgroups are orthogonal to each other under the bilinear pairings e, i.e. for $\forall h_i \in \mathbb{G}_{p_i}, h_j \in \mathbb{G}_{p_j}, i \neq j$, there is $e(h_i, h_j) = 1$, where 1 is the identity element of $\mathbb{G}_T$.

Definition 2. *Given $g \in \mathbb{G}, g^a$, where $g \in \mathbb{G}, a \in_R \mathbb{Z}_N^*$, the discrete logarithm (DL) problem is to compute a.*

Assumption 1. *The advantage of an algorithm $\mathcal{A}$ in solving the DL problem is defined to be $Adv_{DL}(\mathcal{A}) = \Pr[\mathcal{A}(g, g^a) = a : g, g^a \leftarrow_R \mathbb{G}]$. We say that $\mathbb{G}$ satisfies the DL assumption if $Adv_{DL}(\mathcal{A})$ is a negligible function of security parameter λ for any polynomial algorithm $\mathcal{A}$.*

Definition 3. *Given g, g^a, g^b, where $g \in \mathbb{G}, a, b \in \mathbb{Z}_N$, the computational Diffie-Hellman (CDH) problem is to compute g^{ab}.*

Assumption 2. *The advantage of an algorithm in solving the CDH problem is defined to be $Adv_{CDH}(\mathcal{A}) = \Pr[\mathcal{A}(g, g^a, g^b) = g^{ab} : g, g^a, g^b \leftarrow_R \mathbb{G}]$. We say that $\mathbb{G}$ satisfies the CDH assumption if $Adv_{CDH}(\mathcal{A})$ is a negligible function of security parameter λ for any polynomial algorithm $\mathcal{A}$.*

3   Definition and Security Model

3.1   Definition

An MCP-AABE scheme consists of seven polynomial time algorithms.

Global Setup$(\lambda) \rightarrow GPP$. The global setup algorithm takes the security parameter λ as input, and outputs the global public parameters GPP.

Authority Setup$_{A_{i,j}}(GPP) \rightarrow SK_{A_{i,j}}, PK_{A_{i,j}}$. For $i = 1, ..., n$, each authority $A_{i,j} \in \mathbb{A}_i$ takes GPP as input, and outputs its master secret key $SK_{A_{i,j}}$ and public key $PK_{A_{i,j}}$.

Key Gen$(GPP, at, gid, SK_{A_{i,j}}) \rightarrow K_{A_{i,j},gid,at}$. For $i = 1, ..., n$, each authority $A_{i,j} \in \mathbb{A}_i$ takes GPP, a global identifier gid, an attribute at managed by $A_{i,j}$, master secret key $SK_{A_{i,j}}$ as input, and outputs a secret key $K_{A_{i,j},gid,at}$.

Key Agg$(GPP, \{K_{A_{i,j}}, gid, at\}_{i \in [n]}) \to D_{gid,at}$. The key aggregate algorithm takes GPP, secret keys $\{K_{A_{i,j},gid,at}\}_{i \in [n]}$ as input, and outputs an aggregate decryption key $D_{gid,at}$ of attribute at and identity gid.

Encrypt$(GPP, M, (\mathbb{W}, \rho)) \to CT$. The encryption algorithm takes GPP, a message M, an access structure $(\mathbb{W}, \rho)$ as input, and outputs a ciphertext CT.

Decrypt$(GPP, CT, \{D_{gid,at}:at \in S_{gid}\}) \to M$. The decryption algorithm takes in GPP, a ciphertext CT, a set of aggregate decryption keys $\{D_{gid,at}:at \in S_{gid}\}$, and outputs a plaintext M if S_{gid} satisfies the access policy; else, outputs a reject symbol $\bot$.

Audit$(GPP, \{D_{gid,at}:at \in S_{gid}\}) \to gid$ or $\bot$. The auditing algorithm takes GPP and a set of aggregate decryption keys $\{D_{gid,at}:at \in S_{gid}\}$ (or corresponding secret keys $\{K_{A_{i,j},gid,at}\}_{i \in [n]}$ for each $at \in S_{gid}$) as inputs, it outputs identity gid or a reject symbol $\bot$.

3.2   Full Security Model

The adversary in full security model, called **Type-I** adversary, is allowed to corrupt authorities, but it is naturally restricted that the corrupted authority can't directly decrypt the challenge ciphertext. The full security of MCP-AABE is defined by the following game run between a challenger $\mathcal{C}$ and an adversary $\mathcal{A}$. Similarly with the security model in [18], we assume that $\mathcal{A}$ can corrupt authorities only statically, i.e. $\mathcal{A}$ should tell $\mathcal{C}$ the public keys of corrupted authorities after receiving the global parameters.

Setup. $\mathcal{C}$ runs the Global Setup(λ) algorithm and sends the global public parameters to $\mathcal{A}$. For $i = 1, ..., n$, $\mathcal{A}$ specifies sets $S_i \subset \mathbb{A}_i$ of corrupted authorities. For non-corrupted authorities in $\mathbb{A}_i - S_i$, $\mathcal{C}$ runs the Authority Setup$_{A_{i,j}}$ (GPP) algorithm to obtain master keys and gives public keys to $\mathcal{A}$.

Query Phase 1. The adversary $\mathcal{A}$ is given access to the following oracles which are simulated by the challenger $\mathcal{C}$.

- KQ(gid, at) Query: $\mathcal{A}$ submits an identity gid, an attribute at belonging to $A_{i,j} \in \mathbb{A}_i - S_i$ to $\mathcal{C}$, $\mathcal{C}$ returns $\{K_{A_{i,j},gid,at}\}_{i \in [n]}$ to $\mathcal{A}$.
- KA$(\{K_{A_{i,j},gid,at}\}_{i \in [n]})$ Query: $\mathcal{A}$ submits secret keys $\{K_{A_{i,j},gid,at}\}_{i \in [n]}$ of attribute at to $\mathcal{C}$, $\mathcal{C}$ returns aggregate decryption key $D_{gid,at}$ of at.

Challenge. $\mathcal{A}$ submits two messages M_0, M_1 of equal length, an access structure $(\mathbb{W}, \rho)$ to $\mathcal{C}$. $\mathcal{C}$ flips a random coin $b \in_R \{0, 1\}$ and generates the challenge ciphertext CT. At last, $\mathcal{C}$ returns CT to $\mathcal{A}$.

Query Phase 2. $\mathcal{A}$ further queries as in Query Phase 1.

Guess. $\mathcal{A}$ outputs a guess bit $b' \in_R \{0, 1\}$.

For an identity gid, a set W_{gid} is defined as $W_{gid} = \{at|$KQ(gid, at) *is made by* $\mathcal{A}\}$. $\mathcal{A}$ wins the game if $b = b'$ under the restriction that for $i = 1, ..., n$ no W_{gid} such that $W_{gid} \cup \bigcup_{A_{i,j} \in S_i} \mathcal{T}_i^{-1}(A_{i,j})$ can satisfy the challenge access policy $(\mathbb{W}, \rho)$. The advantage of $\mathcal{A}$ is defined to be $Adv(\mathcal{A}) = |\Pr[b' = b] - 1/2|$.

Definition 4. *An MCP-AABE is full secure if all polynomial time adversaries have at most a negligible advantage in above game.*

3.3   Key Escrow Security Model

Key escrow security concerns about the attack from the authorities, which can be divided into two types, **Type-II** adversary and **Type-III** adversary.

Type-II adversary is defined as a dishonest authority, denoted by DA, colluding with corrupted authorities. Let $S_i \subset \mathbb{A}_i, i = 1, ..., n$ be corrupted authorities sets. Such an adversary is allowed to ask for master keys of corrupted authorities. But it is restricted that these authorities have no common attribute, i.e.

$$\bigcap_{DA,A_{i,j} \in S_i, i=1,\cdots,n} \mathcal{T}_i^{-1}(A_{i,j}) = \emptyset.$$

Type-III adversary is defined as a dishonest authority colluding with dishonest users. Such an adversary owns an authority's master key, and is allowed to ask for secret keys of dishonest users. But it is restricted that corrupted authorities and dishonest users have no common attribute, i.e. $\bigcap_{A_{i,j} \in S_i, i=1,\cdots,n} \mathcal{T}_i^{-1}(A_{i,j}) \cap W_{gid} = \emptyset$, where $W_{gid} = \{at | KQ(gid, at)$ *is made by* $\mathcal{A}\}$.

The goal of an adversary in key escrow attack is to generate an illegal secret key which is prevented by signatures signed by authorities. Thus, the key escrow security of MCP-AABE can be defined by the following unforgeability game run between a challenger $\mathcal{C}$ and an adversary $\mathcal{A}$.

Setup. $\mathcal{C}$ runs the Global Setup(λ) algorithm and sends the global public parameters to $\mathcal{A}$. For $i = 1, ..., n$, $\mathcal{A}$ specifies sets $S_i \subset \mathbb{A}_i$ of corrupted authorities. For non-corrupted authorities, $\mathcal{C}$ runs the Authority Setup$_{A_{i,j} \in \mathbb{A}_i - S_i}(GPP)$ algorithm to obtain the master keys and gives public keys to $\mathcal{A}$.

Query Phase 1. The adversary $\mathcal{A}$ is given access to the following oracles which are simulated by the challenger $\mathcal{C}$.

- KQ(gid, at) Query: $\mathcal{A}$ submits an identity gid, an attribute at belonging to $A_{i,j} \in \mathbb{A}_i - S_i$ to $\mathcal{C}$, $\mathcal{C}$ returns $\{K_{A_{i,j}, gid, at}\}_{i \in [n]}$ to $\mathcal{A}$.
- KA$(\{K_{A_{i,j}, gid, at}\}_{i \in [n]})$ Query: $\mathcal{A}$ submits secret keys $\{K_{A_{i,j}, gid, at}\}_{i \in [n]}$ of attribute at to $\mathcal{C}$, $\mathcal{C}$ returns an aggregate decryption key $D_{gid, at}$ of at.

Forge. $\mathcal{A}$ outputs a decryption key D_{gid^*, at^*} for some gid^*, at^*. $\mathcal{A}$ wins if D_{gid^*, at^*} can pass the Audit algorithm and $\bigcap_{A_{i,j} \in S_i, i=1,\cdots,n} \mathcal{T}_i^{-1}(A_{i,j}) \cap W_{gid^*} \neq at^*$, where $W_{gid^*} = \{at | KQ(gid^*, at)$ *is made by* $\mathcal{A}\}$. The advantage of $\mathcal{A}$ is defined to be $Adv(\mathcal{A}) = \Pr[\mathcal{A} \, wins]$.

Definition 5. *An MCP-AABE is without key escrow if all polynomial time adversaries have at most a negligible advantage in the above game.*

3.4   Key Abuse Security Model

The key abuse of authority can be prevented if the CP-ABE scheme is without key escrow. Thus, we only consider the key abuse of user. It is defined as a dishonest user, denoted by DU, colluding with corrupted authorities. Let $S_i \subset \mathbb{A}_i, i = 1, ..., n$ be corrupted authorities sets. Such an adversary is allowed to ask for master keys of corrupted authorities. But it is naturally restricted that they have no common attribute, i.e. $\bigcap\limits_{A_{i,j}\in S_i, i=1,\cdots,n} \mathcal{T}_i^{-1}(A_{i,j}) \cap W_{DU} = \emptyset$, where W_{DU} is the attributes belongs to DU.

The key abuse security for MCP-AABE can be defined through following game between a challenger $\mathcal{C}$ and an adversary $\mathcal{A}$.

Setup. $\mathcal{C}$ runs the Global Setup(λ) algorithm and sends the global public parameters to $\mathcal{A}$. For $i = 1, ..., n$, $\mathcal{A}$ specifies sets $S_i \subset \mathbb{A}_i$ of corrupted authorities. For non-corrupted authorities in $\mathbb{A}_i - S_i$, $\mathcal{C}$ runs Authority Setup$_{A_{i,j}\in\mathbb{A}_i-S_i}$ (GPP) algorithm to obtain the master keys and gives the public keys to $\mathcal{A}$.

Query Phase 1. The adversary $\mathcal{A}$ is given access to the following oracles which are simulated by the challenger $\mathcal{C}$.

- KQ(gid, at) Query: $\mathcal{A}$ submits an identity gid, an attribute at belonging to $A_{i,j} \in \mathbb{A}_i - S_i$ to $\mathcal{C}$, $\mathcal{C}$ returns $\{K_{A_{i,j},gid,at}\}_{i\in[n]}$ to $\mathcal{A}$.
- KA($\{K_{A_{i,j},gid,at}\}_{i\in[n]}$) Query: $\mathcal{A}$ submits secret keys $\{K_{A_{i,j},gid,at}\}_{i\in[n]}$ of attribute at, $\mathcal{C}$ returns an aggregate decryption key $D_{gid,at}$ of attribute at.

Forge. $\mathcal{A}$ outputs a decryption key D_{gid^*,at^*} for some gid^*, at^*. $\mathcal{A}$ wins if D_{gid^*,at^*} can pass Audit algorithm and $\bigcap\limits_{A_{i,j}\in S_i, i=1,\cdots,n} \mathcal{T}_i^{-1}(A_{i,j}) \cap W_{DU} \neq at^*$, where W_{DU} is the attributes belongs to dishonest user DU. The advantage of $\mathcal{A}$ is defined as $Adv(\mathcal{A}) = \Pr[\mathcal{A}\ wins]$.

Definition 6. *An MCP-AABE can resist key abuse of dishonest users if all polynomial time adversaries have at most a negligible advantage in above game.*

An MCP-AABE is accountable if it can both resist key abuse of dishonest users and authorities.

4   Our Construction

Global Setup(λ) $\rightarrow GPP$: The algorithm runs the group generator with security parameter λ and obtains $(\mathbb{G}, \mathbb{G}_T, e, N = p_1p_2p_3)$, where p_1, p_2, p_3 are three distinct primes, $\mathbb{G}$ and $\mathbb{G}_T$ are two cyclic groups of order N, $e : \mathbb{G}\times\mathbb{G} \rightarrow \mathbb{G}_T$ is a bilinear map. Let $\mathbb{G}_{p_1}$ be the subgroup of order p_1 in $\mathbb{G}$, and $g \in \mathbb{G}_{p_1}$ be a random generator of $\mathbb{G}_{p_1}$. Let $\mathbb{U}$ be the attribute universe, $\mathbb{A}_1, ..., \mathbb{A}_n$ be n sets of authorities, and all the authorities in each set $\mathbb{A}_i$ manage the attribute universe $\mathbb{U}$. For $i = 1, ..., n$, let $\mathcal{T}_i : \mathbb{U} \rightarrow \mathbb{A}_i$ be a map from each attribute $at \in \mathbb{U}$ to an authority $A_{i,j} \in \mathbb{A}_i$, and let $\mathcal{T}_i^{-1}(A_{i,j}) = \{at \in \mathbb{U} : \mathcal{T}_i(at) = A_{i,j}\}$, where $A_{i,j} \in \mathbb{A}_i$. Let $\mathcal{F} : \mathbb{U} \rightarrow \mathbb{G}$ be a map from each attribute $at \in \mathbb{U}$ to an element of $\mathbb{G}$. Let $H : \{0,1\}^* \rightarrow \mathbb{G}$ be a secure Hash function modeled as random oracles. The global public parameters $GPP = \{N, \mathbb{G}, \mathbb{G}_T, e, g, \mathbb{U}, \mathbb{A}_1, ..., \mathbb{A}_n, \mathcal{T}_1, ..., \mathcal{T}_n, \mathcal{F}, H\}$.

Authority Setup$_{A_{i,j}}(GPP) \rightarrow SK_{A_{i,j}}, PK_{A_{i,j}}$: For $i = 1, ..., n$, each authority $A_{i,j} \in \mathbb{A}_i$ randomly chooses $\alpha_{i,j}, x_{i,j} \in_R \mathbb{Z}_N^*$, keeps $SK_{A_{i,j}} = \{\alpha_{i,j}, x_{i,j}\}$ as its master key, and publishes its public key $PK_{A_{i,j}} = (e(g,g)^{\alpha_{i,j}}, g^{x_{i,j}})$.

Key Gen($GPP, at, gid, SK_{A_{i,j}}$) $\rightarrow K_{A_{i,j},gid,at}$: The secret key $K_{A_{i,j},gid,at}$ of attribute at and identity gid, where $\mathcal{T}_i(at) = A_{i,j}$, can be generated as follows.

- The user submits identity gid and attribute at to authority $A_{i,j}$, and the authority $A_{i,j}$ verifies the correctness of gid, at;
- If attribute at belongs to gid, $A_{i,j}$ chooses $r_i \in_R \mathbb{Z}_N^*$ randomly, and computes $K_{A_{i,j},gid,at}^{(1)} = g^{\alpha_{i,j}} H(gid)^{x_{i,j}} \mathcal{F}(at)^{r_i}$, $K_{A_{i,j},gid,at}^{(2)} = g^{r_i}$, and returns $(K_{A_{i,j},gid,at}^{(1)}, K_{A_{i,j},gid,at}^{(2)})$ to user secretly.

Key Agg$(GPP, \{K_{A_{i,j},gid,at}\}_{i\in[n]}) \rightarrow D_{gid,at}$: Receiving $\{K_{A_{i,j},gid,at}\}_{i\in[n]}$ from $A_{i,j}$, for $i = 1, ..., n$, the user computes $D_{gid,at}^{(1)} = \prod_{i=1}^{n} K_{A_{i,j},gid,at}^{(1)}$, $D_{gid,at}^{(2)} = \prod_{i=1}^{n} K_{A_{i,j},gid,at}^{(2)}$. Here, gid is indispensable to decryption process, and regarded as part of secret key. At last, the aggregate decryption key $D_{gid,at}$ for identity gid with attribute at formats as $D_{gid,at} = (gid, D_{gid,at}^{(1)}, D_{gid,at}^{(2)})$.

Encrypt$(GPP, M, (\mathbb{W}, \rho)) \rightarrow CT$: Given message M, access structure $(\mathbb{W}, \rho)$, where $\mathbb{W}$ is a $l \times l'$ matrix and ρ is a map from a row $\mathbb{W}_i$ of $\mathbb{W}$ to an attribute $at_{\rho(i)}$. For $i = 1, ..., l$ and $j = 1, ..., n$, let $\mathcal{T}_j(at_{\rho(i)}) = A_{j,\rho(i)}$. Then the ciphertext $CT = (C_0, \{C_{1,i}, C_{2,i}, C_{3,i}, C_{4,i}\}_{i\in[l]})$ can be generated as follows.

- Chooses $s, v_2, ..., v_{l'}, w_2, ..., w_{l'} \in_R \mathbb{Z}_N^*$ randomly, and constructs two vectors: $\vec{v} = (s, v_2, ..., v_{l'})$, $\vec{w} = (0, w_2, ..., w_{l'})$.
- For $i = 1, ..., l$, chooses $t_i \in_R \mathbb{Z}_N$ randomly, computes $\lambda_i = \mathbb{W}_i \cdot \vec{v}$ and $\mu_i = \mathbb{W}_i \cdot \vec{w}$, and computes: $C_0 = M \cdot e(g,g)^s$; $C_{1,i} = e(g,g)^{\lambda_i} \prod_{j=1}^{n} e(g,g)^{\alpha_{j,\rho(i)} t_i}$; $C_{2,i} = g^{t_i}$; $C_{3,i} = \prod_{j=1}^{n} g^{x_{j,\rho(i)} t_i} g^{\mu_i}$; $C_{4,i} = \mathcal{F}(at_{\rho(i)})^{t_i}$.

Decrypt$(GPP, CT, \{D_{gid,at} : at \in S_{gid}\}) \rightarrow M$: If S_{gid} satisfies the access policy specified by $(\mathbb{W}, \rho)$, user gid with attribute set S_{gid} can recover message as follows.

- Computes $\{\omega_i : i \in I\}$ such that $\sum_{i\in I} \omega_i \mathbb{W}_i = (1, 0, ..., 0)$, where $I = \{i : at_{\rho(i)} \in S_{gid}\}$.
- Computes $\dfrac{C_{1,i} e(C_{3,i}, H(gid)) e(C_{4,i}, D_{gid,at_{\rho(i)}}^{(2)})}{e(C_{2,i}, D_{gid,at_{\rho(i)}}^{(1)})} = e(g,g)^{\lambda_i} e(g, H(gid))^{\mu_i}$.
- Computes $\prod_{i\in I} (e(g,g)^{\lambda_i} e(g, H(gid))^{\mu_i})^{\omega_i} = e(g,g)^s$.
- Recovers $M = \dfrac{C_0}{e(g,g)^s}$.

Audit$(GPP, gid, \{D_{gid,at} : at \in S_{gid}\}) \rightarrow gid$ or $\bot$: Given an aggregate decryption key $(gid, \{D_{gid,at} : at \in S_{gid}\})$, any third party can publicly verify whether it belongs to identity gid or not. If and only if $\exists at \in S_{gid}$ such that $e(D_{gid,at}^{(1)}, g) = \prod_{i=1}^{n} PK_{A_{i,j}}^1 \prod_{i=1}^{n} e(PK_{A_{i,j}}^2, H(gid)) e(\mathcal{F}(at), D_{gid,at}^{(2)})$, where $\mathcal{T}_i(at) = A_{i,j}$ for $i = 1, ..., n$, the algorithm output an identity gid, else output $\bot$.

5   Security Analysis and Performance

The proposed MCP-AABE scheme can be proved fully secure based on the full security of the multi-authority CP-ABE scheme [18] by Theorem 1, and can be proved without key escrow based on the unforgeability of the short signature scheme [30] in Theorem 2, and can be proved without key abuse based on the unforgeability of signature schemes [29,30] by Theorem 3.

5.1   Confidentiality

Theorem 1. *If there is an adversary $\mathcal{A}$ that can break full security of the proposed MCP-AABE scheme with advantage ε, there will be an adversary $\mathcal{A}_1$ with advantage ε that can break the multi-authority CP-ABE scheme [18].*

Proof. We will prove that an adversary $\mathcal{A}$ against the proposed MCP-AABE scheme can be used to construct an adversary $\mathcal{A}_1$ against the multi-authority CP-ABE scheme [18] as follows.

Setup. Challenger $\mathcal{C}$ runs the Global Setup(λ) algorithm and sends the global public parameters $\{N, \mathbb{G}, \mathbb{G}_T, e, g, \mathbb{U}, \mathbb{A}_1, ..., \mathbb{A}_n, \mathcal{T}_1, ..., \mathcal{T}_n, \mathcal{F}, H\}$ to $\mathcal{A}$, and sends $\{N, \mathbb{G}, \mathbb{G}_T, e, g, \mathbb{U}, \}$ to $\mathcal{A}_1$. $\mathcal{A}$ and $\mathcal{A}_1$ specifies corrupted authorities. $\mathcal{C}$ runs the Authority Setup$_{A_{i,j}}(GPP)$ algorithm, and gives public keys of uncorrupted authorities to $\mathcal{A}$, computes $(e(g,g)^{\sum_{i=1}^{n} \alpha_{i,j}}, g^{\sum_{i=1}^{n} x_{i,j}})$ which implies the master key of uncorrupted authority is set to be $\alpha_j = \sum_{i=1}^{n} \alpha_{i,j}, x_j = \sum_{i=1}^{n} x_{i,j}$ and sends $(e(g,g)^{\sum_{i=1}^{n} \alpha_{i,j}}, g^{\sum_{i=1}^{n} x_{i,j}})$ to $\mathcal{A}_1$.

Query Phase 1. Given a KQ(gid, at) query from $\mathcal{A}_1$, $\mathcal{C}$ generates an aggregate decryption key $(D_{gid,at}^{(1)}, D_{gid,at}^{(2)})$ of attribute at with $r_i = 0, i = 1, ..., n$, and sends $D_{gid,at}^{(1)} = g^{\sum_{i=1}^{n} \alpha_{i,j}} H(gid)^{\sum_{i=1}^{n} x_{i,j}} \mathcal{F}(at)^{\sum_{i=1}^{n} r_i} = g^{\alpha_j} H(gid)^{x_j}$ to $\mathcal{A}_1$.

Challenge. Given two messages M_0, M_1 and an access structure $(\mathbb{W}, \rho)$. $\mathcal{C}$ generates a challenge ciphertext $CT = (C_0, \{C_{1,i}, C_{2,i}, C_{3,i}, C_{4,i}\}_{i \in [l]})$ for $\mathcal{A}$. $C_{1,i}, C_{3,i}$ can be written as $C_{1,i} = e(g,g)^{\lambda_i} e(g,g)^{\alpha_{\rho(i)} t_i}, C_{3,i} = \prod_{j=1}^{n} g^{x_{j,\rho(i)} t_i} g^{\mu_i} = g^{x_{\rho(i)} t_i} g^{\mu_i}$. Thus, $\mathcal{C}$ sends $(C_0, \{C_{1,i}, C_{2,i}, C_{3,i}\}_{i \in [l]})$ to $\mathcal{A}_1$.

From above simulation, $\mathcal{C}$ can indistinguishably simulate all the queries asked from $\mathcal{A}_1$. Thus, if there is an adversary $\mathcal{A}$ that has advantage ε to have a correct guess $b = b'$, similarly $\mathcal{C}$ has advantage ε to break the multi-authority CP-ABE scheme [18].

5.2   Security Analysis for Problem of Key Escrow

Theorem 2. *Let $Adv_{DL}(\mathcal{A})$ denote the advantage of adversary $\mathcal{A}$ in solving the DL problem, and ε_1 denote the advantage of adversary $\mathcal{A}$ against the short* *signature scheme* [30], *then a Type II or Type III adversary* $\mathcal{A}$ *in the proposed MCP-AABE scheme can generate a valid decryption key with advantage at most* $Adv_{DL}(\mathcal{A}) + \varepsilon_1$.

Proof. The short signature in scheme [30] formats as $H(m)^x$, where x is the secret key. $D_{gid,at}^{(1)} = g^{\sum\limits_{i=1}^{n} \alpha_{i,j}} H(gid)^{\sum\limits_{i=1}^{n} x_{i,j}} \mathcal{F}(at)^{\sum\limits_{i=1}^{n} r_i} = H(gid)^{\sum\limits_{i=1}^{n} x_{i,j}} g'$, can be directly seen as a short signature [30] of identity signed by secret key $\sum\limits_{i=1}^{n} x_{i,j}$.

The short signature scheme [30] is proved to be unforgeable under the CDH assumption. Then, we only need to reduce the key escrow security of our scheme to the unforgeability of scheme [30]. There are two kinds of adversaries in key escrow security model: Type II and Type III adversary.

Type-II adversary is defined as a dishonest authority colluding with corrupted authorities. Let DA denote the dishonest authority and $S_i \subset \mathbb{A}_i, i = 1,...,n$ be corrupted authorities sets. However, it is restricted that corrupted authorities have no common attribute, i.e. $\bigcap\limits_{DA, A_{i,j} \in S_i, i=1,\cdots,n} \mathcal{T}_i^{-1}(A_{i,j}) = \emptyset$. Without loss of generality, we assume authority $A_{1,1}$ denote the dishonest authority, and authorities $A_{i,j}, i \in [2,n], j \in J$, where J is an index set, are corrupted, and assume $at \notin \mathcal{T}_1^{-1}(A_{1,1})$ according to the restriction. Then, a Type-II adversary knows $\sum\limits_{i=2}^{n} x_{i,j}$ and public key $g^{x_{1,1}}$. Owing to the unforgeability of signature scheme [30] and the DL assumption, a Type-II adversary can't generate

$$D_{gid,at}^{(1)} = H(gid)^{x_{1,1}} H(gid)^{\sum\limits_{i=2}^{n} x_{i,j}} g'.$$

Type-III adversary is defined as dishonest authorities colluding with dishonest users. It is naturally restricted that corrupted authorities and dishonest users have no common attribute, i.e. $\bigcap\limits_{A_{i,j} \in S_i, i=1,\cdots,n} \mathcal{T}_i^{-1}(A_{i,j}) \cap W_{gid} = \emptyset$, where $W_{gid} = \{at | KQ(gid, at) \text{ is made by } \mathcal{A}\}$. We assume $at \notin \mathcal{T}_1^{-1}(A_{1,1})$, then a Type-III adversary can get $H(gid)^{\sum\limits_{i=2}^{n} x_{i,j}} g^{\sum\limits_{i=2}^{n} \alpha_{i,j}} \mathcal{F}(at)^{\sum\limits_{i=2}^{n} r_i}$ from corrupted authorities and dishonest users, and public key $g^{x_{1,1}}$. Owing to the unforgeability of scheme [30], a Type-III adversary cannot generate a valid secret key

$$D_{gid,at}^{(1)} = H(gid)^{x_{1,1}} H(gid)^{\sum\limits_{i=2}^{n} x_{i,j}} g'.$$

5.3   Security Analysis for Problem of Key Abuse

Theorem 3. *Let $Adv_{DL}(\mathcal{A})$ denote the advantage of adversary $\mathcal{A}$ in solving the DL problem, and ε_2 denote the advantage of adversary $\mathcal{A}$ against the signature scheme* [29], *then a malicious user $\mathcal{A}$ in the proposed MCP-AABE scheme can generate a forged decryption key with advantage at most $Adv_{DL}(\mathcal{A}) + \varepsilon_2$.*

Proof. The signature scheme in scheme [29] formats as $g_2^{\alpha} \mathcal{F}(at)^r, g^r$, where $g_2 \in_R \mathbb{G}, r \in_R \mathbb{Z}_N^*$ and α is the secret key. The decryption key $D_{gid,at}^{(1)} = g' g_2^{\sum\limits_{i=1}^{n} x_{i,j}}$

$\mathcal{F}(at)^{\overset{n}{\underset{i=1}{\sum}} r_i}$, $D_{gid,at}^{(2)} = g^{\overset{n}{\underset{i=1}{\sum}} r_i}$, where $g_2 = H(gid), g' = g^{\overset{n}{\underset{i=1}{\sum}} \alpha_{i,j}}$, can be directly

seen as a signature [29] of attribute at signed by secret key $\overset{n}{\underset{i=1}{\sum}} x_{i,j}$.

The signature scheme [29] is proved to be unforgeable under the CDH assumption. Then, we will reduce the key abuse security of the proposed scheme to the unforgeability of scheme [29]. The key abuse of authority can be prevented because the CP-ABE scheme is without key escrow. Thus, we only consider the key abuse of user.

The key abuse of user is defined as a dishonest user, denoted by DU, colluding with corrupted authorities. It is restricted that they have no common attribute, i.e. $\underset{A_{i,j} \in S_i, i=1,\cdots,n}{\bigcap} \mathcal{T}_i^{-1}(A_{i,j}) \cap W_{DU} = \emptyset$, where W_{DU} is the attributes belongs to dishonest user DU. We assume $at \notin \mathcal{T}_1^{-1}(A_{1,1})$, then a Type-III adversary can get $H(gid)^{\overset{n}{\underset{i=2}{\sum}} x_{i,j}} \mathcal{F}(at)^{\overset{n}{\underset{i=2}{\sum}} r_i} g^{\overset{n}{\underset{i=2}{\sum}} \alpha_{i,j}}, g^{\overset{n}{\underset{i=2}{\sum}} r_i}$ from corrupted authorities and dishonest users, and the public key $g^{x_{1,1}}$. Thus, owing to the unforgeability of signature scheme [29], a malicious user cannot generate a valid secret key

$D_{gid,at}^{(1)} = g_2^{x_{1,1}} g_2^{\overset{n}{\underset{i=2}{\sum}} x_{i,j}} \mathcal{F}(at)^{\overset{n}{\underset{i=1}{\sum}} r_i} g', D_{gid,at}^{(2)} = g^{\overset{n}{\underset{i=1}{\sum}} r_i}$.

Furthermore, from Theorem 2 and Theorem 3, the key abuse of both dishonest user and authority can be prevented, so it can achieve accountability.

5.4   Feature and Efficiency Comparisons

Table 1 shows comparisons of security properties between multi-authority ABE schemes [18,19,25], traceable ABE schemes [26–28] and the MCP-AABE scheme, where TR denotes traceability and PV denotes public verifiability. The proposed MCP-AABE scheme is adaptively secure in the random oracle model, and is the first multi-authority CP-ABE that is without key escrow and key abuse.

Table 1. Security property comparison with related works

Scheme	Type I	Key Escrow			Key Abuse	
		Type II	Type III	Type IV	TR	PV
[18]	Full	×	×	×	✓	×
[19]	Full	✓	×	✓	×	×
[25]	Selective	✓	✓	×	×	×
[26]	Selective	✓	×	×	✓	✓
[27]	Full	×	×	×	✓	×
[28]	Full	×	×	×	✓	✓
MCP-AABE	Full	✓	✓	✓	✓	✓

We also give a comparison of efficiency with the multi-authority CP-ABE schemes [18,19]. Let $|A|$ denote the number of attributes associated with a secret key, $|W|$ denote the number of attributes related to an access structure, $|D|$ denote the number of attributes needed for decryption, $|N|$ denote the number of CAs in [19].

Table 2. Efficiency comparison with scheme [18]

Scheme	Key	Ciphertext	Encryption		Decryption	
			Pairing	Exponential	Pairing	Exponential
[18]	$|A|$	$3|W|+1$	1	$5|W|+1$	$2|D|$	$|D|+1$
[19]	$2|A|+1$	$2|W|+1$	1	$3|W|+|N|+1$	$3|D|$	$|D|+1$
MCP-AABE	$2|A|$	$4|W|+1$	1	$6|W|+1$	$3|D|$	$|D|+1$

As shown in Table 2, the efficiency of MCP-AABE is comparable to the CP-ABE scheme [18,19]. Actually, if without considering the multiplication operation in group $\mathbb{G}$, the efficiency (including the key and ciphertext size) of the proposed MCP-AABE scheme can be decreased to the same as scheme [18] if we let an attribute relate to a master key instead of a master key managing many attributes, i.e. for $i = 1, ..., n, \forall A_{i,j} \in \mathbb{A}_i, |T_i^{-1}(A_{i,j})| = 1$. Let $r_i = 0, i = 1, ..., n$, then $(D_{gid,at}^{(1)}, D_{gid,at}^{(2)}) = (g^{\alpha_j} H(gid)^{x_j}, g)$ is same as secret key in scheme [18] with master key $\alpha_j = \sum_{i=1}^{n} \alpha_{i,j}, x_j = \sum_{i=1}^{n} x_{i,j}$. Furthermore, in scheme [19], AAs should register itself to the CAs which will need troublesome authenticated interaction, and in MCP-AABE, each authority can independently issue secret keys for users.

6   Conclusion

Key escrow and key abuse are two quite challenging issues in an ABE access control system. We formalize the concept of MCP-AABE and propose a concrete MCP-AABE scheme. In the proposed scheme, authorities who are from different authority sets will independently distribute a secret key for an attribute, and there is no requirement for any global coordination other than the creation of an initial set of common reference parameters. In the proposed scheme, no individual authority can decrypt any ciphertext. Even with the help of any corrupted user, no individual authority can decrypt the ciphertext not intended for the corrupted user. Furthermore, corrupted authorities can't decrypt any ciphertext if they have no common attribute in their domains of attributes. In addition, any third party can publicly verify the identity of an exposed secret key. Thus, it can achieve accountability. At last, the computation cost and communication cost of our scheme is comparable to the decentralizing CP-ABE scheme [18].

Acknowledgment. This work was supported in part by China Postdoctoral Science Foundation of China (No. 2016M591629), in part by the National Natural Science

Foundation of China (No. 61602512, 61632012, 61373154, 61371083, 61411146001), in part by the Prioritized Development Projects through Specialized Research Fund for the Doctoral Program of Higher Education of China (No. 20130073130004).

References

1. Sahai, A., Waters, B.: Fuzzy identity-based encryption. In: Cramer, R. (ed.) EURO-CRYPT 2005. LNCS, vol. 3494, pp. 457–473. Springer, Heidelberg (2005). doi:10.1007/11426639_27

2. Goyal, V., Pandey, O., Sahai, A., Waters, B.: Attribute-based encryption for fine grained access control of encrypted data. In: Proceedings of the 13th ACM Conference on Computer and Communications Security, pp. 89–98. ACM (2006)

3. Bethencourt, J., Sahai, A., Waters, B.: Ciphertext-policy attribute-based encryption. In: IEEE Symposium on Security and Privacy 2007, pp. 321–334. IEEE (2007)

4. Okamoto, T., Takashima, K.: Fully secure functional encryption with general relations from the decisional linear assumption. In: Rabin, T. (ed.) CRYPTO 2010. LNCS, vol. 6223, pp. 191–208. Springer, Heidelberg (2010). doi:10.1007/978-3-642-14623-7_11

5. Lewko, A., Okamoto, T., Sahai, A., Takashima, K., Waters, B.: Fully secure functional encryption: attribute-based encryption and (hierarchical) inner product encryption. In: Gilbert, H. (ed.) EUROCRYPT 2010. LNCS, vol. 6110, pp. 62–91. Springer, Heidelberg (2010). doi:10.1007/978-3-642-13190-5_4

6. Herranz, J., Laguillaumie, F., Ràfols, C.: Constant size ciphertexts in threshold attribute-based encryption. In: Nguyen, P.Q., Pointcheval, D. (eds.) PKC 2010. LNCS, vol. 6056, pp. 19–34. Springer, Heidelberg (2010). doi:10.1007/978-3-642-13013-7_2

7. Lewko, A., Waters, B.: Unbounded HIBE and attribute-based encryption. In: Paterson, K.G. (ed.) EUROCRYPT 2011. LNCS, vol. 6632, pp. 547–567. Springer, Heidelberg (2011). doi:10.1007/978-3-642-20465-4_30

8. Waters, B.: Ciphertext-policy attribute-based encryption: an expressive, efficient, and provably secure realization. In: Catalano, D., Fazio, N., Gennaro, R., Nicolosi, A. (eds.) PKC 2011. LNCS, vol. 6571, pp. 53–70. Springer, Heidelberg (2011). doi:10.1007/978-3-642-19379-8_4

9. Yamada, S., Attrapadung, N., Hanaoka, G., Kunihiro, N.: Generic constructions for chosen-ciphertext secure attribute based encryption. In: Catalano, D., Fazio, N., Gennaro, R., Nicolosi, A. (eds.) PKC 2011. LNCS, vol. 6571, pp. 71–89. Springer, Heidelberg (2011). doi:10.1007/978-3-642-19379-8_5

10. Okamoto, T., Takashima, K.: Fully secure unbounded inner-product and attribute-based encryption. In: Wang, X., Sako, K. (eds.) ASIACRYPT 2012. LNCS, vol. 7658, pp. 349–366. Springer, Heidelberg (2012). doi:10.1007/978-3-642-34961-4_22

11. Lewko, A., Waters, B.: New proof methods for attribute-based encryption: achieving full security through selective techniques. In: Safavi-Naini, R., Canetti, R. (eds.) CRYPTO 2012. LNCS, vol. 7417, pp. 180–198. Springer, Heidelberg (2012). doi:10.1007/978-3-642-32009-5_12

12. Hohenberger, S., Waters, B.: Attribute-based encryption with fast decryption. In: Kurosawa, K., Hanaoka, G. (eds.) PKC 2013. LNCS, vol. 7778, pp. 162–179. Springer, Heidelberg (2013). doi:10.1007/978-3-642-36362-7_11

13. Rouselakis, Y., Waters, B.: Practical constructions and new proof methods for large universe attribute-based encryption. In: Proceedings of the 2013 ACM SIGSAC Conference on Computer and Communications Security, pp. 463–474. ACM (2013)

14. Chase, M.: Multi-authority attribute based encryption. In: Vadhan, S.P. (ed.) TCC 2007. LNCS, vol. 4392, pp. 515–534. Springer, Heidelberg (2007). doi:10.1007/978-3-540-70936-7_28

15. Mller, S., Katzenbeisser, S., Eckert, C.: On multi-authority ciphertext-policy attribute-based encryption. Bull. Korean Math. Soc. **46**(4), 803–819 (2009)

16. Lin, H., Cao, Z., Liang, X., et al.: Secure threshold multi authority attribute based encryption without a central authority. Inf. Sci. **180**(13), 2618–2632 (2010)

17. Chase, M., Chow, S.: Improving privacy and security in multi-authority attribute-based encryption. In: Proceedings of the 16th ACM Conference on Computer and Communications Security, pp. 121–130. ACM (2009)

18. Lewko, A., Waters, B.: Decentralizing attribute-based encryption. In: Paterson, K.G. (ed.) EUROCRYPT 2011. LNCS, vol. 6632, pp. 568–588. Springer, Heidelberg (2011). doi:10.1007/978-3-642-20465-4_31

19. Liu, Z., Cao, Z., Huang, Q., Wong, D.S., Yuen, T.H.: Fully secure multi-authority ciphertext-policy attribute-based encryption without random oracles. In: Atluri, V., Diaz, C. (eds.) ESORICS 2011. LNCS, vol. 6879, pp. 278–297. Springer, Heidelberg (2011). doi:10.1007/978-3-642-23822-2_16

20. Rouselakis, Y., Waters, B.: Efficient statically-secure large-universe multi-authority attribute-based encryption. In: Böhme, R., Okamoto, T. (eds.) FC 2015. LNCS, vol. 8975, pp. 315–332. Springer, Heidelberg (2015). doi:10.1007/978-3-662-47854-7_19

21. Qian, H., Li, J., Zhang, Y., Han, J.: Privacy preserving personal health record using multi-authority attribute-based encryption with revocation. Int. J. Inf. Secur. **14**(6), 487–497 (2015)

22. Chow, S.S.M.: A framework of multi-authority attribute-based encryption with out-sourcing and revocation. In: Proceedings of the 21st ACM on Symposium on Access Control Models and Technologies 2016, pp. 215–226. ACM (2016)

23. Jiang, R., Wu, X., Bhargava, B.: Secure data sharing scheme in multi-authority cloud storage systems. Comput. Secur. **62**, 193–212 (2016). Elsevier

24. Zhong, H., Zhu, W., Xu, Y., et al.: Multi-authority attribute-based encryption access control scheme with policy hidden for cloud storage. Soft Comput. (2016). doi:10.1007/s00500-016-2330-8

25. Zhang, X., Jin, C., Wen, Z., Shen, Q., Fang, Y., Wu, Z.: Attribute-based encryption without key escrow. In: Huang, Z., Sun, X., Luo, J., Wang, J. (eds.) ICCCS 2015. LNCS, vol. 9483, pp. 74–87. Springer, Cham (2015). doi:10.1007/978-3-319-27051-7_7

26. Li, J., Ren, K., Kim, K.: A2BE: accountable attribute-based encryption for abuse free access control. IACR Cryptology ePrint Arch 2009, 118 (2009)

27. Ning, J., Cao, Z., Dong, X., Wei, L., Lin, X.: Large universe ciphertext-policy attribute-based encryption with white-box traceability. In: Kutyłowski, M., Vaidya, J. (eds.) ESORICS 2014. LNCS, vol. 8713, pp. 55–72. Springer, Cham (2014). doi:10.1007/978-3-319-11212-1_4

28. Ning, J., Dong, X., Cao, Z., Wei, L.: Accountable authority ciphertext-policy attribute-based encryption with white-box traceability and public auditing in the cloud. In: Pernul, G., Ryan, P.Y.A., Weippl, E. (eds.) ESORICS 2015. LNCS, vol. 9327, pp. 270–289. Springer, Cham (2015). doi:10.1007/978-3-319-24177-7_14

29. Paterson, K.G., Schuldt, J.C.N.: Efficient identity-based signatures secure in the standard model. In: Batten, L.M., Safavi-Naini, R. (eds.) ACISP 2006. LNCS, vol. 4058, pp. 207–222. Springer, Heidelberg (2006). doi:10.1007/11780656_18

30. Boneh, D., Lynn, B., Shacham, H.: Short signatures from the weil pairing. In: Boyd, C. (ed.) ASIACRYPT 2001. LNCS, vol. 2248, pp. 514–532. Springer, Heidelberg (2001). doi:10.1007/3-540-45682-1_30

Optimization of Cloud Workflow Scheduling Based on Balanced Clustering

Lei Zhang, Dongjin Yu[(✉)], and Hongsheng Zheng

School of Computer Science and Technology, Hangzhou Dianzi University,
Hangzhou, China
yudj@hdu.edu.cn

Abstract. Scientific workflow applications consist of many fine-grained computational tasks with dependencies, whose runtime varies widely. When executing these fine-grained tasks in a cloud computing environment, significant scheduling overheads are generated. Task clustering is a key technology to reduce scheduling overhead and optimize process execution time. Unfortunately, the attempts of task clustering often cause the problems of runtime and dependency imbalance. However, the existing task clustering strategies mainly focus on how to avoid the runtime imbalance, but rarely deal with the data dependency between tasks. Without considering the data dependency, task clustering will lead to the poor degree of parallelism during task execution due to the introduced data locality. In order to address the problem of dependency imbalance, we propose Dependency Balance Clustering Algorithm (DBCA), which defines the concept of dependency correlation to measure the similarity between tasks in terms of data dependencies. The tasks with high dependency correlation are clustered together so as to avoid the dependency imbalance. We conducted the experiments on the WorkflowSim platform and compared our method with the existing task clustering method. The results showed that it significantly reduced the execution time of the whole workflow.

Keywords: Cloud computing · Scientific workflow · Scheduling · Task clustering · Dependency balance

1 Introduction

Scientific workflow applications are generally used for scientific computing in different areas such as astronomy, physics, bioinformatics and earth sciences. These workflows consist of many compute-intensive tasks with data dependencies. Some tasks run only a few seconds while some need tens of minutes. Such intensive computing usually depends on a distributed computing environment with high-performance. Because cloud computing has the characteristics of flexibility, high scalability and economy, many organizations migrate traditional workflow applications to cloud computing environment, which introduces so-called cloud workflow. However, significant scheduling overhead will be generated when performing these workflow tasks in a large, distributed cloud computing environment. Sometimes, the extra time generated by scheduling overhead is even far more than the runtime of the task itself, thus

S. Wen et al. (Eds.): CSS 2017, LNCS 10581, pp. 352–366, 2017.
https://doi.org/10.1007/978-3-319-69471-9_26

affecting the execution time of the entire process [1]. In order to reduce the impact of this overhead, many task clustering techniques have been developed during the recent years. Such techniques usually combine fine-grained tasks into coarse-grained tasks, so as to reduce the number of tasks and increase the computational granularity of the tasks. In this way, the purpose of reducing the scheduling overhead can be achieved and the execution time of the whole process can be optimized.

However, inside a workflow, the tasks on the same level may have different run-time. Merging tasks on the same level into several clusters without considering the variation of their runtime will lead to load imbalances. For example, some clusters may consist of short-runtime tasks, while others consist of long-runtime tasks. Such runtime imbalance problem will delay the release of the tasks on the next level.

On the other hand, the data dependency between tasks also plays an important role in task clustering. Here, data dependency means that there is data transfer between two tasks (the output data of one task is the input data for another task). In the process of task clustering, it is necessary to consider the dependencies between tasks (such as merging the tasks which have the same successor task). If the data dependency is not considered in task clustering, the output data of the upper tasks will be particularly dispersive. A task on one level has to wait for more upper tasks to be finished before it can be executed, which will increase the data transfer time and extend the execution time of the process.

In addition to system overhead, security and privacy are important factors when scheduling and executing workflows in a cloud environment. In fact, during the execution of tasks in a workflow, data are transferred from one task to another task. If the data privacy is not protected, it may lead to data leakage. In other words, clustering tasks according to data dependencies will not only reduce the completion time of workflow, but also the dispersion of data. The child tasks with the same parent task are encapsulated together to ensure the safety and closure of data.

Unfortunately, to the best of our knowledge, the existing task clustering strategies mainly study how to avoid the runtime imbalance, but rarely consider the data dependency between tasks. To address the problem of dependency imbalance, we propose a Dependency Balance Clustering Algorithm (DBCA). DBCA defines the concept of dependency correlation to measure the degree of similarity in terms of data dependencies between tasks. It gradually adds the tasks that maximizes the sum of dependency correlations to the cluster by using incremental method, leading to the maximum of dependency correlations for each cluster, which can better solve the problem of dependency imbalance.

The contributions of this paper are as the follows. (1) We define the dependency correlation which can precisely measures the similarity of the two tasks in terms of data dependencies. (2) We propose a Dependency Balance Clustering Algorithm (DBCA) to solve the problem of dependency imbalance. (3) We compared our clustering algorithm with the existing algorithm through the WorkflowSim simulation platform with extensive experiments.

The rest of this paper is organized as follows. After Sect. 2 gives an overview of the related work, Sect. 3 presents the relevant models and the concept of balanced task clustering. Section 4 details the proposed clustering algorithm called DBCA, whereas Sect. 5 demonstrates experimental results. Finally, Sect. 6 concludes our work and shows the future work.

2 Related Work

System overhead analysis has always been a concerned issue in the workflow community. Several research studies have been conducted in the past in order to analyze system overhead in a distributed environment (such as grid and cloud). Stratan et al. presented a grid workflow engine evaluation method that focuses on five features: overhead, raw performance, stability, scalability and reliability [2]. They pointed out that the main bottleneck of a busy system is the head node, so the resource consumption caused by the head node should not be ignored. In [3], Chen et al. focused on measuring the overlap of major overheads imposed by workflow management systems and execution environments and analyzed how existing optimization techniques improve the workflow runtime by reducing or overlapping overheads. These above works allow researchers to understand the system overhead more deeply and pave the way for the generation of task clustering technology.

Some works applied task clustering to the running of scientific application in distributed environment. Task clustering reduces the scheduling overhead by combining fine-grained tasks in the workflow into coarse-grained tasks, shortening the completion time of process. Muthuvelu et al. proposed a clustering algorithm that cluster tasks based on the runtime of tasks [4]. Later they extended their work in [5] by considering more factors in task clustering such as task file size, CPU time, and resource policies. Recently they proposed policies and approaches to decide the granularity of a task group that obeys the task processing requirements and resource network utilization constraints while satisfying the user's QoS requirements [6]. Other research teams also have done a lot of work. Ang et al. proposed a bandwidth-aware job grouping-based scheduling strategy to maximize the Grid resource utilization and reduce the delay [7]. Liu and Liao proposed an adaptive fine-grained job scheduling algorithm which clusters tasks according to some resource characteristics such as processing capacity and bandwidth [8]. However, these task clustering strategies just study from the runtime balance, but hardly consider the data dependency between tasks.

In recent years, several works considered data dependencies between tasks which reduced the overhead by designing a series of data placement strategies. In [9], Zhao et al. proposed a data placement strategy based on heuristic genetic algorithm to reduce data movements among data centers while balancing the loads of data centers. Deng et al. proposed an efficient data and task co-scheduling strategy which can improve the performance of task scheduling and meanwhile reduce data transfer volume [10]. In [11], Li et al. proposed a novel workflow-level data placement strategy for data-sharing scientific cloud workflows. The strategy is divided into two stages, first pre-allocates initial datasets to proper data centers during workflow build-time stage, and then dynamically distributes newly generated datasets to appropriate data centers during runtime stage.

Different from the current works, we define dependency correlation to precisely characterize the similarity between tasks in terms of data dependencies. On this basis, we further propose a balanced clustering method to solve the problem of data dependency imbalance.

3   Problem Description

3.1   Workflow Model

Workflow is composed of a series of tasks with dependencies, generally described by finite acyclic graphs (DAG). Figure 1 shows a simple workflow example, in which the nodes represent tasks, and the edges represent dependencies between tasks.

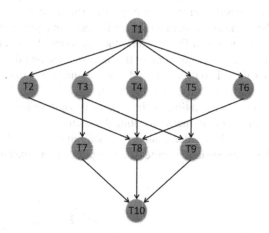

Fig. 1. An example of a workflow.

Workflow can be expressed as a tuple: $W = \{T, E, D\}$. Here $T = \{t_1, t_2, \ldots, t_i, \ldots, t_N\}$ represents a set of tasks, in which N denotes the number of tasks. The initial task is the one without parent node, which is represented by t_{entry}, whereas the final task is a task without any child node, represented by t_{exit}. Besides, E denotes a set of directed edges, and $E = \{(t_i, t_j) \mid t_i, t_j \in T\}$ in which (t_i, t_j) indicates the dependencies between tasks t_i and t_j, that is, task t_i is the predecessor task of task t_j, or task t_j is the subsequent task of task t_i. For simplicity, we use $pre(t_i)$ to denote the set of direct predecessor tasks for task t_i, and $succ(t_i)$ to denote the set of direct successors. $D = \{d_{t_i, t_j} \mid t_i \in T, t_j \in T\}$ represents the size of data transferred between tasks t_i and t_j, which indicates the communication overhead between any two tasks in the workflow. In particular, when the task t_i and task t_j are scheduled on the same virtual machine (VM), the communication overhead can be ignored.

3.2   Task Clustering

In the cloud environment, task clustering algorithm acts on the workflow mapper. Task clustering combines tasks into groups to reduce the number of tasks in the workflow scheduling phase to further shorten the queue waiting time for task scheduling. The workflow engine dispatches the job that are merged by tasks to the cloud resource node. When the job reaches the cloud resource node, the workflow system extracts the tasks in the job and executes them.

In order to analyze the clustering process in a better way, as the work of [12], we extend the DAG model to an overhead aware DAG (O-DAG), because the system overhead plays an important role throughout the execution time of the process. Figure 2 shows the process of extending a DAG model to an O-DAG model. The O-DAG model adds the system overhead S, such as workflow delay and queuing delay.

According to the O-DAG model, we can easily analyze the advantages of clustering. For example, in Fig. 3, there are two tasks without data dependency t_1 and t_2, which needs to be combined into a job j_1. After clustering, tasks t_1 and t_2 in job j_1 will be executed in a specific order, in series or in parallel (in this paper is serial execution). The job parser in the workflow system will parse the tasks in a job, which will cause the clustering delay, c_1, as shown in Fig. 3. Here, the clustering delay refers to the length of time between the actual execution time of the tasks in a job and the execution time of the job. Assume that there is only one cloud resource node, the execution time of the process in Fig. 3(a) is as follows: $runtime1 = s_1 + t_1 + s_2 + t_2$. After clustering, as shown in Fig. 3(b), the execution time of the process is: $runtime2 = s_1 + c_1 + t_1 + t_2$. If $c_1 < s_2$, $runtime1 < runtime2$. In many distributed systems, the clustering delay caused by a single node is much smaller than the scheduling overhead. Therefore, such clustering can reduce the system overhead and optimize the execution time of the process.

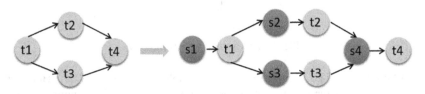

Fig. 2. An example of extending a DAG model to an O-DAG model.

There are two types of task clustering: horizontal clustering and vertical clustering [13]. Horizontal clustering merges the tasks of the same horizontal level into the workflow model, where the horizontal level of a task is defined as the longest distance from the entry task(s) of the workflow model to it. On the other hand, vertical clustering merges the tasks of sequential levels with a single parent task and child task. Figure 4 shows an example of horizontal clustering (HC) and vertical clustering (VC). However, the effect of vertical clustering is largely limited by the structure of workflow. The vertical clustering does not show any improvement for the workflow whose structure has no explicit pipelines. Therefore, only horizontal clustering is discussed in this paper.

3.3   The Problem of Balance Clustering

There will be runtime and dependency imbalance in the process of task clustering [14]. The time imbalance denotes the difference of running time between jobs after task

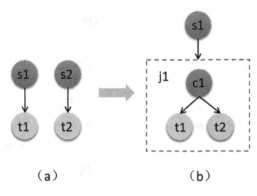

(a)   (b)

Fig. 3. An example of task clustering.

clustering. In the DAG model, job with the longest running time at one level deter-mines when the tasks of the next level will begin. If the difference of running time between jobs at the same level is too large, the execution of jobs at the next level will be delayed, affecting the execution time of the entire workflow. In order to optimize the workflow execution time after task clustering, it is necessary to consider time balance in the process of task clustering. As shown in Fig. 5, for example, there are four tasks t_1, t_2, t_3 and t_4, the running time of t_1 and t_2 is 10 s, and the running time of t_3 and t_4 is 30 s. Using horizontal clustering, the possible result is: t_1 and t_2 are merged into one job, t_3 and t_4 are merged into another job. We can see that the runtime of the two jobs are not balanced. In contrast, Fig. 5(b) shows a runtime-balanced task clustering with a uniform running time distribution between every cluster. However, time-balanced clustering does not take into account the structure and the data dependency of the process, which may lead to dependency imbalance problem.

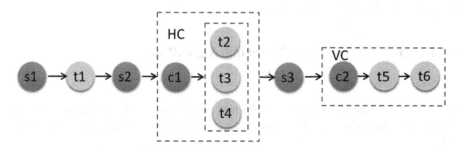

Fig. 4. Horizontal clustering (HC) and vertical clustering (VC).

Dependency imbalance means that a task at one level has to wait for more upper tasks to be finished before it can be executed, which will delay the release of following

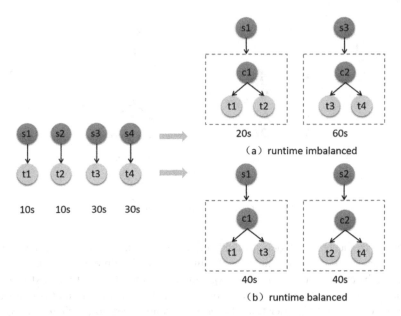

Fig. 5. Different clustering results under runtime balanced and runtime imbalanced.

tasks and thus reduce the parallelism of the workflow. As shown in Fig. 6, there is a workflow model with two levels. The first level has four tasks, while the second level has two tasks. Regardless of the data dependency between tasks, it is possible to combine t_1 and t_2, t_3 and t_4, which will result in t_5 and t_6 receiving data from different data sources and they can be executed only if t_1, t_2, t_3 and t_4 are all finished. The balanced scheduling strategy is to cluster the tasks with the same child tasks as far as possible, as shown in Fig. 6(b), once t_1 and t_2 are finished, t_5 can be executed immediately. The same is true for t_6.

4   Dependency Balance Clustering Algorithm

4.1   Overview

In order to measure the similarity of the two tasks in terms of data dependency, we define $cor(t_i, t_j)$ as the dependency correlation between two tasks t_1 and t_2, as shown in Eq. 1.

$$cor(t_i, t_j) = \sqrt{\frac{|c(t_i)| \bigcap |c(t_j)|}{|c(t_i)|}} = \sqrt{\frac{|c(t_i)| \bigcap |c(t_j)|}{|c(t_i)|}} \cdot \sqrt{\frac{|c(t_i)| \bigcap |c(t_j)|}{|c(t_j)|}} \qquad (1)$$

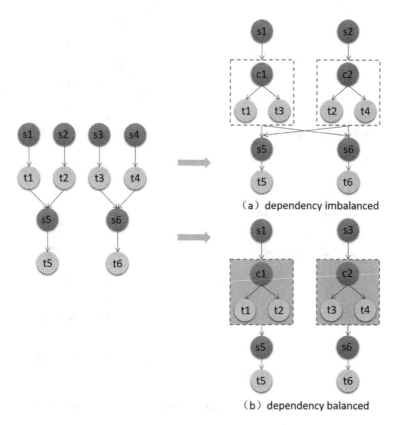

(a) dependency imbalanced

(b) dependency balanced

Fig. 6. Different clustering results under dependency balanced and dependency imbalanced.

Here, $c(t_i)$ represents the set of child tasks of task t_i, and $|c(t_i)|$ represents the number of child tasks of task t_i. The dependency correlation can be seen as the product of two specific proportions, representing the proportion of the shared tasks in the total child tasks of the two tasks respectively. In other words, task clustering does not simply merge the parent tasks with the same child tasks together, but takes into account the child tasks shared by these tasks and their respective child tasks. Sometimes even if two tasks have the same child tasks, they are not always clustered together. We also need to consider the other child tasks of the two tasks. Theoretically, we tend to merge the tasks with high dependency correlation together, so that the clusters and the tasks at the next level will be less relevant, thus reducing data dependency.

Figure 7 illustrates the meaning of merging tasks with high dependency correlation. Tasks t_1, t_2 and t_3 have the same child task t_4, but t_3 also have other child tasks t_5 and t_6. Calculated by the above dependency correlation formula: $cor(t_1, t_2) = 1$, $cor(t_2, t_3) = \sqrt{1/3}$. Because the dependency correlation of t_1 and t_2 is higher than that of t_3 and t_4, t_1 and t_2 are merged together, as shown in Fig. 7(a). If t_2 and t_3 are merged together as shown in Fig. 7(b), then t_5 and t_6 must wait for t_2 and t_3 to be finished and

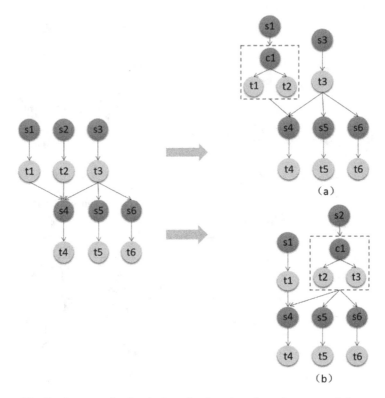

Fig. 7. An example of task clustering based on dependency correlation.

data to be transmitted successfully before they can be executed, which extends the execution time of tasks. At the same time for the workflow in Fig. 6, by applying the concept of dependency correlation we can get: $cor(t_1, t_2) = 1$, $cor(t_2, t_3) = 0$. Because the dependency correlation of t_1 and t_2 is higher than which of t_3 and t_4, we merge t_1 and t_2 together, and t_3 and t_4 together. Similarly, such clustering can avoid the dependence imbalance.

4.2 The Detail of DBCA

Algorithm 1 shows the pseudo-code of DBCA. The input of the algorithm is a set of tasks to be clustered called *taskList* and the number of clusters called *clusterNum*. The output of the algorithm is the result of clustering. The algorithm process is divided into the following steps:

(1) **Initialization:** Input a set of tasks to be clustered on a level in the workflow and number of clusters.

(2) **Calculate the dependency correlation:** Calculate the dependency correlation between every two tasks according to Eq. 1 and use the array *simArr* to store the dependency correlations. According to the number of tasks at this level and the number of clusters, calculate $needNum(C_i)$ which denotes the number of tasks needed to fill each cluster C_i.

(3) **Fill empty cluster C_i:** According to the order of $C_1, C_2, C_3,..., C_{clusterNum}$ and $needNum(C_i)$, fill the cluster C_i with tasks. In particular, when $needNum(C_i)$ equals to 1, each of the remaining unassigned tasks is clustered individually, and skip to Step (6) when the clustering process is over. Otherwise, find two tasks with the highest dependency correlation (i.e., pairs of tasks) from the remaining tasks and add them into cluster C_i. If there are multiple pairs of tasks with the highest dependency correlation, choose two tasks whose the sum of the running time is closest to $\frac{2}{n} \cdot \sum_{i=1}^{n} RT(t_i)$ and add them into cluster C_i, where n denotes the number of tasks at this level and $RT(t_i)$ denotes the running time of task t_i; In other words, the priority is given to the dependency correlation. When the multiple dependency correlations are the same, try to make the clustering time balance as much as possible.

(4) **Continue to fill C_i :** If the number of tasks already in cluster C_i is less than $needNum(C_i)$, add each task in the remaining tasks to cluster C_i and then calculate the sum of dependency correlations for each pair of tasks in cluster C_i separately. Next, choose the task that maximizes the sum of dependency correlations to add it to the cluster. If there are multiple tasks that meet the above condition, choose the task whose running time is closest to the average running time of the remaining tasks in cluster C_i. The average running time of the remaining tasks in cluster C_i is defined as follows:

$$leftTaskTime = \frac{\frac{\sum_{i=1}^{n} RT(t_i)}{clusterNum} - curTaskTime(C_i)}{needNum(C_i) - curTaskNum(C_i)} \qquad (2)$$

(5) **Fill the remaining clusters in turn:** Continue to add tasks to cluster C_i according to step (3) until the end, and then skip to step (2) to continue filling the next cluster, until all the clusters are filled.

(6) **Output the result:** Output the clustering result $C_i, i = 1, 2, \ldots clusterNum$.

Algorithm 1: DBCA

Input: $taskList$ // a list of tasks on a level of the workflow, $clusterNum$ // number of clusters

Output: $C_i, i = 1,2, ..., clusterNum$ // the result of task clustering

```
01: simArr(i, j), 1 ≤ i, j ≤ n // Calculate the dependency correlation between each of the
02:                            two tasks according to Equation 1
03: for i = 1 to clusterNum do
04:     needNum // Calculate the number of tasks required by Cᵢ
05:     if needNum==1 then
06:         Cluster tasks in taskList successively to get Cᵢ, Cᵢ₊₁, ..., C_clusterNum
07:         break
08:     for taskI in taskList do
09:         for taskJ in taskList after taskI do
10:             sim=simArr[taskI][taskJ]
11:             diffTime=abs(taskI.time+taskJ.time - 2 · ∑ⁿᵢ₌₁ RT(tᵢ) /n)
12:             if sim>maxSim||(sim==maxSim&&diffTime<minDiffTime)
13:                 maxSim=sim
14:                 minDiffTime=diffTime
15:                 task1=taskI, task2= taskJ
16:         Cᵢ ← task1, task2
17:         taskList.remove(task1), taskList.remove(task2)
18:         while Cᵢ.size < needNum
19:             leftTaskTime // Calculate the average runtime of the remaining tasks according
20:                            to Equation 2
21:             maxAddSim=−∞
22:             minDiffTime= ∞
23:             bestTask=0
24:             for task in taskList do
25:                 addSim=0; diffTime=abs(task.time-leftTaskTime)
26:                 for taskTmp in Cᵢ do
27:                     addSim+=simArr[task][taskTmp]
28:                 if addSim>maxAddSim||(addSim==maxAddSim&&diffTime<minDiffTime)
29:                     maxAddSim=addSim
30:                     minDiffTime=diffTime
31:                     bestTask=task
32:             Cᵢ ← bestTask
33:             taskList.remove(bestTask)
34: return Cᵢ, i = 1,2, ..., clusterNum
```

5   Experiments

5.1   Experimental Configuration

We implemented the clustering algorithms using two workflow datasets: LIGO and CyberShake. LIGO (Laser Interferometer Gravitational Wave Observatory, shown as Fig. 8), is an astrophysical application that detects the gravitational waves by analyzing the data obtained from binary system such as neutron star and black hole. The tasks generated by LIGO can be generally divided into two types: those with particularly

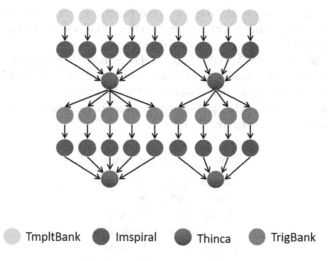

Fig. 8. LIGO workflow model.

short execution time, and those with particularly long execution time. On the other hand, CyberShake is a workflow application that calculates the likelihood of earthquake occurrence, as shown in Fig. 9. It is a data-intensive workflow that consumes huge amount of computing resources.

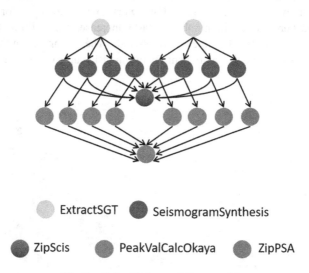

Fig. 9. CyberShake workflow model.

Bharathi et al. developed a workflow generator called WorkflowGenertor [16], to create workflow models of any size that resemble real workflow applications. The workflow model generated by the workflow generator uses XML file format to represent DAG workflow model (DAX). In this paper, the workflow generator is used to generate workflow models with different number of tasks to verify the effectiveness of the algorithm in the workflows with different scale.

In our experiment, the WorkflowSim simulation tool [15] is employed to simulate the real case. The experiments ran on a server with a 3.30 GHz Intel(R) Core(TM) i5-4590 CPU, 8 GB memory and Windows 10 64-bit system.

Similar to the literature [12], we assume that there is a virtual machine cluster of 20 virtual machines, each configured as Table 1.

Table 1. Experiment Parameters.

Parameter name	Setting value
Number of VMs	20
Memory size	512 MB
Calculation speed	1000 MIPS
Bandwidth	15 MB/s

5.2 Results

The experiment takes the process completion time as a criterion for comparing DBCA clustering method and HIFB [12] clustering method. Figures 10 and 11 show the results of using two clustering methods for LIGO and CyberShake workflow models with different number of tasks. In the figure, LIGO_100 represents a LIGO workflow with 100 tasks, all else follows. As they indicate, the process completion time is reduced by an average of 26% for LIGO workflows, and 16% for CyberShake workflows. Furthermore, as the number of tasks increases from 100 to 1000, the gap between the two algorithms becomes more obvious. The reason lies in that in the case of a large number of tasks, the relationship between tasks turns out to be more complex.

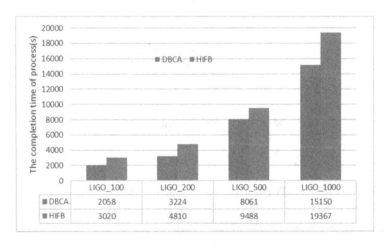

Fig. 10. The comparison of process completion time of two algorithms in different LIGO workflows.

At this point, the problem of dependency imbalance caused by task clustering becomes dominant. Our method takes a more comprehensive consideration of the dependencies between tasks in the process of task clustering, so that it can fairly well solve the problem of dependency imbalance.

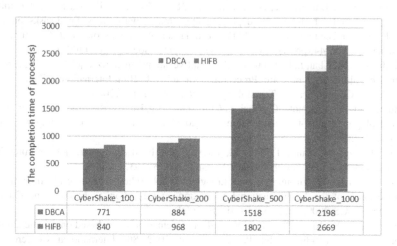

	CyberShake_100	CyberShake_200	CyberShake_500	CyberShake_1000
■ DBCA	771	884	1518	2198
■ HIFB	840	968	1802	2669

Fig. 11. The comparison of process completion time of two algorithms in different CyberShake workflows.

6 Conclusion and Future Work

Task clustering combines fine-grained tasks into coarse-grained tasks. Unreasonable task clustering leads to time imbalance and dependency imbalance, which reduces the parallelism of task execution. To address the problem of dependency imbalance, we propose Dependency Balance Clustering Algorithm (DBCA), which gradually adds the tasks that maximizes the sum of dependency correlations to the cluster by using incremental method, leading to the maximum of dependency correlations for each cluster. In addition, our algorithm also considers the runtime of each task on the basis of the dependency balance, therefore ensuring the runtime balance and dependency balance at the same time.

Although the results show that our algorithm performs well, it does not have universality. The effect of the clustering algorithm is limited by the different workflow structures. In the future, we aim to experiment with more types of workflows and define an evaluation index to measure the scope of our clustering algorithm.

References

1. Da Silva, R.F., Juve, G., Deelman, E., Glatard, T., Desprez, F., Thain, D., Tovar, B., Livny, M.: Toward fine-grained online task characteristics estimation in scientific workflows. In: WORKS@ SC, pp. 58–67 (2013)

2. Stratan, C., Iosup, A., Epema, D.H.: A performance study of grid workflow engines. In: Proceedings of IEEE/ACM 9th International Conference on Grid Computing, pp. 25–32. IEEE Computer Society (2008)
3. Chen, W., Deelman, E.: Workflow overhead analysis and optimizations. In: Proceedings of the 6th workshop on Workflows in Support of Large-Scale Science, pp. 11–20. ACM (2011)
4. Muthuvelu, N., Liu, J., Soe, N.L., Venugopal, S., Sulistio, A., Buyya, R.: A dynamic job grouping-based scheduling for deploying applications with fine-grained tasks on global grids. In: Proceedings of the 2005 Australasian Workshop on Grid Computing and e-Research, vol. 44, pp. 41–48. Australian Computer Society, Inc. (2005)
5. Muthuvelu, N., Chai, I., Eswaran, C.: An adaptive and parameterized job grouping algorithm for scheduling grid jobs. In: Proceedings of ICACT 10th International Conference on Advanced Communication Technology, pp. 975–980. IEEE (2008)
6. Muthuvelu, N., Vecchiola, C., Chai, I., Chikkannan, E., Buyya, R.: Task granularity policies for deploying bag-of-task applications on global grids. Future Gener. Comput. Syst. **29**, 170–181 (2013)
7. Ang, T., Ng, W., Ling, T., Por, L., Liew, C.: A bandwidth-aware job grouping-based scheduling on grid environment. Inf. Technol. J. **8**, 372–377 (2009)
8. Liu, Q., Liao, Y.: Grouping-based fine-grained job scheduling in grid computing. In: Proceedings of the 1st International Workshop on Education Technology and Computer Science, ETCS 2009, pp. 556–559. IEEE (2009)
9. Zhao, E., Qi, Y., Xiang, X., Chen, Y.: A data placement strategy based on genetic algorithm for scientific workflows. In: Proceedings of 2012 8th International Conference on Computational Intelligence and Security (CIS), pp. 146–149. IEEE (2012)
10. Deng, K., Ren, K., Song, J., Yuan, D., Xiang, Y., Chen, J.: A clustering based coscheduling strategy for efficient scientific workflow execution in cloud computing. Concurrency Comput. Pract. Exp. **25**, 2523–2539 (2013)
11. Li, X., Zhang, L., Wu, Y., Liu, X., Zhu, E., Yi, H., Wang, F., Zhang, C., Yang, Y.: A novel workflow-level data placement strategy for data-sharing scientific cloud workflows. IEEE Trans. Serv. Comput., 1 (2016)
12. Chen, W., da Silva, R.F., Deelman, E., Sakellariou, R.: Using imbalance metrics to optimize task clustering in scientific workflow executions. Future Gener. Comput. Syst. **46**, 69–84 (2015)
13. Sahni, J., Vidyarthi, D.P.: Workflow-and-platform aware task clustering for scientific workflow execution in cloud environment. Future Gener. Comput. Syst. **64**, 61–74 (2016)
14. Chen, W., Da Silva, R.F., Deelman, E., Sakellariou, R.: Balanced task clustering in scientific workflows. In: Proceedings of IEEE 9th International Conference on E-Science (e-Science), pp. 188–195. IEEE (2013)
15. Chen, W., Deelman, E.: Workflowsim: a toolkit for simulating scientific workflows in distributed environments. In: Proceedings of IEEE 8th International Conference on E-Science (e-Science), pp. 1–8. IEEE (2012)
16. Bharathi, S., Chervenak, A., Deelman, E., Mehta, G., Su, M.-H., Vahi, K.: Characterization of scientific workflows. In: Proceedings of the third Workshop on Workflows in Support of Large-Scale Science, pp. 1–10. IEEE (2008)

DexPro: A Bytecode Level Code Protection System for Android Applications

Beibei Zhao[1], Zhanyong Tang[1(✉)], Zhen Li[1], Lina Song[1], Xiaoqing Gong[1], Dingyi Fang[1], Fangyuan Liu[1], and Zheng Wang[2]

[1] School of Information Science and Technology, Northwest University, Xi'an, People's Republic of China
zytang@nwu.edu.cn
[2] MetaLab, School of Computing and Communications, Lancaster University, Lancaster, UK

Abstract. Unauthorized code modification through reverse engineering is a major concern for Android application developers. Code reverse engineering is often used by adversaries to remove the copyright protection or advertisements from the app, or to inject malicious code into the program. By making the program difficult to analyze, code obfuscation is a potential solution to the problem. However, there is currently little work on applying code obfuscation to compiled Android bytecode. This paper presents DEXPRO, a novel bytecode level code obfuscation system for Android applications. Unlike prior approaches, our method performs on the Android Dex bytecode and does not require access to high-level program source or modification of the compiler or the VM. Our approach leverages the fact all except floating operands in Dex are stored in a 32-bit register to pack two 32-bit operands into a 64-bit operand. In this way, any attempt to decompile the bytecode will result in incorrect information. Meanwhile, our approach obfuscates the program control flow by inserting opaque predicates before the return instruction of a function call, which makes it harder for the attacker to trace calls to protected functions. Experimental results show that our approach can deter sophisticate reverse engineering and code analysis tools, and the overhead of runtime and memory footprint is comparable to existing code obfuscation methods.

Keywords: Code obfuscation · Reverse engineering

1 Introduction

Unauthorized code reverse engineering is a major concern for Android application developers. This technique is widely used by adversaries to perform various attacks, including removing copyright protection to obtain an illegal copy of the software, taking out advertisement from the app, or injecting malicious code into the program. By making the program harder to be traced and analyzed, code obfuscation is a viable means to protect applications from unauthorized code modification.

© Springer International Publishing AG 2017
S. Wen et al. (Eds.): CSS 2017, LNCS 10581, pp. 367–382, 2017.
https://doi.org/10.1007/978-3-319-69471-9_27

A number of code obfuscation approaches have been proposed to protect applications against reverse engineering [1–4]. Most of the prior work perform code obfuscation on high-level programming languages such as Java and require access to the program source code. However, this requirement has two major drawbacks: (1) source code level code obfuscation provides limited protection as the obfuscated code can removed or optimized out by the compiler; (2) many developers are not willing to disclose their source code. As such, a code protection technique performing on the compiled bytecodes or binary with stronger protection is highly attractive.

The first effort in this direction is SMOG [5] that performs code obfuscation by permuting the instruction opcodes from the compiled Dex bytecode[1]. The permutated opcodes are then interpreted at runtime through a modified VM interpreter. While promising, there is a significant shortcoming of this approach. Programs protected by SMOG must run in a dedicated VM other than the native Android runtime environment, which limits the application of SMOG at larger scale.

In this paper, we present DEXPRO, a novel bytecode level code obfuscation system for Android applications. Unlike prior approaches, our method performs on the Android Dex bytecode and does not require access to high-level program source or modification of the compiler or VM. DEXPRO advances prior work in the following ways. Firstly, DEXPRO performs code obfuscation on the bytecode level, so it does not require accessing to the source code and as a result the obfuscated code will not be optimized out by the compiler. Secondly, it requires no modification to the compiler and runtime environment. Hence the obfuscated code can run on any environment that supports the standard Android bytecode format. DEXPRO exploit two key structures of the Android Dex bytecode definition to protect the program against dynamic and static code analysis, which is explained in Sect. 6.2: (1) all except for floating operands are based on a 32-bit register and (2) the instruction follows a function call is always used to retrieve the return value of the function. Our approach utilizes the register structure of Dex to pack two 32-bit operands into a single 64-bit data item, so that any attempt in decoding the protected operands will receive incorrect information. We leverage the calling conversion of Dex, to insert opaque predicates [6,7] (i.e. code with complex logic but does not get executed) between instructions of the function call and return value retrieval. Doing so not only makes it harder for the attacker to obtain the return value, but also obfuscates the dynamic program behavior. By combining these two techniques, DEXPRO provides stronger protection when compared to existing code obfuscation techniques that target at the source code or bytecode level, with little extra overhead.

The core concept of DEXPRO is obfuscating the access procedure of variables in the registers. However, a naïve solution will lead to illegitimate code as the

---

[1] The Dalvik executable format (Dex) is the executable binary format for Android applications. It was originally designed for the Dalvik VM. It remains to be used as a standard bytecode format for Android applications after the Dalvik VM is replaced by the Android runtime (ART).

Android verify will invalid the generated code [8,9]. Our solution to the problem is to use the Dex dynamic loading mechanism and a Dalvik runtime tampering technology to bypass the verification mechanism.

We have evaluated our approach by using DEXPRO to protect a number of representative Android application operations. Experimental results show that our approach can protect software against sophisticated reverse engineering tools, including *Jeb* [10], *dexdump* [11], *IDA pro* [12] and *Dex2jar* [13] with less than 5% increment in code size and runtime overhead. His paper makes two specific contributions:

- It is the first work to exploit the register structure and calling convention of Android Dex for code protection;
- It is the first byte-code level code obfuscation scheme that protects software against static and dynamic code analysis.
- The obfuscation method is evaluated from potency, resilience, availability and cost.

Structure of the paper: We provide background in Sect. 2. Section 3 presents the overview of our system and Sect. 4 introduce the process of system implementation in detail. In Sect. 5, we discuss the potency, resilience and cost of the obfuscation method, and in Sect. 6 we deliberate evaluation of code obfuscation against current popular reverse tools and the overhead. Most relevant work in Android code obfuscation is discussed in Sect. 7. Finally, the concluding remarks are given in Sect. 8.

2 Background and Attack Scenario

2.1 Dalvik Virtual Machine

Dalvik virtual machine is one of the core parts of the Android mobile device platform. Android applications are written mostly in Java, but run in the DVM. The DVM run-time environment is introduced as follows.

Application Structure. Android applications are shipped as a single Zip archive named with the .apk extension by convention. A.dex is core file in zip file, A.dex file contains multiple Class Definitions each containing one or more Method definition each of those being linked to Dalvik bytecode instructions present int the Data section. Figure 1 provides a conceptual view of the compilation process for DVM application, meanwhile, each class within the .dex file corresponds to a smali file.

Instruction set. The Dalvik bytecode instruction set is substantially different than that of Java. There are 237 opcodes present in the Dalvik opcode constant list [14]. The set of instructions can be divided between instructions which provide the type of the registers they manipulate.

The process of the DVM execution. When an app installed, every installed application gets its own unique user ID by default. This means that every application will be executed as a separate system user. When an Android application is executed by the DVM, the process [3] is interpreted as follows.

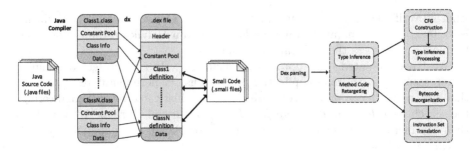

Fig. 1. Compilation process for DVM applications.   **Fig. 2.** Dalvik bytecode retargeting.

In detail, the specific process is as follows:

- **Load a class.** When the DVM loads a class by the function load-ClassFromDex(), the class will have a ClassObject type of data structure in the runtime environment. DVM stores all loaded classes by using gDvm.loadedClassed global hash table;
- **Verify Bytecode.** Bytecode verifier verifies the loaded class by using function dvmVerifyCodeFlow();
- **Find the main class.** The DVM searches the main class in gDvm.loadedClassed global hash table by using function FindClass(). If it can't find the needed class, it will go back to load the class;
- **Execute bytecode flow.** Interpreter is initialized by invoking function dvmInterpret() and then the Dalvik bytecode flow will be executed.

2.2   Attack Scenario

There are a lot of dex opcodes within a Android application and they are very difficult to understand. So attacker required access to source code rather than operate on the Dex opcodes to identify key-positives resulting from automated code analysis, e.g., perform manual confirmation.

The initial stage of decompilation retargets the application .dex file to Java classes [15]. Figure 2 shows this process. The first and most important step is recovering typing information. However, the Dalvik bytecode has two generalized cases where variable types are ambiguous: (1) constant and variable declaration only specifies the variable width (e.g., 32 or 64 bits), but not whether it is a float, integer; and (2) comparison operators do not distinguish between integer and object reference comparison. Reverse tools determine unknown types by observing how variables are used in operations with known type operands. They also infer register types by observing how they are used in subsequent operations with known type operands. Dalvik registers loosely correspond to Java variables. Because Dalvik bytecode reuses registers whose variables are no longer in scope, we must evaluate the register type within its context of the method control flow, i.e., inference must be path-sensitive.

3 Overview of Our Approach

There are two Android virtual machine and the DM was replaced by the Android runtime (ART) [16]. The difference between them is that ART virtual machine will translate the dex bytecode into native machine code when loading the class, so both virtual machines execute the same unmodified Dalvik bytecode file structure, instruction formats (smali), and constrains. Hence, our proposed obfuscation applies to apps run by both DVM and ART. But The difference between them is that the ART is not dex bytecode after loading the apps, and we can't bypass the verifier through backfilling the obfuscated bytecode after it. We should think of an approach to prevent the verifier and decrease the performance overhead as well.

As depicted in Fig. 3, the system is proposed as a software protection system within which an obfuscation engine and solving the conflict problem. It mainly obtain three part.

At the first part, we are mainly introduce to how to obfuscate the smali code. The basic idea is confusing the data-flow for the access procedure of register data, and combining opaque predicates technology to confuse the control-flow.

The next step, because our obfuscation method would cause problems of the register-type conflict, we should make the executable .dex file normally execute by the Dalvik VM. So we need to modify the .dex file, which is explained in Sect. 4.3.

Lastly, we will utilize the dex dynamic loading technology to load the above .dex file, but some bytecode is nop after the class being loaded, so Dalvik runtime tampering technology is used to solve the problem. Meanwhile, To illustrate this, we firstly analyzed the exact nature of the problem, and then describe the details process that is to implement normal running.

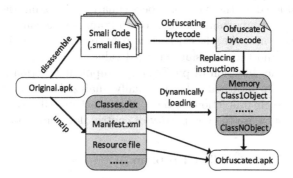

Fig. 3. Workflow of the DexPro system. We can see three part, obfuscate the smali code, nop bytecode within the .dex file, and dynamic load and runtime tamper, which is the background of the light-green. (Color figure online)

4   Implementation Details

Our proposed schemes obfuscate Android apps at Dalvik bytecode level to achieve an expressive control-flow and data-flow obfuscation. Within this paper, our approach combines obfuscation techniques against static and dynamic reverse engineering, which is discussed next.

4.1   The Process of Obfuscation

Dalvik VM's instructions based on the architecture of register and the constant pool is modified to use the index of 32 bits, which can simplify the interpreter. Therefore the constants within smali code are stored in the 32-bit registers. As shown in the Fig. 2, Analyzing CFG and register type inference processing is very important to retarget the application .dex file to Java classes. According to this characteristic we can confuse the type of registers and control flow, they are data flow obfuscation and control flow obfuscation.

Dalvik VM gets the operand from the corresponding register directly based on the type of operation code when performing bytecode flow, regardless of what the type of register is, so we can obfuscate it from two aspects. On the one hand, because the constants of the long and double in smali code are 64-bit, they are stored in the two adjacent 32-bit registers, so we can use a long constant instead of the two constants respectively stored in two 32-bit registers. On the other hand, we will confuse a instruction of capturing the return value of an object reference for a instruction of capturing the return value. The two methods on the above are to confuse on the data access, so that they can make the compiler tools puzzled.

In this paper, we propose a obfuscation method by inserting reinforced opaque predicates [2]. The first step is to judge the position where to insert, which was conducted on the basis of process analysis. Invoking the key function (*self-define*) is very important modules of program, so we can insert reinforced opaque predicates into the place where is between the instruction of invoking the key function and the accessing returned value, and the process is shown in Fig. 4. For example, function of purchasing equipment function is very critical in the game and its returned value is usually analyzed by the attacker. If the developer takes such protection method, the attackers will not get the return value. This way increase the complexity of control flow and data flow.

4.2   Register Type-Conflict Problem

This section elaborates an important problem caused by the Android runtime system, which we encountered while implementing the described obfuscation techniques. It also explains how we modified target apps prior to apply the obfuscation techniques so as to prevent the problem and satisfy the Android runtime system.

```
.method pubilc test()
      ......
      invoke-virtual {p0, v0, v1},
      Lcom/example/test/MarketLogic;
      ->payCallback(II)I

      inject opaque predicates

      move-result v4
      ......
.end method
```

Fig. 4. Control obfuscation. In order to obfuscate the control-flow, we will inject the opaque predicates between two instructions that are invoking and capturing the return value.

Because the Verifier module [8,9] seems to perform a register liveness analysis in each method prior to running it, and ensure that there is no type conflict among live registers at an program point.

Firstly, at each program point, it keeps track of live registers together with the data type they hold. Should it find a register with two different types at the same program point, it will report the register-type conflict problem and the running app will crash.

Secondly, In order to exactly get the return value of the child function which is called, the instruction used to retrieve the return value of the function does not follow a function call. Our approach insert the reinforced opaque predicates into the two instructions. So it will report the conflict information.

From the error information, we can come to the conclusion that the validation fails is reported during the static initialization of the class. It is a new solution that Obfuscated Dalvik bytecode are backfilled in the memory after initializations. However, we now know that when Dalvik VM performs the bytecode flow with in the dex file, it gets out the operand from the corresponding register in terms of the opcode, regardless of what the type of register is. Given this issue, we thus need to find a solution that will bypass the verifier of the evaluated Android runtime systems from deducing any false type conflict in otherwise correctly obfuscated apps.

4.3 App Execution

As described in Sect. 2.1, Dalvik VM verifies the validity of instructions when loading the class, for example, verifying the type of the registers. So executing an obfuscated app must bypass the process of the verifier. To address the problem, we can do the following three things.

Firstly, we will recompile the obfuscated smali into a .dex file. Then we will apply for a memory space to store the obfuscated bytecode, which is in the .dex file can be stored in the ObjMethod structure of showing in Fig. 5. At last, we will fill the junk bytecode in the obfuscated method and get a new.dex file. When attackers statically analysis it, they will get many junk code, so this way resist static analysis successfully.

Secondly, in order to load the executable file new.dex utilizing the technology of loading dex dynamically, we develop our own customized Classloader function to load all the classes in this dex file, before which the default Classloader in the API layer should be replaced to ensure the normal execution of the real dex file.

There exists a system component called Application [13] in Android frame. It will initialize several global variables when establishing Application (i.e. before launching app), and all the Activity within the same app can access the value of these variables. Usually, system will develop an Application automatically and we don't need to develop it specifically, so through designing customized class ProxyApplication that extends Application, the default Classloader in the system will be replaced by the customized MyDexclassloder when initiating ProxyApplication. Moreover, we should configure ProxyApplication in the ApplicationManifest.xml in APP.

Lastly, in order to bypass verification of Dalvik VM for instructions (i.e. register types), we utilize the technology of dynamically loading. As bytecode in the obfuscated methods in new.dex is a zero sequence after loading new.dex, we need to fill the obfuscated bytecode in the corresponding location in the memory before execution.

```
typedef struct {
    String ClassName;
    String MethodNmae;
    Char* newCode;
}ObjMethod;
```

Fig. 5. The structure of ObjMethod. It is used to store the bytecode of the obfuscated method within the .dex file. The bytecode backfill the memory after the class loaded.

Table 1. Count the number of instructions of meting obfuscation criteria.

App	Function	Before obfuscation	After obfuscation
ele_me	Online ordering	24	12
Fileexplorer	Mi file manager	72	36
Photup	Photo album	30	15
v2ex-daily	Exchange community	16	8
Zhihupaper	Zhihu daily	16	8

5 Obfuscation Evaluations

5.1 Evaluations Criteria

Collberg [17] gives an accurate definition on code obfuscation: The i is one of all possible inputting set I which is in the program P. If and only if it is $\forall i$:

$T(P)(i) = P(i)$, we can just think that the transition of the confusion was correct. The obfuscation method is evaluated from potency, resilience and cost by Collberg et al.

Let T be a behavior-conserving transformation, such that $P \xrightarrow{T} P'$ transforms a source program P into a target program P'.

$T_{pot}(P)$, the potency of T with respect to a program P, is a measure of the extent to which T changes the complexity of P. Let $E(P)$ be the complexity of P. It is defined as

$$T_{pot}(P) = E(P')/E(P) - 1 \qquad (1)$$

T is a potent obfuscating transformation if $T_{pot}(P) > 0$.

$T_{res}(P)$ is the resilience of T with respect to a program P. $T_{res}(P) = one - way$ if information is removed from P such that P cannot be reconstructed from P'. Otherwise,

$$T_{res}(P) \triangleq Resilience(T_{Deobfuscaoreffort}, T_{Programmereffort}) \qquad (2)$$

$T_{cost}(P)$ is the extra execution time/space of P' compared to P. That is to say

$$T_{cost}(P) = Cost(C_{time}, C_{size}) \qquad (3)$$

5.2   Evaluations Obfuscation Method

Abouting code obfuscation techniques, Collberg put forward three evaluation indexes: the potency, resilience and cost, We will Make qualitative evaluation for the confusion in this article according to the evaluation index.

Potency. The proposed code confusion method includes both control obfuscation and data obfuscation. In data obfuscation, we can obfuscate the instructions of accessing the values from the registers and calling method that its returned value is object type. The experimental result as shown in Fig. 6, first, we confuse two 32-bit constant definition instructions into a 64-bit constant definition instruction, when the attackers are using reverse tools to reverse, such as dexdump Dex2jar Jeb, the getting result is wrong. In control obfuscation, in order to resist attacker to access the returned values which is after calling the key function, we will insert the opaque predicate between two instructions that are calling and accessing returned value. The above two kinds of method can both resist the attacker to acquire correct program code and increase the complexity of the control flow. Thus, the proposed method has good strength.

Resilience. The obfuscated program has been analyzed in terms of reverse analysis. For example, the attacker can't access correct instructions and analyzing logical construction of program. As shown in Fig. 7, decompilation process is failure and control flow becomes very complicated, so the proposed method has strong slastic.

Cost. The function's time complexity is O(1) after being obfuscated. Firstly, inserting opaque predicate and modifying the instruction format does not change

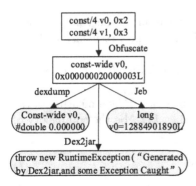

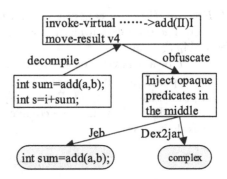

Fig. 6. Two 32-bit constant definition instruction confusion into a 64-bit constant defined instruction,get the wrong results from reverse tool *dexdump, Dex2jar, Jeb*

Fig. 7. The case of reversing engineering. When we inject the opaque predicates after invoking the *add()* method, the attacker can't capture the return-value *sum*.

polynomial of the complexity. Secondly, dex dynamic loading and backfilling the bytecode both increase little time, as shown in Fig. 10. In space consumed, we will only insert opaque predicate into invoking the key function and obfuscated instructions is short. Thus this method has little effect on the time and consumed space.

6   Experiments and Analysis

6.1   Experimental Setup

Hardware. Our approach is evaluated using a Xiaomi 4 phone, which runs the Android 4.4.4 operating system. The device has a processor: a four-core processor at 2.5 GHz. The device has 2 GB of RAM and 16 GB of internal storage.

Benchmarks. Based on the deep research in DEXPRO, as shown in Fig. 2, this paper designed and implemented a prototype system. It can resist the static analysis and dynamic analysis of the process of the reverse engineering. Our approach is evaluated by using the developed tool to protect a set of representative operations of typical Android applications.

In order to prove the practicability of our protection method, we selected five popular apps downloaded from Android Open Source Project, switch can represent different types in the application market, Choosing different function applications can show the feature that exist instructions of defining 32-bit variables preferably in the application market, so it is different with the next experiment cases. Then count the instructions of meting obfuscation criteria that is two adjacent instructions of defining 32-bit variables. So the number of the instruction of this type would decrease 50 percent. It is listed in Table 1. We found that, in all tested apps, there are many instructions meting the conditions of obfuscating some application.

Performance overhead is also very important about code obfuscation and our protection method applied user-definable key functions. So measure the performance overhead and effectiveness of DEXPRO, We have implemented these operations in four applications (listed Table 2). We chose these APP for the following reasons: Data.apk is a constant definition; BubbleSor.apk is a bubble sorting algorithm; Hanoi.apk is a typical representation of the Hanoi algorithm; Contact.apk has all of the above instruction features, Each representing a different character, switch can show effectiveness and performance overhead betterly. So these test cases can completely represent our obfuscation engineering and be tested to evaluate from the effectiveness and performance overhead.

Table 2. A list of apps we selected to test. Column 2 represent the type of instructions of four typical Android apps.

Test case	The characteristics of the instruction
Data.apk	Defining two 32-bit variables
BubbleSor.apk	Returned value of the reference type
Hanio.apk	Key function (self-defined)
Contact.apk	All the above

6.2 Effectiveness

The main purpose of this paper is to protect the executable code of the application, and make it not be easy analyzed by attacker. The below from two aspects of resisting static and dynamic analysis analyze the effectiveness of the protection method based on confusion of smali code.

The some bytecode within executable file is a junk code sequence before executed bytecode flow by DVM. So when attackers want to statically analyze the logical structure of the program, they can't acquire correct bytecode. Before the app running the attackers dump the bytecode through dynamically analyzing, this way is the same with resisting static analysis. If running, they will dump the obfuscated bytecode, which isn't correctly decompiled, as shown in Fig. 4.

In order to the effectiveness of the obfuscated method, we will also utilize reversing tools to reverse executable code of the application. The experiment results is shown in Table 3.

6.3 Performance Overhead

We measured the performance overhead of DEXPRO by comparing the .dex file size, memory use and launch time of applications before and after obfuscated

Table 3. The results of analysis by reversing tools. × represent that the code after reversing is wrong. ∗ represent that it becomes very complicated

Test case	Jeb	Dex2Jar	dexdump	IDA pro
Data.apk	×	×	∗	∗
BubbleSor.apk	×	×	∗	∗
Hanio.apk	×	∗	×	∗
Contact.apk	×	×	×	∗

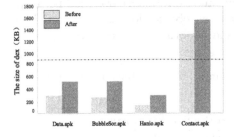

Fig. 8. Describe the changes of the .dex file size. Compare to the D-value of the .dex file size before and after obfuscated.

Fig. 9. Describe the changes of memory use. Compare to D-value of memory use before and after obfuscated.

by DEXPRO. We measured the launch time by capturing the timestamps of logs output by Android Logcat. The size of memory use was measured by using the command procrank, which can get the memory usage of the current system process and read information from the */proc/pid/maps* to count them, including PSS, USS, VSS, RSS.

We can see from Fig. 8 that the dex file size increases more than 13 KB. This increase in file size is mainly due to the packer dex file that is used to load really dex file and inserting the opaque predicates. The results are not obvious, because the application size we selected is relatively small and little difference.

Figure 9 illustrates memory use changes of applications before and after obfuscated. The memory usage increases by an average of 1.95M. We will describe that memory costs are mainly caused by the re-packaging dex file, storing obfuscated bytecode, and native library. But current mobile devices tend to provide more RAM, for example, Huawei Nexus has two processors: a four-core ARM Cortex-A57 processor at 1.95 GHz and a four-core ARM Cortex-A53 processor at 1.55 GHz. The device has 3 GB of RAM and 64 GB of internal storage. So you can ignore the costs.

To measure the app response delay after being protected by DEXPRO, we compared the app launch time for the first, second, third, and fourth run before and after obfuscated. To make it more precisely, we did each experiment 20 times

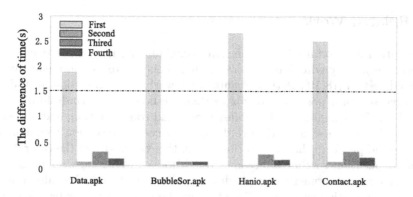

Fig. 10. Describe the changes of launch time D-value. Compare to the first, second, third, and fourth launch time D-value before and after obfuscated. We can see only that the time significantly increase at the first launch

Table 4. Launch time (in seconds) of four apps for the four times launch before and after obfuscated.

Test case		Data.apk	BubbleSor.apk	Hanio.apk	Contact.apk
First(s)	Before	2.175	2.249	2.124	2.912
	After	4.027	4.612	4.677	5.412
Second(s)	Before	0.939	0.923	0.844	0.911
	After	1.027	0.942	0.892	1.017
Third(s)	Before	0.845	0.882	0.797	0.891
	After	1.171	0.959	1.024	1.238
Fourth(s)	Before	0.823	0.862	0.781	0.887
	After	0.994	0.928	0.934	1.099

and used the average value as a final reference. The launch time of four test case is listed in Table 4.

Figure 10 shows the app launch time changers at each time. We can see that the time increase at the first launch, which is mainly caused by: (1) running the obfuscated application needs to replace Classloader; (2) Before running we must find the obfuscated method in the corresponding memory address through parsing the structure of the dex file and then fill the bytecode that is stored in ObjMethod in the address. These classes and libraries will be loaded at the application's first execution and will be kept in the memory so long as the system resources are sufficient. Thus, they do not need to be loaded again in the app's latter launch, which is the reason why they all show a similar launch time as the unprotected apps at the latter launch.

7   Related Work

Obfuscation is a useful and cost effective technique and it does not require any special execution environment. Moreover it is believed to be more effective on Android system [18,19]. Patrick Schulz in his work code Protection in Android [20] discusses some possible code obfuscation methods on the Android platform using identifier mangling, string obfuscation, dead code insertion, and self modifying code. Ghosh et al. [21] have discussed a code obfuscation technique on the Android platform that aims at increasing the complexity of the control flow of the application so that it becomes tough for a reverse engineer to get the business logic performed by an Android application. Kundu has also worked on some obfuscation techniques like clone methods, reordering expressions and loops, changing the arrays and loop transformations [22].

There are various Android obfuscation tools available in the market, such as Proguad [4]. But the current Android obfuscation tools seem to still lack the combination of complex control-flow and data-flow obfuscation techniques. In [1–3] authors presents confusion scheme and algorithm of Android oriented software Java code, combined with the algorithm and improved insertion branch path and flattening the excess flow of control of these two kinds of control flow obfuscation method.

Junliang Shu et al. proposed SMOG [5], a comprehensive executable code obfuscation system to protect Android app. The obfuscation engine is at software vendor's side to conduct the obfuscation on the app's executable code, and then release the obfuscated app to the end-user along with an execution token. SMOG will also modify the code of DVM interpreter. Noor et al. [23] present a protection scheme based on obfuscation, code modification and cryptographic protection that can effectively counter reverse engineering.

Vivek Bala et al. [24] analyzed the need for potent control-flow based obfuscation so as to help protect Android apps. They also have described the design and implementation of three control-flow obfuscations for Android apps at the Dalvik bytecode level, which go beyond simp control-flow transformations used by exiting Android obfuscators. The register-reuse conflict problem raised by the Android runtime system has also been addressed by means of our type separation technique.

8   Conclusion and Future Work

This paper has presented a code obfuscation scheme to protect Android applications against reverse engineering. Our approach combines two techniques for code obfuscation by obfuscating the register load/store instructions and confusing the control flow through opaque predicates. Experimental results show that our approach provides strong protection at low cost. In future work, we intend to exploit control-flow platting techniques to confuse the control-flow of apps to protect native library code, and will extend our approach to the Android ART VM.

Acknowledgment. This work was partially supported by the National Natural Science Foundation of China under grant agreements No. 61672427 and No. 61572402; the International Cooperation Foundation of Shaanxi Province, China under grant agreements No. 2015KW-003 and No. 2017KW-008; the Research Project of Shaanxi Province Department of Education under grant agreement No. 15JK1734; the Service Special Foundation of Shaanxi Province Department of Education under grant agreement No. 16JF028; the Research Project of NWU, China under grant agreement No. 14NW28; the UK Engineering and Physical Sciences Research Council under grants EP/M01567X/1 (SANDeRs) and EP/M015793/1 (DIVIDEND); and the Royal Society International Collaboration Grant (IE161012).

References

1. Zheng Qi, X.A.: The control flow of confusion for android mobile application (2014)
2. Jinliang, L.: Research and realization on Android software protection technology. Ph.D. thesis, Beijing University of Posts and Telecommunications (2015)
3. Qi, Z.: Research and implementation of code obfuscation algorithms for applications of and smartphone terminal. Master's thesis, Beijing University of Posts and Telecommunications (2015)
4. Proguard. http://proguard.sourceforge.net/
5. Shu, J., Li, J., Zhang, Y., Gu, D.: Android app protection via interpretation obfuscation. In: 2014 IEEE 12th International Conference on Dependable, Autonomic and Secure Computing (DASC), pp. 63–68. IEEE (2014)
6. Yang, Y., Fan, W., Huang, W., Xu, G., Yang, Y.: The research of multi-point function opaque predicates obfuscation algorithm. Appl. Math. **8**(6), 3063–3070 (2014)
7. Yuan, Z., Wen, Q., Mao, M.: Constructing opaque predicates for java programs. In: 2006 International Conference on Computational Intelligence and Security (2006)
8. Codeverify.cpp. http://androidxref.com/4.2.2_r1/xref/dalvik/vm/analysis/CodeVerify.cpp
9. Dexverify.cpp. http://androidxref.com/4.2.2_r1/xref/dalvik/vm/analysis/DexVerify.cpp
10. Jeb. http://securitymusings.com/article/4003/android-security-and-the-tools-i-use-jeb
11. dexdump. https://play.google.com/store/apps/details?id=com.redlee90.dexdump
12. Idapro. https://www.hex-rays.com/products/ida
13. Dex2jar. https://sourceforge.net/p/dex2jar/wiki/UserGuide/
14. Bartel, A., Klein, J., Traon, Y.L., Monperrus, M.: Dexpler: converting android dalvik bytecode to jimple for static analysis with soot. In: ACM SIGPLAN International Workshop on State of the Art in Java Program Analysis, pp. 27–38 (2012)
15. Enck, W., Octeau, D., Mcdaniel, P., Chaudhuri, S.: A study of android application security. Br. Med. J. **2**(3859), 1175 (2011)
16. Android runtime. https://en.wikipedia.org/wiki/Android_Runtime
17. Collberg, C., Thomborson, C., Low, D.: A taxonomy of obfuscating transformations. Technical report, Department of Computer Science, The University of Auckland, New Zealand (1997)
18. Venkatesan, A.: Code obfuscation and virus detection. Ph.D. thesis, San Jose State University (2008)

19. Schrittwieser, S., Katzenbeisser, S.: Code obfuscation against static and dynamic reverse engineering. In: Filler, T., Pevný, T., Craver, S., Ker, A. (eds.) IH 2011. LNCS, vol. 6958, pp. 270–284. Springer, Heidelberg (2011). doi:10.1007/978-3-642-24178-9_19

20. Schulz, P.: Code protection in android. Insititute of Computer Science, Rheinische Friedrich-Wilhelms-Universitgt Bonn, Germany 110 (2012)

21. Ghosh, S., Tandan, S., Lahre, K.: Shielding android application against reverse engineering. Int. J. Eng. Res. Technol. **2**, 2635–2643 (2013). ESRSA Publications

22. Kundu, D.: JShield: a java anti-reversing tool. Ph.D. thesis, San José State University (2011)

23. Shoaib, M., Yasin, N., Abbassi, A.G.: Smart card based protection for dalvik bytecode-dynamically loadable component of an android apk. Int. J. Comput. Theory Eng. **8**(2), 156 (2016)

24. Balachandran, V., Tan, D.J., Thing, V.L.: Control flow obfuscation for android applications. Comput. Secur. **61**, 72–93 (2016)

IP Geolocation Base on Local Delay Distribution Similarity

Fan Zhao[1], Xiangyang Luo[1(✉)], Yong Gan[2], Shuodi Zu[1],
and Fenlin Liu[1]

[1] State Key Laboratory of Mathematical Engineering and Advanced Computing,
Zhengzhou 450001, China
zhaofan_123@yeah.net, luoxy_ieu@sina.com,
harmonica_music@163.com, liufenlin@vip.sina.com
[2] School of Computer and Communication Engineering,
Zhengzhou University of Light Industry, Zhengzhou 450001, China
ganyong@zzuli.edu.cn

Abstract. IP geolocation technology can be used to obtain the real-time locations of target Internet hosts especially mobile computers, which can help law enforcement to quickly get the criminal evidence or arrest criminals. Among existing numerous geolocation methods, SLG (Street-Level Geolocation) method can achieve geolocation result with relative higher precision for a target host. However, the geolocation accuracy will be significantly reduced once the common routers that play an important role in geolocation are anonymous, which often happens in paths detection. To solve this problem, this paper proposes an IP geolocation algorithm base on local delay distribution similarity. Firstly, the target's location at city-level granularity is obtained based on traditional SLG method. Secondly, the landmarks connected with the target by common routers are found out by topology analysis. The target's local delay between the nearest common router and the target is gained by multi-measurement and calculation, so do the landmarks'. Thirdly, their local delay distribution is obtained by statistical analysis. Lastly, the landmark whose local delay distribution is the most similar with the target's is selected as the estimated location of the target. Experimental results show that the proposed algorithm obviously improves the geolocation accuracy compared with traditional SLG when the common routers are anonymous.

Keywords: IP geolocation · Mobile computer · Street-Level Geolocation algorithm · Anonymous routers · Local delay distribution similarity

1 Introduction

In recent years, the popularity of mobile computers has brought great convenience to human life, but also provides a new way for the criminals to transmit illegal information or organize criminal activities. They fabricate and spread false information and constantly change their locations by making use of the characteristic of mobile computers which brings great difficulties to determine the criminals' locations for law enforcement. Although law enforcement departments can locate the criminals by

© Springer International Publishing AG 2017
S. Wen et al. (Eds.): CSS 2017, LNCS 10581, pp. 383–395, 2017.
https://doi.org/10.1007/978-3-319-69471-9_28

turning to Internet Service Providers (ISP), but it often requires high approvals and permission approval usually takes a long time. In fact, the illegal activities are often kept in the same place only for a short period of time. Even if the mobile computer that exchanges the illegal information is found out later by ISP, criminals can still give a variety of excuses to evade the legal liability. Therefore, it is important for law enforcement to obtain the real-time locations of the target Internet hosts especially mobile computers which will help to quickly get the criminal evidence or arrest criminals.

Every Internet host that connects to the Internet will be assigned an IP address, and existing geolocation methods usually determine the location of an Internet host with its IP, which often referred to as IP geolocation [1]. Over the last decade, many outstanding achievements about IP geolocation technology have been proposed and existing IP geolocation methods are mainly categorized into two types: Database-based and Measurement-based.

Database-based geolocation methods are widely used because of their less measurement and fast response. Currently, there are several geolocation databases on the Internet that provide query interfaces such as Whois [2], Akamai [3], Maxmind [4], Quova [5], IP2location [6], CQ Counter [7] and so on. The research on several of the databases above in [8, 9] shows that the query results from the databases are usually credible at the national-level granularity. However, it is hard to guarantee the reliability at city-level granularity. Reference [10] confirms that the low accuracy of commercial IP geolocation databases mainly results from selecting a single representative location for a large IP block from the Whois [2] registry database, parsing city names in a naive way, and resolving the wrong geolocation coordinates. In general, these methods can not get the real-time location of the target Internet hosts especially mobile computers.

Measurement-based geolocation methods are the research hotspot currently, which can determine the target' location in real time. They can divided into three categories further: the methods based on delay measurement, probability estimation, and topology analysis. Delay measurement based methods usually try to describe the relationship between delay and geographic distance and convert the measured delay between vantage points and the target to distance constraints. The typical methods include Shortest Ping [11], GeoPing [11], CBG (Constraint-based Geolocation) [12], SPRG (Segmented Polynomial Regression Approach) [13], Geo-RX [14], GeoWeight [15], etc. Probability estimation based methods obtain the probability conversion relationship between delay and distance through statistic for large amounts of data. These methods include LBG (Learning-based Geolocation) [16], ELC (Enhanced Learning Classifier) [17], MLE-based Approach (Maximum Likelihood Estimation based Approach) [18], Spotter [19], GENN [20], etc. The methods based on topology analysis achieve relative high-precision geolocation results by exploiting the target and landmarks' topology information (landmark refers to an IP with known geographical location), or combine with the measured delay sometimes. The representative methods include GeoTrack [11], TBG (Topology-based Geolocation) [21], Octant [22], SLG (Street-Level Geolocation) [23], Topology Mapping and Geolocation [24], Geolocation based on PoP-level [25], etc. In addition, some scholars try to geolocate an IP by data mining methods such as Structon [26], Checkin-Geo [27] and GQL [28].

Most of the methods above can realize the geolocation for a target IP at regional or city-level granularity. SLG [23] is a three-tier geolocation algorithm, which can geolocate IP addresses more accurately than the best previous system in its experimental environment. However, its geolocation precision will be significantly reduced once the common routers that play an important role in geolocation are anonymous, which often happens in paths detection. To solve this problem, we proposed an improved Street-Level Geolocation algorithm base on local delay distribution similarity in this paper. This algorithm first determines the target's location at city-level granularity based on the traditional SLG algorithm and find out the landmarks connected with the target by paths detection. Then, the target and the landmarks' local delay distributions are obtained by multi-measurement, calculation and statistical analysis. Finally, the landmark whose local delay distribution is the most similar with the target's is selected as the estimated location of the target. Experimental results show that the geolocation accuracy of this algorithm is higher common routers are anonymous.

2   Traditional SLG Algorithm and Its Problem

SLG is a typical three-tier high-precision geolocation algorithm based on the idea of successive approximation that gradually narrows the estimated geographic scope of a target IP. The framework is shown in Fig. 1.

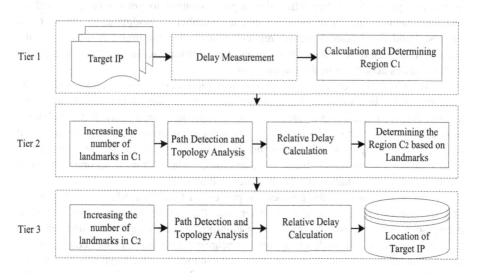

Fig. 1. Framework of the traditional SLG.

SLG can be summarized as the following three steps. (1) In the first tier, the delays between the target and many vantage points are measured and converted to the distance constraint.

The target is geolocated in a coarse-grained region C_1 based on the idea of multi-lateration in CBG [12]. (2) In the second tier, the relative delay is ingeniously exploited.

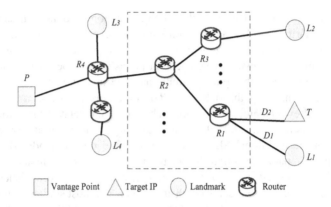

Fig. 2. A schematic of the traditional SLG when the common routers are anonymous.

As shown in Fig. 2, D_1 represents the delay between the router R_1 and the landmark L_1, and D_2 denotes the delay between the router R_1 and the target T, then $(D_1 + D_2)$ is called the relative delay between L_1 and T. After obtaining the region C_1, the number and density of landmarks in region C_1 are increased, and the landmarks connected with the target are found out by paths detection. Then, the minimum relative delays between the landmarks and the target are converted to distance constraints. The landmarks are used as vantage points to further refine the target's location to get region C_2 based on multilateration again. (3) In the third tier, the number of landmarks in region C_2 is increased and the landmark whose relative delay is the minimum is selected as the estimated location of the target. In the process of geolocation, the tier 2 can be repeated multiple times according to the requirement.

Randolph Baden et al. reveal that propagation delay can be neglected in the measured delay in a metropolitan area network [29]. As we all know, only the propagation delay is related to propagation distance in the measured delay. If the traditional SLG could return the target's location at city-level granularity at the first tier, it is hard to get a smaller region at the second tier because the distance constraint will be too loose converted from the relative delay. Therefore, the target's more accurate estimated location is usually obtained by the third tier within a city.

It can be known from the geolocation process of traditional SLG described above that the traditional SLG can only determine the common routers that are non-anonymous in tier 3, but the true nearest common routers cannot be found out once they are anonymous. In such a situation, the nearest common router will connect to the target by at least two hops and the geographical distance between them may be very far. The selected landmark with the minimum relative delay may lead to large errors. As shown in Fig. 2, if the routers $(R_1, R_2,$ and $R_3)$ located within the dashed box are anonymous, the traditional SLG takes common router R_4 as the nearest common router between the target and landmarks $(L_1, L_2, L_3,$ and $L_4)$. It is hard to select L_1 as the estimated location of the target by using the principle of the minimum relative delay.

From the Fig. 2, the true nearest common router between the target and landmarks is R_1, and L_1 should be selected. That is, SLG can hardly select the landmark nearest to the target utilizing the minimum relative delay rule when the common routers are anonymous. In addition, we also find that the landmark with the minimum relative delay is not always the nearest one to the target in repeating the traditional SLG experiments.

To improve the accuracy of the traditional SLG in this case, we propose an IP geolocation algorithm base on local delay distribution similarity.

3 Proposed IP Geolocation Algorithm

The basic idea of the proposed algorithm is that the two hosts' measured delays should present the similar characteristics in the changes of distribution if the packets forwarding through similar routing paths. Reference [30] indicates that the terminal IP is very close to the last-hop router. Hence, there is a high probability that the two hosts are close to each other if they are connected by the last hop router and similar routing paths.

3.1 Framework and Main Steps

The framework includes the following major components: estimated location of target IP at city-level granularity, path detection and topological analysis, local delay measurement, distribution of local delay obtaining, similarity calculation and geolocation, as shown in Fig. 3.

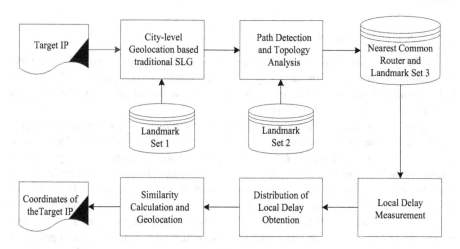

Fig. 3. Framework of improved IP Geolocation algorithm based on local delay distribution.

The main steps of proposed geolocation algorithm based on local delay distribution similarity are as follows:

Input: target IP;

Output: the coordinates of the target IP;

Step 1. City-level geolocation. The target's location at city-level granularity is determined based on the traditional SLG algorithm input by existing landmarks (denoted as landmark set 1).

Step 2. Path detection and topology analysis. Landmarks located in the same city with the target are taken as landmark set 2. Paths detection is carried out for the target and landmarks in landmark set 2 to get their topology. Landmarks connected to the target by the nearest common router are obtained by topology analysis and denoted as landmark set 3.

Step 3. Local delay measurement. Large amounts of the target' local delays are gained by multi-measurement and calculation, so do the landmarks' in landmark set 3. The method of measuring local delay will be described in detail in Sect. 3.2.

Step 4. Distribution of local delay obtaining. Distributions of the target and landmarks' local delay are required by statistical analysis using histogram.

Step 5. Similarity calculation and geolocation. The relative entropy is used to evaluate the similarity of two distributions. The relative entropy of target and landmarks' local delay distributions is calculated and the landmark whose relative entropy with the target is the minimum is selected as the estimated location of the target.

The keys to this algorithm are local delay measurement, distribution of local delay obtaining, similarity calculation and geolocation. These 3 steps are described in detail below.

3.2 Local Delay Measurement

Local delay measurement is one of the key steps in our algorithm. We take the landmarks connected with the target by the nearest common router as $\mathbf{L} = \{L_1, L_2, \cdots, L_n\}$. The local delay is obtained by measuring and calculating the delay of the nearest common router, target, and landmarks.

Figure 4 shows the example of local delay measurement. Three landmarks (L_1, L_2, and L_3) connected with the target T by the nearest common router R. Delay measurement is carried out for T, L_1, L_2 and L_3 from vantage point P. The process of measurement is as follows: at the same time t, we measure the delay of the nodes above multiple times and take the minimum value as their final delay at time t. The delays of landmarks, target and the nearest common router at time t is denoted as $L_{i,t}$ ($i = 1, 2, 3$), T_t, and R_t. Then, the local delay of landmark L_i is gained by $L_{i,t} - R_t$. The target's local delay is $T_t - R_t$. The measurement is repeated many times in a period of time, and the interval among measurement time should be small. Ultimately, we can get a quantity of local delays of landmarks and target.

3.3 Distribution of Local Delay Obtaining

In order to avoid the influence of outliers, we remove the values that too large in local delay and use the histogram to gain their local delay distribution.

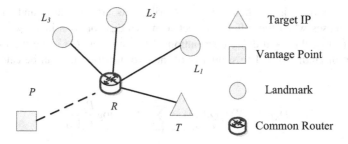

Fig. 4. An example of local delay measurement.

For an IP address, its local delays in ascending order are denoted as $(I_1, I_2, \cdots, I_n)$. We divide the local delays into m numbers of intervals and statistics the count of local delay that presents in each interval, denoted as $M_1, M_2, M_3, \cdots, M_m$. The frequency of every interval is given by $M_1/n, M_2/n, \cdots, M_m/n$. We use the frequency histogram of an IP to represent its local delay distribution. For example, the frequency histogram of 125.41.72.1 is shown in Fig. 5.

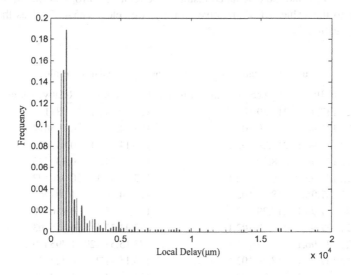

Fig. 5. An example of the frequency histogram.

3.4   Similarity Calculation and Geolocation

We take the relative entropy to measure the similarity of target and landmarks' local delay distribution. The relative entropy, also known as the Kullback-Leibler divergence (called *KLD*), is usually used to measure the similarity between two probability density distribution P and Q. Typically, P represents the true distribution of data, Q represents the theoretical distribution, model distribution, or approximate distribution of P.

The relative entropy is 0 when the two distributions are the same and the relative entropy increases when the differences between two distributions increase.

Let $P_T(X)$ be the local delay distribution of the target T, $Q_i(X)$ be the local delay distribution of landmark i. The similarity of the two distributions can be calculated by formula (1).

$$D_{KL}(P_T(X) \| Q_i(X)) = \sum_{x \in X} P_T(x) \log \frac{P_T(x)}{Q_i(x)} \tag{1}$$

where, X is the range of the local delay that generally determined based on the actual measured values.

Finally, the landmark whose local delay distribution is the most similar with the target (namely, the relative entropy between them is the smallest) is selected as the estimated location of the target, as shown in formula (2).

$$\hat{i} = \arg\min_i D_{KL}(P_T(X) \| Q_i(X)) \tag{2}$$

For instance, for the target 222.137.96.1, we find out the nearest common router's IP is 218.29.102.1 and the calculated result of the relative entropy is shown in Table 1. According to the values of the relative entropy, we select 125.41.72.1 as the target's estimated location.

Table 1. Examples of relative entropy calculation results.

Target IP	The nearest common router	Landmark	Relative entropy
222.137.96.1	218.29.102.1	115.60.144.1	1.081169
222.137.96.1	218.29.102.1	123.14.176.1	0.495614
222.137.96.1	218.29.102.1	123.14.200.1	0.847923
222.137.96.1	218.29.102.1	123.14.24.1	0.833725
222.137.96.1	218.29.102.1	123.14.40.1	0.930192
222.137.96.1	218.29.102.1	123.14.80.1	1.097668
222.137.96.1	218.29.102.1	123.14.96.1	0.956339
222.137.96.1	**218.29.102.1**	**125.41.72.1**	**0.486703**
222.137.96.1	218.29.102.1	123.15.51.129	1.795479
222.137.96.1	218.29.102.1	123.15.47.233	0.725328
222.137.96.1	218.29.102.1	123.6.144.1	1.782708
222.137.96.1	218.29.102.1	123.6.160.1	1.088317

4   Relationship Between Routing Path and Delay Distribution

The proposed algorithm is based on the following assumption: if the two same packets forwarding through two similar paths, their delay distribution should be similar. To verify this hypothesis, the following method is used to examine the relationship between routing path and delay distribution.

Let the number of landmarks be m. The local delay distribution of every IP is obtained by using multi-measurement and the histogram. We calculate the relative entropy between each two IPs. An IP is randomly selected, denoted as IP_0, the relative entropy (called d) between IP_0 and the rest $m - 1$ IPs are sorted from the smallest to the largest, denoted as $\{(d_1, IP_1), (d_2, IP_2), \cdots, (d_{m-1}, IP_{m-1})\}$, where $(d_1 \leq d_2 \leq \cdots \leq d_{m-1})$. n numbers of IPs are selected randomly from the rest $m - 1$ landmarks and their ranking position (starting from d_1 to d_{m-1}) are denoted with $\{r_1, r_2, \cdots, r_n\}$. Formula (3) is used to measure the average distribution similarity of the local delay between IP_0 and the n numbers of IPs, and the small d_{ave} indicates their average similarity is high.

$$d_{ave} = \frac{r_1 + r_2 + \cdots + r_n}{mn} \tag{3}$$

We select 10 IPs randomly from 118 IPs. For each IP, we also randomly select another 5 IPs whose routing paths are similar with it and 5 IPs whose paths are quite different. We use formula (3) to calculate the average relative entropy between each IP selected firstly and the 5 IPs with similar paths as well as the 5 IPs with different paths. The results are shown in Table 2.

Table 2. Relative entropy between IPs with similar and different paths separately.

IPs randomly selected	Relative entropy	
	Similar paths	Different paths
219.155.24.1	0.0814	0.1932
61.168.2.181	0.0763	0.1898
125.41.24.1	0.188	0.397
125.46.152.1	0.0966	0.1407
125.41.208.1	0.1102	0.4186
125.47.17.1	0.1864	0.4746
182.119.232.1	0.3305	0.2136
125.41.72.1	0.2424	0.3085
61.52.203.1	0.2915	0.3881
61.163.144.1	0.2051	0.2237

5 Experiments

5.1 Experimental Settings

To test the effectiveness of the proposed algorithm, experiments are conducted in China Unicom network in Zhengzhou city. Our algorithm aims to solve the problem in the traditional SLG when the common routers are anonymous in the third tier. Thereby, we carry out the experiments within one city and compare the geolocation results under the condition that the common routers are anonymous. We take the last-hop routers as anonymous routers and geolocate the target IPs using the proposed algorithm and the

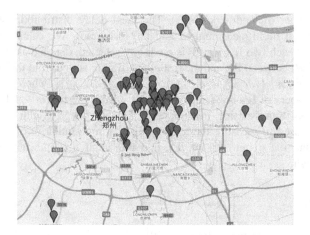

Fig. 6. Geography distribution of 118 landmarks.

traditional SLG algorithm, respectively. 118 landmarks with accurate longitude and latitude are used and their geographical distribution is shown in Fig. 6.

The vantage point is located in Zhengzhou city. The tool used to measure delay is developed based on Winpcap and can return results with microsecond accuracy. The delay of every landmark is measured by 72 groups and the minimum delay of each group is used in experiments. Routing paths are collected by traceroute tool.

5.2   Experimental Results

Due to the limited amount of experimental data, we take the method of Leave-One-Out Cross-Validation, that is, we regard one of the IPs known location as a test target and the rest of the IPs as landmarks.

Table 3 shows the geolocation results of 15 IP that randomly selected. The table includes target IP, the geolocation errors of the proposed algorithm and the traditional SLG, the ranking of the selected landmark in landmarks connected to target by the nearest common router. As Table 3 shows, for the randomly selected 15 targets, most geolocation results of the proposed are more accuracy than the traditional SLG algorithm. But due to the limited times of measurement, the limited delay values cannot fully characterize the delay distribution of an IP. A small number of geolocation results of the proposed algorithm are less accuracy than the traditional SLG's.

Geolocation results of all target IPs are present by Cumulative Distribution Function of errors, as shown in Fig. 7.

We can see from Fig. 7, the median error of the proposed is approximately 5.2 km and the traditional SLG is 6.7 km. Because of the small number, dispersed distribution and large covered area of the landmarks, the geolocation errors are slightly larger. It still proves that our algorithm can get more accuracy geolocation results when the common routers are anonymous.

Table 3. Part of geolocation results of the targets.

Target IP	Landmark	Errors (km)		Ranking of errors	
		Proposed	SLG [23]	Proposed	SLG [23]
218.28.44.81	123.14.96.1	0.4266	6.4089	2/6	5/6
125.41.132.1	61.52.203.1	0.6635	5.5183	1/7	3/7
61.52.88.1	125.41.72.1	1.0616	1.0616	2/9	2/9
123.14.96.1	221.14.192.1	3.6092	6.7725	3/6	6/6
182.119.232.1	125.41.72.1	3.7496	3.7496	5/9	5/9
61.52.144.1	222.137.96.1	4.5217	5.9232	2/9	3/9
125.41.136.1	125.40.24.1	4.7187	6.4534	1/3	2/3
61.163.144.1	222.137.96.1	5.5949	4.0338	6/9	1/9
222.137.68.1	218.28.166.137	6.2425	17.3975	2/5	4/5
125.40.96.149	125.41.72.1	6.3335	6.3335	45/90	45/90
125.42.108.1	218.28.166.137	7.2074	5.9442	4/5	3/5
182.119.176.1	222.137.0.1	8.1075	5.1921	4/4	3/4
222.137.72.1	123.6.144.1	8.4327	12.8584	1/3	3/3
61.168.2.181	125.41.72.1	11.5716	11.5716	72/90	72/90
222.137.188.1	123.6.144.1	15.0114	17.9917	1/3	2/3

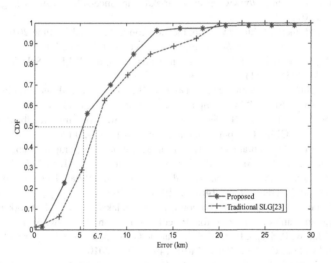

Fig. 7. Geolocation results based on proposed algorithm and the traditional SLG algorithm [23].

6 Conclusion

In this paper, we first introduce the basic idea of the typical high-precision SLG algorithm, and point out its flaw when the common routers are anonymous. Then, to solve this problem, we propose the algorithm based on local delay distribution similarity and elaborate the framework and main steps. Next, we describe the methods of the local delay measurement, distribution of local delay obtaining, and similarity calculation and geolocation. Finally, the effectiveness of the algorithm is proved in experiments. We take 118 IPs located in the Chinese city of Zhengzhou as test targets. Experimental results show that the proposed algorithm obviously improves the geolocation precision compared with the traditional SLG when the common routers are anonymous. In the next research work, we will focus on how to combine more other information to improve geolocation accuracy.

Acknowledgment. The work presented in this paper is supported by the National Natural Science Foundation of China (No. U1636219, 61379151, 61401512, 61572052), the National Key R&D Program of China (No. 2016YFB0801303, 2016QY01W0105) and the Key Technologies R&D Program of Henan Province (No. 162102210032).

References

1. Taylor, J., Devlin, J., Curran, K.: Bringing location to ip addresses with ip geolocation. J. Emerging Technol. Web Intell. **4**(3), 273–277 (2012)
2. Whois Homepage. https://www.whois.com/. Accessed 24 June 2017
3. Akamai Homepage. https://www.akamai.com/. Accessed 24 June 2017
4. Maxmind Homepage. https://www.maxmind.com/zh/home. Accessed 24 June 2017
5. Quova Homepage. https://www.neustar.biz/risk/compliance-solutions/ip-intelligence. Accessed 24 June 2017
6. IP2location Homepage, http://www.ip2location.com/. Accessed 24 June 2017
7. CQ Counter Homepage, http://cqcounter.com/. Accessed 24 June 2017
8. Shavitt, Y., Zilberman, N.: A geolocation databases study. IEEE J. Sel. Areas Commun. **29**(10), 2044–2056 (2011)
9. Poese, I., Uhlig, S., Kaafar, M.A., Donnet, B., Gueye, B.: IP geolocation databases: unreliable? ACM SIGCOMM Comput. Commun. Rev. **41**(2), 53–56 (2011)
10. Lee, Y., Park, H., Lee, Y.: IP Geolocation with a crowd-sourcing broadband performance tool. ACM SIGCOMM Comput. Commun. Rev. **46**(1), 12–20 (2016)
11. Padmanabhan, V.N., Subramanian, L.: An investigation of geographic mapping techniques for internet hosts. ACM SIGCOMM Comput. Commun. Rev. **31**(4), 173–185 (2001)
12. Gueye, B., Ziviani, A., Crovella, M., Fdida, S.: Constraint-based geolocation of internet hosts. IEEE/ACM Trans. Netw. **14**(6), 1219–1232 (2006)
13. Dong, Z., Perera, R.D.W., Chandramouli, R., Subbalakshmi, K.P.: Network measurement based modeling and optimization for IP geolocation. Comput. Netw. **56**(1), 85–98 (2012)
14. Laki, S., Mátray, P., Hága, P., Csabai, I., Vattay, G.: A model based approach for improving router geolocation. Comput. Netw. **54**(9), 1490–1501 (2010)
15. Arif, M.J., Karunasekera, S., Kulkarni, S.: GeoWeight: internet host geolocation based on a probability model for latency measurements. In: Proceeding of the ACSC 2010 33rd Australasian Conference on Computer Science, pp. 89–98 (2010)
16. Eriksson, B., Barford, P., Sommers, J., Nowak, R.: A learning-based approach for IP geolocation. In: Krishnamurthy, A., Plattner, B. (eds.) PAM 2010. LNCS, vol. 6032, pp. 171–180. Springer, Heidelberg (2010). doi:10.1007/978-3-642-12334-4_18
17. Maziku, H., Shetty, S., Han, K., Rogers, T.: Enhancing the classification accuracy of IP geolocation. In: The 31st International Proceedings on Military Communications, pp. 1–6. IEEE, Florida (2012)

18. Arif, M.J., Karunasekera, S., Kulkarni, S., Gunatilaka, A., Ristic, B.: Internet host geolocation using maximum likelihood estimation technique. In: The 24th IEEE International Conference on Advanced Information Networking and Applications, pp. 422–429. IEEE, Perth (2010)
19. Laki, S., Mátray, P., Hága, P., Sebök, T., Csabai, I., Vattay, G.: Spotter: a model based active geolocation service. In: The 30th IEEE International Conference on Computer Communication, pp. 3173–3181. IEEE, Shanghai (2011)
20. Jiang, H., Liu, Y., Matthews, J.N.: IP geolocation estimation using neural networks with stable landmarks. In: The 35th IEEE International Workshops on Computer Communications, pp. 170–175. IEEE, San Francisco (2016)
21. Katz-Bassett, E., John, J.P., Krishnamurthy, A., Wetherall, D.: Towards IP geolocation using delay and topology measurements. In: the 6th ACM SIGCOMM Conference on Internet measurement, pp. 71–84. ACM, Berlin (2006)
22. Wong, B., Stoyanov, I., Sirer, E.G.: Octant: a comprehensive framework for the geolocalization of Internet hosts. In: The 4th USENIX Symposium on Networked Systems Design & Implementation, pp. 313–326. USENIX Association, Berkeley (2007)
23. Wang, Y., Burgener, D., Flores, M., Kuzmanovic, A., Huang, C.: Towards street-level client-independent IP geolocation. In: The 8th USENIX Conference on Networked Systems Design and Implementation, pp. 1–14. USENIX Association, Boston (2011)
24. Tian, Y., Dey, R., Liu, Y., Ross, K.W.: China's internet: Topology mapping and geolocating. In: The 31th IEEE International Conference on Computer Communication, pp. 2531–2535. IEEE, Florida (2012)
25. Siqi, L., Fenlin, L., Fan, Z., Lixiang, C., Xiangyang, L.: IP city-level geolocation based on the PoP-level network topology analysis. In: The 6th International Conference on Information Communication and Management, pp. 109–114. IEEE, Hertfordshire (2016)
26. Chuanxiong, G., Wenchao, S., Helen, J.W., Qing, Y., Yongguang, Z.: Mining the web and the internet for accurate ip address geolocations. In: The 28th IEEE International Conference on Computer Communication, pp. 2841–2845. IEEE, Rio de Janeiro (2009)
27. Hao, L., Yaoxue, Z., Yuezhi, Z., Di, Z., Xiaoming, F., Ramakrishnan, K.K.: Mining checkins from location-sharing services for client-independent IP geolocation. In: The 33rd IEEE International Conference on Computer Communication, pp. 619–627. IEEE, Toronto (2014)
28. Dan, O., Parikh, V., Davison, B.D.: Improving IP geolocation using query logs. In: The 9th ACM International Conference on Web Search and Data Mining, pp. 347–356. ACM, Shanghai (2016)
29. Randolph, B.: IP Geolocation in Metropolitan Area Networks. University of Maryland, College Park (2008)
30. Prieditis, A., Chen, G.: Mapping the internet: geolocating routers by using machine learning. In: The 4th International Conference on Computing for Geospatial Research and Application, pp. 101–105. ACM, San Jose (2013)

Privacy Preserving Authenticating and Billing Scheme for Video Streaming Service

Xingwen Zhao[✉] and Hui Li

School of Cyper Engineering, Xidian University, Xi'an 710071, China
sevenzhao@hotmail.com, lihui@mail.xidian.edu.cn

Abstract. Video streaming service is popular in recent years and it provides numerous information to users all over the region. Since it needs to provide low latency and high quality-of-services (QoS) service to end users, the processing of video flows should be fast and can be finished real-time. As more and more people concern about their privacy in daily life, it is desirable to present privacy-preserving protocols in video streaming service. An authenticating and billing scheme is described in this paper to enable privacy-preserving sequential video streaming services. Two kinds of anonymous certificates are used. When connecting to the network, a pseudonym certificate as the proxy ticket is used to fetch proxy service for user's node so as to request for proxy-based Internet access. Another pseudonym certificate as video subscribing ticket is shown when each user starts a pay-per-video session, and then only a hash value is needed for each sequential video. Pseudonym certificates can hide each user's identity and easily-verifiable hash values enable quick sequential authentications. A temporary random key is selected to protect video streaming data so that the scheme can resist active man-in-middle attacks in many scenarios.

1 Introduction

In recent years, Internet is experiencing a tremendous transformation from browsing widely for resources to pulling on-demand multimedia contents. A study of Netflix [1] shows that on-demand video streaming accounts for up to 30% of the peak download traffic in US. In order to boost the applications, many video streaming clients collect personally identifiable information (PII) [2] when they are used. Some information may be private, such as an individual's name, address, telephone number, social security number, driver's license number, e-mail address, etc. Normally, PII can be used in marketing strategy such as targeted advertising. However, some people may abuse this information such as using it to assess a person's character, deciding whether a person may be a security risk, or embarrassing a person for opposing them. Thus, personal private information should be protected in many circumstances including video streaming service.

Many methods are presented [3,4] to offer low-latency media streaming to users. However, they do not consider the protection of users' privacy. Some

© Springer International Publishing AG 2017
S. Wen et al. (Eds.): CSS 2017, LNCS 10581, pp. 396–410, 2017.
https://doi.org/10.1007/978-3-319-69471-9_29

members in each service provider may collect the interests of its subscribers and sell them to other companies for profits. This may lead to unwanted crimes such as blackmails. It is desirable to design privacy-preserving protocols for these situations to avoid such a problem.

1.1 Our Contributions

We describe an authenticating and billing scheme that enables privacy-preserving sequential video streaming services for pay-per-video scenarios where each end user subscribes a sequential of videos during a period of time. The advantages of the proposed scheme are listed as follows:

- Privacy-preserving feature is achieved because the billed user obtains a set of pseudonym tickets.
- Double spending behaviors can be prevented by employing online double spending checking.
- The scheme is described as a framework which is constructed by several cryptographic tools, so it can take advantage of the advances in the future research.
- Fast authentication is achieved by using hash chain based receiving-and-acknowledging method.
- The scheme can fight against active man-in-middle attacks described in [5].

1.2 Organization

The remainder of this paper is organized as follows. In Sect. 2 we describe the related works. In Sect. 3 we describe the system model and security requirements. In Sect. 4, we describe the proposed privacy-preserving authenticating and billing scheme for video streaming services. Security analysis and features comparisons are discussed in Sect. 5. Conclusion and future extension are given in Sect. 6.

2 Related Works

In this section, we will describe some related works on video authentication and privacy-preserving authentication.

2.1 Authentication Schemes for Video Streaming

Authentication schemes for video streaming aim to provide users with several security features including integrity, source authenticity and non-repudiation. Traditional video streaming authentications [6,7] build authentication graphs on each packet and then sign them with digital signature. These schemes should make a balance between reducing authentication overhead so as to reduce transmission overhead and increasing authentication graph in order to avoid authentication failure due to packet loss. Some scheme [8] considers employing channel coding to achieve high end-to-end quality in lossy networks. The scheme uses content authentication and channel coding separately, so it cannot reach an optimal transmission rate. Some schemes [9,10] consider authentication and coding together to achieve both optimally high verification probability and low authentication overhead.

All above schemes consider the integrity and source authentication of video streaming but do not consider the privacy protection of end users.

2.2 Privacy-Preserving Authentication Schemes

There exist many anonymous payment methods [11,12]. In [11], the authors use a hash chain to improve the efficiency during the payment process, but these methods do not provide anonymity. In [12], the authors use complicated cryptographic tools including zero knowledge proof that need many messages to be exchanged between users and service providers. On the other hand, the timing needed for these protocols will not be appropriate for online video subscription where fast switching amongst short video clips needs quick authentication sequentially.

Several works [13–15] discuss the identical problem of sequential anonymous authentication and present some methods for wireless charging electric vehicles on the move. However, directly using their schemes in video streaming subscription cannot protect users' privacy since several service providers can collude together to break the anonymity of users.

All above schemes cannot be directly used for privacy-preserving video streaming authentication.

There are some other schemes [16–18] designed for anonymous authentication. Authors in [16] discuss that public-key techniques are needed to construct anonymous authencation scheme. The schemes in [17,18] employ the above idea when designing anonymous authentication protocols. The methods in these schemes can help to construct schemes for video streaming service.

3 System Model and Security Requirements

3.1 System Participants and Network Model

The proposed scheme consists of the five main parties, namely a trusted registration authority (RA), the bank, a user's node, the proxy service provider (PSP) and the video streaming service provider (VSSP), as shown in Fig. 1.

First, there is a trustful RA that will generate parameters for the system, public/private keys and signing/verifying keys for other parties.

The second party is the bank. It is trustful that it will not disclose users' privacy and can help to track illegal users if certain user violates the regulations. Each user should have an account in a bank and there should be enough money in this account for booking the tickets. Their deposit value should be enough to cover the ticket fees for a time period of secure proxy service and the fee for a number of video clips. Each user books tickets and use them to obtain a valid

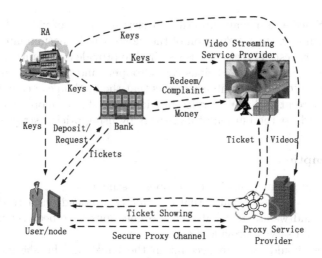

Fig. 1. System model for our privacy-preserving method.

secure proxy connection and subscribe for a list of videos. The money will be frozen and deducted after they use these tickets to enjoy the above services. The money will be returned to the deposits if their unused tickets expired.

The third is the user's node (acts as the user) that connects to Internet via Internet service provider ISP and subscribes a number of video clips from VSSP.

The fourth is PSP who provides secure proxy service to a user. PSP accepts proxy ticket from the user and decides whether it is valid to access the Internet through secure proxy channels. If valid, PSP will use the temporary session key that is negotiated in proxy ticket showing process to protect the data between PSP and the user.

The fifth is VSSP who owns online video service. VSSP accepts video subscribing ticket from the user and decides whether the user can view the claimed sequent videos. If valid, VSSP will use the temporary session key that is negotiated in video subscribing ticket showing process to protect the data between VSSP and the user (actually the proxy server that conceals the user).

3.2 Security Requirements

An Internet payment system should satisfy anonymity, reliability, security, flexibility, efficiency and scalability to support various service providers and various users [19]. We consider some of them in our scheme for the sequential video streaming service.

- Security against double spending. It is harmful to a payment system if double spending cannot be prevented.
- Fast authentication. One of the required features of video streaming service is the fast transaction, as the user may switch from one video clip to another very quickly.

– Privacy. Since a user may subscribe to view a variety of videos from several VSSPs each day, the information of the videos can be accumulated to profile the user's interest. Therefore, it is required to provide anonymity and preserve the privacy against the malicious eavesdroppers and the service providers.
– Price Flexibility. Price flexibility means that the method can change the price of the service at will, so a service provider can attract more customers and optimally adjust the burden of its servers by using pricing strategy.

3.3   Assumption

There are some assumptions for the proposed scheme.

Each bank is a trusted party that can link each issued ticket to the identity of its owner, and we assume that secure connections have been set up between the bank and all service providers.

Each user should have an account in the bank, and he/she can obtain a number of anonymous tickets if he/she has enough money in the deposit. Each ticket should be prepaid with certain amount of money that is consistent with the highest market price.

We need PSP to conceal the network addresses of the users and each user may use several PSPs to protect his/her privacy, so we assume that at least one PSP is not corrupted and it will not provide IP mapping information to VSSP and ISP. Each PSP is assumed to control many different addresses and the mappings for each session are random and different.

3.4   Thread Model

In the model, the following participants (the user, the video service provider, the proxy service provider and the Internet service provider) are assumed to be malicious. Several kinds of behaviors are considered as malicious, namely statement fraudulence, double spending and user privacy infringement. The user may bypass the billing process by reusing the spent tickets multiple times. The video service provider VSSP may refuse to give a video stream to the user after receiving a valid video subscribing ticket. The proxy service provider PSP may still block the proxy channels to Internet after receiving a valid proxy ticket. Besides, VSSP and ISP can abuse each user's privacy by collecting subscribed video lists, network addresses and related identity and sell to a third party, such as information brokers. Furthermore, the adversaries can sniff the interactions between a user and the video service provider to collect ticket information for double spending or for building up the user's interests.

4   The Proposed Scheme for Video Streaming

We present an authenticating and billing scheme for video streaming service. We first describe our idea and define the cryptographic tools that will be used, and then the detailed scheme.

4.1   Our Idea

In traditional cases, a VSSP knows each user's network addresses and the corresponding video list, and an ISP knows each user's identity and the assigned network addresses. VSSPs and ISPs together can recover a specified person's interests by accumulating the above information. In order to protect each user's privacy, video subscription lists and the network addresses should not be linked to any user. We suggest that two methods be used. The prepaid anonymous tickets (the proxy ticket and the video subscribing ticket) are used to protect each user's identity. Each user should always fetch the above two anonymous tickets from a bank by depositing money enough for a period of time of secure proxy-based Internet access and a number of videos. The proxy ticket is shown to a PSP meaning that a user wants to access the Internet via proxy for a period of time. If an unused valid ticket is received, the PSP should assign a proxy channel to the user and the channel will map the user's address no less than two times in PSP's servers so as to avoid the leakage of that address. The time length specified in the ticket can be separated into several time segments. After accessing the proxy service for a segment of time, the user should show proof to PSP that he/she is a valid user and wants to access the proxy service for another segment of time. PSP collects these proofs to redeem money from the bank later. The video subscribing ticket is shown to a VSSP when the user wants to watch a number of videos. If an unused valid ticket is received, the VSSP establishes a secure channel and conveys the video stream to the user. After finishing the current video, the user shows proof to VSSP that he/she is a valid user and wants to obtain another video clip. VSSP collects these proofs to redeem money from the bank later. PSP is used to prevent linking network addresses to identities. The video subscribing ticket is used to prevent linking interests to identities. Thus, each user's identity and his/her interests are not leaked even when ISPs and VSSPs collude together.

4.2   Cryptographic Tools

We need several cryptographic tools to construct the proposed billing scheme, including a hashing function, a public key encryption scheme, a symmetric key encryption scheme and a digital signature scheme.

- **Hash Function.** We need an efficient collusion-resistant one-way hash function (denoted as $H(\cdot)$) that its input values and output values are in the same domain. In other words, the output value can be fed as input. With this feature, we can generate hash chains such as $h_1 = H(h_0)$, $h_2 = H(h_1)$, $h_3 = H(h_2)$ and so on, if the initial value h_0 is given.
- **Public Key Encryption Scheme.** It can be any efficient secure public key encryption scheme which can be denoted as the tuple (ES-SETUP(1^λ), $\text{ENC}_{PK}(\cdot)$, $\text{DEC}_{SK}(\cdot)$). Given a secure parameter λ, ES-SETUP(1^λ) can generate parameters for the scheme and then public/private key pair (PK, SK) for each participant. $\text{ENC}_{PK}(\cdot)$ means encrypting something with key PK.

$DEC_{SK}(\cdot)$ means decrypting something with key SK. For instance, encryption schemes such as Elgamal [20] and elliptic curve cryptography [21] can be used.

- **Symmetric Key Encryption Scheme**. It can be any efficient secure symmetric key encryption scheme which can be denoted as the tuple $(SENC_{KEY}(\cdot)$, $SDEC_{KEY}(\cdot))$. $SENC_{KEY}(\cdot)$ means encrypting something with key KEY. $SDEC_{KEY}(\cdot)$ means decrypting something with key KEY. For instance, symmetric encryption schemes such as AES [22] and IDEA [23] can be used.

- **Signature Scheme**. It can be any efficient secure digital signature scheme. The scheme can be denoted as the tuple $(DS\text{-}SETUP(1^\lambda)$, $SIG_{CK}(\cdot)$, $VER_{VK}(\cdot))$. Inputting a secure parameter λ, $DS\text{-}SETUP(1^\lambda)$ can output parameters for the billing scheme and signing/verifying key pair (CK, VK) for each participant. $SIG_{CK}(\cdot)$ means signing some message with key CK. $VER_{VK}(\cdot)$ means verifying certain signature with key VK. It will be better to choose signature schemes with batch verification ability [24,25] so that we can verify many signatures in one round and detect invalid signatures quickly.

4.3   The Scheme

(1) System Setup
The trusted registration authority (RA) selects a large number λ and generates the system parameters $Params$ by running $ES\text{-}SETUP(1^\lambda)$ and $DS\text{-}SETUP(1^\lambda)$. When each participant is properly authenticated, RA generates its permanent private and public keys and transmits to it securely. A bank with identity $B_i(i = 1, 2, \ldots)$ will receive a pair of public/private keys (PK_{B_i}, SK_{B_i}) and a pair of signing/verifying keys (CK_{B_i}, VK_{B_i}). A service provider (PSP, VSSP etc.) with identity $S_i(i = 1, 2, \ldots)$ will receive a pair of public/private keys (PK_{S_i}, SK_{S_i}) and a pair of signing/verifying keys (CK_{S_i}, VK_{S_i}). A user with identity $U_i(i = 1, 2, \ldots)$ will receive a pair of public/private keys (PK_{U_i}, SK_{U_i}) and a pair of signing/verifying keys (CK_{U_i}, VK_{U_i}). Moreover, each user is equipped with a node (a computer, a mobile phone or likewise smart device) to carry out security related computations. And the keys of each user are securely transferred into the node before operating. We assume that all parties are consistent with the standard time so they do not have any dispute on timestamps.

(2) Ticket Obtaining
Each user should obtain two kinds of tickets by interacting with his/her bank B_j. One is the proxy ticket and the other is the video subscribing ticket. Both tickets are prepaid with some amount of money to cover the intended number of time periods. The proxy ticket is retrieved in three steps as follows:

(1) U_i generates randomly a pair of temporary proxy signing/verifying keys $(TPCK_{U_i}, TPVK_{U_i})$ and a hash chain h_0, $h_1 = H(h_0)$, $\ldots$, $h_n = H(h_{n-1})$ in his/her free time. h_0 should be generated randomly. U_i sends a ticket-requesting message to the bank. The message contains the temporary verifying key $TPVK_{U_i}$, an expected expiration time T, user's identity U_i, the end value

of hash chain h_n, and the number n for the requested ticket. n is the expected number of time segments for the proxy service. A segment means a short period of time for proxy service accounting, e.g. an hour or 10 min. T should be limited according to the application, such as 10 days. The message is signed by the signing key CK_{U_i} of the user and then encrypted with bank's public key PK_{B_j}. Let $M_1 = (TPVK_{U_i}, U_i, T, h_n, n)$. The request message is denoted as

$$U_i \rightarrow B_j : C_1 = \text{ENC}_{PK_{B_j}}(M_1, \text{SIG}_{CK_{U_i}}(M_1)).$$

(2) After receiving the request, the bank B_j recovers the message with its secret key SK_{B_j}. The bank verifies the user's signature and the expiration time T. It also checks whether there is enough money in the user's deposit. If all are qualified, the bank generates the ticket for user and the corresponding amount of money is frozen. The ticket is the bank's signature to $(TPVK_{U_i}, T, h_n, n)$. Let $M_2 = (TPVK_{U_i}, T, h_n, n)$. The returned message to user U_i is denoted as

$$B_j \rightarrow U_i : C_2 = \text{ENC}_{PK_{U_i}}(\text{SIG}_{CK_{B_j}}(M_2)).$$

(3) Obtaining the returned message, U_i decrypts and verifies with the secret key SK_{U_i} and the bank's verifying key VK_{B_j}. If the bank's signature is correct, $\text{SIG}_{CK_{B_j}}(TPVK_{U_i}, T, h_n, n)$ is stored as the ticket.

Similarly, the user obtains the video subscribing ticket from the bank. U_i generates a random pair of temporary video signing/verifying keys $(TVCK_{U_i}, TVVK_{U_i})$ and a hash chain h_0, $h_1 = \text{H}(h_0)$, ..., $h_n = \text{H}(h_{n-1})$ where h_0 is a random value. After similar steps as obtaining the proxy ticket, U_i receives $\text{SIG}_{CK_{B_j}}(TVVK_{U_i}, T, h_n, n)$ as the video subscribing ticket. The details are omitted for brevity.

(3) Ticket Using in Proxy Service
Before a user subscribes for certain video clip, his/her node should connect to PSP firstly. By showing proxy ticket, each user's node obtains a secure proxy channel from the PSP and then accesses the Internet without leaking personally identifiable information. We explain ticket showing interactions as following.

(1) Accessing the proxy service for the first segment of time
When a user U_i attempts to access the Internet via the proxy service provided by PSP S_k, PSP S_k would ask him/her to fulfill the authentication. U_i sends an encrypted message $(TPVK_{U_i}, T, h_n, n, K_1, \text{SIG}_{CK_{B_j}}(TPVK_{U_i}, T, h_n, n),$ $\text{SIG}_{TPCK_{U_i}}(T, S_k, K_1), m)$ to S_k. The number $m(m \leq n)$ is used to show how many time segments he/she needs for using the proxy service. K_1 is randomly selected and will be used to protect later interactions. Then, S_k checks the validity of the signature and the expiration time T, and forwards the ticket to bank B_j. If the signature is valid, T is not expired and bank B_j confirms that the ticket is spent for the first time, S_k replies with an encrypted message $(co,$ $S_k, T_e, \text{SIG}_{CK_{S_k}}(co, S_k, T_e, h_n))$ that contains the price of each time segment co, its identity S_k, a timestamp T_e, a signature to co, S_k, T_e and h_n. The timestamp is served as beginning time of this session and also used to prevent reply attacks. The user computes $\text{SIG}_{TPCK_{U_i}}(m, co, S_k, T_e)$ as message and sends it to S_k.

With this message, PSP S_k checks the validity of this message with $TPVK_{U_i}$. If the signature passes the verification, S_k now assures the authentication of the user and lets it access the proxy service. PSP should guarantee that the proxy service will map the addresses of user's packets no less than twice with different addresses. The service can be maintained and then can be checked by the user easily, so we do not discuss the details further. This interaction can be denoted as

$$U_i \rightarrow S_k : ENC_{PK_{S_k}}(TPVK_{U_i}, T, h_n, n, K_1,$$
$$\text{SIG}_{CK_{B_j}}(TPVK_{U_i}, T, h_n, n), \text{SIG}_{TPCK_{U_i}}(T, S_k, K_1), m);$$
$$S_k \rightarrow U_i : SENC_{K_1}(co, S_k, T_e, \text{SIG}_{CK_{S_k}}(co, S_k, T_e, h_n));$$
$$U_i \rightarrow S_k : SENC_{K_1}(\text{SIG}_{TPCK_{U_i}}(m, co, S_k, T_e)).$$

Later, K_1 is used to protect session data including the video streaming packets after PSP doing the proxy mappings.

The proxy ticket is untraceable anonymous ticket, so the PSP can only know that certain valid user is requiring to access the proxy service and do not know any personally identifiable information about the user.

(2) Authenticating for the next segment of time

If a user wants to access the proxy service continually, he/she should send the next value in the hash chain to PSP sequentially at the end of each time segment. There are two messages during each report interaction. The first message should be $(T_{m-1}, h_{m-1}, TPVK_{U_i})$, where T_{m-1} is current time and the sequential hashing of h_{m-1} should lead to h_n. It means ISP S_k can verify whether the equations $h_m=H(h_{m-1})$, $h_{m+1}=H(h_m)$, ..., $h_n=H(h_{n-1})$ hold or not. If the hash chain is valid, PSP S_k extends U_i's time bound to another time segment, and sends a confirming message to the user $\text{SIG}_{CK_{S_k}}(T_{m-1}, h_{m-1}, TPVK_{U_i})$. At the end of this segment, the user sends a new message $(T_{m-2}, h_{m-2}, TPVK_{U_i})$, where PSP can verify it as $h_{m-1}=H(h_{m-2})$. If valid, PSP extends U_i's time bound to another time segment. PSP also returns a signature $\text{SIG}_{CK_{S_k}}(T_{m-2}, h_{m-2}, TPVK_{U_i})$ with the new time T_{m-2}. The user should reject releasing the next value of the hash chain if he/she cannot access the proxy service in current time segment. Since $H(\cdot)$ is a secure one-way hash function, PSP cannot figure out the input value from the given sequence of output values. Thus, in order to redeem the money from the bank, PSP should treat each user fairly to obtain the whole hash chain. This interaction will continue until the user sends (T_0, h_0, TVK_{U_i}) to PSP and obtains the access to the proxy service for the mth time segment. This interaction can be denoted as

$$U_i \rightarrow S_k : T_{m-1}, h_{m-1}, TPVK_{U_i};$$
$$S_k \rightarrow U_i : \text{SIG}_{CK_{S_k}}(T_{m-1}, h_{m-1}, TPVK_{U_i});$$
$$U_i \rightarrow S_k : T_{m-2}, h_{m-2}, TPVK_{U_i};$$
$$S_k \rightarrow U_i : \text{SIG}_{CK_{S_k}}(T_{m-2}, h_{m-2}, TPVK_{U_i});$$

...

$$U_i \rightarrow S_k : T_0, h_0, TPVK_{U_i};$$
$$S_k \rightarrow U_i : \text{SIG}_{CK_{S_k}}(T_0, h_0, TPVK_{U_i}).$$

As we notice that, it is possible that PSP S_k refuses to offer the proxy access to Internet on any time segment after receiving certain hash value h_i ($0 \leq i \leq m - 1$) from the user, and the user can do nothing. In that case, the user loses a small amount of money for a single time segment and PSP S_k risks ruining its reputation by benefiting from cheating only one time segment. The user loss can be decreased to negligible if the time segment is short enough. We should notice that the user could send several hash values together to PSP to extend his/her time bound to several time segments in one report interaction, if he/she does not care about the risk of bad service.

(3) Ticket Using in Video Subscribing Service

Before a user receives any video streaming, he/she should be authenticated to VSSP (with identity as S_l) with an unused ticket. There are two phases for the authentication: starting a new session and subscribing to a next video clip. As for the first phase, when a user requests to open a new session for video service, the node of the user should connect and show its ticket to the VSSP. After the authentication, VSSP knows how many videos the user is going to watch and a session key for video streaming protection is established between VSSP and the user. As for the second phase, the user should send to VSSP a sequential value of the shown ticket, if he/she wants to subscribe to a new video clip after finishing current clip. We explain these separate interactions in brevity as following.

(1) Start a video session

The user U_i selects a random key K_2 for symmetric encryption scheme and interacts with VSSP S_l to begin the video subscribing process. Since the interactions are similar to accessing the proxy service, the details are omitted and they can be denoted as

$$U_i \rightarrow S_l : ENC_{PK_{S_l}}(TVVK_{U_i}, T, h_n, n, K_2,$$
$$\text{SIG}_{CK_{B_j}}(TVVK_{U_i}, T, h_n, n), \text{SIG}_{TVCK_{U_i}}(T, S_l, K_2), m);$$
$$S_l \rightarrow U_i : SENC_{K_2}(co, S_l, T_e, \text{SIG}_{CK_{S_l}}(co, T, S_l, h_n));$$
$$U_i \rightarrow S_l : SENC_{K_2}(h_{m-1}, \text{SIG}_{TVCK_{U_i}}(m, co, S_l, T_e, h_{m-1})).$$

m ($m \leq n$) is the number of videos that the user is going to subscribe. Later, K_2 is used to protect session data between U_i and S_l.

(2) Continuing the session for a next video

Before receiving a new clip, U_i should report the value of the hash chain to S_l sequentially. The details are omitted and the interactions can be denoted as

$$U_i \rightarrow S_l : T_{m-2}, h_{m-2}, TVVK_{U_i};$$
$$S_l \rightarrow U_i : \text{SIG}_{CK_{S_l}}(T_{m-2}, h_{m-2}, TVVK_{U_i});$$

$\cdots$

$$U_i \rightarrow S_l : T_0, h_0, TVVK_{U_i};$$
$$S_l \rightarrow U_i : \mathrm{SIG}_{CK_{S_l}}(T_0, h_0, TVVK_{U_i}).$$

As we notice that, it is possible that S_l refuses to send a new video after receiving certain hash value h_i ($0 \le i \le m-1$) from the user, and the user can do nothing. In that case, the user loses a small amount of money for a single video clip and the service provider risks ruining its reputation by benefiting from cheating only one clip. The possibility for such a cheating can be decreased to negligible if a video is cut to many clips as short as possible. The assumption that there are several competing service providers and they all can provide enormous videos to each user [15] is also a helpful solution.

(4) Money Retrieval
(1) Money Retrieval for PSP
After accumulating enough tickets, PSP builds a message from those received in proxy service request interactions and sends the message to the bank B_j to redeem the ticket via a secure channel. The message is of the form (M_{E_1}, M_{E_2}, M_{hash}, M_{sig}), where $M_{E_1} = (TPVK_{U_i}, T, h_n, n, \mathrm{SIG}_{CK_{B_j}}(TPVK_{U_i}, T, h_n, n))$, $M_{E_2} = (m, co, S_k, T_e, \mathrm{SIG}_{TPCK_{U_i}}(m, co, S_k, T_e))$, $M_{hash} = (h_0, h_1, \ldots, h_n)$, and $M_{sig} = \mathrm{SIG}_{CK_{S_k}}(M_{E_1}, M_{E_2}, M_{hash})$. The bank verifies all the above signatures, and checks whether it is a transaction between a normal user and the specified PSP. PSP redeems the money for that proxy session and the rest will be returned to the user's deposit. If the M_{hash} is incomplete (such as $M_{hash} = (h_l, \ldots, h_m, \ldots, h_n)$ where $l \le m \le n$), ISP can only get the money for $m-l$ segments. This interaction can be denoted as

$$M_{E_1} = TPVK_{U_i}, T, h_n, n, \mathrm{SIG}_{CK_{B_j}}(TPVK_{U_i}, T, h_n, n);$$
$$M_{E_2} = m, co, S_k, T_e, \mathrm{SIG}_{TPCK_{U_i}}(m, co, S_k, T_e);$$
$$M_{hash} = h_0, h_1, \ldots, h_n;$$
$$M_{sig} = \mathrm{SIG}_{CK_{S_k}}(M_{E_1}, M_{E_2}, M_{hash});$$
$$S_k \rightarrow B_j : M_{E_1}, M_{E_2}, M_{hash}, M_{sig}.$$

(2) Money Retrieval for VSSP
Money retrieval for VSSP can be processed similarly by building a message from those received in Session Starting and Continuing interactions. The details are omitted for brevity.

5   Security Analysis and Comparisons

We first discuss the security of the proposed scheme. Then, we compare our method with several schemes proposed for video streaming authentication and sequential anonymous authentication.

5.1   Security Analysis

According to the security requirements listed in Sect. 3, we will discuss the double spending avoidance, identity and Interests privacy infringement.

(1) Security against double spending

Double spending means an adversary replays a sniffed ticket or certain user shows the already-spent ticket again. The two cases will be discussed respectively as following:

Case 1: An adversary can record the messages interacted between the owner of the tickets and the service provider, but he/she cannot spend the captured ticket at any service provider. The bank will show that the ticket is spent more than once. Moreover, the adversary cannot reply to the service provider correctly since he/she does not hold the secret signing key of that ticket.

Case 2: Each user as the owner of a ticket may spend the ticket several times via different service providers since he/she holds the ticket's private key. However, double spending of a same ticket will be detected by the bank. Since each ticket has a limited validation time period, each local ticket management server of the bank need not store large amount of tickets and the ticket matching is fast.

(2) Identity and Interests Privacy

The user interacts with the bank using encryption and signature schemes, so an adversary cannot obtain any information about ticket received by the specified user. The temporary verification key and the hash value in each ticket are generated randomly by the owner, so an adversary cannot link one ticket to another. The ticket is only valid for one session so the adversary cannot link one session to another and the user is untraceable. The contents from VSSP to each user and the data from PSP to the user are protected by different shared session keys that are fresh for each session, so any eavesdropper except VSSP cannot know the information of each user's interests. Even the colluding ISP and VSSP cannot track the user's identity and interests by analyzing all the interactions. We discuss this colluding issue in two cases.

Case 1: We assume that attackers (including ISP and VSSP) cannot obtain extra information about the users except for the assigned network addresses and the corresponding subscribed videos, which is the ideal case. In this case, they can only obtain that certain user at certain network address has accessed some types of videos, and they can form a profile of interests for this session but cannot link it to other sessions since the tickets are privacy preserving against others except the releasing bank.

Case 2: We assume that the attackers can obtain limited location information about the users that in a specified region there are n known residents or employees who may access the Internet. The information can be gathered from the public investigation or from the mail service provider. We also assume that, in the worst case, the attackers know exactly that m of them are browsing the Internet at the same time. In this case, a user's interests and privacy may be in danger if m is small. For instance, if the attackers know a subscribed list of videos and during that time period only two persons are accessing the Internet, the probability of guessing the right person is about 50 percent. This case will fit in with the k-anonymity model [27]. In the worst case, the probability of guessing the right user is $1/m$ and it will be decreased to a low value when m is increased to a large number.

5.2 Comparisons

We compare several features of our method with the previous methods of some authentication schemes for video streaming [4,10], and some privacy-preserving sequential authentication schemes [12,15]. The comparison is shown in Table 1.

Table 1. Comparison with Previous Works

	Privacy protection	Price flexibility	Detect double spending	Prevent double spending	Avoid fraudulence in service	Track illegal user	Man-in-middle prevention
[4]	×	not concern	×	×	×	×	×
[10]	×	not concern	×	×	×	×	×
[12]	√	√	√	√	√	×	×
[26]	√‡	√	√	√	√	√	×
[15]	√	√	×	√	√	×	×
Proposed scheme	√	√	√	√	√	√	√

‡: weak protection that all authentications of the same user can be linked.

The video streaming schemes in [4,10] are designed for video source authentication over lossy networks and the authors do not consider the privacy protection, the billing and the malicious behaviors of the users, so many features are not achieved. In the scheme of [12], the authority cannot trace illegal users because each user are totally anonymous by using skills of zero-knowledge proof. In the scheme of [15] the service provider authenticates each user in an offline form, so the user can double spend his/her token elsewhere with different service providers.

In our scheme, anonymous tickets are used to protect privacy. Cost for each period of proxy service or each video is sent in each session, so price flexibility is achieved. Online ticket checking is used to detect and stop double spending. Sequential authentication with a hash chain can authenticate quickly while avoiding severe fraudulence. Illegal user that abuses the proxy service or video streaming service can be tracked with help of the ticket-releasing bank. The temporary shared key is used to protect the video data from man-in-middle attacks.

6 Conclusion

We present an efficient privacy-preserving billing scheme for video streaming services. Each user obtains anonymous tickets from the bank and spends them with PSP and VSSP so that even ISP and VSSP collude together cannot fetch useful information about the user's identity and its interests.

Acknowledgment. This work is supported by National Natural Science Foundation of China, Grant (no. 61672411 and U1401251), National Key Research and Development Program of China Grant (no. 2017YFB0802201), Natural Science Basic Research Plan in Shaanxi Province of China, Grant (no. 2016JM6007), Major Basic Research Program of Shaanxi Province Natural Science Foundation Research Project (No. 2016ZDJC-04), China 111 Program (No. B16037) and the Research Fund for the Doctoral Program of Higher Education of China (No. 20130203120003). The authors gratefully acknowledge the anonymous reviewers for their valuable comments.

References

1. Adhikari, V.K., Guo, Y., Hao, F., Varvello, M., Hilt, V., Steiner, M., Zhang, Z.: Unreeling netflix: Understanding and improving multi-cdn movie delivery. In: Greenberg, A.G., Sohraby, K. (eds.) Proceedings of the IEEE INFOCOM 2012, Orlando, FL, USA, 25–30 March 2012, pp. 1620–1628. IEEE (2012)
2. Wikipedia: Personally identifiable information, February 2017. https://en. wikipedia.org/wiki/Personally_identifiable_information
3. Zhu, X., Pan, R., Prabhu, M.S., Dukkipati, N., Subramanian, V., Bonomi, F.: Layered internet video adaptation (LIVA): network-assisted bandwidth sharing and transient loss protection for video streaming. IEEE Trans. Multimedia **13**(4), 720–732 (2011)
4. Zhu, X., Zhu, J., Pan, R., Prabhu, M.S., Bonomi, F.: Cloud-assisted streaming for low-latency applications. In: International Conference on Computing, Networking and Communications, ICNC 2012, Maui, HI, USA, 30 January–2 February 2012, pp. 949–953. IEEE Computer Society (2012)
5. Stojmenovic, I., Wen, S., Huang, X., Luan, H.: An overview of fog computing and its security issues. Concurrency Comput. Pract. Exp. **28**(10), 2991–3005 (2016)
6. Perrig, A., Canetti, R., Tygar, J.D., Song, D.X.: Efficient authentication and signing of multicast streams over lossy channels. In: IEEE Symposium on Security and Privacy, Berkeley, California, USA, 14–17 May 2000, pp. 56–73. IEEE Computer Society (2000)
7. Zhang, Z., Sun, Q., Apostolopoulos, J.G., Wong, W.: Rate-distortion-authentication optimized streaming with generalized butterfly graph authentication. In: Proceedings of the International Conference on Image Processing, ICIP 2008, San Diego, California, USA, 12–15 October 2008, pp. 3096–3099. IEEE (2008)
8. Li, Z., Sun, Q., Lian, Y., Chen, C.W.: Joint source-channel-authentication resource allocation and unequal authenticity protection for multimedia over wireless networks. IEEE Trans. Multimedia **9**(4), 837–850 (2007)
9. Zhu, X., Chen, C.W.: A joint layered scheme for reliable and secure mobile JPEG-2000 streaming. TOMCCAP **8**(3), 30 (2012)
10. Zhu, X., Chen, C.W.: A joint source-channel adaptive scheme for wireless H.264/AVC video authentication. IEEE Trans. Inf. Forensics Secur. **11**(1), 141–153 (2016)
11. Rivest, R.L., Shamir, A.: PayWord and MicroMint: two simple micropayment schemes. In: Lomas, M. (ed.) Security Protocols 1996. LNCS, vol. 1189, pp. 69–87. Springer, Heidelberg (1997). doi:10.1007/3-540-62494-5_6

12. Au, M.H., Liu, J.K., Fang, J., Jiang, Z.L., Susilo, W., Zhou, J.: A new payment system for enhancing location privacy of electric vehicles. IEEE Trans. Veh. Technol. **63**(1), 3–18 (2014)
13. Hussain, R., Kim, D., Nogueira, M., Son, J., Tokuta, A.O., Oh, H.: PBF: a new privacy-aware billing framework for online electric vehicles with bidirectional auditability. CoRR abs/1504.05276 (2015)
14. Zhao, T., Wei, L., Zhang, C.: A secure and privacy-preserving billing scheme for online electric vehicles. In: IEEE 83rd Vehicular Technology Conference, VTC Spring 2016, Nanjing, China, 15–18 May 2016, pp. 1–5. IEEE (2016)
15. Rezaeifar, Z., Hussain, R., Kim, S., Oh, H.: A new privacy aware payment scheme for wireless charging of electric vehicles. Wireless Pers. Commun, 1–18 (2016)
16. Wang, D., Wang, P.: On the anonymity of two-factor authentication schemes for wireless sensor networks: attacks, principle and solutions. Comput. Netw. **73**, 41–57 (2014)
17. Wang, D., Wang, P., Liu, J.: Improved privacy-preserving authentication scheme for roaming service in mobile networks. In: IEEE Wireless Communications and Networking Conference, WCNC 2014, Istanbul, Turkey, 6–9 April 2014, pp. 3136–3141. IEEE (2014)
18. Odelu, V., Banerjee, S., Das, A.K., Chattopadhyay, S., Kumari, S., Li, X., Goswami, A.: A secure anonymity preserving authentication scheme for roaming service in global mobility networks. Wireless Pers. Commun., May 2017
19. Neuman, B.C., Medvinsky, G.: Requirements for network payment: The netcheque perspective. In: COMPCON, pp. 32–36 (1995)
20. ElGamal, T.: A public key cryptosystem and a signature scheme based on discrete logarithms. In: Blakley, G.R., Chaum, D. (eds.) CRYPTO 1984. LNCS, vol. 196, pp. 10–18. Springer, Heidelberg (1985). doi:10.1007/3-540-39568-7_2
21. Cohen, H., Frey, G., Avanzi, R., Doche, C., Lange, T., Nguyen, K., Vercauteren, F. (eds.): Handbook of Elliptic and Hyperelliptic Curve Cryptography. Chapman and Hall/CRC (2005)
22. Fips, N.: Announcing the advanced encryption standard (aes). Nat. Inst. Stand. Technol. (NIST) **29**(8), 2200–2203 (2001). http://csrc.nist.gov/publications/fips/fips197/fips-197.pdf
23. Lai, X., Massey, J.L.: A proposal for a new block encryption standard. In: Damgård, I.B. (ed.) EUROCRYPT 1990. LNCS, vol. 473, pp. 389–404. Springer, Heidelberg (1991). doi:10.1007/3-540-46877-3_35
24. Jiang, Y., Shi, M., Shen, X., Lin, C.: BAT: a robust signature scheme for vehicular networks using binary authentication tree. IEEE Trans. Wireless Commun. **8**(4), 1974–1983 (2009)
25. Bayat, M., Barmshoory, M., Rahimi, M., Aref, M.R.: A secure authentication scheme for vanets with batch verification. Wireless Netw. **21**(5), 1733–1743 (2015)
26. Hussain, R., Kim, D., Nogueira, M., Son, J., Tokuta, A.O., Oh, H.: A new privacy-aware mutual authentication mechanism for charging-on-the-move in online electric vehicles. In: 11th International Conference on Mobile Ad-hoc and Sensor Networks, MSN 2015, Shenzhen, China, 16–18 December 2015, pp. 108–115. IEEE Computer Society (2015)
27. Sweeney, L.: k-anonymity: a model for protecting privacy. Int. J. Uncertainty Fuzziness Knowl. Based Syst. **10**(5), 557–570 (2002)

Secure Role-Based Access Control over Outsourced EMRs Against Unwanted Leakage

Xingguang Zhou[1], Jie Chen[1], Zongyang Zhang[1,2(✉)], Jianwei Liu[1(✉)], and Qianhong Wu[1(✉)]

[1] School of Electronic and Information Engineering, Beihang University, Beijing, China
{zhouxingguang,jonathon_cj,zongyangzhang,liujianwei, qianhong.wu}@buaa.edu.cn
[2] State Key Laboratory of Information Security, Institute of Information Engineering, Chinese Academy of Sciences, Beijing 100093, China

Abstract. Along with large scale deployment of electronic medical record systems, huge amount of health data is collected. To protect the sensitive information, it must be securely stored and accessed. Considering secure storage on cloud servers, we summary a series of attack behaviors and present the security model against many types of unwanted privacy leakage. In this model, the privacy of unleaked medical records is guaranteed, and the influences of privacy leakage are confined in a strict manner. We also propose a role-based access control scheme for hierarchical healthcare organizations to achieve flexible access on these private records. One can access medical records only if his role satisfies the defined access policy, which implies a fine-grained access control. Theoretical and experimental analyses show the efficiency of our scheme in terms of computation and communication.

Keywords: Secure · Medical records · Leakage · Role-based access control

1 Introduction

Outsourcing Electronic Medical Record (EMR) to cloud service providers (CSP) in healthcare organizations becomes more and more common in recent years. For example, the doctors in a country hospital diagnoses a patient, but they are lack of advanced equipment for further treatment. They can outsource the patient's EMR to a cloud server, and immediately contact the municipal hospital. The remote doctors in their duties could download the EMR and prepare the patient for operation timely. This method brings convenience for both patients and hospitals. However, it faces the risk of privacy leakage of EMRs to cloud servers and outsiders. After the EMR owner uploads it to the CSP, he is losing the

© Springer International Publishing AG 2017
S. Wen et al. (Eds.): CSS 2017, LNCS 10581, pp. 411–426, 2017.
https://doi.org/10.1007/978-3-319-69471-9_30

physical control over the data and the cloud server will obtain the access on it. Privacy threats experienced by users of services offered by Google Inc., Apple Inc., and Amazon Inc. [1] clearly indicate that cloud is intrinsically insecure from the user's point of view [2]. Security is very important for not only the measurement to ensure secured communications, but also the precondition for other security services [3]. Healthcare organizations really need secure solutions to store and exchange confidential data and protect its privacy, against unauthorised disclosers or accesses. Besides, these solutions need to be flexible enough to deal with the changes of users' roles and permissions [4]. One promising solution towards data confidentiality is encapsulation of EMR. There are mainly two methods. By using attribute-based encryption (ABE) [5,6], users can decapsulate EMR data if their attributes satisfy the access policy. The other method uses role-based access control scheme (RBAC) [7,8]. In a RBAC scheme, the identity of each user denotes a role, and each user is allowed to gain a specific access permission if his role belongs to a defined policy.

However, the above solution does not consider unexpected leakage in practice, including secret credential leakage [9], encapsulation-related randomness leakage [10], internal files or other records leakage, etc. We summarize three types of risks in a real EMR cloud-storage system: internal information leakage, external adversary corruption and leakage caused by EMR itself. For the first type, since CSP is a semi-trusted organization, it is honest with cloud system rules but does everything possible to spy on stored files. Patients' information might be leaked by internal staff of CSP. For the second type of risk, malicious adversaries keep trying to gain access to the encapsulated communication between EMR owners and recipients. There are lots of ways do this [11]. One way is to break the random-number generator (RNG) [12] and thus gain the randomness used to encapsulate. Another way is to break into the could servers. For instance, Albrecht and Paterson [13] introduces a powerful attack that an adversary runs malicious JavaScript in a targeted browser and completely recovers HTTP session cookies or user credentials such as passwords. The third type of risk is due to EMRs' internal association for a certain patient and his family, i.e. a father's hepatitis-B record may reflect his son with the same kind of disease. Leaking on one record might readily infer unassailed ones.

Contribution. We mainly focus on access control of outsourced EMR and impact of privacy leakage. Specific techniques are highlighted as followings.

- **Privacy Leakage Controllability.** As unexpected privacy leakage always happens in various forms, we propose new security models, called Role-based Access Control Against Unwanted Leakage (RBAC-UL) to capture further leakage on the remaining "unleaked" EMRs. RBAC-UL security is achieved if confidentiality of unassailed EMRs are still guaranteed.
- **Flexible access control.** We offer an efficient approach to support fine-grained access control for a hierarchial hospital organization. A user can comprehend an EMR only if his identity satisfies the associated access policy.
- **Scalable data sharing.** Scalable data sharing is achieved by letting higher-level medical staff delegate access privilege for his subordinates.

Related Work. The essential for the privacy of EMR is represented by the ability to guarantee the data confidentiality and access control. A lot of prominent schemes have been suggested to secure outsourced health data, especially for fine-grained access control. Attribute-based encryption (ABE) [14], a new cryptographic primitive, is the most commonly used method to obtain flexible access control in clouds [15–17]. Applications have been also provided to obtain access control [18,19], and authentication [20] for the outsourced EMRs. Very recently, a role-based access control framework of EMR system [21,22] was proposed by using hierarchical identity-based broadcast encryption (HIBBE) [23], which ensures the security, scalability and flexiblity for outsourced EMRs.

Although the aforementioned schemes devote to securing the outsourced EMRs, they are unable to deal with the situation of unexpected privacy leakage, let alone to minimize its effect. These practical threats include secret credential leakage [9,24], encapsulation-related randomness leakage [10,25], internal files, accounts or other records leakage, etc. The target of our paper is to minimize the impact of leakage in the event that these unexpected issues already happened. We notice that a lot of schemes have been put forward theoretically against these unwanted leakage, including the public-key encryption schemes [26–28] and the identity-based encryption schemes [29–31]. This is different from our RBAC-UL mechanism. The formers mainly guarantee the confidentiality of the remaining "unleaked" records, while ours not only ensures the confidentiality of "unleaked" data, but also achieves scalable sharing and flexible access control of all the outsourced EMRs.

2 Preliminaries

2.1 Bilinear Group

Let $\mathcal{G}$ be a group generation algorithm that takes a security parameter λ as input and outputs the description of a bilinear group $(N, \mathbb{G}, \mathbb{G}_T, e)$. In our case, $\mathcal{G}$ outputs $(N = p_1 p_2 p_3 p_4, G, G_T, e)$ where p_1, p_2, p_3, p_4 are distinct prime factors, $\mathbb{G}$ and $\mathbb{G}_T$ are cyclic groups of order $N = p_1 p_2 p_3 p_4$, and $e : \mathbb{G} \times \mathbb{G} \to \mathbb{G}_T$ is an efficient bilinear map satisfying the two properties: (i) Bilinearity: For all $g, h \in \mathbb{G}$ and all $a, b \in \mathbb{Z}_N$, $e(g^a, h^b) = e(g, h)^{ab}$; (ii) Non-degeneracy: There exists at least a generator g in $\mathbb{G}$ such that $e(g, g)$ generates $\mathbb{G}_T$. We respectively denote the subgroups of order p_1, p_2, p_3, p_4 in $\mathbb{G}$ by $\mathbb{G}_{p_1}, \mathbb{G}_{p_2}, \mathbb{G}_{p_3}$ and $\mathbb{G}_{p_4}$. We use $G_{p_i p_j}$ $(1 \leq i, j \leq 4)$ to denote the subgroup of order $p_i p_j$ in $\mathbb{G}$. These four subgroups additionally satisfy the orthogonality property, i.e., $\forall h_i \in \mathbb{G}_{p_i}$ and $h_j \in \mathbb{G}_{p_j}$ for $i \neq j$, $e(h_j, h_j) = 1$.

2.2 Theoretical Assumptions

Our security analysis is based on the following mathematical assumptions.

Assumption 1. Given a group generator $\mathcal{G}$, we define the following distribution:

$$\mathbb{G} = (N = p_1p_2p_3p_4, G, G_T, e) \xleftarrow{R} \mathcal{G}, g_1 \xleftarrow{R} G_{p_1}, g_3 \xleftarrow{R} G_{p_3}, g_4 \xleftarrow{R} G_{p_4} D = (\mathbb{G}, g_1, g_3, g_4)$$

Assumption 1 determines whether a given element T is randomly chosen from G or from $G_{p_1p_3p_4}$, namely $T \xleftarrow{R} G$ or $T \xleftarrow{R} G_{p_1p_3p_4}$.

The advantage of an algorithm $\mathcal{A}$ that outputs $b \in \{0, 1\}$ in breaking Assumption 1 is defined as

$$Adv1_{\mathcal{A}}(\lambda) = \left| \Pr\left[\mathcal{A}\left(D, T \xleftarrow{R} G \right) = 1 \right] - \Pr\left[\mathcal{A}\left(D, T \xleftarrow{R} G_{p_1p_3p_4} \right) = 1 \right] \right| - \frac{1}{2}$$

Definition 1. $\mathcal{G}$ *satisfies Assumption 1 if* $Adv1_{\mathcal{A}}(\lambda)$ *is a negligible function for any polynomial time algorithm* $\mathcal{A}$.

Assumption 2. Given a group generator $\mathcal{G}$, we define the following distribution:

$$\mathbb{G} = (N = p_1p_2p_3p_4, G, G_T, e) \xleftarrow{R} \mathcal{G}, g_1 \xleftarrow{R} G_{p_1}, g_3 \xleftarrow{R} G_{p_3}, g_4 \xleftarrow{R} G_{p_4}, D = (\mathbb{G}, g_1, g_3, g_4)$$

Assumption 2 determines whether a given element is $T \xleftarrow{R} G_{p_1p_2p_4}$ or $T \xleftarrow{R} G_{p_1p_4}$.

The advantage of an algorithm $\mathcal{A}$ that outputs $b \in \{0, 1\}$ in breaking Assumption 2 is defined as

$$Adv2_{\mathcal{A}}(\lambda) = \left| \Pr\left[\mathcal{A}\left(D, T \xleftarrow{R} G_{p_1p_2p_4} \right) = 1 \right] - \Pr\left[\mathcal{A}\left(D, T \xleftarrow{R} G_{p_1p_4} \right) = 1 \right] \right| - \frac{1}{2}$$

Definition 2. $\mathcal{G}$ *satisfies Assumption 2 if* $Adv2_{\mathcal{A}}(\lambda)$ *is a negligible function for any polynomial time algorithm* $\mathcal{A}$.

Assumption 3. Given a group generator $\mathcal{G}$, we define the following distribution:

$$\mathbb{G} = (N = p_1p_2p_3p_4, G, G_T, e) \xleftarrow{R} \mathcal{G}, g_1 \xleftarrow{R} G_{p_1}, g_3 \xleftarrow{R} G_{p_3}, g_4 \xleftarrow{R} G_{p_4},$$
$$D_{23} \xleftarrow{R} G_{p_2p_3}, A_{12} \xleftarrow{R} G_{p_1p_2}, D = (\mathbb{G}, g_1, g_3, g_4, D_{23}, A_{12})$$

Assumption 3 determines whether a given element is $T \xleftarrow{R} G_{p_1p_2p_3}$ or $T \xleftarrow{R} G_{p_1p_3}$.

The advantage of an algorithm $\mathcal{A}$ that outputs $b \in \{0, 1\}$ in breaking Assumption 3 is defined as

$$Adv3_{\mathcal{A}}(\lambda) = \left| \Pr\left[\mathcal{A}\left(D, T \xleftarrow{R} G_{p_1p_2p_3} \right) = 1 \right] - \Pr\left[\mathcal{A}\left(D, T \xleftarrow{R} G_{p_1p_3} \right) = 1 \right] \right| - \frac{1}{2}$$

Definition 3. $\mathcal{G}$ *satisfies Assumption 3 if $Adv3_{\mathcal{A}}(\lambda)$ is a negligible function for any polynomial time algorithm $\mathcal{A}$.*

Assumption 4. Given a group generator $\mathcal{G}$, we define the following distribution:

$$\mathbb{G} = (N = p_1 p_2 p_3 p_4, G, G_T, e) \xleftarrow{R} \mathcal{G}, g_2 \xleftarrow{R} G_{p_2}, g_3 \xleftarrow{R} G_{p_3}, g_4 \xleftarrow{R} G_{p_4},$$
$$W_{14} \xleftarrow{R} G_{p_1 p_4}, E_{12} \xleftarrow{R} G_{p_1 p_2}, D = (\mathbb{G}, g_2, g_3, g_4, W_{14}, E_{12})$$

Assumption 4 determines whether a given element is $T \xleftarrow{R} G_{p_2 p_4}$ or $T \xleftarrow{R} G_{p_1 p_2 p_4}$.

The advantage of an algorithm $\mathcal{A}$ that outputs $b \in \{0, 1\}$ in breaking Assumption 4 is defined as

$$Adv4_{\mathcal{A}}(\lambda) = \left| \Pr\left[\mathcal{A}\left(D, T \xleftarrow{R} G_{p_2 p_4} \right) = 1 \right] - \Pr\left[\mathcal{A}\left(D, T \xleftarrow{R} G_{p_1 p_2 p_4} \right) = 1 \right] \right| - \frac{1}{2}$$

Definition 4. $\mathcal{G}$ *satisfies Assumption 4 if $Adv4_{\mathcal{A}}(\lambda)$ is a negligible function for any polynomial time algorithm $\mathcal{A}$.*

Assumption 5. Given a group generator $\mathcal{G}$, we define the following distribution:

$$\mathbb{G} = (N = p_1 p_2 p_3 p_4, G, G_T, e) \xleftarrow{R} \mathcal{G}, g_1 \xleftarrow{R} G_{p_1}, g_4 \xleftarrow{R} G_{p_4}, D_{23} \xleftarrow{R} G_{p_2 p_3}, D = (\mathbb{G}, g_1, g_4, D_{23})$$

Assumption 5 determines whether a given element is $T \xleftarrow{R} G$ or $T \xleftarrow{R} G_{p_1 p_2 p_4}$.

The advantage of an algorithm $\mathcal{A}$ that outputs $b \in \{0, 1\}$ in breaking Assumption 5 is defined as

$$Adv5_{\mathcal{A}}(\lambda) = \left| \Pr\left[\mathcal{A}\left(D, T \xleftarrow{R} G \right) = 1 \right] - \Pr\left[\mathcal{A}\left(D, T \xleftarrow{R} G_{p_1 p_2 p_4} \right) = 1 \right] \right| - \frac{1}{2}$$

Definition 5. $\mathcal{G}$ *satisfies Assumption 5 if $Adv5_{\mathcal{A}}(\lambda)$ is a negligible function for any polynomial time algorithm $\mathcal{A}$.*

3   Scenario

As described in Fig. 1, a EMR cloud-storage system is a multi-user setting environment, which displays the real-life interactions among patients and hospital staff. There are five entities: patient, EMR owner, EMR recipient, Trusted Keying Authority (TKA) and Cloud Server Provider (CSP).

The EMR owners are usually out-patient doctors, who are responsible for patients with distinct diseases, and responsible for encapsulating and uploading

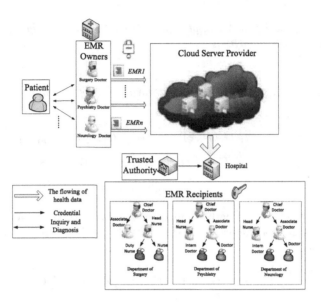

Fig. 1. EMR owners and recipients in a multi-party communication environment

corresponding EMRs to cloud servers. Every EMR is associated with its own access policy and stored on cloud servers for sharing with the entitled staff.

The EMR recipients constitute of groups of medical staff who are entitled to read a patient's EMR and provide services for him. Medical staff are honest but semi-trusted. If they are authorized, they don't reveal any information. Otherwise, they might be a potential adversary. The staff at higher-level is responsible for managing lower-level ones, which derives a tree-like organization.

The CSP provides a large number of servers for many organizations. It is honest but curious, i.e., it obeys rules of cloud system, but could do everything possible to spy on stored EMRs.

The TKA is responsible for generating and distributing system parameters.

Table 1 gives some notations which will be used in the paper. For ease of description, some notations are borrowed from [21].

4   Security Requirement

In practice, all entities except TKA are likely to attack the system. A dishonest party may try to get useful information from the encapsulated EMRs, which is not authorized to access, or derive from the leaked EMRs. In the context of such attack, our scheme is expected to meet the following security requirements.

– **Data Privacy.** EMRs need to be obfuscated before being uploaded and securely stored on cloud servers, until an entitled user downloads and de-obfuscates them.

Table 1. Notations

Notation	Description
λ	Security parameter
R	Atom role for medical staff
$\boldsymbol{R}$	Role for medical staff
$S_{\boldsymbol{R}}$	Atom role set for $\boldsymbol{R}$
P	Access policy
S_P	Atom role set for P
MSK	Master secret key
EMR	Electronic medical
$SC^{\boldsymbol{R}}$	Secret credential for a role $\boldsymbol{R}$
En	The encapsulated EMR
$Pref(\boldsymbol{R})$	Prefix of $\boldsymbol{R}$, defined as $\{(R_1, ..., R_{d'}) : d' \leq d\}$
$Pref(P)$	Prefix of P, defined as $\bigcup\limits_{\boldsymbol{R} \in P} Pref(\boldsymbol{R})$

- **Leakage Controllability.** When unwanted leakage is unavoidable, it must be possible to minimize the leakage effect. That means the privacy of non-leaked EMRs should be guaranteed.
- **Flexible Access Control.** Users are allowed to flexibly specify policies to constrain the access to confidential information.

4.1 Adversary Model for RBAC-UL

The adversary model for RBAC-UL is aimed to achieve **Leakage Controllability**. Since the content of EMRs may be internal related, partially leakage might readily expose information on those EMRs with unleaked status. Therefore, it is necessary to clarify what it means for the unleaked EMRs to remain confidential. In RBAC-UL security model, we assume two roles: adversary and simulator. The adversary's goal is to get as much information from the unleaked EMRs as possible, i.e. the attacked EMRs, the encapsulated EMRs, and the randomness used for encapsulation. The simulator acts like a normal person with neutral characters: he can get the same input as the adversary if the EMR data is leaked, and he has the ability to corrupt the EMR owners to learn their EMRs. Apart from that, the simulator cannot get any further information. We claim that if the adversary who tries to use various means attacking our system cannot benefits more information from the unleaked EMRs than the simulator, then the security of remaining EMRs are guaranteed. In other words, if there is hardly any advantage for the adversary to obtain unexposed messages, we claim that our system achieves RBAC-UL security.

We formally define the adversary model of RBAC-UL in our system. In the model, the attacked EMR is encapsulated with a target access policy set P^*

containing all medical staff who are allowed to decapsulate. The adversary is endowed with great capacity: (a) it can obtain secret credentials associated with roles $R \notin Pref(P^*)$, which implies that the adversary can collude any medical staff with roles that do not satisfy the target access policy; (b) it can obtain all the targeted encapsulated EMRs, $\textbf{En} = \{En_1, En_2, ..., En_n\}$; (c) it can randomly corrupt any encapsulated EMR from $\textbf{En}$, and then obtain their files $\{EMR_i\}_{i \in \{1,2,...n\}}$ with the randomness used for encapsulation $\{r_i\}_{i \in \{1,2,...n\}}$, which implies that the adversary has the ability to corrupt the EMR owners.

We use two security games for further illustration. The first game is played by an adversary $\mathcal{A}$ and a challenger $\mathcal{C}$, and describes what an adversary obtains in a real-world. The second game is played by a simulator $\mathcal{S}$ and a challenger $\mathcal{C}$, and describes what a simulator obtains in an ideal experiment.

Game RBAC-UL-Real

Setup. The challenger $\mathcal{C}$ runs the **Setup** algorithm to obtain a system parameter PK and gives it to the adversary $\mathcal{A}$.

Query Phase 1. $\mathcal{A}$ issues a secret credential query for a medical staff associated with a role $\textbf{R}$. The challenger $\mathcal{C}$ generates a secret credential for $\textbf{R}$ and returns it to $\mathcal{A}$.

Challenge. The adversary $\mathcal{A}$ outputs $\textbf{EMR} = \{EMR_1, EMR_2, ..., EMR_n\}$ on which it wishes to challenge, together with a set of policy $P^* = \{P_1{}^*, P_2{}^*, ..., P_n{}^*\}$ including all the broadcast groups that it wishes to attack. Each access policy $P_i{}^*$ should satisfy that for all the secret credential queries issued in Query Phase 1, $\textbf{R} \notin Pref(P_i{}^*)$. $\mathcal{C}$ randomly chooses $r[i] \leftarrow Z_p$ for each EMR_i, where $p = |\mathbb{G}|$ and $i \in \{1, n\}$. Then the challenger $\mathcal{C}$ executes the following encryptions:

$$En_i \leftarrow Enc(PK, P_i{}^*, EMR_i, r_i)$$

$\mathcal{C}$ returns the encapsulated EMRs $\textbf{En} = \{En_1, En_2, ..., En_n\}$ to $\mathcal{A}$.

Corrupt. The adversary $\mathcal{A}$ outputs a set $I \subseteq \{1, 2, ..., n\}$ to $\mathcal{C}$ on which $\mathcal{A}$ wishes to corrupt. $\mathcal{C}$ corrupts the corresponding EMRs to get $(EMR_i, r_i)_{i \in I}$ and returns them to $\mathcal{A}$.

Output. The adversary $\mathcal{A}$ outputs Out_A.

Game RBAC-UL-Sim

Setup. The simulator $\mathcal{S}$ gets system parameters from challenger $\mathcal{C}$.

Challenge. The simulator $\mathcal{S}$ outputs $\textbf{EMR} = \{EMR_1, EMR_2, ..., EMR_n\}$ on which it wishes to challenge, together with a set of policy $P^* = \{P_1{}^*, P_2{}^*, ..., P_n{}^*\}$ including all the broadcast groups that it wishes to attack. The challenger $\mathcal{C}$ gets these inputs, but gives no feedback to $\mathcal{A}$.

Corrupt. The simulator $\mathcal{S}$ outputs a set $I \subseteq \{1, 2, ..., n\}$ to $\mathcal{C}$. The challenger $\mathcal{C}$ picks up the corresponding EMRs $(EMR_i)_{i \in I}$ and returns them to $\mathcal{S}$.

Output. The simulator $\mathcal{S}$ outputs Out_S.

We claim that if for every adversary there exists a simulator who can generate the same output without seeing any encapsulated EMR and encapsulation randomness, the scheme achieve RBAC-UL security.

Definition 6. *Assume that an adversary is the one who runs with game $Game_{real}$ and a simulator is the one who runs with game $Game_{sim}$. We define the advantage of the adversary $\mathcal{A}$ against an RBAC scheme Γ with the simulator $\mathcal{S}$ as*

$$Adv_{\Gamma,\mathcal{S}}^{RBAC-UL}(\mathcal{A}) = Pr[Game_{real}^{\mathcal{A}} = 1] - Pr[Game_{sim}^{\mathcal{S}} = 1]$$

Definition 7. *Given a RBAC scheme, if no polynomial time distinguisher $\mathcal{D}$ can distinguish the output from Game **RBAC-UL-Real** and that of Game **RBAC-UL-Sim**, namely $|Pr[\mathcal{D}(Out_A = 1)] - Pr[\mathcal{D}(Out_S = 1)]| = \epsilon$. ϵ is a negligible advantage. We claim that the scheme achieves **RBAC-UL** security.*

4.2 Semantic Security Model

In our security analysis, we will apply the full security notion [32,33] to achieve **Data Privacy**. The adversary adaptively decides to output the set of access policy it wishes to challenge during the system interaction. The detailed setting is as follows: the recipient (doctor who wants to get access on EMR) generates a credential pair; the sender (EMR owner) encapsulates one out of two EMRs and send it to the adversary. The adversary tries to find out which one it was. Here, importantly, the adversary has the authority to issue secret credential query. If the adversary cannot distinguish an encapsulation of a challenge EMR from an encapsulation of a random message, we claim that our system achieves RBAC-IND security. RBAC-IND security model is defined by a security game played with a challenger $\mathcal{C}$ and an adversary $\mathcal{A}$ as following.

Setup. The $\mathcal{C}$ runs setup algorithm to obtain public key PK and gives it to $\mathcal{A}$.

Query Phase 1. $\mathcal{A}$ issues a secret credential query for the medical staff with role $\boldsymbol{R}$. The challenger generates a secret credential for $\boldsymbol{R}$ and gives it to $\mathcal{A}$.

Challenge. The adversary $\mathcal{A}$ outputs two equal-length EMR files, EMR_0 and EMR_1 on which it wishes to challenged. $\mathcal{A}$ outputs a challenge access policy P^* either. The access policy P^* should satisfy that for all the secret credential queries for $\boldsymbol{R}$ issued in Query Phase, $\boldsymbol{R} \notin Pref(P^*)$. The challengers flips a random coin $\beta \in \{0,1\}$ and encapsulate EMR_β under the challenge access policy P^*. Then it returns the resulting challenge encapsulated EMR to $\mathcal{A}$.

Guess. The adversary $\mathcal{A}$ output a guess $\beta' \in \{0,1\}$ and wins the game if $\beta = \beta'$.

Definition 8. *We define the advantage of a RBAC-IND adversary $\mathcal{A}$ against RBAC scheme Γ to be $Adv_{\Gamma}^{RBAC-IND}(\mathcal{A}) = 2 \cdot Pr[RBAC - IND_{\Gamma}^{\mathcal{A}} = 1] - 1$.*

Definition 9. *Given a RBAC scheme, if no polynomial-time adversary with the challenge access policy set P^* can distinguish between an encapsulation of the challenge EMR and an encapsulation of random message, then the scheme Γ achieves RBAC-IND security.*

5   Proposed Solution

Our role-based access control solution supports fine-grained access by encapsulating EMRs to any subset of hierarchically organized users, which is based on HIBBE. Furthermore, it resists many types of unwanted leakage, so as to control the leakage effect in a certain scope. The following subsections show how we achieve the targets. In Sect. 5.1, we construct a one-bit RBAC scheme with one-sided public leakage (1SPL) functionality. 1SPL means there exists a public procedure that given the one-bit encapsulation message En^1 of 1 can compute the randomness r under which the encapsulation applied to 1 would generate En^1. The idea comes from the notion of one-side public openability [34]. In Sect. 5.2, we provide security analysis for the proposed one-bit RBAC scheme with 1SPL. In Sect. 5.3, we provide a reduction showing that if a one-bit RBAC scheme with 1SPL functionality is secure, the normal multi-bit scheme with RBAC-UL model is secure. Finally, our solution achieves data privacy, leakage controllability and flexible access control.

5.1   One-Bit RBAC Scheme with 1SPL Functionality

Setup(λ, n). System setup algorithm is run by TKA. It chooses a bilinear group G of order N, random elements g_1, g_2, g_3, g_4 from $G_{p_1}, G_{p_2}, G_{p_3}, G_{p_4}$, random exponents $u_{11}, u_{12}, ..., u_{1n}, u_4, x_1, x_4, \omega_4 \leftarrow Z_N$, and computes $U_{1i} \leftarrow g_1^{u_{1i}}$, $U_4 \leftarrow g_4^{u_4}$, $X_1 \leftarrow g_1^{x_1}$, $X_4 \leftarrow g_4^{x_4}$, $W_4 \leftarrow g_4^{\omega_4}$, $U_{1i,4} \leftarrow U_{1i}U_4$, $W_{14} \leftarrow g_1W_4$, $X_{14} \leftarrow X_1X_4$ for $i \in [1, n]$. It outputs public key $PK = \{N, \{U_{1i,4}\}_{i\in[1,n]}, X_{14}, W_{14}, g_4\}$ and master secret key $MSK = \{g_1, g_3, \{U_{1i}\}_{i\in[1,n]}, X_1\}$.

SCGen$(PK, MSK, \boldsymbol{R})$. Secret credential generation algorithm. For medical staff with role $\boldsymbol{R} = (R_1, ..., R_d)$, we denote $I = \{i : R_i \in S_{\boldsymbol{R}}\}$. When a medical staff at the top-level joins a hospital organization, TKA generates secret credential $SC^{\boldsymbol{R}}$ for him: $K_1 = g_1^r g_3^{r_3}$, $K_2 = (\prod_{i\in I} U_{1i}^{R_i} \cdot X_1)^r \cdot g_3^{r_3'}$, $E_j = \{U_{1j}^r \cdot g_3^{r_j}\}_{j\in[i,n]\setminus I}$. where $r, r_3, r_3', \{r_j\}_{j\in[1,n]\setminus I} \leftarrow Z_N$.

SCDeleg$(PK, SC^{\boldsymbol{R'}}, R)$. Secret credential delegation algorithm. A junior medical staff with role $\boldsymbol{R} = (\boldsymbol{R'}, R)$ is authenticated by a supervisor with role $\boldsymbol{R'}$. His supervisor delegates secret credential for him

$$K_1 = K_1' g_1^{r'} g_3^{\tilde{r}_3}, \quad K_2 = K_2'(\prod_{i\in I} U_{1i}^{R_i} \cdot X_1)^{r'} \cdot (E_i')_{i\in I\setminus I'}^{R} \cdot g_3^{\tilde{r}_3'}$$

$$E_j = \{E_j' \cdot U_{1,j}^{r'} \cdot g_3^{r_j'}\}_{j\in[1,n]\setminus I} = \{U_{1,j}^{r+r'} \cdot g_3^{r_j'+r_j}\}_{j\in[1,n]\setminus I}$$

where $I' = \{i : R_i \in S_{\boldsymbol{R'}}\}$ and $r', \tilde{r}_3, \tilde{r}_3', \{r_j'\}_{j\in[i,n]\setminus I} \leftarrow Z_N$. It can be computed

$$K_1 = g_1^{\hat{r}} g_3^{\hat{r}_3}, \quad K_2 = (\prod_{i\in I} U_{1i}^{R_i} \cdot X_1)^{\hat{r}} \cdot g_3^{\hat{r}_3'}, \quad E_j = \{U_{1j}^{\hat{r}} \cdot g_3^{\hat{r}_j}\}_{j\in[i,n]\setminus I}$$

The credential is well formed as if it is generated by TKA with SCGen algorithm.

EMREnc(PK, P, EMR). EMR encapsulation algorithm. For an access policy P, we denote $\mathbb{I} = \{i : R_i \in S_P\}$. When a single bit 0 from EMR data needs to be encapsulated under P, medical staff chooses random $s, t_4, t'_4 \leftarrow Z_N$ and computes $En_1 = (\prod_{i \in \mathbb{I}} U_{1i,4}^{R_i} \cdot X_{14})^s g_4^{t_4}$, $En_2 = W_{14} g_4^{t'_4}$. When a single bit 1 needs to be encapsulated, medical staff sets $En_1, En_2 \xleftarrow{R} G$.

EMRDec(PK, R, En, SC^R). EMR decapsulation algorithm. The medical staff with role satisfied an access policy P, can use his secret credential to recover all one-bit messages for EMR data. If $e(En_1, K_1) = e(En_2, K_2)$, the medical staff returns bit 0. Otherwise, he returns bit 1.

Correctness. We need to verify when input a well-formed EMR encapsulation $En = (En_1, En_2)$ with a valid credential SC^R for 0 bit, whether $e(En_1, K_1) = e(En_2, K_2)$ holds.

$$e(En_1, K_1) = e((\prod_j U_{1j,4}^{id_j} \cdot X_{14})^s g_4^{t_4}, g_1^r g_3^r)$$

$$e(En_2, K_2) = e(g_1^s \cdot g_4^{\omega_4 s + t'_4}, (g_1^{u_{11} \cdot id_1} \cdots g_1^{u_{1j} \cdot id_j} \cdot g_1^{x_1})^r \cdot g_3^{r'})$$

Due to the orthogonality property, we can get $e(En_1, K_1) = e(En_2, K_2) = e(g_1^s, g_1^{r \cdot (\sum_{i=1}^{j} u_{1i} \cdot id_1 + x_1)})$. Therefore, when $En = (En_1, En_2)$ is a well-formed EMR encapsulation, decapsulation algorithm can correctly recover EMR.

5.2   Security Analysis of One-Bit RBAC Scheme

We prove by contradiction. Assume an adversary can break the one-bit RBAC scheme in polynomial time, then we can solve a series of hard-to-solve problems based on the subgroup decision assumptions. Since no algorithm could solve these problems, we reach a contradiction and conclude our proposed scheme is secure. These hard-to-solve assumptions are mentioned in Sect. 2.2.

Theorem 1. *Let G be a group of composite order $N = p_1 p_2 p_3 p_4$, equipped with an efficient bilinear map. Suppose that Assumptions 1, 2, 3, 4, and 5 hold in G. Then our one-bit RBAC scheme is secure under the formal security model.*

We prove Theorem 1 through a series of game transitions, played between a challenger and an adversary. The fist game is a real security game. The subsequent one is a little different from its previous one, but the difference is negligible from adversary's view. In the last game, all components in the EMR encapsulation are random elements. As all useful information are blinded to adversary, no leakage occurs. Thus the one-bit RBAC scheme is secure.

5.3   From One-Bit RBAC with 1SPL to Multi-bit RBAC-UL

We provide security analysis for the RBAC-UL model. The key point is to reduce its security from a secured one-bit RBAC with 1SPL functionality. We use a specific 1SPL algorithm *LeakToOne* which exposes the randomness as if it is randomly chosen for bit 1, and fails with probability δ when it cannot find out the randomness to 1. In security analysis, we assume that all the roles in the access policy set or its subset are ordered from high-level to lower level one.

Theorem 2. *Let Γ be a one-bit RBAC scheme, and Γ^l be the l-bit RBAC scheme built from it. Let k be the number of leaked EMRs and δ be the failing probability of LeakToOne. Suppose there exists a RBAC-UL adversary $\mathcal{A}$, a RBAC-UL simulator $\mathcal{S}$ and a RBAC adversary $\mathcal{B}$. If Γ is secure with $Adv_\Gamma(\mathcal{B})$, then Γ^l is secure with $Adv_{\Gamma^l,k,\mathcal{S}}(\mathcal{A}) \leq kl \cdot Adv_\Gamma(\mathcal{B}) + kl \cdot \delta$.*

We prove it by a series of game transitions. The proof idea can be sketched as following. $\mathcal{A}$ is a RBAC-UL adversary against Γ^l and $\mathcal{S}$ is a RBAC-UL simulator. We use $Game_{real}^{\mathcal{A}}$ and $Game_{sim}^{\mathcal{A}}$ to describe the games that $\mathcal{A}$ and $\mathcal{S}$ runs respectively. Between $Game_{real}^{\mathcal{A}}$ and $Game_{sim}^{\mathcal{A}}$, there are a series of game transitions. We finally show that there is no algorithm to distinguish $Game_{real}^{\mathcal{A}}$ from $Game_{sim}^{\mathcal{A}}$, which means simulator $\mathcal{S}$ can run identically to $\mathcal{A}$. That is what we claimed in Sect. 4.1 for RBAC-UL security.

Due to space limit, the concrete proofs of Theorems 1 and 2 will be shown in the extended version.

6 Performance Analyses

6.1 Improve User Experience

There are several ways studied for better user experience. For example, the key management schemes [35,36] provide security with low complexity. In our paper, we apply online/offline cryptography [37] to speed up data processing in procedures of credential generation and EMR encapsulation. The offline phase executes most of heavy computations by assuming a set of random roles, while the online phase only performs light computations to produce the EMR encapsulation or secret credential once the true roles are available.

6.2 Theoretical Analysis

Table 2 compares several schemes in different perspectives. We denote t_e as one exponent operation time, t_m as one multiplication time and t_p as one pairing operation time. The maximal depth of the hierarchy for a access policy is $\|P\|$. $\|R\|$ is the number of atom roles in a secret credential. We denote "Our& RBAC" as our scheme with improved efficiency. The properties of scalable sharing, flexible access and leakage controllability support further rendering our scheme with improved efficiency to practical usage.

Table 2. Comparison with related work

	Credential generation time	Encapsulation time	Controllability of leakage	Scalable sharing	Flexible access control
[16]	$(1+4\|\boldsymbol{R}\|)t_e$ $(1+4\|\boldsymbol{R}\|)t_m$	$6t_e + t_m$ $+t_p$	×	✓	✓
[19]	$2(\|\boldsymbol{R}\|+1)t_e$ $+\|\boldsymbol{R}\|t_m$	$5t_e + \|P\|t_m$ $+t_p$	×	✓	✓
[21]	$3(n+4)t_e$ $+(3\|\boldsymbol{R}\|+4)t_m$	$(\|P\|+4)t_e$ $+(\|P\|+4)t_m$	×	✓	✓
[29]	$5t_e + 3t_m$	$5t_e + 3t_m$	✓	×	×
Ours	$(2n-\|\boldsymbol{R}\|+4)t_e$ $+(n+2)t_m$	$(\|P\|+3)t_e$ $+(\|P\|+2)t_m$	✓	✓	✓
Our RBAC	$\|\boldsymbol{R}\|\cdot t_m$	$\|P\|\cdot t_m$	✓	✓	✓

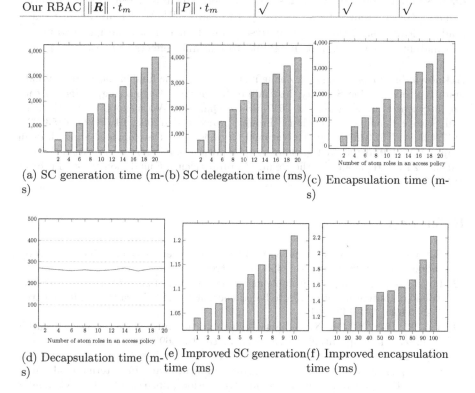

(a) SC generation time (m-s) (b) SC delegation time (ms) (c) Encapsulation time (m-s)

(d) Decapsulation time (m-s) (e) Improved SC generation time (ms) (f) Improved encapsulation time (ms)

Fig. 2. Experimental results for our proposed system

6.3 Performance Analysis

We conduct experiment on Intel Core i7 processor with 8GB RAM and 2.6GHZ CPU. We use elliptic curve type A1 for the Tate symmetric pairing. Both group order of $\mathbb{Z}_N$ and element size in $\mathbb{G}$ are configured as 512 bits. The experiment is executed with jPBC library. As Fig. 2 illustrates, we test the operational time for credential generation, delegation, EMR encapsulation and decapsulation. Figure 2(e) and (f) show the operational time when user experience is improved. The Y-axis represents the operational time in milliseconds. The X-axis in Fig. 2(a)–(f) means the number of related atoms role included in a medical staff's role; the X-axis in Fig. 2(c) and (d) means the number of atom roles in an access policy.

7   Conclusion

We consider a multi-party communication scenario in an EMR cloud-storage system. A diversity of medical records are outsourced by different professional doctors and accessed by medical staff with hierarchical privileges. We summarize behaviors of different adversaries and put forward a RBAC scheme against many kinds of leakages. Performance analyses show that our scheme has advantages in scalability, flexibility, and the ability to minimize effects of privacy leakage.

Acknowledgments. Zongyang Zhang is supported by the fund of the State Key Laboratory of Information Security, Institute of Information Engineering, Chinese Academy of Sciences, under grant No. 2017-MS-02. Qianhong Wu is supported by the Natural Science Foundation of China through projects 61672083, 61370190, 61532021, 61472429, and 61402029, by the National Cryptography Development Fund through project MMJJ20170106, by the planning fund project of ministry of education through project 12YJAZH136 and by the Beijing Natural Science Foundation through project 4132056.

References

1. Boldyreva, A., Goyal, V., Kumar, V.: Identity-based encryption with efficient revocation. In: CCS 2008, pp. 417–426. ACM (2008)
2. Li, M., Yu, S., Zheng, Y.: Scalable and secure sharing of personal health records in cloud computing using attribute-based encryption. IEEE Trans. Parallel Distrib. Syst. **24**(1), 131–143 (2013)
3. Yao, X., Han, X., Du, X.: A lightweight multicast authentication mechanism for small scale iot applications. IEEE Sens. J. **13**(10), 3693–3701 (2013)
4. Mont, M.C., Bramhall, P., Harrison, K.: A flexible role-based secure messaging service: exploiting IBE technology for privacy in health care. In: International Workshop on Database and Expert Systems Applications, pp. 432–437. IEEE Computer Society (2003)
5. Akinyele, J.A., Lehmann, C.U., Green, M.D.: Self-protecting electronic medical records using attribute-based encryption (2010). http://ia.cr/2010/565
6. Narayan, S., Gagné, M., Safavi-Naini, R.: Privacy preserving EHR system using attribute-based infrastructure. In: CCSW 2010, pp. 47–52. ACM (2010)
7. Mao, B.B., Sun, Y.F.: Role based access control model. Comput. Sci. **30**(1), 121–123 (2003)

8. Motta, G.H.M.B., Furuie, S.S.: A contextual role-based access control authorization model for electronic patient record. IEEE Trans. Inf. Technol. Biomed. **7**(3), 202–207 (2003)

9. Qin, B., Liu, S.: Leakage-flexible CCA-secure public-key encryption: simple construction and free of pairing. In: Krawczyk, H. (ed.) PKC 2014. LNCS, vol. 8383, pp. 19–36. Springer, Heidelberg (2014). doi:10.1007/978-3-642-54631-0_2

10. Paterson, K.G., Schuldt, J.C.N., Sibborn, D.L.: Related randomness attacks for public key encryption. In: Krawczyk, H. (ed.) PKC 2014. LNCS, vol. 8383, pp. 465–482. Springer, Heidelberg (2014). doi:10.1007/978-3-642-54631-0_27

11. Hoang, V.T., Katz, J., O'Neill, A., Zaheri, M.: Selective-opening security in the presence of randomness failures. In: Cheon, J.H., Takagi, T. (eds.) ASIACRYPT 2016. LNCS, vol. 10032, pp. 278–306. Springer, Heidelberg (2016). doi:10.1007/978-3-662-53890-6_10

12. Bellare, M., Tackmann, B.: Nonce-based cryptography: retaining security when randomness fails. In: Fischlin, M., Coron, J.-S. (eds.) EUROCRYPT 2016. LNCS, vol. 9665, pp. 729–757. Springer, Heidelberg (2016). doi:10.1007/978-3-662-49890-3_28

13. Albrecht, M.R., Paterson, K.G.: Lucky microseconds: a timing attack on Amazon's *s2n* implementation of TLS. In: Fischlin, M., Coron, J.-S. (eds.) EUROCRYPT 2016. LNCS, vol. 9665, pp. 622–643. Springer, Heidelberg (2016). doi:10.1007/978-3-662-49890-3_24

14. Goyal, V., Pandey, O., Sahai, A., Waters, B.: Attribute-based encryption for fine-grained access control of encrypted data. In: CCS, CCS 2006, pp. 89–98 (2006)

15. Nabeel, M., Bertino, E.: Privacy preserving delegated access control in the storage as a service model. In: International Conference on Information Reuse and Integration 2012, pp. 645–652. IEEE (2012)

16. Wan, Z., e Liu, J., Deng, R.H.: Hasbe: a hierarchical attribute-based solution for flexible and scalable access control in cloud computing. IEEE Trans. Inf. Forensics Secur. **7**(2), 743–754 (2012)

17. Wang, H., He, D., Shen, J., Zheng, Z., Zhao, C., Zhao, M.: Verifiable outsourced ciphertext-policy attribute-based encryption in cloud computing. Soft Comput. 1–11 (2016)

18. Barua, M., Liang, X., Lu, R., Shen, X.: Peace: an efficient and secure patient-centric access control scheme for ehealth care system. In: INFOCOM WKSHPS 2011, pp. 970–975. IEEE (2011)

19. Yeh, L.Y., Chiang, P.Y., Tsai, Y.L., Huang, J.L.: Cloud-based fine-grained health information access control framework for lightweight IOT devices with dynamic auditing and attribute revocation. IEEE Trans. Cloud Comput. 1(1) (2015)

20. Guo, L., Zhang, C., Sun, J., Fang, Y.: Paas: a privacy-preserving attribute-based authentication system for ehealth networks. In: ICDCS 2012, pp. 224–233. IEEE (2012)

21. Liu, W., Liu, X., Liu, J., Wu, Q., Zhang, J., Li, Y.: Auditing and revocation enabled role-based access control over outsourced private ehrs. In: HPCC 2015, pp. 336–341. IEEE (2015)

22. Zhou, X., Liu, J., Liu, W., Wu, Q.: Anonymous role-based access control on e-health records. In: AsiaCCS 2016, pp. 559–570. ACM (2016)

23. Liu, W., Liu, J., Wu, Q., Qin, B.: Hierarchical identity-based broadcast encryption. In: Susilo, W., Mu, Y. (eds.) ACISP 2014. LNCS, vol. 8544, pp. 242–257. Springer, Cham (2014). doi:10.1007/978-3-319-08344-5_16

24. Qin, B., Liu, S.: Leakage-resilient chosen-ciphertext secure public-key encryption from hash proof system and one-time lossy filter. In: Sako, K., Sarkar, P. (eds.) ASIACRYPT 2013. LNCS, vol. 8270, pp. 381–400. Springer, Heidelberg (2013). doi:10.1007/978-3-642-42045-0_20

25. Yilek, S.: Resettable public-key encryption: how to encrypt on a virtual machine. In: Pieprzyk, J. (ed.) CT-RSA 2010. LNCS, vol. 5985, pp. 41–56. Springer, Heidelberg (2010). doi:10.1007/978-3-642-11925-5_4

26. Fehr, S., Hofheinz, D., Kiltz, E., Wee, H.: Encryption schemes secure against chosen-ciphertext selective opening attacks. In: Gilbert, H. (ed.) EUROCRYPT 2010. LNCS, vol. 6110, pp. 381–402. Springer, Heidelberg (2010). doi:10.1007/978-3-642-13190-5_20

27. Hemenway, B., Libert, B., Ostrovsky, R., Vergnaud, D.: Lossy encryption: constructions from general assumptions and efficient selective opening chosen ciphertext security. In: Lee, D.H., Wang, X. (eds.) ASIACRYPT 2011. LNCS, vol. 7073, pp. 70–88. Springer, Heidelberg (2011). doi:10.1007/978-3-642-25385-0_4

28. Zhang, Z., Chow, S.S.M., Cao, Z.: Post-challenge leakage in public-key encryption. Theor. Comput. Sci. **572**, 25–49 (2015)

29. Bellare, M., Waters, B., Yilek, S.: Identity-based encryption secure against selective opening attack. In: Ishai, Y. (ed.) TCC 2011. LNCS, vol. 6597, pp. 235–252. Springer, Heidelberg (2011). doi:10.1007/978-3-642-19571-6_15

30. Lai, J., Deng, R.H., Liu, S., Weng, J., Zhao, Y.: Identity-based encryption secure against selective opening chosen-ciphertext attack. In: Nguyen, P.Q., Oswald, E. (eds.) EUROCRYPT 2014. LNCS, vol. 8441, pp. 77–92. Springer, Heidelberg (2014). doi:10.1007/978-3-642-55220-5_5

31. Chen, Y., Zhang, Z., Lin, D., Cao, Z.: Generalized (identity-based) hash proof system and its applications. Secur. Commun. Netw. **9**(12), 1698–1716 (2016)

32. Gentry, C.: Practical identity-based encryption without random oracles. In: Vaudenay, S. (ed.) EUROCRYPT 2006. LNCS, vol. 4004, pp. 445–464. Springer, Heidelberg (2006). doi:10.1007/11761679_27

33. Gentry, C., Halevi, S.: Hierarchical identity based encryption with polynomially many levels. In: Reingold, O. (ed.) TCC 2009. LNCS, vol. 5444, pp. 437–456. Springer, Heidelberg (2009). doi:10.1007/978-3-642-00457-5_26

34. Canetti, R., Dwork, C., Naor, M., Ostrovsky, R.: Deniable encryption. In: Kaliski, B.S. (ed.) CRYPTO 1997. LNCS, vol. 1294, pp. 90–104. Springer, Heidelberg (1997). doi:10.1007/BFb0052229

35. Du, X., Xiao, Y., Guizani, M., Chen, H.H.: An effective key management scheme for heterogeneous sensor networks. Ad Hoc Netw. **5**(1), 24–34 (2007)

36. Du, X., Guizani, M., Xiao, Y., Chen, H.H.: A routing-driven elliptic curve cryptography based key management scheme for heterogeneous sensor networks. IEEE Trans. Wireless Commun. **2**(5), 1223–1229 (2011)

37. Hohenberger, S., Waters, B.: Online/offline attribute-based encryption. In: Krawczyk, H. (ed.) PKC 2014. LNCS, vol. 8383, pp. 293–310. Springer, Heidelberg (2014). doi:10.1007/978-3-642-54631-0_17

Users' Perceived Control, Trust and Expectation on Privacy Settings of Smartphone

Yun Zhou[1]([✉]), Alexander Raake[2], Tao Xu[3,4], and Xuyun Zhang[5]

[1] School of Education, Shaanxi Normal University,
Xi'an 710062, Shaanxi, People's Republic of China
zhouyun@snnu.edu.cn
[2] Audiovisual Technology Group, Institute for Media Technology,
University of Technology Ilmenau, 98693 Ilmenau, Germany
alexander.raake@tu-ilmenau.de
[3] School of Software and Microelectronics, Northwestern Polytechnical University,
Xi'an 710072, Shaanxi, People's Republic of China
xutao@nwpu.edu.cn
[4] State Key Laboratory for Manufacturing Systems Engineering,
Xi'an Jiaotong University, Xi'an 710054, Shaanxi, People's Republic of China
[5] Department of Electrical and Computer Engineering, University of Auckland,
Auckland 1010, New Zealand
xuyun.zhang@auckland.ac.nz

Abstract. A common issue is that a large number of authorized apps use important and sensitive personal information without arousing users' full awareness. Existing schemes for privacy protection on smartphones try to provide users with privacy settings to control privacy leakage. Privacy settings on smartphone are intended to inform users about risks of privacy leakage and let users take over control of smartphone. Therefore, it is essential to understand and measure how much users perceive and trust these settings. To this end, we design and conduct a fine-grained online survey with 222 respondents. We collect the demographics as well as users' smartphone usage, covering not only participants' basic background information like age, gender, job, but also time of smartphone use per day, respective importance and sensitivity level of personal data, and their smartphone OSs. In this paper, we investigate users' current privacy perception and protection on smartphone in different groups, discussing participants' responses to (1) Rating the importance and sensitivity of personal information; (2) Trust on existing privacy protection; (3) Perceived control on smartphone; (4) Frequency of searching privacy knowledge; (5) Concerns about manufacturer and third-party company's behaviors on personal data and decision.

Keywords: Privacy · Smartphone · Trust · Survey

1 Introduction

The smartphone has penetrated many facets of everyday life, covering work, study, life, and game. It not only transforms people's engagement in daily lives,

© Springer International Publishing AG 2017
S. Wen et al. (Eds.): CSS 2017, LNCS 10581, pp. 427–441, 2017.
https://doi.org/10.1007/978-3-319-69471-9_31

improves the productivity, enables social networking, but also plays the roles of life and health manager, even the companion. All these activities generate a considerable amount of personal data, which contain personal identification and detailed preference. Therefore, smartphone and app usage are always associated with privacy and security threats in the app ecosystem. A large number of authorized apps unprecedentedly use important and sensitive personal information without arousing users' full awareness. To solve this issue, many studies revolve around proposing a comprehensive protection or a specific safeguard integrated in the OS or installed as a privacy application. Current schemes for privacy protection on smartphones try to provide users with privacy settings to control privacy leakage. Although users could take over more control with privacy settings, it is unclear on their perception on protection and trust on such settings. Our purpose is to figure out how people react to manufacturer and third-party company's behavior on users' data, gauge what users expect for privacy control and to what degree privacy settings satisfy users' requirements. It's worthy of understanding how people treat privacy and protect their data, which would inform the design of usable privacy interface rightly.

In this exploratory work, we organize an online survey with more than 200 participants. To understand differences of mobile privacy perception and protection behaviors in different groups, we collect not only the demographics, but also the smartphone usage, covering participants' basic background information like age, gender, job, also time of use per day, respective importance and sensitivity level of personal data, and their smartphone OSs, etc. We present and discuss participants' responses to (1) Rating the importance and sensitivity of personal information; (2) Trust on existing privacy protection; (3) Perceived control on smartphone; (4) Frequency of searching privacy knowledge; (5) Concerns about manufacturer and third-party company's behaviors on personal data and decision.

The rest of the paper is organized as follows: We outline related work and provide the organization of survey in Sects. 2 and 3 respectively. We present results and discussion in Sect. 4, and conclude with future work in Sect. 5.

2   Related Work

Privacy is a complex issue, involving all responsible stakeholders like user, company, policy maker, designer, developer. It is not possible to guarantee fully a total privacy-protected system for users at the current stage. Smartphone accesses to important and sensitive personal information unprecedentedly. Furthermore, a more common issue is that a large number of authorized apps use important and sensitive personal information without arousing users' full awareness. Existing schemes for privacy protection on smartphones try to provide users with privacy settings and profiles to control information leakage [10,13,14]. Different types of users would have different privacy awareness and behaviors, thus it is effective to analyze by splitting users based on types. The work [1] explored the security and privacy awareness of Android and iOS users based on their demographic differences. It is essential to understand and measure how much users perceive and trust these settings. The work [8] found that the sharers trust level in a share strongly influenced the security level that the sharer enforced. Sharers used fewer security precautions to share with trusted shares, whereas sharers used more security precautions with less trusted sharees. Some studies found that people don't care about privacy enough [2,4]. The work [2] involving 60 smartphone users investigates the ways and reasons that users select applications and how they decide to trust applications. The main findings showed that participants often install a large number of applications from unfamiliar brands without reading privacy policies of applications. The results of Android permissions study [4] indicated that respondents paid low attention to permissions during installation and current Android permission warnings do not help most users make correct security decisions. The survey of smartphone users' concerns [3] measured how upset the participants would be if the risks occurred and developed a ranking of risks by user concern, the results of which could be used to guide warning design and classified low, middle and high ranked risks. The study [11] of smartphone users in western European countries found that even users continue using apps, they felt their personal space had been violated in "creepy" ways.

To go a step further, we also explore users' decision based on privacy and their concerns. For example, the work [6] showed people were concerned about their personal data viewed by mobile phone borrowers. OSs have provided multiuser accounts or restriction to eliminate this concern in these two years. However, we don't know whether people really notice this feature and use it. The review [9] discussed approaches to measure privacy concerns. The work [12] conducted a survey data from middle school students revealed that perceived risks of information disclosure increased privacy concerns, whereas perceived benefits offered by information exchange decreased privacy concerns.

The research on user perspective on mobile privacy [5] explored precautions taken, perceptions of control and desire for control overall, conducted in the UK, Singapore and Spain. Results showed that the majority of users felt more in control of their personal information when using a PC than using a mobile. However, most users were not really sure how in control they were of mobile. Overall, users wanted to have control by whatever means they could and the clear evidence suggested that greater controls would increase trust and engagement with services and apps. The work by Kelley et al. [7] showed that representing privacy information checklist to users could help users make the decision. We study the control level of current privacy and security settings, what information they want to get and be notified, and what options of control over privacy settings they prefer to have.

3 Survey Design and Demography

We recruited diverse participants, who were required to be the smartphone owner, using Wenjuan website to collect their answers, which is the one of the largest and influential online crowdsourcing platform in China. In total, we recruited 223 participants and obtained 222 pieces of responses.

The questionnaire is composed of three following sessions:

1. Background information (including age, gender, education level, occupation, income and budget to smartphone, smartphone usage, smartphone activities, and the importance and sensitivity of personal information)
2. Overall attitude on privacy, including trust on privacy protection, concerns and behaviors about leakage, searching activities, etc.
3. Attitude and usage of privacy settings, including perceived control, privacy setting usage, etc.

We listed the variables and their levels of measurement as below:

1. age, ordinal
2. gender, categorical
3. education level, ordinal
4. income, ordinal
5. budget to smartphone, ordinal
6. numbers of years' experience using smartphone, ordinal
7. smartphone OS (Operating System), categorical
8. numbers of apps installed, ordinal
9. the time spent on smartphone per day, ordinal
10. the importance of personal information stored on smartphone, interval
11. the sensitivity of personal information, interval
12. frequency of searching privacy knowledge, interval
13. perceived control level, interval
14. trust on smartphone OS, interval
15. attraction level of having more control over privacy settings, interval
16. concern level on manufacturer and third-party company's behaviors on users' data, interval
17. reaction on manufacturer and third-party company's behaviors on users' data, categorical

3.1 Participants

In total, we had 72.1% males and 27.9% females. Their ages were distributed and covered all age groups while 61.3% were between ages 18–24. There was a bias towards higher education levels and 78.9% were under a higher education. The occupations were variously distributed and participants were consisted of students, IT engineer, financier, project managers, freelancer, lawyer, designer, policeman, etc. 75.7% of participants were using Android OS, and the rest of them using iOS (22.1%), Blackberry OS (0.0%), Windows Phone OS (1.4%), Firefox (0.0%), and others (0.0%).

4   Results and Discussion

In this paper, we present our results based on participants' responses to (1) Rating the importance and sensitivity of personal information; (2) Trust on existing privacy protection; (3) Perceived control on smartphone; (4) Frequency of searching privacy knowledge; (5) Concerns about manufacturer and third-party company's behaviors on personal data and decision.

4.1   Rating the Importance and Sensitivity of Personal Information

In this part, we discuss the correlations between the importance, sensitivity of personal information and other variables. We asked participants to rate the importance and the sensitivity of their personal information stored on their smartphone, using the semantic differential technique with paring of Not important/Very important and Not sensitive/Very sensitive to form the answers in 7-scale with 4 as neutral score.

Table 1. Correlation between importance of personal information and sensitivity of personal information

	r	N	p
Importance-sensitivity of PI[a]	.546	222	.000*

[a]PI is short for Personal Information.
*Correlation is significant at the 0.01 level.

As shown in Table 1, we used Pearson's correlation coefficient to test the correlation between importance of personal information and sensitivity of personal information. The importance and sensitivity of personal information show a significant positive correlation.

Table 2. Correlations between age and importance of personal information, as well as income and importance of personal information

	r_s	N	p
Age-importance of PI	.130	222	.027*
Income-importance of PI	.196	222	.002**

**Correlation is significant at the 0.01 level.
*Correlation is significant at the 0.05 level.

We used Spearman's correlation coefficient to test the correlation between age, education level, income, budget to smartphone, numbers of years' experience using smartphone, numbers of apps installed, the time spent on smartphone per day, and the importance and sensitivity of personal information.

There was the significant positive correlation between age and the importance of personal information, as well as income and the importance of personal information (see Table 2). We did not find significant correlation between other variables. The higher is the age of the participants, the higher the importance of information they rated. The higher is the income of the participants, the more important they rated the stored information.

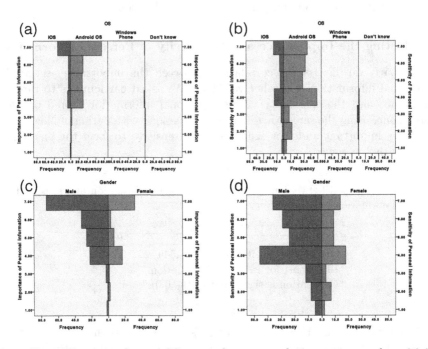

Fig. 1. How different gender and OS types of users rate the importance and sensitivity of personal information.

We also analyzed how different gender and OS types of users rate the importance and sensitivity of personal information. We found that a higher percentage of iOS participants rated their data important than Android OS participants (see Fig. 1). Both iOS (83.7% of iOS participants gave the score from 5 to 7) and Android OS (78.6% of Android OS participants) users regarded their data as important, while less participants (53.0% of iOS and 56.5% Android OS users) regarded their data as sensitive. As shown in Fig. 1(c, d), a higher percentage of male participants (82.6%: rating importance, 55.6%: rating sensitivity) rated their data important and sensitive than female (67.7%: rating importance, 51.6%: rating sensitivity) participants.

4.2   Trust on Existing Privacy Protection

In this part, we discuss users' trust on existing privacy protection from their smartphone OS. We used the semantic differential technique with paring of Not trustworthy/Very trustworthy to form the answers in 7-scale with 4 as neutral score. 48.3% of participants gave score below 4 and only 11.7% gave score above 4. 40.1% of participants expressed a neutral feeling. The median is 4 overall. Thus, current privacy settings and OS did not gain sufficient trust from smartphone participants.

We used Pearson's correlation coefficient to test the correlation between users' trust on existing privacy protection and their perceived control on smartphone. There was the significant positive correlation between users' trust and their perceived control (see Table 3). The less they perceived the control over personal information using privacy settings, the less they trusted on their smartphone privacy protection.

Table 3. Correlation between users' trust on existing privacy protection and their perceived control on smartphone

	r	N	p
Trust-perceived control	.351	222	.000**

**Correlation is significant at the 0.01 level.

4.3 Perceived Control on Smartphone

In this subsection, we explored to what degree users feel in control over private information on smartphone with current privacy settings, and their expectation for advanced privacy settings. We used the semantic differential technique with paring of Not controllable/Fully controllable to form the answers in 7-scale. We found both iOS (75.6% gave score from 1 to 4) and Android users (76.1%) did not feel in control over private information on smartphone.

We used Spearman's correlation coefficient to test correlations between age, education level, income and users' perceived control. We did not find the significant correlation between these variables.

We used Pearson's chi-square test to test associations between gender, smartphone OS, and perceived control. There were no significant associations between gender and perceived control, OS and perceived control. We used only iOS and Android users' responses ($N = 217$) in the test between OS and perceived control.

To go one step further, we asked participants to answer how appealing of having more control over their privacy settings. We used the semantic differential technique with paring of Not attractive/Very attractive to form the answers in 7-scale. Overall, only 9.5% of participants selected score below 4, while up to 70.7% of participants gave scores above 4. 19.8% of them gave the score of 4 and expressed the neutral feeling. The median of attractive level is 6. We found slightly larger numbers of iOS users (77.5% gave scores from 5 to 7) felt appealing than Android users (69.1%) to equip their phones with improved privacy settings.

As shown in Table 4, we used Pearson's correlation coefficient to test correlations between importance of personal information, sensitivity of personal

Table 4. Correlations between importance of personal information and expectation, as well as sensitivity of personal information and expectation

	r	N	p
Importance of PI-attraction[a]	.385	222	.000**
Sensitivity of PI-attraction[a]	.276	222	.000**

[a]How appealing of having more control over their privacy settings.
**Correlation is significant at the 0.01 level.

information, and expectation on having more control over privacy settings. The more important and sensitive information stored, the higher was the participants' expectation on having more control over privacy settings.

Table 5. Correlations between age, education level, income, budget to smartphone, numbers of years' experience using smartphone, numbers of apps installed, the time spent on smartphone per day and expectation

	r_s	N	p
Age-attraction	.065	222	.169
Education level-attraction	.010	222	.440
Income-attraction	.111	222	.050*
Budget-attraction	.036	222	.295
Numbers of years-attraction	−.004	222	.477
Numbers of apps-attraction	−.015	222	.410
Time spent-attraction	.219	222	.001**

*Correlation is significant at the 0.05 level.
**Correlation is significant at the 0.01 level.

As shown in Table 5, we used Spearman's correlation coefficient to test correlations between age, education level, income, budget to smartphone, numbers of years' experience using smartphone, numbers of apps installed, the time spent on smartphone per day and expectation. We did not find the significant correlations between these variables, except income and attraction as well as the time spent on smartphone per day and attraction. The higher is the income of the participants, the more attractive was having more control with privacy settings. The longer participants spent on the smartphone per day, the more they felt attractive of having more control with privacy settings.

We used Pearson's chi-square test to test associations between gender, smartphone OS, and expectation. There were no significant associations between gender and attraction, OS and attraction. We used iOS and Android users' responses (N = 217) in the association test between OS and attraction.

To look into this question, we also asked users which information they would like to get or be notified. A high rate of participants (above 60%) were interested in (1) notifying when information is collecting by apps; (2) notifying what information is shared by apps; (3) information about who is collecting information; (4) information about what type of information is being collected and sending from phone; (5) information about where information are sent to; (6) information about the purpose of use of data by companies; (7) information about the potential risks that would be caused according to the type and usage of data; (8) notifying which settings or options user could use (turn off/on) to fight against data leakage from phone.

We asked participants which options of control over privacy settings that they preferred to have, results showed that almost more than 50% participants were interested in (1) options of giving/not giving permission for user data to be collected by known or unknown companies; (2) options of adjusting accuracy of data (like location information) to be collected by known or unknown companies; (3) options of isolating data to be seen by other people (for example, when lending smart phone to others); (4) options of granting/refusing permissions for apps installed; (5) options of cleaning my histories of application use, browsing websites, etc.; (6) options of encrypting data to be stored and transmitted to some where other than the smartphone.

4.4 Frequency of Searching Privacy Knowledge

To know how frequently users search information on protecting mobile privacy, we used the semantic differential technique with paring of Never/Always to form the answers in 7-scale. Overall, the median of frequency on searching is 4. 25.7% of participants searched with a low frequent level and gave score below 4, 40.1% of participants answered 4, and 34.2% of them above 4 (ranging from score 5 to 7).

We did not find there was a noticeable difference between iOS users and Android users when they searched information about privacy protection (see Fig. 2(a)). We divided participants to information-not-important (importance rating score ranging from 1 to 4) and information-important groups (score ranging from 5 to 7), as well as information-not-sensitive and information-sensitive groups. Information-important and information-sensitive groups searched more often than information-non-important and information-non-sensitive groups respectively (see Fig. 2(c, d)).

As shown in Table 6, we used Pearson's correlation coefficient to test correlations between importance of personal information, sensitivity of personal information, perceived control, attraction and search frequency. There were correlations between importance and search frequency, as well as sensitivity and search frequency. The more important participants rated the information stored on the smartphone, the more frequently they search for the privacy information. Similarly, the more sensitive participants evaluate the personal information, the more frequently they search for the privacy information. We also found correlations between perceived control and search frequency, as well as attraction and search frequency. The participants who felt more in control of personal information would search more frequently. When participants had increased expectation

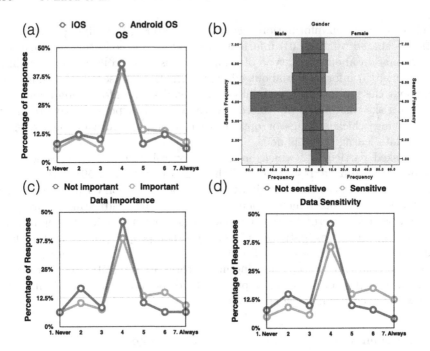

Fig. 2. The frequency at which participants search information on privacy protection of smartphone.

Table 6. Correlations between importance of personal information, sensitivity of personal information, perceived control, attraction and search frequency

	r	N	p
Importance of PI-search frequency	.154	222	.011*
Sensitivity of PI-search frequency	.233	222	.000**
Perceived control-search frequency	.213	222	.001**
Attraction-search frequency	.158	222	.009**

*Correlation is significant at the 0.05 level.
**Correlation is significant at the 0.01 level.

on more control over privacy settings, they would have more frequent searching activities.

As shown in Table 7, we used Pearson's chi-square test to test associations between gender, smartphone OS, and search frequency. No association was found between OS and search frequency. Male participants had privacy information search activities more often (39.4% gave score from 5 to 7) whereas females searched less frequently (see Fig. 2(b)).

As shown in Table 8, we used Spearman's correlation coefficient to test correlations between age, education level, income, budget to smartphone, numbers of years' experience using smartphone, numbers of apps installed, the time spent on

Table 7. Associations between gender, smartphone OS, and trust

	Chi-square	p	phi
Gender-search frequency	12.639	.049*	.239
OS-search frequency	16.939	.527	.276

*Correlation is significant at the 0.05 level.

smartphone per day and searching frequency. There was a negative correlation between age and search frequency. It showed that participants had less search activities with the age increasing.

To know from where they got information on privacy protection of smartphone, we listed six main methods, including tutorials found on smartphone OS websites, personal answers online (like forums, question and answer sites, etc.), reviews of public media (like books, magazines, journals, online media, etc.), previous bad experience, information on smartphone, people surrounding (like friends, families, etc.). We also provided the option of "I never thought that I should know how to protect mobile privacy" and "other ways". Among these, the information on smartphone like help information, notification, and alert message on smartphone was their first choice (26.7%). As shown in Fig. 3, participants were used to obtain protection knowledge from their friends, families, colleagues, and other people surrounding them (17.7%) as the second choice. Thus, we believe it's a right direction to equip smartphone with improved privacy settings, usable privacy notification and help interface.

Table 8. Correlations between age, education level, income, budget to smartphone, numbers of years' experience using smartphone, numbers of apps installed, the time spent on smartphone per day and searching frequency

	r_s	N	p
Age-search frequency	−.119	222	.038*
Education level-search frequency	−.046	222	.246
Income-search frequency	−.090	222	.090
Budget-search frequency	−.014	222	.421
Numbers of years-frequency	−.030	222	.326
Numbers of apps-frequency	.026	222	.348
Time spent-search frequency	.030	222	.329

*Correlation is significant at the 0.05 level.

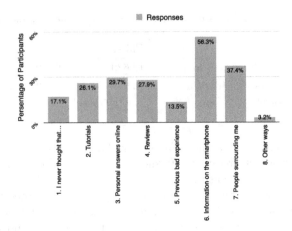

Fig. 3. The methods that participants obtain information on privacy protection of smartphone.

4.5   Concerns About Manufacturer and Third-Party Company's Behaviors on Personal Data and Decision

In this part, we discuss participants' concern on behaviors of manufacturers and third-party companies, and whether they would continue to use apps/services based on manufacturer's and third party company's activities.

We asked participants to express their concerns about the following behaviors:

1. manufacturer collects data
2. manufacturer uses data
3. manufacturer is hacked and leaks the stored users' data
4. third-party (3rd-party) company collects data
5. third-party (3rd-party) company uses data
6. third-party (3rd-party) company is hacked and leaks the stored users' data

Information-important users showed more concern than information-not-important users for all six behaviors (see Fig. 4). Users were more concerned about manufacturer's leaking behavior and third-party company's behavior (collecting, using and leaking users' data) than manufacturer's collecting and using data. Furthermore, participants made decisions on whether continued to use services/apps if they knew six behaviors of companies. We found that participants had more tolerance for manufacturer and third-party collecting and using their data, but most of them decided to quit if the data would be leaked (see Fig. 5).

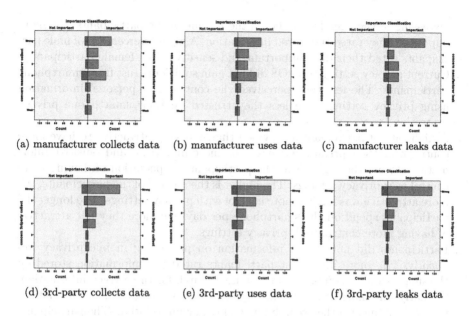

Fig. 4. Participants' concern level based on classification of personal information importance if manufacturer and 3rd-party company collect, use or leak their data.

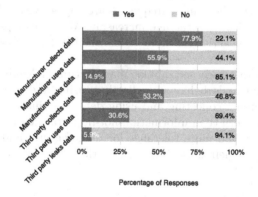

Fig. 5. Percentage of participants who decide to continue to use the services/apps if they know companies' activities.

5   Conclusion and Future Work

This work is motivated on the basis of missing studies in exploration on users' perceived control, trust and expectation on smartphone privacy settings. In this work, we designed and conducted an online survey, collecting 222 pieces of real responses. Overall, results from this evaluation include:

1. The importance and sensitivity of personal information show a significant positive correlation. Participants rated information more important with the

increasing of the age. The higher is the income of the participants, the more important they rated the stored information. A higher percentage of male participants rated their data important and sensitive than female participants.

2. Current privacy settings and OS did not gain sufficient trust from smartphone participants. The less they perceived the control over personal information using privacy settings, the less they trusted on their smartphone privacy protection.

3. A high rate of participants expressed that it is very attractive to have more control over their privacy settings. The more important and sensitive information stored, the higher was the participants' expectation on having more control over privacy settings. The higher is the income of the participants, the more attractive was having more control with privacy settings. The longer the participants spend on the smartphone per day, the more they felt attractive of having more control with privacy settings.

4. Participants did not search information on protecting mobile privacy frequently. The more important participants rated the information stored on the smartphone, the more frequently they search for the privacy information. Similarly, the more sensitive participants evaluate the personal information, the more frequently they search for the privacy information. The participants who felt more in control of personal information would search more often. When participants had increased expectation on more control over privacy settings, they would have more frequent searching activities. Participants had less search activities with the age increasing. Male participants had privacy information search activities more often whereas females searched less frequently.

5. Users were more concerned about manufacturer's leaking behavior and third-party company's behavior (collecting, using and leaking users' data) than manufacturer's collecting and using data. Information-important users showed more concern than information-not-important users for all six behaviors. Participants had more tolerance for manufacturer and third-party collecting and using their data, but most of them decided to quit if the data would be leaked.

In the near future, to explore and understand impacting factors for mobile perception and protection behavior, we are going to analyze with the data obtained from German groups. Then we plan to analyze the privacy behavior regression models. Besides, we will leverage cluster analysis to create privacy user types based on participants responses, which will be used to create personas to inform the design of usable privacy settings and features on smartphone.

Acknowledgment. This work is supported by the Opening Project of State Key Laboratory for Manufacturing Systems Engineering, No. sklms2016001.

References

1. Benenson, Z., Gassmann, F., Reinfelder, L.: Android and IOS users' differences concerning security and privacy. In: CHI 2013 Extended Abstracts on Human Factors in Computing Systems (CHI EA 2013), New York, NY, USA, pp. 817–822. ACM (2013)
2. Chin, E., Felt, A.P., Sekar, V., Wagner, D.: Measuring user confidence in smart phone security and privacy. In: Proceedings of the Eighth Symposium on Usable Privacy and Security, p. 1. ACM (2012)
3. Felt, A.P., Egelman, S., Wagner, D.: I've got 99 problems, but vibration ain't one: a survey of smartphone users' concerns. In: Proceedings of the Second ACM Workshop on Security and Privacy in Smartphones and Mobile Devices, pp. 33–44. ACM (2012)
4. Felt, A.P., Ha, E., Egelman, S., Haney, A., Chin, E., Wagner, D.: Android permissions: user attention, comprehension, and behavior. In: Proceedings of the Eighth Symposium on Usable Privacy and Security, p. 3. ACM (2012)
5. GSMA. User perspectives on mobile privacy. futuresight. Technical report (2011)
6. Karlson, A.K., Brush, A.J., Schechter, S.: Can i borrow your phone? Understanding concerns when sharing mobile phones. In: Proceedings of the SIGCHI Conference on Human Factors in Computing Systems, pp. 1647–1650. ACM (2009)
7. Kelley, P.G., Cranor, L.F., Sadeh, N.: Privacy as part of the app. decision-making process. In: Proceedings of the SIGCHI Conference on Human Factors in Computing Systems, pp. 3393–3402. ACM (2013)
8. Matthews, T., Liao, K., Turner, A., Berkovich, M., Reeder, R., Consolvo, S.: She'll just grab any device that's closer: a study of everyday device & account sharing in households. In: Proceedings of the 2016 CHI Conference on Human Factors in Computing Systems (CHI 2016), New York, NY, USA, pp. 5921–5932. ACM (2016)
9. Preibusch, S.: Guide to measuring privacy concern: review of survey and observational instruments. Int. J. Hum. Comput. Stud. 71(12), 1133–1143 (2013)
10. Seifert, J., Luca, A., Conradi, B., Hussmann, H.: TreasurePhone: context-sensitive user data protection on mobile phones. In: Floréen, P., Krüger, A., Spasojevic, M. (eds.) Pervasive 2010. LNCS, vol. 6030, pp. 130–137. Springer, Heidelberg (2010). doi:10.1007/978-3-642-12654-3_8
11. Shklovski, I., Mainwaring, S.D., Skttir, H.H., Borgthorsson, H.: Leakiness and creepiness in app space: perceptions of privacy and mobile app use. In: Proceedings of the 32nd Annual ACM Conference on Human Factors in Computing Systems, pp. 2347–2356. ACM (2014)
12. Youn, S.: Determinants of online privacy concern and its influence on privacy protection behaviors among young adolescents. J. Consum. Affairs 43(3), 389–418 (2009)
13. Zhou, Y., Piekarska, M., Raake, A., Xu, T., Wu, X., Dong, B.: Control yourself: on user control of privacy settings using personalization and privacy panel on smartphones. Procedia Comput. Sci. 109, 100–107 (2017). 8th International Conference on Ambient Systems, Networks and Technologies (ANT-2017), 16–19 May 2017, Madeira, Portugal
14. Zhou, Y., Xu, T., Raake, A., Cai, Y.: Access control is not enough: how owner and guest set limits to protect privacy when sharing smartphone. In: Stephanidis, C. (ed.) HCI 2016. CCIS, vol. 617, pp. 494–499. Springer, Cham (2016). doi:10.1007/978-3-319-40548-3_82

A New Way for Extracting Region of Interest from Palmprint by Detecting Key Points

Zhiqiang Gao[1], Yong Ding[2(✉)], Huiyong Wang[1], and Jilin Wang[3]

[1] School of Mathematics and Computing Science, Guilin University of Electronic Technology, Guilin, Guangxi, People's Republic of China
[2] Guangxi Key Laboratory of Cryptography and Information Security, School of Computer Science and Information Security, Guilin University of Electronic Technology, Guilin, Guangxi, People's Republic of China
stone_dingy@126.com
[3] Information School, Zhejiang University of Finance and Economics, Hangzhou, Zhejiang, People's Republic of China

Abstract. Extracting region of interest (ROI) from palmprint is the important and key link of palmprint recognition. The quality of ROI directly determines the recognition rate. We propose a new algorithm for extracting palm ROI, and show the validity of our algorithm with numerical experiments on PloyU database and CASIC database, achieving recognition rates respectively 100% and 99.527%. The core idea of our algorithm is to obtain the key points from the palmprint. To get the first key, we firstly construct a circle with radius r slide along the edge of the palm, then calculate the center of the circle when the intersection area of the circle and the palmprint reaches maximum, so that the center is the first key point we need. To get the second key, we remove the first key point and its neighborhood, then detect the second key point using the same method. Other key points are obtained using the same method. In the step of generating ROI, the length of sides of the square ROI is based on the approximate half width of the palm.

Keywords: Region of interest (ROI) · Palmprint recognition · Key point detection

1 Introduction

Traditionally, personal identification can be divided into two categories: token-based, such as a physical key, an ID card, and a passport, and knowledge-based, such as a password. However, these approaches both have some limitations. In the token-based approach, the token can be easily stolen or lost. In the knowledge-based approach, to some extent, the knowledge can be guessed or forgotten. Thus, biometric personal identification is emerging as a powerful means for automatically recognizing a persons identity [1]. Biometric characteristics include fingerprint, iris, retina, gait, voice, palm vein, face and hand geometry. The human

© Springer International Publishing AG 2017
S. Wen et al. (Eds.): CSS 2017, LNCS 10581, pp. 442–451, 2017.
https://doi.org/10.1007/978-3-319-69471-9_32

palm means the inner area between the fingers and wrist [2]. As relatively new biometric features, palmprints have several advantages compared with other currently available features: palmprints contain more information than fingerprints, so they are more distinctive; palmprint acquisition devices are much cheaper than iris devices; palmprints also contain additional distinctive features such as principal lines and wrinkles, which can be extracted from low-resolution images; a highly accurate biometrics system can be built by combining all features of palms, such as palm geometry, ridge and valley features, and principal lines and wrinkles, etc. [3]. As a result, palmprint based recognition has the potential to achieve reliable performance [4]. The palmprint is defined as the inner surface of a palm, which possesses not only fingerprint-like feature such as minutiae points, singular points and texture but also some other special discriminative features such as principal lines, wrinkles and patterns of ridges. We often choose a stable region from the palmprint, namely the region of interest (ROI), to represent the whole palmprint. Extracting the feature of palmprint is the key link in the process of palmprint recognition, which determines the recognition rate. There are several typical algorithms of palmprint at present: recognition method based on line feature and method based on subspace and method based on spatial-frequency domain [5].

1.1   Related Work

The main steps in extracting palmprint ROI are three stages: obtaining palmprint images, locating palmprint images, establishing Cartesian coordinate systems and extracting ROI. Some literatures used constrained devices to acquire palmprint images. In 2003, the palmprint acquisition device of Zhang et al. included ring source, CCD camera, lens, frame grabber, and A/D (analogue-to-digital) converter [6]. In 2004, Chin-Chuan Han designed a CCD camera-based capturing device to grab hand images [7]. Some used unconstrained devices. In [8], the appearance of the image capturing device had two common CMOS web cameras placed in parallel. [9] used an Android mobile device to capture palmprint images.

About locating palmprint, some literatures [1–3,10–14] applied the valley point between the index finger and the middle finger and the valley point between the ring finger and the pinky to locate palmprint. [1] obtained the boundaries of the gaps between the fingers using a boundary tracking algorithm, and then used the rightmost tangent line to locate the two key points. [12,15,16] computed local minimums from the signal to find the key points used to align hand image. [3] computed the bisector of the lines which was decided by the first finger and middle finger and the bisector of the lines which is decided by the third finger and little finger, and computed intersections of the two bisectors and the boundary of palmprint, the two intersections are key points. [11,14] used Harris corner algorithm to detect the two corner points. [13] detected the key points by using a modified Harris corner detection algorithm. [17] used 25 key points to locating palmprint. [8] used the direction of middle finger as the main direction of palmprint to locate palmprint. [18] detected the region of interest in palmprint from a highly noisy image by locating the disk with maximum possible radius, [19] used a fixed circle rolling along the outer edge of the palmprint, by calculating the slope variation of the adjacent center to locate the key points. [20] detected key point candidates for extracting a palm region by using a radial distance function. In [6], the first step was tracking the acquired palmprint edge, the second step was taking the center of gravity of palmprint contour as a reference point, the third step was calculating the distance between each point on the edge and the center of gravity, and the final step was searching the minimum distance between the convergence points of index-finger and middle-finger and the center of gravity, the first key point K_1 could be extracted. Using the same way, the next key point K_2 between the convergence points of ring-finger and little-finger could be searched. [21] detected all the finger tips and valley points between fingers. [22] used the palm print to split the image into seven parts, through calculating the core of each part to detect the valley points. [23] used the holes between palmprint borders to decide the key points.

When the key points have been found, the next work is to build the coordinate system and extract ROI. Zhang's method was that lined up the key points to get the Y-axis of the palmprint coordinate system, and used a line passing through the midpoint of these two points, which was perpendicular to the Y-axis, to determine the origin and X-axis of the coordinate system, extracted a subimage of a fixed size based on the coordinate system. The subimage is located at a certain area of the palmprint image for feature extraction. [1–3,10,11,13,14] used this method. [15,16] after finding the valley point between index finger and middle finger and the valley point between ring finger and pinky, namely A_1 and A_2, there was a line through the two points, two straight lines whose angles between these two lines and line A_1A_2 were respectively 45° and 60° were made, the two lines intersect with the border of palm at two points, namely B_1 and B_2, find the midpoint C_1 of A_1B_1 and the midpoint C_2 of A_2B_2 ,the square area whose length is C_1C_2 is extracted as ROI. [17] after the selecting the key points, parallel lines were made between the valley point on the upper border of the palmprint and the peak point at the lower boundary, take the two parallel lines for reference to select ROI. [8] after deciding the main direction, cut up the fingers and extracted a sub-image from palmprint as ROI. [7] used the six poles of their device to locate the palmprint and extract ROI.

1.2   Our Contribution

We propose a new algorithm of obtaining the key points and a new method of constructing a coordinate system. In obtaining the key points, by firstly constructing a circle with radius r slide along the edge of the palm, then calculating the center when the intersection area of the circle and the palmprint reaches maximum, the center of the circle is the first key point; remove the first key and its neighborhood, and then the second key will be got, other key points are obtained using the same method. In the step of generating ROI, we extract a square area whose length is approximately equal to half width of the palm from the palmprint as the ROI. We propose a new algorithm of obtaining the key points and a new method of constructing a coordinate system. In obtaining the key points, by firstly constructing a circle with radius r slide along the edge of the palm, then calculating the center when the intersection area of the circle and the palmprint reaches maximum, the center of the circle is the first key point; remove the first key and its neighborhood, and then the second key will be got, other key points are obtained using the same method. In the step of generating ROI, we extract a square area whose length is approximately equal to half width of the palm from the palmprint as the ROI.

2   Our Algorithm

There are seven main steps in the algorithm: (1) Select the palmprint image. (2) Smooth the original image. (3) Use a threshold to convert the smoothed image to a binary image. (4) Trace the boundary of the binary image. (5) Find the key points. (6) Make a palmprint coordinate system. (7) Crop a subimage with fixed size from the center of the image as ROI. The flow chart of the algorithm is shown in Fig. 1.

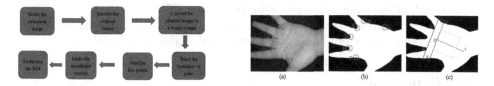

Fig. 1. The flow chart of the algorithm.   **Fig. 2.** Our ideal palmprint image.

The details of each step are described in the following:

(1) Select the palmprint image I. The most ideal palmprint image we select should look like Fig. 2(a), and satisfies that $\angle 1 < \angle 2$, $\angle 1 < \angle 4$, $\angle 3 < \angle 2$, $\angle 3 < \angle 4$. We will explain the specific reasons at (5). In this paper we take the palmprint image from CASIA and PolyU databases.

(2) Smooth the original image. Smooth the original image by a Low-pass filter. The purpose is to make the image smoother and convenient for binarization. $I_{SmoothMap} = I * A$ (where A is the low-pass filter).

(3) Binarize the image. Use a threshold α, to convert an original gray image into a binary map, i.e.

$$I_{binarymap} = \begin{cases} 1, I_{SmoothMap} > \alpha \\ 0, I_{SmoothMap} \leqslant \alpha \end{cases}.$$

(4) Trace the boundary of the palmprint. Use the boundary tracking operator to obtain the boundary of palmprint. $I_{bounbary} = I_{binarymap} * B$ (where B is the boundary tracking operator).

(5) Detect the key points of the palmprint. Observing the binary image of the palmprint, we will find the following characteristics: As shown in the Fig. 2(b), let the area of the circle is S, and when the center of the circle is at the A, B, F, the area of the intersection of the circle and the palm is approximately $1/2S$. When the center is at C, D, E, the intersection of the circle and the palm is approximately $3/4S$. If the input of the palmprint is the ideal image we want, when the appropriate radius is chosen so that the center of the circle moves along the edge of the palm to compute the area where the circle intersects with the palm, when the area reaches maximum, the center of the circle is the first key point and then the neighborhood of the key point is removed and the second key point will be detected using the same way.

(6) Create Cartesian coordinate system. Through the last step, the key points C and E, that is, the valley point between the index finger and the middle finger and the valley point between the ring finger and little finger have been found. Connect CE, make a line parallel to line CE on the right side and intersect at two points C_1E_1 with the boundary of palms, the midpoint of E_1C_1 is the origin of the coordinates, the direction of E_1C_1 is the y-axis, the direction perpendicular to E_1C_1 is the x-axis (Fig. 2(c)). The reason why we did this because CE due to individual differences, some people of this segment is too long or too short and may lead to false ROI captured and E_1C_1 whose length is approximate to the length of the palm has better robustness than EC.

(7) Extract ROI. With reference to the length of E_1C_1, a square area whose length is equal to half of E_1C_1 is extracted as the ROI (Fig. 2(c)).

3 Experiment

3.1 Experiments on the PloyU Database

The palmprint database provided by Hong Kong Polytech University is PolyU Palmprint Database which contain 600 palmprint images of 100 person (every person has 6 palmprint images), and the resolution of each image is 75 dpi, the size of each image is 384×284 [19]. Their palmprint capture device includes ring source, CCD camera, lens, frame grabber, and A/D (analogue-to-digital) converter [1]. Images were collected by a special equipment, the thumbs have been removed from, and their brightness are uniform and valley points of them are very obvious. The specific steps are as follows:

(1) Read the original image $original\_I$ (Fig. 3(a)).

(2) Smooth the image with the sequential statistics filter (Fig. 3(b)).

$$ord\_I = ordfilt2(original\_I, 300, ones(20, 40)).$$

(3) Set the threshold, binarize the smoothed images (Fig. 3(c)).

$$I_{binarymap} = \begin{cases} 1, I_{ord} > 8 \\ 0, I_{ord} \leqslant 8 \end{cases}.$$

(4) Extract the edge of the image, we use four edge detection operators ($[11], [110], [11]', [110]'$)to detect the boundary of $I_{binarymap}$, then we get I_{edge} (Fig. 3(d)).

(5) Detecting the key points. A circle C with a radius r along the edge image I_{edge} scans the binary image $I_{binarymap}$, when the area which the circle C intersect with the binary image $I_{binarymap}$ is maximal, the center of the circle is the first key K_1(Fig. 3(e)), remove this point and its neighborhood (Fig. 3(f)), the second key point K_2 is got with the same method (Fig. 3(g)).

(6) Building coordinate system and extract ROI from palmprint. Connect K_1K_2, calculate the length of K_1K_2 l and the slope of K_1K_2 k, rotate the original image $original\_I$ $tan^{-1}k$ to get $original\_I'$ (Fig. 3(h)), correspondingly K_1K_2 rotate to $K_1'K_2'$, the line $K_1'K_2'$ moves $1/4l$ units to the right and intersect with the edge of the image at A and B, the length of the line segment AB is d, the midpoint of AB is the coordinate origin, the direction of BA is the y-axis, the x-axis is perpendicular to the BA direction, and then we extract $[0, d] \times \left[-\frac{d}{2}, +\frac{d}{2}\right]$ in rotated image as ROI (Fig. 3(i)).

The result of this experiment: when the radius is 20, five ROIs from palmprints are not correctly extracted, when the radius is 25, ROIs from all of palmprints are correctly extracted. Table 1 gives the comparison results of our algorithm with the previous algorithms.

Table 1. Comparison results of different algorithms

Algorithms	Published year	Correction rate of location (%)
Proposed by [3]	2004	97.8
Proposed by [19]	2012	98.83
Proposed by this paper	2017	100

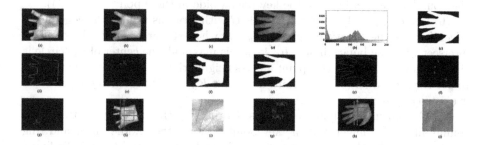

Fig. 3. The program runs on the ployU database.

Fig. 4. The program runs on the CASIC database.

3.2 Experiments on the CASIC Database

In test, the Chinese Academy of Sciences (CASIA) palmprint database was used. This database contains 5,502 palmprint images captured form 310 subjects. Each image is a 8-bit gray-level image and is the size of 480×640 pixels. For each person, the palmprint images were collected from both left and right palms [13]. Compared with PolyU database, palmprint images in the CASIA database contain whole hands, and they were collected in the random direction, thumb form some palmprints were not captured, and some samples cut off the fingertips, the brightness of the images is not uniform, so, the steps of extracting ROI from CASIA palmprint images are more complex than those of PolyU palmprint images. The specific steps are as follows:

(1) Read the original image $original\_I$ (Fig. 4(a)).

(2) Binary the image using bimodal method.

Drawing a histogram of the image (Fig. 4(b)), firstly the average of gray image a can be calculated, then the first peak point b_1 can be calculated from $[1, a]$, the second peak b_2 can be calculated from $[a + 1, 255]$, the valley point c from $[b_1, b_2]$ can be got, if the value in gray image is less than c, it equals 0, otherwise it equals 1 (Fig. 4(c)).

$$I_{binarymap} = \begin{cases} 1, I_{original\_I} > c \\ 0, I_{original\_I} \leqslant c \end{cases}.$$

(3) Smooth the binary image, the purpose of doing this is to make the border of the image smoother. In this step, we use the sequential statistics filter (Fig. 4(d)).

$$ord\_I = ordfilt2(I_{binarymap}, 300, ones(20, 40)).$$

(4) Extract the edge of the image by using four edge detection operators ([11], [110], [11]′, [110]′) to get $edge\_I$ (Fig. 4(e)).

(5) Optimizing the edge of palmprint. Using a circle whose radius is r along the border of binary image to scan binary image, set a threshold, we get the concave part $edge\_I'$ between fingers, the purpose of doing this is to optimize the boundary image, because the key points hide in these points (Fig. 4(f)).

(6) Detecting the key points. A circle C with a radius r along the edge image $edge\_I'$ scans the binary image $I_{binarymap}$, when the area which the circle C intersect with the binary image $I_{binarymap}$ is maximal, the center of the circle is the first key K_1, remove this point and its neighborhood, with the same method to get the second key K_2, the third key point K_3 and the forth key point K_4 if it exists (Fig. 4(g)).

(7) Computing the final key points. Optimizing the key point between the thumb and index finger and the key point between the middle finger and ring finger, and finally the key point between the index finger and the middle finger and the key point between the ring finger and little finger will be got, namely K_1' and K_2' (Fig. 4(g)).

(8) Building coordinate system and extract ROI from palmprint. Connect $K_1' K_2'$, calculate the length of $K_1' K_2'$ l and the slope of $K_1' K_2'$ k, rotate the

original image $original\_I$ $tan^{-1}k$ get $original\_I'$ (Fig. 4(h)), correspondingly $K_1'K_2'$ rotate to $K_1''K_2''$, the line $K_1''K_2''$moves $1/4l$ units to the right and intersect with the edge of the image at A and B, the length of the line segment AB is d, the midpoint of AB is the coordinate origin, the direction of BA is the y-axis, the x-axis is perpendicular to the BA direction, and we extract $[0, d] \times \left[-\frac{d}{2}, +\frac{d}{2}\right]$ in rotated image as ROI (Fig. 4(i)).

Experimental results: there are 26 images not correctly extracted, the reasons for which are the following: (1) 13 images because of opening angle between fingers is too small; (2) 10 images because of missing the key points; (3) 4 images because of the input of palmprint not meeting our requirements; 2 image because of the program not correctly identified. Table 2 gives the comparison results of our algorithm with the previous algorithms.

Table 2. Comparison results of different algorithms

Algorithms	Published year	Correction rate of location (%)
Proposed by [14]	2008	94.8
Proposed by [13]	2012	96
Proposed by [17]	2015	99.42
Proposed by this paper	2017	99.527

4 Conclusion

The recognition rate is satisfactory, the correct recognition rate is 100% on the PloyU database and the correct recognition rate is 99.527% on the CASIA database. It shows that the recognition rate is higher while the shape of hand is more uniform. So as long as the input of the palmprint images conform to the requirements of our algorithm, the recognition rate of our algorithm will increase. In addition, the algorithm uses the maximum area of the circle intersect with palm image to detect the valley point, otherwise, uses the minimum value will detect the fingertip point. We hope that the algorithm is applied to other areas of image recognition.

Acknowledgment. This research was supported by National Science Foundation Grant (61772150), planning fund project of ministry of education (12YJAZH136) and China password development fund (JJ20170217).

References

1. Zhang, D., Kong, W., You, J., Wong, M.S.: Online palmprint identification. IEEE Trans. Pattern Anal. Mach. Intell. **25**(9), 1041–1050 (2003)
2. Ali, M.M.H., Yannawar, P., Gaikwad, A.T.: Study of edge detection methods based on palmprint lines. In: International Conference on Electrical, Electronics, and Optimization Techniques (2016)
3. Wu, X., Wang, K., Zhang, D.: HMMs based palmprint identification. In: Zhang, D., Jain, A.K. (eds.) ICBA 2004. LNCS, vol. 3072, pp. 775–781. Springer, Heidelberg (2004). doi:10.1007/978-3-540-25948-0_105
4. Fei, L., Xu, Y., Zhang, D.: Half-Orientation Extraction of Palmprint Features. Elsevier Science Inc., New York (2016)
5. Feng, J., Wang, H., Li, Y., Liu, F.: Palmprint feature extraction method based on rotation-invariance. In: Yang, J., Yang, J., Sun, Z., Shan, S., Zheng, W., Feng, J. (eds.) Biometric Recognition. LNCS, vol. 9428, pp. 215–223. Springer, Cham (2015). doi:10.1007/978-3-319-25417-3_26
6. Wu, Q.E., Chen, Z., Han, R., Yang, C., Du, Y., Zheng, Y., Cheng, W.: A palmprint recognition approach based on image segmentation of region of interest. Int. J. Pattern Recognit. Artif. Intell. **30**(02) (2016)
7. Han, C.C.: A hand-based personal authentication using a coarse-to-fine strategy. Image Vis. Comput. **22**(11), 909–918 (2004)
8. Han, Y., Sun, Z., Wang, F., Tan, T.: Palmprint recognition under unconstrained scenes. In: Yagi, Y., Kang, S.B., Kweon, I.S., Zha, H. (eds.) ACCV 2007. LNCS, vol. 4844, pp. 1–11. Springer, Heidelberg (2007). doi:10.1007/978-3-540-76390-1_1
9. Cox, A.: Palmprint biometric data acquisition: extracting a consistent region of interest (ROI) for method evaluation (2014)
10. Hong, D., Jian, S., Hong, Q., Pan, Z., Wang, G.: Blurred palmprint recognition based on stable-feature extraction using a Vese–Osher decomposition model. Plos One **9**(7), e101866 (2014)
11. Chen, M., Chen, Y.M., Huang, S.H., Yao, Z.W.: A palmprint recognition algorithm based on harris synthetically method. IEEE Computer Society (2008)
12. Saliha, A., Karima, B., Mouloud, K., Nabil, D.H., Ahmed, B.: Extraction method of region of interest from hand palm: application with contactless and touchable devices. In: International Conference on Information Assurance and Security, pp. 77–82 (2015)
13. Shang, L., Chen, J., Su, P.-G., Zhou, Y.: ROI extraction of palmprint images using modified Harris corner point detection algorithm. In: Huang, D.-S., Ma, J., Jo, K.-H., Gromiha, M.M. (eds.) ICIC 2012. LNCS, vol. 7390, pp. 479–486. Springer, Heidelberg (2012). doi:10.1007/978-3-642-31576-3_61
14. Chen, J., Han, M., Yang, S., Chang, Y.: A fingertips detection method based on the combination of centroid and Harris corner algorithm. In: IEEE/ACIS International Conference on Software Engineering, Artificial Intelligence, Networking and Parallel/Distributed Computing, pp. 225–230 (2016)
15. Babu, B.V., Nagar, A., Deep, K., Pant, M., Bansal, J.C., Ray, K., Gupta, U. (eds.): Proceedings of the Second International Conference on Soft Computing for Problem Solving (SocProS 2012), December 28-30, 2012. AISC, vol. 236. Springer, New Delhi (2014). doi:10.1007/978-81-322-1602-5
16. Badrinath, G.S., Gupta, P.: Palmprint based recognition system using phase-difference information. Fut. Gener. Comput. Syst. **28**(1), 287–305 (2012)

17. Aykut, M., Ekinci, M.: Developing a Contactless Palmprint Authentication System by Introducing a Novel ROI Extraction Method. Butterworth-Heinemann, Guildford (2015)
18. Liambas, C., Tsouros, C.: An algorithm for detecting hand orientation and palmprint location from a highly noisy image. In: IEEE International Symposium on Intelligent Signal Processing, pp. 1–6 (2007)
19. Wu, G., Zhang, H., Li, Y., Zhang, B.: A contour extraction algorithm of palmprints based on corner point features. In: IEEE International Conference on Automation and Logistics, pp. 501–505 (2012)
20. Ito, K., Sato, T., Aoyama, S., Sakai, S.: Palm region extraction for contactless palmprint recognition. In: International Conference on Biometrics, pp. 334–340 (2015)
21. Yrk, E., Konukolu, E., Sankur, B., Darbon, J.: Shape-based hand recognition. IEEE Trans. Image Process. **15**(7), 1803–1815 (2006). A Publication of the IEEE Signal Processing Society
22. Vijilious, M.A.L., Ganapathy, S., Bharathi, V.S.: Palmprint feature extraction approach using nonsubsampled contourlet transform and orthogonal moments. In: International Conference on Advances in Computing, Communications and Informatics, pp. 735–739 (2012)
23. Li, W., Zhang, D., Xu, Z.: Palmprint identification by Fourier transform. Int. J. Pattern Recognit. Artif. Intell. **16**(04), 417–432 (2008)

Efficient Privacy-Preservation Multi-factor Ranking with Approximate Search over Encrypted Big Cloud Data

Jing He[1], Yiming Wu[2], Guangli Xiang[3], Zhendong Wu[4], and Shouling Ji[2(✉)]

[1] Department of Computer Science, Kennesaw State University,
30060 Marietta, GA, Georgia
jhe4@kennesaw.edu
[2] School of Computer Science and Technology, Zhejiang University,
Hanzhou, China
yiming96510@163.com, sji@zju.edu.cn
[3] School of Computer Science and Technology, Wuhan University of Technology,
Wuhan, China
glxiang@whut.edu.cn
[4] School of Cyberspace, Hangzhou Dianzi University, Hanzhou, China
wzd@hdu.edu.cn

Abstract. Encrypting data before outsourcing data has become a challenge in using traditional search algorithms. Many techniques have been proposed to cater the needs. However, as cloud service has a pay-as-you-go basis, these techniques are inefficiency. In this paper we attack the challenging problem by proposing an approximate multi keyword search with multi factor ranking over encrypted cloud data. Moreover, we establish strict privacy requirements and prove that the proposed scheme is secure in terms of privacy. To the best of our knowledge, we are the first who propose approximate matching technique on semantic search. Furthermore, to improve search efficiency, we consider multi-factor ranking technique to rank a query for documents. Through comprehensive experimental analysis combined with real world data, our proposed technique shows more efficiency and can retrieve more accurate results and meanwhile improve privacy by introducing randomness in query data.

1 Introduction

In order to provide on-demand access to resources, many companies are migrating services to cloud. However, there are huge amount of data in many places because the users can use them in remote location [1]. Researches have proposed some techniques on encrypting and outsourcing data into the cloud [2]. Given the expensive bandwidth cost, it's impossible to download and decrypt all the data locally, while we can search on encrypted data firstly and then download exact information. However, meeting requirements of performance such as accuracy, privacy and efficiency through this method can be quite challenging.

Particularly, we summarize our contribution of the paper as follows.

© Springer International Publishing AG 2017
S. Wen et al. (Eds.): CSS 2017, LNCS 10581, pp. 452–459, 2017.
https://doi.org/10.1007/978-3-319-69471-9_33

- Using Stemming Algorithm for approximate matching to reduce search time complexity;
- Considering multiple factors to calculate approximating scores for ranking results more accurately;
- Efficient index construction by eliminating unimportant words to achieve optimized storage;
- Improving privacy-preservation by including dynamic dummy fields in the index and the query;
- Comparing experimental results with the state-of-the-art technique [3] in terms of searching time, accuracy, and privacy-preservation.

2   Problem Definition

2.1   System Model

The system model is illustrated in Fig. 1. In this paper, we use vector space model to model the documents stored in cloud server in which each data is represented as data vector when we refer data and document vectors. We explain the concept of multi keyword search in high dimensional space that has a particular data in dimensional matrix can be termed as data vector. In the context of multi keyword search algorithm, we model the data as dimensional matrix to perform ranking and retrieving ranking score for a particular query. Remember that we don't store index in matrix form but use binary tree index [3] technique to create index.

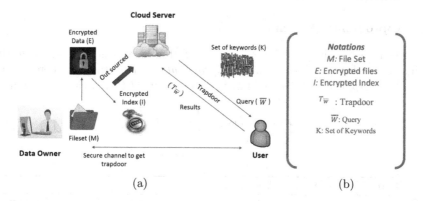

Fig. 1. System Architecture for search over encrypted data in cloud computing

2.2   Notations

In this section we summarize the notations used in the paper. We follow the same notations in entire paper:

- M: The plain text document collection denoted as set of n data documents M:$\{m_1, m_2...., m_n\}$. Where n is the number of files in the document collection.

- E: Encrypted documents stored in cloud server that can be denoted as E: $\{e_1, e_2, ...e_n\}$.
- W: The distinct keywords extracted from document collection M, denoted as $W = \{w_1, w_2, ..., w_n\}$.
- I: Searchable Encrypted index associated with E denoted as E:$\{i_1, i_2, i_3.i_n\}$, where each index i_i is built for each document m_i in document collection.
- $\overline{W}$: Represents keyword set in a search query that can also be considered as subset of W and denoted by $\overline{W}$:$\{\overline{w}_{j1}, \overline{w}_{j2}, \overline{w}_{j3}......\overline{w}_{ji}\}$, where j represents the jth keyword in the query, and $i=1,2,3,n$ represents the ith letter in j^{th} keyword.
- $T_{\overline{W}}$: The trapdoor generated for $\overline{W}$.
- $M_{id\overline{W}}$: The ranked id $list$ of all documents for $\overline{W}$, where the subscript represents the id of the document retrieved for $\overline{W}$.
- K: Initial Keyword set created based on stem condition that can be represented as K: $\{k_1, k_2, k_m\}$ where m is the number of keywords in a the set.
- S_k: Secrete key generated by data owner used to encrypt, decrypt and to perform secure hash operations.
- T_1, T_2: They are the matrices to create secrete key.
- V, Q: Represents the data vector and query vector that can be multiplied to calculate to get the ranking score while searching.
- P_{score}: Score added to the term frequency rule by considering multiple factors.

3   Approximate Matching and Multi-factor Based Ranking Scheme

3.1   Approximate Matching

Trying to measure the similar between the created keywords with regard to the original query keyword, we propose *Approximation Score* to rank them. To be specific, the *Approximate Score* of k_i is denoted by *APP(k_i)*, can be formulate as follows:

$$APP(k_i) = Log_{10}((\frac{L_{ij}}{Q_j})) * ((\frac{U_{ij}}{Q_j}))$$ (1)

Algorithm 1. Create Stem Words

1: Procedure **createstem**($\overline{w}_j$, m, n) //$\overline{w}_j$ represents single keyword in the given multiple keyword query;
2: **for** j $= 0$ to length of $\overline{w}_j$ **do**
3:    **if** j $< $ m **then**
4:       $p^{'} = +\overline{w}_{ji}$;
5:    **else if** j $< $ (length($\overline{w}_j$) $- n$) **then**
6:       $s^{'} = +\overline{w}_{ji}$;
7:    **end if**
8: **end for**

The pseudo-codes of the whole process are summarized as follows. The stem words are created based on pre-defined conditions as shown in Algorithm 1. And then basic keyword sets are created on the basis of pre-created stem words (shown in Algorithm 2). Finally, the final keyword set is constructed by retrieving top l keywords in the basic keyword set (shown in Algorithm 3).

Algorithm 2. Basic Keyword Set Creation

1: Procedure keyword set traverse(I, $p^{'}$, $S^{'}$);
2: **if** $\overline{w}_{ji}$==nil **then**
3:    return -1;
4: **else**
5:    return 1 + Math.max(height(I.root.left),height(I.root.right));
6:    //compute height of tree;
7: **end if**
8: **if** I.root == nil **then**
9:    return
10: **end if**
11: **for** i = 0 to height of tree **do**
12:    traverse(I.root.left, $p^{'}$, $S^{'}$);
13: **end for**
14: **if** I.root.left == $p^{'}$ **then**
15:    save in K_i;
16: **else if** I.root.left == $S^{'}$ **then**
17:    traverse(I.root.right, $p^{'}$, $S^{'}$);
18: **end if**

3.2 Ranking Similarity Measure

We consider two additional factors in calculating ranking score to further improve the precision. One the position of the keyword with respective to other documents and the other is the distance between the keywords in a sentence. The multi-factor based ranking score denoted by $Score(m_i,\overline{W})$ is formulated in Eq. 2.

$$Score(m_i, \overline{W}) = \frac{1}{|m_i|} \sum_{W_j \in W} (1 + ln(f_{m_i,w_j})) * ln(1 + \frac{|M|}{f_{w_j}}) + P_{score} \qquad (2)$$

P_{score} is the padding score, which can be calculated by Eq. 3.

$$P_{score} = (\frac{f_{m_i,w_j}}{|m_i|})(1 - \frac{positon(w_j)}{|m_i|}) \qquad (3)$$

4 System Framework and Efficient Search Mechanism

In this section we describe the basic framework of how our system works on encrypted data. The overview of the system framework is summarized in Fig. 2.

Algorithm 3. Final Keyword Set Creation

1: Procedure Set buildfinalset(K,l).//l represents the top keyword that needs to be searched;
2: **if** length of K <0 **then**
3:    Generate trapdoor on K;
4: **else**
5:    **for** i =0 to length of K **do**
6:       **for** j = 0 to j < i **do**
7:          **if** letter of i at j is matched with query of letter j **then**
8:             count = count+1;
9:          **else if** letter matched with position **then**
10:             temp = temp+1;
11:             Compute approximate score for each k_i;
12:          **end if**
13:       **end for**
14:    **end for**
15:    SORT(K); //keyword collection is sorted based on the approximate score;
16: **end if**
17: Return Set;

4.1   Random Dummy Field Insertion Mechanism

Trapdoor calculates the dummy fields with Eq. 4, and matches the keyword with the ranking score.

$$I_i * T_{\overline{W}} = T_1^T * \overrightarrow{V_l}', T_2^T * \overrightarrow{V_l}'' * T^{-1}\overrightarrow{Q_l}', T_2^{-1} * \overrightarrow{Q_l}'$$
$$= (\overrightarrow{V_l} * \overrightarrow{Q_l}) * (\overrightarrow{V_l}'' * \overrightarrow{Q_l}'') \Rightarrow V_i * Q_i$$
$$= Score(m_i, \overline{W}) + \sum \mu^{(U)} + t \tag{4}$$

4.2   Security Analysis

To provide privacy, dummy values are inserted by extending the dimension of data vector of trapdoor and the query. These random values can be inserted dynamically in the extended dimensions. Each time the trapdoor is generated dimension extensions can be different and random dummy fields would be different. Introducing dummy fields can produce different equations for each query. However, performance might could be compromised when introducing dummy fields in the extended dimension and differentiating from actual data vector. However, improving privacy is a tradeoff to loose performance in terms of computational speed and accuracy.

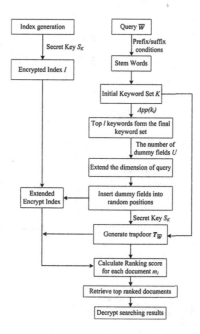

Fig. 2. Approximate searching process.

5   Performance Analysis

5.1   Simulation Settings

We build our own simulator through J2EE to simulate the cloud scenario. We used *Enron dataset* [4] that contains email information taken from *60000* users and randomly select subsets to form our testing dataset. Experiments are done for *700* files in a dataset and having *800* keywords in each file. To make smooth output, we averaged the values for every *100* instances. Three different schemes are implemented: (1) Our proposed scheme, noted by Approximation Search. (2) Privacy-Preserving Scheme in Known Ciphertext Model proposed in [5], noted by MRSE1. (3) Privacy-Preserving Scheme in Known Background Model proposed in [5], noted by MRSE2. We compare them in terms of the index creation time, trapdoor generation time, the query execution time.

5.2   Simulation Results

Index Construction Time. Index is created by extracting words from the document and each letter in the word forms a node. The index construction time includes the time to scan documents and create nodes in the index tree. Figure 3(a) shows the results of index construction time for all there algorithms.

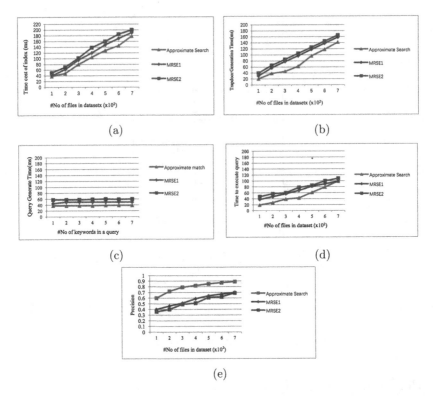

Fig. 3. Simulation results

Trapdoor Generation Time. Generating trapdoor requires the query and a secrete key. Figure 3(b) illustrates the time cost for trapdoor generation when a user gives a query to the server.

Query Generation and Execution Time. Query execution in server consists of creating and matching the hash values to differentiate the randomness from actual data, and ranking the order of the document. Figure 3(c) shows the results of query execution time with regard to the number of keywords in a query. Figure 3(d) shows the results of query execution time with regard to the number of files. Figure 3(e) summarizes the accuracy comparison results among three schemes.

6   Conclusion

In this paper we first introduce an approximate matching that can work on encrypted cloud data to improve searching efficiency. Subsequently, a multi-factor based ranking scoring technique is proposed to improve the accuracy of the searching results. Finally, to improve preserve privacy, a dynamic random dummy value insertion scheme is proposed, so that it can withstand scale analysis attacks.

Acknowledgement. This work was partly supported by the Kennesaw State University College of Science and Mathematics the interdisciplinary Research Opportunities Program (IDROP), and the Office of the Vice President for Research (OVPR) Pilot/Seed Grant.

This was also partly supported by NSFC under No. 61772466, the Provincial Key Research and Development Program of Zhejiang, China under No. 2017C01055, the Fundamental Research Funds for the Central Universities, the Alibaba-Zhejiang University Joint Research Institute for Frontier Technologies (A.Z.F.T.) under Program No. XT622017000118, the CCF-Tencent Open Research Fund under No. AGR20160109, the National Key Research and Development Program of China (2016YFB0800201), and the Natural Science Fundation of Zhejiang Province (LY16F020016).

References

1. Chapman, C., Emmerich, W., Clayman, S.: Software architecture definition for on-demand cloud provisioning. Cluster Comput. **15**(2), 79–100 (2012)
2. Li, M., Yu, S., Cao, N., Lou, W.: Authorized private keyword search over encrypted data in cloud computing. In: 2011 31st International Conference on Distributed Computing Systems (ICDCS), pp. 383–392. IEEE (2011)
3. Ji, S., Li, W., He, J., Srivatsa, M., Beyah, R.: Poster: Optimization based data de-anonymization2014. In: Poster Presented at the 35th IEEE Symposium on Security and Privacy, May, vol. 18, p. 21 (2014)
4. Wang, C., Wang, Q., Ren, K., Cao, N., Lou, W.: Toward secure and dependable storage services in cloud computing. IEEE Trans. Serv. Comput. **5**(2), 220–232 (2012)
5. Cao, N., Wang, C., Li, M., Ren, K., Lou, W.: Privacy-preserving multi-keyword ranked search over encrypted cloud data. IEEE Trans. Parallel Distrib. Syst. **25**(1), 222–233 (2014)

Cloud Data Integrity Checking with Deduplication for Confidential Data Storage

Hongyu Liu[1]([⊠]), Leiting Chen[1], and Liyao Zeng[2]

[1] School of Computer Science and Engineering, University of Electronic Science and Technology of China, Chengdu 611731, China
gaintsky@126.com
[2] Institute of Electronic and Information Engineering, UESTC, Dongguan 523808, Guangdong, China
lyzeng@alu.uestc.edu.cn

Abstract. Data loss is a severe issue in cloud storage due to a number of confidential files stored on the cloud and thus, cloud servers have become the target of attackers. In this paper, we propose a cloud data integrity checking protocol with deduplication, which can guarantee the remote data integrity while achieving secure deduplication within the same framework. Another bonus of our construction is privacy preserving of the outsourced data, which is denoted as zero-knowledge data privacy, indicating that the third party auditor learns nothing about the stored data during the auditing process. In addition, we demonstrate the performance of our construction by developing a prototype of the protocol.

Keywords: Cloud storage · Data deduplication · Proof of ownership

1 Introduction

Cloud computing has been envisioned as the next-generation information technology architecture for enterprises, due to its highlighted advantages: on-demand self-service, location independent resource pooling etc. [1]. As one of the dominate services in cloud computing, cloud storage has been increasingly prevalent because of its advantages [2]. Currently, commercial cloud storage services such as Microsoft Skydrive, Amazon S3 have attracted millions of users.

However, there are many barriers before cloud computing can be widely deployed in reality. One of the major security concerns of cloud users is the integrity of outsourced files, since the data are outsourced to cloud servers, users lose the physical control of their data. Cloud users are at the mercy of their storage providers for the continuous availability of their data. The existing malware infection, social engineering and Advanced Persistent Threat [3] have caused financial damages, disruption of services. Nowadays, widely used mobile devices may produce vast quantities of confidential personal data information [4–6].

© Springer International Publishing AG 2017
S. Wen et al. (Eds.): CSS 2017, LNCS 10581, pp. 460–467, 2017.
https://doi.org/10.1007/978-3-319-69471-9_34

Once these data are stolen, it might cause huge disaster to users since these data may expose personal and social behavior patterns to attackers [7–9]. Data loss is one of the most serious threat in cloud storage because cloud servers have become the target of the attackers due to many confidential cloud files. The investigation of the cloud security Alliance [10] showed that the incidents of data Loss & Leakage accounted for 25% of all cloud security incidents, ranked the second only to "Insecure Interfaces & APIs". Moreover, the cloud server might not be fully trusted. It may also intend to hide data loss or damage accidents or attacks to maintain a good reputation [11]. Sometimes it is insufficient to detect data corruption when accessing the data because it might be too late to recover the corrupted data.

Ateniese et al. [12] proposed two concrete PDP constructions by making use of RSA-based homomorphic linear authenticators. The PoR has also been enhanced and extended in multiple dimensions [13]. Due to the necessity and practicability, remote data integrity checking has attracted extensive research interest, and a number of cloud data auditing schemes [14–16] been proposed so far. The integrity of the outsourced data is important for cloud users and at the same time, the high storage efficiency is required as well for cloud providers.

According to the survey in [17], only 25% of the data may be unique. Data deduplication is an attractive technology that eliminates duplicate copies of data and keeps only one copy in the storage, which can reduce the consumption of both network bandwidth and server storage dramatically. However, the trivial deduplication approach is vulnerable to various attacks and leads to the fact that a malicious cloud user can claim it has certain data while it does not. To deal with the issue above, the notion of Proof of Ownership (PoW) [18,19] was proposed. Nevertheless, these schemes only disposed of the issue of PoW but did not consider the issue of cloud data integrity.

Our contribution: In this paper, we propose a construction of cloud data integrity auditing protocol with deduplication by evolving SW scheme [13] to realize cloud data integrity checking and secure data deduplication within a framework. Another merit of the concrete protocol is perfect data privacy preserving, that is, the auditor learns nothing about the stored data during the integrity auditing process. Inspired by the contributions due to Zheng et al. [20] and Wang et al. [21], we simplify our auditing protocol and apply it again to realize the deduplication. We prove the soundness of the auditing scheme in the generic group model and uncheating of the deduplication. We also analyze the performance of our construction, which indicates the efficiency of the protocol.

2 The System Statement

2.1 System Model

A cloud storage system involves the following the participants, as illustrated in Fig. 1.

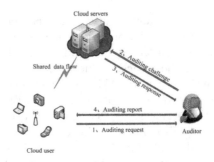

Fig. 1. System model of digital evidence auditing in cloud storage

1. Cloud server, denoted by S, provides storage service and computation resources to cloud users, by which the users can check the integrity of their data stored on the cloud and the servers can save storage space via data deduplication in a secure manner.
2. Cloud user or client, denoted by C, has limited storage space but large amount of data files to be stored, while allowing the cloud server to conduct data deduplication operations.
3. Third party auditor, denoted by $Auditor$, can be a trusted organization that has expertise and capacities that cloud users do not have is to offer the data auditing service. It is trusted by the user to check the integrity of its outsourced data.

2.2   System Components

A privacy preserving public cloud auditing with deduplication protocol consists of the following algorithms.

1. *KeyGen*: This is the key generation algorithm. It takes as input a security parameter λ, and outputs two pairs of public/private keys (PK_{int}, SK_{int}) and (PK_{dup}, SK_{dup}).
2. *UploadStore*: This protocol is run by a user C and a server S. On input a file F with a unique identifier fid and the secret key SK_{int}, it produces authentication tag Tag_{int} that can be used to audit the integrity of F.
3. *AuditINT*: This algorithm is executed between the server S and an $Auditor$. The $Auditor$ uses the file identifier fid and the corresponding client's PK_{int} to produce a challenge $Chal$, and forwards $Chal$ to the server. The server generates a response $resp$ by imputing the file F, the identifier fid, the challenge $chal$ and the authentication tag Tag_{int} associated with F. Then the $Auditor$ checks the $resp$.
4. *ReplicaVer*: This is executed between the server S and the cloud user C.the server S sends a challenge $chal$ to C, which returns a response $resp$ that is produced using data file F and possibly other information. S verifies the validity of $resp$ using possibly Tag_{dup} and PK_{dup}, if the verification is successful outputs 1, meaning that the client indeed has data file F, and 0 otherwise.

3   Our Construction

3.1   The Construction

The details of the construction are as follows. Let G and G_T be multiplicative cyclic groups of prime order p and g is a generator of group G. $\hat{e} : G \times G \rightarrow G_T$ denotes a billinear map. We use hash functions $H(\cdot): \{0,1\}^* \rightarrow G$ and $h(\cdot) : G_T \rightarrow Z_p$. Choose a random $g_1 \in G$. The system parameters is $pp = (e, p, g, g_1, G, G_T)$

KeyGen: The cloud user generates a pair of signing key (spk, ssk). Then choose a random $x \in Z_p$ and compute $v = g^x$. Thus the secret key is $sk = (x, ssk)$, and the public key is $pk = (spk, v)$.

UploadStore: Given a File F, the user splits the file into n blocks, each s sectors long, and obtains $F = \{m_{ij}\}_{1 \leq i \leq n, 1 \leq j \leq s}$. Then choose a unique file name Fid from Z_p and compute $t = Fid\|Sign_{ssk}(Fid)$, $Sign$ is a secure digital signature algorithm. Choose s elements $u_1, \cdots, u_s$ and make them as public parameters. Compute authenticators Tag_{int} for each block m_i for file F as $\sigma_i = \left(H(Fid\|i) \cdot \prod_{j=1}^{s} u_j^{m_{ij}} \right)^x \in G$. Then, the cloud user uploads $(F, \{\sigma_i\}_{1 \leq i \leq n}, t)$ to the cloud.

AuditInt: The cloud server first checks the validity of the signature $Sign_{ssk}Fid$. The TPA can execute auditing process by a challenge-response interaction. TPA chooses a subset I of $[1, n]$, which contains c elements. For each $i \in I$, TPA chooses a random v_i. Then TPA forwards $chal = (i, v_i)_{i \in I}$ to cloud server. Upon receiving the challenge chosen by TPA, cloud server generates a response in the following way.

1. Choose random r_σ and r_{m_j} for $1 \leq j \leq s$, then compute $R_j = e(u_j, v)^{r_{m_j}}$ and $R' = e(g_1, g)^{r_\sigma}$. Let $\gamma = h(R'\|R_1\| \cdots \|R_s) \in Z_p$.
2. Let $\mu'_j = \sum_{i \in I} v_i m_{ij}$ and $\sigma' = \prod_{i \in I} \sigma_i^{v_i}$.
3. Blind μ'_j and σ' with the random values denoted in step 1. Specifically, choose a random $\rho \in Z_p$, and compute $\sigma = \sigma' \cdot g_1^\rho$. Let $\mu_j = r_{m_j} + \gamma \mu'_j$.
4. Define $\xi = r_\sigma + \gamma \rho \bmod p$.

Then, cloud server sends $\{\xi, \sigma, R', \{\mu_j, R_j\}_{1 \leq j \leq s}\}$ as response value to TPA. Upon receiving the response from cloud server, TPA first checks the validity of $\gamma = h(R'\|R_1\| \cdots \|R_s)$ and then checks whether the following verification equation holds.

$$\cdot\ R'R_1 \cdots R_s \cdot e(\sigma^\gamma, g) \stackrel{?}{=} e\left(\left(\prod_{i=1}^{c} H(Fid\|i)^{v_i} \right)^\gamma \cdot \prod_{j=1}^{s} u_j^{\mu_j}, v \right) \cdot e(g_1, g)^\xi$$

ReplicaVer: Once receiving a file identifier that is already existed on the cloud server, the cloud server will audit the integrity of user's file by executing the following interactions with the user.

- The cloud server chooses a random set $I \in [1, n]$ with c elements and a set of coefficients $v = \{v_1, v_2, \cdots, v_c\}$. Then cloud forwards $chal = \{(i, v_i)\}_{i \in I}$ to cloud user.
- The cloud user executes the $UploadStore$ algorithm and obtains $Tag_{dup} = \{\sigma_i\}_{1 \le i \le n}$. Then compute $\mu_j = \sum_{i \in chal} v_i m_{ij}$ and forward $resp = (\{\mu_j\}_{1 \le j \le s}, \{\sigma_i\}_{1 \le i \le n})$ to cloud server.
- Upon receiving the $resp$ from cloud user, the cloud server gets the corresponding challenged $\{\sigma_i\}_{i \in chal}$ from Tag_{dup} and computes $\sigma = \prod_{i \in chal} \sigma_i^{v_i}$ and checks whether $e(\sigma, g) \stackrel{?}{=} e\left(\prod_{i \in chal} H(name\|i)^{v_i} \cdot \prod_{j=1}^{s} u_j^{\mu_j}, v \right)$ holds.

3.2 Correctness

The correctness of this protocol is shown as follows.

$$R'R_1 \cdots R_s \cdot e(\sigma^\gamma, g) = e(g_1, g)^{r\sigma} \prod_{j=1}^{s} e(u_j, v)^{r m_j} e((\sigma' g_1^\rho)^\gamma, g)$$

$$= e(g_1, g)^{r\sigma} \prod_{j=1}^{s} e(u_j, v)^{r m_j} e(\sigma'^\gamma, g) e(g_1, g)^{\rho\gamma} = e(g_1, g)^{r\sigma + \rho\gamma} \prod_{j=1}^{s} e(u_j, v)^{r m_j} e\left(\prod_{i=1}^{c} \sigma_i^{v_i \gamma}, g \right)$$

$$= e(g_1, g)^\xi \prod_{j=1}^{s} e(u_j, v)^{r m_j} e\left(\prod_{i=1}^{c} \left(H(Fid\|i)^{v_i \gamma} \prod_{j=1}^{s} u_j^{\mu_j' \gamma} \right), v \right)$$

$$= e(g_1, g)^\xi e\left(\prod_{i=1}^{c} \left(H(Fid\|i)^{v_i} \right)^\gamma \cdot \prod_{j=1}^{s} u_j^{\mu_j}, v \right)$$

3.3 Soundness

The soundness of this protocol relies on the underlying SW scheme [13], in which the security is reduced to the computational Diffie-Hellman assumption and the discrete logarithm assumption in bilinear groups.

3.4 Zero-Knowledge Privacy

Intuitively, we can see from our $AuditInt$ algorithm, the response value $\{\mu_j\}_{1 \le j \le s}$ and σ are masked with some selected random values, which prevents them leaking information of file blocks $\{m_{ij}\}_{1 \le i \le c, 1 \le j \le s}$ and the corresponding authenticators $\{\sigma_i\}_{1 \le i \le c}$. Additionally, our proposed cloud data protocol can achieves zero-knowledge privacy against TPA. Here, TPA is treated as an adversary and suppose there is a simulator, who can execute some interaction with TPA. Specifically, first define $R = R'R_1 \cdots R_s$ and randomly choose $\gamma, \xi, \{\mu_j\}_{1 \le j \le s} \in Z_p$, $\sigma \in G$. Set $R = e((\prod_{i=1}^{c} H(Fid\|i)_i^v)^\gamma \prod_{j=1}^{s} \mu_j^{m_{ij}}, v) \cdot e(g_1, g)^\xi / e(\sigma^\gamma, g)$. Then backpatch $\gamma = h(R)$, since the simulator controls the random oracle $h(\cdot)$.

Now rewind and set $h(R)$ to be $\gamma* \neq \gamma$. Finally, output $\{\xi, \{\mu_j\}_{1 \leq j \leq s}, \sigma, R\}$ and $\{\xi, \{\mu_j^*\}_{1 \leq j \leq s}, \sigma, R\}$. Then we can extract μ_j' from the simulation and likewise, σ' can be recovered from σ. Clearly, a pair of valid μ_j' and σ' can be extracted.

4   Implementation

In this section, we will show the performance results of the experiment. All the implementation is conducted on a laptop with windows 8-64 bit operate system, 4 GB RAM and Intel(R) Core(TM) i5-4300 CPU @1.90G Hz.

The security level is fixed as AES-80 bit, which implies that $|p| = 160$ bits and $p = 3 \pmod 4$. The implementation results are shown as follows.

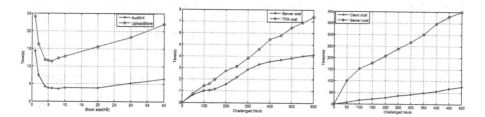

Fig. 2. Tradeoff   **Fig. 3.** Server & TPA cost   **Fig. 4.** Server & Client cost

In the first section, we fix the file size to be 1 MB and test the tradeoff between *UploadStore* and *AuditInt* algorithm to find the optimal block size. As shown in Fig. 2, the best performance is between 4 KB to 8 KB. We choose the optimal block size to be 6 KB. The time consumption is 3.67 s and 11.355 s respectively when the block size is 6 KB.

In the second part, we choose a file with 10,000 blocks and each block 6 KB, to test the server cost and TPA cost in an auditing phase. As can be seen from Fig. 3, the time cost increases as the number of challenged blocks increase. The time cost of cloud server and TPA is 2.8 s and 3.8 s respectively when the number of challenged block is 300 [12]. And for 460 challenged blocks, the time consumption is 3.7 s and 5.8 s for cloud server and TPA.

In the third part, we test the client and server time consumption in a deduplication phase. As shown in Fig. 4, the time consumption increases when the number of challenged blocks increase for both cloud user and server. We can also easily to find that, the time cost and computational overhead of user side is low, which shows that the proof of ownership does not impose too much burden for the user.

5   Conclusion

A number of protocols for cloud data security have been proposed based on the concepts of POR, PDP, POW and POSD. However, most of them focus only on one aspect, which not to fulfill the two important requirements of cloud storage: data integrity and storage efficiency. We present a concrete construction of zero-knowledge privacy preserving public cloud data auditing protocol with deduplication which achieves data integrity and deduplication simultaneously. The proposed scheme can protect the privacy of the stored data, which is suitable for auditing the integrity of the confidential cloud data. The theoretical analysis and the implementation show that the proposed protocol is secure and practical.

References

1. Mell, P., Grance, T.: Draft NIST Working Definition of Cloud Computing, June 2009, http://csrc.nist.gov/groups/SNS/cloudcomputing/index.html
2. Timothy, G., Peter, M.M.: The NIST definition of cloud computing, vol. NIST SP-800-145, September 2011
3. Frankie, L., Anthony, L., Ddl, D.: Evidence of advanced persistent threat: a case study of malware for political espionage. In: 6th International Conference on Malicious and Unwanted Software (2011)
4. Du, X., Xiao, Y., et al.: An effective key management scheme for heterogeneous sensor networks. Ad Hoc Netw. $5(1)$, 24–34 (2007). Elsevier
5. Du, X., Guizani, M., Xiao, Y., Chen, H.H.: A routing-driven elliptic curve cryptography based key management scheme for heterogeneous sensor networks. IEEE Trans. Wireless Commun. $8(3)$, 1223–1229 (2009)
6. Du, X., Lin, F.: Maintaining differentiated coverage in heterogeneous sensor networks. EURASIP J. Wireless Commun. Netw. $5(4)$, 565–572 (2005)
7. Xiao, Y., Chen, H.H., Du, X., Guizani, M.: Stream-based cipher feedback mode in wireless error channel. IEEE Trans. Wireless Commun. $8(2)$, 662–666 (2009)
8. Du, X., Zhang, M., et al.: Self-healing sensor networks with distributed decision making. Int. J. Sensor Netw. $2(5/6)$, 289–298 (2007)
9. Yao, X., Han, X., Du, X., Zhou, X.: A lightweight multicast authentication mechanism for small scale IoT applications. IEEE Sens. J. $13(10)$, 3693–3701 (2013)
10. Cloud Security Alliance. Top threats to cloud computing (2010), http://www.cloudsecurityalliance.org
11. Yu, Y., Zhang, Y., Ni, J., Au, M.H., Chen, L., Liu, H.: Remote data possession checking with enhanced security for cloud storage. Future Gener. Comput. Syst. 52, 77–85 (2015)
12. Ateniese, G., Burns, R., et al.: Provable data possession at untrusted stores. In: Proceedings 14th ACM Conference Computer and Communications Security, New York, NY, USA (2007)
13. Shacham, H., Waters, B.: Compact proofs of retrievability. In: Pieprzyk, J. (ed.) ASIACRYPT 2008. LNCS, vol. 5350, pp. 90–107. Springer, Heidelberg (2008). doi:10.1007/978-3-540-89255-7_7
14. Yu, Y., Au, M.H., Ateniese, G., et al.: Identity-based remote data integrity checking with perfect data privacy preserving for cloud storage. IEEE Trans. Inf. Forensics Secur. 4, 767–778 (2017)
15. Yu, Y., Li, Y., Ni, J., Yang, G., Mu, Y., Susilo, W.: Comments on public integrity auditing for dynamic data sharing with multiuser modification. IEEE Trans. Inf. Forensics Secur. $11(3)$, 658–659 (2016)

16. Li, Y., Yu, Y., Susilo, W., et al.: Fuzzy identity-based data integrity auditing for reliable cloud storage systems. IEEE Trans. Dependable Secure. Comput. (2016). doi:10.1109/TDSC.2017.2662216
17. The digital universe decade - are you ready? International Data Corporation (2010), http://idcdocserv.com/925
18. Pinkas, B., Shulman-Peleg, A., Halevi, S., Harnik, D.: Proofs of ownership in remote storage systems. Cryptology ePrint Archive, Report (2011), http://eprint.iacr.org/
19. Di Pietro, R., Sorniotti, A.: Boosting efficiency and security in proof of ownership for deduplication. In: ASIACCS 2012, pp. 81–82 (2012)
20. Qingji, Z., Shouhuai, X.: Secure and efficient proof of storage with deduplication. In: Proceedings of the 2nd ACM Conference on Data and Application Security and Privacy, pp. 1–12, New York, USA (2012)
21. Wang, C., Chow, S.S., Wang, Q., et al.: Privacy-preserving public auditing for secure cloud storage. IEEE Trans. Comput. **62**(2), 362–375 (2013)

Supporting User Authorization Queries in RBAC Systems by Role-Permission Reassignment

Jianfeng Lu[✉], Yun Xin, Hao Peng, Jianmin Han, and Feilong Lin

Department of Computer Science and Engineering,
School of Mathematics-Physical and Information Engineering,
Zhejiang Normal University, Jinhua, Zhejiang, China
lujianfeng@zjnu.cn

Abstract. The User Authorization Query (UAQ) Problem is a key issue related to efficiently handling users' access requests in RBAC systems. In practice, there may not exist any solution for the UAQ problem, as missing any requested permissions may make the failure of this task, while any extra permissions may bring the intolerable risk to the system. Hence, making a desirable update of the RBAC system state to support the UAQ problem is desirable. However, this task is generally complex and challenging as usually the resulting state is expected to meet various necessary objectives and constraints. In this paper, we study a fundamental problem of how generate a valid role-permission assignment to satisfy all objectives and constraints, such as reassignment objectives, prerequisite constraints and permission-capacity constraints. The computational complexity result shows that it is intractable (NP-complete) in general. We also propose an approach to reduce it to SAT that benefit from SAT solvers to reduce the running time. Experiment results show that the proposed approach scales well in large RBAC systems.

Keywords: RBAC · User authorization query · Computational complexity · Constraint · SAT solver

1 Introduction

Role based access control (RBAC) has received considerable attention over the past two decades, and established itself as the predominant model for advanced access control in many organizations and enterprises [1]. Several beneficial features, such as policy neutrality, support for least privilege and efficient self-management are associated with RBAC models. Such features make RBAC better suited for handling access control requirements of diverse organizations [2]. A fundamental problem in RBAC is to determine whether there exists an optimum set of roles to be activated to provide a particular set of permissions requested by a user, which is introduced as the user authorization query (UAQ) problem by Zhang et al. [3]. UAQ has been the subject of considerable research in recent years, and is widely accepted as a key issue related to efficiently handing users' access requests in RBAC [4–8]. Ideally, the chosen set of roles to be activated to exactly satisfy a user's permissions request. However, this is not

© Springer International Publishing AG 2017
S. Wen et al. (Eds.): CSS 2017, LNCS 10581, pp. 468–476, 2017.
https://doi.org/10.1007/978-3-319-69471-9_35

always possible since we cannot find any combination of roles that can activate only requested permissions in many situations. Hence we have to find a set of roles to activate a set of permissions that is as close as possible to those requested permissions. Wickramaarachchi et al. [5] specified the UAQ problem by considering a lower bound P_{LB} and an upper bound P_{UB} for the set of requested permissions. There are two possible optimization objectives that should be included in the UAQ problem. One is prefer to minimize the number of extra permissions beyond the requested permissions, which is motivated by the principle of least privilege, as too many extra permissions may bring the intolerable risk to the system. The other is prefer to minimize the number of missing permissions, as the unavailability of too many of the requested permissions may make it difficult for a user to carry out the required task. Existing approaches to the UAQ problem primarily focus on how to design approximate or exhaustive solutions [5–7]. However, there may not exists any solution for UAQ as we cannot find any combination of roles that have permissions between P_{LB} and P_{UB}. Hence, a novel approach for supporting the UAQ problem by making a desirable update of the RBAC system state is desirable.

An RBAC system state is determined by three types of assignments: *user-role* assignment (UA), *role-role* assignment (RH), and *permission-role* assignment (PA). To make the most RBAC benefits, proper considerations should be taken in the entire life cycle of roles, which includes four stages: role analysis, role design, role management, and role maintenance. Particularly, the role maintenance stage concerns the changes related roles in access control system. Hu et al. [9] refer to the updating of UA, RH and PA in the role maintenance stage as *role updating*. In our observation, UA is business-driven, since user's role memberships are determined by their attributes, such as jobs, titles, and etc. Hence, in this paper, we focus on the updating of RH and PA, which we refer to as *role-permission reassignment* (RPR). It should be noted that role hierarchy play crucial roles in policy specification and security management in an organization, by allowing permission-inheritance, role hierarchies reduce overhead associated with the permission administration. When the role-permission assignments are renewed, administrators can accomplish the role-role assignments and permission-role assignments straightforwardly, so do the user-role assignments.

RPR is demanded not only for the UAQ problem when there doesn't exist any solution for it, but also needed in many access control scenarios, such as misconfig-uration repair, proper satisfaction and role hierarchy transformation. However, RPR is generally complex and challenging, especially for large-scale RBAC systems. This is because the resulting state usually is expected to meet a variety of constraints, which makes it impossible to assign permissions to roles. For example, an objective of RPR may require that the chosen set $\mathcal{R}$ of roles can activate permissions between a lower bound P_{LB} and an upper bound P_{UB}. Obviously, such an objective states an overall request that must be satisfied, the set $\mathcal{R}$ of selected roles together activate the requested permissions, rather than restrict which roles are allowed to activate the individual permissions. Moreover, a prerequisite constraints require that the permissions can be activated by a role set $\mathbb{R}$ must also be activated by some other roles, can be used in cases, where a number of responsibilities are prerequisites for a certain task [10]. In addition, a permission-capacity constraint is satisfied in an RBAC system if and only if all the permission in $\mathbb{Z}$ can be activated by the set R_{LB} of roles, and any role not included in R_{UB} cannot activate any permission in $\mathbb{Z}$. Here, R_{LB} and R_{UB} are the lower bound and the upper bound role sets of $\mathbb{Z}$, such that $R_{LB} \subseteq R_{UB}$ [11].

To help system managers understand and manage RBAC policies, various RBAC policy analysis tools have been developed [10, 11], which focus on whether the given state-change rules can be satisfied, and do not care what the resulting states look like. In addition, they focus on user-role assignments rather than role-permission assignments. Meanwhile, there also exists a wealth of literature on role engineering [12]. However, RAR has two main differences from role engineering. First, role engineering focus on how to generate an appropriate set of roles, whereas RAR aims to determine whether an update can achieve with the request without violating any security constraints. Second, RAR works when RBAC states have been defined and possibly deployed, whereas role engineering usually define roles from scratch. The most similar work with RAR is RBAC updating. Ni et al. [13] studied the role adjustment problem (RAP) in the context of role-based provisioning based on machine learning algorithms. The main difference between our work to Ni's is that, RAR is request-driven, whereas RAP is a learning process. Specially, the administrator submits a specific reassignment objective, which tries to find the expected update. On the contrary, RAP is supplied by administrators with provisioning data and output a set of mappings from roles to entitlements. Hu et al. [9] proposed an approach for assistanting administrators with the updating of user-role, role-role, and permission-role relations. They also presented a tool, named RoleUpdater, which answers administrator's high-level update request for role-based access control systems. However, it is worth observing that there appears to be no good reason to assume that user's privilege escalation is forbidden, that is, the update will make the user's permission sets remain the same or deplete. In addition, they made sure that users' permission set varies from a lower bound to former, did not consider any security constraint.

In the above work, the system manager may change the system configuration in a trial-and-error way, which is effort-consuming, inefficient, and most importantly counter productive to security. Therefore, in this paper, we advocate for an automatic approach to RPR. The system manager needs only to specify the objectives and constraints: an RPR solution, if any, is automatically generated so that the system managers can follow to accomplish reassignment. In order to achieve this aim, we reduce the RPR to SAT that benefit from several decades of research in designing SAT solvers to reduce the running time. In general, if a truth assignment is found for the SAT instance, we can construct a valid *role-permission* (RP) assignment for the system configuration. We propose an approach for RGP by reducing RGP to the Boolean satisfiability (SAT) that to resolve it, which enables us benefit from several decades of research in designing SAT solvers to reduce the running time. Experiment results show the effective of our proposed approach.

2   Definition of the Reassignment Generation Problem

An RBAC state determines the set of permissions for which a role is assigned and the user can acquire the associate permissions via roles to take the associated tasks [1]. We assume that an RBAC state builds upon three countable infinite sets: U (the set of all possible users), R (the set of all possible roles) and P (the set of all possible permissions). The formal definition of an RBAC state is defined as follows.

Definition 1 (RBAC State). *An RBAC state γ is a tuple $\langle U, R, P, UR, RP \rangle$, where U, R, P denote the set of all users, the set of all roles, the set of all permissions, respectively. $UR \subseteq U \times R$ associates users with roles, $RP \subseteq R \times P$ associates roles with permissions.*

Given a UAQ problem, ideally, the chosen set of roles should activate the permissions not beyond the scope of $[P_{LB}, P_{UB}]$. However, this is not always possible when any combinations of roles fail to active any permission set P' such that $P_{LB} \subseteq P' \subseteq P_{UB}$. In this case, it is necessary to change the RP assignments that make sure there exists at least a solution for the UAQ problem. Given a requested permission region $[P_{LB}, P_{UB}]$, and a set $\mathcal{R} \subseteq R$ of roles, we write $RO\langle \mathcal{R}, P_{LB}, P_{UB} \rangle$ to express the RPR objective that we can find at least a combination of roles that have permissions between P_{LB} and P_{UB}. In the following, we give the definition of the reassignment objective, which determines whether the reassignment achieves the request.

Definition 2 (Reassignment Objective). *A reassignment objective is represented as $RO\langle \mathcal{R}, P_{LB}, P_{UB} \rangle$, where $\mathcal{R} \subseteq R$ is a role set, and P_{LB}, P_{UB} ($P_{LB} \subseteq P_{UB} \subseteq P$) are called the lower bound and upper bound for the set of requested permissions.*

A reassignment objective $RO\langle \mathcal{R}, P_{LB}, P_{UB} \rangle$ is satisfied if and only if $P_{LB} \subseteq Perm(\mathcal{R}) \subseteq P_{UB}$. In other words, every permission in P_{LB} must be assigned to at least one role in $\mathcal{R}$, and any permission in $P \backslash P_{UB}$ can not be assigned to any role in $\mathcal{R}$. In the remainder of this section, we introduce two types of security constraints, such as prerequisite and permission-capacity. These two constraints (or their special forms) have been considered in existing literature [9–11].

Definition 3 (Prerequisite constraint). *A prerequisite constraint is represented as $PRE\langle cond, \mathbb{R} \rangle$, where $\mathbb{R} \subseteq R$ is a role set, cond is called prerequisite condition on $\mathbb{R}$ that it is an expression consisting of roles, conjunctive operator $\wedge$, disjunctive operator $\vee$, and negation operator $\neg$.*

A prerequisite constraint $PRE\langle cond, \mathbb{R} \rangle$ is satisfied if and only if for any member p of roles in $\mathbb{R}$, the role membership of p satisfies $cond$. Prerequisite constraints state that if a role takes a certain responsibility, she is also required to take some other responsibilities. In particular, role hierarchy can be represented and enforced using prerequisite constraints.

Definition 4 (Permission-Capacity Constraint). *A permission-capacity constraint is represented as $PC\langle \mathbb{Z}, R_{LB}, R_{UB} \rangle$, where $\mathbb{Z}$ is a permission set, and $R_{LB} \subseteq R_{UB} \subseteq R$ are called the lower bound and the upper bound role sets of all the permissions in $\mathbb{Z}$ is a member of, respectively.*

$PC\langle \mathbb{Z}, R_{LB}, R_{UB} \rangle$ is satisfied if and only if $\mathbb{Z} \subseteq Perm(R_{LB})$ and $\forall r \notin R_{UB}$ such that $Perm(r) \cap \mathbb{Z} = \emptyset$. In practice, many permissions are related to security or privacy focus, these permissions should be assigned to a few key roles. In contrast, we require a set of permissions be assigned to at least a certain number of roles so as to meet workload or resiliency requirement. When $R_{LB} = \emptyset$, there is no limitation on the minimum roles that the permissions in $\mathbb{Z}$ must be a member of, and $R_{UB} = R$ means there is no limitation on the maximum roles that should be assigned to.

Definition 5 (Reassignment Configuration). *Given an RBAC state γ, an RPR configuration is denoted as a 3-tuple $\langle \gamma, C, O \rangle$, where γ is an RBAC state, C is a set of constraints where each constraint takes one of the form of prerequisite and permission-capacity constraint, and O is a set of reassignment objectives.*

When the reassignment configuration $\langle \gamma, C, O \rangle$ is given, a interesting problems arise, such as "How to generate a valid RP assignment under $\langle \gamma, C, O \rangle$?". We define it as and Reassignment Generation Problem (RGP) as follows.

Definition 6 (RGP). *Given an reassignment configuration $\langle \gamma, C, O \rangle$, the Reassignment Generation Problem (RGP) returns a valid role-permission assignment relation RP under $\langle \gamma, C, O \rangle$.*

3   The Complexity of the Reassignment Generation Problem

Theorem 1. *RGP is NP-complete*

Proof. On one hand, we show that it is efficient to check whether the returned RP relation is valid under the reassignment configuration $\langle \gamma, C, O \rangle$. We only need to check two things: (1) each reassignment objective in O is satisfied; (2) no constraint in C is violated. It is obvious that there exist many efficient algorithms to check them, and hence RGP is in NP.

On the other hand, we show that RGP is NP-hard by reducing the NP-complete monotone SAT problem to its subcase that determines whether such a valid role-permission assignment exists. In monotone SAT, given an expression ϕ in conjunctive normal form (CNF) and ask whether there exists a truth assignment for variables appeared in ϕ such that ϕ is evaluated to true. Let $\phi = \phi_1 \wedge \cdots \wedge \phi_m$, where $\phi_i = l_{i_1} \vee \cdots \vee l_{i_l}$ is a clause and l_{i_j} is a literal, each clause contains either only positive literal or only negative literal. Let $\{v_1, \cdots, v_n\}$ be the set of variables appeared in ϕ. Without loss of generality, assume that no clause contains both v and $\neg v$. Given a monotone SAT instance, we call a clause with only positive literals a positive clause, denoted as ϕ^+, and otherwise a negative clause, denoted as ϕ^-, and construct an reassignment configuration $\langle R, P, C, O \rangle$ as follows: For each clause $\phi^+ \in \phi$, create a permission p_{ϕ^+}; for each clause $\phi^- \in \phi$, create a permission p_{ϕ^-}. Denote $P^+ = \bigcup_{\phi^+ \in \phi} p_{\phi^+}, P^- = \bigcup_{\phi^- \in \phi} p_{\phi^-}$, and $P = P^+ \bigcup P^-$. For each variable $v \in V$, create a corresponding role r_v, let $R = \bigcup_{v \in V} r_v$. Let $(r_v, p_{\phi^+}) \in RP$ if and only if ϕ^+ contains the variable v, and $(r_v, p_{\phi^-}) \in RP$ if and only if ϕ^- contains the variable $\neg v$. For each ϕ^+, let $R_{\phi^+} = \{r_v | \phi^+ \text{ contains the variable } v\}$, and construct an RO objectives $RO \langle R_{\phi^+}, P_{LB}^+, P_{UB}^+ \rangle$, where $P_{LB}^+ = P_{UB}^+ = \bigcup_{r_v \in R_{\phi^+}} \text{Perm}(r_v) \cap P^+$. For each ϕ^-, let $R_{\phi^-} = \{r_v | \phi^- \text{ contains the variable } \neg v\}$, and construct an RC constraint $RO \langle R_{\phi^-}, P_{LB}^-, P_{UB}^- \rangle$, where $P_{LB}^- = P_{UB}^- = \bigcup_{r_v \in R_{\phi^-}} \text{Perm}(r_v) \backslash P^+$. We construct a PC constraint $PC \langle \mathbb{Z}, R_{LB}, R_{UB} \rangle$ as follows: let $R_{LB} = R_{\phi^+}$, $R_{UB} = R$, and $\mathbb{Z} = P^+$. Now, we prove that ϕ is satisfiable if and only if there exists a valid role-permission assignment RP under $\langle \gamma, C, O \rangle$.

For the "only if" part, suppose that τ is a truth assignment that makes ϕ true. Then RP consists of: removing all (r_v, p) from RP where $\tau(v) = 1$ and $p \in P^-$, or $\tau(v) = 0$ and $p \in P^+$. Since ϕ is true, all ϕ^+ is true. For each ϕ^+, there must exists a variable v such that $\tau(v) = 1$. Then $\{r_v | \tau(v) = 1\}$ is a role in R_{ϕ^+} whose permission set is exactly P^+. Thus $PC\langle \mathbb{Z}, R_{LB}, R_{UB} \rangle$ is fulfilled. For each $RO\langle R_{\phi^-}, P_{LB}^-, P_{UB}^- \rangle$, and for each $r \in R_{\phi^+}$ and any permission $p \in P^-$ that (r, p) has been removed from RP, and any permission $p \in P^+$, (r, p) is still unchanged. Hence, $RO\langle R_{\phi^+}, P_{LB}^+, P_{UB}^+ \rangle$ is satisfied. Similarly, for each $RO\langle R_{\phi^-}, P_{LB}^-, P_{UB}^- \rangle$, for each $r \in R_{\phi^-}$ and any permission $p \in P^+$ that (r, p) has been removed from RP, that means $P^+ \cap Perm(R_{\phi^-}) = \emptyset$, hence, $RO\langle R_{\phi^-}, P_{LB}^-, P_{UB}^- \rangle$ is also satisfied. For the "if" part, suppose RP is valid under $\langle \gamma, C, O \rangle$. We construct a truth assignment τ over $\{v_1, \cdots, v_n\}$ that makes ϕ be evaluated to true as follows: $\tau(v) = 1$ if and only if $Perm(r_v) \subseteq \mathbb{Z}$, otherwise, $\tau(v) = 0$. We now show that τ is a truth assignment that makes ϕ true as follows. Suppose, for the sake of contradiction, that there exists $\phi^+ = v_1 \vee \cdots \vee v_k$ is false under τ, it means that $\tau(v_i) = 0$ $(1 \le i \le k)$, by the above constructions, $Perm(r_{v_i}) \not\subseteq \mathbb{Z}(1 \le i \le k)$. $RO\langle R_{\phi^+}, P_{LB}^+, P_{UB}^+ \rangle$ requires that $Perm(R_{\phi^+}) = \bigcup_{1 \le i \le k} Perm(r_{v_i}) \subseteq P_{UB}^+ \subseteq \mathbb{Z}$, Thus, we reach a contradiction. On the other hand, suppose there exists $\phi^- = \neg v_1 \vee \cdots \vee \neg v_l$ is false under τ, that means $\tau(v_i) = 1$ $(1 \le i \le l)$, hence $Perm(r_{v_i}) \subseteq \mathbb{Z}(1 \le i \le l)$ by the above constructions. However, $RO\langle R_{\phi^-}, P_{LB}^-, P_{UB}^- \rangle$ requires that $Perm(R_{\phi^-}) = \bigcup_{1 \le i \le l} Perm(r_{v_i}) \subseteq P_{UB}^- \backslash \mathbb{Z}$, that means $Perm(r_{v_i}) \not\subseteq \mathbb{Z}(1 \le i \le l)$, which reachs a contradiction, and hence RGP is NP-hard. $\square$

4   An Approach for the Reassignment Generation Problem

In this section, we describe an approach for RGP by reducing the RGP to SAT, that is, we can benefit from several decades of research on the design of SAT solvers to reduce the running time. For each $(r_i, p_j) \in RP$, we specify a variable v_{ij} in our SAT instance. Variable v_{ij} being set to true indicates that $(r_i, p_j) \in RP$. If no satisfying truth assignment is found, then ϕ is unsatisfiable. Otherwise, we get a truth assignment A, we can construct a valid RP for $\langle \gamma, C, O \rangle$ in the following way: $RP = \{(r_i, p_j) | (v_{ij} = true) \in A\}$. Given a fixed RP $(r_i, p_j) \in RP$, we just need to specify a clause v_{ij}, which forces any truth assignment that satisfies $(r_i, p_j) \in RP$.

Reassignment objectivests: given a reassignment objective $RO\langle \mathcal{R}, P_{LB}, P_{UB} \rangle$, we can reduce it to Conjunctive Normal Form (CNF) in efficiently. (1) For every permission p_j in P_{LB}, and every role r_i in $\mathcal{R}$, we specify a clause $\phi = \bigvee_{r_j \in \mathcal{R}} v_{ij}$; (2) For every permission p_j in $P \backslash P_{UB}$, and every role r_i in $\mathcal{R}$, we specify a clause $\phi = \bigwedge_{r_j \in P \backslash P_{UB}} \neg v_{ij}$.

PRE constraints: given a prerequisite constraint $PRE\langle cond, \mathbb{R}\rangle$, such a constraint essentially states that $\mathbb{R} \rightarrow cond$, which can be equivalently written as $\neg\mathbb{R} \vee cond$. For every permission p_j in P, we construct a clause $\phi = f(\neg\mathbb{R} \vee cond)$, where the function f constructs a clause from $\neg\mathbb{R} \vee cond$ by replacing every role with a variable: any role r_i in $\neg\mathbb{R} \vee cond$ is replaced with v_{ij}.

PC constraints: given a permission-capacity constraint $PC\langle \mathbb{Z}, R_{LB}, R_{UB}\rangle$, we can reduce it to CNF in efficiently: (1) For every role r_i in R_{LB}, and every permission p_j in $\mathcal{R}$, we specify a clause $\phi = \bigvee_{r_j \in R_{LB}} v_{ij}$; (2) For every role r_i in $R \backslash R_{UB}$, and every permission p_j in $\mathcal{R}$, we specify a clause $\phi = \bigwedge_{p_j \in P_{PC}} \neg v_{ij}$.

We have prototyped the proposed approach and performed some experiments using randomly generated instances. Our prototype is written in Java and use sat4j [14]. To generate the reassignment configuration $\langle \gamma, C, O\rangle$, we adapt data generation algorithm motivated by [7]. In order to compare our experimental results in different cases in convenient, we set the ratio of $|R| : |P|$ is 1:2 and 1:10 in each test case. All the experiments are carried out on a standard desktop PC with an Intel Core i7-4790 running at 3.6 GHz, and with DDR3 8 GB 1600 MHz, running the 64-bit Windows 7 operating system.

The following experimental results show the CPU time taken by each test case. Figure 1(a) shows our performance for different number of roles (i.e., no.R). We observe that our approach is highly resilient to an increase in no.R. On the one hand, the running time will increase as the number of roles increases. The main reason behind this phenomenon is that the computational complexity increase with the number of roles, and the larger range of optional collections, such as $\mathcal{R}, R_{LB}, R_{UB}$. On the other hand, the running time increases with the ratio of permissions and roles. The reason is that the larger of the ratio, the larger number of permissions, that the optional scope of the sets such as $P_{LB}, P_{UB}, \mathbb{Z}$ will get larger to increase the computational complexity. Figure 1(b) shows the performance for different number of RO constraints (i.e., no. RO). The time taken is almost polynomial to no.RO. We tried for up to no.RO = 20 and our approach goes only up to fewer than 0.22 s when $|R| : |P|$ equals 1:10 and 0.13 s when $|R| : |P|$ equals 1:2. Figure 1(c) shows the performance of different number of PRE constraints (i.e., no.PRE). The CPU time taken is almost polynomial to no.PRE. We tried for up to no.PRE = 20 and our approach goes only up to fewer than 0.25 s when $|R| : |P| = 1:10$, and 0.14 s when $|R| : |P|$ is 1:2. The higher ratio of permissions to roles, the more running time will be spent. This is due to fact that the more no. RO or no.PRE, the larger size and the higher complexity of the problem is, thereby, increasing the CPU time. Figure 1(d) shows the performance of different number of PC constraints (i.e., no.PC). The CPU time increases as no.PC increases in both of the two cases. Our approach is also resilient with the increasing of no.PC. The major difference is that the increasing range is smaller than the former three cases obviously. Our experimental results show that our approach scales reasonably well with the larger RBAC system when no.R, no.P, no.RC,no.PC and no.PRE is large. In particular, our approach turns more effective when the ratio of permissions to roles is small.

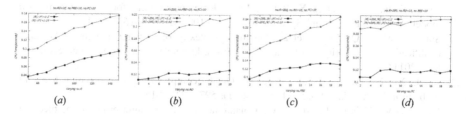

Fig. 1. Performance for different number of (a) roles (i.e., no.R); (b) RO constraints (i.e., no. RO); (c) PRE constraints (i.e., no.PRE); (d) PC objectives (i.e., no.PC).

5 Conclusion

We have introduced reassignment objective, prerequisite constraint, and permission-capacity constraint to role-permission reassignment, formally defined, studied the computational complexity, and proposed an approach for RGP. Our work will assistant administrators to answer whether the rule updates can achieve the request.

Acknowledgment. This work is supported by National Natural Science Foundation of China under Grant 61402418, 61503342, 61672468, 61602418, Social development project of Zhejiang provincial public technology research under Grant 2017C33054, 2016C3316.

References

1. ANSI.: American national standard for information technology-role based access control, ANSI INCITS 359-2004 (2004)
2. Xu, D., Kent, M., Thomas, L., et al.: Automated model-based testing of role-based access control using predicate/transition nets. IEEE Trans. Comput. **64**(9), 2490–2505 (2015)
3. Zhang, Y., Joshi, J.B.D.: UAQ: a framework for user authorization query processing in RBAC extended with hybrid hierarchy and constraints. In: 13th ACM Symposium on Access Control Models and Technologies, New York, USA, pp. 83–92 (2008)
4. Lu, J., Joshi, J.B.D., Jin, L., Liu, Y.: Towards complexity analysis of user authorization query problem in RBAC. Comput. Secur. **48C**, 116–130 (2015)
5. Wickramaarachchi, G.T., Wahbeh, H.Q., Li, N.: An efficient framework for user authorization queries in RBAC systems. In: 14th ACM Symposium on Access Control Models and Technologies, Stresa, Italy, pp. 23–32 (2009)
6. Armando, A., Ranise, S., Turkmen, F., Crispo, B.: Efficient run-time solving of RBAC user authorization queries: pushing the envelope. In: 17th ACM Conference on Data and Application Security and Privacy, San Antonio, Texas, USA, pp. 241–248 (2012)
7. Mousavi, N., Tripunitara, Mahesh V.: Mitigating the intractability of the user authorization query problem in role-based access control (RBAC). In: Xu, L., Bertino, E., Mu, Y. (eds.) NSS 2012. LNCS, vol. 7645, pp. 516–529. Springer, Heidelberg (2012). doi:10.1007/978-3-642-34601-9_39
8. Chen, L., Crampton, J.: Set covering problems in role-based access control. In: Backes, M., Ning, P. (eds.) ESORICS 2009. LNCS, vol. 5789, pp. 689–704. Springer, Heidelberg (2009). doi:10.1007/978-3-642-04444-1_42

9. Hu, J., Khan, K. M., Zhang, Y., Bai, Y., Li, R.: Role updating in information systems using model checking. Knowl. Inf. Syst. (2016). doi:10.1007/s10115-016-0974-4

10. Sun, Y., Wang, Q., Li, N., et al.: On the complexity of authorization in RBAC under qualification and security constraints. IEEE Trans. Dependable Secure Comput. **8**(6), 883–897 (2011)

11. Lu, J., Xu, D., Jin, L., Han, J., Peng, H.: On the complexity of role updating feasibility problem in RBAC. Inf. Process. Lett. **114**(11), 597–602 (2014)

12. Verde, N.V., Vaidya, J., Atluri, V., Colantonio, A.: Role engineering: from theory to practice. In: 2nd ACM Conference on Data and Application Security and Privacy, San Antonio, Texas, USA, pp. 181–192 (2012)

13. Ni, Q., Lobo, J., Calo, S.B., Rohatgi, P., Bertino, E.: Automating role-based provisioning by learning from examples. In: 14th ACM Symposium on Access Control Models and Technologies, Stresa, Italy, pp. 75–84 (2009)

14. SAT4 J: A satisfiability library for Java, January 2006, http://www.sat4j.org/

An Information Theory Based Approach for Identifying Influential Spreaders in Temporal Networks

Liang Luo, Li Tao, Hongyi Xu, Zhenyun Yuan, Hong Lai, and Zili Zhang[✉]

College of Computer and Information Science, Southwest University,
Chongqing, China
{luoliang,tli,hlai,zhangzl}@swu.edu.cn,
{xhy603213557,yuanzhenyun5}@email.swu.edu.cn

Abstract. Identifying the most influential nodes in computer networks is an important issue in preventing the spread of computer viruses. In order to quantify the importance of nodes in the spreading of computer viruses, various centrality measures have been developed under an assumption of a static network. These measures have limitations in that many network structures are dynamically change over time. In this paper, we extend an entropy-based centrality from time-independent networks to time-dependent networks by taking into account the temporal and spatial connections between different nodes simultaneously. We also propose an algorithm for ranking the influences of nodes. According to the experimental results on three synthetic networks and a real network for susceptible-infected-recovered (SIR) spreading model, our proposed temporal entropy-based centrality (TEC) is more accurate than existing temporal betweenness, and closeness centralities.

Keywords: Temporal networks · Influential nodes identification · Temporal entropy-based centrality · Information theory · SIR model

1 Introduction

Finding the most influential spreaders is of critical importance in preventing and controlling the spread of computer viruses over email networks, computer networks, or social networks [1]. At present, a lot of centrality measures have been presented to identify the most influential spreaders in networks such as the degree centrality, closeness centrality, betweenness centrality, K-shell centrality, and eigenvector centrality [2]. However, most of these measures are defined based on a static network model with the assumption that nodes and edges in the network are fixed. However, many networks in the real world such as email networks are time-awareness and not static. New nodes or edges in the networks

This work is supported by the Fundamental Research Funds for the Central Universities (No. XDJK2015C153 and SWU114112).

S. Wen et al. (Eds.): CSS 2017, LNCS 10581, pp. 477–484, 2017.
https://doi.org/10.1007/978-3-319-69471-9_36

may appear at any time, and old nodes or edges may disappear as well. The networks that contain a series of time-ordered graphs over a set of nodes are often named as temporal networks. Figure 1 shows a toy temporal network with six nodes as an example. Due to the dynamics of topological structures in temporal networks, the traditional centrality measures do not suit to quantify the influences of nodes.

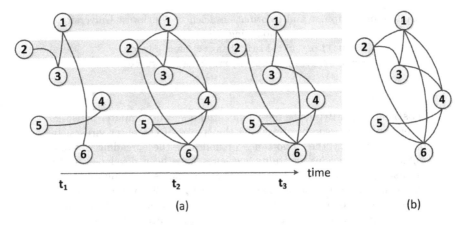

Fig. 1. A toy temporal network which includes 3 snapshot graphs with 6 nodes (a), and the corresponding aggregated static network (b).

Although temporal networks are ubiquitous, there are few metrics for locating the most influential spreaders in such temporal networks. Tang et al. [3] proposed a temporal closeness centrality (TCC) and a temporal betweenness centrality (TBC) to identify important nodes in time-dependent networks from a communication perspective. The temporal closeness centrality aims to find nodes with a fastest speed to spread a piece of information, while the temporal betweenness centrality focuses on the classification of nodes that behave as key mediators in the communication over time. Takaguchi et al. [4] defined fastest temporal paths on a network and based on which they defined temporal coverage centrality and temporal boundary coverage centrality. Rocha et al. [5] and Estrada et al. [6] estimated the roles of nodes in propagation process based on the random walk theory. Praprotnik and Batagelj [7] extended the matrix-based centralities in time-independent network such as eigenvector centrality and Katz centrality to temporal networks. Taylor et al. [8] further generalized the eigenvector centrality. They also presented two additional metrics, namely as marginal and conditional centralities, with the aim of facilitating the capture of centrality trajectories. However, these measures seldom consider the relationships between nodes' influences at different time snapshot. Intuitively, if a node connects to more nodes that have more neighbors in the subsequent time snapshots, the node may be a more important spreader.

From this point of view, this paper contributes to extend the entropy-based centrality [9] from a static network to a temporal network based on the information theory. As defined by Shannon [10], entropy is an effective way to measure the uncertainty of the outcomes when an event happens. In the scenario of computer virus spreading, a node may have a higher uncertainty on its outcome if it connects to more nodes in a snapshot. That means, if an infected node has more uninfected neighbors, it is more difficult to predict how many neighbors it will infect. Thus the node has a larger entropy. Furthermore, based on the observation on the propagation process of computer viruses, we have found that if a node has more neighbors in a snapshot, and its neighbors have more neighbors in the future, the node may be more influencing. This is easy to understand because if the neighbors of an infected node will connects to more nodes in the subsequent time snapshots, the node may have a higher probability to infect more nodes after several time steps. Furthermore, we also propose a recursion algorithm, namely as "Information Theory-based Temporal Centrality Calculation" ITTCC algorithm to calculate the influence for each node in a temporal network.

The proposed temporal entropy-based centrality (TEC) estimates the importance of a node by considering both the magnitude of its degree in each snapshot as well as the influences of its neighbors in the subsequent time. In order to examine the effectiveness of TEC in identifying vital nodes, we apply it to a toy temporal network (as shown in Fig. 1) to demonstrate its calculation process. Based on the classic SIR spreading model, we also compare the proposed metric on three synthetic temporal networks and a real-world temporal email network with other two centrality measures, i.e., temporal betweenness centrality (TBC) and temporal closeness centrality (TCC) [3]. The experiment results show that our method is able to find more influential spreaders in temporal networks.

The remainder of this paper is organized as follows. Section 2 introduces the TEC and the corresponding ITTCC algorithm. Section 2 also presents a numerical example to show the calculation process of the TEC based on the toy temporal network as shown in Fig. 1. Section 3 evaluates our method based on three synthetic networks and a real-world email network. Section 4 concludes the whole work and highlights the main contribution.

2 Temporal Entropy-Based Centrality and ITTCC Algorithm

2.1 Definitions for Temporal Entropy-Based Centrality

The metric of TEC is defined based on a temporal network model. Incorporating the definitions given from [3], a temporal network G can be defined as an ordered sequence of undirected and unweighted graphs $\{G_1, G_2, ..., G_T\}$ with a node set $V = \{v_1, v_2, ...v_N\}$ and a given time period T, where $G_t = (V, E_t)$ $(t \in T)$. Here, $E_t = \{(v_i, v_j, t)\}$ $(\forall i, \forall j \in V)$ is the edge set with the timestamp t.

The TEC measures the amount of randomness that a node may infect. That is, if a node v_i has a greater number of directly connected neighbors, the node has more possible outcomes, and thus the information of v_i will be larger. In this case, a possible outcome means node v_i infects a specific number of neighbors. In this paper, we define L_i^t as the neighbor set of v_i at snapshot t. L_i^t contains all the directly connected nodes of v_i at snapshot t. Let $|L_i^t|$ be the number of neighbors of v_i at t, the information of v_i, denoted as H_i^t, can be estimated by the following equation:

$$H_i^t = -\sum_{m=1}^{|L_i^t|} \frac{C_{|L_i^t|}^m}{2^{|L_i^t|}} \log_2 \frac{C_{|L_i^t|}^m}{2^{|L_i^t|}} \tag{1}$$

In Eq. 1, $C_{|L_i^t|}^m$ denotes the number of m-combinations from $|L_i^t|$ number of neighbors of v_i, and thus $\frac{C_{|L_i^t|}^m}{2^{|L_i^t|}}$ is the probability that node v_i may infect m number of neighbors. For each timestamped graph, the centrality of a node v_i can be normalized as follows:

$$\tilde{H}_i^t = \frac{H_i^t}{\sum_{j \in V} H_j^t} \tag{2}$$

In the computer virus propagation process, a node's influence at snapshot t is not only determined by the number of its current neighbors, but also affected by its neighbors' influences in the future. Taking into account this aspect, the influence of a node v_i at snapshot t, as denoted as I_i^t in this paper, can be defined as follows:

$$I_i^t = \frac{pI_i^{t+1} + \frac{\sum_{k \in L_i^t} I_k^{t+1}}{\sum_{j \in V} I_j^{t+1}}}{\sum_{q \in V}(pI_q^{t+1} + \frac{\sum_{k \in L_q^t} I_k^{t+1}}{\sum_{j \in V} I_j^{t+1}})} \tag{3}$$

where $p \in [0,1]$ is a parameter to denote how node v_i at $t+1$ determines its influence at time t. Specifically, for node v_i in the last timestamped graph, we assume that its influence is only determined by its infection uncertainty, i.e., $I_i^T = \tilde{H}_i^T$, because we do not know its neighbors' influences in the subsequent snapshot. When $t = 1$, the influence of each node has considered the cumulative effects of its neighbors over the whole time period. That means, we can use the influence of each node at $t = 1$ to measure its importance in computer virus propagation process on a temporal network.

2.2 ITTCC Algorithm

Based on the definitions for TEC, we propose ITTCC algorithm for calculating node influences. The ITTCC algorithm is an recursive algorithm in which the influence of a node v_i at t is calculated based on its current neighbors' influences at $t + 1$. The ITTCC algorithm is given as follows.

Input: The temporal network $G = \{G_1, G_2, ..., G_T\}$
Output: Node influences $\{I_1^1, I_2^1, ..., I_N^1\}$
initialization;
for $t \leftarrow T$ **down to** 1 **do**
    if $t == T$ **then**
        for $v_i \in V$ **do**
            calculate its information using Equ.1;
        end
        for $v_i \in V$ **do**
            calculate its influence:$I_i^T = \frac{H_i^T}{\sum_{j \in V} H_j^T}$;
        end
    else
        for $v_i \in V$ **do**
            calculate its influence using Equ. 3;
        end
    end
end

2.3 A Numerical Example

To demonstrate the estimating process of our proposed method, Table 1 presents the centralities for nodes in the toy temporal network (as shown in Fig. 1) based on TEC. For this calculation, we assume the parameter p is 0.05. As shown in Table 1, the most influential spreaders as identified by the degree centrality on the aggregated static network are nodes 1, 4, and 6 because the three have more neighbors than other nodes. The nodes' centralities are quite different by using the measures of TBC and TCC. TBC and TCC find that node 6 is the most influential node. However, the top influential node as located by TEC is node 3. This is perhaps because node 4, one of the neighbors of node 3 at t_2, has a connection with node 6 at t_3, which has the largest number of neighbors and thus has the highest influence.

3 Experiments and Results

In order to demonstrate the effectiveness of TEC in identifying important nodes, we examine it on three synthetic temporal networks and a real email network. Two well-known metrics, i.e., TBC and TCC, are employed as benchmark methods for comparison. On each network, we first utilize TEC, TBC, and TCC to identify the most influential node, respectively. Then, we set the identified most influential node as the infection source in the corresponding network and run simulations based on the classic SIR model. The spreading of each identified infection source node is quantified by the number of new infected nodes in total. During the simulation, we set the virus spreading rate $\beta = 0.9$, and the recovery rate $\mu = 0.2$. Each simulation runs 100 times to eliminate the bias caused by the random number.

Table 1. Temporal entropy-based centralities versus degree centralities.

NodeID	$TEC = I_{t_1}$	I_{t_2}	I_{t_3}	TBC	TCC	SC
1	0.22	0.14	0.15	0.11	0.60	0.8
2	0.11	0.18	0.07	0.03	0.50	0.6
3	0.25	0.15	0.14	0.09	0.57	0.6
4	0.13	0.23	0.21	0.17	0.58	0.8
5	0.18	0.16	0.15	0	0.48	0.6
6	0.11	0.14	0.27	0.23	0.62	0.8

3.1 Synthetic and SWU-Email Networks

We generate a temporal random (TR) network, a temporal small-world (TSW) network, and a temporal scale-free (TSF) network by repetitively utilizing the Erdös-Rényi random network model [11], the Watts-Strogatz small-world network model [12], and the Barabási-Albert scale-free network model [13], respectively. In this work, each temporal network contains 365 timestamped graphs with 500 vertices. In our research scenario, each timestamped graph represents the interaction structures between individuals in a day.

The email data used in this study is supported by the Southwest University (SWU), China. This dataset includes 167545 emails that sent or received by campus users in January, 2013 (29 days in total). To ensure that the data do indeed reflect the interactions between campus users, we filtered out the emails that were not sent or received from SWU email server. To construct a network based on SWU-email dataset, we used the window size of 24 h (from 0am to 12pm in a day) to preprocess the complete temporal network into 29 timestamped, undirected, and unweighted graphs. That is, campus users are regarded as the nodes in each timestamped graph. If two campus users exchanged at least one email in a specific day, there will be an undirected edge added between the two nodes on the corresponding timestamped graph.

3.2 Results

Figure 2 shows the spread of computer viruses based on SIR model in the TR network, TSW network, TSF network, and SWU-email network respectively. Please note that in the TSF network, the most influencing nodes as identified by the three measures are the same. In this case, we set the second most influencing node that is identified by each measure as the infection source. From Fig. 2, we can see that the total number of infected nodes each day in the case of using TEC to set the infection source is higher than that employing TBC and TCC. This finding is also supported by the inner small figures in Fig. 2, which shows that at the initial few days, the infection source that is recognized by the measure of TEC infects more susceptible nodes. This reveal that our method is more accurate than the TBC and TCC.

In ITTCC algorithm, we have to calculate the entropy for each node in the last snapshot graph, and based which to calculate the influences of nodes

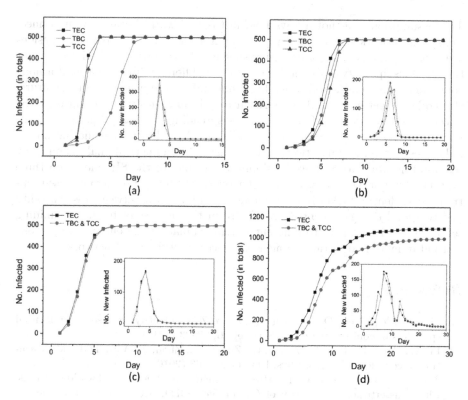

Fig. 2. The accuracy of three centrality measures in evaluating the nodes' spreading influences according to the SIR model in the temporal random network (a), temporal small-world network (b), temporal scale-free network (c), and temporal SWU-email network (d).

backwards along time. Thus the time complexity of the proposed algorithm is the time complexity of computing the node entropy multiplied by the number of nodes in the network, and then multiply the number of snapshots in a temporal network. Therefore, the time complexity of ITTCC algorithm can be represented as $O(g(k) * n * T)$. Here, $g(k)$ is the time complexity of calculate the entropy for a node; k is the largest number of neighbors for a node in the last snapshot graph; and $n = |V|$. The complexity of the fastest method for calculating the combination in Eq. 1 is $O(k)$. Therefore, the time complexity of the proposed algorithm is $O(n^2 * T)$ if $k = n$.

4   Conclusions

Identifying influential nodes is a fundamental problem before any control strategies on the spread of computer viruses. To address this problem, most existing studies only consider the topological structure of a static network.

This assumption does not always hold in the real world because most connections in a network are dynamically changing over time. In this paper, besides the topological structure of each snapshot graph, we further take into account the relationships between nodes' influences at different time. That is, if a node connects to more nodes and which have more influential neighbors in the future, this node will get higher influence. As entropy is an effective way to measure the uncertainty of a node's influence in virus spreading, we has proposed an temporal entropy-based centrality and an ITTCC algorithm for calculating nodes' influences in a temporal network. According to the numerical analysis on a toy temporal network, as well as the simulation results of the SIR model on three synthetic temporal networks and a real network, the temporal entropy-based centrality can identify higher influence nodes than temporal betweenness centrality and temporal closeness centrality. We are in the process of further examining sensitivities with respect to different p, and evaluating the effectiveness of our method in more real world propagation process and temporal networks.

References

1. Zhang, J.X., Chen, D.B., Dong, Q., Zhao, Z.D.: Identifying a set of influential spreaders in complex networks. Sci. Rep. **6**, 27823 (2016)
2. Lü, L., Chen, D., Ren, X., Zhang, Q., Zhang, Y., Zhou, T.: Vital nodes identification in complex networks. Phys. Rev. **650**, 1–63 (2016)
3. Tang, J.K.: Temporal network metrics and their application to real world networks. Ph.D. dissertation, Univeristy of Cambridge (2011). https://www.cl.cam.ac.uk/~cm542/phds/johntang.pdf
4. Takaguchi, T., Yano, Y., Yoshida, Y.: Coverage centralities for temporal networks. Eur. Phys. J. B **89**, 35 (2016)
5. Rocha, L.E.C., Masuda, N.: Random walk centrality for temporal networks. New J. Phys. **16**, 063023 (2014)
6. Estrada, E.: Communicability in temporal networks. Phys. Rev. E **88**, 042811 (2013)
7. Praprotnik, S., Batagelj, V.: Spectral centrality measures in temporal networks. Ars Math. Contemp. **11**, 11 (2015)
8. Taylor, D., Myers, S.A., Clauset, A., Porter, M.A., Mucha, P.J.: Eigenvector-based centrality measures for temporal networks. Multiscale Model. Simul. **15**(1), 537–574 (2017)
9. Alexander, G.N., Raihan, R., Ashwin, K.: On effcient use of entropy centrality for social network analysis and community detection. Soc. Netw. **40**, 154–162 (2014)
10. Shannon, C.E.: A mathematical theory of communication. Bell Syst. Tech. J. **27**(3), 379–423 (1948)
11. Newman, M.E.J., Strogatz, S.H., Watts, D.J.: Random graphs with arbitrary degree distributions and their applications. Phys. Rev. E **64**(2), 026118 (2001)
12. Watts, D.J., Strogatz, S.H.: Collective dynamics of 'small-world' networks. Nature **393**(6684), 440–442 (1998)
13. Barabási, A., Albert, R.: Emergence of scaling in random networks. Science **286**(5439), 509–512 (1999)

TICS: Trusted Industry Control System Based on Hardware Security Module

Yu Qin[✉], Yingjun Zhang, and Wei Feng

Trusted Computing and Information Assurance Laboratory, Institute of Software
Chinese Academy of Science, Beijing, China
{qin_yu,zhangyingjun,fengwei}@tca.iscas.ac.cn

Abstract. The new attack technologies have caused great security threats to industry control system, especially APT attacks such as Stuxnet, BlackEnergy, WannaCrypt. Traditional protection methods fail to defend the hackers attacks on the cyber and physical components of ICS. This paper propose an ICS terminal defense solution in establishing the trustworthiness of with trusted execution environment. The check attestation method is employed to optimize ICS software attestation, and the whitelist mechanism is used to enforce the process execution in terminal. We design and implement a trusted terminal defense system in industry control network. The test results shows that the performance of hardware security module and process enforcement meets the real-time requirements. *abstract* environment.

Keywords: Trusted execution environment · Industry control system · Software attestation · Policy enforcement · Hardware security module

1 Introduction

It becomes the future trend to integrate Internet and Internet of things deeply with industry control system (ICS). It promotes intelligence and information technology of ICS significantly, but it also brings a series of new security challenges. These new attack technologies like Stuxnet, Flame, BlackEnergy cause the serious threats to ICS such as electric power generation, oil refineries, wastewater treatment, and chemical, food automotive production, which lead to serious effluences for national security, economic development and social stability.

1.1 Related Work

In aspect of ICS standards, the most important standards are NIST SP800-82 [1] and IEC 62443 [2]. These standards define generic architecture in ICS, specify

---

Y. Qin—The research presented in this paper is supported by National Natural Science Foundation of China (No. 61402455, No. 61602455).

S. Wen et al. (Eds.): CSS 2017, LNCS 10581, pp. 485–493, 2017.
https://doi.org/10.1007/978-3-319-69471-9_37

the typical threats and vulnerabilities, and propose security guides and evaluation methods. Risk assessment specifications of ICS network had also been released for information security enforcement in China [3]. The various industry has its own specific process, so there are many concrete information security guides for different industries. In other special industry system such as electricity, nuclear energy, there are smart grid security standards NISTIR7628 in North American, security guides RG5.71 for nuclear facilities network.

In aspect of ICS security architecture, the researchers in Darmstadt University of Technology, Germany leverage the hardware security features SMART [4] in embedded system, design and implement the TrustLite [5], TyTAN [6] security architecture to ensure the trusted execution environments of the codes, resistant the malicious codes attack. Furthermore, they summarize the security and privacy challenges in Industrial IoT systems, and give an overall outlook on possible solutions to ICS [7]. The researchers in University of Cagliari, Italy use RFID to identify and authenticate the devices and hosts, and take the active countermeasures to prevent unknown intrusion in industrial network and system [8]. Researchers carry out an in-depth analysis of the communication security solutions for industrial IoT, adopt the technology of datagram transport layer security to realize the network authentication of the terminal devices [9].

In aspect of key security technologies in ICS, these technologies include software attestation, system vulnerability detection, and active defense etc. Software attestation is key technology to prove trust of code execution in embedded devices. Early representative work was Pioneer system developed by CMU. After that, researchers propose many software attestation methods based on the integrity checksum and time limit. The software attestation for peripherals is proposed to verify the integrity of firmware in embedded devices [16], so that the malicious code injection can be detected while peripheral firmware is updated. The Germany researcher proposed a security framework of software attestation in combination of ICS software integrity authentication [17], gave out the attacker model, the definition of security properties, design the concrete the attestation protocol and scheme, and analyze its security in details. CMU researchers presented a key establishment protocol for software attestation (SAKE) [13] for industrial sensor network by using ICE (Indisputable Code Execution) technique. The scheme can build the trust execution environment dynamically on remote sensors, and resistant the attacks during the key establishment. CyberDNA research center in America proposed a secure software attestation method for military robot system [18]. It implemented a secure communication protocol among military robot, remote doctor, the verifier, reducing the time delay of attestation.

1.2 Our Contributions

Against the ICS security threats, we propose a terminal defense solution of trusted execution environment based on a hardware security module. In summary, we make the following contributions in this paper.

- The check-attestation method is utilized to improve monitor performance significantly for ICS terminal environment. It has low communication costs, only one hmac check for periodic attestation. It overcomes the defections of universal attestation against TOCTOU (Time-to-Check, Time-to-Use) attack.
- Trusted execution environment is built based on a hardware security module in trusted computing. The runtime environment is enforced with whitelist policies. So that It assures that only trusted programs can run in ICS terminal, and illegal programs will be prevented from executing.
- Three concurrent threads with tri-state ring buffer are designed to deal with a great quantity of risk alarm reports. While a lot of exceptional events occur in terminal stations, the methods can efficiently handle the heavy loads in the monitor server.
- We implement the trust terminal system in ICS, evaluate the whitelist enforcement, and give out trade-off between performance and security according to testing results.

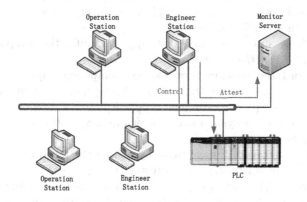

Fig. 1. Industry control system architecture

2   Our Scheme for ICS

2.1   Architecture

The main participants involved in ICS are following parties: the operation station and engineer station ($\mathcal{ST}$ for short), the monitor server $\mathcal{S}$, and $\mathcal{PLC}$ devices as shown in Fig. 1.

- $\mathcal{PLC}$ is the solid-state devices running embedded system that controls industrial equipment and processes, and it is used extensively in almost all industrial systems. While PLCs are control system components used in SCADA and DCS (Distributed Control System), they are often managed by configuration software in operation stations $\mathcal{ST}$.

– ST is the distributed control computers running industrial configuration software. These stations are connected through LAN to complete data collection and process control such as electric power generation, oil refineries.
– S is the control center performs centralized monitoring and control for ST and PLC. ICS manager manually supervises the states of industrial system, responding the emergent operations to the system exceptions.

2.2   Attestation Protocol

The stations ST must attest the current system states to monitor server based on hardware security module M. The measurement agent (MA) collects the integrity of application components, especially the integrity of ICS software, and then attestation service (AS) proves the runtime states of whole station ST with the M's signature on system fingerprint. The attestation protocol is as follows:

1. The monitor server challenge ST with nonce.
2. MA collects n application components with algorithm $CollectInt(App_x)$
   (1) Initialize integrity log as $log := \{\}$, state fingerprint as $\chi := 0$
   (2) FOR each $j = 1$ TO n DO
       (a) MA measures the component App_j computes the component fingerprint $\omega_j := Hash(App_j)$
       (b) Record the measurement log for component App_j, $log := log \cup \{(desc_j, \omega_j\}$, where $desc_j$ is the description information of component, e.g. application name, type, corporation, version.
       (c) Aggregate the system state fingerprints, $\chi := Hash(\omega_j||\chi)$
   (3) MA sends χ, log to AS
3. AS signs the aggregation fingerprint by calling the hardware security module M at the moment t_i. The attestation signature is $s = Sign(sk_M, Hash(\chi||nonce||t_i))$, where (sk_M, pk_M) is private and public key of M.
4. AS responses to monitor server with (s, log) for system state attestation.
5. Monitor server verifies the signature and aggregation fingerprint according to log.

The attestation protocol ensures the ST trusted states, but it will fail if ICS software is attacked. This is $TOCTOU$ (time to check, time to use) problem on state attestation. Periodic attestation can alleviate the weakness, but it is inefficient. As ICS has relatively constant configurations and states, we design the check-attestation method to improve performance. To avoid repeatedly sending a lot of attestation logs, the server only checks the message authentication code of the state. When the HMAC check failed, it will find out ST state had been changed before.

1. ST sends nonce n_t to monitor server S for challenge response.
2. S challenge ST with nonce n_s.
3. ST measures the application components with algorithm $CollectInt(App_x)$, and acquires the fingerprint aggregation $\chi = Hash(\omega_n||Hash(\omega_{n-1}||...Hash(\omega_1||0)))$.

4. ST derives the HMAC key from the system state fingerprint.

$$k = KDF(HMAC - SHA - 256, Hash(pk_M || \chi))$$

It computes $h = HMAC(k, n_t || n_s)$, and send h to S.

5. ST use the former χ_0 in initial attestation to compute HMAC key k, and verifier whether the message h is correct.

The HMAC key is bound with the system state fingerprint χ. Once the station has changed the system states, the monitor server will immediately detect the failure of check-attestation. The Fig. 2 gives the derivation method of attestation key. The check-attestation has some advantages compared with the traditional attestation. Firstly the protocol utilizes the efficient key derivation and message authentication method, so it has the better computation performance. The measurement for all application components is only executed in the check-attestation, and it ensures realtime performance. Secondly the attestation message is very short, only a HMAC. Thirdly it has enough security to resist the intruder, eavesdropper and middleman attacker, because the attestation key is shared between the station and server.

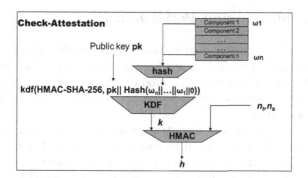

Fig. 2. Key derivation flow of check attestation

2.3   Policy Enforcement

The ICS server makes the security policies to enforce each station by the whitelist mechanism. The Policies can be categorized into four types: system, application, network, USB device.

$policy := \{policy_{sys}, policy_{app}, policy_{net}, policy_{usb}\}$

$policy_{sys} := \{type, corporation, version, hardware, HSM\}$

$policy_{app} := \{name, corporation, version, path, filetype, measurement, desc\}$

$policy_{net} := \{IP, MAC, HSM, domain, right\}$, where $right = \{reject, permit, isolate\}$

$policy_{usb} := \{deviceID, HSM, domain, right\}$, where $right = \{block, approve\}$

The server checks IP address, MAC address and HSM, and determine the network access right; The local reference monitor check the USB device ID, HSM, and enforce the USB devices connection by the policy. The policy of application components is a complex security policy, because the application states are often changed in system runtime. The server must verify the application measurement besides HSM's attestation signature. The measurement agent collects the information on the system, applications, network, USB device, and HSM attests these data to the server. The system manager extracts the critical information to generate the security policy by online attestation. Another way to generate policy is offline submission by the collection tools. Owing to the same configuration for major stations, the manager can make up batch policies. That is, reusing the same policy can reduce the deployment cost for the similar configuration.

The station ST must enforce the whitelists after deploying security policy. The reference monitor is in charge of policy enforcement in the station ST. It decides the security of the current system state according to the policy database. Every process will be intercepted before it is initialized, and the reference monitor checks its image integrity and signature. If something does not comply with the security policy, the system will reject its running.

3   Implementation and Performance

Current mainstream industry control platform is mostly Windows system, so we implement trusted terminal on windows by plugging PCI hardware security module TCM (trusted cryptographic module) enhancing system security. The PCI security module supports trust bootstrap, terminal authentication, system measurement and so on.

Our system consists of two subsystems: trusted terminal and trusted server. The trust terminal is installed on engineering station and operation system. The kernel service in trusted terminal hooks the process creation API NtCreateSection. It utilizes hardware security module to measure the process image, and enforce the process running according to whitelist. The trusted server is deployed on the monitor server, managing the security policy for all terminals, and giving the alarms of terminal security events.

In our solution hardware security module is introduced to enhance the windows security, so we evaluate TCM's cryptographic performance in trusted terminal. The major commands only execute once when system initializes. The software hash algorithm is used at the frequency of 99.3% in windows kernel mode, but its time cost is just 0.9 ms without any performance impact. In our system TCM are utilized to hash the process image, and extend the integrity value to TCM registers. It only cost 31 ms at the frequency of 0.69%. TCM_Sign cost 642 ms at the attestation protocol, but its use frequency is very low at 0.01%. From the performance test, we can conclude that the hardware security module has no influence on real time of industry control system.

The ICS terminal execution environment is so complex that it will trigger the exception or attack while some files are modified. Therefore we evaluate the

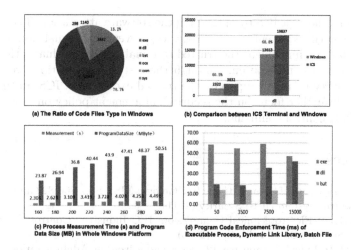

Fig. 3. ICS code test samples and their enforcement performance

executable codes in terminal runtime environment. From code file samples of ICS terminal shown in Fig. 3, we found that the OS has the significant effects to ICS terminal in the aspect of code executions with the ratio of approximately 60.8% in whitelist. The dynamic link library (dll) dominates the code execution with the ratio of approximately 78.7% in whitelist, which is far beyond the execution files (exe) 15.2%. So that it is the important choice that the trade-off between enforcement and efficiency on the dll files.

The reliability is very important index in industry control system, so we conduct the system stress test and periodic test on the process measurement (see Fig. 3(c)). Generally windows system runs approximately 100 processes, less than 150. The time period is chosen in 10 min, and the number of processes ranges from 160 to 300. It is quite complex windows system in 300 processes. In the stress test, the general system in 160 processes costs processes measurement of whole system at 2.306 s, and the complex system of 300 processes costs at 4.491 s. So that our solution can spend 2–4 s to check processes states of the whole windows, and it has no interference to normal operations in the stress and periodic test. Finally the influences are evaluated between whitelist size and enforcement time. In Fig. 3(d) X-axis indicates whitelist size, and Y-axis indicates process enforcement time. The enforcement time of the executable process (exe) is 58.42 ms in whitelist size 50, 46.99 ms in whitelist size 15000. The enforcement of dynamic link library (dll) and batch file (bat) has the similar test result. Consequently the whitelist retrieval does not affect the whitelist enforcement.

4   Outlook and Conclusion

The trusted execution environment is built to ensure the trustworthiness of ICS terminal based on hardware security module in our paper. We propose a check attestation method for ICS by optimizing the software attestation. The whitelist mechanism is utilized to enforce the processes, preventing the malicious code execution. At last we implement the trusted terminal system, evaluates the system performance and configuration. Through the test and evaluation, we give the effective security policy to supervise the trusted execution of ICS. In the future work, we will further focus on the security enforcement policy on network data flow and PLC control commands.

References

1. National Institute of Standards and Technology: NIST Spp. 800-82 Guide to Industrial Control System (ICS) Security (2011)
2. International Electrotechnical Commission: IEC Industrial Control Network and System Security Standardization (2013)
3. National Technical Committee 124 on Standardization Administration of China (SAC/TC124): Evaluation Specification for Security in Industrial Control Network (2010)
4. Defrawy, K.E., Francillon, A., Perito, D., Tsudik, G.: SMART: secure and minimal architecture for (establishing a dynamic) root of trust. In: Network and Distributed System Security Symposium (NDSS). Internet Society (2012)
5. Koeberl, P., Schulz, S., Sadeghi, A.-R., et al.: Trustlite: a security architecture for tiny embedded devices. In: Proceedings of the Ninth European Conference on Computer Systems (EuroSys 2014) (2014)
6. Brasser, F., El Mahjoub, B., Sadeghi, A.-R., et al.: TyTAN: tiny trust anchor for tiny devices. In: Proceedings of the 52nd Annual Design Automation Conference (DAC 2015) (2015)
7. Sadeghi, A.R., Wachsmann, C, Waidner, M.: Security and privacy challenges in industrial internet of things. In: Proceedings of the 52nd Annual Design Automation Conference, vol. 54. ACM (2015)
8. Da Xu, L., He, W., Li, S.: Internet of things in industries: a survey. IEEE Trans. Ind. Inform. **10**(4), 2233–2243 (2014)
9. Keoh, S.L., Kumar, S.S., Tschofenig, H.: Securing the internet of things: a standardization perspective. Internet Things J. IEEE **1**(3), 265–275 (2014)
10. Kil, C., Sezer, E.C., Azab, A.M., Ning, P., Zhang, X.: Remote attestation to dynamic system properties: towards providing complete system integrity evidence. In: IEEE/IFIP DSN (2009)
11. Seshadri, A., Perrig, A., Van Doorn, L., Khosla, P.: SWATT: software-based attestation for embedded devices. In: IEEE S&P (2004)
12. Li, Y., McCune, J.M., Perrig, A.: VIPER: verifying the integrity of PERipherals firmware. In: ACM CCS (2011)
13. Seshadri, A., Luk, M., Perrig, A.: SAKE: software attestation for key establishment in sensor networks. Ad Hoc Netw. **9**(6) (2008)
14. Seshadri, A., Luk, M., Perrig, A., Doorn, L.V., Khosla, P.: SCUBA: secure code update by attestation in sensor networks. In: ACM WiSec (2006)
15. Seshadri, A., Luk, M., Perrig, A., van Doorn, L., Khosla, P.: Using FIRE & ICE for detecting and recovering compromised nodes in sensor networks. Technical report, DTIC Document, December 2004

16. Li, Y., McCune, J.M., Perrig, A.: SBAP: software-based attestation for peripherals. In: Acquisti, A., Smith, S.W., Sadeghi, A.-R. (eds.) Trust 2010. LNCS, vol. 6101, pp. 16–29. Springer, Heidelberg (2010). doi:10.1007/978-3-642-13869-0_2

17. Armknecht, F., Sadeghi, A.R., Schulz, S., et al.: A security framework for the analysis and design of software attestation. In: Proceedings of the 2013 ACM SIGSAC Conference on Computer & Communications Security, pp. 1–12. ACM (2013)

18. Coble, K., Wang, W., Chu, B., et al.: Secure software attestation for military telesurgical robot systems. In: Proceedings of Military Communications Conference (MILCOM 2010), pp. 965–970. IEEE (2010)

On Using Wearable Devices to Steal Your Passwords: A Fuzzy Inference Approach

Chao Shen$^{(\boxtimes)}$, Ziqiang Ren, Yufei Chen, and Zhao Wang

Xi'an Jiaotong University, Xi'an, Shaanxi, China
{cshen,yfchen,zhaowang}@sei.xjtu.edu.cn, chiang1208@sina.com

Abstract. The security of wearable devices user's privacy data has become more and more concerned because of the high accuracy of the embedded sensors. Existing methods of obtaining privacy data often rely on installations of dedicated hardware, or accurate numerical calculation of sensor data, which do not have flexible adaptability. In this paper we utilize a multi-SVM and a KNN classifier using only accelerometer data and fuzzy coordinates to get the privacy data such as password directly with a higher accuracy.

Keywords: Motion sensor · Side-channel attacks · Privacy leakage

1 Introduction

The various functions of wearable devices are stimulating the growth of the market of smart devices [1]. Wearable devices have the function of acquiring user motion and other kinds of data, such as the acceleration of the hand [2]. There has been active study on sensitive information leakage when using both key-based security systems and wearable devices. Traditional attacks rely on either shoulder surfing or hidden cameras [3,4]. Furthermore, Shukla et al. propose a side-channel attack utilizing a camera-based method to recover smartphone lock PINs from the user's spatial-temporal hand dynamics without directly seeing the keypad on screen [5]. Some recent works [6] propose to utilize sensors in smartwatches to infer user's typed words or passwords.

Different from the previous methods, we build a model of the user's password inputting activity, which does not depend on the precise hand movement distance calculation and requires only relatively inaccurate hand movement data to carry out analysis. We use machine learning methods to get the password. The structure and data flow of our system is shown in Fig. 1. The main purpose and contributions of this paper are summarized as follows:

- We present a method of using the built-in motion sensors of the wearable devices such as Microsoft Band to obtain the privacy password entered by the user and analyze its feasibility and applicability.
- We use numerical integration to process the acceleration data, but our classification method such as kNN does not depend on the exact numerical integration and uses some fuzzy, scale-level information that the integral data shows instead.

© Springer International Publishing AG 2017
S. Wen et al. (Eds.): CSS 2017, LNCS 10581, pp. 494–502, 2017.
https://doi.org/10.1007/978-3-319-69471-9_38

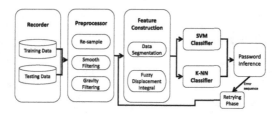

Fig. 1. System architecture.

2   Related Work

Recent studies show that embedded sensors on mobile devices, such as accelerometers and touch screens, can capture user's motion and leak their sensitive information [8–10]. And wearable devices, such as smartwatches and fitness bands, extend the sensing capability to limbs and enable many useful applications [11–13]. The studies above show that the latest sensors have reliable accuracy, which encourages us to infer 6-digits passwords based on the sensor data.

Toward this end, there are some preliminary research work. Researchers show that it is possible to recognize users' keystrokes by using acoustic approaches. Berger et al. [15] demonstrate that by using linguistic models and recorded typing sound on a keyboard, an attacker can successfully reconstruct the typed words. Zhu et al. [16] present a context-free and geometry-based approach to recover keystrokes by using multiple smartphones to record acoustic emanations from the keystrokes.

The most related work to ours are two current studies, which analyze the leak of users' passwords or typed words from smartwatches [6,20]. Liu et al. [6] apply sensors in a smartwatch to infer users' inputs on a keyboard or POS terminal by utilizing machine-learning based techniques. Wang et al. [20] develop a distance estimation and direction derivation schemes that capture the fine-grained hand movements at mm-level precision, and their method is training-free.

3   Attack Model and Feasibility Study

Acceleration sensor can be read out as three vertical acceleration of x, y, z axis. To some extent these data is hinted by the user when entering the password so we can get the possible passwords according the order of keys' inputting.

3.1   Attack Model

We assume a situation in which the criminals can determine the type of the device worn by the user. Because wearable devices often need to pair with the smart phones, they often transmit sensor data to the smart phones through the bluetooth. Bluetooth transmission has possibility of privacy data leakage, criminals

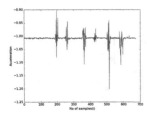

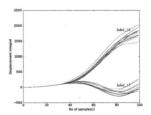

Fig. 2. The vibration in Z-axis when pressing keys.

Fig. 3. Success percentage of the top-k candidates.

can gain access to sensor information through this vulnerability. Because passwords are input in different scenarios, the outline of the keyboard and the relative location of each key are different, we take the following two scenarios.

ATM keyboard: ATM machines usually use metal keyboard with the purpose of preventing criminals using the thermal imaging camera to get the user's password and other privacy data [16]. However, the high-performance sensors of smart wear devices make it possible to crack passwords entered through the ATM machine keyboard.

General numeric keypad: In the more general cases, the user maybe use POS machines or other numeric keypad for password input in the supermarket and other similar places.

3.2 Feasibility Study

When accessing a key-based security system, passwords are entered one by one by keystrokes. In this process, the user's wrist maintain the status of wearing the devices. The stroke of a particular key is divided into three states: press, release, and movement between the keys from the previous key to the current one press.

See Fig. 2, the z-direction acceleration output of the acceleration sensor produces a significant jitter during the key depression and release, since the acceleration does not rise and fall strictly during the key press, there exists a shock. During the hand movement above the keys, the change of the acceleration in the x and y directions is more obvious than the z direction one, so we use this clue to get the sequence of user's input.

In the feasibility, one challenge is the credibility of the acceleration integral. Due to the limitation of the accuracy of the acceleration sensor, the displacement after two integrals is often inaccurate in numerical terms. We set up the following experiment, moving from 0 to 2 for 10 times, moving from 2 to 0 for 10 times. The displacement data were obtained by integrating the acceleration data in these total 20 times of motion. Obviously, we find that based on the inaccurate value of the displacement integral, it can still reflect the different motion direction and scale disparity. As shown in Fig. 3. As the time (number of samples) increases, the two sets of different displacements (0 to 2, 2 to 0) eventually converge to different values, therefore the two displacements can be distinguished by some certain methods.

4   Wristband-Sensor Behaviour Analysis

We model the displacements of movements in 2-dimensional Cartesian coordinate system and set the center of each key as the true point on the coordinate system. We model a keyboard with 10 numeric keys and an 'Enter' key, with a motion vector between each two keys. For vectors (such as 1 to 2, and 5 to 6 vectors, which are both (0, 1) vectors on the x and y coordinate axes, we set the same vector with the same label, and similarly, different motion vectors are labeled with different labels. Finally we get 31 labels including cases like 2 to 2 where there is no significant motion in the x and y axes.

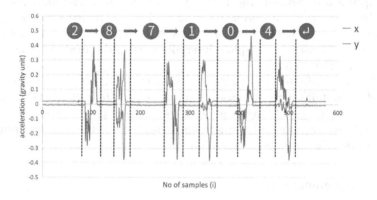

Fig. 4. Result of segmentation when user inputs '287104' as password.

4.1   Data Pre-processing

We use the following two methods to remove the effects of gravity in the original acceleration data and improve the signal-to-noise ratio (SNR).

Gravity Filtering. In general, the sensor data obtained directly from the movement of the wearable devices contains certain noise, and the Microsoft Band accelerometer data contains the component of gravity acceleration. Under normal circumstances, this kind of component will be linearly superimposed on the z-axis vertically to the ground, but in general, when the user is in the process of using Microsoft Band, a series of wrist movement makes the z-axis difficult to maintain the statue of keeping vertical to the ground. In this way, the acceleration component will produce components in the x-axis and y-axis, so we need to use a low-pass filter to remove the impact of gravity acceleration.

Here we employ the Kalman filter method, which is a recursive way of estimating optimal value of state variables, to obtain an unbiased estimated value of motion-sensor data (that refers to as linear acceleration $linear\_acc[n]$, and for x-axis, that is $linear\_acc_x[n]$). The acceleration due to band orientation with respect to gravity $g[n]$, and for x-axis, that is $g_x[n]$. Specifically, the gravitational component embedded in raw sensor data can be reduced in each of three axes (X, Y, Z) of the sensors (i.e., accelerometer and gyroscope sensors) by following steps [15]:

step1:

$$g_x[n] = \alpha * g_x[n] + (1 - \alpha) * acc_x[n] \tag{1}$$

step2:

$$linear\_acc_x[n] = acc_x[n] - g_x[n] \tag{2}$$

Re-sampling and Smoothing Filtering. The maximum sampling frequency of the Microsoft Band Accelerometer is 62 Hz, but this frequency does not capture enough sample points when user enters password quickly. Therefore, we apply the widely used cubic spline interpolations in the related studies to re-sample the acceleration data.

Because of the limited accuracy of the acceleration sensor, the acquired acceleration data contains inherent noise. Also there exists slight shock when the user press keys and makes additional noise. In order to improve the signal-to-noise ratio (SNR) of the acquired acceleration data, we use the wavelet transform method to denoise the acceleration data.

4.2   Data Segmentation

Since the process of user's password input is continuous, we need to segment the acceleration data sequence to extract data fragments. Here, we propose a segmentation method in which the z-axis acceleration data does not participate in the calculation of short-term energy. The mathematical expression for calculating the short term energy and the energy per frame is as follows:

$$E\_xy[i] = linear\_acc_x[i]^2 + linear\_acc_y[i]^2 \tag{3}$$

$$A\_xy[i] = \sum_{n=i}^{i+10} E\_xy[n] \tag{4}$$

We first frame the acceleration data by windowing the original data and calculate the short-term energy according to the formulas listed above. For the sum of the short-term energies in each frame, based on the empirically determined threshold, Frames above this threshold have valid acceleration data. In this way we get the acceleration of the segmentation. As shown in Fig. 4. For each segment of acceleration we obtain its quadratic integration, and get the approximate motion displacement.

4.3   Classify Analysis

In this section, we have obtained the approximate displacement which has obvious group-difference according to our experiment, so it is possible to apply classifiers. Figure 5 shows the distribution of the motion vectors (whose labels are from 11 to 17). It can be found that the kNN and the multi-SVM can be used ideally.

kNN (k-nearest neighbor): The basic idea of kNN is that in the distance domain, if the most k neighbors of a sample belong to a certain category, the samples belong to this category. In our work, the displacement data obtained by integrating the acceleration data twice are mapped in the two-dimensional Cartesian coordinate system, and our experiments show that the two same motion vectors are similar in distance after mapping, so we apply kNN. We set k as 6 in our experiments empirically.

Multi-SVM (multi-class support vector machine): Ordinary binary support vector machine (SVM) method maps the training samples into high dimensional space for classification. In our work, since the objects of classification are more than 30 different label vectors, we use a multi-class support vector machine method: libsvm. Considering the non-linearity of multi-classification, we choose Radial Basis Function (RBF) as the kernel function of libsvm method.

4.4   Password Inference

From the previous analysis we can see that for each particular movement, there is a label corresponding to it. For each successive password input, the user must press the key 'Enter' at the end of inputting, so we use this as the starting point for the backward inference.

As the user's hand moves from one key to another, its speed and sensitivity affect the peak value of the acceleration. Although mathematically, as long as the actual hand movement distance is constant, the change in acceleration waveform does not affect the shift of the position value. However, after several tests, we found that there is a large deviation due to the inaccuracy of the acceleration data. For example, from key '8' to key '5', the corresponding motion vector is (1, 0), corresponding to label '6'. However, if the movement of the user's wrist has a large fluctuation or abrupt acceleration, the displacement data obtained by the actual integration may be closer to (2, 0), which is corresponding to the label '16' in dead. With this in mind, we are doing clustering analysis of labels. A new method is used to produce the deviation between the possible clustering result and the ground-truth.

5   Experimental and Evaluation Methodology

5.1   Devices Chosen and Data Collection

As the password input device, we use the Lenovo ThinkPad 33L3225 numeric keypad which has 17 keys. We only consider the keys from 0 to 9, as well as the

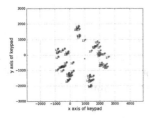

Fig. 5. Classify diagram.   **Fig. 6.** ATM and numeric keypad.

'Enter' key, a total of 11. Also we choose Microsoft Band as wearable device. Microsoft Band has a higher sensor accuracy than its similar devices. In the data acquisition phase, the acceleration sensor sampling rate is set to the 62 Hz.

We chose 200 testers, the gender, age, wrist width and other features of the which are random. We asked each tester to enter 10 groups of 6-bit password on the keypad randomly and click the 'Enter' key to confirm the input. In the experiment we also use Android smart phone Red Mi 3S, which has been installed an APP named Microsoft Health Applications. When the user inputting passwords, acceleration data will be transmitted to the phone through the Bluetooth application. We use Microsoft's official APIs to capture and store acceleration data from Microsoft Health Applications, which can also be sent over the Internet to our computers. In this way, we can read out the acceleration data we care about (Fig. 6).

5.2   Evaluation Methodology

Similar to the paper [20], we only use the following two evaluation indicators.

- **Top-k Success Rate.** Our method can return multiple top candidates of key entry sequence in an ascending order of the accumulated Euclidean distance. We define that the inference algorithm is a Top-k Success Hit if the first k candidates of key-entry sequence returned from our algorithm contain the target user's key-entry sequence. We further define the Top-k Success Rate as the ratio of the number of Top-k Success Hits over the total number of experimental runs when applying key-entry sequence inference to recover the target user's password sequence.

- **Tries Until Success.** The adversary has the chance to try out each key sequence returned in the candidate list to recover the target user's password sequence. We define the Number of Tries Until Success as the number of candidate key-entry sequence the adversary has tried (starting from the candidate with the smallest accumulated Euclidean distance) until he/she breaks the key-based security system, suggesting a success recovery of the target user's password sequence. Thus, the Number of Trails Until Success indicates the possible efforts that an attack needs to take to break the key-based security system.

6   Performance of Backward PIN-Sequence Inference

The results are shown in Fig. 8. For a typical 6-digit password entry on the ATM machine's keyboard, the correct rate of the top-1 option is approximately 78%, considering that most key based security systems allow a limited number of entries, for the top-3 option, The accuracy rate is more than 84%. For normal numeric keypad, the distance of key pressing down to the lowest position is larger than the general ATM machine keyboard, resulting in a larger magnitude of the acceleration numerical vibration, therefore the accuracy of the password inference is slightly lower, and the top-1 and top-3 options are 72% and 82% correct, respectively. The number of retries before the input is correct for the ATM machine keyboard and ordinary numeric keypad also have nuances, as shown in Fig. 7.

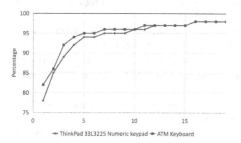

Fig. 7. Success percentage of the increasing try times.

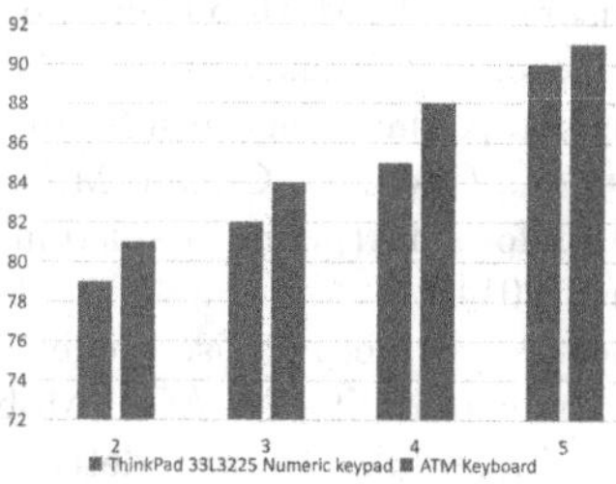

Fig. 8. Success percentage of the top-k candidates.

7   Conclusion

In this paper, we establish a hardware-based sensor system and a software-based fuzzy password inference system using on machine learning. The results show that our system is reasonable and feasible, and has a high accuracy rate. Based on the consideration of privacy security, a suggestion for the future development of wearable devices is that to make it more difficult to obtain the original sensor data in the process of data transmission and readout. We hope that our work will contribute to the improvement of the privacy of intelligent devices.

Acknowledgments. This work was supported in part by the National Natural Science Foundation of China under Grant 61403301 and Grant 61773310, in part by the China Postdoctoral Science Foundation under Grant 2014M560783 and Grant 2015T81032, in part by the Natural Science Foundation of Shaanxi Province under Grant 2015JQ6216, and in part by the Fundamental Research Funds for the Central Universities under Grant xjj2015115.

References

1. Worldwide smartwatch market will see modest growth in 2016 before swelling to 50 million units in 2020, according to IDC. https://www.idc.com/getdoc.jsp?containerId=prUS41736916

2. Live healthier and achieve more: this is Microsoft Band. https://www.microsoft.com/microsoft-band/en-us

3. Balzarotti, D., Cova, M., Vigna, G.: Clearshot: eavesdropping on keyboard input from video. In: IEEE S&P, pp. 170–183 (2008)

4. Maggi, F., et al.: A fast eavesdropping attack against touchscreens. In: IEEE IAS, pp. 320–325 (2011)

5. Shukla, D., Kumar, R., Serwadda, A., Phoha, V.V.: Beware, your hands reveal your secrets! In: ACM CCS, pp. 904–917 (2014)

6. Liu, X., Zhou, Z., Diao, W., Li, Z., Zhang, K.: When good becomes evil: keystroke inference with smartwatch. In: ACM CCS, pp. 1273–1285 (2015)

7. Wang, H., Lai, T.T.-T., Choudhury, R.R.: Mole: motion leaks through smartwatch sensors. In: ACM MobiCom, pp. 155–166 (2015)

8. Miluzzo, E., Varshavsky, A., Balakrishnan, S., Choudhury, R.R.: Tapprints: your finger taps have fingerprints. In: ACM MobiSys, pp. 323–336 (2012)

9. Ren, Y., Chen, Y., Chuah, M.C., Yang, J.: User verification leveraging gait recognition for smartphone enabled mobile healthcare systems. IEEE Trans. Mob. Comput. (2014)

10. Sherman, M., et al.: User-generated free-form gestures for authentication: security and memorability. In: ACM MobiSys, pp. 176–189 (2014)

11. Liu, L., et al.: Toward detection of unsafe driving with wearables. In: ACM WearSys, pp. 27–32 (2015)

12. Parate, A., et al.: RisQ: recognizing smoking gestures with inertial sensors on a wristband. In: ACM MobiSys, pp. 149–161 (2014)

13. Xu, Z., Bai, K., Zhu, S.: Taplogger: inferring user inputs on smartphone touchscreens using on-board motion sensors. In: ACM WISEC, pp. 113–124 (2012)

14. Friedman, N., Rowe, J.B., Reinkensmeyer, D., Bschman, M.: The manumeter: a wearable device for monitoring daily use of the wrist and fingers. IEEE J Biomed. Health Inform. **18**(6), 1804–1812 (2014)

15. Using the accelerometer: isolate the force of gravity with the low-pass filter and remove the gravity contribution with the high-pass filter. https://developer.android.com/guide/topics/sensors/sensor_motion.html

16. Researchers show ATM theft by thermal imaging. https://phys.org/news/2011-09-atm-theft-thermal-imaging.html

17. Wang, J., Zhao, K., Zhang, X., Peng, C.: Ubiquitous keyboard for small mobile devices: harnessing multipath fading for fine-grained keystroke localization. In: ACM Mobysis, pp. 14–27 (2014)

18. Liu, J., Wang, Y., Kar, K., Chen, Y., Yang, J., Gruteser, M.: Snooping keystrokes with mm-level audio ranging on a single phone. In: ACM Mobicom (2015)

19. Marquardt, P., Verma, A., Carter, H., Traynor, P.: (sp)iphone: decoding vibrations from nearby keyboards using mobile phone accelerometers. In: ACM CCS, pp. 551–562 (2011)

20. Wang, C., Guo, X., Wang, Y., Chen, Y., Liu, B.: Friend or foe? Your wearable devices reveal your personal pin. In: The ACM, pp. 189–200 (2016)

An Efficient Privacy-Preserving Palmprint Authentication Scheme Based on Homomorphic Encryption

Huiyong Wang[1], Yong Ding[2(✉)], Shijie Tang[3], and Jilin Wang[4]

[1] School of Mathematics and Computing Science, Guilin University of Electronics Technology, Guilin, Guangxi, People's Republic of China
why6082015@gmail.com
[2] Guangxi Key Laboratory of Cryptography and Information Security, School of Computer Science and Information Security, Guilin University of Electronics Technology, Guilin, Guangxi, People's Republic of China
stone_dingy@126.com
[3] Guangxi Key Laboratory of Intelligent Integrated Automation, School of Electronic Engineering and Automation, Guilin University of Electronics Technology, Guilin, Guangxi, People's Republic of China
[4] Information School, Zhejiang University of Finance and Economics, Hangzhou, Zhejiang, People's Republic of China

Abstract. In order to provide protection for biometric features in palmprint authentication, we propose a palmprint authentication scheme suitable for personal environments with privacy-preserving trait using the ElGamal encryption scheme which is mulplicatively homomorphic. To achieve faster running speed, we use binary vectors to represent palmprint features and use Hamming distance to indicate the similarity of different feature vectors. We give security and performance analysis, and use Matlab to implement some key modules of the proposed scheme. Theoretical analysis and experimental results show that the proposed scheme achieves confidential computations of palmprint feature vectors. The recognition accuracy can meet practical requirements and the overall performance transcends existing relative schemes.

Keywords: Palmprint · Privacy-preserving · Authentication · ElGamal

1 Introduction

With the continuous development of Internet and information technology, biometric identifications are increasingly needed in peoples' lives, such as the company face swiping systems, fingerprint authentication systems for mobile phones, and the bank's identification systems. However, biometrics are unchangeable, which means one leakage might bring permanent and irrevocable trouble for the owner. In the mean time, most of the current biometric identification systems transmit and store user's biometrics in plain-texts, which poses a significant risk

S. Wen et al. (Eds.): CSS 2017, LNCS 10581, pp. 503–512, 2017.
https://doi.org/10.1007/978-3-319-69471-9_39

to user's biometric security. Therefore, it is an urgent need to construct biometric systems with privacy-preserving trait.

Ratha [1] and Jain et al. [2] argue that the key to secure biometric systems is the safety of bioinformatics templates. They divide traditional protection methods for biometric templates into two categories: feature transformation methods and cryptographic methods.

In recent years, homomorphic encryption (HE) has shown great potential in biometric authentication. The idea of fully homomorphic encryption (FHE) was to construct encryption schemes with the capability of computing arbitrary functions confidentially, which is in line with the need for privacy protection in cloud computing environments. Partial homomorphic (or homomorphic) encryption schemes allow only one homomorphic operation (The BGN scheme [3] permits homomorphic additions and once homomorphic multiplication), and thus have limited applications. But in some special scenes, some homomorphic schemes can also play a very good role.

Among the existing biometric methods, palmprint authentication has several obvious advantages: palm area is larger than the fingerprint, which may provide a greater amount of information, so that the authentication accuracy is more likely to improve; palmprint acquisition is generally non-contact, so that the original palmprints are less likely to be left on the equipment; palmprint acquisition equipments ares generally much cheaper than iris equipments, and so on. Therefore, we use palmprint as a carrier to construct privacy-preserving biometric schemes.

1.1 Related Work

In June 2014, Luo [4] studied the existing biometric-based remote identification schemes and proposed a new identity authentication scheme based on the RSA scheme [5] as well as a prototype system based on palmprint authentication. The system includes a client, a server, and a trusted third-party certificate authority (TA). This framework has been adopted by multiple schemes [6,7] and has been extended to applications of face [8] and iris [9] authentication.

In 2015, Qu [10] designed and implemented an ElGamal [11] based palmprint authentication system. In communications between the client and the server, one-way hash functions are used to verify the legitimacy of both identities. The communication contents are encoded using the ElGamal scheme or the AES. However, as each stage of the program requires multiple communications between the client and the server, the computational and communicational complexity are high.

In 2016, Im et al. [12] constructed a simple palmprint authentication scheme, which consists of three entities: user, a portable device (with a camera, such as a mobile phone) and a server. The user uses the mobile phone to capture a palm print image and get the region of interest (ROI) and the palmprint feature vector. Then the feature vector is encrypted using the Paillier system [13]. In calculating the Euclidean distance between two palmprint feature vectors, a transformation method proposed by Catalano et al. [14] was used, which can convert a scheme with linear homomorphic property (such as ElGamal, Paillier, and GM [15], etc.) into a scheme that supports homomorphic operations of degree 2 polynomials. But as the overall efficiency of the program and the recognition accuracy is low, the practicality is poor.

1.2 Contribution

We propose a palmprint authentication scheme for personal environments based on the above work, which is suitable for protecting equipments in distributed networks [16], particularly portable devices. We use Matlab to implement several key algorithms for the proposed scheme, including "original image processing", "ROI area extraction", "palmprint feature vector generation, dimensionality and encryption", "ciphertext multiplication", and "Seeking Hamming distance". The ElGamal scheme is used to encrypt palmprint feature vectors and the Hamming distance is used to measure the similarity of different palmprint feature vectors. Theoretical analysis and experimental results show that the proposed scheme can realize private matching of palmprint feature vectors and the overall performance is an enable to practical needs.

1.3 Organization

The rest of this paper is organized as follows. Section 2 introduces some basic notations and concepts essential for later discussion. In Sect. 3, we give the main construction of the palmprint authentication scheme. Security analysis and performance comparisons with existing relative schemes are given in Sects. 4, and 5 is devoted to implementations of some key algorithms and a palmprint recognition framework. Conclusions and prospects are given in Sect. 6.

2   Preliminaries

In this section, we describe some concepts for later discussion.

2.1   The ElGamal System

ElGamal is an cryptography system that supports unlimited homomorphic multiplications, which is the trait we will use for our main constructions.

> **Setup**: Let p be a big prime; $g < p$ be a generator of a circular group Z_p^*.
> **KeyGen**: Choose randomly a number $x \in Z_p^*$, calculate $y = g^x mod p$, then output the public key $pk = \{y, g, p\}$ and the secret key x.
> **Encryption**: For a message m, choose a random number k co-prime with $p - 1$, compute and output $c = E(m) = (a, b) = (g^k mod p, my^k mod p)$ as the ciphertext.
> **Decryption**: For a ciphertext $c = (g^k mod p, y^k m mod p)$, compute and output $b(a^x)^{-1} mod p$ as the plaintext.

2.2 Palm Identification

1. Main structure

A palmprint authentication system consists of four modules: registration, authentication, data update and data revocation. It typically includes a client and a server-side. The client is responsible for collecting the user's palmprint information, preprocessing the data, extracting the ROI and the eigenvector, and sending it to the server. The server is responsible for storing data and adding, comparing, updating, and deleting data as required. Detailed contents can refer to [17].

2. Image preprocessing and ROI extraction

The extraction of ROI is the most important part in image preprocessing, for the quality of ROI is critical for the final authentication accuracy. There are many ways to pre-process palmprint images, while since we focus on encrypted comparisons, we follow a usual way to extract palm ROI, which mainly includes denoising, location of key points, translation and rotation corrections.

3. The Random Projection reduction method

There are many ways for data reduction, such as the PTA [18], LDA [19], and so on. In 2001, Bingham et al. [20] proposed the Random Projection (RP) method. The projection matrix for the RP method does not need to be changed with samples, which makes RP more generalized and efficient than other methods. Achlioptas [21] shows that if the elements of the projection matrix U satisfies the following conditions, the RP method will be made more efficient:

$$U_{i,j} = \begin{cases} 1 & p = \frac{1}{6} \\ 0 & p = \frac{2}{3} \\ -1 & p = \frac{1}{6} \end{cases} \tag{1}$$

The basic steps of dimension reduction of palmprint ROI using this method are as follows:

First, the random projection matrix U of dimension $m \times n^2$ is constructed. Then, the ROI is adjusted to $n \times n$ size, and the gray image is transformed into a vector x of n^2 dimension. Finally, the eigenvector is computed by $y = Ux^T$.

3 Main Construction

To facilitate narration, we first describe several algorithm modules.

3.1 Some Key Modules

1. Palmprint acquisition and feature extraction module (CVRM):

Step1: Generate and store a $m \times n^2$ projection matrix U.
Step2: The user i inputs his palmprint P_i by a palmprint acquisition device.

Step3: Preprocess the original palm picture and extract the region of interest ROI_i from P_i and saves it as a $n \times n$ matrix, then turn the matrix into a n^2 dimensional vector α_i by sequencialization.

Step4: Compute $y_i = U\alpha_i^T$ to get a palmprint feature vector y_i of dimension m, where U is the projection matrix in [20].

Step5: If $y_{ij} > 0$, set it to 1; otherwise, set it to 0, then we get a binary palmprint feature vector y_i, where y_{ij} is the j'th element of y_i.

2. Encryption module (ENCM): Let $\boldsymbol{\omega} = \{\omega_1, \omega_2, \ldots, \omega_k\}$ be a binary feature vector of dimension k.

Step1: Choose two different prime numbers $a, b \in \mathbb{Z}_p^*$, where p is the prime modulus used in the ElGamal scheme.

Step2: Set $\boldsymbol{\omega}' = \{\omega_1', \omega_2', \ldots, \omega_k'\}$, where $\omega_i' = \begin{cases} a, \ if \ \omega_i = 1 \\ b, \ if \ \omega_i = 0 \end{cases}$.

Step3: Encrypt $\boldsymbol{\omega}': Enc(pk, \boldsymbol{\omega}') = (Enc(pk, \omega_1'), Enc(pk, \omega_2'), \ldots, Enc(pk, \omega_k'))$.

Step4: Compute $y_i = U\alpha_i^T$ to get a m dimensional feature vector y_i.

3. Ciphertext multiplication module (CMM): Let

$$Enc(pk, \boldsymbol{\omega}') = (Enc(pk, \omega_1'), Enc(pk, \omega_2'), \ldots, Enc(pk, \omega_k'))$$

be the encryption of a k dimensional binary feature vector $\boldsymbol{\omega} = \{\omega_1, \omega_2, \ldots, \omega_k\}$, and let

$$Enc(pk, \boldsymbol{\varphi}') = (Enc(pk, \varphi_1'), Enc(pk, \varphi_2') \ldots, Enc(pk, \varphi_k'))$$

be the encryption of $\boldsymbol{\varphi} = \{\varphi_1, \varphi_2, \ldots, \varphi_k\}$.

Step1: The server computes

$$\begin{aligned} &Enc(pk, \boldsymbol{\omega}') \otimes Enc(pk, \boldsymbol{\varphi}') \\ =&(Enc(pk, \omega_1') \otimes Enc(pk, \varphi_1'), \ldots, Enc(pk, \omega_k') \otimes Enc(pk, \varphi_k')) \\ =&(Enc(pk, \omega_1'\varphi_1'), Enc(pk, \omega_2'\varphi_2'), \ldots, Enc(pk, \omega_k'\varphi_k')) \end{aligned}$$

4. Hamming distance calculation module (from encrypted vectors) (HDM)

Step1: User or TA uses sk to decrypt $Enc(pk, \boldsymbol{\omega}') \otimes Enc(pk, \boldsymbol{\varphi}')$, and sends the result

$$\left(\omega_1'\varphi_1', \omega_2'\varphi_2', \ldots, \omega_k'\varphi_k'\right)$$

to the server.

Step2: The server computes $\omega_i'\varphi_i' \ mod \ ab$ to get a vector $\boldsymbol{\alpha} = (\alpha_1, \alpha_2, \cdots, \alpha_k)$, where

$$\begin{cases} \alpha_i = 0 \ if \ \omega_i'\varphi_i' \ mod \ (ab) = 0 \\ \alpha_i = 1 \ if \ \omega_i'\varphi_i' \ mod \ (ab) \neq 0 \end{cases}$$

Step3: The server records the number of zeros in $\boldsymbol{\alpha}$ as σ, and computes the Hamming distance $d_h = \sigma/k$.

Step4: The server compares d_h and a threshold τ. If $d_h < \tau$, the authentication succeeds; otherwise, it fails.

3.2   A Palmprint Authentication Scheme

We now give a palmprint authentication scheme for private environments similiar to that described in [12], where palmprints are encrypted and stored in remote severs, but no calculations are needed between palmprints belonging to different users. Its typical usage is to protect portable devices, such as mobile phones. In the process, the server is only responsible for the storage of encrypted palmprint templates, which means that keys used for encryption and decryption can be generated and stored by the user. The general process is as follows.

1. The registration phase

Step1: The portable device P (uses a program, such as an App) generates a public key pk and a corresponding secret key sk and store them in a secure manner, for example, in an encrypted area of its storage.

Step2: P calls the palmprint acquisition and feature vector extraction module CVRM to get the palmprint eigenvector y.

Step3: P calls the encryption module ENCM to encrypt y and get the ciphertext $Enc(pk, \omega')$ and sends it to the server.

2. The authentication phase

Step1: P calls the palmprint acquisition and feature vector extraction module CVRM to get the palmprint eigenvector x.

Step2: P calls the encryption module ENCM to encrypt x and get the ciphertext $Enc(pk, \varphi')$ and sends it to the server.

Step3: The server finds the palmprint template y^* belonging to the user according to the ID of the portable device or the user, then calls the ciphertext multiplication module CMM to compute $Enc(pk, \omega') \otimes Enc(pk, \varphi')$.

Step4: The server returns $Enc(pk, \omega') \otimes Enc(pk, \varphi')$ to P.

Step5: P calls the Hamming distance calculation module HDM to get the Hamming distance d_h and the verification result.

4   Security and Performance Analysis

4.1   Security

A typical use for the proposed palmprint authentication scheme is to protect portable devices in a personal environment. That is, if the scheme is integrated into the mobile phone or other portable devices hardware, the owners' palmprint can not be found in the device in the case of device theft, so that the illegal owner can not get access to the device. While the palmprint template stored in the cloud is also encrypted so that it can not be stolen by external and internal attacks from the server. As keys for our scheme are stored in the device, they are possible to be cracked. This problem can be alleviated by saving the keys in the protected area of the devices' storage.

The scheme assumes that the server is semi-honest, that is, it will faithfully perform the specified operations, but may collect information for guessing the user's palmprint data. In addition, in order to achieve better speed, the above programs didn't consider the confidentiality issue of communications among the user and the server. For example, before the communication of the user and the server, we can use one-way hash functions and random numbers to verify the legitimacy of data from both sides [22].

4.2 Performance

Theoretically, the overall performance of the proposed scheme is significantly higher than that of the literature [10,12] for we use Hamming distance as the metric to evaluate the similarity of vectors. Table 1 lists the main advantages and disadvantages of the two schemes compared to [10,12].

Table 1. Characteristics of the proposed scheme compared to existing schemes

Schemes	Advantages	Typical use	Major security risk
Our scheme	Easy to implement	Portable devices	Key theft
[10]	Better security	Bank authentication	Authentication only
[12]	Easy to implement	Portable devices	Key theft; low efficiency

5 Implementation

We now implement some of the key steps for the proposed scheme, which includes "original image processing", "ROI region extraction", "palmprint feature vector generation, dimensionality reduction and encryption", "ciphertext multiplication", and "Hamming distance calculation", and so on. On the basis of these algorithms, it is easy to realize the whole scheme.

We use windows 10 and Matlab 2016 as the software platform, and choose the Hong Kong Polytechnic University palmprint library (a total of 600 palmprint images belonging to 100 people) as a test object. To facilitate operations, all palmprint images are firstly assigned into 100 folders according to their identities in the eigenvector extraction phase, where each folder contains 6 pictures.

Subsequently, all ROI pictures are processed using the random projection method (Sect. 2.2), and the eigenvectors of each ROI are extracted. The projection matrix is of size 100×16384, and is constructed by 1. The palmprint vectors after dimension reduction is of 100 dimension. Then we let $y_{ij} = \begin{cases} 1 & y_{ij} \geq 0 \\ 0 & y_{ij} < 0 \end{cases}$, and get the i'th feature vector $y = (y_{i1}, y_{i2}, \cdots, y_{i,100})$, where j is an index of the weight in the vector.

Before encryption, we first compare the binary eigenvectors in the plaintext form and find that the Hamming distances between the eigenvectors belonging to the same person are less than 0.1, while for different persons, they are all above 0.3. Thus, by setting a threshold $\tau = 0.2$, the accuracy of the (plaintext) authentication can be made satisfactory for practical needs. In the experiment, only 2 out 600 matches fail for improper ROIs, which means the authentication accuracy is above 98%.

Then, we let $y_{ij} = \begin{cases} 3, & if \ y_{ij} = 1 \\ 5, & if \ y_{ij} = 0 \end{cases}$, and use the ElGamal scheme to encrypt the feature vectors.

We first generate the private key and public key for ElGamal. In the experiment, we use the private key $sk = 9$, the prime $p = 19$, and the generator $a = 2$. So we get the public key $y = 2^9 mod 19 = 18$. According to the ciphertext multiplication CMM and the Hamming distance calculation module HDM, some of the comparison results (Palmprints of the first two persons) are shown in Fig. 1.

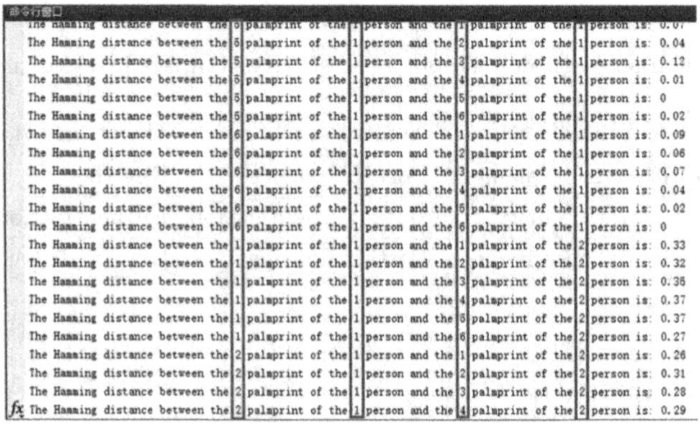

Fig. 1. Part of the comparison results

As can be seen from Fig. 1, the authentication results for the first two persons are basically consistent with the results of non-encrypted comparisons. As long as the threshold τ is set to be 0.2, the accuracy of the identification process is above 95%. This adequately validates the effectiveness of the proposed algorithms.

6 Conclusions and Prospects

We have designed and implemented a palmprint authentication scheme for private uses. The feasibility of the proposed scheme is verified by simulations of the key modules.

Although the proposed scheme is applicable in specific scenes, there are still weaknesses, such as security risks introduced by keys. Designing a palmprint (and other biometrics) identification scheme with perfect privacy-preserving trait is still an important task for the future.

Acknowledgements. This work is partially supported by the National Natural Science Foundation of China "Research on Key Technologies of Secure Cloud Data Storage Based on (Fully) Homomorphic Encryption" (Grant No. 61772150), the Crypto

Development Fund of China (Grant No. MMJJ20170217) and the open subject project "Palmprint feature protection research based on homomorphic encryption" of Guangxi Key Laboratory of cryptography and information security (Approval No. GCIS201622) and the planning fund project of ministry of education (12YJAZH136).

We thank Diongxiong WU and Zhiqiang Gao for helpful comments and discussions.

References

1. Ratha, N.K., Connell, J.H., Bolle, R.M.: Enhancing security and privacy in biometrics-based authentication systems. IBM Syst. J. **40**(3), 614–634 (2001)
2. Jain, A.K., Nandakumar, K., Nagar, A.: Biometric template security. EURASIP J. Adv. Signal Process. **113** (2008)
3. Boneh, D., Goh, E.-J., Nissim, K.: Evaluating 2-DNF formulas on ciphertexts. In: Kilian, J. (ed.) TCC 2005. LNCS, vol. 3378, pp. 325–341. Springer, Heidelberg (2005). doi:10.1007/978-3-540-30576-7_18
4. Luo, Z.: Research on blind identity authentication protocol based on biometrics. Ph.D. thesis, Beijing Jiaotong University, Beijing (2014)
5. Rivest, R.L., Shamir, A., Adleman, L.: A method for obtaining digital signatures and public-key cryptosystems. Commun. ACM **21**(2), 120–126 (1978)
6. Upmanyu, M., Namboodiri, A.M., Srinathan, K., Jawahar, C.V.: Blind authentication: a secure crypto-biometric verification protocol. IEEE Trans. Inf. Forensics Secur. **5**(2), 255–268 (2010)
7. Schoenmakers, B., Tuyls, P.: Computationally secure authentication with noisy data. In: Tuyls, P., Skoric, B., Kevenaar, T. (eds.) Security with Noisy Data, pp. 141–149. Springer, London (2007). doi:10.1007/978-1-84628-984-2_9
8. Erkin, Z., Franz, M., Guajardo, J., Katzenbeisser, S., Lagendijk, I., Toft, T.: Privacy-preserving face recognition. In: Goldberg, I., Atallah, M.J. (eds.) PETS 2009. LNCS, vol. 5672, pp. 235–253. Springer, Heidelberg (2009). doi:10.1007/978-3-642-03168-7_14
9. Blanton, M., Gasti, P.: Secure and efficient protocols for iris and fingerprint identification. In: Atluri, V., Diaz, C. (eds.) ESORICS 2011. LNCS, vol. 6879, pp. 190–209. Springer, Heidelberg (2011). doi:10.1007/978-3-642-23822-2_11
10. Qu, Y.: Research on palmprint authentication based on homomorphic encryption. Ph.D. thesis, Southwest Jiaotong University (2015)
11. ElGamal, T.: A public key cryptosystem and a signature scheme based on discrete logarithms. In: Blakley, G.R., Chaum, D. (eds.) CRYPTO 1984. LNCS, vol. 196, pp. 10–18. Springer, Heidelberg (1985). doi:10.1007/3-540-39568-7_2
12. Im, J.H., Choi, J.C., Nyang, D.H., Lee, M.K.: Privacy-preserving palm print authentication using homomorphic encryption. In: IEEE International Conference on Dependable, Autonomic and Secure Computing, International Conference on Pervasive Intelligence and Computing, International Conference on Big Data Intelligence and Computing and Cyber Science and Technology Congress, Auckland, pp. 878–881 (2016)
13. Paillier, P.: Public-key cryptosystems based on composite degree residuosity classes. In: Stern, J. (ed.) EUROCRYPT 1999. LNCS, vol. 1592, pp. 223–238. Springer, Heidelberg (1999). doi:10.1007/3-540-48910-X_16
14. Catalano, D., Fiore, D.: Using linearly-homomorphic encryption to evaluate degree-2 functions on encrypted data. In: Proceedings of the 22nd ACM SIGSAC Conference on Computer and Communications Security, Denver, pp. 1518–1529. ACM (2015)

15. Goldwasser, S., Micali, S.: Probabilistic encryption. J. Comput. Syst. Sci. **28**(2), 270–299 (1984)
16. Du, X., Zhang, M., Nygard, K.E., Guizani, S., Chen, H.-H.: Self-healing sensor networks with distributed decision making. Int. J. Sens. Netw. **2**(5–6), 289–298 (2007)
17. Yue, F., Zuo, W., Zhang, D.: A survey of palmprint recognition. J. Autom. **36**(3), 353–365 (2010)
18. Yang, J., Zhang, D., Yang, J.-Y., Niu, B.: Globally maximizing, locally minimizing: unsupervised discriminant projection with applications to face and palm biometrics. IEEE Trans. Pattern Anal. Mach. Intell. **29**(4), 650–664 (2007)
19. Connie, T., Jin, A.T.B., Ong, M.G.K., Ling, D.N.C.: An automated palmprint recognition system. Image Vis. Comput. **23**(5), 501–515 (2005)
20. Bingham, E., Mannil, H.:. Random projection in dimensionality reduction: applications to image and text data. In: Proceedings of the Seventh ACM SIGKDD International Conference on Knowledge Discovery and Data Mining, San Francisco, pp. 245–250. ACM (2001)
21. Achlioptas, D.: Database-friendly random projections: Johnson-lindenstrauss with binary coins. J. Comput. Syst. Sci. **66**(4), 671–687 (2003)
22. Yao, X., Han, X., Xiaojiang, D., Zhou, X.: A lightweight multicast authentication mechanism for small scale IoT applications. IEEE Sens. J. **13**(10), 3693–3701 (2013)

An Improved Authentication Scheme for the Integrated EPR Information System

Pei Wang[1,2], Hua Guo[1(✉)], and Yuanfei Huang[2]

[1] Beijing Key Laboratory of Network Technology, Beihang University,
Beijing 100191, China
hguo@buaa.edu.cn
[2] National Computer Network Emergency Response Technical
Team/Coordination Center, Beijing 100029, China

Abstract. Over the past few years, in order to protect patient privacy and increase efficiency and security of integrated electronic patient records(EPR) system, numerous biometric-based user authentication schemes for the integrated EPR system have been proposed. Recently, Jung *et al.* proposed a remote user authentication scheme for the integrated EPR system to remedy the flaws of Li *et al.*'s scheme. After careful analysis, we found that Jung's protocol still has some security problems, in order to fix the existing problems, we propose an authentication scheme. We also demonstrate the completeness of the proposed scheme using the BAN-logic. Besides, informal and formal security analysis exhibits that the proposed scheme conquers the flaws.

Keywords: Integrated EPR information system · User authentication · Biometric-based · Multi-sever

1 Introduction

The goal of electronic patient records(EPR) is to turn the patient's medical records into the electronic record. Integrated EPR system emphasizes the integration of patient-centered medical information within a healthcare facility, it can help medical staff to make the correct clinical decisions based on electronic medical records. Registered users can access a variety of services from the medical server. However, once the information is leaked, it would cause a lot of problems to patients. During the past few years, a lot of authentication schemes have been proposed for the integrated EPR information system [1–9].

In 2012, Wu *et al.* [1] proposed an efficient authentication key protocol based on user passwords for an integrated EPR information system. They claimed that the proposed scheme resists various malicious attacks. Later, Lee *et al.* [2] showed that Wu *et al.*'s scheme was insecure against lost smart card attack and stolen verifier attack. In addition, they proposed an improved lightweight scheme which does not require verifier tables, and they claimed that their solution satisfies all the desired security requirements. Later, Wen *et al.* [3] demonstrated that

© Springer International Publishing AG 2017
S. Wen et al. (Eds.): CSS 2017, LNCS 10581, pp. 513–522, 2017.
https://doi.org/10.1007/978-3-319-69471-9_40

Lee *et al.*'s scheme was vulnerable to off-line password guessing attack, and could not resist user impersonation attack. In order to improve Lee *et al.*'s scheme, Wen *et al.* introduced a novel scheme based on the quadratic residues which provides user anonymity. After that, Li *et al.* [4] showed that Wen *et al.*'s scheme [3] was vulnerable to password disclosure attack and was not efficient in password change phase, then they proposed an improved scheme. However, Das *et al.* [5] found that Lee *et al.*'s scheme and Wen *et al.*'s scheme have the same weakness such as formal security analysis was not conducted, vulnerable to insider attack and didn't verify the old password during the password change phase. Then they proposed a new scheme to fix the weakness. Later, Mir *et al.* [6] pointed out that Das *et al.*' scheme could not resist stolen smart card attack and off-line password guessing attack. To overcome these weaknesses, they proposed an improved secure authentication scheme. Unfortunately, Li *et al.* [7] recently also demonstrated that Das *et al.*' scheme could not protect against user duplication attack and modification attack. Then they suggested an enhanced new authentication mechanism. Recently, Jung *et al.* [8] showed that Li *et al.*'s scheme couldn't prevent off-line password guessing attack and server spoofing attack and further proposed a new scheme to eliminate the drawbacks of Li *et al.*'s.

However, we have found that Jung's protocol is vulnerable to user impersonation attacks, server spoofing attack. Moreover, the password change phase of their scheme is incorrect. In this paper, we cryptanalyze Jung *et al.*' scheme and describe the weakness of their scheme. Then we propose an improved scheme to fix their design flaws. We show our scheme is not only an efficient authentication scheme which only uses the nonce and hash function, but also satisfies all of the known security properties.

2 Security Analysis of Jung *et al.*'s scheme

In this section, we analyze Jung *et al.*'s scheme, and show the weakness of their scheme.

- **User impersonation attack.** In a remote user communication scheme, anyone is considered as a legal user if a user has valid authentication credentials or could be capable of constructing an valid authentication request message. Assume that the adversary E is a legal user registered in RC. In Jung *et al.*'s protocol, an adversary can impersonate a valid user as described below.
  - E gets the value of v from the login request information. Then he computes $RPW_E = h(PW_E||H(B_E))$, $N_E = h(ID_E||RPW_E)$. Moreover he can get the secret key $K = N_E \oplus v_E$ shared between RC and the server using the values of N_E and v_E.
  - When a legal user U_i communicates with a sever, E intercepts the login request information $< DID_i, v, C_1, C_2 >$ from public channel. Then he computes $ID_i = DID_i \oplus v \oplus K$, $N_i = v \oplus K$. He forges the login request information and communicates with S_j.
  - E generates a random nonce r_{1m}, and calculates $C_{2m} = h(ID_i||N_i||r_{1m})$, $C_{1m} = ID_i \oplus r_{1m}$. Then he sends the message $< DID_i, v, C_{1m}, C_{2m} >$ to S_j.

- On receiving the login request information, S_j computes $ID'_i = DID_i \oplus v \oplus K$ and verifies ID_i. S_j also retrieves $r'_1 = C_{1m} \oplus ID'_i$, $C'_{2m} = h(ID_i||N_i||r'_1)$ and verifies $C'_{2m}? = C_{2m}$. They are equal obviously, and S_j generates a random number r_2 and computes $a = r_2 \oplus h(r'_1||C'_2)$, $b = h(C'_2||r_2||r'_1)$, then responds with the message $< a, b >$ to the adversary who is masquerading as U_i.
- The masquerading adversary verifies the received value of $< a, b >$ because he knows the values of r_{1m} and K. Then the masquerading user U_i computes $r'_2 = a \oplus h(r_1||C_2)$, $C_3 = h(r_1||r'_2||C_2||h(ID_i||RPW_i))$ and sends the message $< C_3 >$ back to S_j.
- When receiving the message $< C_3 >$, S_j computes and verifies $h(r'_1||r_2||a||b||ID_i)? = C_3$. It is obvious that they are equal, so the sever and the adversary agree on the common session key $SK_{ij} = h(r_1||r'_2||a||b||ID_i)$.

- **Server spoofing attack.** In Jung $et\ al.$'s protocol, a legal user can obtain the secret key K of the server as described in the user impersonation attack, then he performs the following masquerade attack.

  - E intercepts the login request information $< DID_i, v, C_1, C_2 >$ and computes $ID'_i = DID_i \oplus v \oplus K$, $r'_1 = C_1 \oplus ID'_i$, $C'_2 = h(ID_i||v \oplus K||r'_1)$ and verifies $C'_2? = C_2$. If it holds, E generates a random number r_2, and computes $a = r_2 \oplus h(r'_1||C'_2)$, $b = h(C'_2||r_2||r'_1)$, then masquerades as S_j and delivers the message $< a, b >$ to the smart card.
  - Upon receiving the message $< a, b >$, the user calculates $r'_2 = a \oplus h(r_1||C_2)$, $b = h(C_2||r'_2||r_1)$, and verifies if $b' = b$. It is obvious that it is true. The user computes $C_3 = h(r_1||r'_2||C_2||h(ID_i||RPW_i)$ and delivers the message $< C_3 >$ to E who masquerades as S_j. Therefore, an adversary can fool the legal user U_i and establish a session key with U_i.

- **Incorrect password change phase.** During password change phase, the user U_i enters ID_i and PW_i and biometrics B_i. The smart card SC_i then computes $e' = h(ID_i||PW_i||H(B_i))$ and compares e' with the stored e. If they are the same, SC_i accepts U_i to enter a new password PW_{inew} and replaces PW_i with PW_{inew}. However, the value of $v = N \oplus K = h(ID_i||h(PW_i||H(B_i))) \oplus K$ also contains old password PW_i which has not been updated in the password change phase. So the password change phase of Jung $et\ al.$'s protocol is incorrect.

3   Our Proposed Scheme

In this section, we propose a biometric-based remote user authentication scheme to fix the drawbacks in Jung $et\ al.$'s schemes.

- **Registration phase.** When the remote user authentication scheme starts, the user U_i and the server S_j need to perform the following steps to register with the registration center RC:

1. U_i freely selects his identity ID_i which uniquely identifies the user's identity, password PW_i and scans his biometrics B_i. Then U_i computes $RPW_i = h(PW_i||H(B_i))$, and sends $< ID_i, RPW_i >$ to RC.
2. Upon reception, RC computes $A_i = h(ID_i||K)$, $v_i = RPW_i \oplus h(A_i)$, $N_i = A_i \oplus K \oplus h(K)$ and stores $< V_i, N_i, h(\cdot), H(\cdot) >$ in the smart card.
3. RC sends SC to U_i over a secure channel and the registration phase is therefore complete.
4. Upon receiving the smart card, U_i computes $e_i = h(ID_i||PW_i||H(B_i))$ and stores it in the smart card. Finally, the smart card includes the information $< v_i, N_i, h(\cdot), H(\cdot), e_i >$.

- **Login phase.** When a user (U_i) wants to access the services of server S_j, he must perform the following steps:
    1. U_i sends the login request by inserting smart card (SC), and inputting ID_i, PW_i and B_i.
    2. SC computes $RPW_i = h(PW_i||H(B_i))$ and then checks whether the condition $e_i' = h(ID_i||PW_i||H(B_i))$ holds or not. If the result is negative, the login session can be aborted. Otherwise, SC generates a random number n_1 and computes $RPW_i = h(PW_i||H(B_i))$, $h(A_i) = v_i \oplus RPW_i$, $DID_i = ID_i \oplus h(r_1)$, $C_1 = h(A_i) \oplus r_1$, $C_2 = h(ID_i||RPW_i||r_1)$, and sends $< DID_i, V_i, N_i, C_1, C_2 >$ to S_j as the login request message.

- **Mutual authentication with key-agreement phase.** In this phase, U_i and S_j authenticates each other and compute a session key for further secure communication. The steps of the verification phase are as follows:
    1. On getting login message, S_j computes $A_i = N_i \oplus K \oplus h(K)$, $RPW_i = v_i \oplus h(A_i)$, $ID_i = DID_i \oplus h(r_1)$, $r_1 = h(A_i) \oplus C_1$ and verifies if $C_2' = h(ID_i||RPW_i||r_1)$ holds or not. If they are same, S_j authenticates U_i and generates a random r_2 and calculates $a = r_2 \oplus h(r_1'||C_2'||RPW_i)$, $b = h(a||r_2||r_1')$. Then the sever sends the message $< a, b >$ to U_i.
    2. Upon receiving the message $< a, b >$, U_i computes $r_2 = a \oplus h(r_1||C_2'||RPW_i)$ and verifies $b? = h(a||r_2'||r_1)$. If they are equal, U_i computes $C_3 = h(r_1||r_2'||RPW_i)$ and submits $< C_3 >$ to S_j.
    3. S_j verifies $C_3? = h(r_1||r_2||RPW_i)$ on receiving the message $< C_3 >$. If the condition holds, U_i and S_j would share with the computed session key $SK_{ij} = h(r_1||r_2'||RPW_i||ID_i)$ for further communication.

- **Password changing phase.** In this procedure, U_i changes his password without the involvement of the registration center RC as follows:
    1. U_i inserts the smart card SC and inputs ID_i, PW_i and B_i.
    2. SC verifies the condition $e_i? = h(ID_i||PW_i||H(B_i))$. If the condition doesn't hold, S_j rejects the request.
    3. U_i chooses a new password PW_i^{new} and then computes $RPW_i = h(PW_i||H(B_i))$, $h(A_i) = RPW_i \oplus v_i$, $RPW_i^{new} = h(PW_i^{new}||H(B_i))$, $v_i^{new} = RPW_i^{new} \oplus h(A_i)$, $e_i^{new} = h(ID_i||PW_i||H(B_i))$. Then the smart card replaces v_i, e_i with v_i^{new}, e_i^{new}, finally contains the parameters $< v_i^{new}, N_i, h(\cdot), H(\cdot), e_i^{new} >$.

4   Security Analysis of the Proposed Scheme

In this section, we first use Burrows-Abadi-Needham (BAN) Logic to verify the completeness of the proposed scheme, then prove the security of the scheme through informal and formal analysis.

4.1   Verifying the Proposed Scheme with BAN Logic

The BAN logic introduced by Burrows et $al.$ [11] is a formal method of analyzing the security features of the information exchange protocol. We use BAN logic to prove that a user and a server share a session key in our scheme.

1. Establishment of security goals

   g1:$U_i| \equiv U_i \overset{SK_{ij}}{\longleftrightarrow} S_j$

   g2:$S_j| \equiv U_i \overset{SK_{ij}}{\longleftrightarrow} S_j$

2. Initiative premises

   p1.$U_i| \equiv \#r_1$. p2.$U_i| \equiv \#r_2$.

   p3.$S_j| \equiv U_i \overset{h(A_i)}{\longleftrightarrow} S_j$.

   p4.$U_i| \equiv U_i \overset{h(A_i)}{\longleftrightarrow} S_j$.

   p5.$S_j| \equiv U_i| \equiv U_i \overset{h(A_i)}{\longleftrightarrow} S_j$.

   p6.$U_i| \equiv S_j| \equiv U_i \overset{h(A_i)}{\longleftrightarrow} S_j$.

3. Scheme analysis

   Based on Message $< DID_i, v_i, N_i, C_1, C_2 >$, we derive:

   $a_1.$ $S_j \triangleleft (r_1)_{ID_i}$, $S_j \triangleleft (r_1)_{h(A_i)}$, $S_j \triangleleft < ID_i, r_1 >_{h(A_i)}$.

   We employ Message-meaning rule according to p_5 and a_1 to drive:

   $a_2.$ $S_j| \equiv U_i| \sim r_1$.

   We employ Message-meaning rule according to p_5 and a_1 to drive:

   $a_3.$ $S_j| \equiv U_i| \sim ID_i$

   According to a_1 and p_1, we apply the Freshness-conjuncatenation rule to get the following information:

   $a_4.$ $S_j| \equiv \#(r_1)_{ID_i}$

   According to a_3 and a_4, we apply Nonce-verification rule to obtain:

   $a_5.$ $S_j| \equiv U_i| \equiv (r_1)_{ID_i}$.

   Finally, based on a_2, a_5, we employ Jurisdiction rule to obtain:

   $a_6.$ $S_j| \equiv r_1$.

   Based on Message $< a, b >$, we derive:

   $a_7.$ $U_i \triangleleft (r_1, r_2)_{h(A_i)}$ and $U_i \triangleleft < r_2 >_{h(A_i)}$.

   According to p_6 and a_7, we apply Message-meaning rule to derive:

   $a_8.$ $U_i| \equiv S_j| \sim r_2$.

   According to p_2, we apply Freshness-conjuncatenation rule to derive:

   $a_9.$ $U_i| \equiv \# < r_2 >_{h(A_i)}$.

   According to a_8 and a_9, we apply Nonce-verification rule to derive:

   $a_{10}.$ $U_i| \equiv S_j| \equiv < r_2 >_{h(A_i)}$.

   According to a_9 and a_{10}, we apply Jurisdiction rule to derive:

$a_{11}.$ $U_i| \equiv r_2.$

Based on a_{11}, p1 and $SK_{ij} = h(r_1||r_2||v_i \oplus h(A_i)||ID_i)$, we derive:

$a_{12}.$ $U_i| \equiv U_i \overset{SK_{ij}}{\longleftrightarrow} S_j.$ (g_1)

Based on message $< C_3 >$, we derive:

$a_{13}.$ $S_j \triangleleft < r_1, r_2 >_{h(A_i)}.$

Based on message $SK_{ij} = h(r_1||r_2||v_i \oplus h(A_i)||ID_i)$, a_3 and a_6, we derive:

$a_{14}.$ $S_j| \equiv U_i \overset{SK_{ij}}{\longleftrightarrow} S_j.$ (g_2)

From the above description, we can see that U_i and S_j achieve mutual authentication and share the session key SK_{ij}, they authenticate each other based on the security goals g_1 and g_2.

4.2   Informal Security Analysis

This subsection describes the security analysis of the improved scheme and discuss the main security features of our proposed protocol in details:

- **Off-Line password guessing attack.** $< v_i, N_i, h(\cdot), H(\cdot), e_i >$ can be obtained by means of power analysis and various other ways [10]. The stored parameter contains the password PW_i in the form $v_i = RPW_i \oplus h(A_i)$ where $RPW_i = h(PW_i||H(B_i))$. An adversary tries to check the condition $e_i? = h(ID_i||PW_i||H(B_i))$ while constantly guessing PW_i, the adversary needs ID_i and B_i in order to execute this. However, the value of B_i is nowhere stored and an adversary cannot get the value of ID_i without knowing the private key K. So the adversary cannot guess the correct password PW_i.

- **Stolen smart card attack.** Assume a user's smart card is stolen by an adversary and stored parameters $< v_i, N_i, h(\cdot), H(\cdot), e_i >$ on it are extracted. However, the adversary undeniably cannot obtain any valuable information from these values $v_i = RPW_i \oplus h(A_i)$, $N_i = A_i \oplus K \oplus h(K)$ and $e_i = h(ID_i||PW_i||H(B_i))$, since all the important parameters such as ID_i, PW_i are protected by a one-way hash function. The adversary cannot obtain any login information using the smart card stored parameters v_i, N_i, e_i. At the same time guessing the real identity ID_i and password PW_i is impractical. So the proposed protocol is secure from smart card stolen attack.

- **User masquerade attack.** If an adversary forges messages to impersonate as U_i, he needs to build a login request message $< DID_i, v_i, N_i, C_1, C_2 >$ firstly, where $DID_i = ID_i \oplus h(r_1)$. Conversely, the adversary cannot compute one parameter C_1 and C_2 without user's identity ID_i, PW_i and B_i which are unobtainable. On the other hand, SC checks whether the condition $e'_i = h(ID_i||PW_i||H(B_i))$ is correct during login phase. Unless the adversary enters the correct credentials, he cannot be allowed to further phases. Therefore, the adversary certainly requires legitimate identity ID_i, password PW_i and biometrics B_i for any furthermore computations. However, the probability of obtaining correct ID_i, PW_i, B_i is negligible.

- **Server impersonation attack.** In our protocol, the adversary or the legal user cannot calculate K through all the information they get. Consider a scenario where an adversary captures $< DID_i, v_i, N_i, C_1, C_2 >$ and tries to impersonate a valid server by responding with computed message $< a, b >$. However, RPW_i, ID_i and r_1 are prerequisite, thus the adversary cannot yield either of the values without having the knowledge of K. Note that the adversary cannot get the right values of RPW_i, ID_i and r_1. Assume that the adversary forges the massage $< a, b >$. Upon receiving the response message $< a, b >$, U_i can identify it as a malicious attempt due to the non-equivalence of message $b? = h(a||r'_2||RPW_i)$. Thus, our proposed protocol can withstand server impersonation attack.

- **Replay attack.** In our scheme, different random numbers are used in each session. Assume an adversary has intercepted all the communication message $< DID_i, v_i, N_i, C_1, C_2 >$, $< a, b >$, $< C_3 >$ and resends the transmitted message, the receiver would immediately detect the attack through the authenticated message. Hence, our scheme is secure against replay attack.

4.3   Formal analysis

In this subsection, we use formal security to prove the security of our scheme. We define an oracle as follows:

Reveal: This oracle will unconditionally output the value of x from the corresponding hash function $y = h(x)$.

Theorem 1. Assuming that the one-way hash function $h(\cdot)$ closely behaves like an oracle, considering one way hash function, our proposed scheme is proved to be secure against the attacker to derive the identity ID_i, PW_i, $H(B_i)$ of the legitimate user U_i and the private key K hold by the server.

Proof. In this proof, we construct an adversary E who have the ability to export the identity ID_i, PW_i, $H(B_i)$ and the secret key K hold by the server. The adversary E uses oracle Reveal to run experimental algorithms, $EXP1_{E,BMAKAS}^{HASH}$, for our biometric-based multi-server authentication and key agreement scheme, say BMAKAS, which is provided in Algorithm 1.

We define the success probability of $EXP1_{E,BMAKAS}^{HASH}$ as $Success1 = |pr[EXP1_{E,BMAKAS}^{HASH} = 1] - 1|$. The advantage function for this experiment becomes $Adv1(et_1, q_R) = max_E\{Success1\}$, where the maximum is taken over all of adversary E with the execution time et_1 and the number of queries q_R made to Reveal Oracle. Our scheme is proved to be reliable against adversary E derived ID_i, PW_i, $H(B_i)$ and K, if $Adv1(et_1, q_R) \leqslant \varepsilon_1$ for any sufficiently small $\varepsilon_1 > 0$. According to the experiment, if the adversary can reverse x from hash function $y = h(x)$, then he/she can easily derive $(ID_i, PW_i, H(B_i), K)$ to win the game. However, it is a computationally infeasible problem to retrieve the input of one-way hash function. So $max_E\{Succcess1\} = Adv1(et_1, q_R) \leqslant \varepsilon_1$ for any sufficiently small $\varepsilon_1 > 0$. As a result, there is no way for E to discover the complete connections between U_i and S_j by deriving $(ID_i, PW_i, H(B_i), K)$. Therefore our proposed scheme is provably secure against an adversary.

Algorithm 1. $EXP_{E,BMAKAS}^{HASH}$

1: Eavesdrop the login message $\{DID_i, v_i, N_i, C_1, C_2\}$
2: Apply the Reveal oracle on C_2 , let $(ID_i', RPW_i', r_1') \leftarrow$ Reveal(C_2)
3: Eavesdrop the login message $\{a, b\}$
4: Apply the Reveal oracle. Let $(a, r_2', r_1'') \leftarrow$ Reveal(b)
5: **if** $(r_1'' = r_1')$ **then**
6:    Calculate $ID_i'' = DID_i \oplus h(r_1')$
7:    Calculate $h(A_i)' = r_1' \oplus C_1$
8:    Calculate $RPW_i'' = h(A_i)' \oplus v_i$
9:    **if** $(RPW_i' = RPW_i'')$ and $(ID_i'') = (ID_i')$ **then**
10:      Apply the Reveal oracle. Let $(PW_i', H(B_i)') \leftarrow$ Reveal(RPW_i'')
11:      Apply the Reveal oracle. Let $(A_i') \leftarrow$ Reveal($h(A_i)'$)
12:      Apply the Reveal oracle. Let $(ID_i', K') \leftarrow$ Reveal(A_i')
13:      Calculate $N_i'' = A_i' \oplus K' \oplus h(K')$
14:      **if** $(N_i'' = N_i)$ **then**
15:        Accept the values of $ID_i', PW_i', H(B_i)'$ as the correct $ID_i, PW_i, H(B_i)$, and K' as the correct secret value holds by server.
16:        return 1
17:      **else**
18:        return 0
19:      **end if**
20:    **else**
21:      return 0
22:    **end if**
23: **else**
24:    return 0
25: **end if**

---

5   Functional and Performance Analysis

In this section, we compare the functionality and performance of the proposed scheme with other related authentication and key agreement schemes.

- **Functional analysis.** We first examine the security of our proposed scheme against various attacks, and the suitability of the basic requirements are evaluated. We also perform a comparative analysis of previous schemes, which is illustrated in Table 1. From the table, we can find that the proposed scheme achieves all security and functionality requirements while other relevant protocols can't resist user impersonation attack or other kind of attacks. It demonstrates that our protocol is more secure than other relevant protocols.
- **Performance analysis.** For the evaluation of the computational cost, we define the computational parameter T_h refers to the execution time of one-way hash. According to Kilinc et al.'s [12] experiments on a personal computer, the computation cost for T_h is approximately 0.0023 ms. From Table 2, we find that the proposed scheme requires less computation to accomplish mutual authentication and the key agreement than other three relevant schemes. Although Jung et al.'s protocol [8] requires only $21T_h$, it has some serious

Table 1. Functionality comparison

Scheme	Wen [3]	Li [4]	Das [5]	Mir [6]	Li [7]	Jung [8]	our
Provide mutual authentication	Yes	Yes	Yes	Yes	Yes	No	Yes
User anonymity	Yes	Yes	No	No	No	No	Yes
Resist insider attack	No	No	Yes	Yes	Yes	Yes	Yes
Resist off-line guessing attack	Yes	No	No	Yes	No	Yes	Yes
Resist smart card theft attack	No	Yes	No	Yes	Yes	No	Yes
Resist replay attack	Yes	Yes	Yes	Yes	Yes	Yes	Yes
Resist user Impersonation attack	No	No	No	No	No	No	Yes
Session key agreement	Yes	Yes	Yes	Yes	Yes	Yes	Yes
Efficient password change phase	No	No	No	Yes	No	No	Yes
Resist server Impersonation attack	Yes	Yes	No	Yes	No	No	Yes

weakness which badly impact the user's experience and even cause serious security mistakes. Li *et al.*'s scheme [4] requires only $19T_h$, but their protocol is vulnerable to insider attack and didn't verify the old password during the password change phase. To sum up, our proposed scheme is the only one which is efficient and secure against known attacks, while the rest of the schemes [3–8] are vulnerable to impersonation or other related attacks.

Table 2. Computation costs comparison

Scheme	Registration	Login	Authentication	Password change	Total	Time(ms)
Li *et al.*'s [4]	$4T_h$	$2T_h$	$10T_h$	$3T_h$	$19T_h$	0.0437
Das *et al.*'s [5]	$4T_h$	$3T_h$	$11T_h$	$7T_h$	$25T_h$	0.0575
Mir *et al.*'s [6]	$5T_h$	$7T_h$	$10T_h$	$5T_h$	$27T_h$	0.0621
Li *et al.*'s [7]	$4T_h$	$3T_h$	$11T_h$	$8T_h$	$26T_h$	0.0598
Jung *et al.*'s [8]	$4T_h$	$5T_h$	$9T_h$	$3T_h$	$21T_h$	0.0483
Our scheme	$5T_h$	$5T_h$	$9T_h$	$4T_h$	$23T_h$	0.0529

6   Conclusion

In this paper, we have cryptanalyzed a biometric based authentication scheme proposed by Jung *et al.* We have shown their scheme is vulnerable to user impersonation attack and server impersonation attack. Furthermore, the password change phase is not correct. Then we proposed an improved biometric-based three factor authentication scheme which is suitable for the integrated EPR information system and is demonstrated to satisfy all the essential security requirements. In comparison with other related protocols, our protocol is more efficient and provides more security properties.

Acknowledgements. This work was supported by the National Natural Science Foundation of China (No. 61572027, U1636208, 61402037).

References

1. Wu, Z.Y., Chung, Y., Lai, F., et al.: A password-based user authentication scheme for the integrated EPR information system. J. Med. Syst. **36**(2), 631–638 (2012)
2. Lee, T.F., Chang, I.P., Lin, T.H., et al.: A secure and efficient password-based user authentication scheme using smart cards for the integrated EPR information system. J. Med. Syst. **37**(3), 9941 (2013)
3. Wen, F.: A more secure anonymous user authentication scheme for the integrated EPR information system. J. Med. Syst. **38**(5), 42 (2014)
4. Li, C.T., Weng, C.Y., Lee, C.C., et al.: Secure user authentication and user anonymity scheme based on quadratic residues for the integrated EPRIS. Proc. Comput. Sci. **52**(1), 21–28 (2015)
5. Das, A.K.: A secure and robust password-based remote user authentication scheme using smart cards for the integrated EPR information system. J. Med. Syst. **39**(3), 204 (2015)
6. Mir, O., Weide, T.V.D., Lee, C.C.: A secure user anonymity and authentication scheme using AVISPA for Telecare medical information systems. J. Med. Syst. **39**(9), 265 (2015)
7. Li, C.T., Weng, C.Y., Lee, C.C., et al.: A hash based remote user authentication and authenticated key agreement scheme for the integrated EPR information system. J. Med. Syst. **39**(11), 144 (2015)
8. Jung, J., Kang, D., Lee, D., et al.: An improved and secure anonymous biometric-based user authentication with key agreement scheme for the integrated EPR information system. Plos One **12**(1), e0169414 (2017)
9. Wen, F., Guo, D.: An improved anonymous authentication scheme for telecare medical information systems. J. Med. Syst. **38**(5), 26 (2014)
10. Messerges, T.S., Dabbish, E., Sloan, R.H.: Examining smart-card security under the threat of power analysis attacks. IEEE Trans. Comput. **51**(5), 541–552 (2002)
11. Burrows, M., Abadi, M., Needham, R.: A logic of authentication. Proc. Roy. Soc. Math. Phys. Eng. Sci. **8**(5), 18–36 (1990)
12. Kilinc, H.H., Yanik, T.: A survey of SIP authentication and key agreement schemes. IEEE Commun. Surv. Tutorials **16**(2), 1005–1023 (2014)

KGBIAC: Knowledge Graph Based Intelligent Alert Correlation Framework

Wei Wang$^{(\boxtimes)}$ [ORCID], Rong Jiang, Yan Jia, Aiping Li, and Yi Chen

School of Computer, National University of Defense Technology,
Changsha 410073, China
{wangwei15a, jiangrong, chenyi15a}@nudt.edu.cn,
jiayanjy@vip.sina.com, 13017395458@163.com

Abstract. Alert Correlation is a key part of intrusion detection technique. Traditional methods based on the situation awareness techniques usually store the different dimensions of security information in separate knowledge bases, which leads to the lack of synergies between the various dimensions. For complex attacks, it is difficult to integrate all context information quickly to launch real-time and accurate analysis. To address these issues, we proposed an integrated intelligent security event correlation analysis system, named KGBIAC, which uses knowledge graph to represent and store the network security information. We explain the structure of KGBIAC and conduct an experiment on the DARPA 2000 dataset. Performance evaluation shows that the KGBIAC performs potentially effective.

Keywords: Alert correlation · Knowledge graph · Vulnerability · Cyber security situation awareness

1 Introduction

With the rapid development of computer technology, network viruses, Dos/DDos and other cyber-attacks are also growing. In order to deal with the increasingly complex and hidden network security threats, it is necessary to integrate the heterogeneous information generated by multi-source security devices with the technology of network security situation to aware the whole network environment. Security event correlation technology provides a solution for the problems above, which integrates the isolated low-level network security event information, and through particular methods to explore the real contact between events [1]. The alert correlation process mainly consists filtering, aggregation and attack scene reconstruction [2]. Security event correlation analysis in traditional Cyber Security Situation Awareness (CSSA) takes into account multiple dimensions of information, such as network infrastructure dimension, vulnerability dimension, and cyber threat dimension [3]. However, there are a number of problems with such systems. First of all, the traditional CSSA systems store the different dimensions of security information in separate relational database, the coordination between the various dimensions of poor ability to launch real-time and accurate analysis. Second, relational database storage is not efficient enough for joint search of multiple dimension information. Third, the traditional rule-based association

© Springer International Publishing AG 2017
S. Wen et al. (Eds.): CSS 2017, LNCS 10581, pp. 523–530, 2017.
https://doi.org/10.1007/978-3-319-69471-9_41

analysis needs to rely on expert knowledge to construct the attack scene which lack of ability of reasoning automatically.

To this purpose, in this paper, we present KGBIAC that constructs a network security knowledge graph to fuse independent data into higher-level knowledge. Our framework mainly includes two parts, knowledge graph construction and the use of knowledge graph for correlation analysis. Initially, we fuses network knowledge from a variety of data sources to build a unified knowledge graph based model, which is composed of vulnerabilities kb, network infrastructure kb, cyber threat kb and alerts kb. We also detail the data sources for each dimension. Furthermore, we explain how to connect these sub knowledge graph together to form an intelligent and useful kb. Finally, we conduct experiment on DARPA 2000 dataset and prove the feasibility of our framework.

The remainder of this paper is organized as follows. In Sect. 2, we briefly review relate works. Then, in Sect. 3 we present our proposed framework in detail and present a case study that illustrates the powerful analytic capabilities in KGBIAC, followed by performance analysis in Sect. 4. Finally, we draw our conclusion in Sect. 5.

2   Related Works

For the correlation process, the input data can only one data source or multiple data sources [4]. Obviously, the cost of getting better results using multiple data sources is increasing the complexity of alert correlation systems due to the heterogeneity different input. Y Zhang et al. introduces a simple data fusion technology which prepares a large number of raw security data [5]. These data obtains a standardized asset data set, threat data set, vulnerability data set and network structure data set. They analyzes the relationship between assets, threats, vulnerabilities and security events. Xin Zhuang et al. propose a system Unified Security Information Management Platform (USIM) [6]. In this system, they focus on alerts fusion to reduce the number of alerts, alerts verifying by applying contextual information such as vulnerability information, and alerts correlation with statically built knowledge bases. There is no unified knowledge base model for the description of these elements. To some extent, it limits the flexibility and expansibility of the alert correlation and other CSSA components.

Recent years, some researchers proposed some novel approaches for CSSA based on ontology model. GAO J provides an ontology-based attack model [7]. They categorize attacks into five dimensions, which include attack impact, attack vector, attack target, vulnerability and defense. Afterwards they build an ontology according to these five dimensions and populate the attack ontology with information from many open source information, like NDV, CVE and etc. Finally they propose an ontology-based framework for security assessment and describe the utilization of ontology in the security assessment. Alireza S et al. propose ONTIDS, an ontology-based alert correlation framework that store four dimensions security knowledge, including alert information, current networks context, vulnerability information and attack information in ontologies [8]. They describe the structure of the designed ontology and the detailed attributes for each sub ontology. ONTIDS use SQWRL to correlate and remove non-relevant alerts. Sumit M et al. propose an ontology which comprises three fundamental classes: means, consequence and targets [9]. And they apply reasoned logic language to find relevant information. However, the common problem of these method is the definition of security elements and indicators is too abstract. In order to ensure that the ontology has good flexibility and versatility, many researchers can only broadly define the concepts and ontology framework, resulting in the practicality and operability are poor.

3   KGBIAC Framework

Our correlation framework includes four layers, multi-source alert collection layer, alert normalization layer, alert correlation layer and correlation results display layer. The alert collection layer collects multi-source security evidence by deploying different security devices such as NIDS Snort, HIDS OSSEC, firewall, and vulnerability scanning tool NMAP and et al. However, the alerts are usually heterogeneous, cannot be used directly. Alert normalization layer converts them to a unified format, usually IDMEF format [10]. Alert correlation layer is the core component of KGBIAC, which includes alert fusion, alert verification and attack thread correlation analysis. Correlation results display layer receives the analysis result and uses front-end framework D3. js to show the final result [11].

Here we will start from the following four aspects. First, we illustrate the knowledge graph tool and query language of our system. Then we introduced in detail the significance of the sub knowledge bases and the source knowledge of them. Furthermore, we integrate the sub knowledge bases as a unified knowledge map. Finally, we describe how to correlate security events based on our knowledge graph.

3.1   Knowledge Graph Tool and RDF Query Language

Knowledge Graph is a knowledge base used by Google to enhance its search engine's search results with semantic-search information gathered from a wide variety of sources. The current Knowledge Graph has been used to refer to various large-scale knowledge bases. Triples is a general representation of a KG. $G = (E, R, S)$ represents whole KG and $E = e_1, e_1, \ldots, e_n$ is the collection of entities in the KG, which includes n types entities. $R = r_1, r_2, \ldots, r_m$ is the collection of relations in the KG, which includes $|R|$ types relations. $S \subseteq E \times R \times E$ represents the collection of triples in the KG. There is an edge connection between entities and each entity has a set of attributes. Common open KG such as Freebase [12], Wikidata [13] and DBpedia [14].

We employ Blazegraph for our knowledge base tool. Blaze- graph is a high-performance graph database which support for RDF/SPARQL APIs. It supports large scale edges on single server and SPARQL as knowledge query tool. SPARQL (SPARQL Protocol and RDF Query Language) is an RDF query language which has the ability to retrieve and manipulate data stored in Resource Description Framework (RDF) format [15].

3.2 Sub Knowledge Bases

Network infrastructure Knowledge Base collects and stores the overall configuration information of current system environment, including static information and dynamic information. Static information mainly refers to the information that does not change frequently, mainly contains hardware and software. The Official Common Platform Enumeration (CPE) collects the currently known software and hardware specifications and uniquely identifies it through a unified resource descriptor, which is a useful tool to represent the particular operating system or application software. Besides dynamic network infrastructure includes IP address, mac address in the current network environment also need to be saved in KG.

Vulnerability Knowledge Base organizes all the vulnerabilities that have been announced through the form of knowledge graph. Vulnerability is often an important basis for attackers to launch attacks. First, we get all the known vulnerabilities from the National Vulnerability Database (NVD), which contains a lot of CVE items. In addition, we also put Common Vulnerability Scoring System (CVSS) along with the CVE items to KG. CVSS gives a risk score for all vulnerabilities, thus determining the severity of the vulnerability. Almost every CVE entry points to a Common Weakness Enumeration Specification (CWE) entry, which indicates single vulnerability type.

Cyber Threat Knowledge Base enumerates known attack patterns which usually used for exploiting vulnerabilities within the network infrastructure by attackers. CAPEC (Common Attack Pattern Enumeration and Classification) is an important source of knowledge for attack threats. Each CAPEC item describe the attack mode, attack steps, attack threat level and attack response measures. Figure 1 shows the CAPEC Knowledge Graph. Every node represents each attack pattern and the edge indicates the parent-child relationships between the attack patterns.

Fig. 1. CAPEC knowledge graph

Alert Knowledge Base. Alert sensors generate alerts based on the abnormal behavior by IDS. Normally used IDS sensors include NIDS and HIDS. NIDS is used more frequently than HIDS. Common NIDS includes snort, Bro, AIDE and etc. We only add Snort alert rules to the Knowledge Graph by now. In future we will fuse more knowledge of the other IDS rules.

3.3 Knowledge Graph Fusion

We have described all of the sub Knowledge Bases in this system, including the Network Infrastructure Knowledge Base, the Vulnerability Knowledge Base, the Cyber Threat Knowledge Base and the Alert Knowledge Base. Next we will illustrate how we can integrate these independent Knowledge Bases into a unified Cyber Security Knowledge Graph.

Each vulnerability refers to a set of CPE items, so there are edges between these two KBs' nodes. In addition, through the vulnerability scanning tools can scan the existence vulnerabilities of the hosts. So we can also connect Vulnerability KB with dynamic Network Infrastructure KB.

Each vulnerability has a reference to CWE and each CAPEC is associated with a number of CWE entries. So we can establish the connection between CAPEC and CVE through CWE, and there is a one-to-many relationship between CAPEC and CVE, because there are many vulnerabilities related to the same type of attack.

Currently, we only store the Snort alert rules, part of them have a clearly reference to particular CVE items. So we can create indirect relationships in the two bases. In the future, we will find others ways to extend the associations between this two KBs.

Figure 2 shows a part of our Knowledge Graph of the system, which depicts the association of these KBs and the attributes of each KB. On the basis of the Knowledge Graph, we can carry out a lot of work on Cyber Security Situation Awareness, such as situation assessment, correlation analysis and etc.

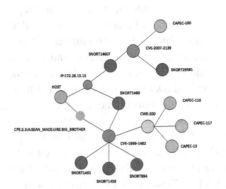

Fig. 2. System knowledge graph framework

3.4   Knowledge Graph Based Event Correlation

Alert Normalization is an important task for tidying the alerts into a unified format and extracting required information. In response to this requirement, the system uses regular expressions for log normalization and information extraction. And then call the detector's information extraction engine. Use the engine to extract important information, such as alert generation time, alert source IP, destination IP, and log description.

Alert Fusion. The main purpose of this phase is to combine alert logs from different detectors but for the same event. The principle of fusing two or more alerts is that if the alerts are generated within a time window, and the attributes of the alerts are consistent. These alert attributes include source IP, destination IP and so on.

Alert verification. The purpose of this step is to filter those unrelated alerts generated by unsuccessful attack. At this point we can use the SPARQL statement, combined with the established Knowledge Graph to query useful knowledge quickly. Assuming the host at this time has a Snort alert, numbered 14607. First through the SPARQL to retrieving all the vulnerabilities of the target host, and then retrieving the vulnerability related to the alert. If the vulnerability in the host vulnerability set, then the alert is the correct alert. Otherwise the alert will be filtered as false alert.

Attack Thread Correlation Analysis. The process of attack thread correlation analysis is based on the existing alerts to predict the real purpose of attackers. Assuming there is an alert Snort-14607, we can intelligently analyze the CVE items associated with the alert as well as other related snort alerts and CAPEC information. Through the Fig. 2 we can find Snort-14607 has a direct reference to CVE-2007-2139 and has an indirect relationship with CAPEC-100 and Snort-29581.

4   Performance Evaluation

We use known DARPA 2000 as experiment data set and replay LLDDOS 1.0 attack scene. MIT official gives the number of alarms they have collected. In addition, we use Snort to sniff the attack scene. Table 1 lists the number of this two parts alerts. We test the performance of our framework on this dataset and compare with Attribute Similarity Method and D-S Evidential Theory method. These two methods are classical alert correlation methods. Table 2 shows the number of remaining alerts after analysis by three methods. Figure 3 shows the effectiveness of these methods. From the figure we can clearly find our framework achieves the best. Also during the correlation process, Snort sensor detects Snort-1918 which means the event is generated when a scan is detected and Snort-1957 which means an attacker attempts to ping the Remote Procedure Call (RPC) sadmind. Through KGBIAC we found these alerts are related to CVE-1999-0977. This CVE indicates buffer overflow in Solaris sadmind allows remote attackers to gain root privileges. At this point we can infer the attacker's real purpose is through buffer overflow in Solaris sadmind to gain root privileges.

Table 1. MIT alerts number and Snort alerts number

Stage	Attack description	MIT alerts	Reduction ratio
1	Host detection	31	38
2	Vulnerability scanning	32	160
3	System intrusion	35	70
4	Trojan installation	22	32
5	DDos launching	1754	3201

Table 2. Remaining alerts after reduction

Stage	Attribute-Similarity method	D-S Evidential Theory	Our method
1	19	12	3
2	32	26	13
3	30	22	8
4	13	11	5
5	650	130	37

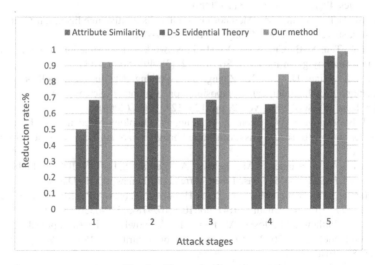

Fig. 3. Alert reduction rate

5 Conclusion

In this paper, we proposed an alert correlation framework based on Knowledge Graph. We mainly introduce how to build a cybersecurity knowledge graph and how to use the KG to carry out alert correlation analysis.

In order to make up for the problem of the different dimensions of security information stored in separate knowledge bases, which leads to the lack of synergies between the various dimension, we prosed our KGBIAC framework. Our proposed framework is generic, easy to be adapted by other systems. And can be very flexible to expand the knowledge base. But we only integrate the open source structured cyber security knowledge by now. In future, we will dig more security related knowledge to expand our Knowledge Graph. Such as by extracting the attack scene from the natural description information. In addition, we will further optimize the alert correlation method to improve accuracy, precision and recall.

Acknowledgements. This work is supported by the National Key Research and Development Program No. 2016YFB0800804, No. 2016YFB0800803, No. 2016YFB0800802

References

1. Liao, H., Lin, C., Lin, Y.: Intrusion detection system: a comprehensive review. J. Network Comput. Appl. **36**(1), 16–24 (2013)
2. Valeur, F., Vigna, G., Kruegel, C., Kemmerer, R.A.: Comprehensive approach to intrusion detection alert correlation. IEEE Trans. Dependable Secure Comput. **1**(3), 146–169 (2004)
3. Stanton, N.A., Stewart, R., Harris, D., Houghton, R.J., Baber, C., McMaster, R., Salmon, P., Hoyle, G., Walker, G., Young, M.S., et al.: Distributed situation awareness in dynamic systems: theoretical development and application of an ergonomics methodology. Ergonomics **49**(12–13), 1288–1311 (2006)
4. Elshoush, H.T., Osman, I.M.: Alert correlation in collaborative intelligent intrusion detection systemsłasa survey. Appl. Soft Comput. **11**(7), 4349–4365 (2011)
5. Zhang, Y., Tan, X.-B., Cui, X.-L., Xi, H.-S.: Network security situation awareness approach based on Markov game model. J. Software **22**(3), 495–508 (2011)
6. Zhuang, X., Xiao, D., Liu, X., Zhang, Y.: Applying data fusion in collaborative alerts correlation. In: International Symposium on Computer Science and Computational Technology, ISCSCT 2008, vol. 2, pp. 124–127. IEEE (2008)
7. Gao, J.-B., Zhang, B.-W., Chen, X.-H., Luo, Z.: Ontology-based model of network and computer attacks for security assessment. J. Shanghai Jiaotong Univ. (Science) **18**(5), 554–562 (2013)
8. Sadighian, A., Fernandez, J.M., Lemay, A., Zargar, S.T.: ONTIDS: a highly flexible context-aware and ontology-based alert correlation framework. In: Danger, J.-L., Debbabi, M., Marion, J.-Y., Garcia-Alfaro, J., Zincir Heywood, N. (eds.) FPS-2013. LNCS, vol. 8352, pp. 161–177. Springer, Cham (2014). doi:10.1007/978-3-319-05302-8_10
9. More, S., Matthews, M., Joshi, A., Finin, T.: A knowledge-based approach to intrusion detection modeling. In: 2012 IEEE Symposium on Security and Privacy Workshops (SPW), pp. 75–81. IEEE (2012)
10. Carey, N., Clark, A., Mohay, G.: IDS interoperability and correlation using IDMEF and commodity systems. In: Deng, R., Bao, F., Zhou, J., Qing, S. (eds.) ICICS 2002. LNCS, vol. 2513, pp. 252–264. Springer, Heidelberg (2002). doi:10.1007/3-540-36159-6_22
11. Zhu, N.Q.: Data Visualization with D3.js Cookbook. Packt Publishing Ltd., Birmingham (2013)
12. Bollacker, K., Evans, C., Paritosh, P., Sturge, T., Taylor, J.: Freebase: a collaboratively created graph database for structuring human knowledge. In: Proceedings of the 2008 ACM SIGMOD International Conference on Management of Data, pp. 1247–1250. ACM (2008)
13. Vrandečić, D., Krötzsch, M.: Wikidata: a free collaborative knowledgebase. Commun. ACM **57**(10), 78–85 (2014)
14. Auer, S., Bizer, C., Kobilarov, G., Lehmann, J., Cyganiak, R., Ives, Z.: Dbpedia: a nucleus for a web of open data. The semantic web, pp. 722–735 (2007)
15. Prud, E., Seaborne, A., et al.: SPARQL query language for RDF (2006)

Author Index

Printed in the United States
By Bookmasters